CONTEMPORARY REAL ESTATE FINANCE

Selected Readings

Edited by:

John B. Major and **Fung-Shine Pan**
California State University at Hayward

SOUTH-WESTERN
THOMSON LEARNING

Australia · Canada · Mexico · Singapore · Spain · United Kingdom · United States

Contemporary Real Estate Finance: Selected Readings
Edited by
John B. Major
Fung-Shine Pan

COPYRIGHT © 2001 by South-Western Publishing, a division of Thomson Learning.
The Thomson Learning logo is a registered trademark used herein under license.

All Rights Reserved. No part of this work covered by the copyright hereon may be reproduced or used in any form or by any means – graphic, electronic, or mechanical, including photocopying, recording, taping, or information storage and retrieval systems – without the written permission of the publisher.

Printed in the United States of America
1 2 3 4 02 01

For more information contact South-Western Publishing, 5101 Madison Road, Cincinnati, Ohio, 45227. Or you can visit our Internet site at http://www.swcollege.com

For permission to use material from this text or product contact us by
- **telephone: 1-800-730-2214**
- **fax: 1-800-730-2215**
- **web: http://www.thomsonrights.com**

ISBN
0-324-13753-2

Brief Contents

Part 1. Introduction *1*
Part 2. Mortgages *38*
Part 3. Mortgage-Related Securities *73*
Part 4. Real Estate Investment Performance *115*
Part 5. Portfolio Management and Real Estate *198*
Part 6. Inflation and Real Estate *250*
Part 7. Finance Theory and Real Estate *277*
Part 8. Real Estate Decision Models *330*
Part 9. Real Estate Derivative Markets *373*

Contents

Note: For author's current affiliations, please see page 405.

Preface   *ix*

Part 1. Introduction   *1*

1. **The Theory and Evidence on Real Estate Financial Decisions: A Review of the Issues**   *1*
   Austin J. Jaffee and C.F. Sirmans

2. **Real Estate: The Whole Story**   *19*
   Paul M. Firstenberg, Stephen A. Ross, and Randall C. Zisler

Part 2. Mortgages   *38*

3. **Mortgage Choice**   *38*
   James R. Follain

4. **Adjustable-Rate and Fixed-Rate Mortgage Choice: A Logit Analysis**   *52*
   Michael Tucker

5. **The Value of Mortgage Assumptions: An Empirical Test**   *62*
   Mark A. Sunderman, Roger E. Cannaday, and Peter F. Colwell

Part 3. Mortgage-Related Securities   *73*

6. **Valuation of GNMA Mortgage-Backed Securities**   *73*
   Kenneth B. Dunn and John J. McConnell

7. **Prepayments on Fixed-Rate Mortgage-Backed Securities**   *90*
   Scott F. Richard and Richard Roll

8. **Duration Estimates on Mortgage-Backed Securities**   *107*
   Paul DeRosa, Laurie Goodman, and Mike Zazzarino

Part 4. Real Estate Investment Performance   *115*

9. Toward Indices of Real Estate Value and Return   *115*
James W. Hoag

10. The Historical Perspective of Real Estate Returns   *127*
G. Stacey Sirmans and C. F. Sirmans

11. What Does the Stock Market Tell Us About Real Estate Returns?   *141*
Joseph Gyourko and Donald B. Keim

12. Transactions-Driven Commercial Real Estate Returns: The Panacea to Asset Allocation Models?   *161*
R. Brian Webb, Mike Miles, and David Guilkey

13. Some Additional Evidence on the Performance of Commingled Real Estate Investment Funds: 1972-1991   *184*
W. B. Brueggeman, A. H. Chen, and T. G. Thibodeau

Part 5. Portfolio Management and Real Estate   *198*

14. Diversification Works in Real Estate, Too   *198*
Terry V. Grissom, James L. Kuhle, and Carl H. Walther

15. Institutional Portfolios: Diversification through Farmland Investment   *207*
David A. Lins, Bruce J. Sherrick, and Aravind Venigalla

16. Real Estate Portfolio Diversification Using Economic Diversification   *224*
Glenn R. Mueller and Barry A. Ziering

17. A Look at Real Estate Duration   *236*
David J. Hartzell, David G. Shulman, Terence C. Langetieg, and Martin L. Liebowitz

Part 6. Inflation and Real Estate   *250*

18. Real Estate Returns and Inflation   *250*
David Hartzell, John S. Hekman, and Mike E. Miles

19. The Inflation-Hedging Effectiveness of Real Estate   *266*
Jack H. Rubens, Michael T. Bond, and James R. Webb

Part 7. Finance Theory and Real Estate   *277*

20. Capital Asset Pricing and Real Estate Valuation   *277*
Dennis W. Draper and M. Chapman Findlay

21. Public Information and Abnormal Returns in Real Estate Investment *303*
    George W. Gau

22. Capital Structure and the Cost of Capital for Untaxed Firms: The Case of REITs *316*
    Brian A. Maris and Fayez A. Elayan

Part 8. Real Estate Decision Models *330*

23. Integrating Research on Markets for Space and Capital *330*
    Jeffrey D. Fisher

24. The Markets for Real Estate Assets and Space: A Conceptual Framework *343*
    Denise DiPasquale and William C. Wheaton

25. Modeling the Corporate Real Estate Decision *355*
    Mike Miles, John Pringle, and Brian Webb

Part 9. Real Estate Derivative Markets *373*

26. Mortgage-Backed Futures and Options *373*
    David C. Ling

27. Index-Based Futures and Options Markets in Real Estate *388*
    Karl E. Case, Jr., Robert J. Shiller, and Allan N. Weiss

    Index of Authors *401*

    Index of Terms *402*

    List of Authors *405*

Preface

In the last two decades, modern finance theory has been applied to the various real estate topics. The transmission of theory to real-world practice has flourished. This book attempts to provide students with a synthesis of financial theory and its application in a variety of real estate topics. The text contains 27 readings of historical interest and state-of-the-art studies. Topics include mortgages, mortgage-related securities, real estate investment performance, real estate portfolio management, inflation hedging, and real estate decision models.

The text is designed for use by upper-division undergraduate students, by graduate students, and as a source for doctoral courses. The collection of readings addresses the application of finance theory to real estate. This book is ideal for use with either undergraduate or graduate real estate seminar courses. This text is also designed to complement a standard textbook presentation of real estate finance and investment.

We wish to thank the authors and publishers who have given permission for their works to be reprinted. We are grateful to the staff of Prentice Hall for their assistance in the publication process.

John B. Major

Fung-Shine Pan

Part 1. Introduction

1 The Theory and Evidence on Real Estate Financial Decisions: A Review of the Issues

Austin J. Jaffe and C. F. Sirmans

There has developed a growing body of literature, both theoretically and empirically based, on real estate financial decisions. Despite these advances, there are a number of important issues that remain unanswered. The purpose of this paper is to provide a review and analysis of where research on real estate financial decisions has been, where it stands today, and where it is likely to be headed in the future. Some of the unresolved issues in real estate investment analysis are also discussed. The hope is that this review will provide the stimulus for solving some of these complex issues.

INTRODUCTION

Despite a growing academic literature, both theoretically and empirically grounded, as well as new interest in real estate as an investment vehicle by a vast array of institutional investors, a number of important issues exist and numerous questions remain unanswered about real estate investment theory and the evidence of real estate investment experience and investor behavior. This topic has concerned the authors previously[1] but recent developments in the field, motivated by scholars and practitioners alike suggest a reevaluation and new look at several important issues.

The real estate investment literature has expanded rapidly in the last twenty years.[2] Since the publication of the seminal work by Wendt and Wong in 1965,[3] the use of financial models for investment valuation has become widespread.[4] Academic and practicing authors have provided considerable insights over the years in an area of interest to numerous types of readers. Real estate as an investment continues to enjoy a wide following and in recent years, this interest has spread from equity investors in small apartment projects to a new generation of syndicators to pension fund managers seeking an outlet for investment funds. In the last few years, real estate has become a serious interest for the institutional real estate community.[5] Finally, numerous journals have come into existence as further indications of the development of real estate as a discipline and real estate research as a growth industry.[6]

From *AREUEA Journal*, Vol. 12, No. 3, 1984.

The purpose of this paper is to provide a review and analysis of where real estate research has been, where the field stands today, and where it seems likely to be headed in the future. In addition, we provide a list of important but "unresolved issues" in the area of real estate investment analysis. While we lay claim that these issues are pressing, we do not mean to claim that this list is all-inclusive. The hope is that this survey will place these concerns into focus among the professional and academic groups and provide some additional impetus for solving some of the complex issues facing the real estate communities. This attempt to introduce and highlight these issues hopefully will provide some insights into answers that have not been provided to date.

WHERE WE HAVE BEEN

The history of real estate investment analysis as a formal discipline is a relatively short one. Although investment analysis dates back to the establishment of private property in land, it was generally not recognized as a formal body of knowledge until relatively recently with the development of several types of real estate professional institutions at the end of the 19th and the beginning of the 20th centuries.[7] In the history of the development of real estate trade associations, investment analysis did not appear to have had a strong political contingent among real estate practitioners for some time. It was not until the 1950s that real estate counselors established their own association called the Society of Real Estate Counselors.[8] It is also interesting to note that the demand for real estate research also began during this period.[9]

During the 1930s, preoccupation with affordability, tax burdens and problems with housing finance prevailed among real estate practitioners and therefore, researchers. In addition, this was the period of new governmental institutions of a magnitude unforeseen prior to that time. Organizations that would fundamentally shape governmental policy in housing included the Federal Reserve Bank System (originally created in 1913), Federal Home Loan Bank System (1932), Home Owners Loan Corporation (1933), Federal Housing Administration (1934), Federal National Mortgage Association (1938), and others.[10] Real estate investment as an area of study necessarily took a back seat to the substantial changes that were taking place within the financial system.

Indeed, real estate valuation thought in the 1930s concentrated on the estimation of market values for appraisal purposes. Classic works were produced, several of which continue to be regarded as the conceptual foundations for modern practice.[11] But the necessary focus and perspective of market valuation procedures and theoretical relationships neglected real estate investment as an area of formal interest. In effect, appraisal was an art; investing was common sense.

Even in the post-WWII period, investing continued to be an ad hoc procedure. A well-cited article in *The Appraisal Journal* in 1945 entitled "Why Buy Real Estate?" failed to provide any assistance for the serious investor.[12] Few other articles dealt with investment issues in the real estate literature.

During the 1950s and early 1960s, more consideration was paid to real estate as an investment.[13] Although all of the studies lacked methodological grounding, this literature represents the beginning of the professional real estate investment literature. By 1964, one author, after completing what is likely to be a similar survey of the then existing literature on real estate as an investment, concluded that a general theory of real estate investment was virtually absent and that the only conclusions available from real estate texts about "real estate as an investment" were that land was indestructible and improvements suffer from physical and functional obsolescence.[14]

The development of mortgage-equity capitalization for use in market value appraising dramatically affected real estate valuation. The "Ellwood Revolution" changed the nature of real estate analysis.[15] In addition, it is likely that mortgage-equity capitalization beginning in the late 1950s and extending into the 1970s provided a solid foundation for financial analysis for investment purposes, even though it can be amply argued that Ellwood capitalization is not very well suited to investment applications.[16] The fact remains that the Ellwood algorithm is a specialized discounted cash flow model,[17] a model that the next generation of students and practitioners would heartily endorse and simultaneously, reject the Ellwood model as "obsolete," "outdated," or simply, "incorrect."

It can be argued that 1) by the late 1960s, the field of real estate investment analysis was ready for a new methodology, 2) the equity valuation model used in the Wendt and Wong study was an excellent choice for the forthcoming normative real estate investment literature, (although the main thrust of the 1965 study was to empirically compare returns from common stock with real estate), and 3) the introduction of this model and the subsequent appearance of the model in a widely read text built the foundation for modern real estate investment analysis.[18] In many ways, the publication of the Wendt and Wong study (as well as the study by Ricks[19]) can be viewed as articles that appeared "in the right place at the right time." The literature was ready for applications of well-established capital budgeting techniques. Mortgage-equity capitalization had gained a fair amount of acceptance in the appraising literature, as well as in practice, and since the approaches were found to be similar, an added degree of respectability was given to the "new" financial applications. In any case, these articles fundamentally changed real estate investment analysis in direction alone, if not in interest, rigor, or method.

The subsequent years witnessed an explosion of interesting real estate analysis "by the numbers." By the mid-1970s, real estate computerization had become the latest development.[20] Quantitative analysis of real estate projects was "in"; qualitative real estate studies were "out". It is interesting that the development of the microcomputer seems to have begun this process once again in the past few years. It seems as if investors believe that computerized real estate investment analysis was discovered when microcomputers were invented and marketed during the early 1980s!

But perhaps the most dominant theme in the area of real estate investing since World War II is the ex ante expectations of abnormally high returns associated with real estate investing, even across relatively lengthy time periods such as twenty years. While the ex post results in this area are less than conclusive, the consensus seems to be that risk-adjusted returns in real estate *have* been superior to the returns to other assets, despite deeply rooted neoclassical hypotheses to the contrary in the areas of investor pricing behavior and the appeal to the theory of rational expectations in application to market participants.[21] One hypothesis is that the federal tax subsidies and unexpected growth in housing support programs account for the continued high returns to real estate during this period. These institutional developments, coupled with the economic growth over the past thirty years, in a society with below-market energy costs for homeownership and a tax structure that strongly discriminates against renters in favor of investors and especially, owner-occupied "investors," may help explain the real estate investment frenzy in this country since the late 1940s until, at least, the most recent period.[22]

SOME IMPORTANT AND LARGELY UNRESOLVED ISSUES IN REAL ESTATE INVESTMENT ANALYSIS

In this section, we highlight some of the major and largely unresolved issues, in our opinion, surrounding real estate financial decision making. While we are not suggesting that these are the only unresolved matters, it appears to us that these are major topic areas that future researchers must examine to fully understand the decisions facing the participants in the real estate market.

Real Estate as an Investment. Perhaps the most sought-after answer in the entire area of real estate financial analysis is the one that tells the investor whether he/she can expect to receive abnormally high returns by investing in real estate. Many investors act as if real estate outperforms other vehicles and as such provides opportunities for superior investment rates of return.

Despite considerable efforts to the contrary, there is not conclusive evidence about the overall performance of real estate as an investment relative to common stocks, corporate bonds, or other portfolio asset choices. However, there is developing a new empirical literature that explicitly has attempted to provide answers to these queries.[23]

For example, recent studies of real estate as a portfolio asset indicate the likelihood of market inefficiencies in pricing high quality real estate assets.[24] At least, pension fund managers act as if such inefficiencies exist, even in the absence of market evidence. Other studies, however, found that the rate of return to holding land over the long term was no higher than holding long-term corporate bonds.[25] Other empirical work typically falls somewhere in between.[26]

Of course, another way of evaluating performance is to investigate whether markets price risk correctly. Indeed, this is really the same issue and often it is easier to estimate risk premiums than to measure hypothetical returns. The relationship between risk and return is a theoretical one and subject to empirical verification. A number of questions remain unanswered about the relationship in real estate markets between risk and return as posited in modern capital market theory. For real estate markets with considerable transaction and information costs, it is certainly possible, if not likely, that the capital market line would be more roughly approximated by market behavior in real estate than in securities.

Investor Objectives. One of the most debated topics in the business literature is the issue of what is the objective of the investor.[27] One of the more intuitive notions advocated by many real estate analysts is that investors should adopt several different goals based upon personal preferences and objectives. Another version of this view is that the appropriate goal of a real estate investor is determined by the characteristics of each individual investor.

We have argued that the basic objective, in the absence of peculiar and special requirements on the part of the investor, "should" be wealth maximization of the equity position rather than any of the competing objectives.[28] If the investor adopts this objective, the net present value decision rules become valuable tools since maximization of (expected) net present value will ensure wealth maximization. At this point, we contend that wealth maximization is the only logical investment objective when markets are competitive.

In competitive markets, property rights are allocated to those users who bid the most for the rights. Investors bidding for the rights will evaluate opportunities according to preferences, beliefs, information sets and incentives (strengths of beliefs). (It is interesting to note that implicit in this argument is the presumption that valuable property rights will gravitate to the highest bidder since the highest bidder will not purposely bear the opportunity loss of remaining silent.) If the investor seeks to maximize wealth, an array of projects will be produced in the order in which the investor would be expected to benefit.

Since the net present value rule would provide an array of projects identical to those ranked by the investor in terms of wealth maximization preferences, investors who adopt approaches producing inconsistent rankings will, by definition, choose an array of projects at a lower level of incremental wealth. Therefore, those investors who bid for property rights based upon a wealth maximization strategy, will, over time, force others to do so as well, as long as market competition exists. Failure to adopt this objective by competing investors implies the existence of structural market inefficiencies, asymmetric information sources (a different type of market failure), or a reduction in the number of market participants through an arbitrage process.

However, there remains considerable doubt about the degree of market efficiency in many real estate markets. Empirical studies of market efficiency are limited, but some effort in this direction is being made.[29] Researchers are plagued by poor data sources, a lack of generality of market behavior, and an incomplete theoretical basis about the operation and institutions of real property markets. Until the issue of market efficiency can be addressed more adequately, the extent to which wealth maximization can be prescriptively advocated remains a matter of conjecture.

In addition, it is certain that we know very little about the characteristics of investors who own property. There is a general presumption about clienteles in various segments of the real estate market. One of the few studies that has addressed this problem identified the characteristics of individuals holding vacant urban land.[30] The study found that the holders of vacant land "were primarily residents of the city where the land is located, were very likely to be in professions directly or indirectly related to real estate, were quite likely to have high stable income, high net worth and were for larger parcels (≤ 10 acres) likely to be in the prime working years (36-55)."[31]

Another issue associated with investor objectives is the optimal form of business organization for holding real estate investments.[32] Each of the various forms (e.g., proprietorships, general and limited partnerships, corporations, REITs and others) are used in the real estate market.[33] Each of these also have varying degrees of liability, tax considerations, ease of disposition and other parameters for consideration. It is likely that some clientele effects are associated with each form and numerous questions remain. For example, how does the market decide which are the preferable forms of organization? Does one form dominate? Are there favorites for certain types of property? Or does the value of the asset vary with the set of ownership forms available? How are the objectives of investors constrained by the regulations permitting and prohibiting certain business organizations? These and similar questions remain subjects for further research and investigation.

Market Analysis. Many investors, developers and appraisers pay traditional lip service to the importance of market analysis. Many reports, for example, contain considerable amounts of data, statistics, exhibits and tables with little attention paid to the analysis of economic behavior.[34] Given current practice, some might argue that market analysis has little essential value in decision making except as window dressing for interested readers. The question yet to be resolved is if market analysis is as essential as nearly every text and monograph on the subject presumes, why has it been neglected in the academic investment literature?[35]

It is not certain that we can provide a satisfactory answer to this question. However, the danger in adopting this position is apparent. The goal of market analysis is to identify and thus, reduce the risk associated with choosing projects in an uncertain environment. A framework can be provided to permit investors to analyze different types of risk and their impacts on decision making. The difficulty lies in the fact that we are only beginning to understand the linkages between activities in the marketplace and their impact on the riskiness of real estate projects.

Perhaps one reason why market analysis is often discarded or given its nominal place in formal analysis is because we know very little about these behavioral relationships. This does not mean that these relationships are unimportant; on the contrary, our inability to fully understand market analysis suggests that it is one of the most important areas within which we continue to grapple.

It has been said that social science will not be treated as seriously as physical sciences for a long time since the social scientist cannot describe the system in which he/she works. In the case of real estate markets, it is unlikely that we will have an adequate description of the interrelationships of all factors for many years, if ever. As a result, it seems likely that the analysis of the market environment will continue to perplex investors seeking linkages between economic units when making decisions and is likely to remain the primary source of uncertainty for many types of real estate users.

One area that has recently received increased attention has been the examination of the supply and demand factors for different types of real estate. Of particular importance is the price elasticity of demand estimates for real estate services such as rental housing. The price elasticity provides information about the percentage changes in quantity demanded for a given percentage change in rent. This result is obviously important in determining the expected cash flows from an investment.

Another relationship is also important in the market environment. This is the relationship between rent adjustments and vacancy.[36] Standard economic theory suggests that an inventory of empty apartment units (or office or commercial space) is not necessarily idle or wasted. Since real estate is produced at a fairly slow rate, a reserve (inventory) is often held in the event of unexpected demand increases. As a result, both the holders (landlords) and the consumers (tenants) are better off. Although the real estate services per unit may be somewhat higher in price in order to cover the inventory costs, the vacancies permit lower search costs and enable tenants to move without committing themselves to a long lead time.

As a matter of policy, investors could reduce rental costs by building less structures, but that would force tenants to bear more costs by requiring more critical planning with longer lead times. This policy would also prevent tenants from adapting quickly to new situations. This type of analysis of rental/vacancy trade-off suggests that there is an "optimal" level of vacancies and that a portion of the rent paid to the lessee is intended to cover the cost of holding units off the market for inventories.[37]

However, as a practical matter, we know very little about the magnitude of the inventory cost. In addition, we often observe the stock-flow adjustment process in the real estate market is complicated by the production cycle. Before we can understand investment analysis very well, it is necessary to develop better predictive models of industry structure and especially, derive estimates of the important interrelationships.

Much of the standard real estate literature has taken the view that real estate markets are characterized by monopolistic competition. In effect, this means employing economic models based upon some characteristics of monopolies and some characteristics of competition. Unfortunately, this type of economic theory has largely been abandoned and indeed, the use of the standard, competitive model may yield the best predictive results. Further work must be done on empirically testing the various standard economic theories of market structure.

If real estate investment analysis is rapidly growing out of the era where the calculation of accounting entries was facilitated due to new developments in computer technologies, the future will mean substantially different values will be placed on types of analysis within the investment process. In this case, a low value is likely to be placed upon the measurement and accounting of cash flows since nearly all regular investors will have computer access; the higher values will be placed upon estimates above net operating income rather than below it. Thus market analysis is likely to become critical in the years ahead.

Legal Environment. To some investors, real estate investment analysis can be effectively described as an analysis of the legal environment. While this may be partially true, especially at some states of the investment decision, there exists a general lack of understanding of the impact of the legal environment on values and decisions.

In recent years, empirical work has begun to reveal the effects of legal institutions on property values.[38] This growing list of studies is subject to a host of methodological problems but serves as a first step toward a firm understanding of the linkage between legal rules, social entitlements and property values. Prior to this type of work, the impact of the legal environment on real estate decision makers and users was virtually unknown.

Another type of analysis in this area involves the differing perspective of lawyers who practice law in the area of real estate (i.e., attorneys who are available on a fee basis to employ the legal institutions for the betterment of their clients) and analysts who regard and view the law as a set of constraints (i.e., investors who view the law as limiting as well as protecting and choose to employ legal counsel to ensure that all of the constraints are satisfied). This difference in perspective can account for the difference in attitude toward legal institutions.

For example, investors may choose a passive attitude toward legal rules. In effect, the investor presumes the law is exogenous to the decision-making process and views the law as a limit to the domain of action. On the other hand, an active perspective tends to be favored by attorneys who view legal decisions as endogenous to investing activity as any other investment decision. In these cases, choices such as the quality of legal estate, the types of covenants in leases, and the expected land use controls are explicit decision variables. If so, there are likely to be models that can be developed to analytically evaluate legal rules and institutions.

In recent years, there has been considerable research in this area, especially employing what has become known as the property rights paradigm.[39] This approach, evolving out of institutional economics, has permitted the analysis of institutions in numerous areas. In the area of real estate investing, the promise is there for considerably new insights. It is expected that the future will provide substantial benefits.

Financing Environment. Most real estate investments are financed with debt and equity. Both sources are available at some cost to the investor. Since there is reason to believe that the costs will vary according to market conditions, investor, and/or investment riskiness, and other factors, an important question is how much of each type of investment should be used in financing the investment. In other words, how should the investor substitute between debt and equity as the relative price of each source changes? Or, how does the relative price change over time with different financing methods and techniques?

This area is one that has attracted considerable interest in finance for nearly fifty years.[40] The determination of the optimal capital structure is one of the most fundamental questions in the theory of the firm. Yet, despite a wealth of research, theoretically, little is really known about the relevance of financing choice. Empirically, we probably know even less.

In the area of real estate financing, it becomes an even tougher battle. Theory is weakened by long-term institutions that preclude elegant model development. For example, the use of the mortgage constant as a cost of borrowing is well ingrained in real estate, probably because nearly all long-term debt is self amortizing. It remains unknown if the valuation of financing can be separated from the valuation of the assets.

Under some conditions, it is possible to increase investor wealth by choosing types of financing that produce gains due to financial leverage. As in the traditional view, investors should thereby borrow as much as possible in order to maximize the gains from leverage.

The problem with this position is that increasing the proportion of debt relative to equity also increases financial risk. The financial risk is likely to be observed by the lender and priced prior to loan origination. If so, the borrower bears the full cost of the financial risk. Lenders would view their positions as riskier and would expect the cost to be higher to the borrower than before the additional risk was assumed. In general, we would expect the market to assess a higher level of risk when a financing gain is anticipated, given a strong relationship between risk and return.

If financial markets assess risk very well, it is more reasonable to expect that investors would not be better off by using debt finance. Riskier investments would be allocated with more costly debt instruments; safer investments would be able to be financed with cheaper sources of funds. However, the important point is that in such a world, the means of financing would not matter since it would not affect the investor's wealth position.

The understanding of capital structure theory can, in an oversimplified sense, be viewed as an analysis of the efficiency of the debt and equity markets for finance. As with other issues of this type, we simply do not know how efficient these markets are. Empirical work related to this topic is likely to provide evidence here as well.[41]

To complicate the financing decision further is the multitude of financing methods and techniques from which the investor must choose. Casual empirical evidence suggests that the variety of methods is large and that there does not exist an "optimal" method. There appears to be a unique method for each project, but how does the market make the selection? Certainly the behavior of lenders and borrowers must be understood if we are to develop better models of investment decision making.

Finally, the issue of separation of financing and investing remains open to debate.[42] Almost all current models of investor behavior act as if the two decisions are made jointly. Conceptually, however, there are numerous problems with this approach.[43]

Taxation Environment. Many people are of the opinion that tax planning generally forms the entire basis of real estate investment decision making. The high visibility of items such as depreciation method selection, tax shelter valuation, and the preferential treatment of capital gains income suggests that the analysis of taxation *is* the core of investment analysis. However, while taxes are important, they remain only one aspect of the investment decision.

Furthermore, despite considerable efforts and insights, tax effects remain perplexing. Since many of these effects are implicit, their impacts tend to be hidden. The economist seeking to identify tax-included behavior is forced to infer behavior in the absence of readily available data.

In order to understand the influence of taxes on the expected cash flow from an investment and therefore, on the value of equity, the measurement of tax liability is required. In an accounting sense, the "analysis" of taxes enables the investor to make better choices given that the specification of tax burdens are fully described.

However, if the tax effects are perfectly anticipated by participants in the market, the value of equity would completely reflect these expectations and lead the analyst to conclude, quite correctly, that after-tax returns fully reflect the tax effects. In some cases, this would mean that the attraction of real estate as a tax shelter would be illusory, since the tax effect would be priced out by the market. For this investor, in effect, it would mean that the investor has paid for the opportunity to shelter his/her taxes.

What is generally unknown about real estate markets is *how* tax effects are capitalized into market prices. While we can say that prices reflect the tax effects, we do not know exactly how this is achieved. For example, if the market value is set by investors in a 50% tax bracket, would an investor in a 40% bracket be worse off? In effect, what we would really like to know is the tax rates at which market values would be maximized.

Another example is the hypothesis that real estate investments are differentially valued according to their capital gains tax treatment. For some investors, the possibility of preferential treatment of capital gains offers incentives to acquire assets with likely capital gains. Since the tax treatment of capital gains varies with income level, the value of the expected capital gains will vary among taxpayers. But who are these taxpayers? How do investor characteristics change with different types of properties?

These questions are important to the equity investor. One line of research in this area has developed the idea of "clientele effects".[44] This concept suggests that investments are priced by particular investors for whom the benefits are more valuable. But how do these clienteles develop? What characteristics distinguish various groups from each other? What types of investments are worth more to investors in various tax brackets? We are only beginning to understand these and other questions.

In recent years, we have seen a radical shift in tax policy. For example, the 1981 tax act (ERTA) sharply reduced the uncertainty associated with tax decisions by specifying the recovery period (useful life) and by limiting the depreciation methods available for investors. We still don't have, however, the answer to the impact of taxes on investor behavior. For example, do the tax effects have an influence on the turnover of real estate investments? Also, how important is the relative impact of a change in tax policy on real estate versus other depreciable assets?

From a valuation perspective, there are three major claims on the net income from an investment: the claims of the debt holder, the governmental tax authority, and the equity investor. The latter represents the residual claim and therefore, bears the most risk associated with variability of the income stream. The question that arises is how can these claims be divided such that they have the greatest impact on total value? For example, suppose we could devise a form of ownership, such as syndication, such that we could reduce the claim that government has on the cash flows. If we were the only investors who could employ this device and if the market price were determined by investors employing other ownership forms with greater government claims, we could earn excess profits since we could buy properties at lower equity prices. However, if other investors learned of the device, competition might also drive up market values.[45]

Role of Specialized Actors. In the daily operations of real estate markets, there are several actors who assume highly specialized roles. In many other markets, the number and specialized nature of the participants is not nearly as great. The interesting aspect of these observations is to attempt to explain why real estate markets employ such specialized participants.

Traditionally, it has generally been argued that specialized participants are found in response to the complex needs of clients. These clients have chosen to deal in a market with complex assets, extensive legal entitlements, dynamic financing and taxation institutions, and considerable uncertainty about future returns. As a result, it has been argued that specialized entrepreneurs offer risk reduction on a fee basis.

Another argument is that it may be cheaper to contractually negotiate with specialists rather than, as an investor, bear the full cost of a wide range of activities. While the issue of which services to contract externally and which to internalize is an important and difficult question to answer in practice, it also serves as the fundamental view of the relationship between individual and specialists, specialists and firms, and firms and firms.[46]

Finally, in a world where it is costly to obtain information about market prices and future economic parameters, specialized agents may be viewed as services to provide superior information. In the case of real estate appraisers, these individuals are more likely to be valued for their information sources than for their technical analysis. In the case of attorneys, employed as a part of the real estate transaction, they are likely to be regarded as service units, who are contractually employed to reduce legal risks prior, during and after ownership. In the case of property managers, their managerial skills may be dominated by their experience and knowledge of maintenance and building systems and thus, reduce the uncertainty associated with business risk arising from the physical operation of the improvements. Finally, real estate brokers are likely to be similarly valued based upon their knowledge of local market conditions, familiarity with market conventions, and information about financing sources, title assurance methods and availability of housing over time. It is the reduction in information costs that makes these participants "worth" their fees.

However, what is unknown is how effectively these participants are able to price their fees and what impact governmental regulation has on the production of services in housing and investment markets. These are difficult questions to answer, but it is hoped that research in the next few years will provide some answers.

Future Developments. Presently, real estate investment analysis has been confronted with important technological changes resulting from developments in computerization and the accompanying reduction of information costs in data processing. This has had an important impact on the tools available for analysis as well as the methods used by real estate practitioners.[47]

In the not so distant past, the methodological debate in real estate investment analysis centered on the type of investment model to be used. One of the parameters of the debate was the ease and complexity of operational usage. It seemed one of the points upon which a defense of the traditional methods was based was the disadvantages associated with the complex calculations required using the newer models. In effect, discounted cash flow models, as well as Monte Carlo simulations, were impressive "state-of-the-art" methods but unless the analyst and perhaps more importantly, the client, were capable of deriving results from these models (i.e., had access to hardware and decision manuals for interpretation), these models were placed on the shelf. Real estate investment modeling was regarded as a growing field with practitioners trying to get out fancy algorithms from useful techniques.

However, the emergence of the microcomputer industry has changed the rules of the game. Such algorithms can now be put to the test; users can accept or reject alternative approaches based upon their appropriateness in making actual decisions. Methods including linear and mathematical programming, decision trees and simulation are now available for almost any professional investor. It is more likely that the binding constraint is technical education rather than technical access.

Another major development is the emergence of national data sources for real estate. Accompanied by changes in the financial environment stemming from the federal deregulation legislation in 1980 and 1982, the real estate investment community finds itself in the midst of fundamental institutional changes. For example, national real estate firms are taking shape after a decade of franchising and networking.[48] The so-called "third party" real estate brokerages are developing, with some opposition from traditional real estate institutions such as the National Association of Realtors, but appear to have support in several states.[49] The financial services industry has exploded with new opportunities such that the nature of real estate brokerage, finance, insurance, legal services and investment counseling are markedly different today than a few short years ago. These developments point to a substantially altered set of firms involved with real estate in the future.

From the point of view of real estate research, these changes are likely to result in major developments. Corporate involvement in real estate analysis and acquisitions, on a systematic basis, is likely to bring forth the resources for massive data collection and acquisition. Corporate interest can be seen by observing the large and growing membership in the National Association of Corporate Real Estate Executives and other groups.

For the first time, national data sources are being developed by these firms and organizations. In the future, real estate researchers will have access to improved data sources, including micro data on property characteristics, financing, values and locational attributes. By implication, this will lead to empirical verification of return experience, risk exposure and the ex post usefulness of real estate as a portfolio asset.

In fact, the expectation is that real estate research is likely to resemble a major portion of the security market research of the past generation during the next few years, but for different reasons. In the former case, new methodologies enabled researchers to test important theoretical hypotheses about asset pricing and portfolio construction. In the case of real estate, new data sources will permit researchers to repeat the same tests applied to corporate securities for the first time as tests of more general propositions about inter-market efficient pricing as well as real estate mythology as superior investment assets.

Finally, these changes are certain to alter society's view of real property. While land and improvements may retain its importance in our society, the nature of the institutions affecting real estate may be dramatically changed. For example, increases in operational efficiency resulting from improved data sources and more widely and fully developed investment markets may reduce the incentive for special financing and tax treatment of investments in land. At the same time, local governments are likely to increase their role in deciding what may or may not be done with land held by private owners. In the end, the environment for real estate investing in the future may be substantially different than in the past.

Changing concepts of property is not a new development.[50] Such recognitions may best be viewed as the latest in a long line of modifications in response to changes in society's institutions. Real estate retains its primacy in our culture. What has changed are the methods in which property in land is distributed and utilized.

WHERE WE ARE HEADED

Despite the noted contributions to the field in recent years, it is unlikely that all of the real estate investment issues will be solved in the near future. At this point, it is important to identify some critical issues that are fundamental cornerstones to future agendas for real estate investment research.

A list of the most important characteristics most likely would include both the normative and descriptive relationships between risk and return. This suggests that future researchers may seek a better understanding of risk analysis and measurement. New developments in risk measurement such as the option pricing theory and the arbitrage pricing model may be the next models on the real estate researcher's agenda. The interest in the capital asset pricing model and real estate portfolio construction for institutional investors is now taken quite seriously in practice. Not surprisingly, research in these areas has begun to blossom.

Another important area for the future is likely to be in the area of financial markets. For example, the use of joint ventures as a form of financing suggests that the relationship between organizational form and the theory of finance is a gray area. It is difficult, given the current state of knowledge, to value joint ventures such as pension funds or developers as they enter into these contractual arrangements with traditional lenders.

The broadening of the mortgage market in the deregulatory environment of the 1980s has brought a plethora of new financing methods and instruments. The key to understanding these approaches seems to rest with valuing the option claims in the covenants of the mortgage or other financing instrument. The use of option pricing theory has begun to be used to understand the new instruments. It is not an understatement that these instruments have dramatically affected all mortgage markets during the last several years.

In addition, a new market has grown up, almost overnight, in the area of mortgage-backed securities. Once regarded as a specialized type of Ginnie Mae instrument, today, securities that use real property as collateral are changing the methods and ways in which property is financed. The mortgage brokerage business has benefited tremendously from these developments, and most observers agree that consumers have shared and will continue to share in the gains.

Finally, government, especially at the state and local levels, continues to take an active role in the attenuation of property rights. As implied earlier in the paper, changes in land use controls are likely to continue. Investors are likely to regard the governmental impact as an increasingly important consideration in any analysis.

In the future, solutions to these and other problems may come from the adaptation of theoretical models in finance, economics, planning and other disciplines. This has generally been a fruitful route for researchers and other investigators to take in the past. It also seems likely that in the future, the keys to better understanding will come from improved model construction, superior data sources, and a greater number of resources devoted to basic and applied research at colleges and universities throughout the United States, Canada and the rest of the world.

CONCLUSIONS

Real estate investment analysis has progressed in the last two decades. What was once a relatively undeveloped, ad hoc process has moved toward an economic science and a complex practice. The valuation of real property remains a fundamental and essential aspect of our society; the new methods and findings seek more accurate and more responsible answers to valuation questions.

At the same time, investors in other markets often look toward real estate for comparative purposes and in search of new investment opportunities. Similarly, real estate investors frequently look toward national securities markets for comparisons. It is unfortunate that many investors are myopic and tend to think that the best opportunities are always in one market: the one they are trading in. It is likely that some of the issues raised in this review will take several attempts to address over the next several years. Some are likely to evade analysis, despite considerable interest and expertise on the parts of investigators and practitioners. Others are hopefully in the process of being answered as this goes to press. In the end, one can expect a new set of questions and proposed new answers as we learn more about market behavior and economic institutions.

NOTES

1. See Jaffe and Sirmans [39, pp. 505-515].

2. For a detailed review of the modern history of real estate investment analysis, see Jaffe and Sirmans [39, pp. 44-65].

3. See Wendt and Wong [86].

4. See also Ricks [63].

5. See, for example, Ellis [22]; Nelson [57]; Updegrave [81]; and Downs [20].

6. For a recent critique and history of real estate as a field of research, see Webb [82].

7. For a general history of the development of the real estate industry in the United States, including interesting, personal accounts of individual contributions as well as a close and sympathetic look at the growth of real estate institutions, see Davies [16].

This definitive historical study reports, for example, the first trade association was founded in Baltimore in 1858 (p. 26), the first real estate firm was founded in Atlanta in 1865 (p. 32), the first real estate boards can be traced to the 1860s in Cleveland and San Jose (p. 32), the first title insurance company in New York in 1883 (p. 36), and in 1892, the "first national voice of real estate" was implemented with the forming of the National Real Estate Association (p. 43).

The Association lasted only until 1894, but served as the forerunner for the National Association of Real Estate Exchanges founded in 1908 (p. 59). In 1916, the name was changed to the National Association of Real Estate Boards, and subsequently changed again, in the 1970s, to the National Association of Realtors. With the development of the automobile, Davies reports dramatic effects on city structure and an increased demand for city planning, such that by 1913, about twenty American cities had established planning commissions (p. 74). In addition, the expanding real estate profession became concerned with urban housing problems (p. 76), zoning (p. 78), property taxation (p. 80), uniform state property laws (p. 81), and other issues.

Also, Davies reports the first real estate courses were offered at the West Side YMCA in New York City in 1904, followed by university courses at the University of Pennsylvania and New York University in 1905, the University of Pittsburgh in 1908, [Case] Western Reserve University in 1913, and the University of Wisconsin and the University of Washington in 1915 (pp. 121-22).

8. The modern name is now the American Society of Real Estate Counselors.

9. Davies [16] cites 1909 as the date that marks the formal beginning of real estate research (p. 124). It is interesting that the impetus for research was in the investment area:

[the] need to determine real estate value and if possible get at the principles that govern value was the first spur to...action. The great hope at this time was that a sufficiently wide body of facts could be gathered on the behavior of real estate values to make it possible not only to appraise with scientific accuracy but also to forecast future values with a sureness that would be gratifying to real estate investors. (pp. 124-25)

Davies also notes that Richard T. Ely's founding of the Institute for Research in Land Economics and Public Utilities at the University of Wisconsin established the first research organization devoted to real estate economics (p. 126), by 1926, and the first real estate professorship was established at the University of Michigan (p. 154). Also Ernest M. Fisher began the process of data collection and reporting of economic activity on a national basis for the first time in the 1920s.

10. A review of the history of these agencies is given in Bloom, Weimer and Fisher [6, pp. 290-317].

11. A survey of the classic valuation books is likely to include Hurd [36]; Zangerle [89]; Pollock and Scholz [60]; Babcock [3]; Bonbright [7]; Wendt [84]; Ratcliff [61]; Kinnard [47]; Wendt [85].

12. See Bedford [5].

13. See Landauer [48]; Case [8]; Recht and Loewenstein [62]; Graham [30]. See also Grebler [31]; Smith [79]; and Hayes and Harlan [33].

14. See Ricks [65].

15. For a complete listing of the Ellwood literature, see Jaffe and Sirmans [39, pp. 49-51].

16. For example, one argument used against it is that taxes are explicitly ignored. However, see Fisher [28] and Sirmans and Newsome [75].

17. See Wendt [83] and Dasso [15].

18. See Jaffe and Sirmans [39, pp. 51-52].

19. See Ricks [63].

20. Several of the articles are listed in Jaffe and Sirmans [39, pp. 53-54].

21. For a somewhat outdated analytical survey, see Roulac [70].

22. This, of course, recognizes that there have been cycles in the real estate investment business as well.

23. The standard reference is Roulac [70].

24. See, for example, Miles and McCue [50].

25. See Kau and Sirmans [42, 44].

26. See Achtenhagen [1] and also Ricks [64].

27. This question manifests itself in several different forms. For example, in neoclassical economics, the goal of the firm is profit maximization. The goal of the individual is utility maximization. With market im-

perfections such as agency costs, conflicts are likely to arise. See Jensen and Meckling [41] and also the excellent survey of this literature by Barnea, Haugen and Senbet [4].

28. The reason for investing in real estate often includes arguments such as the procurement of a positive cash flow, tax shelters, inflation hedge possibilities, and numerous others.

29. See Hoag [35] and Gau [29]. It should be noted that the concept of an efficient market is synonymous with a competitive market.

30. See Witte and Bachman [88].

31. See Witte and Bachman [88, p. 556].

32. See Corley and Black [12] for a discussion of these characteristics for each form.

33. Recent tax law changes have even made the Subchapter S corporation a potentially viable option.

34. See Eldred and Zerbst [21].

35. The introduction of "space" into standard economic models by urban and regional economists may be viewed as market analysis.

36. See Eubank and Sirmans [24].

37. For a recent study of the office building market in sixteen cities over the 1960-75 time period, see Shilling, Sirmans and Corgel [72].

38. See, for example, Ridker and Henning [66]; Nelson [58]; Maser, Riker and Rosett [49]; Ihlanfeldt and Jackson [37]; Rosen [68]; Correll, Lillydahl and Singell [13]; Hellman and Naroff [34]; and others.

39. The seminal work is generally cited as Coase [11]; Demsetz [18, 19]; and Alchian and Demsetz [2].

40. See Williams [87]. The modern literature begins with Modigliani and Miller [53, 54]. See also Stiglitz [80]; Hamada [32]; Rubenstein [71]; Kim [45]; Miller [51]; Myers [55]; Jensen and Meckling [41]; DeAngelo and Masulis [17]; Fama [25, 26]; Ross [69]; Modigliani [52]; and others.

41. For example, in the market for single-family homes, several research papers have examined the degree of capitalization of creative financing into home prices. For example, see Sirmans, Smith and Sirmans [78]; Findlay and Fischer [27]; Rosen [67]; Clauretie [9]. We do not know of any literature on the income property market.

42. See Jaffe [38].

43. For a proposed solution, see Myers [56].

44. See Kim, Lewellen and McConnell [46].

45. Casual observation tends to confirm this statement. For example, there has been much written lately that syndications are "paying to much" for properties.

46. See Coase [10].

47. See, for example, the recent survey by Page [59].

48. Legal issues are beginning to arise for national real estate firms. See Epley and Banks [23].

49. For example, see Jaffe and Woolridge [40].

50. See Cribbet [14].

REFERENCES

[1] P. Achtenhagen. An Investor-Based Marketing Plan for Sale of Real Property Investment Securities to Individuals. Unpublished PhD dissertation, Stanford University, 1974.

[2] A. Alchian and H. Demsetz. The Property Rights Paradigm. *Journal of Economic History* 33: 16-27, March 1973.

[3] F.M. Babcock. *The Valuation of Real Estate*. McGraw-Hill, 1932.

[4] A. Barnea, R. A. Haugen, L. W. Senbet. Market Imperfections, Agency Problems, and Capital Structure: A Review. *Financial Management* 10: 7-22, Summer 1981.

[5] E. W. Bedford. Why Buy Real Estate? *The Appraisal Journal* 13: 135-137, April 1945.

[6] G. F. Bloom, A. M. Weimer, J. D. Fisher. *Real Estate,* pp. 290-317. John Wiley and Sons, 8th edition, 1982.

[7] J. C. Bonbright. *The Valuation of Property.* McGraw-Hill, 1937.

[8] F. Case. Comparative Real Estate Investment Experience. *The Appraisal Journal* 28: 337-344, July 1960.

[9] T. M. Clauretie. Creative Financing, Housing Costs and the Consumer Price Index: 1978-1982. Paper presented at the American Real Estate and Urban Economics Association meeting in San Francisco, California, December 1983.

[10] R. H. Coase. The Nature of the Firm. *Economica* 10: 567-590, November 1937.

[11] ———. The Problem of Social Cost. *Journal of Law and Economics* 3: 1-44, October 1960.

[12] R. N. Corley and R. A. Black. *Principles of Business Law.* Prentice-Hall, 8th edition, 1981.

[13] M. R. Correll, J. H. Lillydahl, L. D. Singell. The Effects of Greenbelts on Residential Property Values: Some Findings on the Political Economy of Open Space. *Land Economics* 54: 207-217, May 1978.

[14] J. E. Cribbet. Changing Concepts in the Law of Land Use. *Iowa Law Review* 50: 246-259, Winter 1965.

[15] J. Dasso. From Inwood to Ellwood: Derivation and Analysis of the Mortgage Equity Capitalization Technique. *Assessors Journal* 3: 27-33, April 1968.

[16] P. J. Davies. *Real Estate in American History.* Public Affairs Press, 1958.

[17] H. DeAngelo and R. W. Masulis. Optimal Capital Structure Under Corporate and Personal Taxation. *Journal of Financial Economics* 8: 3-30, March 1980.

[18] H. Demsetz. The Exchange and Enforcement of Property Rights. *Journal of Law and Economics* 7: 11-26. October 1964.

[19] ———. Toward a Theory of Property Rights. *American Economic Review* 57: 347-373, May 1967.

[20] A. Downs. Should Pension Funds Own Real Estate Equities. *National Real Estate Investor:* 26-28, 42, 254, October 1982.

[21] G. W. Eldred and R. H. Zerbst. A Critique of Real Estate Market and Investment Analysis. *The Appraisal Journal* 46: 443-452, July 1978.

[22] C. D. Ellis. On Pension Funds and Real Estate. *Pension World* 56, September, 1981.

[23] D. R. Epley and W. Banks. National Real Estate Firms and Antitrust Avoiding Liability. *Real Estate Law Journal* 12: 243-260, Winter 1984.

[24] A. A. Eubank, Jr. and C. F. Sirmans. The Price Adjustment Mechanism for Rental Housing in the United States. *Quarterly Journal of Economics* 93: 163-168, February 1979.

[25] E. F. Fama. Agency Problems and the Theory of the Firm. *Journal of Political Economy* 88: 288-307, April 1980.

[26] ———. The Effects of a Firm's Investment and Financing Decisions on the Welfare of Its Security Holders. *American Economic Review* 68: 272-284, June 1979.

[27] M. C. Findlay and F. E. Fischer. On Adjusting the Price of 'Creatively Financed' Residential Sales: Cash Equivalency vs. FFVA. *Housing Finance Review* 2: 63-80, January 1983.

[28] J. D. Fisher. Ellwood After Tax New Dimensions. *The Appraisal Journal* 45: 331-342, July 1977.

[29] G. W. Gau. Public Information and 'Abnormal' Returns in Real Estate Investment. Paper presented at the American Real Estate and Urban Economics Association meetings in San Francisco, California, December, 1983. Forthcoming in *AREUEA Journal.*

[30] D. H. Graham, Jr. Owner's Analysis of Yields on Major Real Estate Investments. *The Appraisal Journal* 33: 541-548, October 1965.

[31] L. Grebler. *Experience in Urban Real Estate Investment.* Columbia University Press, 1955.

[32] R. S. Hamada. Portfoilio Analysis, Market Equilibrium, and Corporation Finance. *Journal of Finance* 24: 13-31, March 1969.

[33] S. L. Hayes and L. M. Harlan. Real Estate as a Corporate Investment. *Harvard Business Review* 45: 144-160, July/August 1967.

[34] D. A. Hellman and J. L. Naroff. The Impact of Crime on Urban Residential Property Values. *Urban Studies* 16: 105-112, February 1979.

[35] J. Hoag. Toward Indices of Real Estate Value and Return. *Journal of Finance* 35: 569-580, May 1980.

[36] R. M. Hurd. *Principles of City Land Values*. Real Estate Record Association, 1903.

[37] K. R. Ihlanfeldt and J. D. Jackson. Systematic Assessment Error and Intrajurisdiction Property Tax Capitalization. *Southern Economic Journal* 49: 417-427, October 1982.

[38] A. J. Jaffe. On the Theory of Finance, Equity Models, and Optimal Financing Decisions of Real Property. In *Research in Real Estate*, Vol. 1, pp. 275-303. JAI Press, Inc., 1982.

[39] A. J. Jaffe and C. F. Sirmans. *Real Estate Investment Decision Making*. Prentice-Hall, 1982.

[40] A. J. Jaffe and J. R. Woolridge. Expanding the Products and Services of Financial Institutions: The Case of Third Party Real Estate Brokerages. Working Paper, The Pennsylvania State University, March 1984.

[41] M. C. Jensen and W. H. Meckling. Theory of the Firm: Managerial Behavior, Agency Costs and Ownership Structure. *Journal of Financial Economics* 4: 305-360, November 1976.

[42] J. B. Kau and C. F. Sirmans. Changes in Urban Land Values: 1936-1970, *Journal of Urban Economics* 15: 18-25, 1984.

[43] ———. *Tax Planning for Real Estate Investors*. Prentice-Hall, 2nd edition, 1982.

[44] ———. Urban Land Value Functions and the Price Elasticity of Demand for Housing. *Journal of Urban Economics* 6: 112-121, January 1979.

[45] E. H. Kim. A Mean-Variance Theory of Optimal Capital Structure and Corporate Debt Capacity. *Journal of Finance* 33: 45-64, March 1978.

[46] E. H. Kim, W. G. Lewellen, J. J. McConnell. Financial Leverage Clienteles: Theory and Evidence. *Journal of Financial Economics* 7: 83-109, March 1979.

[47] W. N. Kinnard, Jr. *Income Property Valuation*. Lexington Books, 1971.

[48] J. D. Landauer. Real Estate as an Investment. *The Appraisal Journal* 38: 426-434. October 1960.

[49] S. M. Maser, W. H. Riker, R. N. Rosett. The Effects of Zoning and Externalities on the Price of Land: An Empirical Analysis of Monroe County, New York. *Journal of Law and Economics* 20: 111-132, April 1977.

[50] M. Miles and T. McCue. Historic Returns and Institutional Real Estate Portfolios. *American Real Estate and Urban Economics Association Journal* 10: 184-199, Summer 1982.

[51] M. H. Miller. Debt and Taxes. *Journal of Finance* 32: 261-275, May 1977.

[52] F. Modigliani. Debt, Dividend Policy, Taxes, Inflation and Market Valuation. *Journal of Finance* 37: 255-273, May 1982.

[53] F. Modigliani and M. H. Miller. Corporate Income Taxes and the Cost of Capital. *American Economic Review* 53: 433-443, June 1963.

[54] ———. The Cost of Capital, Corporation Finance, and the Theory of Investment. *American Economic Review* 48: 261-297, June 1958.

[55] S. Myers. Determinants of Corporate Borrowing. *Journal of Financial Economics* 5: 147-176, November 1977.

[56] ———. Interactions of Corporate Financing and Investment Decisions - Implications for Capital Budgeting. *Journal of Finance* 29: 1-25, March 1974.

[57] J. F. Nelson. Pension Fund Investment in Real Estate. *United States Banker*: 58-60. May 1983.

[58] J. P. Nelson. Airports and Property Values: A Survey of Recent Evidence. *Journal of Transport Economics and Policy* 14: 37-52, January 1980.

[59] D. E. Page. Criteria for Investment Decision Making: An Empirical Study. *The Appraisal Journal* 60: 498-508, October 1983.

[60] W. W. Pollock and K. W. H. Scholz. *The Science and Practice of Urban Land Valuation*. Pollock, 1926.

[61] R. U. Ratcliff. *Modern Real Estate Valuation, Theory and Application*. Democrat Press, 1965.

[62] J. R. Recht and L. K. Loewenstein. Variations in Rates of Return. *The Appraisal Journal* 33: 243-248, April 1965.

[63] R. B. Ricks. Imputed Equity Returns on Real Estate Financed with Life Insurance Company Loans. *Journal of Finance* 24: 926-937, December 1969.

[64] ———. Real Estate Investment: The Investment Process, Investment Performance and Federal Tax Policy. Report of the Real Estate Investment Project for the U. S. Treasury Department, 1968.

[65] ———. Recent Trends in Institutional Real Estate Investment. Research Report No. 23, 1. Center for Real Estate and Urban Economics, Unversity of California, 1964.

[66] R. G. Ridker and J. A. Henning. The Determinants of Residential Property Values with Special Reference to Air Pollution. *Review of Economics and Statistics* 49: 246-257, May 1967.

[67] K. T. Rosen. Creative Financing and House Prices: A Study of Capitalization Effects, Working Paper, University of California, August 1982.

[68] ———. The Impact of Proposition 13 on House Prices in Northern California: A Test of the Interjurisdictional Capitalization Hypothesis. *Journal of Political Economy* 90: 191-200, February 1982.

[69] S. A. Ross. The Determination of Financial Structure: The Incentive-Signaling Approach. *Bell Journal of Economics* 8: 23-40, Spring 1977.

[70] S. E. Roulac. Can Real Estate Outperform Common Stocks? *Journal of Portfolio Management* 2: 26-43, Winter 1976.

[71] M. E. Rubenstein. A Mean-Variance Synthesis of Corporate Financial Theory. *Journal of Finance* 28: 167-181, March 1973.

[72] J. D. Shilling, C. F. Sirmans, J. B. Corgel. Inventories, Price Adjustments, and Optimal Vacancies: An Examination of the Market for Rental Office Space. Working Paper, Louisiana State University, March 1984.

[73] C. F. Sirmans. The Minimum Tax, Recapture, and Choice of Depreciation Method. *AREUEA Journal* 7: 255-267, Fall 1980.

[74] C. F. Sirmans and A. J. Jaffe. *The Complete Real Estate Investment Handbook.* Prentice-Hall, 2nd edition, 1984.

[75] C. F. Sirmans and B. Newsome. After Tax Mortgage Equity Valuation. *The Appraisal Journal* 52: 250-269, April 1984.

[76] C. F. Sirmans and J. R. Webb. Expected Returns on Real Estate Financed with Life Insurance Company Loans: 1966-1977. *AREUEA Journal* 8: 218-228, Summer 1980.

[77] ———. Investment Yields in the Money, Capital and Real Estate Markets: A Comparative Analysis for 1951-1976. *The Real Estate Appraiser and Analyst* 44: 40-46, November/December 1978.

[78] G. S. Sirmans, S. D. Smith, C. F. Sirmans. Assumption Financing and Selling Prices of Single Family Homes. *Journal of Financial and Quantitative Analysis* 18: 307-317, September 1983.

[79] W. F. Smith. *The Low-Rise Speculative Apartment.* Research Report No. 25. Center for Real Estate and Urban Economics, University of California, 1964.

[80] J. E. Stiglitz. A Re-Examination of the Modigliani-Miller Theorem. *American Economic Review* 59: 784-793, December 1969.

[81] W. L. Updegrave. Small Pension Plans—A New Source of Equity for Real Estate. *Housing:* 56-58, July 1981.

[82] J. R. Webb. Real Estate Research: Past, Present, and Future. *The Appraisal Journal* 52: 135-142, January 1984.

[83] P. F. Wendt. Ellwood, Inwood, and IRR. *The Appraisal Journal* 35: 561-574, October 1967.

[84] ———. *Real Estate Appriasal—A Critical Analysis of Theory and Practice.* Holt and Co., 1956.

[85] ———. *Real Estate Appraisal Review and Outlook.* University of Georgia Press, 1974.

[86] P. F. Wendt and S. N. Wong. Investment Performance: Common Stocks Versus Apartment Houses. *Journal of Finance* 20: 623-646, December 1965.

[87] J. B. Williams. *The Theory of Investment Value.* Harvard University Press, 1938.

[88] A. D. Witte and J. E. Bachman. Vacant Urban Land Holdings: Portfolio Considerations and Owner Characteristics. *Southern Economic Journal* 45: 543-558, October 1978.

[89] J. A. Zangerle. *Principles of Real Estate Appraising.* Stanley McMichael, 1924.

2 Real Estate: The Whole Story

Paul M. Firstenberg, Stephen A. Ross, and Randall C. Zisler

We allocate too little to it and pay too little heed to real estate diversification.

Investors traditionally have thought of equity real estate as an inefficient market in which the key to success is in the skill with which an individual investment is selected and negotiated. The general approach seems to be to buy properties when they become available if they look like "good deals," with little regard for the equally important issue of how the acquisition fits with the other holdings in the portfolio and what effect, if any, it will have on the overall risk and return objectives of the portfolio. Only recently have some investors begun to think of the aggregate of their real estate investments as a *portfolio*, with its own overall risk and return characteristics, and to adopt explicit strategies for achieving portfolio goals.

This article takes the view that investors should examine equity real estate investments not only on their individual merits but also for their impact on the investor's overall real estate portfolio. In addition, investors need to assess how the real estate segment fits into their entire portfolio. In turn, this means:

- setting risk and return objectives for the equity real estate portfolio as a whole that are compatible with the goals for the investor's entire portfolio,
- devising a strategy for achieving these objectives, and
- evaluating the extent to which individual transactions conform to the strategy and are likely to further portfolio objectives.

These processes are, of course, familiar to anyone in the business of managing security portfolios. By contrast, there has been a nearly complete neglect of such theory and techniques in the management of real estate portfolios and in their integration into institutional portfolios. This, in turn, has deprived managers of the modern tools that they now employ when considering other financial decisions. Often, for example, the pension fund asset allocation process that results in a decision to "put 10% of the portfolio into real estate" seems governed at least as much by hunch as by any rational mechanism.

Again by way of contrast, probably there is not a single major institutional portfolio in the common stock area that does not make serious use of modern portfolio techniques to continually monitor overall portfolio risk and to assess portfolio performance. These techniques are often the central mechanism for determining management strategy and selecting managers.

While some funds rely much more heavily on quantitative techniques than others do, the implementation of these procedures clearly has moved well beyond the cosmetic and lip service stage. Furthermore, a good general rule is that the larger the portfolio, the greater the reliance on such techniques. This is no doubt a consequence of the realization that even a few good stock picks will have less of an influence on the performance of a $5 billion portfolio than overall structuring decisions will. These decisions include how much to put into different categories of assets or stocks and the overall risk level of the portfolio.

Moreover, within an asset category, the selection of sectors in which to invest is likely to have more impact on results than the choice of individual investments. These types of decisions for real estate are likely to be as critical for performance as a few good individual property "investments" and individual property asset management will be.

Our intention is to show how pension funds and other large investors can use modern portfolio techniques both to construct real estate portfolios and to allocate funds to asset categories including real estate. Our concern, however, is not with a cookbook application of some handy formulas to the real estate market.

Because the real estate market is not an auction market offering divisible shares in every property, and information flows in the market are complex, these features place a premium on investment judgment. Managers who want to own some of IBM simply buy some shares. Managers who want to participate in the returns on, say, a $300 million office building must take a significant position in the property. One alternative is to purchase a share of a large commingled real estate fund, but that does not relieve the fund's managers from the problems of constructing their portfolio.

Our aim is not to eliminate the analysis of each individual property acquisition, but rather to supplement it with a thorough consideration of its contribution to overall portfolio performance. Modern portfolio analysis provides the tool for examining the risk and return characteristics of the overall portfolio and the contribution of the individual elements. The result of its application is a method for selecting properties whose inclusion in the portfolio is of overall benefit.

Before we consider this point in more detail, we examine how real estate performance results compare with those for stocks and bonds. In this analysis, the absence of the large and continuous data record available in the securitized markets presents some special problems.

TOTAL RETURN AND REAL ESTATE DATA

In all modern investment work, the focus of interest is on the total rate of return on assets, that is, the return inclusive of both income and capital gain or loss. The logic underlying this is the basic philosophy of "cash is cash." An investment with a total return of 10%, all from capital gains, is equivalent to one with a total return of 10%, all from income, because the sale of 9% of the shares in the investment that has risen in value will realize for the holder the same cash as the all-income investment provides. This basic truth, though, does not deny the possibility that, for some holders, there may be an advantage to receiving the return in one form or another.[1]

A real estate fund might rationally have an income as well as a total return objective, yet the transaction cost of selling appreciated property to realize income is particularly severe for real estate. While we recognize that this is an important issue, space considerations do not permit us to deal with it explicitly. Fortunately, too, this is not a serious limitation to our analysis, because the income component of large real estate funds is relatively insensitive to the decision as to how to allocate the funds across different types of real estate.

To determine the total return on real estate or any other asset, we just add the income component and the capital gain or loss. The income component of an asset's return is relatively straightforward to determine, as it is just a cash flow, and good data generally are available for the computation.

The price appreciation component, however, is much more difficult to assess. If an asset is traded in a continuous auction market, like the common stock of a major company, price quotes in the market provide a good method for valuing the asset. Most real estate assets trade infrequently, however, and valuation is more problematic. For some of the commingled funds, appraisals are the only source of property valuations.

The appraisal process merits a paper of its own, but a few points are sufficient for our purposes. Appraisals usually are conducted annually and are based on one of two methods or a combination of the two. If comparable properties have recently been bought or sold, then the appraisal can use their prices as benchmarks for estimating the value of properties that have not been traded. Comparability is increasingly difficult to achieve as the number and complexity of leases increases. Alternatively, the property can be valued by the discounted cash flow (DCF) method of discounting the projected net cash flows at some discount rate determined by prevailing market conditions. Neither of these methods can be as accurate as an actual market price, but there is also no reason to think that they will be biased in the long run. Furthermore, even if appraisals are biased, the appreciation computed from appraisals will not be biased as long as the bias is constant over time.

Although appraisals are not necessarily biased, there is evidence of considerable sluggishness or inertia in appraised values. By any of the common measures of the volatility of returns, real estate returns from appraisals appear to vary far less over time than other asset return series. Standard deviation is a measure of the spread or volatility of investment returns, and we will use the standard deviation also as a measure of the riskiness of real estate returns.[2]

The data below reveal that the standard deviation of stock returns, for example, is over five times greater than that of real estate returns. The extent to which this difference is a consequence of real estate returns actually being far less volatile than stock returns or a consequence of the use of appraisal values is not really known. In the data that follow, we make a correction that raises the volatility of the real estate returns to a level that seems more reasonable to us.

The major sources of data on real estate returns come from commingled funds. We have made use of three series of aggregate real estate returns and a separate series of the returns on different subcategories of real estate. For comparison purposes, we also use returns on other assets such as stocks and bonds. The data and the sources appear in the Appendix.

Table 1 describes how real estate returns have compared with the returns on stocks and bonds and with inflation. As the Frank Russell (FRC) and Evaluation Asso-

Table 1 Real Estate Series and Other Assets

Index	Annualized Total Return (%)	Standard Deviation (%)	Series Begins (°)
Real Estate			
FRC	13.87	2.55	6/78
FRC (cap-rate est.)	13.04	11.28	6/78
FRC (appraisal adj.)	13.87	4.37	6/78
EAFPI	10.78	2.80	3/69
EREIT	22.26	19.71	3/74
Other Assets			
S&P 500	9.71	15.35	3/69
Small Stocks	14.51	23.90	3/69
Corporate Bonds	8.38	11.29	3/69
Government Bonds	7.91	11.50	3/69
T-Bills	7.51	0.82	3/69
Inflation	6.64	1.19	3/69
Risk Premium (spread over T-Bills)			
EAFPI	3.27	2.43	
FRC	4.36	1.29	
S&P 500	1.48	17.54	
Small Stocks	7.38	18.04	

° All series end in December 1985. For details and full titles of each series, see the Appendix.

ciates (EAFPI) series are based on appraisals, they might move more sluggishly than a true market value series—if one were available. The two adjusted series under the FRC heading report the result of alterations in the FRC data designed to recognize this weakness. The "cap-rate adjusted" series estimates the change in value from a DCF model, and the "appraisal adjusted" series adjusts the standard deviation of the series upward.[3]

Even when the standard deviation of real estate returns is adjusted upward, both the return and the standard deviation make real estate an attractive asset category in comparison with stocks and bonds. Its lower risk and its comparable return partially offset the lack of liquidity inherent in real estate investments.[4]

We turn now to the issues involved in managing an equity real estate portfolio and the implications of modern portfolio analysis for real estate.

REAL ESTATE PORTFOLIOS: THE BASIC PRINCIPLES

In an imperfect real estate market, the skill with which individual assets are acquired, managed, and disposed of will be a major determinant of total return. Portfolio management is not a substitute for, nor should it divert attention from, property-specific management. Nevertheless, the composition of the portfolio as a whole will impact both the level and the variability of returns.

The twin considerations of individual property-specific management and portfolio analysis require different human skills and make use of different information. This leads naturally to a two-tiered approach to management:

- A macro analysis that employs portfolio management concepts and focuses on the composition and investment characteristics of the portfolio as a whole, identifying major strategic investment options and their long-run implications. Each property that is a candidate for acquisition or disposition should be analyzed for its impact on overall portfolio objectives.
- A micro analysis that employs traditional real estate project analysis, and focuses on the selection of the individual properties that make up the portfolio, evaluating a property's specific risk–reward potential against the investor's performance targets.

We will not have much to say here about the micro analysis; it is the traditional focus of real estate analysis. We make suggestions for it, but we do not propose changing it. Our interest is in the macro analysis.

Macro analysis derives the characteristics of risk and return for the portfolio as a whole from different combinations of individual property types and geographic locations. It establishes the trade-off between the given level of return and the volatility of return that result from different mixes of assets. Selecting the particular risk-return trade-off that best meets an investor's requirements is the most crucial policy decision one can make and is one of our major concerns.

The macro policy is implemented only through the individual selection of properties at the micro level. A thorough analysis of a property should involve an analysis of its marginal contribution to overall portfolio return, volatility, and risk exposure. The difficulty in conducting such an analysis at the individual property level is what gives rise to the separation between the micro and macro analyses. In general, the macro goals are implemented at the micro level by choosing categories of properties to examine with the micro tools, rather than by examining each individual property's marginal effect on the portfolio.

We will employ some familiar principles from modern portfolio theory as guides in portfolio construction:

- To achieve higher-than-average levels of return, an investor must construct a portfolio involving greater-than-average risk. An investor whose risk tolerance is lower than that of the average investor in the market must expect relatively lower returns. Risk may be defined as the variability or dispersion from the mean of future returns or, simply put, the chance of achieving less-than-expected returns. The variability of returns usually is measured by the standard deviation.
- It is possible and useful to measure risk and return and to develop, in an approximate manner, a portfolio strategy that balances the trade-off between these two performance criteria. Because of the difficulty and costs of transacting in the real estate market, and because of the resulting lack of precise "marked-to-market" prices for real estate, it is unrealistic to attempt to fine-tune actual investment decisions in response to risk-return estimates. Even if an investor specifies a preference for a mean return of 15% with a standard deviation of 2.5%, translating that preference into a precise strategy is probably not feasible. Broader relationships between risk and return must guide real estate investment strategy.
- The total risk on any investment can be decomposed into a systematic and an unsystematic component. Unsystematic risk will largely disappear as an influence on the re-

turn of a well-diversified portfolio. To the extent that the return on an individual property is influenced by purely local events, it is unsystematic and washes out in a large diversified portfolio.[5] A regional shopping center, for example, might find its sales adversely affected by a plant closing. A chain of shopping centers spread across the country, however, would find total revenues unaffected by such local influences. Its revenues would depend on the overall economic conditions that affect costs and consumer demand. An investor who owned many such centers would not be subjected to the ups and downs of individual industries and markets and would be affected only by the general economic conditions that influence all retail businesses simultaneously.

- The risk from changes in economic conditions throughout the country is systematic and will influence any portfolio, no matter how large and well-diversified, because it influences each of the parts. For example, a downturn in consumer demand and a rise in wages will probably adversely affect all business, which means that even a conglomerate would suffer a decline in profits. Systematic risk can be lowered only by lowering long-run average returns. A conglomerate might attempt to lower such risks by implementing a strategic decision to sell some businesses and invest the proceeds in cash securities. The resulting revenues will have less sensitivity to the business cycle but also will have a lower average return. An investor could do the same.

In the sections that follow we will illustrate how investors can apply these principles in portfolio construction by examining how different combinations of property types and economic regions affect the risk and return characteristics of a portfolio.

Investors can reduce the unsystematic and, therefore, the overall risk level of the portfolio without sacrificing return by diversifying real estate investments among property types that have non-covariant returns and across geographic areas of leaseholds that are not subject to the same macroeconomic variables. Diversification also protects the investor from overemphasizing a particular asset class or area of the country that then falls victim to unforeseen, or more often unforeseeable, negative developments.

Spreading assets geographically has been a commonly used rough proxy for selecting areas that are economically non-covariant.[6] A more detailed analysis, however, is required to determine whether geographically separate areas are actually subject to the same macroeconomic variables. The economic base of a particular geographic area may be broad-based, with multiple and widely diversified sources of revenues, or its economy may be largely dependent on a single economic activity. The latter is obviously a riskier area in which to invest, but much of its risk is unsystematic.

As a consequence, a diversified portfolio of areas, each of which is influenced by a different industry-specific risk, can avoid such risk at no cost in returns. For instance, the economies of Houston, Denver, and New Orleans were all highly vulnerable to one variable—oil prices; San Jose, California, Austin, Texas, and Lexington, Massachusetts, are all vulnerable, to a lesser degree, to the fortunes of the high-tech industries. A portfolio made up of properties in these cities is diversified geographically, but subject to significant systematic risks. By contrast, a portfolio made up of properties in Lexington, New Orleans, and, say, New York and Reno would have less overall risk.

This line of reasoning explains the power of diversification across geographic areas whose economies are independent. Within a given city, the same economic forces that influence the business demand for industrial and office space also affect the demand of workers for residential space, the demand of customers for hotel room nights, and the

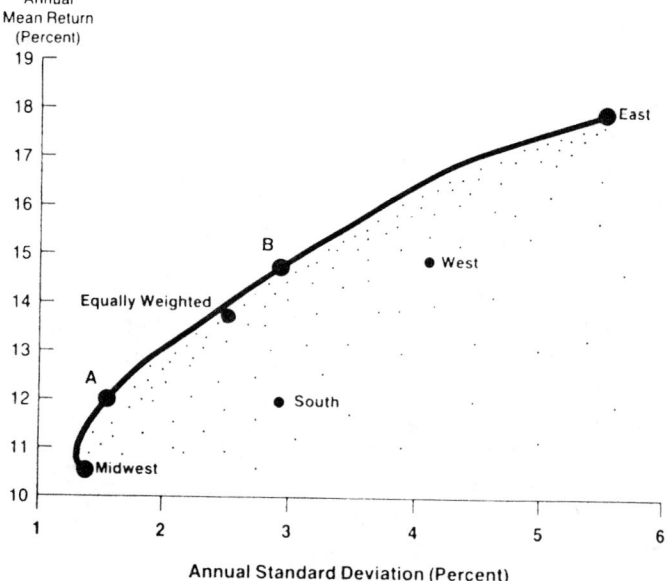

Figure 1 Efficient Regional Portfolio Mixes

demand of retailers who sell to the workers. Too often, casual real estate market research leads to a claim of urban or regional diversification without an adequate analysis of the inter-industry and inter-occupational linkages affecting returns. Diversifying across different areas lowers risk to the extent to which the economies of the areas are independent of each other. Ultimately, the goal of diversifying a real estate portfolio should be to diversify across leaseholds.

Intuition also suggests that international diversification would be a powerful tool for accomplishing this goal. The question of whether a portfolio with London and New York properties is more economically diverse than a portfolio of Boston and New York is really the question of whether the underlying economy of Boston will move more or less with that of New York than with London.

REGIONAL DIVERSIFICATION

Figure 1 illustrates the trade-off between risk and return that is available when we break real estate investment into different regions and examine various portfolio possibilities for diversifying holdings across the regions. The four regions are the East, the Midwest, the South, and the West.[7] Figure 1 displays all the possible combinations of return and risk available from the different combinations of holdings across these four regions.

The expected return is graphed on the horizontal scale in Figure 1, and the vertical scale gives the standard deviation. The data are all historical. History is a guide to the future, but this is not to say that the next ten years will mimic the last ten. Rather, we are asking how different portfolios would have performed in the past. We contend that an intelligent look at past risk and return patterns is necessary for an understanding of the future. This, of course, is a weakness of all analysis, whether quantitative or not, but what else can we use to study the future if not the past?

By choosing different combinations of the four regions, all the points in the shaded part of Figure 1 are available. The labeled points describe the four pure regional portfolios. The East alone, for instance, shows a return of 17.9% and a standard deviation of 5.6%. The equally weighted portfolio in Figure 1 gives the return and the risk of a portfolio that puts one-quarter of its investment in each of the four regions.

Table 2 gives the background data underlying Figure 1. Here we have listed the return and standard deviation for each of the regions as well as the correlations in the returns across the four regions. Correlations are interpreted in the usual fashion. A positive correlation between two regions indicates that the returns tend to rise and fall together, and, as the table shows, all the regional correlations are positive. A zero correlation means that the returns tend to move independently of each other. All the correlations are low, and the correlation between the Midwest and the South is nearly zero. Combining asset categories that are only weakly correlated with each other greatly lowers overall portfolio risk. Figure 1 certainly reveals that this is the case for regional diversification.[8]

Using Figure 1, we can show that investing the entire portfolio in any single region is unnecessarily risky. For three of the regions, there is a superior alternative that involves combining the regions. The only exception is the all-East portfolio. As it had the highest return in the period used to construct Figure 1 (see Table 2), putting the entire portfolio into the East would have been the best choice, but, if course, we have no basis for assuming that the next ten years would still put the East on top.

As for the other three choices, take, for example, the South. The South had a mean return of 11.96% and a standard deviation of 2.92%. Compare these results with those of Point A, directly above the South on the curve that bounds the possible combinations of return and risk. This point has the same standard deviation of 2.92% as that of the all-South portfolio, yet its return is nearly 15%, or 300 basis points, greater than that of the all-South portfolio. Similarly, Point B, just to the left of the South, is also superior to the all-South portfolio. It has the same return of 11.96% as the all-South portfolio, but its risk level is about 1.5%, or nearly half that of the all-South portfolio. The points on the curve of Figure 1 are called efficient portfolios, because they give the best possible returns for their levels of risk. The points between A and B are efficient portfolios that dominate the all-South portfolio.

Table 2 Returns by Region, 1978-1985

Region	Annualized Mean Return (%)	Standard Deviation (%)
East	17.91	5.58
Midwest	10.49	1.44
South	11.96	2.92
West	14.83	4.11

Regional Correlation Matrix

Region	East	Midwest	South	West
East	1.00	0.16	0.25	0.32
Midwest	0.16	1.00	0.04	0.14
South	0.25	0.04	1.00	0.46
West	0.32	0.14	0.46	1.00

Table 3 lists the efficient regional portfolios for each level of return and shows their risk level. These portfolios are the ones that give the returns and standard deviations on the curve in Figure 1. Table 3 provides a great deal of valuable information on the optimal regional diversification of a real estate portfolio.

As we move from low returns to high returns—and higher risk—we see that in the range from an 11.3% return with a 1.4% standard deviation to a 15.8% return with a 3.6% standard deviation, the efficient portfolios diversify to include all the regions. In other words, as we avoid the extremes of the highest returns and risks and the lowest returns and risks, a characteristic of the efficient portfolios is that they are fully diversified. Indeed, as Figure 1 shows, the equally weighted portfolio that puts exactly the same investment into each region is essentially an efficient portfolio with its return of 14% and its standard deviation of 2.3%.

This is as far as this quantitative analysis can take us. At this point judgment takes over. The quantitative analysis can weed out the inferior choices, but, in the end, it cannot make the final choice for the manager. The manager is left with the central question: What combination of risk and return should be chosen and, therefore, which efficient portfolio?[9] Each investor will have particular requirements for establishing the trade-off between risk and return.

We offer here only some broad considerations. For a publicly-held fund, the basic issue is one of marketing; the combination of return and risk and, therefore, the regional diversification should be chosen according to an evaluation of the clients' demands. For a pension fund, the decision should be based on how the real estate portfolio is expected to contribute to the overall objectives of the fund. We will look at this matter more closely when we consider allocating funds across asset classes including real estate. When regional diversification and property type diversification are combined, the resulting reduction in risk is considerable.

Table 3 Efficient Portfolio Mixes by Region (Proportions, %)

East	Midwest	South	West	Mean (%)	Portfolio Standard Deviation (%)
	99		1	10.50	1.43
0%	81	18%	1	10.80	1.31
5	74	17	5	11.30	1.36
9	66	15	9	11.80	1.49
14	59	13	13	12.30	1.67
19	52	12	18	12.80	1.89
23	45	10	22	13.30	2.14
28	38	8	26	13.80	2.41
32	31	7	30	14.30	2.70
37	23	5	35	14.80	2.99
41	16	3	39	15.30	3.30
46	9	2	43	15.80	3.60
51	2	0	47	16.30	3.91
64			36	16.80	4.28
80			20	17.30	4.80
96			4	17.80	5.43

PROPERTY TYPE DIVERSIFICATION

Figure 2 illustrates the trade-off between risk and return that is available from forming portfolios of the five different property types, and Table 4 gives the data underlying Figure 2. The properties are classified into five major property types: apartments, hotels, office buildings, retail properties including shopping centers, and industrial properties such as warehouses. This classification corresponds both to the available data and to an a priori sensible breakdown into non-covariant business groupings. As we would expect, the efficient portfolios are diversified by property type, but here the results are different from those obtained when we consider regional diversification.

As Table 5 reveals, the efficient portfolios can have as few as two asset types in them. For returns above 16.3%, the efficient portfolios are dominated by hotels and office properties. For the low-risk alternatives, apartments, industrial properties, and retail dominate. At all levels of risk and return, though, some diversification is appropriate.

It is difficult to say to what extent these results predict future patterns and to what extent they are the consequence of the relatively short statistical history. There is reason to believe, though, that we should depend less on the property diversification results than on the regional analysis. For one thing, the numbers themselves are less reliable. The hotel category, for example, is based on a relatively small number of properties, and they are unduly concentrated in New York City. For another, it may well be that some of these returns reflect the economics of relatively tight leasing markets in the late 1970s and early 1980s. Furthermore, fundamental changes in the tax laws since 1986 probably will affect these property types differently.

For these reasons, we would advocate using Table 5 as a rough guide and tend to give greater weight to the middle region where all property types are represented. The

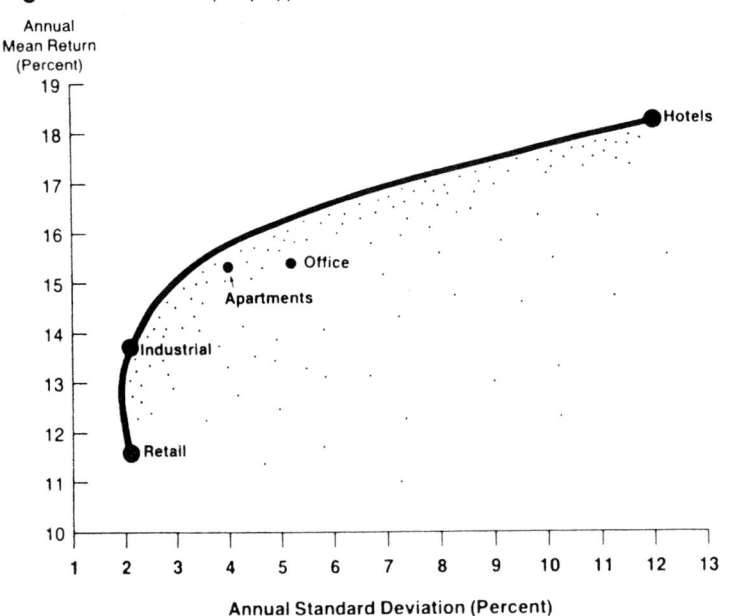

Figure 2 Efficient Property Type Mixes

Table 4 Returns by Property Type, 1978-1985

	Annualized Mean Return (%)	Standard Deviation (%)
Apartments	15.29	3.97
Hotels	18.25	12.08
Industrial	13.63	2.27
Office	15.38	4.72
Retail	11.56	2.19

Property Type Correlation Matrix

	Apartments	Hotels	Industrial	Office	Retail
Apartments	1.00	0.56	0.41	0.21	0.13
Hotels	0.56	1.00	0.17	0.11	−0.01
Industrial	0.41	0.17	1.00	0.65	0.59
Office	0.21	0.11	0.65	1.00	0.21
Retail	0.13	−0.01	0.59	0.21	1.00

final choice of a risk and return trade-off, as with regional diversification, rests with the manager and is governed by the same considerations as affect the regional choice.[10]

IMPLICATIONS FOR PORTFOLIO MANAGEMENT

We conclude from the foregoing analysis of the risk-return characteristics of portfolios constructed with different mixes of property types and geographic regions that:

- There is a trade-off between the riskiness (as measured by standard deviation) of a real estate portfolio and the total expected return it generates. Consistent with experience with financial assets, the degree of risk an investor is willing to assume will be the single most important factor in determining return.

Table 5 Efficient Portfolio Mixes by Property Type (Proportions, %)

Apartments	Hotels	Industrial	Office	Retail	Mean (%)	Portfolio Standard Deviation (%)
4		4		92	11.80	2.10
9		20		71	12.30	1.97
13		36		51	12.80	1.94
18		50	1	31	13.30	2.01
23		61	3	13	13.80	2.18
30		61	9		14.30	2.43
41	2	34	24		14.80	2.81
53	3	7	38		15.30	3.29
38	16		46		15.80	4.03
15	33		53		16.30	5.23
	49		51		16.80	6.67
	67		33		17.30	8.40
	84		16		17.80	10.29
	98		2		18.20	11.88

- Diversifying the composition of a portfolio among geographic locations and property types can increase the investor's return for a given level of risk. Diversification among holdings with non-covariant returns will reduce risk without sacrificing return. To construct such a portfolio, each investment category identified as offering diversification potential should be represented; the goal should be to have a substantial minimum threshold investment across property types and geographic regions (e.g., no property type or region should be below, say, 15% of the total portfolio).
- There are at least two alternative strategic approaches to diversifying a real estate portfolio. One approach calls for all investments to be made in strict accordance with diversification criteria, even though the assets allocated to different categories may exceed the minimums necessary to gain significant benefits. Under such a strict policy, an investor would not shift allocations because of perceived future changes in the payoffs from different allocations. The investor would modify the initial diversification slowly and generally only in response to some sort of significant long-term change in the marketplace. The assumption underlying this approach is that such modifications always create additional risk and that the investor lacks the forecasting ability to earn sufficient additional return to compensate for the risk.

    The second approach allows for strategic deviations from the strict plan, provided that the threshold minimum allocations are met. Such an approach could reflect an investor's confidence in the ability to project changes in the risk-return differential of various geographic areas or property types. Or it could stem from pursuing a high risk-return strategy of, say, investing in development projects or in less than fully leased properties in currently out of favor markets in the hope of producing results outside of the efficient frontier of Figures 1 and 2. In such cases, the portfolio will reflect the strategic investment selections that deviate from a strict diversification policy, with the expectation that the added risk will be compensated for by additional return. One way to implement such a strategy is to divide the portfolio into a strictly diversified component (a core portfolio) and a higher risk/higher return portion (an opportunity portfolio), with the blend between the two reflecting an overall risk-return target.

    In sum, an investor can target a real estate portfolio to lie at any point along the risk-return continuum; the crucial step is to articulate and explicitly adopt an investment strategy that fits this goal and that both the investor and the investment manager fully understand and agree upon. The strategies to be pursued in managing a real estate portfolio should be explicit, not unspoken.
- We need to learn a good deal more about the factors that, in fact, produce genuine diversification (i.e., non-covariant returns). Present categories of broad geographic regions or property types provide only crude guidelines for achieving efficient mixes. This lack of the proper economic classifications and the accompanying data are the most serious weakness of our analysis.

ASSET ALLOCATION: STOCKS, BONDS, AND REAL ESTATE

In principle, the same considerations that govern the construction of the all-real estate portfolio apply to the asset allocation decision. Table 1 gives the basic return and risk information, while Table 6 gives the correlations between real estate and other asset categories.

Table 6 Correlations Among Asset Classes*

	FRC	EAFPI	EREIT	S&P 500	Government Bonds	T-Bills	Inflation
FRC	1.00	0.71	−0.14	−0.26	−0.38	0.30	0.38
EAFPI	0.71	1.00	−0.20	−0.28	−0.10	0.54	0.48
EREIT	−0.14	−0.20	1.00	0.78	0.36	−0.23	0.03
S&P 500	−0.26	−0.28	0.78	1.00	0.49	−0.43	−0.15
Government Bonds	−0.38	−0.10	0.36	0.49	1.00	−0.09	−0.35
T-Bills	0.30	0.54	−0.23	−0.43	−0.09	1.00	0.41
Inflation	0.38	0.48	0.03	−0.15	−0.35	0.41	1.00

*For details and full titles of each series, see Appendix.

In constructing Table 6, we have treated real estate as a single category, even though different regions or property types will have different relations with other assets. Whenever we aggregate asset classes and consider their relationship with each other as classes, we always lose some of the fine detail. This is true of stocks as well as real estate. As these asset categories are managed as individual classes, however, the separation of management forces the separation of our analysis.[11]

From a portfolio perspective, the great attractive feature of real estate is its lack of correlation with other assets. Even if real estate risk is understated, the lack of correlation makes real estate a particularly attractive feature of a well-diversified portfolio.

Look first at the correlations among the three real estate indexes FRC, EAFPI, and EREIT. The two appraisal-based indexes, FRC and EAFPI, are highly correlated with each other, and both are negatively correlated with the stock market-traded REIT index, EREIT. This striking difference points up the difficulty with the real estate data. Indeed, both FRC and EAFPI are negatively correlated with the stock market as well, while EREIT with a 0.78 correlation with the S&P 500 actually looks like a stock index rather than the other two real estate indexes. (A closer look reveals that individual REITs can behave like the other real estate indexes; it all depends on the particular REIT.) Presumably, the truth lies somewhere between these two, and we can conclude that real estate returns, if not negatively correlated with those on stocks, are at least far from perfectly correlated with them.

One point with which all of the real estate indexes agree, however, is that real estate hedges against increases in inflation. All three indexes are positively correlated with changes in inflation. By contrast, the S&P 500 index has responded negatively to inflation.

Our argument for including real estate as a substantial portion of an overall investment portfolio is, thus, based on its significant diversification value in reducing risk, whatever the goal for returns.

Using the correlation data from Table 6 and the return data from Table 1, we created the efficient frontier of real estate, stocks, and bonds displayed in Figure 3 and tabulated in Table 7. We used the upward adjustment in the standard deviation of real estate in constructing Table 7 so as to avoid any possible underemphasis of its risk. The efficient portfolios in Table 7 display the same characteristics as the efficient portfolios of the real estate categories. In the middle ranges of return and risk, the portfolio is evenly diversified among the three categories, although real estate has the major share. Insofar as the risk of real estate is still understated by the 11.3% standard deviation, these numbers will overstate real estate's role in an efficient asset allocation.

Figure 3 Mixes of Real Estate, Stocks and Bonds

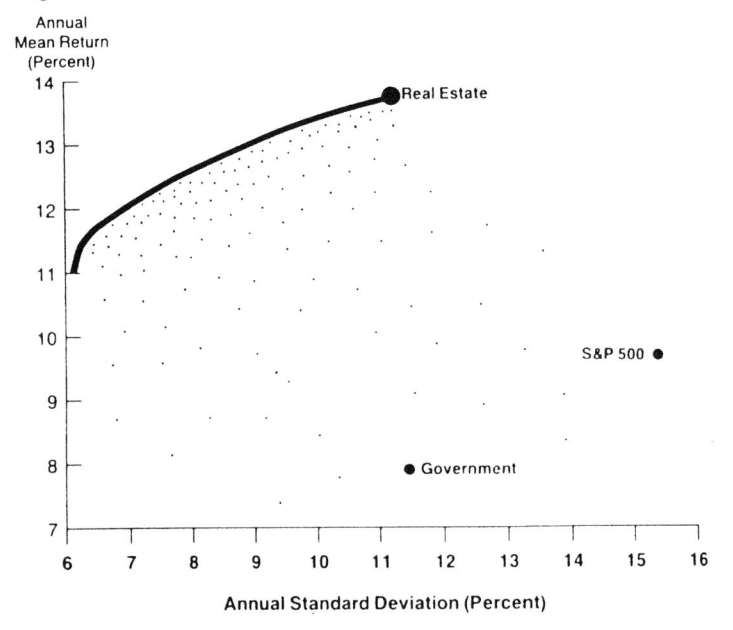

To examine this matter further, we raised real estate's standard deviation to be the same as that for the S&P 500, 15.4%. The resulting efficient portfolios are given in Table 8. Although the increase in the risk level of real estate lowers its contribution to the efficient portfolios and raises the proportion of bonds, the amount of the change is surprisingly small. For example, the efficient portfolio with a 12% mean return has a 61% holding in real estate when real estate is assumed to be as risky as stocks and a 65% holding when real estate is assumed to have a risk level below that of stocks but above its measured level. Of course, this result is dependent upon the limitations of the data and our model.

The important conclusion to draw from this analysis is that, even with an upward risk adjustment, real estate belongs in efficient portfolios at significantly higher levels than the 3.6% allocation for the top 200 public and private funds in 1986. Taking a pragmatic perspective, we feel that pension funds should seek initial real estate asset allocations of between 15 and 20%.

A second level of consideration in choosing among these possible asset allocations makes use of the additional data presented in Table 6, the correlations between asset returns and inflation and interest rates. Similar data can be collected for other major economic variables that influence asset returns, such as real productivity and investor confidence (see Chen, Roll, and Ross, 1986). We can see from Table 6 that real estate is positively correlated with inflation and, at least for the FRC and the EAFPI indexes, it is also positively correlated with interest rates. This is in marked contrast to stock returns, which are negatively correlated with the inflation variable and with interest rates.

This means that real estate returns have been a superior hedge against an increase in inflation or in interest rates, as compared with the experience of the stock market. As inflation or interest rates have risen, the stock market historically has tended to fall, and real estate returns have tended to rise. Of course, this will depend on the source of the

Table 7 Efficient Portfolio Mixes of Real Estate, Stocks, and Bonds. Real Estate Standard Deviation 'Cap-Adjusted' = 11.28% (Proportions, %)

Real Estate (FRC Index)	Stocks (S&P 500)	Government Bonds	Mean (%)	Portfolio Standard Deviation (%)
49	11	40	11.00	6.16
52	12	36	11.20	6.20
55	13	32	11.40	6.29
58	14	28	11.60	6.44
61	15	24	11.80	6.65
65	16	19	12.00	6.91
68	17	15	12.20	7.22
71	18	11	12.40	7.56
74	19	7	12.60	7.94
77	20	3	12.80	8.35
80	20		13.00	8.79
85	15		13.20	9.30
90	10		13.40	9.89
95	5		13.60	10.56
100	0		13.80	11.28

increase in inflation and interest rates. The Monday, October 19, 1987, crash in the stock market produced the opposite result, where sellers of stock ran to the bond market, pushing these prices up. Rather, we are primarily concerned here with a change in stock prices accompanied by a change in inflationary expectations. This differs from a once-and-for-all shift in prices, such as a jump in commodity prices because of formation of a cartel.

Table 8 Efficient Portfolio Mixes of Real Estate, Stocks, and Bonds. Real Estate Standard Deviation = Stock Standard Deviation = 15.35% (Proportions, %)

Real Estate (FRC Index)	Stocks (S&P 500)	Government Bonds	Mean (%)	Portfolio Standard Deviation (%)
38	13	49	10.40	7.05
41	15	44	10.60	7.09
44	17	39	10.80	7.19
47	18	35	11.00	7.37
50	20	30	11.20	7.61
53	21	26	11.40	7.91
56	23	21	11.60	8.26
58	25	17	11.80	8.66
61	26	12	12.00	9.10
64	28	8	12.20	9.57
67	30	3	12.40	10.80
71	29		12.60	10.61
76	24		12.80	11.22
80	20		13.00	11.92
85	15		13.20	12.70
90	10		13.40	13.54
95	5		13.60	14.42
100	0		13.80	15.35

A corporate pension fund that is funded ultimately by the earnings of the company would find real estate a relatively attractive asset category if its earnings tend to be negatively related to inflation. For example, suppose that a manufacturing company believes that an increase in inflation brings about a more rapid rise in its wage and material costs than in the prices of its products. A fund with a tilt toward real estate would tend to offset this profit squeeze by rising when corporate earnings fell off.

This does not mean that companies whose earnings rise and fall with inflation should shun real estate. For example, a natural resource company with relatively fixed costs would find its earnings down in a period of low inflation. But the analysis of Tables 7 and 8 is still relevant, and the pension fund of such a company should still hold a significant proportion of its assets in real estate, simply to take advantage of the return and risk diversification characteristics. The proper conclusion to draw is that such a company should hold relatively less real estate than the manufacturing company.

In the end, the allocation decision among the three categories we have studied involves a judgment that is associated with the particular needs of the fund being considered. If, in addition to the considerations of risk and return on which we have focused, there is also a concern for liquidity, this will tend to push the fund toward marketed assets such as stocks and bonds and out of real estate.[12] There is no single answer that is best for all portfolios, only a range of desirable choices. Modern portfolio analysis limits this range to the manageable alternatives presented in Tables 7 and 8.

CONCLUSION

We have shown how modern portfolio analysis can be used both to optimally diversify a real estate portfolio and to allocate overall fund assets among real estate, stocks, and bonds. Real estate is an enormous percentage of world assets, and, as our final tables show, even with an upward risk adjustment, it may belong in efficient portfolios at significantly higher levels, such as 15 to 20%, compared to the 3.6% allocation in 1986 for the top 200 public and private pension funds.

NOTES

[1] Regulatory and accounting conventions may lead to preference for income over capital gains. Tax issues also influence this preference. Furthermore, some funds may be precluded from realizing income through sales, and, even if they can sell appreciated assets to generate income, the transaction costs of doing so will detract from the return. On the other side, some investors actually may prefer capital gains to income (ignoring tax effects) to avoid being faced with the need to reinvest the cash.

[2] A rule of thumb is that two-thirds of the returns tend to fall within one standard deviation of the mean return and 95% of the returns fall within two standard deviations. The higher the standard deviation, the greater the range of the effective returns, and the greater the probability or likelihood of loss.

[3] The first correction uses a "cap-rate" proxy in place of appraisal returns. Net operating income is a commonly used yardstick for the valuation of real estate. By treating changes in the current income stream as indications of changes in the market value of the asset, we can estimate an appreciation return. Although this approach has a number of problems, at least it allows us to base the estimate of appreciation on known data. The result is an FRC series with an annual standard deviation of 11%.

We generated a series of appreciation returns on the change of an estimated value of the real estate index, where the value is given by the present value of a perpetual stream of income flows. The income flows are taken to be the current period income, and the discount rate can be modeled either as a spread over T-bills, or simply as a fixed rate.

$$Cr_t = \frac{(Ve_{t-1} - Ve_t)}{(Ve_{t-1})},$$

$$Ve_t = D_t r_t,$$

where:

- Cr = cap-rate return
- Ve = cap-rate value
- D = income per invested dollar
- r = discount rate
- Y = income return
- I = appreciation index value

This simplifies to:

$$Cr_t = \left[\frac{I_t}{I_{t-1}} \cdot \frac{Y_t}{Y_{t-1}} \cdot \frac{r_{t-1}}{r_t} \right] - 1.$$

This method may have some validity, insofar as a similar procedure on the stock market produces estimates near the true value for volatility.

The appraisal-adjusted series is derived from an analysis of the appraisal process and estimates a volatility of returns based on the reported data. This method is an attempt to correct returns by removing any inertia or sluggishness inherent in the appraisal process. True rates of return should be uncorrelated with each other across time. Insofar as there is excessive correlation in the FRC returns, they will not accurately reveal the true return on real estate.

To model the appraisal process, we assumed that a property's appraised value is a mixture of the series of previous appraised values and the appraiser's estimate of the current market price the property would bring if sold. In other words, the appraiser incorporates past appraisals into the current appraisal.

The basis of this estimation is as follows. An estimated mean return can be expressed as the true mean, M_t, and some random error term, e_t:

$$M_t = R_t + e_t,$$

where the standard deviation of e_t is the true standard deviation of returns.

The appraiser can be thought of as combining the true mean return with a lagged return to make the following estimation:

$$E[R_t] = (1 - A)M_t + AR_{t-1}.$$

More generally, the process might use a whole year's worth of past returns in combination with the true mean to produce the current estimation:

$$E[R_t] = (1 - A)M_t + a_1 R_{t-1} + a_2 R_{t-2} + a_3 R_{t-3} + a_4 R_{t-4},$$

where

$$A = a_1 + a_2 + a_3 + a_4.$$

A linear regression based on this model yields the following information:

$$R_t = b_0 + b_1 R_{t-1} + \ldots + b_4 R_{t-4} + z_t,$$

where z_t is the residual error term.

Combining these two equations, we can solve for the true mean and standard deviation from the estimates of b_1, b_2, b_3, and b_4 as follows:

$$b_1 = a_1, b_2 = a_2, b_3 = a_3, \text{ and } b_4 = a_4,$$

and, therefore, the true mean:

$$M = b_0/(1 - A), b_0/(1 - A),$$

where

$$A = b_1 + b_2 + b_3 + b_4,$$

and the true standard deviation of returns is given by:

$$\sigma = \sigma(z_t)/(1 - A),$$

where $\sigma(z_t)$ is the standard deviation of the regression residual, z_t.

[4] We know very little about the effect of illiquidity on investment returns beyond the intuition that liquidity is certainly no worse than illiquidity. As we do not know much more than this, we will adopt the sensible policy of not saying much more.

[5] In practice, real estate managers spend most of their resources investigating local market conditions and negotiating terms of sale. Little if any attention is directed toward the role of a property in the overall portfolio. This is not as misdirected as it might seem. While diversification removes individual and unsystematic property risk, it does not help portfolio returns if misunderstanding the local markets results in overpaying for every property. Nevertheless, without understanding the marginal contribution that properties make to overall portfolio goals, the whole can be less than the sum of the parts.

[6] It is important that property returns be noncovariant, that is, that they not move together, or the risk will be systematic and the advantages of diversification will be lost. For example, a $100-million stock portfolio with 100 holdings of $1 million each will not be terribly well diversified if all of the stocks are utilities.

[7] Data are reported by the Frank Russell Company on a quarterly basis.

[8] We have used the appraisal based returns and have not adjusted the resulting standard deviations in Table 2 and Figure 1, but the possible low volatility of appraisal returns has no effect whatsoever on our analysis. If we were to increase all of the standard deviations by, for example, a factor of two, then this would double all of the numbers on the vertical scale of Figure 1, but all of the points would remain in the same position relative to each other. The analysis of Figure 1 would change only if the appraisals distort volatility by different amounts in the different regions. However, that seems unlikely (not to mention unknowable).

[9] This is probably a good place to dispel another notion that sometimes surfaces in discussions of risk and return. Often a manager will say that "Risk is important, but over the long run, the risk will wash out and all that will matter is the expected return." This is a misunderstanding of risk and its relation to return and, in fact, both the return and the risk increase over time. The exact form this takes depends on various technical features, but generally over very long periods, the greater the standard deviation of a portfolio's returns, the more likely it is that the value of the portfolio will fall below a given level.

[10] It might have occurred to the reader that we should consider breaking real estate into twenty classifications according to both property type and region. For example, hotels in the West would be one of the twenty classes. This is possible, but we have chosen not to do so because of the small number of properties in some of these classes and the resulting lack of reliability of the figures.

[11] A subtle technical point arises from our focus on constructing efficient real estate portfolios. Because of the different interactions between individual stock categories and real estate, we are not assured that an efficient portfolio of stocks and real estate will make use of an efficient real estate portfolio. In practice, though, the difference will be small and the data are not accurate enough to discern the difference.

[12] Liquidity concerns, however, generally should not be a cause to forgo the diversification of benefits of real estate, because real estate constitutes a small percentage of most portfolios. Other assets can better serve as sources of ready liquidity.

REFERENCES

The two modern portfolio techniques used in the paper are the Capital Asset Pricing Model (CAPM) and the Arbitrage Pricing Theory (APT). Expositions of these approaches can be found in most textbooks on corporate finance. Two references are:

Brealey, Richard, and Steward Myers. *Principles of Corporate Finance*, 2nd ed. New York: McGraw-Hill Book Company, 1984.

Copeland, Thomas, and J. Fred Weston. *Financial Theory and Corporate Policy*, 2nd ed. Reading, Mass.: Addison-Wesley Publishing Company, 1983.

The following article outlines the APT approach to strategic planning:

Roll, Richard, and Stephen A. Ross. "The Arbitrage Pricing Theory Approach to Strategic Portfolio Planning." *Financial Analysts Journal*, May/June 1984.

Other articles of interest include the following:

Chen, Nai Fu, Richard Roll, and Stephen Ross. "Economic Forces and the Stock Market." *Journal of Business*, July 1986.

Hoag, J. "Toward Indices of Real Estate Value and Return." *Journal of Finance,* May 1980.

Miles, M., and T. McCue. "Commercial Real Estate Returns." *Journal of the American Real Estate and Urban Economics Associations,* Fall 1984.

Zerbst, R. H., and B. R. Cambon. "Historical Returns on Real Estate Investments." *Journal of Portfolio Management,* Spring 1984.

APPENDIX

Data Series and Sources

Source	Data Description
Frank Russell Company (FRC Indexes)	A quarterly time series of equity real estate returns extending from 1978 to the present. The series is broken down by income and capital gains and also by region and property type. Currently, the data base has approximately 1000 properties owned by real estate funds with an average value of about $10 million per property.
Evaluation Associates (EAFPI)	A quarterly time series extending from 1969 to the present. It is an index constructed by an equal weighting of the returns on a number of largely all-equity real estate funds. The data base currently includes about thirty-three tax-exempt funds with a total asset value of about $25 billion.
Gs & Co. Equity REIT Returns (EREIT)	A monthly time series extending from 1974 to the present. It is an equally-weighted index constructed from thirty-three REITs holding more than 80% equity assets. In comparison with the FRC index, EREIT is more heavily concentrated in shopping centers and apartments and less in office properties.
Stock, Bond, and Inflation Data	Ibbotson and Associates provide a comprehensive monthly data base that begins in 1926.

Part 2. Mortgages

3　Mortgage Choice

James R. Follain

Mortgage choice refers to a set of problems faced by a homeowner that includes the choice of a loan-to-value ratio, the refinancing and default decisions, and the choice of mortgage instrument. This paper reviews much of the literature that has been written on the topic. It begins with a listing of the major stylized facts the literature seeks to explain. Models used to explain mortgage choice are categorized and discussed. It is argued that the relatively simple certainty model that incorporates liquidity constraints seems capable of explaining some of the stylized facts, but is unable to explain some others. The paper concludes with a discussion of three policy questions that require a better understanding of mortgage choice before they can be answered. The paper is based upon the author's Presidential Address to the American Real Estate and Urban Economics Association, which was delivered in Atlanta, Georgia on December 29, 1989.

INTRODUCTION

My first publication, which appeared in the *AREUEA Journal* in 1977, analyzes the demand for alternative mortgage instruments (AMIs) [16]. My most recent publication also addresses the issue of mortgage choice; Jan Brueckner and I [9] consider its effect on housing demand. In between these two papers, I published several others about mortgage choice, which is defined broadly to include the choice of mortgage instrument as well as the loan-to-value, refinancing, and default decisions facing owner-occupants. Mortgage choice is also the topic of this address because it is a challenging problem ripe for additional study.

Lest you think that my knowledge of this topic is limited only to academic experiences, let me assure you this is not the case. Barbara and I obtained our first mortgage in 1974 and it was a classic thirty-year FHA-FRM. Since then we have had nine mortgages including one-month, six-month, and twelve-month ARMs, assumable loans, home improvement loans, home equity loans, and even a ten-year FRM from the seller of the house. Our LTV has varied from 97% to 50%. Given time I might be able to concoct a model that explains this behavior, but I have found it easier to focus my research on the "typical" consumer, who we know makes rational mortgage choices without being privy to the academic literature on this topic.

From *AREUEA Journal*, Vol. 18, No. 2, 1990. The comments of Patric Hendershott, Donald Haurin and Jan Brueckner are appreciated.

I begin with a set of stylized facts, which our models of mortgage choice should seek to explain. I then present a broad characterization of the models used to explain mortgage choice. One group is labeled certainty models; they assume interest rates and housing prices are known and that mortgage choices are driven by transactions costs, liquidity constraints, and taxes. Uncertainty models are more recent and include mean-variance utility maximization models as well as option pricing models of mortgage choice. After reviewing the stylized facts and the models used to explain mortgage choice, I conclude with a discussion of several policy questions that await a better understanding of mortgage choice.

The focus of this address is the homeowner as opposed to the real estate investor. The homeowner's problem may be more complex than the investor's because the typical homeowner has to worry about all of the issues an investor does—the cost of debt and equity, default, diversification, transactions costs—and also has to think bout the possibility of moving, liquidity constraints, and whether non-housing expenses are sufficient to take full advantage of the mortgage interest deduction. Of course, the homeowner is also less informed than the investor because the homeowner, unlike many investors, has another job.

DIMENSIONS OF MORTGAGE CHOICE

Mortgage choice is more general than mortgage demand, although both refer to the demand side of the market. A basic component of mortgage choice is the loan-to-value (LTV) decision. Although much has been written about the aggregate demand for mortgages, housing economists do not seem to have picked up on what many financial economists have made a career of doing: explaining debt-equity ratios. Hendershott and Hsieh [20] and Jones [24] are rare papers that address this issue directly. More typically, mortgage demand is viewed as a multiple of housing demand, a multiple that receives little attention.

A second component of mortgage choice is the choice of mortgage instrument. Many have analyzed the choice between the FRM and the ARM; recent examples include Brueckner and Follain [8], Dhillon et al, [12] Sa-Aadu and Shilling [27], and Sa-Aadu and Sirmans [28]. Other mortgage instruments also have been studied including the PLAM, the GPM, the RAM, and more; for example, Jim Alm and I forecast the demand for PLAMs, GPMs and some subsidized mortgage instruments like FHA 235 [1,2].

The third component of mortgage choice includes the decisions to prepay or default. These decisions may be considered special cases of the loan-to-value decision, but they are unique enough to justify separate classification. Prepayment may be caused by a household's decision to move, by refinancing to obtain a lower rate, or to obtain more money. Wall Street analysts have devoted much attention to prepayment lately hoping to gain some advantage in the pricing of mortgage securities. Default is also of interest to such analysts as well as to private and government mortgage insurers. Indeed, default is probably going to receive even more attention based upon recent reports on the status of the FHA insurance fund. Sa-Aadu [26] surveys some of this literature.

Another choice that is relevant but does not fit neatly into these categories is the coupon-points choice. Should a household select a mortgage with a high coupon and a low number of points or a low coupon with a high number of points? This might be considered a special case of the instrument choice, but I think it better fits into the third category, especially if one views points and the spread between the mortgage and the current treasury as payments for the prepayment and the default options embedded in the mortgage. Little has been written on this topic.

Implicit in much of this literature is the belief that the supply of funds to any one capital market is perfectly elastic; as a result, the price or yield on a mortgage is determined by supply. However, the price at which supply is perfectly elastic can depend on mortgage choice. One example of this involves the ARM-FRM choice. If households with longer expected holding periods are more likely to choose FRMs, then the value of the prepayment and default options implicit in a mortgage will be greater because the period until expiration is longer for FRMs in a world in which ARMs exist than in one without ARMs. More generally, the determinants of the default and prepayment decisions are key inputs into any pricing model for mortgages on owner-occupant housing units. The better our understanding of these decisions, the better will be our pricing models.

STYLIZED FACTS

Any model of mortgage choice should be consistent with several stylized facts about mortgage choice. What follows is a list that seems reasonable to me.

Loan-to-Value Decision (LTVs)

A1. LTVs for the population as a whole are quite low, around 30%; indeed, over one-third of owners have no mortgage at all. The American Housing Survey, the Survey of Consumer Finances, and the recent Michigan Survey on Home Mortgage Debt confirm these numbers.

A2. LTVs among recent homebuyers are much higher. National Association of Realtors survey data indicate that the average ratio is about 0.7, a number also substantiated by FHLBB data on new loans. Although the ratio is higher for first-time homebuyers, the difference is not nearly as stark as the difference between recent homebuyers and existing homebuyers.

A3. LTVs decline rapidly with length of stay in the house. Amortization is one obvious reason, but appreciation in the value of the house is another. It does not seem to be the case that the ratio at the time of purchase is anything like an intertemporal optimum that households seek to maintain.

A4. LTVs among the elderly are especially low; 83% of those 65 years of age or older have no mortgage debt whatsoever. Those who promote the Reverse Annuity Mortgage would especially like to know why this is true.

A5. Lending rules limit mortgage payment to income ratios and loan-to-value ratios. These rules vary over time and among markets and individuals.

Explaining variations in the loan-to-value ratios among households is difficult based upon my own experience. I have made attempts using several different surveys including the 1977 and 1983 Surveys of Consumer Finances, the National Association of Realtor's Survey of Mortgage Finance, and the Annual Housing Survey. All of the work is unpublished because I have never found it easy to market papers that say, "Please publish my paper that shows I cannot explain what I set out to explain, especially with data that are questionable and omit some important variables." About the only variables I find to matter are length of stay, age and income. I usually find a modest positive relationship between income and LTV whereas the LTV decreases as age and length of stay increase.

Mortgage Instrument Choice

B1. The FRM works well during noninflationary times and it remains extremely popular.

B2. The surge in ARM originations in the 1980s was demand driven, being strongly related to movements in the level of interest rates and the FRM ARM rate spread, e.g., Brueckner and Follain [8,9].

B3. Some household characteristics affect the demand for ARMs, but their influence is modest. Demand increases modestly with income, although this may represent the fact that FHA did not insure ARMs until recently. The variable most likely to matter is expected length of stay—short-timers prefer the use of ARMs, especially during periods of an upward sloping yield curve and teasers—yet only proxies for this variable have been used in the empirical studies with which I am familiar.

B4. The demand for other instruments is weak. Jack Guttentag and Susan Wachter once counted over 100 AMIs, but few have been successful on a large scale. The GPM had some limited success, but the PLAM has not done well despite some projections by me in the early '80s that it would.

B5. The demand for the home equity loan is modest. A recent survey by the Michigan Survey Research Center [11] finds that only 6% of homeowners have obtained home equity loans in 1988. High-income households are most likely to have such loans.

Explanation of the demand for specific ARM features is as difficult as the explanation of the LTV ratio. Usually these involve estimating "demand" equations for characteristics such as cap size and adjustment period. I have made some attempts and I know of others, but no important conclusions have been generated by this research, to my knowledge.

Refinancing and Default

C1. Refinancing does not take place as rapidly as pure option pricing models would suggest. Recent work by Louis Scott, Tai-le Yang, and me [15] support this claim, but others have done so, too.

C2. Default seems to depend upon the LTV. Foster and Van Order [18] find that default occurs most often when housing equity is substantially negative and below what a purely financial model of default would predict. This is similar to the result stated above that prepayment is less sensitive to the interest-rate spread than the pure financial model suggests.

C3. Foreclosure is relatively uncommon.

I am unable to identify other information about prepayments and defaults that is both general enough and known with enough certainty to label as "stylized facts"; however, I would like to introduce another category labeled as "suspicions" (S) or my own educated guesses. Empirical support or rebuttal might be useful information in our search to develop better models of prepayment and default. These include:

S1. Many lenders state as fact that refinancing should occur when the current market rate is 200 basis points below the existing contract rate. Prepayment models do show severe nonlinearity; little occurs with a differential below 100 basis points or above 400 basis points.

S2. Refinancing usually involves increasing the LTV ratio. I am not confident of this at all, but it represents a suspicion that many people refinance not just to obtain a lower rate but also to obtain more debt.

S3. Short-time stayers choose high coupon rates and low points.

S4. Personal bankruptcy is common when foreclosure does occur. This would occur if people have all of their wealth in their homes, so lenders had little to gain by suing for a share of their non-housing wealth. It would be interesting to know whether foreclosure is more common in states that allow recourse than in those that do not.

MODELS OF MORTGAGE CHOICE

Two broad categories of models are used to explain mortgage choice. The first is labeled certainty models because the future movements of interest rates, housing prices, and other economic variables are assumed known. Uncertainty models treat interest rates and housing price as stochastic variables.

Certainty Models. The simplest certainty model assumes the borrower faces a fixed cost of debt and equity; the homeowner chooses a high LTV if debt is cheaper than equity, and vice versa. If the cost of debt increases more rapidly with the LTV than the cost of equity does, then an optimal LTV can be defined as the LTV at which the marginal cost of one more dollar of debt just equals the marginal cost of one more dollar of equity. This model is found in many textbooks on real estate finance. More elaborate versions of the model introduce taxes, varying holding periods, and liquidity constraints.

Modigliani and Miller (MM) have taught us that this simple model is not appropriate in perfect capital markets characterized by the absence of transactions costs and liquidity constraints, but the model does yield insights about some aspects of mortgage choice. Consider the case of the ARM-FRM choice. If a household expects to remain in a house for only a few years, then this model may be all one needs to explain why mobile households choose a capped ARM with a first-year teaser over an FRM during periods of upward sloping yield curves. In such a case, the ARM debt is absolutely cheaper than FRM debt over the expected holding period; more complex financial analysis adds little.

Although this may have been the case for some of the early demand for ARMs, to my knowledge, only proxies for expected holding periods have been used to test the role of expected holding period. Some explicit testing of the role of expected holding period is required. In any event, this model is unlikely to be important if first-year discounts become less common and the yield curve flattens. Also, the models yield little insight about mortgage choice among households with long expected holding periods because the model does not take into account uncertainty about the future course of interest rates.

The addition of taxes to the simple model increases its explanatory power and may provide a partial explanation as to why many high income households have large LTVs. High income households with tax rates above the rate at which tax-exempts dominate taxables have an arbitrage opportunity if they borrow at the mortgage rate and itemize deductions. These households should have large LTVs and invest any available equity in tax-exempts. The profit per dollar of debt can easily be in excess of 2% for households in the 50% tax bracket when the tax-exempt rate equals 75% of the taxable rate (see Hendershott and Ling [21]).

Strictly speaking, this arbitrage is illegal, although it is difficult to identify the source of investments in commingled portfolios. This also makes empirical tests of this hypothesis difficult; no empirical studies exist that examine the importance of the arbitrage, to my knowledge. Even if one believes this arbitrage opportunity was a factor in the past, it is probably less important in the current market and tax environment, which feature lower marginal tax rates and a higher ratio of the returns to a tax-exempt versus a taxable security.

The simple model also has been used to shed light on the refinancing decision. The simple model suggests that refinancing will not occur until the savings in mortgage payments associated with refinancing exceed the cost of refinancing, the savings being discounted by the current market rate. Tzang and I [17] compute the savings associated with refinancing under a variety of assumptions regarding tax rate, origination costs, holding period, and transactions costs to examine the validity of the 200-basis-point rule mentioned above. If one interprets transactions costs broadly to include the cost of the prepayment option a borrower forgoes upon prepayment, then the analysis yields some insights about refinancing. Otherwise, this type of analysis of the refinancing decision understates the interest-rate differential needed to justify refinancing because it does not take into account the value of the prepayment option. To do this requires a model with uncertainty.

Another issue for which the simple model may yield insights concerns the LTV choices of elderly households and the demand for RAMs. As noted above, most elderly households choose corner solutions, not only in terms of zero LTVs but also in terms of high portions of wealth in housing equity. Such corner solutions seem to expose the elderly to financial risks because all of their assets are in one basket, but the simple model suggests why their decisions may be quite sensible.

First, because most elderly probably take the standard deduction, interest payments are not taxable but interest receipts may be; consequently, their cost of debt exceeds the after-tax return they earn on their wealth, assuming the before-tax cost of debt and equity are equal. This argument suggests the optimal LTV for these elderly is zero if diversification benefits are ignored. Second, the before-tax cost of debt may exceed the return an elderly household can earn by investing its equity in non-housing assets. This is probably quite possible for elderly households with small loans; in such a case transactions costs may by themselves generate a substantial spread between the cost of debt and the return to equity investments. If so, then the optimal LTV for an elderly household is zero, and the demand for RAMs will be very small.

Tax considerations and transactions costs may also explain the generally low level of LTVs among households. If many households believe that the cost of debt they face exceeds the returns they can earn on their equity investments, then many would be expected to have low LTVs. In fact, such a possibility is consistent with the existence of substantial transactions costs in the debt and equity markets in which these households operate. Taking account of income tax considerations increases the possibility that households face a positive spread between the cost of debt and equity, especially possible for those who do not itemize deductions. The only data I have seen on this subject indicates that many owners do not itemize. The recent Michigan survey [11] indicates that only 57% of homeowners itemize; among these, 35% have no home mortgage debt. This suggests that a strong link exists between a household's decision to itemize and the amount of mortgage debt it owes; the recent Michigan survey could be useful in exploring this linkage further.

Constrained Demand. The most general model in this category incorporates liquidity constraints into the mortgage choice problem. Alm and Follain [1,2], and Schwab [29] present models of the consumer's intertemporal utility maximization problem subject to various types of liquidity constraints. Alm and Follain consider payment-to-income constraints, downpayment constraints, and positive net worth constraints in their mathematical programming treatment of the problem and compute household willingness to pay measures for various AMIs that circumvent the liquidity constraints. Schwab obtains interesting analytical results about the effect of inflation and the potential benefits of the PLAM in the presence of net worth constraints. Both build on earlier models developed by Tobin and Dolde [30] and Dolde [13]. Brueckner [7] also presents a model that focuses upon the downpayment constraint.

These approaches yield several insights about mortgage choice. First, they easily explain why LTVs among first-time homebuyers are high; they borrow as much as possible in the early years in order to smooth their intertemporal housing consumption path. Second, the role of general inflation is clarified and shown to exacerbate the "tilt" problem not just for first-time homebuyers, but for all households with rising nominal incomes and modest amounts of wealth. Third, they indicate the positive net worth constraint by itself can lead to a large LTV among households and a substantial willingness to pay for AMIs that combat the tilt problem.

Much empirical work also has been done to examine the role of these liquidity constraints in housing demand and tenure choice, although less has been done on the issue of mortgage choice. Brueckner and Follain [8,9] attribute the strong role of the level of interest rates in the ARM-FRM choice to liquidity constraints. Zorn [32] estimates that the housing consumption choices of 66% of the population in 1986 would have been affected by such constraints; their tenure decisions would be much less affected. Most of the evidence presented is indirect; more direct tests that take explicit account of the constraints are needed. One puzzling aspect of the literature is the modest link between the liquidity constraint literature in housing and that in the larger macroeconomic literature. Numerous papers going back to Tobin and Dolde [30] and recent papers by Hayashi [19] argue that liquidity constraints may be important in the macroeconomy. The literature often alludes to housing as a market in which liquidity constraints are likely to occur, but then goes on to estimate the impact of these constraints using aggregate consumption data. It seems to me the role of liquidity constraints can be more easily identified by studying the market in which they are most prevalent—housing and mortgages—than by studying broad aggregates. We should take more steps to link our results to the broader debate in the macroeconomics literature.

In sum, the simple model can explain a portion of the demand for ARMs versus FRMs, the portion attributable to homebuyers with very short expected holding periods. With taxes and liquidity constraints, the model can explain large LTVs among first-time homebuyers and many other younger households during inflationary periods and, perhaps, the low LTVs among the elderly and the overall population.

Uncertainty Models. The main reason to introduce uncertainty into a model of mortgage choice is because entire classes of problems cannot otherwise be addressed. The ARM-FRM choice is the best example because the selection of the ARM increases the interest-rate risk experienced by the borrower, a risk that can only be assessed in a model that takes explicit account of interest-rate uncertainty. A complete treatment of refinancing, default, the selection of the point-coupon combination, and selecting the optimal LTV requires the application of the type of uncertainty models found in the modern literature in financial economics.

Another reason for using uncertainty models is related to the larger debate about the efficiency of financial markets. Strict versions of efficient markets imply that households are indifferent about the LTV and the choice of mortgage instrument. If empirical evidence shows that some mortgage choices and LTVs are not random, then proponents of the efficient markets model will want to find out why. Hard core proponents might argue, for example, that hedging instruments exist to allow a borrower to hedge any risk associated with an ARM. Also, purists are not pleased by explanations of mortgage choice that resort to imperfections in the mortgage market such as transactions costs and liquidity constraints. Analyzing mortgage choice in the context of a sophisticated financial model with uncertainty offers an opportunity to counter the arguments that mortgage choice is driven by transactions costs and liquidity constraints.

The standard mean-variance expected utility model has been often employed to analyze mortgage choice. Jim Alm and I [3] develop a model in which households maximize a utility function that depends upon the mean and variance of wealth at the end of the second period in a two-period model. The wealth constraint depends upon initial wealth, income and its growth rate, the cost of mortgage debt, the return on a risky asset, housing prices and a terminal wealth condition. The household can choose between a mortgage in which the interest rate is stochastic and one in which the rate is fixed. Comparative statics are computed numerically to indicate the sensitivity of willingness to pay measures for the FRM to changes in income, the covariance matrix of returns, preferences toward risk, and other variables. Although the results are quite sensitive to the parameterization of the problem, it provides a framework for thinking about the problem.

Brueckner [6] offers a different approach in which the ARM-FRM choice is made continuous. The borrower chooses the size of the cap associated with interest-rate movement. If the cap is zero, then the mortgage is essentially an FRM. An infinite cap is equivalent to a pure ARM. A price function is developed that indicates the market price for each cap amount, and borrowers maximize utility subject to this price function. An important result is that borrowers usually choose finite cap amounts and, effectively, agree to share interest-rate risk with the lender, depending upon the preferences for risk of both the borrower and lender.

Using the same type of framework Arvan and Brueckner [4,5] analyze optimal risk-sharing between lender and borrower, deriving the features of the optimal ARM contract. They show that the margin-cap structure of current ARMs is not optimal. A superior arrangement involves a more continuous type of risk-sharing in which the borrower shares part of any cost-of-funds increase experienced by the lender, with no cap used.

More specific insights from these models are difficult to obtain because so little is known about the parameters that shape the problem; indeed, estimation of the parameters is extremely demanding in terms of data. Brueckner and Follain [8,9] are able to test some of the ideas, but many more are untested because variables such as the size and composition of non-housing wealth and expectations about returns to various investments are not included. More work on these questions is needed, especially during periods with a flatter term structure and smaller first-year discounts.

A second type of uncertainty model of mortgage choice draws upon the option pricing literature. In these models the mortgage is viewed as an asset with two implicit options, a default and a prepayment option. Borrowers are assumed to take the value of the options into account in their refinancing or default decisions. Hendershott and Van Order provide a thorough review of this literature [23].

The refinancing decision demonstrates the value of the option pricing model to mortgage choice. A borrower refinances if the savings from refinancing exceed incidental transactions costs plus the value of the call option implicit in the existing mortgage. The call should be included as a cost because it represents an opportunity cost of refinancing. Follain, Scott and Yang [15] use a binomial option pricing model to compute the interest-rate differentials needed to justify refinancing. They find general support for the 200-basis-point rule and show how the certainty approach to refinancing understates the differential. Many others have developed models along these lines including Kau, et al. [25] and Chen and Ling [10].

Wall Street has invested many resources into the development of econometric models of prepayment loosely based upon the pure option-pricing model. Although many of these models are proprietary, my sense is they do show modest support for the option-pricing approach to prepayment. They find that prepayments depend upon the spread between the existing mortgage rate and the current market rate, but the pattern of response is generally slower than the pure option-pricing model suggests. These models also include seasonal and regional variables and aggregate measures that explain household mobility. To my knowledge, none of these models incorporate information about the *expected* holding period of the borrower, a variable that surely affects the borrower's perception of the value of the call option and, hence, his or her refinancing decision.

The default decision is modeled similarly. A borrower is assumed to default if the value of the house exceeds the value of the mortgage inclusive of the default option and any relevant transactions costs. Most applications of this approach either focus on pricing the default option or testing its relevance empirically. A recent example is Foster and Van Order [18], who estimate a default function for FHA data. Like earlier studies they find that default to be more a function of equity in the house than income and household characteristics; however, households default at lower housing prices than the pure model suggests.

More work on default is needed and two additional improvements seem especially important. First, the cost of default should be studied carefully, especially the costs of bankruptcy, which are themselves stochastic. Perhaps some after-the-fact interviews of those who defaulted in Texas during the mid-1980s might yield some interesting information. Second, default behavior in recourse and nonrecourse states should be studied.

Although this will require information about the non-housing wealth of households in recourse states, this is really necessary before the option-pricing approach can be accepted as empirically important in recourse states.

Development of the uncertainty models along the lines of the certainty models calls for the inclusion of liquidity constraints. Unfortunately, this is quite difficult to do in a multiperiod framework. Alm and Follain [3] do so in a two-period model, but their approach does not apply to the multiperiod problem. One indirect way of doing so in a multiperiod model is to use a utility function that is not defined at negative values, but, to my knowledge, no one has explicitly introduced the net worth restriction. Until this is done, the uncertainty models seem to offer little guidance to some problems in mortgage choice, such as how to design mortgage instruments to aid first-time homebuyers.

Uncertainty models have not been applied to study the LTV problem of the general population or the elderly. Some simply assert that the optimal LTV in a properly specified portfolio model is indeterminate, e.g., Woodward and Weicher [31]. I would like to see a model developed to indicate the potential diversification benefits of a portfolio that includes mortgage debt and investments in non-housing assets relative to a portfolio that includes no debt or non-housing assets, the latter being representative of the typical household portfolio. It seems to me that the diversification benefits must be modest to be consistent with the low LTVs among the population, especially among the elderly.

In summary, the introduction of uncertainty models produces substantial insights about mortgage choice. The uncertainty models allow the analysis of whole classes of problems that cannot be explored by the certainty model. Option-pricing models are especially revealing, even though the empirical models suggest they are insufficient by themselves to explain fully refinancing and default behavior. Nonetheless, due to the difficulty of solving uncertainty models with liquidity constraints they are not very useful in analyzing the tilt problem and AMIs designed specifically to address it, e.g., GPMs and PLAMs. The uncertainty models may be able to shed light on the LTV decisions among the general population, especially the elderly, but little has been done in this direction so far.

POLICY QUESTIONS

Much progress has been made since we first started examining mortgage choice fifteen years ago. The simpler certainty models seem to provide insights about situations affected by taxes and liquidity constraints, while the uncertainty models are essential to understanding refinancing and default. Both provide insights about the ARM-FRM choice.

Despite the progress we still lack a comprehensive model that covers all choices for all households. The lack of such a model and the stringent data demands associated with the problem hinder careful empirical analysis. Progress can be enhanced by the development of better databases; information about expected holding periods and non-housing assets is especially important. More analysis of the basic LTV decision, especially among the elderly, would be useful.

Such information would be of more than academic interest. Indeed, there are several important policy questions that await better analysis of mortgage choice. I would like to close with a discussion of some of these policy questions.

How Would the Elimination of the Mortgage Interest Deduction Affect the LTV Decisions of Households? David Ling and I [14] presented a paper at this year's AREUEA meetings in which we show the value of the mortgage interest deduction has been greatly diminished in value by the 1986 Tax Reform Act, which increased the standard deduction and reduced the number of non-housing expenses that can be itemized. In fact, the mortgage deduction is virtually worthless to many middle-income households. The primary beneficiaries of the deduction are recent homebuyers and higher-income households with enough non-housing deductions to take full advantage of their mortgage interest deductions.

If the subsidy is of little value to middle-income homeowners, especially the elderly, then why not eliminate the deduction altogether. First-time homebuyers can be compensated for any loss they might incur from its elimination with a more targeted subsidy to them. High-income households with large mortgage debt might suffer, but this suffering might be minimized if the elimination is phased in over a number of years.

Indeed, some (e.g., Woodward and Weicher [31]) argue that high-income households would not be hurt at all; they would simply eliminate their use of debt. According to this version of the MM hypothesis, high-income households are indifferent to their LTV in the current tax environment, but if interest is no longer deductible the playing field would then favor equity and high-income households would rush out to sell stocks and bonds and pay off their mortgage debt.

Is this really true? Is it feasible to think that the housing choices of high-income households above, say $60,000 would be unchanged by the elimination of the interest deduction? At a minimum a reduction in their LTVs would produce a less diversified portfolio, which might generate a decline in housing consumption. Also, if the tax-exempt arbitrage argument stated above has any merit, housing consumption would decline. Unfortunately, little empirical evidence exists on this issue. A related question is whether we will see a dramatic reduction in LTV ratios among middle-income households in the next decade who no longer obtain any benefit from the interest deduction. Possibly, but, again, little hard evidence is available to draw upon for guidance.

My own guess is that the elimination of the interest deduction would probably increase the cost of housing but actually improve the distribution of the subsidy, especially if a new form of aid is targeted to first-time homebuyers. I would also guess that such a package would represent an improvement over the current situation because the existing subsidy is so large and heavily skewed toward high-income households; however, it is hard to be dogmatic without more evidence as to how households might adjust their LTVs and housing choices in response to such a change. Better models and more empirical evidence on these points would be welcome additions to the debate.

What Will Happen to the Demand for ARMs if the Term Structure Flattens, Inflation Continues its Decline, and the Baby-boomers Decline in Importance? The early portion of the 1980s was characterized by higher than normal long-term mortgage rates and substantial spreads between long and short rates. The slope of the yield curve and the level of long-term rates have declined somewhat in recent years as inflation has diminished (Hendershott and Peek [22]). Also, lenders are not using "teaser" rates to entice households toward ARMs as they did in much of the 1980s. Will these changes reduce the demand for ARMs by recent homebuyers and lead existing households to refinance their ARMs with FRMs?

Another factor that may reduce the demand for ARMs is the aging of the baby-boom population, those born in the late 1940s and 1950s. Younger households are probably more mobile and liquidity constrained than older households and, as a result, are probably more attracted to ARMs, especially during periods of inflation and steep term structure curves.

My own guess is that ARM demand will decrease under these conditions because much of the demand for ARMs represents a response to the tilt problem and a demand by mobile households who took advantage of teasers and capped ARMs to reduce their cost of debt. If this is true, then we might see many current ARM borrowers refinancing in the 1990s with FRMs to reduce their interest-rate risk.

One reaction to these questions might be, Who cares? One group who might care includes those concerned about the S&Ls and deposit insurance. If regulators are counting on a strong ARM demand and a continuance of interest-rate risk sharing by households, they may be in for a surprise. If households shun ARMs during periods of lower interest rates, we may see a return to the same set of circumstances that immediately preceded the 1980s, a set of circumstances that led to one of the greatest financial disasters in history, the collapse of the S&L industry. Taxpayers will have to be on guard; otherwise we might see our "defense dividend" chewed up by another S&L collapse.

Is Housing Policy Better Served by Explicit Interest Subsidies or Mortgage Guarantees? More specifically, are mortgage insurance subsidies like some of the FHA 202 programs preferred in any way to explicit mortgage interest subsidies, e.g., FHA 235? The two programs are equivalent if the borrower can borrow at the risk-neutral rate. If one believes the federal government can borrow at the risk-neutral rate, then the distinction between a guarantee and an explicit subsidy is probably not important to it unless guarantees are used to bypass contrived federal budget restrictions. In such a situation, guarantees are desirable to those who wish to avoid the day of reckoning.

Most citizens, I would think, would not advocate such a policy. Instead, housing policy should seek to provide whatever housing assistance the citizenry deems appropriate as cheaply as possible and with a minimum of distortions. In such case, it is not obvious which of the two policy alternatives is optimal. Neither is the choice obvious for state and local governments because they do not borrow at the risk-neutral rate.

Much has been written about the proper pricing of guarantees and about the costs and benefits of interest-rate subsidies. To my knowledge, little has been written that compares guarantees to interest-rate subsidies. Indeed, this is an example of a case in which the certainty and the uncertainty approaches must be combined. The uncertainty approach sheds light on the effects and the deadweight loss associated with interest-rate subsidies, but the uncertainty approach is needed to evaluate guarantee programs like mortgage insurance.

Although I do not claim to have thought through this issue completely, it strikes me as a problem similar to the ARM-FRM choice facing households. A system of interest-rate subsidies is similar to an FRM in that the payments are known with certainty; whereas the guarantees are similar to an ARM contract. An uncertainty model is needed to make a comparison. If policy-makers are assumed to be risk neutral and the risks of a guarantee program can be completely hedged, then a contingent claims approach is needed. Otherwise, a more general choice model under uncertainty is needed that takes account of risk aversion and imperfect capital markets. The problem becomes even messier if liquidity constraints—e.g., Gramm-Rudman—are taken into account.

REFERENCES

[1] James Alm and James R. Follain. Alternative Mortgage Instruments: Their Effects on Consumer Housing Choices in an Inflationary Environment. *Public Finance Quarterly* 10: 134–57, April 1982.

[2] ———. Alternative Mortgage Instruments, the Tilt Problem, and Consumer Welfare. *Journal of Financial and Quantitative Analysis* 19(1): 113–26, March 1984.

[3] ———. Consumer Demand for Adjustable Rate Mortgages. *Housing Finance Review* 6: 1–16, 1987.

[4] Lanny Arvan and Jan K. Brueckner. Efficient Contracts in Credit Markets Subject to Interest Rate Risk: An Application of Vaviv's Insurance Model. *American Economic Review* 76: 259–63, March 1986.

[5] ———. Risk Sharing in the Adjustable-Rate Loan Market: Are Existing Contracts Efficient? *Economics Letters* 22: 361–64, 1986.

[6] Jan K. Brueckner. The Pricing of Interest Rate Caps and Consumer Choice in the Market for Adjustable-Rate Mortgages, *Housing Finance Review* 5: 119–36, 1986.

[7] ———. The Downpayment and Housing Tenure Choice: A Simplified Exposition. *Regional Science and Urban Economics* 16: 519–25, 1985.

[8] ——— and James R. Follain. The Rise and the Fall of the ARM: An Economic Study of Mortgage Choice. *Review of Economics and Statistics:* 92–103, February 1988.

[9] ———. ARMs and the Demand for Housing. *Regional Science and Urban Economics* 19: 164–87, 1989.

[10] Andrew Chen and David Ling. Optimal Mortgage Refinancing with Stochastic Interest Rates. *AREUEA Journal* 17: 278–99, Fall 1989.

[11] Richard T. Curtin. National Survey of Home Equity Loans. Survey Research Center, University of Michigan, 1989.

[12] Upinder S. Dhillon, James D. Shilling and C. F. Sirmans. Choosing between Fixed and Adjustable Rate Mortgages. *Journal of Money, Credit, and Banking* 19: 260–67, May 1987.

[13] Walter Dolde. Capital Markets and the Short-Run Behavior of Life Cycle Savers. *Journal of Finance* 33: 413–28, May 1978.

[14] James R. Follain and David C. Ling. The Federal Tax Subsidy to Housing and the Reduced Value of the Mortgage Interest Deduction. Department of Economics Discussion Paper No. 40, Syracuse University, January 1990.

[15] James R. Follain, Louis O. Scott and Tai-Le Yang. Micro Foundation of a Mortgage Prepayment Function. ORER Paper No. 69, University of Illinois Office of Real Estate Research, 1988.

[16] James R. Follain and Raymond Struyk. Homeownership Effects of Alternative Mortgage Instruments. *AREUEA Journal:* 1–37, May 1977.

[17] James R. Follain and Dah-nein Tzang. The Interest Rate Differential Needed to Justify Refinancing a Mortgage. *Appraisal Journal:* 243–51, April 1987.

[18] Chet Foster and Robert Van Order. FHA Terminations: A Prelude to Rational Mortgage Pricing. *AREUEA Journal* 13(3): 273–91, 1985.

[19] Fumio Hayashi. Tests for Liquidity Constraints: A Critical Survey. National Bureau of Economic Research Paper No. 1720, 1985.

[20] Patric H. Hendershott and Chang-tseh Hsieh. Inflation and the Growth in Home Mortgage Debt. *The Journal of Financial Research* 3(2): 189–202, Fall 1980.

[21] Patric H. Hendershott and David C. Ling. Prospective Changes in the Tax Law and the Value of Depreciable Real Estate. *AREUEA Journal* 12: 297–317, Fall 1984.

[22] Patric H. Hendershott and Joe Peek. Treasury Bill Rates in the 1970s and 1980s. National Bureau of Economic Research Paper No. 3036, 1989.

[23] Patric H. Hendershott and Robert Van Order. Pricing Mortgages: An Interpretation of the Models and Results. National Bureau of Economic Research Paper No. 2290, 1987.

[24] Lawrence D. Jones. Determinants of Home Mortgage Debt. Unpublished manuscript, University of British Columbia, 1985.

[25] James B. Kau, Donald C. Keenan, Walter J. Muller, James F. Epperson. Pricing Fixed Rate Mortgages with Default and Prepayment. Unpublished manuscript, University of Georgia, 1989.

[26] J. Sa-Aadu. Legal Restrictions, Credit Allocation, and Default Risk Under Fixed and Adjustable Rate Mortgages. *Housing Finance Review* 7: 225–47, 1988.

[27] ——— and James Shilling. Testing for Self-Selection in Adjustable-Rate Mortgage Markets. Working paper, University of Florida, 1989.

[28] J. Sa-Aadu and C. F. Sirmans. The Determinants of Mortgage Contract Choice: A Multinomial Logit Approach. Working paper, University of Florida, 1989.

[29] Robert M. Schwab. Inflation Expectations and the Demand for Housing. *American Economic Review* 72: 143–53, March 1982.

[30] James Tobin and Walter Dolde. Wealth, Liquidity, and Consumption. In *Consumer Spending and Monetary Policy.* Federal Reserve Bank of Boston, 1971.

[31] Susan E. Woodward and John C. Weicher. Goring the Wrong Ox: A Defense of the Mortgage Interest Deduction. *National Tax Journal* 62: 301–13, September 1989.

[32] Peter M. Zorn. Mobility-Tenure Decisions and Financial Credit: Do Mortgage Qualification Requirements Constrain Home Ownership? *AREUEA Journal* 17: 1–16, Spring 1989.

4 Adjustable-Rate and Fixed-Rate Mortgage Choice: A Logit Analysis

Michael Tucker

Logit analysis is used to determine if financial variables are significant in determining borrower selection between fixed-rate and adjustable-rate mortgages. The results support the hypothesis that mortgage choice is a function of the consumer price index, Treasury bill rates, and differences in the initial interest rates offered by the competing mortgages.

INTRODUCTION AND THEORY

Adjustable-rate mortgages (ARMs) have been widely available since 1981 when the Federal Home Loan Bank Board (FHLBB) allowed their use under its auspices. They have fluctuated in popularity among borrowers since that time. Changes in lender pricing of ARMs is likely more responsible for these fluctuations than individual borrower characteristics.

The efficient market hypothesis suggests that borrowers will select the least expensive mortgage. Determining the least expensive mortgage is not a simple analysis because uncertain future interest-rate changes in the ARM are as important as actual initial rate differentials between it and comparable FRMs. While it is likely that greater favorable differentials between introductory ARM rates and FRM rates increase the probability borrowers will select ARMs, their choice may also be influenced by signals gleaned from other pricing variables. The borrower's expectations of future ARM interest-rate changes based upon the level of the current underlying benchmark interest rate against which ARMs are adjusted and the consumer price index (CPI), as a measure of current inflation and a predictor of future inflation, may also play a role in mortgage choice. The current benchmark rate provides a market price for the mortgage rates as compared to the below-market rate offered by the lender. The CPI can be seen as an ad hoc predictor of future interest rates.

An increasing CPI that reflects higher housing prices relative to income may generate a greater demand for lower initial interest-rate ARMs that enable buyers to qualify for larger loans. Rising prices may initially create greater demand as buyers rush to purchase before they are priced out of the market. They buy as much home as they can afford, learning that they will not be able to do better in the future. Those same rising prices also inspire buyer confidence in the value of his purchase. He is more willing to

From *The Journal of Real Estate Research*, Vol. 4, No. 2.

accept the greater interest-rate risk inherent in ARMs in the expectation of greater returns in the form of price appreciation. Buyers with incomes more likely to adjust upward quickly with a rising CPI, will have the added confidence of being able to afford any subsequent mortgage payment increases.

Mobility may also motivate choice. Borrowers expecting short-term home ownership would likely benefit from the lower initial interest rates offered by ARMs. They will avoid later rate escalation by exercising their option to sell and pay off their ARMs prior to rate escalation.

Higher current benchmark rates will have a dampening effect on ARM selection. Introductory ARM rates are typically priced below market, i.e., the current benchmark rate plus the loan's specified spread above that rate. If benchmark rates are currently rising and/or already high, borrower choice of mortgage may be more greatly influenced by expected future interest rates than the initial below-market rate. Expectations of higher payments could increase the number of borrowers selecting FRMs.

It is the premise of this paper that while individual borrower characteristics may play some role in mortgage selection, pricing variables such as interest-rate differentials between fixed and adjustable-rate mortgages, benchmark interest rates against which adjustable-rate mortgages are set and the CPI are of greater importance in determining mortgage choice. The importance of pricing variables can be demonstrated by using them to predict mortgage choice. Results of the logit analysis conducted below support this hypothesis.

LITERATURE REVIEW

Two studies have attempted to reveal the underlying borrower preferences for ARMs versus FRMs by focusing on variables descriptive of individual borrowers, pertinent financial characteristics of the mortgages themselves and geographical differences [3, 5].

Dhillon, Shilling and Sirmans, using data from a lender doing business in one city over one year, were unable to find a strong relationship between mortgage choice and individual borrower characteristics [5]. While none of the variables were statistically significant, pricing variables were considerably more important in constructing a probit model that was able to predict borrower preference than were borrower characteristics. Brueckner and Follain [3], using a national database from a single year (1985), found only one variable descriptive of borrower characteristics that was statistically significant. A borrower's income was positively related to the selection of ARMs. Pricing variables, however, were more important in determining which mortgage a borrower selected, with the difference between the initial interest rates of ARMs and FRMs the most important and significant factor in borrower decisionmaking.

The actual ARM and FRM rates offered by lenders may be affected by the yield curve prevailing at that time [11]. Examining borrower mortgage preferences across several years, as is done in this study, allows for greater variability in yield curve behavior and will give a more complete picture of the importance of pricing and economic variables examined.

HYPOTHESIS

Borrower expectations of future interest-rate movement as well as the actual initial interest rates of ARMs and FRMs are likely to be crucial factors in arriving at a decision of mortgage preference. The greater the favorable differential between an ARM and FRM, the greater the probability a borrower will select an ARM.

Housing prices, as a constituent of the CPI, are likely to be highly correlated with general price increases. When already high-priced housing continues to rise at a rate greater than income, some buyers may be more motivated to enter the market as quickly as possible. These buyers will be less likely to qualify for FRM financing for housing of their choice predicating a tilt toward ARMs. Selection of ARMs may be made out of necessity. A positive relationship between the CPI and ARM selection would support this hypothesis.

The CPI may be used by borrowers as a proxy measure to indicate the relative risk of future interest-rate hikes. With the Federal Reserve's stated goal the containment of inflation, a rising CPI implies future hikes in interest rates. For some borrowers, the increased likelihood of a more rapid rise in interest rates associated with a rising CPI will be of more importance than the lower initial rate offered by the ARM. A negative relationship between CPI and ARM selection will support the hypothesis that rate hike apprehension dominates mortgage selection. A positive relationship will support the hypothesis that borrowers seek to borrow the greatest amount their income levels will allow, i.e., ARMs, in order to purchase the most house they can possibly afford when the market is dominated by more rapidly escalating prices.

The one-year constant maturity Treasury bill rate is used by the lender supplying data for this study. This rate plus the lender's stipulated spread (2.75%) represents a fully priced ARM. While lenders offer introductory rates priced below this rate, the fully priced ARM rate may be a buyer's best indication of the future affordability of the loan. The higher that benchmark rate is, the more certain the borrower will be that the initial lower rate offered will in one year adjust upward at the maximum amount allowable. The perceived probability of that maximum adjustment is a function of the current benchmark rate. As such, the one-year constant maturity Treasury bill rate will likely be negatively related to the probability of choosing an ARM, i.e., the higher it is the less likely a borrower will be to select an ARM.

The actual rate offered by either type of mortgage could play a role in determining which is selected. Dhillon, et al., and Brueckner and Follain found that higher levels of FRM interest rates were positively related to the selection of ARMs. The Brueckner study found this variable to be statistically significant. Higher fixed rates would likely increase the difficulty of borrowers qualifying for loans, causing them to opt for lower interest-rate ARMs in order to be able to obtain a mortgage. The high correlation between ARM rates and FRM rates ($r = .90$) eliminates the need to use both rates in separate models. Statistically, it is not possible to incorporate both FRM and ARM rates in the same model with a variable measuring the difference between the two rates because the Gaussian transformation could not be performed. The FRM rate is included in one model for purposes of comparison with the results of the earlier studies.

The rates of thirty-year FRMs and ARMs (one year adjustable) offered and the number of mortgage loans of each type approved monthly from January 1985 through February 1989 were provided by a Connecticut savings and loan institution. While the loans were made throughout the state of Connecticut, most of the mortgages were for the eastern part of the state, an area considered to be part of the New York metropolitan area. Over the fifty-month period 20,697 thirty-year mortgages were granted of which 9,161 were FRMs and 11,536 ARMs. The rates offered for fixed-rate mortgages for each of the fifty months, percentage changes in the New York metropolitan area CPI and one-year constant maturity Treasury bill rates are used to build a logit statistical model.

The margin above the one-year constant maturity Treasury bill benchmark assigned by the lender over all but the first six months of the period was 2.75%. Borrowers paid 2 1/2 points for FRMs and 2 points for ARMs for the last forty-four of the fifty months. The ARMs had a lifetime cap of 6% above the initial rate and an annual adjustment cap of 2%.

The hypothesis is that the probability of borrowers selecting ARMs over FRMs increases as the interest-rate margin between the two types of mortgages increases, decreases with increases in one-year constant maturity Treasury bill rates, and increases with FRM rate increases. The sign of the CPI variable is uncertain.

The hypothesis may be stated as:

Probability of selecting ARM = INTDIFF – T-bill? CPI + FIXINT

where:

INTDIFF = FRM interest rate – ARM interest rate,
CPI = consumer price index at time of loan,
T-bill = one-year constant maturity Treasury bill rate at time of loan,
FIXINT = FRM interest rate offered.

METHODOLOGY

Logit analysis is used to estimate the probability of a borrower selecting an ARM and measures the significance of the variables incorporated in the model. An advantage of the logit distribution over probit is that changes in the value of independent variables will have the greatest impact at the midpoint of the distribution. This is due to the fact that the slope of the logit curve is greatest where *Probability* = ½ [12]. If there are only slight differences between the FRM and ARM selection groups, they are more likely to be detected by logit analysis than by probit.

Logit also imposes fewer restrictions on the statistical properties of the sample distribution than does probit [6, 14]. There is no need for the distribution to be normal. The logit model is specified as [12]:

$$P_i = 1/(1 + e^{-Z_i}) \qquad (1)$$

where:

$$Z_i = a + B_i°X_i \qquad (2)$$

The equation used to estimate the coefficients is:

$$ln(p_i/(1 - p_i)) = a + B_i°X_i \qquad (3)$$

Two models are estimated:

Model 1

$$P_i = f(\text{INTDIFF, T-bill, CPI}) \qquad (4)$$

Model 2

$$P_i = f(\text{T-bill, CPI, FIXINT}) \qquad (5)$$

INTDIFF = (FRM interest rate) − (ARM interest rate),
T-bill = one-year constant maturity Treasury bill rate,
CPI = percent change in the New York metropolitan consumer price index from one year prior,
FIXINT = the FRM interest rate.

As in ordinary least squares regression analysis, the signs of the individual coefficients may be directly interpreted. If the CPI contributes to the probability of a borrower selecting an ARM, the CPI coefficient in the logit model will be positive. The contribution of the variable to the probability of a borrower selecting an ARM will be a function of the CPI value multiplied by the CPI coefficient. If the CPI is higher, the borrower's ex ante probability of selecting an ARM will be greater. A chi-square test measuring the significance of each variable coefficient can also be performed to determine its level of significance. The probability of borrowers selecting an ARM in any given month as generated by the specifications of the model can be compared to the actual percentage of ARMs for that month. Statistical Analysis Software (SAS) is used to estimate the logit models.

EMPIRICAL RESULTS AND DISCUSSION

INTDIFF, CPI and T-bill are significant at better than the .0001 level on chi-square tests in both models and the models overall attain the same high level of significance. R, the proportion of variability explained, a measure similar to R^2, is .302 and .301 (See Exhibit 1).

The importance of the INTDIFF variable follows the findings of Dhillon, et al., and Brueckner and Follain. The greater the difference between FRM interest rates and ARM rates, the greater the probability of choosing an ARM. Borrower preference for immediate economic gain is demonstrated. It can also be stated that the greater the interest-rate disparity, the greater the margin of "safety," i.e., the longer period of time it will take for the ARM to adjust to a rate greater than the FRM. Greater initial interest-rate disparity provides the borrower with both initial gains as well as a longer lead time during which to increase income in order to meet future higher payments, sell the house or refinance.

The positive relationship between a rising CPI and the selection of ARMs supports the hypothesis that the borrower is purchasing prior to further price increases that

Exhibit 1 Coefficients of Variables under Different Models

Variable	Model 1	Model 2
INTERCEPT	−2.2224	2.2528
	(458.53)°	(153.11)°
T-BILL	−18.3247	18.8272
	(137.03)°	(41.42)°
INTDIFF	101.8549	101.3148
	(717.53)°	(477.12)°
CPI	39.19	39.5245
	(456.04)°	(258.55)°
FIXINT		0.6062
		(.04)
OVERALL CHI-SQUARE	2950.5°	2590.54°
R	.302	.301

Figures in parenthesis are chi-square results.
°denotes chi-square test is significant at greater than .0001 level.

will either price him out of the market or force him to purchase a less desirable house. In an escalating price environment selection of ARMs will increase as buyers strain to meet lenders' loan-qualifying income levels. For some borrowers, a rising CPI provides greater confidence in their ability to increase future income. Those buyers with incomes that move up with inflation may be more comfortable selecting ARMs when prices are rising. Baesel and Biger [2] postulated that buyers with index-linked income would prefer index-linked mortgages. Those buyers will be able to meet possible increases in payments as well as gaining from rising housing values.

While the positive sign for the FIXINT coefficient is in agreement with prior studies, its lack of statistical significance differs from Brueckner's findings [3]. The high correlation between ARM rates and FRM rates in this study indicates that increases in FRM rates would likely be closely followed by ARM increases. As rates increase, marginal homebuyers, those more likely to require the lower interest ARMs to meet lender income qualifications, are eliminated from the market. Higher income buyers remaining in the market were shown by Brueckner to have a somewhat greater propensity to choose ARMs. In this study, the average price paid for houses purchased with ARMs was $139,135 and $114,338 for those bought with FRMs. Wealthier buyers, those buying higher-priced houses, may counterbalance the elimination from the market of those lower income buyers who would have, out of economic necessity, chosen ARMs.

Higher T-bill rates are associated with a decrease in the probability of borrowers selecting ARMs. At higher rates, borrowers' risk aversion toward ARMs may increase. It is a simple matter for the borrower to determine the amount the payment would be if the mortgage were fully priced, making the nature of the risk inherent in ARMs more readily apparent. Exhibit 2 examines the sensitivity of the probability of choosing an ARM to increases of fifty basis points in each of the three significant variables used in Model 1 while holding the other two variables constant. For INTDIFF, the probability of choosing an ARM increased by 11.82% in this study. In the Brueckner study, a fifty-basis point increase resulted in an increase of 43.2%. The reduced sensitivity may in part be explained by the larger sample size employed in this study, 20,697 versus 475 by Brueckner and the longer observation period (50 months versus 12 months).

The sensitivity of the probability function to changes in the parameters shows that INTDIFF has the greatest impact, followed by CPI and T-bill rates (Exhibit 2). The sensitivity to the probability of choosing ARMs to changes in each of the three variables from their minimum to maximum values is shown in Exhibits 3, 4 and 5.

Exhibit 2 Changes in Probability of Choosing ARM with Addition of 50 Basis Points to Mean Parameter Values

	All at Mean	Mean T-BILL +.005	Mean INTDIFF +.005	Mean CPI +.005
MEAN		0.0709	0.0217	0.0404
STANDARD DEVIATION		0.0103	0.0052	0.0103
PCTGE CHANGE FROM MEAN		7.06%	23.00%	12.36%
PROB OF CHOOSING ARM	56.88%	54.62%	68.70%	61.61%
CHANGE IN PROB		−2.26%	11.82%	4.73%
PCTGE CHANGE IN PROB		−3.97%	20.79%	8.31%
ELASTICITY°		−0.5631	0.9036	0.6724

°(δProbability/δParameter) ÷ (Probability/Parameter)

Exhibit 3 Sensitivity of Probability of Choosing an ARM to Changes in INTDIFF

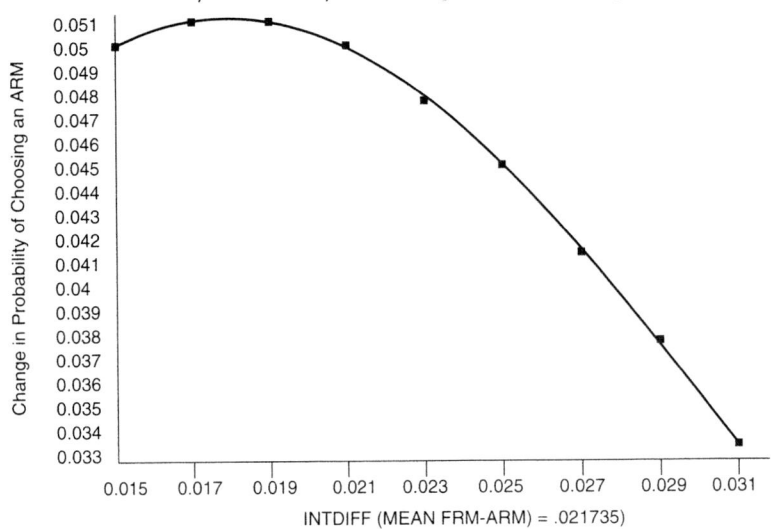

[Graph: Change in Probability of Choosing an ARM vs. INTDIFF (MEAN FRM-ARM) = .021735]

The predicted probability of choosing an ARM was highly correlated with the percentage of ARMs actually chosen over the fifty-month period ($r = .7906$). Exhibit 6 demonstrates that actual and predicted ARM probability track quite closely. A similar analysis by Brueckner found a correlation of $r = .563$ when their model was matched with the actual percentage of ARMs selected.

Exhibit 4 Sensitivity of Probability of Choosing an ARM to Changes in T-Bill

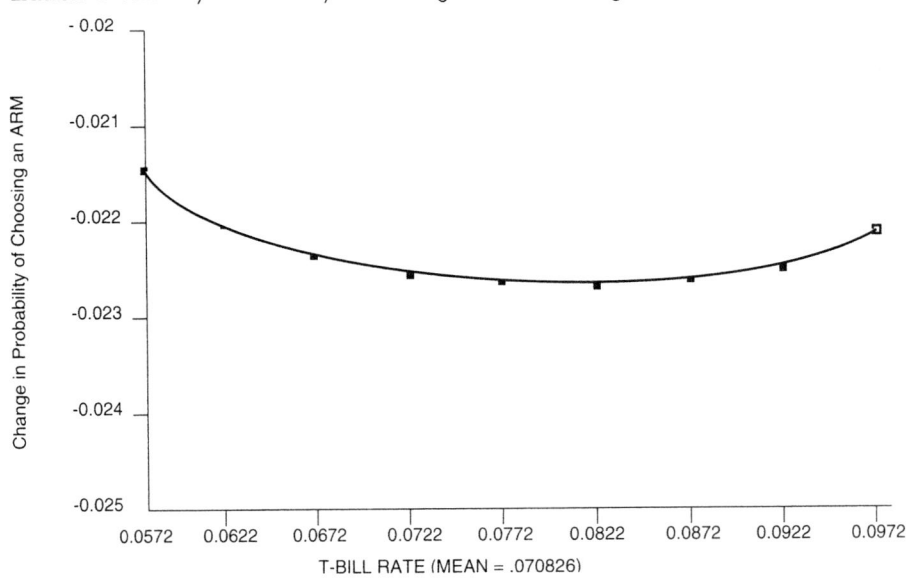

[Graph: Change in Probability of Choosing an ARM vs. T-BILL RATE (MEAN = .070826)]

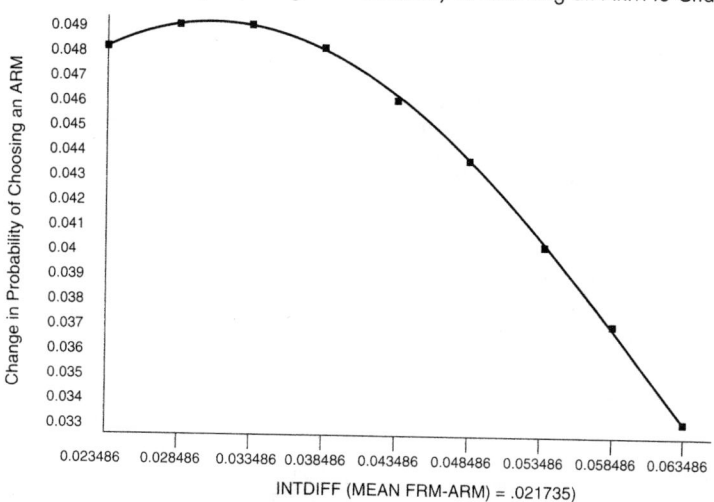

Exhibit 5 Sensitivity of Changes in Probability of Choosing an ARM to Changes in CPI

[Chart: X-axis labeled "INTDIFF (MEAN FRM-ARM) = .021735" ranging from 0.023486 to 0.063486; Y-axis labeled "Change in Probability of Choosing an ARM" ranging from 0.033 to 0.049. Curve rises slightly then declines from about 0.048 to 0.033.]

CONCLUSION AND IMPLICATIONS

This paper demonstrates the importance of economic and pricing variables in determining mortgage choice. The differential in interest rates between ARMs and FRMs was the most important factor but changes in the CPI and the one-year constant maturity Treasury bill rate were also statistically significant in building a logit model. Unlike earlier studies, the interest-rate level of the FRM was not significant in mortgage choice. The model performed well when the probability of selecting an ARM simulated over the fifty-month period was compared with actual ARM selection. The greater accuracy of prediction across the sample of the pricing model compared to a model used in a prior study employing more detailed individual borrower characteristics supports the efficient market hypothesis that borrowers select the lowest cost mortgage as specified by pricing variables.

An implication of the findings is that the added risk of the ARM is more acceptable when prices are rising as demonstrated by the positive relationship between ARM choice and the CPI. This follows from the efficient market hypothesis; greater risk is acceptable in the presence of greater expected returns. The borrower expects rapid housing value appreciation subsequent to purchase given a rising CPI and is therefore more willing to accept the added interest-rate risk of the ARM. The implication is that when prices rise less rapidly, hold steady or decline, greater returns will not accrue to borrowers and they will therefore be more reluctant to assume the risk of ARMs.

Higher benchmark rates discourage ARM borrowing because buyers expect their ARM to adjust more rapidly to levels exceeding prevailing FRM rates, i.e., greater risk is perceived. A CPI rising less rapidly and higher interest rates may occur in tandem. The higher rates will precede the lower CPI and these higher rates are likely to have followed a period of higher CPI and lower rates. Higher rates will have a dampening effect on the overall economy thereby slowing price increases, i.e., CPI. Buyers will be less willing to take on the added risk of ARMs because the perceived risk is greater due

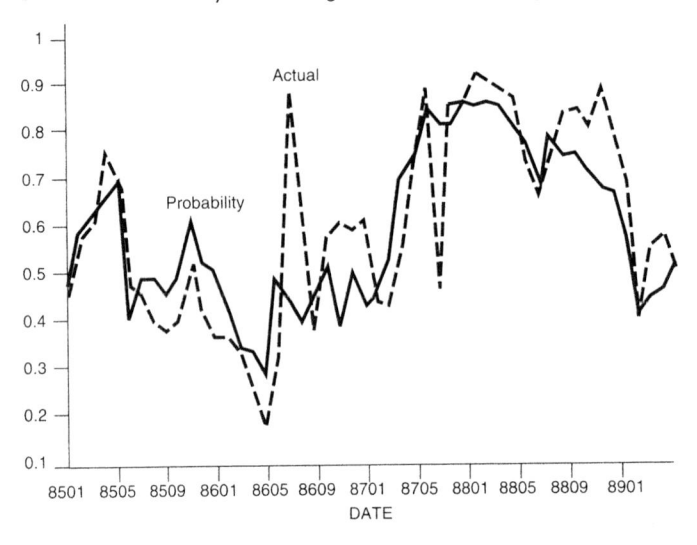

Exhibit 6 Probability of Selecting an ARM vs. Percentage of Actual ARMs Selected

to higher rates, particularly in conjunction with a slower growth economy, and a decline in expected returns implied by the lower CPI. Lenders will respond to higher rates imposed by the Federal Reserve by raising rates for both ARMs and FRMs. If they also narrow the spread between FRMs and ARMs in order to pass on more of the interest-rate risk to borrowers, they will motivate borrowers to select FRMs instead of ARMs. While interest rates are historically cyclical, borrowers may be unwilling to risk a further rise in rates by selecting an ARM at a time when ready rising rates have sensitized them to the possibility of further increases. Rising rates may also increase risk of job loss or, at least, the risk of reduced income increases they would need to meet rising ARM payments.

Interest-rate pricing variables are effected by economic cyclicality, specifically the Federal Reserve's responses to changes in the economy. Housing prices, as a constituent of the CPI, may in turn have a feedback effect. As prices rise, the Federal Reserve intervenes by raising interest rates which in turn changes the types of mortgages selected by borrowers while at the same time dampening housing demand and eventually curtailing price increases.

Individual borrower characteristics, while of interest microeconomically in mortgage choice, are diversified away over large sample sizes, leaving pricing variables as the deciding factors. The most economically efficient mortgage is selected based on perceived risk and expected return. The results of this study support this view.

REFERENCES

[1] James Alm and James Follain. Alternative Mortgage Instruments, the Tilt Problem, and Consumer Welfare. *Journal of Financial and Quantitative Analysis* 19 (March 1984), 113-26.

[2] Jerome Baesel and Nahum Biger. The Allocation of Risk: Some Implications of Fixed Versus Index-Linked Mortgages. *Journal of Financial and Quantitative Analysis* 15 (June 1980), 457-68.

[3] Jan Brueckner and James Follain. The Rise and Fall of the ARM: Analysis of Mortgage Choice. *Journal of Economics and Statistics* (February 1988), 93-102.

[4] William Celsis. Homing Devices: Some Hungry Thrifts Offer Rates Below Prime, and the Risk Is All Theirs. *Wall Street Journal,* May 19, 1989, R12.

[5] Upinder Dhillon, James Shilling and C. F. Sirmans. Choosing between Fixed and Adjustable Rate Mortgages. *Journal of Money, Credit and Banking* 19 (February 1987), 260-67.

[6] J. Kimball Dietrich and Eric Sorensen. An Application of Logit Analysis to Prediction of Merger Targets. *Journal of Business Research* 12 (1984), 393-402.

[7] Robert Edelstein and Jack Guttentag. The Alternative Mortgage Instrument: A Suggested Analytic Approach. Special Publication Series, Federal Home Loan Bank of San Francisco, December 1982.

[8] Al Field and Henry Cassidy. Simulation Analysis of Alternative Mortgage Instruments. *AREUEA Journal* 5 (1977), 411-33.

[9] Patric Hendershott. Pricing the Adjustable Rate Mortgage: Federal Home Loan Bank. *Quarterly Review* (1983), 1-4.

[10] ——— and James D. Shilling. Valuing the ARM Rate Caps: Implications of 1970–84 Interest-Rate Behavior. *AREUEA Journal* 13 (1985), 317-32.

[11] Michael Lea. An Empirical Analysis of the Value of ARM Features. *Housing Finance Review* 4 (January 1985), 467-81.

[12] Robert Pyndick and D. Rubinfeld. *Econometric Models & Economic Forecasts.* McGraw-Hill, second edition, 1981.

[13] Meir Statman. Fixed Rate or Index-Linked Mortgages from the Borrower's Point of View: A Note. *Journal of Financial and Quantitative Analysis* 17 (September 1982), 451-57.

[14] Henri Theil. *Principles of Econometrics.* John Wiley & Sons, 1971.

[15] George Von Furstenberg. The Equilibrium Spread Between Variable and Fixed Rates on Long-Term Financing Instruments. *Journal of Financial and Quantitative Analysis* (December 1973), 807-19.

5 The Value of Mortgage Assumptions: An Empirical Test

Mark A. Sunderman, Roger E. Cannaday, and Peter F. Colwell

This study provides an empirical test of the two main techniques for calculating the financing premium for assumption financed sales, cash equivalence adjustment (*CEA*) and financed-fee valuation adjustment (*FFVA*). The results indicate that both the *CEA* and *FFVA* computational techniques overvalue the premium associated with assumption financing. A variation of the empirical test is considered that differentiates this study from previous studies. This variation allows for a test of the hypothesis that the proportion of the financing premium capitalized into the sales price is a function of the loan-to-price ratio. It is concluded that this hypothesis cannot be rejected.

INTRODUCTION

It is commonly accepted that the assumption of an existing mortgage has an effect on the sales price of a single-family house. If the seller is successful in capturing the value attributed to a mortgage assumption (or any form of seller financing) in the sales price, this would result in a sales price that is inflated in relationship to a conventionally financed sale. Unless an adjustment is made, this will create problems whenever sales price of an assumption financed sale is used as a proxy for market value in the absence of special financing.

The overall purpose of this paper is to examine the effect assumption financing has on the sales price of a single-family house. Both of the adjustment techniques suggested in the literature are empirically tested. They are: (1) the traditional cash equivalence adjustment (*CEA*); and (2) the financed-fee valuation adjustment (*FFVA*). The empirical test utilizes residential sales data and a hedonic model.

A specific purpose of this paper, which differentiates it from previous studies, is to test the following hypothesis:

The proportion of the financing premium (as calculated by *CEA* or *FFVA*) that is capitalized into the price of the house is a function of the loan-to-price ratio.

From *The Journal of Real Estate Research*, Vol. 5, No. 2. This research was in part funded through a University of Wyoming Faculty Development Award. The authors acknowledge the helpful comments of three anonymous reviewers.

This paper is organized into four sections. The section following this introduction includes a discussion of the *CEA* and *FFVA* adjustment techniques. An empirical test of these techniques is presented in the third section. The final section is a summary of major conclusions.

ADJUSTMENT TECHNIQUES

The traditional cash equivalence adjustment (*CEA*) is the most frequently recommended approach to adjust for non-standard financing. The *CEA* approach has been a topic in the literature at least since 1972 when Garcia [10] suggested its use. However, the *CEA* approach was not empirically tested until Sirmans, et al. [12] did so in 1983. Sirmans, et al. found that, on average, only 32.2% of the calculated *CEA* financing premium was capitalized in the sales price of the house purchased with an assumption, thus raising questions about the validity of the *CEA* approach.

The *CEA* financing premium can be calculated by finding the present value of the monthly savings accruing to the buyer by taking the assumption mortgage rather than obtaining conventional financing at the current mortgage rate, as shown in equation (1):

$$P = a_{in}(f_{in}L - f_{kn}L) \qquad (1)$$

where:

- P = financing premium,
- a_{rt} = present worth of 1 per period; r indicates the discount rate and t indicates number of periods,
- f_{rt} = mortgage constant; r indicates the mortgage interest rate and t indicates number of periods,
- i = current interest rate available on conventional first mortgages,
- k = contract interest rate on the assumption,
- n = periods remaining on the assumption, and
- L = balance due on the assumption (or the book value).

See Clauretie [4], Smith, et al. [14], and Sirmans, et al. [11].[1]

In examining the literature, all of the empirical evidence indicates that (on average at least) some of the value attributed to assumption financing is capitalized into the sales price of the house; however, *CEA* appears to over-value it.[2] To explain why *CEA* does not appear to work, authors have developed modified versions of *CEA* or have entered other financing factors into the analysis. These attempts are typically centered on four main criticisms of the *CEA* approach. They are: (1) *CEA* makes no provision for the larger downpayment often required with an assumed mortgage, (2) *CEA* is a before-tax measure and therefore ignores the effect of income taxes, (3) interest-rate risk is ignored by the *CEA* approach, and (4) the holding period of the buyer is not considered.[3]

Most modified versions of *CEA* have received little attention. The exception has been the financed-fee valuation adjustment or *FFVA*, first introduced in 1983 by Findlay and Fischer [9]. The *FFVA* approach has been suggested as a means to overcome one of the potential problems with the *CEA* approach; specifically, that the *CEA* technique makes no provision for the additional downpayment often required with an assumption mortgage (that is, a potential buyer is indifferent to the loan-to-value ratio of the assumable loan). This would imply that the buyer's opportunity cost associated with an additional downpayment is equal to the market rate or that he has the opportunity to borrow the additional downpayment at the same rate as that available on conventional first mortgages. Findlay and Fischer argue that the interest rate on the second mortgage used to make up the difference in downpayments is likely to be higher than the rate on first mortgages because of the additional risk. However, if the combination of the assumed first mortgage and the second mortgage result in a "blended" rate lower than the market rate available on a conventional first mortgage, the potential buyer should be willing to pay a higher purchase price for this special opportunity.

The formula for $FFVA$, as presented by Dale-Johnson, et al. [6, p. 392], is $FFVA$ = maximum $(SP_a - SP_c, 0)$ where SP_c is computed as follows:[4]

$$SP_c = \frac{SP_a - L(1 - a_{sn}/a_{kn})}{1 - M(1 - a_{sm}/a_{im})} \qquad (2)$$

where:

SP_a = observed sales price of a given house with assumption financing,
SP_c = true price of the same house with conventional financing,
M = the loan-to-value ratio available on conventional financing,
s = interest rate on second mortgage,
m = periods in amortization schedule of new conventional first mortgage, and remaining terms are defined as before.

Whereas CEA has been extensively tested, it appears that $FFVA$ has only been tested three times. All of these tests have attempted not only to determine whether 100% of the $FFVA$ premium was capitalized into the sales price, but also how $FFVA$ compares to the CEA approach. Two of these tests used matched-pair analysis while the third used hedonic pricing. The two studies using matched pairs, Dale-Johnson, et al. [6] and Dale-Johnson and Findlay [5], found that the coefficient on the $FFVA$ variable was not significantly different from one, whereas, the coefficient on the CEA variable was. This implied that $FFVA$ was a superior model and that it did not overvalue the financing premium capitalized into the sales price. However, the study using hedonic pricing by Sirmans, et al. [13], found that the financing premium variable for $FFVA$ was not significant in explaining pricing behavior. They also found that a financing dummy variable outperformed the $FFVA$ approach.

In summary, there are very few conclusions with which all investigators would agree. However, it does appear clear that some adjustment is needed for sales including assumption financing. Further, it appears that the computational CEA approach overvalues this premium. Whether or not the $FFVA$ technique is the solution is still unclear.

EMPIRICAL TEST

An appropriate data set and a properly specified model are needed to compare the CEA and $FFVA$ approaches. After the data set is described and the specification of the model is discussed, the empirical results are presented.

Data. The data used for the empirical tests are derived from information included in Multiple Listing Service comparable books on sales of single-family detached houses located in a cluster of subdivisions (a section) in the southwest portion of Champaign, Illinois, known as the Southwood area. The sample consists of 386 sales that occurred during the period from January 1979 to August 1984. The sample contains 103 sales using assumption financing and 283 using conventional financing. These were the only forms of financing included in the sample, thus avoiding the simultaneity bias problem associated with some of the earlier empirical studies (see Clauretie [3, p. 522]).

Summary statistics for the variables to be included in the hedonic model are presented in Exhibit 1. In order to calculate the magnitudes of the financing variables, a schedule of the prevailing interest rates available on conventional mortgages (at the time of sale) with an amortization of thirty years and a loan to value of 80% was utilized along with the balance due, remaining term, and interest rate on the assumption loans.

Specification of the Model. The specification of the model includes selection of the dependent and explanatory variables to be included, determination of the overall functional form, and specification of the form of the explanatory variables, particularly the finance variables.

Since the concern is the effect that assumption financing has upon the sales price of a house, the actual sales price is used as the dependent variable. This is consistent with previous studies that use a hedonic price model.

Selection of explanatory variables for the model is based on an attempt to incorporate all the physical, locational, financing, and date of sale (to allow for changes in market conditions) variables that would be required to minimize specification bias. In addition, the selection of variables was guided by the results of previous studies and the availability of data. The form of the date-of-sale variable suggested and used by Bryan and Colwell [2] is used here.

The functional form chosen for the model is linear. A linear model is chosen because it allows direct comparison with models developed in many other studies, particularly the one by Sirmans, et al. [13] to which we refer subsequently. Also, linear models have been found to be acceptable in some instances even though nonlinear models would be superior in certain respects (see Donnelly [7, p. 10]). The model can be stated as follows:

$$SP_j = \beta_0 + \beta_1 X_{1j} + \beta_2 X_{2j} + \ldots + \beta_\lambda X_{kj} + \mu_j \tag{3}$$

where:

SP_j = sales price of the jth property.
X_{1j} to $X_{\lambda j}$ = explanatory variables defined in Exhibit 1.
$\beta's$ = parameters to be estimated, and
μ_j = the random error term.

Two different variables are used to capture the value of the financing premium. They are the traditional cash equivalence (*CEA*), presented in equation (1), and the financed-fee valuation adjustment (*FFVA*), presented in equation (2). These two approaches provide the same computational result when the loan-to-sales price ratio on the assumption is equal to the loan-to-sales price ratio available on conventional first mortgages. As the loan-to-sales price ratio declines, the difference between the calculated *CEA* and *FFVA* premiums increases.

A strictly linear model only allows for a constant percentage of the financing premium variable to be capitalized into the sales price. Therefore, the proportion of the financing premium variable capitalized into the sales price will be unaffected by the loan-

Exhibit 1 Description of Variables and Summary Statistics

Variable	Description of Variable	Mean	Standard Deviation	Minimum	Maximum
Dependent Variable:					
SP	Sales Price	60004.0	11838.0	27500.0	94600.0
Independent Variables:					
Physical Characteristics:					
BSQF	Square feet of living area	1495.1	347.32	820.00	2500.0
AGE	Building age (years)	9.0518	7.0624	1.0000	25.000
BATH	Number of bathrooms	1.7565	0.46740	1.0000	3.0000
FIRE	1 if a fireplace is present	0.57513	0.49496	0.0	1.0000
CARS	Number parking spaces available	1.6334	0.55451	0.0	2.5000
CENTRAL	1 if central air is present	0.85751	0.35000	0.0	1.0000
RANCH	1 if building style is ranch	0.62694	0.48424	0.0	1.0000
D15STORY	1 if building style is 1.5-story	0.77720D-02	0.87930D-01	0.0	1.0000
D2STORY	1 if building style is 2-story	0.44041D-01	0.20545	0.0	1.0000
DBILEVEL	1 if building style is bi-level	0.82902D-01	0.27609	0.0	1.0000
DTRLEVEL	1 if building style is tri-level	0.21762	0.41316	0.0	1.0000
DCONTY	1 if building style is contemporary	0.20725D-01	0.14265	0.0	1.0000
NGARAGE	1 if there is no garage	0.31088D-01	0.17378	0.0	1.0000
DATTACH	1 if garage is attached to building	0.88342	0.32134	0.0	1.0000
DDETACH	1 if garage is detached from building	0.75130D-01	0.26394	0.0	1.0000
DCARPT	1 if garage is a carport	0.10363D-01	0.10140	0.0	1.0000
LSQF	Lot square feet	7897.2	1604.8	5460.0	19160.0
Locational Characteristics:					
GMS	1 if in Green Meadow subdivision	0.95855D-01	0.29477	0.0	1.0000
SP1	1 if in Stratford Park No. 1 through No. 3	0.80311D-01	0.27213	0.0	1.0000
SP2	1 if in Stratford Park No. 4 through No. 6	0.18135D-01	0.13361	0.0	1.0000
SPNS	1 if in Stratford Park North	0.67358D-01	0.25097	0.0	1.0000
SPSS	1 if in Stratford Park South	0.64767D-01	0.24643	0.0	1.0000
SVS	1 if in Southwood Village	0.38860D-01	0.19351	0.0	1.0000
SW1	1 if in Southwood No. 1 through No. 20	0.50518	0.50062	0.0	1.0000
SW21	1 if in Southwood No. 21	0.12953	0.33623	0.0	1.0000
Date-of-Sale Characteristics:					
B79	Beginning of 1979	0.16872	0.28621	0.0	1.0000
B80	Beginning of 1980	0.23111	0.27754	0.0	1.0000
B81	Beginning of 1981	0.16893	0.28528	0.0	1.0000
B82	Beginning of 1982	0.81174D-01	0.19944	0.0	1.0000
B83	Beginning of 1983	0.15026	0.26364	0.0	1.0000
B84	Beginning of 1984	0.16462	0.27673	0.0	1.0000
B85	Beginning of 1985	0.35190D-01	0.11484	0.0	1.0000
Financing Characterics (assumptions only):					
CEA	Value for traditional premium	7878.4	4217.7	105.40	21725.0
FFVA	Value for the *FFVA* premium	5823.9	4537.0	0.0	20984.0
LTP	Loan-to-price ratio	0.66401	0.15422	0.18392	0.94947
LTPCEA	(*LTP*) (*CEA*)	5373.9	3513.1	68.938	17625.0
LTPFFVA	(*LTP*) (*FFVA*)	4236.5	3793.9	0.0	17024.0

to-sales price ratio of the assumption loan. Since it is this variable that causes computation of the *CEA* and the *FFVA* variable to differ, it is hypothesized that the coefficient, β, on the financing premium variable (*FIN*), in particular for the *CEA* model, is a function of the loan-to-price ratio (*LTP*). This relationship can be expressed as

$$\beta = \chi_0 + \chi_1 \, LTP. \tag{4}$$

Equation (4) can be rewritten as

$$\beta \, FIN = \chi_0 \, FIN + \chi_1 \, (LTP)(FIN). \tag{5}$$

Equation (5) suggests that an added variable is needed, the product of *LTP* and the financing premium variable. As a result, two new variables were created. The first, *LTPCEA*, is the product of *LTP* and *CEA*. The second, *LTPFFVA*, is the product of *LTP* and *FFVA*. For the *FFVA* model, this is in a sense taking the loan-to-price ratio into account two ways; once in the computation of the *FFVA* variable and again as a variable in the regression model. By including the loan-to-price ratio in the computation of the *FFVA* variable this assumes a given relationship exists. However, by including the loan-to-price ratio in the regression model it is possible to ascertain the relationship that is determined by the market.[5] In addition, this may help explain the unusual results found by Sirmans, et al. [13] as noted subsequently in our Note 6.

Empirical Results. The null hypothesis for our empirical test is that the proportion of the financing premium capitalized into the sales price is *not* a function of the loan-to-price ratio. A discussion of the results when the loan-to-price ratio is ignored is followed by a presentation of the results when the loan-to-price ratio is included as a variable.

The regression results, based on ordinary least squares estimation using a linear functional form without a loan-to-price ratio variable, are presented for two models in Exhibit 2. Model 1 includes the *CEA* variable and Model 2 includes the *FFVA* variable.

Both of these models have high explanatory power with an R^2 adjusted for degrees of freedom of approximately 0.90. All physical characteristics variables (building style is taken as a group and garage type is taken as a group), subdivision location variables (taken as a group), and date-of-sale variables (taken as a group) have coefficients that are considered statistically significant from zero at the 95% level of confidence. Further, for each of these variables the sign on the coefficient is as expected. For both of the models the financing premium variables have coefficients that are also statistically significant. The coefficient of the *CEA* variable has a positive sign and its magnitude is between zero and unity, which is consistent with the theory presented in a recent paper by Sunderman, et al. [15, p. 17]. We also expected the *FFVA* coefficient to be positive, but with a magnitude higher than that for the *CEA* variable, the opposite of the results reported in Exhibit 2. The results indicate that, on average, just over 18% of the calculated *CEA* premium is incorporated into the price while only about 14.5% of the *FFVA* premium is incorporated.[6]

The regression results when *LTPCEA* and *LTPFFVA* are included in the models are presented in Exhibit 3. Model 3 includes the *CEA* and the *LTPCEA* variables. Model 4 includes the *FFVA* and the *LTPFFVA* variables. The *t*-statistics for the coefficients on both financing premium variables in these two models allow us to reject the null hypoth-

Exhibit 2 OLS Regression Results
Sales Price as Dependent Variable Using *CEA* and *FFVA* Only

	Model 1 with CEA		Model 2 with FFVA	
Variable	Estimated coefficient	t-statistic (356 DF)	Estimated coefficient	t-statistic (356 DF)
BSQF	15.013°	12.721	14.946°	12.528
AGE	−364.04°	−6.5421	−370.64°	−6.6111
BATH	2008.6°	2.7924	2049.5°	2.8269
FIRE	1157.2	2.3028	1172.7°	2.3120
CARS	1873.5°	2.9901	1863.0°	2.9485
CENTRAL	2555.0°	3.5598	2557.2°	3.5327
D15STORY	2291.7	0.96706	2212.9	0.92588
D2STORY	3316.8°	3.0158	3287.5°	2.9653
DBILEVEL	−2356.1°	−2.0825	−2209.4	−1.9376
DTRLEVEL	633.20	0.98108	674.24	1.0349
DCONTY	7659.7°	4.9428	7508.3°	4.8098
DATTACH	3373.7°	2.1709	3406.8°	2.1742
DDETACH	90.981	0.57186D-01	59.684	0.37213D-01
DCARPT	1082.1	0.46154	964.90	0.40821
LSQF	0.17464	1.2542	0.17750	1.2644
GMS	−6043.1°	−4.2236	−5788.7°	−4.0238
SP1	−7203.9°	−6.7365	−7074.4°	−6.5667
SP2	−9397.0°	−5.5313	−9174.2°	−5.3643
SPNS	−898.86	−0.93377	−839.22	−0.86470
SPSS	−702.44	−0.68963	−423.14	−0.41466
SVS	−627.43	−0.52267	−443.54	−0.36719
SW1	−1754.0°	−2.2964	−1539.7°	−2.0093
B80	741.18	0.59725	929.17	0.74335
B81	4030.8°	4.3755	4318.1°	4.6605
B82	3886.8°	2.9450	4164.5°	3.1167
B83	3960.0°	3.6518	4073.8°	3.7243
B84	8708.8°	7.6489	8739.0°	7.6138
B85	6381.5°	2.8790	6322.6°	2.8278
CEA	0.18142°	3.3087	—	—
FFVA	—	—	0.14516°	2.2476
INTERCEPT	25308.0°	11.229	25183.0°	11.079
Adjusted R-square	0.8955		0.8938	
Standard error	3827.3		3858.5	

° significantly different from zero at the 95% level of confidence

esis at the 0.05 level of significance. In comparing these models to Model 1 and Model 2, Model 3 and Model 4 provide a better fit since the adjusted R^2 is higher (standard error is lower).

After the parameters for these two models are estimated, the coefficients for *CEA* and *FFVA* can be calculated for a range of loan-to-price ratios with equation (4). These results for both *CEA* and *FFVA* are presented in Exhibit 4. Exhibit 4 shows that the coefficient on the financing premium variable increases as the loan-to-price ratio decreases. The coefficient on *FFVA* is greater than the coefficient on *CEA* except when the loan-to-price ratio is greater than 0.80.[7] In fact, for loan-to-price ratios below 0.80 the

Exhibit 3 OLS Regression Results
Sales Price as Dependent Variable Effect of Loan-to-Price Ratio

	Model 3 with CEA and LTPCEA		Model 4 with FFVA and LTPFFVA	
Variable	Estimated coefficient	t-statistic (355 DF)	Estimated coefficient	t-statistic (355 DF)
BSQF	14.880°	12.686	14.988°	12.637
AGE	−359.30°	−6.4993	−358.49°	−6.4035
BATH	1926.5°	2.6946	1953.9°	2.7065
FIRE	1287.8°	2.5667	1295.3°	2.5546
CARS	2014.6°	3.2248	2011.2°	3.1851
CENTRAL	2522.0°	3.5384	2609.3°	3.6242
D15STORY	2628.8	1.1154	2449.8	1.0301
D2STORY	3260.3°	2.9851	3264.1°	2.9615
DBILEVEL	−2403.8°	−2.1396	−2392.9°	−2.1058
DTRLEVEL	653.02	1.0190	603.38	0.93061
DCONTY	7859.9°	5.1014	7693.9°	4.9513
DATTACH	3120.7°	2.0181	3183.3°	2.0397
DDETACH	−54.495	−0.34475D-01	−120.37	−0.75407D-01
DCARPT	881.37	0.37840	813.66	0.34614
LSQF	0.14921	1.0763	0.14691	1.0480
GMS	−6199.0°	−4.3595	−5911.1°	−4.1305
SP1	−7183.2°	−6.7652	−7088.9°	−6.6193
SP2	−9575.6	−5.6718	−9279.5°	−5.4562
SPNS	−777.77	−0.81271	−706.47	−0.73094
SPSS	−1053.3	−1.0315	−763.06	−0.74432
SVS	−703.15	−0.58976	−597.09	−0.49648
SW1	−1797.2°	−2.3692	−1651.5°	−2.1636
B80	697.30	0.56587	786.89	0.63249
B81	3903.9°	4.2615	4030.4°	4.3359
B82	4081.8°	3.1094	4123.6°	3.1042
B83	3911.4°	3.6323	3887.2°	3.5649
B84	8665.8°	7.6650	8687.0°	7.6121
B85	6512.3°	2.9583	6234.0°	2.8043
CEA	0.73435°	3.1954	—	—
LTPCEA	−0.77394°	−2.4765	—	—
FFVA	—	—	0.99454°	2.6445
LTPFFVA	—	—	−1.0928°	−2.2922
INTERCEPT	25793.0°	11.482	25431.0°	11.242
Adjusted R-square		0.8970		0.8950
Standard error		3800.0		3835.6

° significantly different from zero at the 95% level of confidence

difference between the coefficient on *FFVA* and on *CEA* increases as the loan-to-price ratio decreases. This is expected since the difference between *FFVA* and *CEA* increases as the loan-to-price ratio decreases. Now it can be seen that the unexpected results regarding the relative magnitudes of the coefficients for *CEA* and *FFVA*, as presented in Exhibit 2 as well as those found by Sirmans, et al. [13] (as noted in our Note 6), are likely due to the fact that the influence of the loan-to-price ratio on the proportion of the financing premium capitalized into price was not taken into account.

Exhibit 4 Proportion of Financing Premium Paid Varying with Loan-to-Price Ratio

Loan to Price	β on CEA	β on FFVA
0.90	0.037804	0.011020
0.85	0.076501	0.065660
0.80	0.115198	0.120300
0.75	0.153895	0.174940
0.70	0.192592	0.229580
0.65	0.231289	0.284220
0.60	0.269986	0.338860
0.55	0.308683	0.393500
0.50	0.347380	0.448140
0.45	0.386077	0.502780
0.40	0.424774	0.557420
0.35	0.463471	0.612060
0.30	0.502168	0.666700
0.25	0.540865	0.721340
0.20	0.579562	0.775980

β is defined in equations (4) and (5) on page 67.

The findings reported in Exhibit 4 suggest that the buyer is paying an increasing percentage of the calculated financing premium as the loan-to-price ratio decreases. There are several possible explanations for why this may be occurring. One possibility is that the higher loan-to-price ratio assumptions (perhaps being more recently acquired by the seller) have the highest interest rates and that buyers anticipate falling interest rates in the near future. The time period covered by this data includes just such an episode. Another possibility is that the lower loan-to-price ratio assumptions have been outstanding for a longer period of time and have lower interest rates. Perhaps, buyers expect to realize more of the financing premium under these circumstances since they will not have to hold the loan as long.

SUMMARY OF MAJOR CONCLUSIONS

The overall purpose of this paper is to empirically test the cash equivalence adjustment and financed-fee valuation adjustment techniques for calculating financing premiums. One additional specific purpose is to examine the impact of the loan-to-price ratio on the proportion of the financing premium incorporated in the price.

When loan-to-price ratio is not included as a variable, the empirical results in Exhibit 2 indicate that not only the *CEA* computational technique, but also the *FFVA* technique overvalues the premium associated with assumption financing. Based on the results presented in Exhibit 3, the null hypothesis that the loan-to-price ratio has no impact on the proportion of the financing premium included in the sales price is rejected. This in itself is not surprising; however, it appears that as the loan-to-price ratio declines the proportion of the financing premium paid increases. The reason for this result is theorized to be a function of the market conditions during the time period covered by the data. In summary, we find that results are improved when the loan-to-price ratio is included as a variable in the model.

NOTES

[1] A second method to calculate the *CEA* financing premium is to find the difference between the balance due on the assumption loan and the present value of the payments on the assumption loan discounted at the current market rate, as shown in the following equation:

$$P = L - a_m(f_{kn}L).$$

See Agarwal and Philips [1] and Sirmans, et al. [12]. It is a simple matter to show that the above equation and equation (2) are equivalent using the notion that $a_{in}f_m = 1$.

[2] For a review of the literature see Sirmans, et al. [11].

[3] See Agarwal and Philips [1], Clauretie [4], Ferreira and Sirmans, [8], Sirmans, et al. [12], and Smith, et al. [14].

[4] The notation used by Dale-Johnson, et al. [6] has been changed to match the notation being used in this paper.

[5] If the loan-to-price ratio has no impact on the amount of the *CEA* financing premium capitalized into sales price then the coefficient on *LTPCEA* should be statistically insignificant. If the loan-to-price ratio has been correctly considered in the computation of the *FFVA* financing premium then the coefficient on *LTPFFVA* should be statistically insignificant.

[6] It should be noted that these results are similar to those of Sirmans, et al. [13] who also compared *CEA* and *FFVA* with a hedonic pricing model. They found that the proportion of *CEA* and *FFVA* capitalized into the sales price was higher than these findings (i.e., 32.2% versus 18.1% for *CEA* and 29% versus 14.5% for *FFVA*); however, they also found that the *CEA* performed better in explaining the effect of assumption financing than *FFVA*. This was based on the model's R_2 and the *t*-statistic of the financing variable. Further, they also found that the coefficient on *FFVA* was smaller than that on the *CEA* variable, the opposite of what one would expect.

[7] Since the computed *FFVA* and *CEA* are equal for all observations with a loan-to-price ratio greater than 0.8, it would be expected that the coefficient on *FFVA* and *CEA*, for that range of loan-to-price ratios, would be equal. However, as Exhibit 4 indicates, this is not the case. It is believed that these results (i.e., the coefficient of *FFVA* is not equal to that for *CEA* when the loan-to-price ratio is greater than 0.8) are an artifact of the functional form chosen.

REFERENCES

[1] Vinod B. Agarwal and Richard A. Philips. The Effects of Assumption Financing Across Housing Price Categories. *AREUEA Journal* 13 (Spring 1985), 48–57.

[2] Thomas B. Bryan and Peter F. Colwell. Housing Price Indexes. In C. F. Sirmans, editor. *Research in Real Estate*, 57–84. Greenwich, CT: JAI Press, 1982.

[3] Terrence M. Clauretie. A Note on the Bias in House Price Capitalization Models. *AREUEA Journal* 11 (Winter 1983), 521–24.

[4] ———. Capitalization of Seller-Supplied Financing Implications for Assessment. *Property Tax Journal* 3 (December 1984), 229–38.

[5] David Dale-Johnson and M. Chapman Findlay. Valuation and Efficiency in the Market for Creative Financing: Extensions of a Working Model. *Property Tax Journal* 4 (December 1985), 329–44.

[6] ———, A. L. Schwartz, Jr. and S. Kapplin. Valuation and Efficiency in the Market for Creatively Financed Houses. *AREUEA Journal* 13 (Winter 1985), 388–403.

[7] William A. Donnelly. The Methodology of Housing Value Assessment: An Analysis. *The Journal of Real Estate Research* 4 (Summer 1989), 1–12.

[8] Eurico J. Ferreira and G. Stacy Sirmans. Assumption Loan Value in Creative Financing. *Housing Finance Review* 3 (April 1984), 139–47.

[9] M. C. Findlay and F. E. Fischer. On Adjusting the Price of 'Creatively Financed' Residential Sales: Cash Equivalence vs. FFVA. *Housing Finance Review* 2 (January 1983), 63–80.

[10] Ken Garcia. Sales Prices and Cash Equivalents. *The Appraisal Journal* 40 (January 1972), 1–10.

[11] G. Stacy Sirmans, C. F. Sirmans and Stanley D. Smith. The Issues and Implications of Creative Financing and House Prices: A Survey. *Property Tax Journal* 4 (December 1985), 383–415.

[12] G. Stacy Sirmans, Stanley D. Smith, and C. F. Sirmans. Assumption Financing and Selling Price of Single-Family Homes. *The Journal of Financial and Quantitative Analysis* 18 (September 1983), 307–17.

[13] ———. Valuation of Creative Financing: An Empirical Test of Financed Fee Valuation Adjustment Versus Cash Equivalence. *Housing Finance Review* 5 (Fall 1986), 151–58.

[14] Stanley D. Smith, G. Stacy Sirmans and C. F. Sirmans. The Valuation of Creative Financing in Housing. *Housing Finance Review* 3 (April 1984), 129–38.

[15] Mark A. Sunderman, Peter F. Colwell and Roger E. Cannaday. The Microeconomics of Valuing Mortgage Assumptions. Unpublished manuscript, November 1989.

Part 3. Mortgage-Related Securities

6 Valuation of GNMA Mortgage-Backed Securities

Kenneth B. Dunn and John J. McConnell

GNMA mortgage-backed pass-through securities are supported by pools of amortizing, callable loans. Additionally, mortgagors often prepay their loans when the market interest rate is above the coupon rate of their loans. This paper develops a model for pricing GNMA securities and uses it to examine the impact of the amortization, call, and prepayment features on the prices, risks and expected returns of GNMAs. The amortization and prepayment features each have a positive effect on price, while the call feature has a negative impact. All three features reduce a GNMA security's interest rate risk and, consequently, its expected return.

INTRODUCTION

In this paper we present a model for the valuation of Government National Mortgage Association (GNMA) mortgage-backed pass-through securities. We then use the model to evaluate various facets of the pricing, returns, and risks of GNMA securities relative to those of other types of fixed rate securities. The paper is motivated by the considerable interest among portfolio managers, financial analysts, security dealers, and government officials in the pricing and investment performance of GNMA securities ([9], [17], [19], [20], [22], [23]).

In Section I we describe the unique characteristics of the GNMA security. In Section II we summarize and recapitulate the essential features of the generic model for pricing interest dependent securities developed by Brennan and Schwartz [2] and Cox, Ingersoll, and Ross [5]. In Section III we extend the generic bond pricing model to incorporate the unique characteristics of GNMA mortgage-backed pass-through securities. In Section IV we present numerical solutions for the prices of three types of default-free bonds: (1) nonamortizing, noncallable coupon bonds; (2) nonamortizing, callable coupon bonds; and (3) amortizing, noncallable bonds. We then compare these with solutions for GNMA mortgage-backed pass-through securities. The solutions are presented for alternative assumptions about the shape of the term structure of interest

---

From *The Journal of Finance*, Vol. XXXVI, No. 3 (June 1981). This paper has benefited from helpful comments by J. Ang, M. Brennan, P. Hendershott, R. Johnson, W. Kracaw, M. Long, G. Schlarbaum, C. Spratt, R. Thompson, and Eduardo Schwartz. We are especially grateful to J. Ingersoll, S. Richard, and G. Wright for many helpful discussions and suggestions.

rates, the remaining terms to maturity of the securities, and the rate at which the individual mortgage loans that back the GNMA security are expected to be "prepaid." These comparisons are designed to highlight the impact of the call, amortization, and prepayment features on the pricing, returns, and risks of GNMA securities. A final section contains a conclusion.

I. GNMA MORTGAGE-BACKED PASS-THROUGH SECURITIES

GNMA mortgage-backed pass-through securities are issued by mortgagees, generally mortgage bankers, who are approved by the Federal Housing Administration (FHA). Prior to issuing the security, a mortgage banker must generate a pool of new individual residential mortgage loans. GNMA requires that all the loans in a pool have the same coupon interest rate and original term to maturity and that each be insured by the FHA or guaranteed by the Veterans Administration (VA). Once GNMA approves the mortgage loans in the pool, the issuer can either sell GNMA securities (i.e. participations in the pool) directly to individual investors or sell the entire issue to a GNMA dealer. Subsequently, the issuer is responsible for servicing the loans in the pool. For providing this service the issuer receives a monthly administration fee of .0367 percent per month (.44 percent per year) of the remaining principal balances of the loans in the pool. For guaranteeing the pool GNMA charges a fee of .005 percent per month (.06 percent per year) of the remaining principal balances of the loans in the pool. Thus a GNMA security is issued with an annual coupon interest rate that is .50 percent less than the contract rate on the underlying mortgage loans.

Each month the issuer of a GNMA security must "pass through" the scheduled interest and principal payments on the underlying mortgage loans to the holder of the security, whether or not the issuer has actually collected those payments from the individual mortgagors. Each month the issuer must also pass through any additional amounts which are received from the mortgagors for loan prepayments and/or from the FHA or VA for settlements on those loans in the pool which have been foreclosed. If the security issuer defaults on the monthly payments, GNMA assumes responsibility for the timely payment of principal and interest. Because GNMA monitors the performance of the security issuers and because the securities are backed by the "full faith and credit" of the U.S. Treasury, GNMA pass-through securities are generally considered to be riskless in terms of default.

The mortgage loans which back GNMA securities are fully amortizing. Each of the equal monthly payments on the loans includes interest on the outstanding principal balance and a partial repayment of principal.[1] Because the fee for servicing and guaranteeing the loans is a fixed percentage of the declining principal of the loans, the scheduled monthly payment to the holders of the security increases slightly through time, approaching the total monthly payment on the underlying loans at maturity.

All FHA and VA mortgage loans can be prepaid (i.e. called by the mortgagor) at any time without a prepayment penalty (i.e. without the payment of a call premium). Furthermore, the loans are assumable. That is, the mortgagor may transfer his obligation for the debt. Hence, with FHA and VA mortgage loans there are not contractual restrictions which limit mortgagors' call strategies. Thus, when markets are frictionless, mortgagors will exercise their call option only when they can refinance their existing loan with a similar loan that has a lower contract interest rate.

One of the notable characteristics of mortgagors is that, in practice, many of them call their loans even when the market interest rate is above the contract rate on their existing loans. These prepayments are generally associated with one of the following events: (1) a mortgagor changes his residence and the obligation for the existing mortgage is not assumed by the purchaser of his house; (2) the present house is refinanced so that the owner can withdraw equity; or (3) the mortgagor defaults on his loan.[2]

The fact that GNMA requires all loans in a pool to be approximately homogenous is especially convenient for our purposes. This requirement allows us to value a GNMA security as if it were a single default-free mortgage loan.[3]

II. THE GENERIC PRICING MODEL

The model for valuing GNMA mortgage-backed pass-through securities is based on the generic model for pricing interest contingent securities developed in [2] and [5]. The generic model is derived from the following assumptions:

A.1: *The value of a default-free fixed interest rate security, $V(r, \tau)$, is a function only of the current value of the instantaneous risk-free rate, $r(t)$, and its term to maturity τ.*

A.2: *The interest rate for instantaneous riskless borrowing and lending follows a continuous stationary Markov process given by the stochastic differential equation*

$$dr = \mu(r)\,dt + \sigma(r)\,dz \quad (1)$$

where

$\mu(r) \equiv k(m - r), \quad k, m > 0,$
$\sigma(r) \equiv \sigma\sqrt{r}, \sigma \text{ constant, and}$

dz is a Wiener process with $E(dz) = 0$ and $dz^2 = dt$ with probability 1. The function $\mu(r)$ is the instantaneous drift of the process, k is the speed of adjustment parameter, m is the steady-state mean of the process, and the function $\sigma^2(r)$ is the instantaneous variance. Negative interest rates are precluded with this mean reverting interest rate process and the variance of the process increases with the interest rate.

A.3: *The risk adjustment term, $p(r)\sigma\sqrt{r}$ is proportional to the spot interest rate, i.e.*

$$p(r)\sigma\sqrt{r} = qr, \quad (2)$$

where q is the proportionality factor and $p(r)$, the price of interest rate risk, equals the equilibrium expected instantaneous return in excess of the riskless return per unit of risk for securities which satisfy A.1.

A.4: *Individuals are nonsatiated, have risk preferences consistent with (2), and agree on the specification of Equation (1).*

A.5: *The capital market (including the market for individual junior and senior mortgage loans) is perfect and competitive; trading takes place continuously.*

A.6: *The cash flows $C(\tau)$ from any security (including a GNMA security) are paid continuously.*

Assumption A.1 means that a single state variable, the current risk-free interest rate, completely summarizes all information which is relevant for the pricing of fixed-rate securities. Because changes in the value of all default-free fixed-rate securities are governed by the same random variable, the returns on all fixed-rate securities are locally perfectly correlated. Assumptions A.1 to A.5 lead to the model of the term structure of interest rates derived by Cox, Ingersoll, and Ross [5] in a general equilibrium framework for an economy with a single source of uncertainty.[4] This model of the term structure provides the foundation for the GNMA pricing model.

Assumptions A.4 and A.5 ensure that a borrower will prepay his loan according to the optimal call policy. Specifically, a borrower will never let the market value of this existing loan exceed its outstanding principal balance. If this condition were violated, the loan could be refinanced with an otherwise identical loan which has a lower effective rate of interest than the rate on the existing loan.

Although the cash payments from most fixed-rate securities occur at discrete intervals, most securities are traded with interest that accrues daily. Thus, the assumption of continuous cash flows, A.6, is a convenient means of approximating the way in which fixed-rate securities (including GNMAs) are actually traded.

Given the assumptions above and the hedging arguments developed by Black and Scholes [1] and Merton [15], it follows that the value of a default-free security must satisfy the nonstochastic parabolic partial differential equation (PDE)

$$\tfrac{1}{2}\sigma(r)^2 V_{rr} + [\mu(r) - p(r)\sigma(r)]V_r - V_\tau - rV + C(\tau) = 0, \qquad (3)$$

where subscripts on V denote partial derivatives. This equation is a special case of the fundamental valuation equation derived by Cox, Ingersoll, and Ross [5] for the value of any contingent claim and differs from the PDE derived by Brennan and Schwartz [2] for valuing several types of bonds only with respect to the functional forms of $\sigma(r)$, $\mu(r)$, and $p(r)$.

According to the generic bond pricing model, differences among interest-dependent claims are reflected in the form of their cash flows and the boundary conditions which Equation (3) must satisfy. At maturity, $\tau = 0$, the value of a default-free bond must equal its face value or remaining principal balance $F(0)$. This provides the initial condition

$$V(r, 0) = F(0). \qquad (4)$$

For a bond with continuous amortization payments, $F(0)$ is zero. For a nonamortizing bond, $F(0)$ is equal to the face value of the bond.

The value of an interest-dependent security goes to zero as the interest rate approaches infinity. This yields the boundary condition

$$\lim_{r \to \infty} V(r, \tau) = 0. \qquad (5)$$

With the assumed interest rate process, $r = 0$ is a natural boundary. Setting $r = 0$ in (3) and substituting from (1) for $\sigma(0) = 0$ and $\mu(0) = km$, we obtain

$$kmV_r + C(\tau) = V_\tau \qquad (6a)$$

which is the boundary condition for noncallable bonds at $r = 0$.

For callable bonds, the region of the interest rate is limited by the optimal call policy. Optimal calls are driven by the stochastic process governing the risk-free interest rate. For each τ there is some level of the risk-free interest rate, say $r_c(\tau)$, for which $V[r_c(\tau), \tau] = F(\tau)$ and the call option will be exercised. Risk-free interest rates below $r_c(\tau)$ are not relevant for pricing callable bonds. The effect of the optimal call policy is to preclude the market value of a bond from exceeding its remaining principal balance; therefore, the boundary condition for a callable bond is

$$V(r, \tau) \leq F(\tau). \tag{6b}$$

Given the boundary conditions above and the relevant functional form of the cash flows, Equation (3) can be solved for the value of any default-free interest-dependent security for which Assumptions A.1 through A.6 are appropriate.

III. THE GNMA PRICING MODEL

As we discussed above, one of the notable characteristics of mortgagors (or at least those whose loans are pooled to support GNMA securities) is that they often call their loans at times other than those that would be dictated by the optimal call policy. We differentiate between the two types of prepayments by referring to those which occur when r is above r_c as "suboptimal" prepayments.[5] In an efficient market, the price of a GNMA security will reflect the possible occurrence of suboptimal prepayments and the generic pricing model must be modified to incorporate them. To do so, we add the following two assumptions:

A.7: *Prepayments which occur when the value of a GNMA security is less than its remaining principal balance follow a Poisson-driven process. The Poisson random variable, y, is equal to zero until the loan is called suboptimally. If y jumps to one, there is a suboptimal prepayment and the security ceases to exist. The Poisson process, dy, is given by*

$$dy = \begin{cases} 0 \text{ if a suboptimal prepayment does not occur} \\ 1 \text{ if a suboptimal prepayment occurs} \end{cases}$$

where

$$E(dy) = \lambda(r, \tau)\,dt \tag{7}$$

and $\lambda(r, \tau)$ is the probability per unit of time of a suboptimal prepayment at a time to maturity τ and interest rate r.

A.8: *Prepayments which occur when the value of a GNMA security is less than its remaining principal balance are uncorrelated with all relevant market factors and are, therefore, purely nonsystematic.*

With the addition of Assumption A.7, the value of a GNMA security $V(r, \tau, y)$, is a function of two state variables, r and y, and is governed by the mixed process

$$dV = [a(r, \tau)V - C(\tau) - \lambda(r, \tau)(F(\tau) - V)]\,dt + s(r, \tau)V\,dz + [F(\tau) - V]\,dy. \tag{8}$$

In (8), $a(r, \tau)$ is the total instantaneous expected rate of return on the security and $s(r, \tau)$ is the instantaneous standard deviation of the return, conditional on the Poisson event not occurring. From Ito's lemma and an analogous lemma for Poisson processes (Merton [14]), we obtain

$$a(r, \tau) = [\tfrac{1}{2}\sigma(r)^2 V_{rr} + \mu(r)V_r - V_\tau + C(\tau) + \lambda(r, \tau)(F(\tau) - V)]/V$$

and

$$s(r, \tau) = \sigma(r)V_r/V. \tag{9}$$

A portfolio containing a GNMA security and any other interest-dependent security can be constructed so that the uncertainty due to unexpected changes in the interest rate is completely eliminated. Let $b(r, \tau)$ denote the instantaneous expected rate of return and $g(r, \tau)$ denote the standard deviation of the return on the other security. The interest rate risk can be eliminated by investing the proportion $g/(g-s)$ in the GNMA security and by investing the proportion $-s/(g-s)$ in the other security. The rate of return on this portfolio is

$$\frac{dP}{P} = \left(\frac{g}{g-s}\right)\left[\left[a - \lambda\left(\frac{F-V}{V}\right) - \frac{s}{g} b\right] dt + \left(\frac{F-V}{V}\right) dy\right]. \quad (10)$$

Most of the time the realized return on this portfolio will equal the coefficient of dt in (10), but, when there is a suboptimal prepayment, there will be an unexpected return equal to the proportion of the portfolio invested in the GNMA security times $(F - V)/V$.

Because of the importance of Assumption A.8 to our model, some additional discussion is appropriate. From A.7 the prepayment probabilities depend only on the time to maturity and the interest rate at that time. By introducing the dynamics for other market factors, the prepayment probabilities could be made to depend on additional state variables. Assumption A.8 means that given the state of the economy at the beginning of any time interval, the Poisson process is uncorrelated with changes in the state variables during that time interval. Therefore, prepayments are unique to each security and the uncertainty due to the suboptimal prepayments can be costlessly diversified away. As a consequence, there is not a risk premium associated with the suboptimal prepayments and the expected return on the portfolio must be the riskless rate of return, r.[6] Setting the expected value of dP/P equal to $r\,dt$ and rearranging, we obtain

$$\frac{a-r}{s} = \frac{b-r}{g} \equiv p(r). \quad (11)$$

Thus, if the risk associated with suboptimal prepayments is diversifiable, a GNMA security must be priced so that its equilibrium expected excess return per unit of risk equals the price of interest rate risk, $p(r)$, for interest-dependent securities.

The partial differential equation for the value of a GNMA security is obtained by substituting from (9) for $a(r, \tau)$ and $s(r, \tau)$ in (11). Making these substitutions and rearranging yields

$$\tfrac{1}{2}\sigma(r)^2 V_{rr} + [\mu(r) - p(r)\sigma(r)]V_r - V_\tau - rV + C(\tau) + \lambda(r, \tau)[F(\tau) - V] = 0.[7] \quad (12)$$

Comparing (12) with (3) shows that (12) contains the additional term $\lambda(r, \tau)[F(\tau) - V(r, \tau, y)]$. This additional term is the expected value of a suboptimal prepayment when the remaining time to maturity is τ and the riskless interest rate is r. If the Poisson event occurs, investors will receive $F(\tau)$. At that point, the market value of the security will "jump" by the amount $F(\tau) - V(r, \tau, y)$. Hence, $\lambda(r, \tau)[F(\tau) - V]$ is an additional component of the expected change in the value of the GNMA security. Like (11), (12) requires that the expected risk-adjusted return on a GNMA security be equal to the instantaneous risk-free return.

Substituting for $\mu(r)$ and $\sigma(r)$ from (1) and for $p(r)$ from (2), we obtain

$$\tfrac{1}{2}\sigma^2 r V_{rr} + [km - (k+q)r]V_r - V_\tau - rV + C(\tau) + \lambda(r, \tau)[F(\tau) - V] = 0. \quad (13)$$

With the initial condition, (4), the boundary conditions, (5) and (6b), (13) can be solved for the value of a GNMA mortgage-backed pass-through security.

IV. COMPARISON OF GNMA MORTGAGE-BACKED SECURITIES WITH OTHER TYPES OF FIXED-RATE BONDS

A. Preliminaries

The mean of the Poisson process driving suboptimal prepayments is equal to zero for all securities except a GNMA security with suboptimal prepayments. Further, with $\lambda = 0$, (13) coincides with (3). Thus, by setting $\lambda = 0$ in (13) and changing either the boundary conditions and/or the functional form of the future cash flows, (13) can be solved for the prices of each of the other fixed-rate securities of concern. We use an implicit finite difference method, as described by Brennan and Schwartz [2], to solve (13) with the boundary conditions (4) through (6a) or (6b) for the price of: (1) a nonamortizing, noncallable coupon bond; (2) a nonamortizing callable coupon bond; (3) an amortizing, noncallable bond; (4) a GNMA security when the optimal call policy is followed; and (5) a GNMA security with suboptimal prepayments. Comparison of the solutions for the various types of securities illustrates the effects of the amortization feature, the call option, and the suboptimal prepayments on the value, risk, and expected return of a GNMA security.

For the models presented in this paper, the value of every interest-dependent security is a function of the risk-adjustment parameter, q, and the parameters k, m, and σ^2 of the stochastic process which governs the instantaneous interest rate. From Cox, Ingersoll, and Ross [5] we know that the price of every interest-dependent security and, therefore, the price of a GNMA security decreases with increases in the instantaneous interest rate, r, the long run mean of the current interest rate, m, and the risk premium (which is the product of the risk-adjustment parameter, q, and the interest rate elasticity of the security's price). Further, the price of a noncallable security increases with increases in the variance of the current interest rate, σ^2. Because of the call option, however, an increase in σ^2 can either increase or decrease the value of a callable security such as a GNMA. When the term structure is falling (rising), prices increase (decrease) as the speed of the adjustment parameter, k, increases. For the numerical solutions presented, we assume $k = .8$, $m = .056$, $\sigma^2 = .008$, and $q = .247$.[8] The value of q is calculated by assuming that the long run interest rate, $R(\infty)$ is .08 per year.[9] When $k = .8$ the current interest rate is expected to revert halfway back to m in 10.4 months.

In the numerical illustrations we assume that the mean of the Poisson process driving the suboptimal prepayments, $\lambda(r, \tau)$, is a function only of the remaining term to maturity of the loans supporting to the GNMA security. The $\lambda(\tau)$'s are estimated from the historical FHA actuarial data in [17]. With those data it is not possible to estimate the expected prepayment rates as a function of both r and τ.

Tables I and II contain selected numerical solutions for the four types of interest-dependent securities described above. To facilitate comparisons among the securities, the prices shown are stated per $100 of remaining principal balance. Each of the securities is assumed to have an original term to maturity of 30 years and a coupon interest rate of 8 percent per year. The probabilities of a suboptimal prepayment are stated relative to the historical FHA experience. For example, 100 percent FHA experience indicates that the $\lambda(\tau)$'s equal the historical FHA prepayment rates, while 200 percent FHA experience means that they are twice the FHA rate.

In Table I the current instantaneous interest rate, which determines the entire term structure, is varied from zero to 20 percent per year. When the current interest

Table 1 Prices of Various Fixed-Rate Securities as a Function of the Current Interest Rate when the Coupon Rate of the Bonds is 8 Percent and the Term to Maturity is 30 Years

(1) Percentage Current Interest Rate	(2) Percentage 30 Year Interest Rate	(3) Nonamortizing Noncallable Bond	(4) Nonamortizing Callable Bond	(5) Amortizing Noncallable Bond	(6) GNMA Security with the Optimal Call Policy	(7) GNMA Security with Suboptimal Prepayments at 100% of FHA Experience	(8) GNMA Security with Suboptimal Prepayments at 200% of FHA Experience
0.0000	7.5268	113.29805	100.00000	113.11888	100.00000	100.00000	100.00000
1.0000	7.5863	111.52800	100.00000	111.37348	100.00000	100.00000	100.00000
2.0000	7.6459	109.78614	100.00000	109.65568	100.00000	100.00000	100.00000
3.0000	7.7054	108.07378	100.00000	107.96676	100.00000	100.00000	100.00000
4.0000	7.7649	106.38961	100.00000	106.30542	100.00000	100.00000	100.00000
5.0000	7.8244	104.73284	99.98574	104.67093	100.00000	100.00000	100.00000
6.0000	7.8840	103.10400	99.27023	103.06378	99.37159	99.62100	99.75924
7.0000	7.9435	101.50229	98.13678	101.48319	98.29127	98.69237	98.92891
8.0000	8.0030	99.92686	96.85764	99.92836	97.05001	97.55658	97.86710
9.0000	8.0625	98.37738	95.51956	98.39893	95.74209	96.33082	96.70242
10.0000	8.1221	96.85347	94.15900	96.89456	94.40717	95.06459	95.48951
11.0000	8.1816	95.35476	92.79359	95.41488	93.06444	93.78187	94.25497
12.0000	8.2411	93.88086	91.43269	93.95950	91.72411	92.49552	93.01308
13.0000	8.3006	92.43135	90.08169	92.52803	90.39207	91.21296	91.77215
14.0000	8.3602	91.00581	88.74380	91.12006	89.07187	89.93571	90.53723
15.0000	8.4197	89.60381	87.42101	89.73514	87.76572	88.67562	89.31155
16.0000	8.4792	88.22487	86.11456	88.37284	86.47499	87.42552	88.09717
17.0000	8.5387	86.86852	84.82519	87.03268	85.20054	86.18959	86.89548
18.0000	8.5982	85.53428	83.55332	85.71419	83.94289	84.96857	85.70734
19.0000	8.6578	84.22222	82.29961	84.41745	82.70275	83.76333	84.53372
20.0000	8.7173	82.93240	81.06464	83.14252	81.48074	82.57460	83.37541

Selected Interested Rate Elasticities of the Bond Prices

6.0000	− 0.09398	− 0.05968	− 0.09277	− 0.05557	− 0.04376	− 0.03650
8.0000	− 0.12508	− 0.10862	− 0.12346	− 0.10565	− 0.09755	− 0.09180
12.0000	− 0.18683	− 0.17803	− 0.18434	− 0.17488	− 0.16673	− 0.16026

Note—The prices equal to $100.00 in Columns 4, 6, 7, and 8 indicate that the securities have been called optimally at their call prices of $100.00.

rate, r, is below the long run interest rate of 8 percent per year, the term structure is ascending. The term structure is humped when r is between $R(\infty)$ and $km/(k + q)$ and falling when r is above $km/(k + q)$. This table indicates the impact of the amortization feature, the call option, and the suboptimal prepayments on the price of a GNMA security at different levels of the current interest rate when the remaining term to maturity of each security is 30 years.

Column 1 of Table I gives the level of the current interest rate. For each level of the current interest rate, Column 2 shows the corresponding yield-to-maturity on a pure discount bond with a 30-year term to maturity. Together, these two columns provide an impression of the term structure of interest rates, given the assumed market parameters. Column 3 gives the values of the nonamortizing, noncallable bond. Column 4 shows the prices of the nonamortizing, callable bond. Column 5 presents the prices of the amortizing, noncallable bond. Columns 6, 7, and 8 contain the prices of GNMA securities under the optimal call policy and when the prepayment rates are 100 and 200 percent of the FHA experience, respectively.

B. The Shape of the Term Structure

B. 1. The Call Option. Table I shows that the noncallable bonds are more valuable than the otherwise identical callable ones. The price of each bond declines as the current interest rate is increased from zero to 20 percent. However, the magnitude of the decrease in value is greater for the noncallable than for the callable securities. Unlike a noncallable bond, the value of a callable bond cannot exceed its call price, here $100. With 30 years to maturity, the level of the current interest rate at which the 8 percent nonamortizing callable bond (Column 4) will be called, r_c, is between 4 and 5 percent. For each of the GNMA securities (Columns 6, 7, and 8), r_c is between 5 and 6 percent. When the current interest rate is below r_c, a callable security will have been called at its call price of $100.

At every level of the instantaneous interest rate the value of the call option can be computed by subtracting the value of a callable security from the value of an otherwise identical noncallable one. At "high" levels of the current interest rate, the call option has a smaller impact on the total value of the security than when the interest rate is low. This is because there is a smaller probability that the option will eventually be exercised optimally when the current interest rate is high. For example, when the current interest rate is zero the difference in the values of otherwise identical callable and noncallable bonds (i.e. Column 3 less Column 4 and Column 5 less Column 6) is about $13.00. When the current interest rate is 20 percent, the difference in values is about $2.00.

B. 2. The Amortization Feature. The impact of the amortization feature on value can be seen by comparing the nonamortizing, noncallable bond (Column 3) with the amortizing, noncallable bond (Column 5) and by comparing the nonamortizing, callable bond (Column 4) with the GNMA security under the optimal call policy (Column 6). With the assumed market parameters, the amortization feature has a relatively small impact on the values of the securities when their remaining terms to maturity are 30 years.[10] The differences between the prices in Columns 2 and 4 and between those in Columns 3 and 5 range in absolute value from about $.01 to about $.42.

Note, however, (by comparing Columns 3 and 5) that for high levels of the current interest rate an amortizing, noncallable bond is more valuable than a nonamortizing, noncallable one, but the difference in value declines as the current interest rate declines so that the value of the nonamortizing bond eventually exceeds the value of the amortizing one. This phenomenon occurs because the level cash flows from the amortizing bond are always greater than those from the nonamortizing one until maturity when the total principal of the nonamortizing bond is repaid. When the current interest rate is high, relative to the contract rate on the securities, the final payment on the nonamortizing bond is severely discounted so that the amortizing bond is more valuable than the nonamortizing one.

The valuation relationship is reversed when the current interest rate passes below the long-term interest rate of 8 percent (which is the coupon rate of the bonds). In other words, the amortizing, noncallable bond is more (less) valuable than the nonamortizing, noncallable one when the discount rates given by the term structure are above (below) the coupon rate on the securities. However, for equal absolute differences between the current interest rate and 8 percent, the absolute value of the differences in the prices of the two bonds are, in general, smaller when r is above 8 percent than when it is below 8 percent. For example, the absolute value of the difference in the prices is .08419 when r is 4 percent and .07864 when r is 12 percent. This is because when $k = .8$, the current interest rate is expected to revert rapidly to its steady-state mean of 5.6 percent. Thus, the term structure has a "natural" tendency to be ascending and below the 8 percent coupon rate of these securities. Hence, there is a "natural" tendency for a nonamortizing, noncallable bond to be more valuable than an amortizing, noncallable one.

We should note, however, that there is an interactive effect between the amortization feature and the call option. The nonamortizing, noncallable security is more valuable than the amortizing, noncallable one when both of them are selling at a premium to their face values. However, when they are both selling at a discount, the amortizing security is more valuable. Because the call option prevents a callable security from selling at a premium, an amortizing, callable security is more valuable than an otherwise identical nonamortizing, callable security. Comparing Columns 6 and 4 shows that the GNMA security with the optimal call policy is more valuable than the nonamortizing callable bond for all relevant levels of the current interest rate. Further, comparing the difference between Columns 3 and 4 with the difference between Columns 5 and 6 shows that a call option on a nonamortizing security is more valuable than a call option on an amortizing security.

A comparison of Columns 6 and 3 shows that the GNMA security with the optimal call policy is less valuable than the nonamortizing, noncallable bond for all levels of the current interest rate. As discussed above, most of the difference in value is due to the callability feature and very little is due to the amortization feature.

B. 3. Suboptimal Prepayments. The last three columns of Table I show that the effect of suboptimal prepayments is to increase the value of a GNMA security and that the effect is greater the higher the current interest rate. This occurs because the increase in an investor's wealth due to a suboptimal prepayment is greater the larger the discount of the security's price from face value. The increase in value due to suboptimal prepayments also increases with increases in the expected rate of suboptimal prepayments.[11]

For example, as the current interest rate rises from 5 percent to 20 percent, the difference between the value of the GNMA security with the optimal call policy and the one with an expected prepayment rate that is 100 percent of the FHA experience (i.e.

Column 6 vs. Column 7) increases from zero to slightly over $1.00. When the expected prepayment rate is 200 percent of the FHA experience, the additional value due to suboptimal prepayments (i.e. Column 6 vs. Column 8) increases from zero to almost $2.00 as the interest rate rises from 5 percent to 20 percent.

C. Risk and Return. The information contained in Table I can also be used to examine the effect of the call option, the amortization feature, and the suboptimal prepayments on the risk and instantaneous expected return of the GNMA security. Let $a(r, \tau)$ denote the expected return of the securities. From Equations (2), (9), and (11), $a(r, \tau) = r + q[rV_r/V]$. Thus, the expected return equals the current risk-free rate plus a risk premium proportional to the interest rate elasticity of a security's price. Because the interest rate elasticity of each bond and the risk-adjustment parameter, q, are both negative, the expected return increases with increases in the absolute value of a security's interest rate elasticity. By using a centered finite difference approximation V_r, the interest rate elasticity of the price of each security, can be computed at any level of the current interest rate. The interest rate elasticity of each security is given at the bottom of Table I for current interest rates of 6 percent, 8 percent, and 12 percent.[12]

C. 1. The Amortization Feature. The impact of the amortization feature on the risk and expected returns of amortizing bonds relative to otherwise identical nonamortizing ones can be seen by comparing the elasticities in Columns 5 and 6 with those in Columns 3 and 4, respectively. These comparisons show that the prices of amortizing securities are slightly less sensitive to interest rate fluctuations than their nonamortizing counterparts, but the impact of the amortization feature on expected return is small (for the assumed parameters of the interest rate process and when the term to maturity of the securities is 30 years).

When the current interest rate is 12 percent, the absolute value of the interest rate elasticity of the GNMA security with the optimal call policy is .00315 less than that of the nonamortizing, callable bond. This means that the expected return on the GNMA security is 8 basis points per year (.00315 × .247) less than the expected return on the nonamortizing, callable bond.

C. 2. The Call Option. Comparison of Column 5 with Column 6 shows that the effect of the call option is to reduce the risk and expected return of the GNMA security. This phenomenon occurs because the price of a callable security equals the price of an otherwise identical noncallable security less the value of the call option. The values of the noncallable security and the call option both decrease with increases in the current interest rate; therefore, the price of a callable security is less sensitive to changes in the current interest rate than the price of an otherwise identical noncallable one. This effect is smaller for higher levels of the current interest rate because the call feature has less effect on the value of the callable security at higher levels of the current interest rate. Again, this is because the bond is less likely to be called when the current interest rate is high.

The difference between the elasticities in Columns 5 and 6 imply that the expected return on the GNMA security with the optimal call policy is 23 basis points lower than the expected return on the noncallable, amortizing bond when the current interest rate is 12 percent and the difference is 92 basis points when the current interest rate is 6 percent.

C. 3. Suboptimal Prepayments. An increase in the expected rate of suboptimal prepayments decreases the interest rate elasticity and, therefore, the interest rate risk and expected return of the GNMA security. This phenomenon occurs because the risk associated with the suboptimal prepayments is unsystematic and, therefore, unrewarded by the capital market. Further, the suboptimal prepayments reduce the relevant risk of the security, i.e., $s(r, \tau)$ in Equation (9), because they reduce the sensitivity of the security's price to changes in the interest rate. This can be seen by comparing the elasticities in Columns 6, 7, and 8. When the current interest rate is 12 percent (6 percent), the expected return on the GNMA security with suboptimal prepayments at 200 percent of FHA experience is 36 (47) basis points less than the expected return on the GNMA security with the optimal call policy.[13]

D. Term to Maturity. Table II presents the solutions for the four types of securities when the term to maturity is varied from zero to 30 years and when the current interest rate is 12 percent. Column 1 of the table gives the remaining term to maturity of each security. Column 2 shows the yield-to-maturity of a pure discount bond whose term to maturity is the same as that shown in Column 1. Thus, Column 2 gives the term structure of interest rates resulting from the assumed market parameters when the current interest rate is 12 percent. Columns 3 through 8 correspond to the Columns in Table I and, for each term to maturity, Column 9 gives the mean of the Poisson process generating prepayments at 100% of FHA experience.

Table II shows that when the term structure is descending and everywhere above 8 percent, the prices of the noncallable bonds (Columns 3 and 5) and the callable bonds with the optimal call policy (Columns 4 and 6) decline and eventually approach an asymptote as the remaining term to maturity increases. However, this behavior is sensitive to the combination of the coupon interest rate and the parameters of the interest rate process considered.

We do not report the results here, but other numerical solutions show that the prices of noncallable securities which have coupon rates that are above the long run interest, but below the current interest rate, first decline and then increase with increases in the remaining terms to maturity of the bonds. This occurs because the current interest rate is expected to decrease far enough and fast enough so that a noncallable security will eventually sell at a premium. However, because the call feature precludes callable bonds from selling at a premium, the prices of nonamortizing, callable bonds and GNMA securities with the optimal call policy decline and approach an asymptote as the term to maturity is lengthened.

Examination of Columns 7 and 8 shows that the value of the GNMA security with suboptimal prepayments does not approach an asymptote as the term to maturity is lengthened to 30 years. Instead, the prices decrease rapidly as the remaining term to maturity is increased from 25 to 30 years. This phenomenon occurs because the value of a GNMA security depends on the expected rate of future prepayments and, as shown in Column 9, the empirically estimated prepayment probabilities are low in the first two years of the security's life and then increase dramatically in Years 3 and 4.

D. 1. The Amortization Feature. When the term structure is downward sloping, the values of the amortizing securities increase relative to the values of nonamortizing ones as the remaining term to maturity becomes shorter. This result occurs because the final

Table 1. Prices of Various Maturity Securities as a Function of Term to Maturity when the Coupon Rate of the Bonds is 8 Percent and the Current Interest Rate is 12 Percent Per Year

(1)	(2)	(3)	(4)	(5)	(6)	(7)	(8)	(9)
Years to Maturity	Percentage Yield-to-Maturity of a Discount Bond	Nonamortizing Noncallable Bond	Nonamortizing Callable Bond	Amortizing Noncallable Bond	GNMA Security with the Optimal Call Policy	GNMA Security with Suboptimal Prepayments at 100% of FHA Experience	GNMA Security with Suboptimal Prepayments at 200% of FHA Experience	Annual Prepayment Probabilities at 100% of FHA Experience
0	12.0000	100.00000	100.00000	100.00000	100.00000	100.00000	100.00000	.00000
1	11.0864	97.12317	97.08360	98.27117	98.25939	98.43507	98.57899	.32444
2	10.4334	95.60206	95.37638	97.19669	97.12534	97.50224	97.79363	.24495
3	9.9622	94.79564	94.28749	96.44427	96.26721	96.74149	97.10418	.15885
4	9.6170	94.36739	93.55308	95.90570	95.59501	96.20273	96.66045	.15037
5	9.3597	94.13973	93.03641	95.51170	95.05344	95.79050	96.33231	.14224
6	9.1644	94.01863	92.66152	95.21722	94.60796	95.45815	96.07090	.13459
7	9.0133	93.95418	92.38434	94.99257	94.23701	95.18049	95.85009	.12733
8	8.8942	93.91988	92.17448	94.81783	93.92274	94.94301	95.65635	.12049
9	8.7987	93.90162	92.01275	94.67944	93.65248	94.73589	95.48189	.11399
10	8.7208	93.89190	91.88702	94.56804	93.41841	94.55234	95.32201	.10785
11	8.6562	93.88673	91.78890	94.47703	93.21484	94.38657	95.17380	.10208
12	8.6021	93.88398	91.71218	94.40169	93.03722	94.21396	95.00179	.09174
13	8.5560	93.88251	91.65214	94.33860	92.88167	94.04752	94.83072	.08358
14	8.5165	93.88173	91.60513	94.28521	92.74407	93.89050	94.66681	.07665
15	8.4821	93.88131	91.56832	94.23962	92.62090	93.74542	94.51423	.07099
16	8.4520	93.88109	91.53949	94.20040	92.51009	93.61551	94.37781	.06687
17	8.4255	93.88098	91.51692	94.16640	92.41020	93.50229	94.26041	.06408
18	8.4018	93.88092	91.49923	94.13676	92.32010	93.40574	94.16281	.06235
19	8.3807	93.88089	91.48537	94.11079	92.23880	93.32517	94.08464	.06145
20	8.3617	93.88087	91.47437	94.08791	92.16540	93.25891	94.02380	.06112
21	8.3444	93.88086	91.46553	94.06768	92.09910	93.20172	93.97206	.06053
22	8.3288	93.88086	91.45835	94.04972	92.03918	93.16005	93.94139	.06159
23	8.3145	93.88086	91.45250	94.03373	91.98499	93.12710	93.92032	.06221
24	8.3014	93.88086	91.44772	94.01945	91.93594	93.09666	93.89900	.06202
25	8.2893	93.88086	91.44382	94.00665	91.89151	93.06893	93.87892	.06189
26	8.2782	93.88086	91.44062	93.99516	91.85125	93.02219	93.82418	.05774
27	8.2679	93.88086	91.43801	93.98483	91.81473	92.95124	93.72754	.05128
28	8.2583	93.88086	91.43587	93.97552	91.78159	92.86122	93.59875	.04431
29	8.2494	93.88086	91.43412	93.96711	91.75148	92.72596	93.39147	.03172
30	8.2411	93.88086	91.43269	93.95950	91.72411	92.49552	93.01308	.00840

85

balloon payment on a nonamortizing security is discounted at higher interest rates as the remaining term to maturity becomes shorter and the current interest rate is held constant at 12 percent. At each term to maturity, the value of the GNMA security with the optimal call policy is greater than the value of the nonamortizing, callable bond. With 30 years to maturity, the difference in values (Column 6 less Column 4) is only $.29. This difference increases to $2.05 when the term to maturity is four years and then declines to $1.18 when the term to maturity is one year. The difference between the values of the amortizing, noncallable bond (Column 5) and the nonamortizing, noncallable bond (Column 3) increases from $.08 to $1.64 as the term to maturity declines from 30 years to 3 years. This difference then declines to $1.15 when the term to maturity is one year.

D. 2. The Call Option. The effect of changes in the term to maturity on the value of the call option can be seen by comparing the noncallable bonds with their callable counterparts (i.e., Column 3 less Column 4 and Column 5 less Column 6). These comparisons show that the value of the call option declines as the term to maturity becomes shorter and that a call option on a nonamortizing security is more valuable than a call option on an amortizing one. The latter effect is due to the fact that the call option prevents the security from selling at a premium. As discussed above, the call option has a larger impact on the value of a GNMA security than the amortization feature when the remaining term to maturity is long. However, the amortizing feature has a larger impact on price than the call option when the remaining term to maturity is short. In this case the crossover occurs when the term to maturity becomes less than eight years.

D. 3. Suboptimal Prepayments. As the term to maturity is varied from 0 to 30 years, the effect of the suboptimal prepayments on the value of the GNMA security can be seen by comparing Columns 6, 7, and 8. In general, the effect of the suboptimal prepayments is positive and larger the longer the term to maturity. However, because this effect depends on both the pattern of the prepayment probabilities and the extent to which the security is selling at a discount, the effect increases rapidly as the term to maturity is increased from zero to five years and then decreases as the remaining term to maturity is lengthened from 25 to 30 years.

As the remaining term to maturity decreases, the impact of suboptimal prepayments eventually becomes greater than the impact of optimal prepayments so that the GNMA security becomes more valuable than the amortizing, noncallable bond. For example, with prepayments at 100 percent of the historical FHA experience, the GNMA security is more valuable than the amortizing, noncallable bond when the remaining term to maturity is less than 10 years. This effect probably is somewhat overstated, however, because in practice we would expect the prepayment probabilities to decrease with increases in the risk-free interest rate.[14]

CONCLUSION

In this paper we develop a model for the pricing of GNMA mortgage-backed pass-through securities. The model is based on the general model for the pricing of interest-contingent claims developed by Brennan and Schwartz [2] and Cox, Ingersoll, and Ross [5]. A GNMA security is backed by homogenous, fully-amortizing, callable mortgage loans. Additionally, mortgagors often prepay their loans even when the market value of the loan is less than the call price. We model each of the characteristics of the GNMA security and use a numerical solution technique to analyze the impact of each feature on the price, risk, and expected return of the security.

In general, the amortization and prepayment features increase the price of a GNMA security and the callability feature decreases it. In terms of the absolute magnitude, the callability feature has a greater impact on the value of the security than either of the other two features when the remaining term to maturity is long. However, the amortization feature has the largest impact on value when the term to maturity is short. The effect of all three features is to reduce the interest rate risk and, consequently, the expected return of a GNMA security relative to other securities which do not have these features.

The analysis was undertaken with the hope that it would answer questions raised by portfolio managers, financial analysts, security dealers, and government officials about the pricing and investment performance of GNMA securities. A further pressing need is an empirical study to determine if the prices generated by the model are consistent with observed market prices. If the answer is affirmative, then the model presented here should be useful to all active participants in the GNMA market.

NOTES

[1] Recently GNMA began guaranteeing securities backed by graduated mortgage loans. Although the pricing model derived in this paper can price securities backed by graduated payment loans and other non-standard mortgage loans, we focus on securities backed by standard 30-year amortizing loans because they are by far the most widely issued securities to date.

[2] Because of the mortgage insurance, default of an individual loan is equivalent to a loan prepayment from the perspective of a GNMA security holder.

[3] The mortgage loans which back a GNMA security are composed of three values—default-free financing, default insurance, and servicing. With a GNMA security, the servicing is provided by the security issuer, while the U.S. Government provides the default protection. As a consequence, the value of a GNMA security is the value of the default-free financing.

[4] Cox, Ingersoll, and Ross [5] derive a general equilibrium model of the term structure for an economy with many sources of uncertainty of which the model assumed in this paper is a special case. In a preliminary report on their joint work, Ingersoll [10] derives the model where the risk-free interest rate is the only state variable. Brennan and Schwartz [3], Dothan [6], Langetieg [13], Richard [18], and Vasicek [21] also derive continuous time models of the term structure of interest rates.

[5] We use the term "suboptimal" in a casual sense. The prepayments are suboptimal only in the sense that the amount of the prepayment (i.e. the outstanding balance of the loan) exceeds the market value of the debt. Mortgagors cannot repurchase the debt at its market value and a perfect market for the "capital gain" (i.e. the face value less the market value) does not exist; therefore, the "suboptimal" prepayments are constrained maximum. Hence, the prepayment decisions of mortgagors are not suboptimal, but the prepayments are a suboptimal relative to those which would be observed if mortgagors had direct access to the capital market or if there were a perfect market for the capital gain on mortgage loans.

[6] Ingersoll [11] and Merton [16] have used this approach previously to deal with similar problems.

[7] This is similar to equation (7.15) in Brennan and Schwartz [4].

[8] These parameters are similar to those estimated by Ingersoll [12].

[9] The absence of arbitrage requires that the expected excess return per unit of risk, $p(r)$, be the same for all interest-dependent securities. Therefore, the risk adjustment term, $p(r)\sigma\sqrt{r} \equiv qr$, is not a function of maturity and one maturity is as good as another for the purpose of estimating q. Cox, Ingersoll, and Ross [5] show that the yield-to-maturity on a discount bond, $R(r, \tau)$, approaches a limiting value which is independent

of the current interest rate as the time to maturity goes to infinity. This limiting yield is $R(\infty) = 2km/(g + k + q)$ where $g = \sqrt{(k + q)^2 + 2\sigma^2}$. Solving for q we obtain

$$q = k\left(\frac{m}{R(\infty)} - 1\right) - \frac{\sigma^2 R(\infty)}{2km}.$$

[10] The difference in the prices of an amortizing bond and a nonamortizing bond would be larger if we had assumed a lower value for the speed of adjustment parameter k or if we also allowed for uncertainty in the long run interest rate (e.g. see [3], [5] and [18]).

[11] If the prepayment probabilities were assumed to decrease with increases in the interest rate, the increase in value due to suboptimal prepayments would be reduced somewhat. This is because there would be an interactive effect between the prepayment probabilities and the security's discount from face value as the current interest rate increased.

[12] For a given change in the current interest rate, the change in the yield of pure discount bonds with longer terms to maturity is larger the smaller the speed of adjustment parameter, k. Therefore, the absolute values of the interest rate elasticities increase with decreases in k.

[13] Evidence on the historical rate of return experience of GNMA securities is available in Dunn and McConnell [7] and in Waldman and Baum [23].

[14] Numerical solutions for the value of a GNMA security when the mean of the Poisson process generating suboptimal prepayments is assumed to decrease with increases in the risk-free interest rate are presented in Dunn and McConnell [8].

REFERENCES

[1] F. Black and M. Scholes. "The Pricing of Options and Corporate Liabilities." *Journal of Political Economy* Vol. 8 No. 1 (May–June 1973), 637–59.

[2] M. J. Brennan and E. S. Schwartz. "Savings Bonds, Retractable Bonds, and Callable Bonds." *Journal of Financial Economics* Vol. 5 No. 1 (August 1977), 67–88.

[3] M. J. Brennan and E. S. Schwartz. "A Continuous Time Approach to the Pricing of Bonds," *Journal of Banking and Finance* Vol. 3 No. 3 (September 1979), 133–55.

[4] M. J. Brennan and E. S. Schwartz. *Savings Bonds: Theory and Empirical Evidence.* Monograph Series in Finance and Economics, Solomon Brothers Center for the Study of Financial Institutions, Monograph 1979–4. N.Y.: New York University, 1979.

[5] J. C. Cox, J. E. Ingersoll, and S. A. Ross. "A Theory of the Term Structure of Interest Rates." Unpublished manuscript: Stanford University, August, 1978.

[6] L. U. Dothan. "On the Term Structure of Interest Rates." *Journal of Financial Economics* Vol. 6 No. 1 (March 1978), 59–69.

[7] K. B. Dunn and J. J. McConnell. "Rate of Return Indexes for GNMA Securities." *Journal of Portfolio Management*, Vol. 7 No. 2 (Winter 1981), 65–74.

[8] K. B. Dunn and J. J. McConnell. "A Comparison of Alternative Models for Pricing GNMA Mortgage-backed Securities." *Journal of Finance* Vol. 36 No. 2 (May 1981).

[9] *The Ginnie Mae Manual.* Homewood, IL: GNMA Mortgage-backed Security Association, 1978.

[10] J. E. Ingersoll. "Interest Rate Dynamics, the Term Structure, and the Valuation of Contingent Claims." Unpublished manuscript: University of Chicago, 1976.

[11] J. E. Ingersoll. "An Examination of Corporate Call Policies on Convertible Securities." *Journal of Finance* Vol. 32 No. 2 (May 1977), 463–78.

[12] J. E. Ingersoll. "Forward Rates and Expected Spot Rates: The Effects of Uncertainty." Unpublished manuscript: University of Chicago, 1977.

[13] T. Langetieg. "A Multivariate Model of the Term Structure." *Journal of Finance* Vol. 35 No. 1 (March 1980), 71–98.

[14] R. C. Merton. "Optimum Consumption and Portfolio Rules in a Continuous Time Model." *Journal of Economic Theory* Vol. 3 No. 4 (December 1971), 373–413.

[15] R. C. Merton. "Theory of Rational Option Pricing." *Bell Journal of Economics and Management Science* Vol. 4 No. 1 (Spring 1973), 143–83.

[16] R. C. Merton. "Option Pricing When Underlying Stock Returns are Discontinuous." *Journal of Financial Economics* Vol. 3 No. 1/2 (January 1976), 125–44.

[17] *Pass-Through Yield and Value Tables for GNMA Mortgage-Backed Securities.* Publication #715, Fifth Edition. Boston, MA: Financial Publishing Company, 1979.

[18] S. F. Richard. "An Arbitrage Model of the Term Structure of Interest Rates." *Journal of Financial Economics* Vol. 6 No. 1 (March 1978), 33–57.

[19] D. Seiders. *The GNMA Guaranteed Pass Through Security.* Washington, D.C.: Board of Governors of the Federal Reserve System, 1979.

[20] D. E. Senft. *Pass-Through Securities.* New York: First Boston, 1978.

[21] O. Vasicek. "An Equilibrium Characterization of the Term Structure of Interest Rates." *Journal of Financial Economics* Vol. 5 No. 2 (November 1977), 177–88.

[22] M. Waldman. *Introducing the Salomon Brothers Total Rate-of-Return Index for Mortgage Pass Through Securities.* New York: Salomon Brothers, 1979.

[23] M. Waldman and S. Baum. *The Historical Performance of Mortgage Securities: 1972–1980.* New York: Salomon Brothers, 1980.

7 Prepayments on Fixed-Rate Mortgage-Backed Securities

A model with innovations and attributes to extend the understanding of mortgage prepayments.

Scott F. Richard and Richard Roll

Mortgage-backed securities (MBSs) are increasingly a part of the financial scene. To assess their relative value and the value of their derivatives, it is essential to predict mortgage prepayments accurately. It is important to understand how mortgage pass-through securities will prepay in today's interest rate environment as well as how prepayments will fluctuate as interest rates fluctuate.

This paper introduces our latest work on prepayment modeling. Recognizing that work in this area is never completed, we feel nevertheless that our model includes certain innovations and attributes that extend the understanding of mortgage prepayments. We begin by analyzing the economic theory underlying a homeowner's decision to prepay a mortgage. This option-theoretic analysis serves as the basis for our empirical model of prepayment rates.

Three aspects of our model are novel. First, we measure the mortgagor's refinancing incentive as the ratio of the mortgage coupon to the current refinancing rate, not as the difference between these two rates. This idea comes from our economic analysis of the mortgagor's prepayment decision. Second, we show that the seasoning process for mortgages depends importantly on this same ratio, the coupon relative to the refinancing rate. In particular, premium mortgages season more rapidly than current coupon mortgages, which, in turn, season more rapidly than discount mortgages. Finally, we examine the tendency of premium mortgages to slow or "burn out" over time. We introduce a measure of premium burnout that depends on the entire interest rate history since the mortgage was issued.

We try to provide sufficient details so that readers can understand how the model works. Examples in the figures explain the Goldman Sachs prepayment model, without bogging readers down with unnecessary mathematical detail. We also report a detailed summary of our model's predictions in relation to actual prepayment data.

From *The Journal of Portfolio Management*. This copyrighted material is reprinted with permission from *The Journal of Portfolio Management*, 488 Madison Avenue, New York, NY 10022.

PREPAYMENT THEORY

A homeowner with a new thirty-year fixed-rate mortgage has committed to make 360 fixed monthly payments. This stream of fixed payments is known as an annuity. As the mortgage ages, the market value of the annuity changes for two reasons: first, there are fewer payments left in the stream; second, the capitalization rate, as measured by the current mortgage rate, fluctuates.

The present value of the annuity, A, in month t, per dollar of monthly payment is given by the formula:

$$A = [1 - (1 + R)^{-360 + t}]/R,$$

where R is the mortgage refinancing rate in month t.[1]

We measure the homeowner's economic incentive to refinance by computing the annuity value per dollar of principal outstanding. In month t the outstanding principal, P, per dollar of monthly payment is given by

$$P = [1 - (1 + C)^{-360 + t}]/C,$$

where C is the coupon rate. Hence the annuity value per dollar of principal in month t is

$$A/P = (C/R)\{[1 - (1 + R)^{-360 + t}]/[1 - (1 + C)^{-360 + t}]\}.$$

The value of A/P is well-approximated by C/R, the mortgage coupon rate divided by the mortgage refinancing rate, over a wide range of maturities. For small values of t (i.e., relatively new mortgages), the term in braces is trivial, so the dollar amount of refinancing incentive is nearly equal to C/R. Even for larger values of t, the term in braces is not very large. For example, for a fifteen-year-old mortgage (t = 180) with an 8% coupon (C = 0.08/12 = 0.00667) and a current mortgage rate of 10% (R = 0.1/12 = 0.00833), we find that the term in braces is 1.11. It is only as the mortgage nears maturity that the term in braces becomes large; for t = 359, C = 0.00667, and R = 0.00833, the term is 1.25.

The more commonly used measure of the refinancing incentive, the coupon rate less the refinancing rate C − R, is a poor approximation to A/P for most coupons and maturities. In fact, it is only as the mortgage nears maturity that A/P approximately equals 1 + C − R. For example, when t = 359, C = 0.00667, and R = 0.00833, we find that A/P = 0.99835, which is very nearly equal to 0.99833 = 1 + C − R. When t = 30, however, A/P = 0.842, and C/R = 0.800, but 1 + C − R still equals 0.998.

To understand why A/P measures the homeowner's refinancing incentive, we must turn to option pricing theory. Mortgagors have the option to prepay their mortgages. In order to decide whether to exercise this option, they must compare the cost of continuing the monthly payments to the cost of refinancing at the current rate. The cost of refinancing includes both explicit costs, such as title insurance and points, and implicit costs, such as qualifying difficulties if, for example, the mortgagor is currently unemployed. The costs of refinancing can actually be negative if the homeowner has a large incentive to move, as might occur with incentives offered by a new employer.

If mortgagors exercise the prepayment option, they retire their annuity with value A, but must repay the principal P plus the explicit and implicit costs of refinancing. In addition, they lose the right to exercise the option at a future date. This means that the homeowner's prepayment option is an American option on the annuity with strike price equal to the current principal plus the refinancing costs. If refinancing costs are proportional to the principal amount, then the option value per dollar of current principal depends on A/P. Hence the mortgage value per dollar of principal depends on A/P as well.

Standard option pricing theory for American options implies that it is rational for the mortgagor to prepay when A/P exceeds some critical value. This critical value of A/P in turn implies a critical value of refinancing costs, stated as a fraction of the principal. Because costs of refinancing are heterogeneous within a mortgage pool, not all mortgagors will find it optimal to prepay simultaneously.[2] The number of mortgagors in a particular pool with refinancing costs below the critical value will determine the fraction of the pool that prepays. Hence the speed of prepayment in otherwise identical pools (in terms of maturity and coupon) will differ because of heterogeneous refinancing costs for mortgagors within the pools, even if every mortgagor is behaving rationally.

Furthermore, the data indicate that refinancing costs are time varying. To see this, consider a scenario where interest rates fall and then rise. As interest rates fall, A/P rises, causing some households to prepay because their refinancing costs are below the critical value of refinancing costs implied by the current A/P. When interest rates reach their (ex post) minimum, both A/P and the implied critical level of refinancing cost reach their maximum; denote this maximum refinancing cost, M. All households with prepayment costs below M will have prepaid, so only those households with prepayment costs above M will remain in a pool. Now assume interest rates rise so that A/P falls and the implied cost necessary to trigger a prepayment also falls.[3] If prepayment costs did not change over time, there would be no households with prepayment costs below M. As we continue to observe prepayments in this rising interest rate environment, however, we conclude that household prepayment costs must vary over time.

THE GOLDMAN SACHS PREPAYMENT MODEL

Our prepayment model is an empirical estimation of the mortgagor's financing decision. We try to uncover an explanation for prepayments by observing actual prepayments and relating them to the measurable factors suggested by our economic theory of prepayments.

Even a cursory empirical examination reveals that outstanding mortgages with very high coupons relative to current mortgage refinancing rates still do not entirely prepay. At the other end of the spectrum, some borrowers prepay when they could clearly receive higher returns by investing the same cash in safe money market instruments. These are both manifestations of the fact that the mortgagors have heterogeneous refinancing costs.

Factors That Explain Prepayments. The Goldman Sachs prepayment model captures four important economic effects:

1. The refinancing incentive;
2. Seasoning or age of the mortgage;
3. The month of the year (seasonality); and
4. Premium burnout.

We discuss the form and empirical measurement of each of these effects in turn.

The Refinancing Incentive. We measure the refinancing incentive as the weighted average of recent values of C/R, the mortgage coupon rate divided by the mortgage refinancing rate.[4] Two comments are in order about this choice to measure the refinancing incentive. First, we use C/R instead of A/P because of the out-of-sample properties of these two measures. As a mortgage matures, A/P converges to one. This causes the refinancing incentive for premium mortgages to fall automatically and for discount mortgages to rise automatically. As we have no data on the end-of-life behavior of mortgage-backed security pools, we chose not to use A/P out of sample to avoid a possible source of bias. Within our sample, as we have noted, A/P is well approximated by C/R.

Second, we use a weighted average of recent values of C/R to capture the fact that homeowners exhibit varying delays in responding to refinancing incentives because of differences in processing times by mortgage lenders and, perhaps, differences in the time they need to react to a favorable interest rate environment. For convenience we will call this weighted average C/R. The lower recent interest rates have been, the higher the value of C/R. We know from our analysis of the homeowner's prepayment option that the higher C/R is, the higher prepayments will be.

We model the relationship between prepayments and C/R by using a curve-fitting technique. Figure 1 shows monthly prepayment rates (expressed in % CPR) for seasoned thirty-year GNMA single-family pools. The curve in Figure 1 reflects only the pure refinancing incentive for a seasoned pool without adjustment for path-dependent burnout. Notice that there is a highly non-linear relationship between the prepayment rate and C/R, which is typical of option pricing models.

For values of C/R below one, the homeowner's prepayment option is out-of-the money, and the refinancing incentive is relatively small. If C/R is 0.8, for example, representing a seasoned 8% mortgage (with a pass-through rate of 7.5%) in a current mortgage refinancing rate environment of 10%, the prepayment rate is approximately 5% CPR. Conversely, when C/R exceeds one, the coupon is above the refinancing rate, and the incentive to refinance increases dramatically. A seasoned 13% mortgage in a 10% refinancing rate environment (C/R = 1.3), for example, has a base prepayment rate of about 36% CPR without adjusting for premium burnout.

We estimated the refinancing incentive independently for mortgage-backed securities besides GNMA (FNMA and FHLMC). The basic shape is similar across sectors, although the exact values differ to a certain extent.

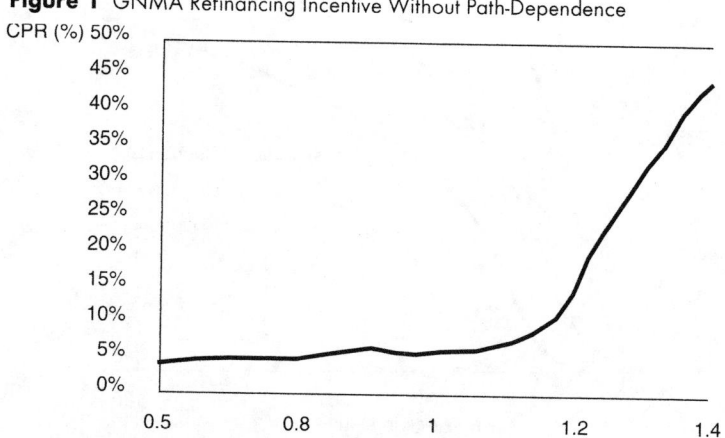

Figure 1 GNMA Refinancing Incentive Without Path-Dependence

Seasoning. It is well known that mortgage prepayment rates rise from very low levels at issue to much higher levels as the mortgages age. This is the rationale for the PSA Standard Prepayment Model, whose base case models mortgage prepayment rates as increasing linearly from 0% CPR at issue to 6% CPR at thirty months and then remaining constant.

It is less well known that the mortgage process differs markedly depending on the coupon rate relative to current refinancing rates. Slight premium GNMA pools, for example, are typically fully seasoned in about thirty months, as suggested by the PSA standard. Current coupon pools, on the other hand, take nearer to five years to season fully, and discount pools can take considerably longer.

Our model captures the interaction between seasoning and coupon by making the seasoning effect a function of the mortgage's current C/R. In Figure 2 we show the relative seasoning effects for a discount pool with C/R = 0.8, a par pool with C/R = 1.0, and a premium pool with C/R = 1.2. Our model shows that these pools season at remarkably different rates.

The discount pool (C/R = 0.8) takes about nine years to season fully, although it is 75% seasoned in about five years. This is not hard to understand in terms of the disincentive for homeowners to move when their mortgage rate is low compared to rates currently available. Moreover, the seasoning process for discount GNMA pools is slowed further by the fact that FHA/VA mortgages are assumable and that the incentive to assume is greater, the smaller C/R is. The par pool with C/R = 1.0 typically takes almost five years to fully season.

Even faster to season fully are premium pools; at a C/R value of 1.2, a pool typically seasons in just over thirty months, as prescribed by PSA. Unfortunately, the seasoning process is decidedly non-linear, and PSA is only an approximation throughout. Again we can see why premium pools season relatively quickly if we look at the homeowner's incentives: Homeowners will not be deterred from moving because they hold a premium mortgage, and it is implausible that anyone will want to assume a high premium mortgage.

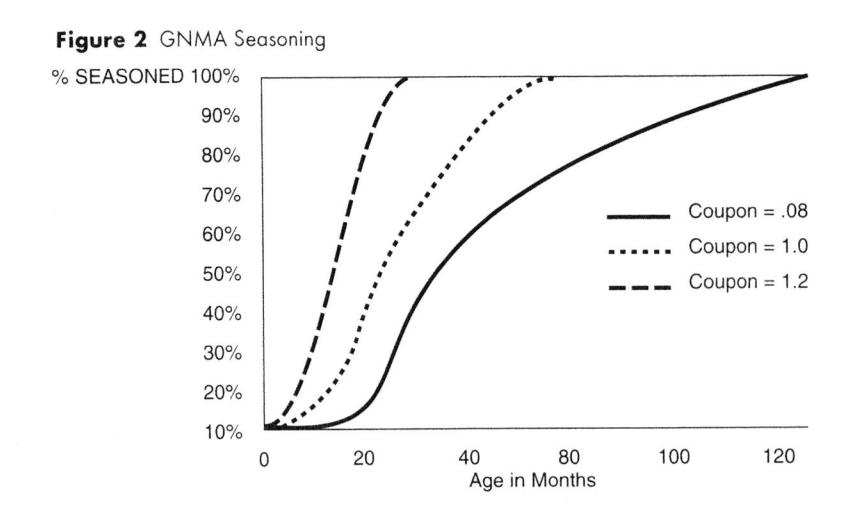

Figure 2 GNMA Seasoning

After mortgages season fully, we assume that aging has no further effect on mortgage prepayment rates, as we have no data on the end-of-life prepayment behavior of mortgage-backed security pools. In the absence of a model of household prepayment costs, economic theory gives little guidance as to whether prepayments should increase or decrease as a mortgage nears maturity. In the absence of theory and data, we have made the neutral choice to assume no further aging effect.

Month of the Year. The seasonal pattern of mortgage prepayments is both important and somewhat surprising. It is commonly believed that prepayments peak in the summer months and trough in the winter because household moves follow a seasonal pattern. Figure 3 shows our model's estimate of the relative month-of-the-year effect in the reporting month for GNMA thirty-year single-family MBSs. There is an obvious winter trough in February-March, but the peak occurs in the autumn in October-November. This is probably due to lags in passing through prepayments. The pattern for FNMAs and FHLMCs is similar to that of GNMAs.

Premium Burnout. Because prepayment costs, both explicit and implicit, differ across households, not all mortgagors in a given pool prepay identically. When a given critical level of C/R is reached, only some of the households will have costs below that critical level, and only these households will choose to prepay. The other households will wait for interest rates to fall farther or for their prepayment costs to drop.

At different times households evidently face different prepayment costs. The first time a critical level of C/R is reached, all the households with prepayment costs below that level will prepay. If interest rates then rise and subsequently fall, this same critical level may be reached again. This will cause some more households to prepay, although not as many as the first time the critical level was reached.[5] Because they choose to prepay the second time a critical level of C/R is reached, but not the first time, we know that the households' costs have fallen over time. Of course, household costs can also rise

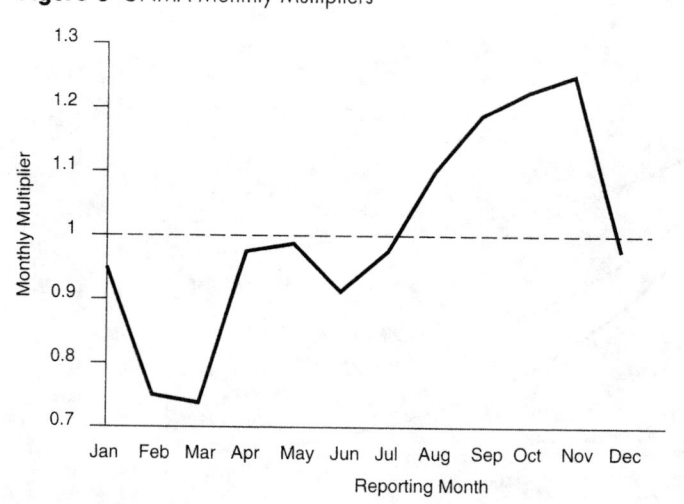

Figure 3 GNMA Monthly Multipliers

over time. For example, the household may no longer qualify for a replacement mortgage because someone in the household may have become unemployed, or the value of the house may have decreased. While it is impossible to measure directly different household prepayment costs, it is certainly possible to estimate empirically the effect of these differing costs on prepayments.

The main empirical effect of household heterogeneity is "premium burnout," by which we mean the tendency of prepayments from premium pools to slow over time, all other things being equal. In the Goldman Sachs prepayment model we capture the effect of premium burnout through a complicated non-linear function. This function depends on the entire history of C/R since the mortgage was issued.

Roughly, we try to measure how much the option to prepay has been deep in-the-money since the pool was issued. The more the prepayment option has been deep in-the-money, the more burned out the pool is, and the smaller prepayments are, all other things being equal.

Figures 4A through 4C illustrate the effect of the adjustment for premium burnout. They show the burnout multiplier as a function of time for hypothetical, newly issued 11.5%, 12%, 12.5%, and 13% coupon GNMA pools (with underlying mortgage rates of 12%, 12.5%, 13%, and 13.5%, respectively) in constant 10%, 10.5%, and 11% mortgage refinancing rate environments, respectively.

To understand the effect of premium burnout, examine Figure 4A. We see that, in a constant 10% mortgage refinancing rate environment, newly issued GNMA pools with 13%, 12.5%, and 12% coupons will all experience premium burnout, but at decreasing rates, and that an 11.5% pool will not. The prepayment options for the higher coupon pools are more in-the-money than for the lower coupon pools.

From Figure 1, we know that the higher coupon pools have a higher refinancing effect. Over time, however, the households with lower prepayment costs in the 13% pool

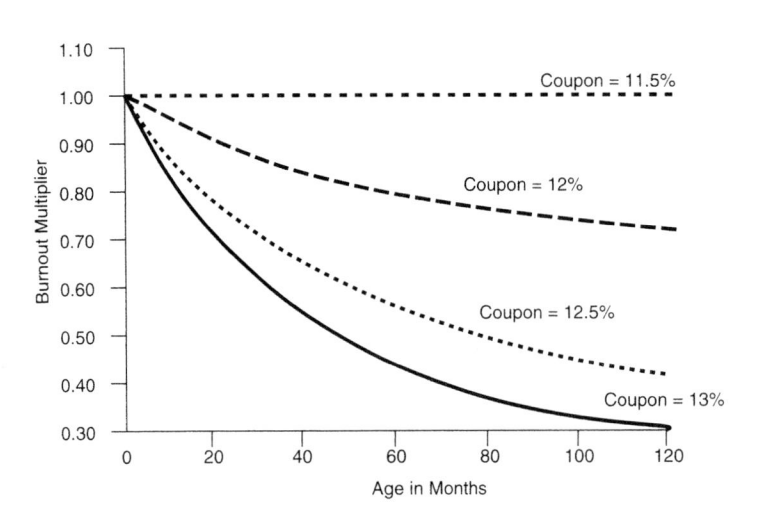

Figure 4A Premium Burnout for New Issues
Mortgage Refinancing Rate = 10.0%

choose to prepay, leaving only the households with higher costs remaining in the pool. A similar effect occurs among households in the 12.5% and 12% coupon pools.

The reason the 11.5% pool experiences no premium burnout is that options for this group of homeowners are not as deeply in-the-money. After forty months in a constant 10% refinancing rate environment, the 13% pool has burned out to the point that prepayments are about half of what they would have been otherwise. Of course, this decline in prepayments is offset somewhat by the seasoning of the pool. For the same reasons, the 12.5% pool has a burnout multiplier of about 0.65, and the 12% pool a multiplier of about 0.85.

Turning now to Figures 4B and 4C, we see that the effect of premium burnout is very sensitive to the assumed refinancing rate. Figure 4B recasts Figure 4A in a 10.5% refinancing rate environment, omitting the 11.5% coupon line that experiences no burnout. We see that the 13% pool will experience burnout, but to a lesser extent than at a mortgage refinancing rate of 10%. The burnout multipliers therefore are higher in Figure 4B than in Figure 4A. For example, after forty months, a 13% pool has a burnout multiplier of about 0.7, and a 12.5% pool has a multiplier of about 0.9; at this higher refinancing rate coupons of 12% and below do not experience burnout.

Finally, Figure 4C shows that, in a constant 11% refinancing rate environment, only the 13% pool experiences burnout; pools of 12.5% and below are unaffected. The effect on the 13% pool is greatly diminished, however, as the prepayment option is not as deeply in-the-money. For example, after forty months the prepayment multiplier is about 0.95 for a 13% pool with an 11% refinancing rate.

We have experimented with other measures of heterogeneity besides the path-dependent measure of burnout. One obvious measure is the "pool factor," the fraction of the original aggregate balance of all mortgages in the pool that remains outstanding. Because the combined effects of scheduled amortization and prepayments reduce the factor, it is not an adequate measure of pool heterogeneity. That is, a well-seasoned dis-

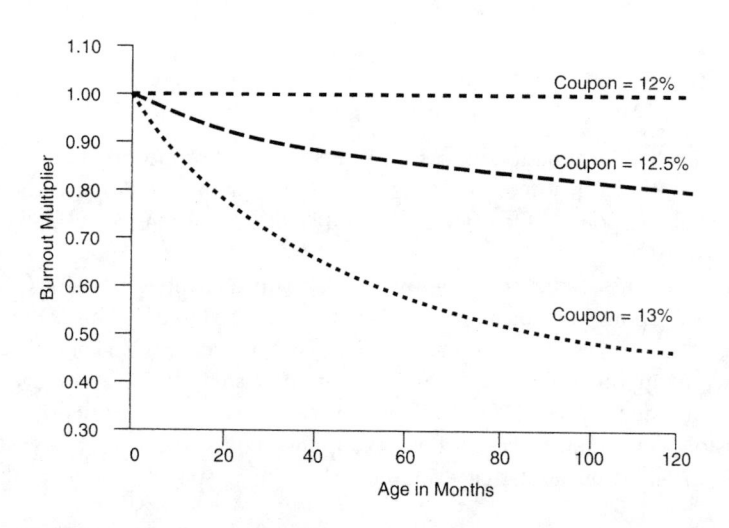

Figure 4B Premium Burnout for New Issues
Mortgage Refinancing Rate = 10.5%

Figure 4C Premium Burnout for New Issues
Mortgage Refinancing Rate = 11.0%

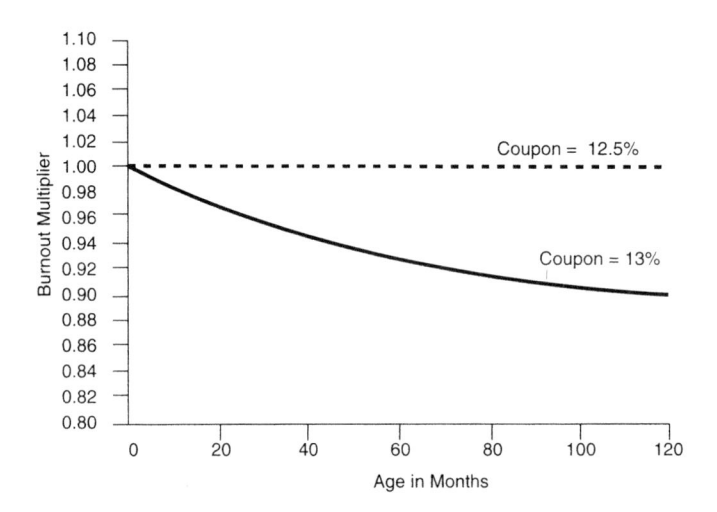

count pool and a relatively new premium pool could have the same factor, which would be attributable mainly to the effect of scheduled amortization in the case of the discount pool and to the effect of prepayments in the case of the premium pool. Yet the two pools would have very different compositions, the discount pool retaining a representative sample of households at all levels of prepayment costs, but the premium pool retaining only those with relatively high costs. We would not expect these two pools to behave in the same way because of this difference. Our empirical experiments on GNMA prepayments bear out these expectations, as the explanatory power of the model is reduced if we use the pool factor as a measure of burnout.

Multiplicative Model. We combine the four effects—the refinancing incentive, seasoning, month of the year, and burnout—in a multiplicative formula to determine prepayment rates:

$$\text{CPR} = (\text{Refinancing Incentive}) \times (\text{Seasoning Multiplier}) \times (\text{Month Multiplier}) \times (\text{Burnout Multiplier}).$$

This multiplicative formulation makes the effects interact proportionately. For example, with the monthly adjustment 10% higher in October than in August, the prepayment rates on all coupons in October will be 110% of their August levels, all other things being equal.

We can see how the effects combine by calculating prepayment rates for GNMA pools with various coupons in a constant refinancing rate environment. This is illustrated in Figure 5, which shows seasonally adjusted CPRs for hypothetical, newly issued GNMA pools with coupons between 8% and 13% in a constant 10.5% mortgage refinancing rate environment (i.e., a GNMA coupon of 10% priced at its parity price). Notice that speeds of prepayment increase for all coupons due to seasoning, but that the 13% coupon experiences burnout that eventually slows its prepayment rate so that it falls below the prepayment rate on the 12% pool. In actuality, prepayment rates over time are much less smooth because of monthly multipliers and interest rate fluctuations, as we discuss in the next section.

Other Possible Explanatory Variables. In constructing our model, we investigated other possible explanatory variables either used by others or reputed to be important. We discuss some of them here and explain why we decided not to include them.

Volatility. It is well known that volatility is an important determinant of option prices: the higher the total return volatility of an asset, the more valuable an option on that asset, all other things being equal. With homeowners retaining an option to prepay an annuity, we would expect an increase in the volatility of interest rates to cause an increase in the value of this option and a decrease in prepayments. Why, then, do we not include interest rate volatility as an explanatory variable?

The answer is that the model incorporates interest rate volatility implicitly through use of the current coupon mortgage rate. It turns out that the logarithm of the mortgage rate is well-approximated as a linear function of the logarithm of the yield on a ten-year zero coupon bond and the logarithm of the volatility of the ten-year zero's yield. Hence, an increase in interest rate volatility causes a proportional increase in mortgage rates, all other things being equal. As we use the mortgage rate to calculate C/R, an increase in mortgage rates causes C/R to decrease, which means prepayments will fall.

Macroeconomic Variables. We explored the potential explanatory effect of several macroeconomic variables by regressing our model's residuals on them. Two of them had weak, but statistically significant, explanatory power in these regressions: industrial production and housing sales. We chose not to include them in our model for several reasons.

Industrial production measures aggregate economic activity. If it is higher than average, we would expect more prosperity than average and hence a greater propensity to

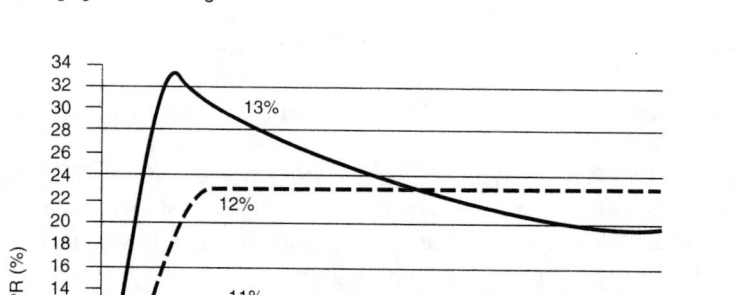

Figure 5 Prepayments of Selected GNMA Coupons All Assumed to be Newly Issued Mortgage Refinancing Rate = 10.5%

trade up in housing. This should increase prepayments, at least for mortgages with a due-on-sale clause. In fact we found just the opposite effect: Industrial production has negative partial correlation with prepayments. The reason for this anomaly can be found by examining our model's residuals,[6] which have trended down over the sample period. (Our coefficient estimates were corrected subsequently for serial correlation.) Industrial production, of course, trends upward, and it is this act that explains the negative correlation. In fact, substituting a time trend for industrial production produces a regression with the same explanatory power.

Other researchers have found that lagged housing sales help explain prepayments. Hence, it is not surprising that lagged housing sales have some explanatory power for our model's residuals. It is also completely uninteresting and useless in forecasting. House sales *cause* prepayments, either because there is a due-on-sale clause (and the below-market rate mortgage cannot be assumed), or the mortgage is at a premium. Because of payment and reporting lags, house sales cause prepayments with a lag, however. Using house sales to explain prepayments is simply using prepayments to explain prepayments.

In general, we have avoided using macroeconomic variables in our prepayment model because they would not aid us in the long-term forecasts required for valuation. Our valuation model simulates interest rates over thirty years to generate prepayments over a pool's lifetime. If the prepayment model were to include a macroeconomic variable, we would have to simulate its behavior over thirty years also. By observing the term structure of interest rates, we can use the market's expectations to simulate possible interest rate scenarios, but we have no such guidance from the market in simulating other variables over a thirty-year horizon. Macroeconomic variables may have some limited use in short-term forecasting, but they cannot be useful in the long-range forecasts required for valuation purposes.

ESTIMATION AND EMPIRICAL RESULTS

The model is estimated using non-linear least squares. Data for each sector come from the Goldman Sachs Mortgage Database aggregated into cohorts each month. We form cohorts by taking the weighted average of all pools in a sector with equal average underlying mortgage rates (WACs) and remaining terms (WAMs). The weights are the outstanding pool balances. In each case, all cohort-months are included in the non-linear regression estimation.

The choice of weights in the non-linear regression has important effects on the estimated coefficients and in sample predictions. The weights we use are the outstanding pool balances adjusted for the age of the observation. Older observations receive less weight than newer observations: observations from one year ago receive 50% of the weight of an otherwise identical current observation; observations from two years ago receive 25% of the weight, and so on.

The purpose of this weighting scheme is twofold. First, we want our prepayment predictions to be more accurate for larger pools, so we use the outstanding pool balance as a weight. Second, we suspect there has been a secular change in prepayment rates and that recent observations have more validity for prediction than do other observations, which we discuss after reporting our results.

Consider the results for the GNMA single-family thirty-year MBSs for the period May 1979 through May 1988, inclusive. There are 103,694 observations in the Goldman Sachs data base for the period. The R-squared is 94.6%, which is the proportion of cross-cohort and cross-month variability in prepayment rates explained by the four effects in the regression. That is, in the GNMA thirty-year sector, roughly 95% of the prepayment differences over time and across coupons can be attributed to refinancing incentives, seasoning, seasonality, and premium burnout.

The table compares our model's in-sample predictions to the actual prepayment rates. For each coupon and each range of mortgage refinancing rates we show five statistics: our prediction of the weighted average prepayment rate (weighted by the outstanding principal balance in the cohort), the actual weighted average prepayment rate, the standard deviation of the actual prepayments in the cell, the number of observations, and the weight of each observation. In general, our predictions are close to the actual observed prepayment rates in each cell. Our prediction is within two standard deviations of the actual prepayment rate in all but two cells and within one standard deviation in all but four of the cells.

We now return to the issue of a possible secular change in prepayment rates. If we recast the table without using the time-dependent portion of the weighting scheme, we find that the comparison of actual versus predicted results changes in a systematic way. Generally, the model then substantially underpredicts prepayment rates for pools with coupons of 7.5% and 8%. This indicates that prepayments on discount GNMA pools have slowed recently compared to the last decade. This secular slowing of prepayment rates on discount GNMA pools may be attributable to two changes in the mortgage market.

First, adjustable rate mortgages (ARMs) have become more readily available over the last decade. Home buyers with more chance of moving soon may be more inclined to finance with an ARM because of the lower initial interest rate. This self-selection will reduce observed prepayments on fixed-rate mortgages. Second, the market for home equity credit lines has become well organized. Where once the second mortgage market was poorly organized and reputed to be expensive, now a homeowner who wants to increase a mortgage balance, but does not want to move, can borrow in the home equity credit market. This will reduce observed prepayments on discount mortgages, as homeowners no longer need to sacrifice the gain on their discount mortgages in order to increase their mortgage borrowing.

Our model's very high degree of explanatory power was obtained in a sample that includes all coupons and all maturities of thirty-year GNMA single-family pools. Another approach is to estimate a separate model for each coupon and for each maturity year, a procedure apparently followed by some other investigators. We have examined the differences and found that explanatory power can be increased to as much as 99% if a separate model is estimated for each coupon and maturity year. These separate models, however, have different coefficients in each case, and we suspect they would fit poorly out-of-sample. Furthermore, estimating separate models ignores much useful information because pools with equal C/R, age, and burnout should behave similarly. (Our high R-squared shows that, in fact, they do behave similarly.) Hence there is important information about the prepayment characteristics of a 12% pass-through in a 10% refinancing rate environment that can be inferred from the prepayment behavior of a 10% pass-through in an 8.25% refinancing rate environment.

Table Prepayments for GNMAs in Years 1979–1988

| Coupon | Statistic | Refinancing Rate Range |||||
		8.5%–9.5%	9.5%–10.5%	10.5%–11.5%	11.5%–12.5%	12.5%–13.5%
7.5%	Predicted CPR (%)	4.6	4.1	3.2	4.1	2.4
	Actual Average CPR (%)	6.2	4.9	3.2	4.3	2.8
	Standard Deviation of CPR (%)	4.5	3.7	2.8	1.6	1.3
	Number of Observations	593	1448	663	716	1877
	Weight	19	24	21	4	2
8%	Predicted CPR (%)	3.8	3.3	2.4	4.8	2.9
	Actual Average CPR (%)	4.7	3.7	2.4	4.4	3.0
	Standard Deviation of CPR (%)	4.5	3.4	2.5	1.3	1.2
	Number of Observations	809	2031	918	1003	2601
	Weight	47	66	60	8	4
8.5%	Predicted CPR (%)	2.0	2.0	1.5	5.4	3.4
	Actual Average CPR (%)	1.9	2.4	1.6	4.7	3.3
	Standard Deviation of CPR (%)	3.4	2.4	1.8	2.2	2.0
	Number of Observations	597	1467	622	650	1666
	Weight	48	69	66	2	1
9%	Predicted CPR (%)	2.6	3.0	2.3	5.5	3.3
	Actual Average CPR (%)	2.3	3.2	2.2	3.9	2.6
	Standard Deviation of CPR (%)	2.9	2.3	1.6	1.2	1.0
	Number of Observations	629	1621	639	650	1462
	Weight	207	210	208	10	6
9.5%	Predicted CPR (%)	5.4	3.5	2.8	6.2	3.5
	Actual Average CPR (%)	4.5	3.9	2.9	3.6	2.5
	Standard Deviation of CPR (%)	4.1	3.1	2.0	1.0	0.8
	Number of Observations	475	1236	459	417	850
	Weight	109	168	153	13	8
10%	Predicted CPR (%)	9.5	4.1	3.4	6.1	3.5
	Actual Average CPR (%)	7.5	4.6	3.6	3.4	2.3
	Standard Deviation of CPR (%)	4.5	3.5	2.2	2.2	1.5
	Number of Observations	580	1445	577	556	992
	Weight	52	83	71	3	2
10.5%	Predicted CPR (%)	17.7	6.0	3.8	3.6	1.8
	Actual Average CPR (%)	18.8	7.1	4.3	2.3	1.6
	Standard Deviation of CPR (%)	11.1	5.3	3.6	3.6	2.9
	Number of Observations	452	1103	458	386	551
	Weight	24	36	36	1	1
11%	Predicted CPR (%)	29.6	13.3	7.0	5.2	4.2
	Actual Average CPR (%)	27.2	13.7	7.6	3.5	3.2
	Standard Deviation of CPR (%)	9.0	5.4	3.6	2.6	1.6
	Number of Observations	589	1445	530	617	1056
	Weight	75	82	83	16	8
11.5%	Predicted CPR (%)	38.0	22.7	10.8	5.9	2.7
	Actual Average CPR (%)	38.3	25.3	12.5	5.0	2.8
	Standard Deviation of CPR (%)	8.0	9.6	4.7	2.6	1.6
	Number of Observations	546	1359	491	573	1003
	Weight	56	60	58	26	15

Table Prepayments for GNMAs in Years 1979–1988 *(continued)*

		Refinancing Rate Range				
Coupon	Statistic	8.5%-9.5%	9.5%-10.5%	10.5%-11.5%	11.5%-12.5%	12.5%-13.5%
12%	Predicted CPR (%)	41.2	29.2	13.4	4.7	2.1
	Actual Average CPR (%)	41.1	30.3	15.3	4.2	2.4
	Standard Deviation of CPR (%)	6.4	10.1	5.4	3.1	2.0
	Number of Observations	469	1166	407	463	862
	Weight	50	53	53	27	10
12.5%	Predicted CPR (%)	41.8	34.9	18.3	8.2	4.1
	Actual Average CPR (%)	41.4	34.3	18.9	7.8	4.2
	Standard Deviation of CPR (%)	6.8	11.6	5.6	3.8	3.1
	Number of Observations	504	1239	430	510	996
	Weight	26	28	28	15	7
13%	Predicted CPR (%)	41.1	38.2	22.5	12.2	4.7
	Actual Average CPR (%)	41.9	37.0	22.0	12.9	5.3
	Standard Deviation of CPR (%)	7.8	12.7	7.2	5.8	3.7
	Number of Observations	434	1061	374	434	840
	Weight	15	17	17	10	6

This cross-coupon information is particularly important when using a prepayment model for valuation purposes. Valuation models consider prepayments in many different interest rate scenarios, usually through Monte Carlo simulations. Frequently the prepayment model is forced to forecast out-of-sample because the simulated interest rate scenario lies outside the bounds of observed interest rates. For example, we have no observations on 7.5% GNMA pools in a 6.5% refinancing rate environment (C/R = 8/6.5 = 1.23), although these are frequently observed in simulation models. We have, however, many observations of 11.5% coupons with a 9.75% refinancing rate or a 12% coupon with a 10.2% refinancing rate (both also have C/R = 1.23). Guided by our analysis of the homeowner's prepayment option, and lacking any data to the contrary, we anticipate that the 7.5% coupon pool in a 6.5% mortgage refinancing rate environment will behave much as an 11.5% coupon pool does in a 9.75% mortgage refinancing rate environment.

USING THE RESULTS TO PREDICT PREPAYMENTS

To predict prepayments over the remaining life of a mortgage-backed security, the model requires two sets of inputs: 1) the characteristics of the MBS itself, i.e., its sector, WAC, and WAM; and 2) the actual historical path of the mortgage refinancing rate since origination and its assumed path from now to maturity. The actual path since origination is a matter of public record, but, of course, the assumed path could take any shape.

One commonly used assumption in generating prepayment forecasts is that the refinancing rate will remain constant at its current level. This is called a static scenario. The static scenario forecasts for generic GNMA coupons are shown in Figure 6 for a constant 10.55% mortgage refinancing rate. (These forecasts are seasonally adjusted by removing the effect of the monthly multiplier). The assumed remaining terms are 348, 350, 348, 296, 276, and 282 months for the 8%, 9%, 10%, 11%, 12%, and 13% generic coupons, respectively.

Static scenarios are highly unrealistic, because interest rates do not follow simple, deterministic paths over time, let alone constant paths. In a model such as ours, with path-dependent prepayment rates, a constant interest rate scenario will not generate the proper behavior of premium burnout. Hence, if prepayments are forecast under the unrealistic assumption that the refinancing rate is not random, then we cannot expect to obtain very realistic forecasts.

Figure 7 illustrates prepayment behavior along a random path. It shows prepayment rates for the same generic GNMA pools with 8%, 10%, and 12% coupons as shown in Figure 6, but with a particular random path for the refinancing rate. The random path was generated by letting the refinancing rate follow a random walk with 8% annual variance. Other random paths will generate very different prepayment rates over time.

The contrast between the paths in Figures 6 and 7 is striking. The prepayment rates in the static scenario are monotonically ordered by coupon. No such simple order prevails in the random scenario because of premium burnout. In fact, the 12% coupon experiences substantial burnout when interest rates first fall below 10% and its CPR climbs to over 40%. The next time interest rates fall, they fall to about 6% (in month 50), and again the CPR for a 12% coupon soars to over 40%. But these CPRs are eclipsed by the prepayment rates on the 8% and 10% coupons, which have experienced no burnout since issue. In the third rally, interest rates again fall to about 7% in month 110, but this time the 12% GNMAs prepay at only a 30% CPR. Clearly, the static interest rate scenario does a poor job of capturing the type of fluctuations in prepayments that we anticipate will actually occur.

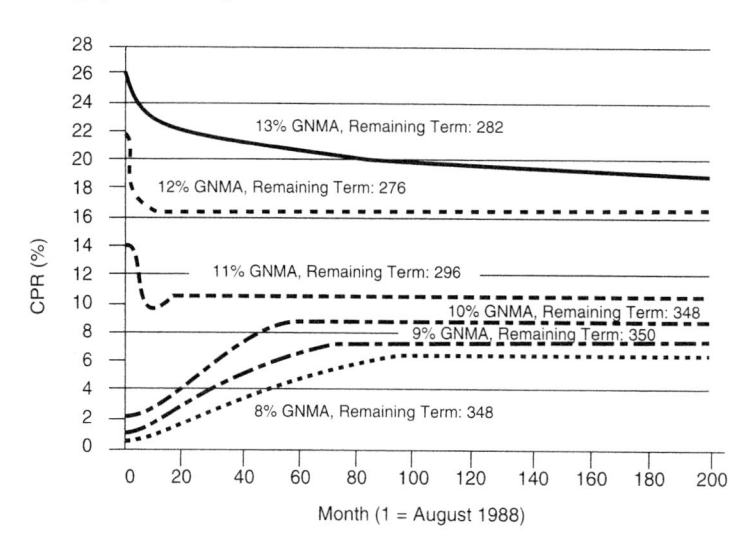

Figure 6 Prepayments of Generic GNMA Coupons
Mortgage Refinancing Rate = 10.55%

Figure 7 Prepayments of Generic GNMA Coupons
Random Mortgage Refinancing Rates

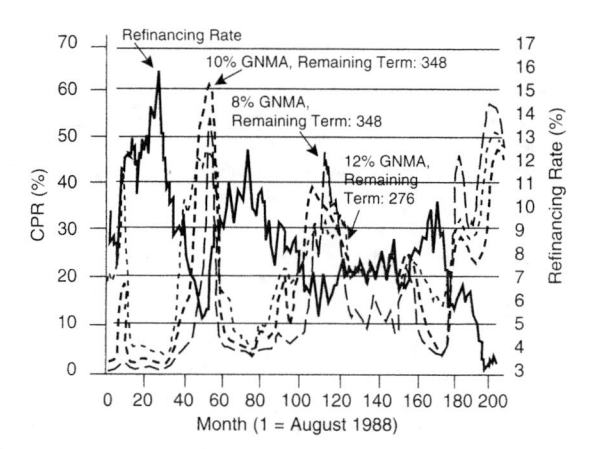

CONCLUSION

We have presented a model of prepayments for mortgage-backed securities that has some unique features and a high level of explanatory power. Among the novel features, three are key in understanding mortgage prepayments.

First, we have shown that option pricing theory suggests that the homeowner's incentive to refinance is best measured in our sample by the ratio of the mortgage coupon rate to the mortgage refinancing rate. By measuring this refinancing incentive properly, we find that the empirically measured effect of the refinancing incentive corresponds well with the type of effect predicted by option pricing theory.

The other two key effects modify the pure refinancing incentive. We have shown that the rate of seasoning of a mortgage pool depends importantly on whether it is a premium, par, or discount pool. Specifically, premium pools season quickly, typically in thirty months or less. GNMA current coupon pools take longer to season, about five years. Finally, discount pools can take substantially more time to season fully, even as long as ten years.

The third key effect is premium burnout, and it is the most difficult to measure empirically. We have offered an explanation in terms of household refinancing costs for why prepayment rates for premium coupon mortgage pools tend to burn out or slow over time (relative to prepayment rates on lower coupon pools). This effect is measured by the cumulative refinancing incentive experienced by the mortgage pool when homeowners' prepayment options are deep in-the-money. Proper measurement and use of premium burnout are vital for explaining mortgage prepayments accurately.

The Goldman Sachs mortgage prepayment model has a good fit to the data available over the last ten years. A note of caution is in order, nevertheless. There are no reliable data on some aspects of mortgage-backed security prepayments, such as end-of-life prepayment rates or burnout on slight premium mortgages over longer periods. We must extrapolate out-of-sample to forecast these effects. While we feel the extrapolations are sensible, we look for the passing of time to produce further data to refine the model.

NOTES

[1] Actually this formula understates the market value of the homeowner's annuity because the mortgage rate is determined for new loans with the right to prepay. Ideally, we should use the rate that would prevail for new loans without the right to prepay, i.e., mortgages with lifetime lockouts. In equilibrium, the lockout mortgage rate would be lower than the actual mortgage rate, as the homeowner gives up the prepayment option in return for a lower interest cost. Capitalizing the mortgage cash flows at the lower lockout mortgage rate would give a higher annuity value.

[2] For an option-theoretic model of household prepayment decisions based on prepayment costs, see K. B. Dunn and C. S. Spatt, "The Effect of Refinancing Costs and Market Imperfections on the Optimal Call Strategy and Pricing of Debt Contract," Carnegie-Mellon University Working Paper, March 1986; and G. C. Timmis, "Essays in Applied Economics," Unpublished Doctoral Dissertation, Carnegie-Mellon University, 1988.

[3] There is an offsetting effect caused by the aging of the mortgage. As the mortgage ages, the prepayment option's maturity becomes shorter. This shortening can make it optimal to exercise an in-the-money prepayment option, even if refinancing costs do not change. Experiments with rational option pricing models indicate that this effect is small for thirty-year mortgages with more than fifteen years to maturity.

[4] The term "refinancing rate" refers to the mortgage refinancing rate and not the yield on the current coupon GNMA. The mortgage refinancing rate would be fifty basis points above the yield on the current coupon GNMA trading at its parity price.

[5] As we noted, there is an alternative explanation that has to do with the aging of the mortgage. See footnote 3.

[6] The model's residuals are the differences between the actual and predicted prepayment rates in our data set.

8 Duration Estimates on Mortgage-Backed Securities

Simple and accurate techniques that can help managers overcome fear of mortgages.

Paul DeRosa, Laurie Goodman, and Mike Zazzarino

It is increasingly apparent that targeting duration can be one of the most successful approaches to managing a portfolio of mortgage-backed pass-throughs. But duration analysis of these securities can be tricky; this discourages too many managers, who either avoid mortgages entirely or limit themselves to the PACs (planned amortization classes) of CMOs, with their known lives over wide prepayment bands.

We attempt here to streamline the issue of duration analysis, outlining and evaluating some of the different methods. We explore in particular two simple and useful methods of measuring mortgage pass-through durations: 1) option-adjusted duration, a theoretical measure, and 2) empirical duration, a functional approach for which we develop methodology.

MEASURING DURATION

Modified duration, which measures the percent change in price for a given change in yield, ordinarily takes the form given in Equation (1):

$$\frac{\Delta P}{P} = D\Delta i \text{ or } D = \frac{-\Delta P}{\frac{P}{\Delta i}} \qquad (1)$$

where P is the price of the security, D is the duration, and Δi is the change in interest rates. The percent change in price for a given change in yield is more difficult to establish for mortgages than for Treasury securities, because prepayments change as interest rates change. In general, durations will be lower when the change in prepayments is taken into account.

Three different estimates are used for mortgage durations. The first of these is the cash flow duration, or static duration. Cash flow duration calls for treating the mortgage

---

From *The Journal of Portfolio Management*. This copyrighted material is reprinted with permission from *The Journal of Portfolio Management,* 488 Madison Avenue, New York, NY 10022.

security as a bond with a fixed amortization schedule, ignoring the effect of changes in prepayment rates due to changes in interest rates.

To figure the cash flow yield, the yield on the bond is calculated assuming a fixed prepayment rate. This yield is then moved up and down 1 basis point, with the average price change calculated. This average price change as a percent of the original price gives the static duration.

We can demonstrate the methodology in calculation of the cash flow duration of a GNMA 9.

1. Calculate the yield of the security at the current price.
2. Price: 104-26 (104.8125)
   WAM: 26 years, 11 months
   Settle: 3/17/92
   Accrued Interest: 0.40
   Speed: 155 PSA
   Yield: 8.133
   Change the yield by 1 basis point and recalculate price.
   Up 1 basis point:
   Yield: 8.143
   Price: 104.7594
   Down 1 basis point:
   Yield: 8.123
   Price: 104.864
3. Calculate durations.
   Price change (±1 bp) = 104.864 − 104.7594 = 0.1046
   Average price change per basis point = 0.0523
   Duration = average price change per basis point, divided by original price plus accrued interest, divided by 0.0001 = 4.97

This methodology is obviously inaccurate in that it ignores shifts in prepayment rates caused by yield changes. For mortgages not subject to refinancing, cash flow duration will not be significantly different from any other duration measure. For mortgages that are refinanceable, however, the cash flow duration will be very distorted.

The second method of calculating duration attempts to take into account effects of changes in the prepayment rate as interest rates change within the confines of a cash flow model. The methodology is similar to that of cash flow duration, except that a 50-basis point up or down move is used, and the prepayment rates associated with sister coupons are then imputed to arrive at the price in the ±50 bps scenarios.

To illustrate application of this methodology, we use the GNMA 9, which has a street consensus prepayment speed of 155 PSA. The GNMA 9.5 has a consensus PSA of 211, while the GNMA 8.5 has a consensus prepayment speed of 130 PSA. The calculation assumes that if rates drop 50 basis points, the 9s would prepay where the 9.5s are now. Furthermore, it is assumed that the security would yield 50 basis points less than the present yield on the GNMA 9. Similarly, if rates rise 50 basis points, the 9s are assumed to prepay where the 8.5s are now, and the security would yield 50 basis points more than the present yield on the GNMA 9.

1. Calculate the yield on the GNMA 9 exactly as in the previous example.
2. Change the yield by 50 basis points, using projected prepayment rates from sister coupons and recalculate price.
   Up 50 basis point:
   Yield: 8.633
   Speed: 130
   Price: 102.4758
   Down 50 basis points:
   Yield: 7.633
   Speed: 211
   Price: 106.2609
3. Calculate duration.
   Price change (±50 bps) = 106.2609 − 102.4758 = 3.7851
   Average price change per basis point = 0.037851
   Duration = 3.5976

Note that this duration is significantly shorter than the cash flow duration, as it includes the impact of the changes in prepayments as interest rates change. It assumes that as Treasury rates move up or down 50 basis points, the static yield on the mortgages will move as well.

In reality, as rates move down 50 basis points, and the mortgage comes closer to being refinanceable, one would expect the required yield to increase. Similarly, as rates move up 50 basis points, and the security moves farther away from being refinanceable, it may trade at a narrower yield spread relative to Treasury securities. This would imply that the security would trade as if the durations are lower than this measure.

Offsetting this effect, however, the Treasury yield curve is steeply upward-sloping, and higher prepayment speeds shorten the average life and duration of the security; hence it is appropriate to price off a shorter part of the Treasury curve. How these two effects net is unclear.

The third measure of duration is the option-adjusted duration measure, derived from an option-adjusted spread (OAS) model. An OAS model calls for construction of an arbitrage-free interest rate tree (see Ho and Lee [1986]). Prepayments are given at each node of the tree as a function of the spread between the gross weighted-average coupon on the mortgage and the Treasury rates. A mortgage priced according to this tree will have a higher price than the actual mortgage price. The OAS is the spread to the Treasury tree that will price the mortgage correctly.

Once this OAS is obtained, it is raised and lowered 1 basis point, and new prices on the mortgages are computed. These price changes for a 1-basis point OAS change are then used to calculate the duration. The OAS duration takes into account both the effect of the Treasury yield curve and the effect of interest rate changes on prepayment rates.

The disadvantage of this approach is that many assumptions are embedded in the model, and different dealers using OAS models may arrive at quite different answers, as Exhibit 1 shows, where estimated durations on the GNMA 9 range from 4.69 to 5.8 years. The range is even wider for securities such as FNMA 10s, with the lowest duration at 1.1 years and the highest at 3.0 years. It is not clear which duration a portfolio manager should rely on, and the differences can be substantial.

Exhibit 1 Street Duration Estimates (January 1992)

Security	Goldman	DLJ	Pru	Shearson	Bear	Kidder
GNMA 8	6.45	5.85	6.9	6.6	6.5	5.98
GNMA 9	4.96	4.69	5.8	4.9	5.2	5.04
GNMA 10	3.26	2.84	3.3	2.4	3.2	3.71
GNMA 11	1.74	2.03	3.4	2.1	1.9	2.93
FHLMC 8	4.81	4.89	5.2	5.4	6.0	5.22
FHLMC 9	3.92	3.69	3.6	3.9	4.1	4.34
FHLMC 10	2.40	1.91	2.2	1.3	3.0	3.03
FHLMC 11	1.50	1.49	2.6	2.2	0.7	2.53
FNMA 8	5.50	5.41	5.9	5.7	5.9	5.73
FNMA 9	3.87	3.94	4.2	4.0	4.0	4.51
FNMA 10	2.17	1.90	2.0	1.1	2.8	3.00
FNMA 11	1.28	1.53	2.5	0.7	0.6	2.47

EMPIRICAL DURATION

Empirical measurement is another way to derive duration. We know that duration simply reflects the change in price for a given change in yield. The duration for a given security will be different at different price levels, as prepayment expectations change. The methodology we use says, in effect, that there is a market consensus on the impact of yield changes on prepayment rates that is reflected in the behavior of market prices.

An empirical measure of duration differs from other measures in another important respect. Other measures are mathematical identities; given assumptions about cash flows, there is only one number that relates yield change to price change. An empirical measure is a functional relationship: it relates changes in mortgage prices to changes in the general level of market yields as measured by Treasury securities.

The equation we use is:

$$\frac{\Delta P}{P} = c + b_1 \Delta yield + b_2 (P - 100) \Delta yield + b_3 \begin{bmatrix} (P - 100)^2 \Delta yield \text{ if } P > 100 \\ 0 \text{ otherwise} \end{bmatrix} + \tilde{e} \quad (2)$$

The first term (c) is a constant term. The second term (b_1) measures the percent change in price that is captured by the change in yields. The third and fourth terms (b_2 and b_3) modify the second term, allowing durations to vary depending on the price level of the mortgages. The third term (b_2) would allow only for a linear relationship. The fourth term (b_3), applicable over par, allows for non-linearity.

For a Treasury security, the C, b_2, and b_3 terms would be expected to be insignificantly different from 0, and the b_1 term would be negative. The absolute value of b_1 would be the estimated duration. With the mortgage securities, the c term would be expected to be zero, the b_1 term would be expected to be negative, and the b_2 and b_3 terms would be expected to be positive.

The results for our regressions are given in Exhibit 2 for GNMA and FNMA 8s, 9s, 10s, and 11s. The regressions are run on five years of daily data: November 19, 1986, through November 18, 1991 (1,264 observations). The yield measure in Equation (2) on which Exhibits 3 and 4 are based is the change in yield on the ten-year

Exhibit 2 Regression Results (T-Statistics in Parentheses)

Dependent Variable	c	b_1	b_2	b_3	R^2	D-W
ΔP/P (GNMA 8)	0.000 (0.77)	−5.210 (−28.21)	0.067 (3.96)	—	0.855	2.09
ΔP/P (GNMA 9)	0.000 (1.18)	−4.945 (−40.83)	0.065 (3.31)	0.059 (1.924)	0.850	2.07
ΔP/P (GNMA 10)	0.000 (1.03)	−4.492 (−69.24)	0.121 (4.48)	0.024 (3.72)	0.823	2.09
ΔP/P (GNMA 11)	0.000 (1.14)	−4.432 (−29.78)	0.350 (5.53)	−0.006 (0.97)	0.747	1.81
ΔP/P (FNMA 8)	0.000 (0.92)	−4.736 (−22.89)	0.056 (2.73)	—	0.818	2.09
ΔP/P (FNMA 9)	0.000 (0.78)	−4.588 (−34.07)	0.032 (1.31)	0.079 (1.98)	0.805	2.01
ΔP/P (FNMA 10)	0.000 (1.01)	−3.932 (−56.46)	0.076 (2.29)	0.029 (3.02)	0.761	2.00
ΔP/P (FNMA 11)	0.000 (1.03)	−3.635 (−27.39)	0.487 (6.97)	−0.026 (−2.93)	0.650	1.90

Number of observations: 1,264.

Treasury. Nearly identical results were obtained using the seven-year Treasury. In all cases, the constant term is zero. Note that the GNMA and FNMA 8s do not have a b_3 term, as there were only two observations over par for the GNMA 8s and none for the FNMA 8s.

The regression results on the FNMA and GNMA 8s, 9s, and 10s are as expected. The constant term is insignificantly different from zero in all the regressions. The b_1, b_2, and b_3 coefficients are of the correct sign, and all but one coefficient are significant. The R^2 on all these regressions is quite high—over 0.80 in five of the six regressions. The GNMA results, as measured by the R^2, are marginally better than the FNMA results. The Durbin-Watson statistics are encouraging in that they detect no serial correlation, which one would encounter were the model seriously misspecified.

The fit on the GNMA and FNMA 11 regressions is worse than on the other regressions. The b_2 term is larger than one would have expected, and the b_3 term is of the wrong sign (insignificant in the case of the GNMA 11). The R^2 is worse than in the lower-coupon regressions.

We use the fit on these equations in order to develop durations for different coupons at different price levels. The equation is:

$$\frac{\frac{\Delta P}{P}}{\Delta y} = \text{Duration} = b_1 + b_2(P - 100) + b_3 \begin{bmatrix} (P - 100)^2 \text{ if } P > 100 \\ 0 \text{ otherwise} \end{bmatrix} \quad (3)$$

This is simply the regression results obtained from (2), divided through by Δy. As c is zero, it does not appear in Equation (3).

Exhibit 3 Empirical Duration Estimates on GNMAs

Price	GNMA 8	GNMA 9	GNMA 10	GNMA 11	Price	GNMA 8	GNMA 9	GNMA 10	GNMA 11
80	6.554				96	5.479	5.205	4.977	
80.5	6.520				96.5	5.445	5.172	4.917	
81	6.487				97	5.412	5.140	4.856	5.481
81.5	6.453				97.5	5.378	5.108	4.795	5.307
82	6.420				98	5.344	5.075	4.735	5.132
82.5	6.386				98.5	5.311	5.043	4.674	4.957
83	6.352				99	5.277	5.011	4.614	4.782
83.5	6.319				99.5	5.244	4.978	4.553	4.607
84	6.285				100	5.210	4.946	4.492	4.432
84.5	6.252				100.5	5.176	4.899	4.425	4.259
85	6.218	5.917			101	5.143	4.822	4.346	4.089
85.5	6.184	5.885			101.5		4.716	4.254	3.922
86	6.151	5.852			102		4.580	4.150	3.759
86.5	6.117	5.820			102.5		4.415	4.034	3.599
87	6.084	5.788			103		4.220	3.905	3.441
87.5	6.050	5.755			103.5		3.996	3.763	3.287
88	6.016	5.723			104		3.742	3.609	3.137
88.5	5.983	5.691			104.5		3.458	3.443	2.989
89	5.949	5.658			105		3.145	3.264	2.845
89.5	5.916	5.626			105.5			3.073	2.704
90	5.882	5.593			106			2.870	2.566
90.5	5.848	5.561			106.5			2.654	2.431
91	5.815	5.529			107			2.425	2.300
91.5	5.781	5.496	5.523		107.5			2.184	2.172
92	5.748	5.464	5.462		108			1.931	2.047
92.5	5.714	5.432	5.402		108.5			1.665	1.925
93	5.680	5.399	5.341		109			1.387	1.806
93.5	5.647	5.367	5.280		109.5				1.691
94	5.613	5.334	5.220		110				1.579
94.5	5.580	5.302	5.159		110.5				1.470
95	5.546	5.270	5.099		111				1.364
95.5	5.512	5.237	5.038		111.5				1.262
					112				1.162

The empirical duration measures are shown in Exhibit 3 for GNMAs and Exhibit 4 for FNMAs. The results for all coupons, including the 11s, are quite reasonable. At a price of 90, a GNMA 9 would have a duration of 5.59. At a price of par, the duration is 4.95, and at a price of 104, the duration is 3.74 years.

There are several interesting things to note about these results. First, at prices higher than par, mortgages lose duration quickly, as would be expected.

Second, at a price of 100, a GNMA 8 has a longer duration than a GNMA 9, which has a longer duration than a GNMA 10 or 11. This is true for the FNMAs as well. This pattern makes sense, as the higher coupon contributes to a marginally shorter duration. More importantly, market participants have an easier time imagining interest rates dropping 150 basis points when the GNMA 11 is the current coupon and the Treasury ten-year is 9.75, as opposed to when the GNMA 8 is the current coupon and the ten-year yields 6.75.

Exhibit 4 Empirical Duration Estimates on FNMAs

Price	FNMA 8	FNMA 9	FNMA 10	FNMA 11	Price	FNMA 8	FNMA 9	FNMA 10	FNMA 11
81	5.808				95.5	4.990	4.732	4.273	
81.5	5.780				96	4.962	4.716	4.235	
82	5.752				96.5	4.933	4.700	4.197	
82.5	5.724				97	4.905	4.684	4.159	
83	5.695				97.5	4.877	4.668	4.121	4.852
83.5	5.667				98	4.849	4.652	4.083	4.609
84	5.639				98.5	4.820	4.636	4.046	4.365
84.5	5.611				99	4.792	4.620	4.008	4.122
85	5.582				99.5	4.764	4.604	3.970	3.879
85.5	5.554				100	4.736	4.588	3.932	3.635
86	5.526				100.5	4.708	4.552	3.887	3.398
86.5	5.498				101	4.679	4.477	3.827	3.175
87	5.470	5.004			101.5		4.363	3.753	2.964
87.5	5.441	4.988			102		4.209	3.664	2.767
88	5.413	4.972			102.5		4.017	3.560	2.583
88.5	5.385	4.956			103		3.785	3.442	2.412
89	5.357	4.940			103.5		3.513	3.309	2.254
89.5	5.328	4.924			104		3.203	3.162	2.110
90	5.300	4.908			104.5		2.853	3.000	1.978
90.5	5.272	4.892			105		2.463	2.823	1.860
91	5.244	4.876			105.5			2.632	1.755
91.5	5.216	4.860			106			2.426	1.663
92	5.187	4.844			106.5			2.206	1.584
92.5	5.159	4.828			107			1.971	1.518
93	5.131	4.812	4.462		107.5			1.721	1.466
93.5	5.103	4.796	4.424		108			1.457	1.427
94	5.074	4.780	4.386		108.5				1.401
94.5	5.046	4.764	4.348		109				1.388
95	5.018	4.748	4.310		109.5				1.388
					110				1.402

Third, at high prices, mortgage durations are much shorter than the street estimates shown in Exhibit 1. This will not come as a surprise to market participants. Finally, FNMA durations for the same coupon at the same price are roughly half a year shorter than their GNMA counterparts.

RELATIONSHIP TO EARLIER STUDIES

There is one earlier attempt by Pinkus and Chandoha [1986] to measure empirical (or implied) durations, which uses data from January 1, 1984, to September 30, 1985. The study estimates the relative volatility of GNMAs at various price levels relative to a current coupon GNMA series, where the current coupon is defined as the mortgage security selling between 99.5 and 100. The authors find that a mortgage selling at a price of 90 has 15% more price volatility than a mortgage selling at par, and a mortgage selling at a price of 108 has 50% less price volatility than the current coupon. FHLMCs have significantly less volatility than GNMAs of the same coupon. These results are broadly consistent with our results.

Pinkus and Chandoha then estimate the relative price volatility between the current coupon mortgage and the ten-year Treasury in order to compute the implied duration of the GNMA current coupon series. They obtain a duration estimate of 4.09 years, somewhat shorter than our estimate. When we expand our data sets to include earlier data, we obtain re-estimated results that are consistent with this earlier work.

This is not surprising, given the volatility of the mortgage-Treasury spread over the Pinkus-Chandoha estimation period. The mortgage market has developed considerably since the mid-1980s, however, and with the market for collateralized mortgage obligations that ties the mortgage and Treasury markets closer together, it is not surprising that mortgages move more closely with Treasuries than they did during that earlier period.

CONCLUSION

Our results in developing empirical mortgage durations are very encouraging. There are two likely directions for future research. The first is to develop empirical duration measures for pass-throughs using more than one interest rate to see how this can improve hedging effectiveness. The second possibility is to apply this empirical duration methodology to interest-only and principal-only securities, where observed durations are often very different from theoretical durations.

REFERENCES

Ho, Thomas S. Y., and Sang Bin Lee. "Term Structure Movements and Pricing Interest Rate Contingent Claims." *Journal of Finance*, Vol. 41, 5 (1986), pp. 1011-1030.

Pinkus, Scott M. and Marie A. Chandoha. "The Relative Price Volatility of Mortgage Securities." *Journal of Portfolio Management*, Vol. 12, 4 (Summer 1986), pp. 9-22.

Part 4. Real Estate Investment Performance

9 Towards Indices of Real Estate Value and Return

James W. Hoag

§1. INTRODUCTION

In this paper, the construction of an index of value and return for non-owner occupied industrial property is chronicled. Although real estate is an important investment vehicle (aggregate value is large in comparison to the stock market), relatively little is known of the historical holding period risk and return for equity owners of real property. In a related paper [Hoag, 1979], current empirical knowledge of real estate returns is summarized and found to be meager. Practically, there are *no available indexes* which attempt to measure price appreciation, cash flow or return from real estate. Actually, many observers question the existence of one national real estate market. With no easily observable market transaction prices, there is little wonder about the paucity of index numbers. Worse yet, with no information available on investment returns it is very difficult to utilize current investment management technology (the Capital Asset Pricing Model—CAPM) to estimate the risk entailed in a real estate investment.

In Section §2, a conceptual framework for estimating real estate value and return is developed and related to methods currently utilized in common stock risk/return analysis.

The method of analysis expounded herein leads naturally to a consideration of a property valuation function based on a vector of fundamental microeconomic and macroeconomic variables which affect property value. With certain reasonable approximations, the valuation model leads directly to an estimate of the market rate of return on real estate, the risk and return associated with each property and the market risk. In this paper, the analysis focuses on time series properties of risk and return estimates for real estate. Coefficients of responsiveness to the fundamental valuation characteristics which are analogous to a multifactor analysis of common stock risk and return can be computed. The responsiveness coefficients are analyzed further in Hoag [1979].

This technique is specialized to one particular property classification in Section §3: industrial real estate (consisting primarily of warehouses with some light manufacturing and distribution.) The valuation factors relevant to these properties are detailed and the sample is discussed in Section §4. Section §5 presents the estimated valuation function and the returns on a subsample of carefully checked observations. The estimates of the

From *The Journal of Finance*, Vol. XXXV, No. 2 (May 1980).

valuation function are performed using pooled cross-section time-series regressions with generalized least squares estimators. Many measurement and errors-in-variables problems are alleviated using these techniques which allow unbiased, consistent and efficient estimates of the market return. The results in Section §6 indicate that equity investment in industrial real estate over a short period in the recent past had risk and return comparable to the stock market.

A discussion of future development in Section §7 finishes this paper. Both the methodology and the empirical results will improve as additional data items on a wider class of properties become available. These developments should begin to fill the vacuum of knowledge and paucity of empirical investigation with respect to investment in real estate.

§2. CONCEPTUAL FRAMEWORK FOR INDEX CONSTRUCTION FROM PROPERTY VALUATION

Analysis of historical common stock returns typically calculates before tax holding period returns using transaction prices and actual cash disbursals for uniquely identifiable assets. Methodological issues in construction of market indexes usually involve discussions of sample size and representatives, appropriate holding periods relative to investor horizons, policies for rebalancing, techniques for aggregating or averaging returns across time or cross-sectionally and rules for weighting individual sample returns (see, for instance, Fisher [1966]). There are a wide variety of indexes available for the stock and bond markets. Most of these indexes are transaction based and many are calculated at daily and sometimes hourly intervals. The same situation does not exist in real estate. Individual transactions are infrequent and information on their number is unavailable. The investment holding period is purported to be very long (on the order of several years, at minimum).

The rapidly growing presence of more institutional investors in the real estate market coincides with other evidence that suggests that a national market has developed in investment real estate (Wendt and Haney [1979]). This development motivates the construction of a real estate index.

The focus is on the holding period returns for investment real estate. One often hears the contrary argument suggesting that if the investment horizon is long, then intermediate fluctuations in value are not very important. Perhaps this holds true for investors who don't sell frequently, have complete discretion in timing their sales *and* match the maturity structure of their liabilities to these long-lived assets. Alternatively, consider any intermediary which sells participations in pooled real estate funds. The effective holding period is the (typically) quarterly period for reporting to investors. Since investors can increase or decrease positions at this time, they are interested in quarterly values and hence quarterly holding period returns.

Initially, return computations are estimated before tax as returns to tax-free investors. Later the nontaxable and taxable portions can be broken out analogously to unrealized capital gains and dividends in common stocks. Thus, our intention is to calculate quarterly before tax holding period compound rates of return. Given that the holding period and investment horizon are not known with certainty, compound returns are robust with respect to the relative lengths of these intervals (see Rosenberg and Marathe [1979]).

Note carefully that a real estate investment fund still has grave difficulties at the quarterly valuation point. A stock fund can easily value their assets, unless the stocks are infrequently traded.[1] Real estate funds faced with this valuation problem hire an appraiser who provides a (subjective) estimate of value, and thus a subjective estimate of return.

The technique proposed here uses fundamental characteristics to (objectively) estimate the value for a property at any point in time. The techniques used herein have been thoroughly developed for common stocks and have proved both useful and intuitively understandable for market participants. The technique outlined in Figure I requires fundamental valuation characteristics (such as location, property type, size and age), economic and demographic variables (such as business inventories, construction costs, transportation access and population), transaction prices and cash flows. This information is used to *estimate* a valuation function which is composed of weights for the value of each fundamental characteristic, that is, the responsiveness of property value to changes in the fundamental factors.

A real estate appraiser would call this the market comparison technique (see, for instance, Wendt and Cerf [1979]). But the technique is actually much broader than pure market comparison. Since the fundamental descriptors include cash flows, property type and location, all the raw elements are available for the equivalent of an income capitalization appraisal. Since construction cost indexes are included the data for a replacement cost appraisal are also provided. Clearly then, a sufficient amount of information is available for an appraiser to make a judgment of value. The objective judgment of the valuation model simply supplants the subjective judgment of the appraiser.

Figure I Conceptual Framework for Index Construction from a Property Valuation Function

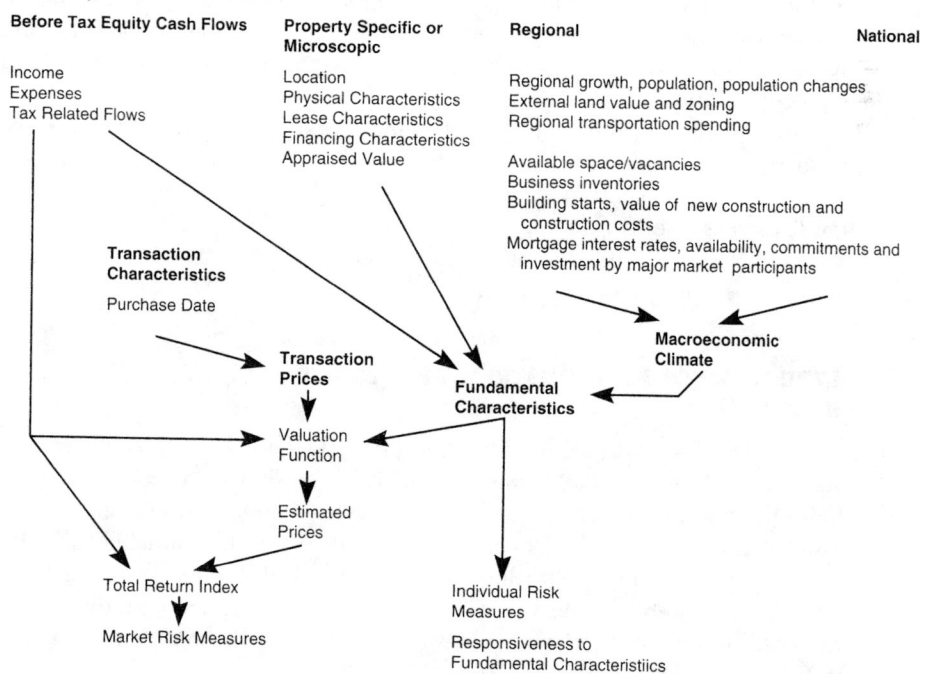

Before Tax Equity Cash Flows	Property Specific or Microscopic	Regional	National
Income Expenses Tax Related Flows	Location Physical Characteristics Lease Characteristics Financing Characteristics Appraised Value	Regional growth, population, population changes External land value and zoning Regional transportation spending Available space/vacancies Business inventories Building starts, value of new construction and construction costs Mortgage interest rates, availability, commitments and investment by major market participants	

Transaction Characteristics

Purchase Date

Transaction Prices

Fundamental Characteristics

Macroeconomic Climate

Valuation Function

Estimated Prices

Total Return Index

Market Risk Measures

Individual Risk Measures

Responsiveness to Fundamental Characteristiics

This type of fundamental analysis is accomplished on a daily basis by security analysts in the stock market. Macroeconomic variables plus firm specific data (such as leverage and industry) are used to estimate the value of the firm. Furthermore, it is possible to use similar techniques to those proposed below to establish the contribution to security risk and return of various common factors (see, for instance, King [1966], Rosenberg [1974] and Rosenberg and Marathe [1976]).

Thus, the analogy is complete. Appraisers and security analysts use fundamental information to establish the *value* of their respective investments: real estate properties and common stocks and bonds. Portfolio managers bid on these investments based on these individual assessments of value, establishing a marketwide consensus[2] of value. If consensus expected returns reflect unbiased estimates of realized returns (rational expectations), then statistical techniques (such as those proposed below) should discern the elements of fundamental characteristic values.

Consider one potential improvement for the valuation scheme. If subjective evaluations of property values are available, consider adding them as a fundamental characteristic for the valuation function. If appraisers can systematically estimate value,[3] then these estimates will improve the valuation function.[4]

The valuation function is estimated using a sample of actual transaction prices from individual assets (data are described in Section 4), and fundamental characteristics collected about these properties (see Figure I, and Section 3 for a description of the fundamental characteristics).

At any point in time, a value for each nontransacting property is estimated from the valuation function applied to the fundamental characteristics at that time. From the valuation function, the individual compound rate of return can be estimated and the aggregate market value is estimated. From the aggregate market value and the cash flows, the total return index is calculated.[5] With the return estimate also comes an estimate of the standard deviation of market return. Further, it is possible to calculate the responsiveness of an individual property's risk and return to the fundamental characteristics of property valuation.[6]

In this section, the technique of fundamental valuation for properties has been compared to the same process in the stock market. The fundamental valuation process leads up to a market return estimate. Utilizing techniques developed from risk estimation for stocks (see King [1966], Sharpe [1973], Rosenberg [1974] and Rosenberg and Marathe [1979]), a fundamental valuation function is estimated in Section 5. (For details of the estimation process, see Hoag [1979, 1980]).

§3. CONSTRUCTION OF AN INDUSTRIAL REAL ESTATE RETURN INDEX

The success of the estimation of market return depends upon the choice of valuation characteristics. Any variable which estimates value should improve the efficiency of the estimation procedure. Indeed, econometric parsimony is *not* required here unless the model is unstable. Furthermore, intuitively understandable value measures should be preferred to technical value measures. Initially, the list of valuation characteristics should be very broad, but as experience grows, many candidate characteristics will be cast aside. Figure I lists a number of important characteristics for industrial properties.

One broad class of variables describes the general economic climate. These values fluctuate through time and provide a texture of time variation in the market rates of return for real estate (in conjunction with transaction prices). These variables attempt to capture the supply and demand for warehouse services, replacement costs and potential profits of warehouse ownership.

For industrial real estate, a number of specific or microeconomic characteristics can be examined. The physical characteristics literally describe the building, its surroundings and location. Notice that the location interacts with specific regional macroeconomic variables such as transportation spending to provide a context for regional valuation if it is warranted.

Next, the actual transaction price and any qualifications are analyzed. The qualifications are used to screen out any swaps or any partial transactions which are not reflective of the price paid for the property. At least initially, swaps and joint purchases (or packages) are avoided so that pure valuation characteristics for industrials can be identified.[7] In addition, any transaction costs paid to locate or purchase this property are included as part of the fundamental characteristics.

If financing exists, a number of variables which are fundamental to the valuation process can be examined. Although leveraging for tax purposes is *not* common among institutional investors, these investors participate in a market which may include taxable investors. Therefore, it is possible that the tax effects, credit availability, and borrowing restrictions for other purposes influence the valuation of real estate properties. Another area where these effects are apparent (and potentially useful in valuation) is in the depreciation and amortization schedules. Although the main concern is with before tax rates of return, it is very possible that overall value is affected by the participation of individuals and institutions with diverse marginal tax rates.[8]

The cash flow stream is a very important part of the valuation process. Not only is the cash flow included directly in return calculations, but its components are potentially useful in the valuation function itself. For instance, a building with large maintenance expenses may be in need of massive repairs. Finally, it is necessary to examine the stability and variability of the cash flow stream. Crude measures of maturity and lessee credit ratings potentially provide useful valuation information.

The purpose of examining the fundamental characteristics of property valuation is to provide insight into the underlying valuation process. Many of the characteristics which seem to be intimately related to the valuation process may not have any empirical importance, whatsoever.

§4. INDUSTRIAL PROPERTY SUBINDEX: SAMPLE SELECTION AND CHARACTERISTICS

The need to concentrate on one homogeneous property type is apparent when the number of potential real estate investments is considered. Of the many property types, industrial properties seem to be the most homogeneous and their valuation characteristics seem readily discernible. It is difficult to check this sample for representativeness. Any extrapolation to population parameters should be made with great care and attention must be paid to the problem of retrospective inclusion and survivorship bias. These problems tend to inflate the values of return estimated from a sample, and it is likely that our sample suffers from these biases to some (currently unknown) degree.

The sample used for calculations in the next section consists of 463 properties with transaction prices at some time during the twenty four quarter interval from first quarter 1973 through the fourth quarter 1978. This subsample was chosen because only these observations have been verified for accuracy and completeness. Only those locations and time periods where sufficient data existed could be used in the estimation process. As more information on industrial properties becomes available, the estimates of return and risk will change—perhaps dramatically at first. As the sample size increases, further changes should be small. From the little information analyzed from the *Site Selection Handbook* and *Western Real Estate News* (see Sand [1978]), the sample does not look wholly unrepresentative, but the results must be treated with care. A complete description of the sample appears in Table I.

§5. THE FUNDAMENTAL VALUATION FUNCTION FOR INDUSTRIAL PROPERTIES

To alleviate problems of substantial pointwise error in any cross-section, pooled cross section time series regressions can be estimated over the entire ensemble of observations of transaction prices. Essentially, estimation of the pooled data implies a stationary valuation function. It is relatively simple to decide on the validity of this procedure for any particular sample.

In Table II estimates of the parameters of the valuation function for industrial properties appear. The sign and magnitude of most of the coefficients in this model are reasonable. In particular, a great deal of importance is attached to the income capital-

Table I Industrial Property Sample Characteristics*

$\overline{P}_{it}$ = $1,167,000
$\sigma(P_{it})$ = $1,039,000
$Max\{P_{it}\}$ = $8,241,000
where P_{it} = the price paid for i industrial property at time t ($i = 1, ..., 463.$)

Temporal Distribution of Transactions

Quarter	1973	1974	1975	1976	1977	1978
1	21	13	18	14	16	47
2	6	24	35	5	14	8
3	13	23	22	9	39	6
4	9	14	34	9	55	9
Annual	49	74	109	37	124	70

Geographic Distribution of Transactions

North East	40
Central	59
South	168
Mountain	13
West	183
	463

* The Industrial Property Sample at the University of California, Berkeley currently has information on 800 industrial properties with at least one transaction each over a period from 1970 through today. Institutional donors of this data have been especially generous with their time and information. This data base will be expanded and updated in future years.

Table II Relative Asset Valuation Function for Industrial Properties*

$$P_{it} = \alpha_0 + \alpha_f \underline{f} + \alpha_n \underline{n} + \alpha_r \underline{r} + \alpha_l \underline{l} + \alpha_q \underline{q} + \epsilon_{it}$$
$$\overline{R}^2 = .89 \quad S(\epsilon) = 352. \quad F(33, 429) = 108.6$$

		α Coefficient	Standard Error
	$\underline{f}$ Fundamental Characteristics of Value		
f_1:	income in year of purchase	9.8	0.42
f_2:	expenses in year of purchase	−1.65	.90
f_3:	net lease variable	79.3	41.8
f_4:	capital improvements in year of purchase	−.58	.14
f_5:	size measure	−.0081	.00086
f_6:	expense measure	.013	.00297
f_7:	lease attractiveness measure	.0086	.001
	$\underline{n}$ National Economic Concomitants of Value		
n_1:	business inventories in quarter of purchase	−3.1	.43
n_2:	nationwide volume of sales of industrial properties	6.22	2.06
	$\underline{r}$ Regional Economic Concomitants of Value		
r_1:	$ value of loans committed in the region of the property	3.09	2.85
r_2:	measured capitalization rate on property in the region	−65.5	62.3
r_3:	capitalization rate dummy variable for credit availability	722.8	633.8
r_4:	regional volume of sales of industrial properties	−8.4	2.8
	$\underline{l}$ Locational Characteristics of Value° °		
	$\underline{q}$ Temporal Characteristics of Value° °		

° The micro and macroeconomic characteristics of value are described in more detail in Hoag [1979] and the estimation of the valuation function for industrial properties is described in detail in Hoag [1980].

° ° See the discussion for a description of these variables and their effects on property value.

ization rate which is also very significant (20 times its standard error[9]) in our regressions. All of the fundamental financial characteristics add to the explanatory power of the model. Additionally, the macroeconomic (regional and national) variables add further to the model. The locational variables detracted somewhat from the regional economic concomitants since each represents essentially a localized measure of value. The existence of significant coefficients for the location variables can be attributed to a lack of strong regional concomitants for industrial properties in the model or segmentation in the real estate market.

The overall performance of the model is quite reasonable with an adjusted R^2 = .89. Quite a large portion of the variance in transaction price can be explained through the relationship in the model in Table II. The goodness of fit of the fundamental valuation model improves the chances of providing reasonable estimates of the value and return of industrial real estate.

§6. HISTORICAL RISK AND RETURN ESTIMATES FOR INDUSTRIAL REAL ESTATE

Results based on the sample described in Table I and the valuation function estimates in Table II indicate that the average compound returns for the industrial real estate value weighted subindex over the period 1Q73 through 4Q78 were 3.38%/quarter with a quarterly standard deviation of 8.61%. The return is high and the risk is comparable to that obtainable on stocks and corporate bonds during that period, as can be seen in Table III.

As is commonly observed in common stock portfolios, the equally weighted industrial real estate index has a larger variance than the value weighted industrial real estate index.

It appears from this evidence that the cross correlations provide a sound basis for fulfilling the inflation hedge and diversification motives of investors. In Figure II, the time series behavior of the total rate of return on industrial real estate is displayed. There appear to be sizeable fluctuations which are, of course, corroborated by the 18% annual standard deviation for industrial real estate over this period. It does *not* appear that real estate was substantially *less* risky than common stock. However, the sample period was one of relative uncertainty in the investment real estate industry due to the virtual collapse of a number of Real Estate Investment Trusts (REITs). More definitive results on real estate investment characteristics await further data collection and analysis.

§7. POTENTIAL APPLICATIONS AND FUTURE DEVELOPMENTS

Perhaps the best indication of the importance of this work is the breadth of potential applications in the real estate investment management arena. The availability of an index of returns permits the evaluation of realized returns on individual properties on an objec-

Table III Comparative Historical Summary Statistics for Quarterly Compound Returns, 1973–1978*

	Mean	Standard Deviation°°
i_t	.0196	.0061
r_{ft}	.0152	.0031
r_{Bt}	.0155	.0402
r_{St}	.0092	.1038
r_{REt}^{EW}	.0211	.0953
r_{REt}^{VW}	.0338	.0861

Cross Correlation Coefficients°°	i_t	r_{ft}	r_{Bt}	r_{St}	r_{REt}^{EW}	r_{REt}^{VW}
i_t	1	.68	−.50	−.41	.79	.50
r_{ft}		1	−.36	−.33	.39	.28
r_{Bt}			1	.64	−.49	−.31
r_{St}				1	−.21	−.07
r_{REt}^{EW}					1	.99
r_{REt}^{VW}						1

where
- i_t = the rate of inflation as measured by changes in the Bureau of Labor Statistics Consumer Price Index
- r_{ft} = the rate of return on U.S. Treasury Bills with 3-month maturity
- r_{Bt} = the total rate of return on corporate bonds measured by the Salomon Brothers High Grade Long-Term Corporate Bond Index
- r_{ST} = the total rate of return on the Standard & Poors' value weighted 500 Stock Index
- r_{REt}^{EW} = estimated total rate of return on an equally weighted portfolio of industrial properties
- r_{REt}^{VW} = estimated total rate of return on a value weighted portfolio of industrial properties

° Historical returns for bonds, stocks, treasury bills and the rate of inflation were obtained from Ibbotson and Sinquefield [1979].

°° The variances and covariances presented have been adjusted for serial correlation due to random pricing errors. For details, see Hoag [1980].

Figure II Historical Market Value Weighted Equity Returns for Industrial Properties

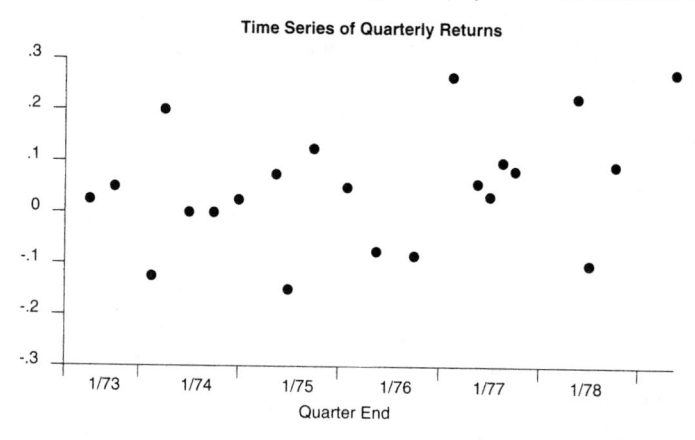

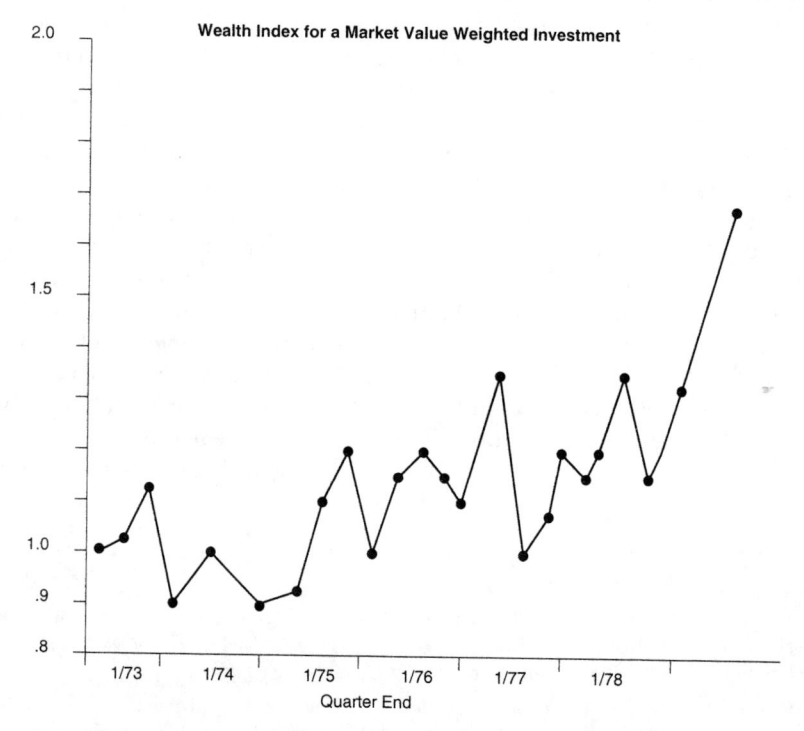

Time Series of Quarterly Returns

Wealth Index for a Market Value Weighted Investment

tive basis. The fundamental valuation characteristics permit measurement of historical risk characteristics for each property. When properties are sold, it is possible to objectively evaluate performance compared to a broad based sample of industrial properties.

One classic objection to previous market indexes has been the lack of real estate representation. With the inclusion of our real property indexes, major objections to missing assets in the "market" portfolio are alleviated.[10]

Further, this new market index and its associated portfolio lead naturally to a redefinition of a passive investment strategy which would include market value weighted portions of all real estate assets. To say that this would be a change in investment strategy for institutions is an understatement. In addition to pursuing the passive strategy, it will be possible *to analyze* asset allocation strategies which differ from the passive strategy. Since industrial real estate appears to have a low correlation with stock returns, it should be a good diversifying asset. Once the matrix of covariances of returns between stocks, bonds *and* all real estate is available, investment managers can rationally explore the efficient frontier.

Last, but not least, the availability of this technique and the fundamental valuation parameters permits investment managers to perform objective evaluations of properties in their portfolio. Thus, in addition to hiring an appraiser, the valuation function can provide a computer based "appraisal." Clearly the fundamental valuation technique embraces *all three* commonly used appraisal strategies and combines these techniques with a broad data base for reference. It would only be natural to compare these two estimates of value to cross check and confirm the valuation. In fact, it would be interesting to look for appraisers that choose properties with positive abnormal returns, much as stock portfolio managers attempt to identify security analysts that pick winners. Regardless of the availability of superior selection ability in real estate, the index and valuation techniques can help in the active management process.

Finally, the real estate indexes are an indispensable tool in valuing contingent claims upon the equity of real property. For instance, mortgages, mortgage bonds, mortgage backed bonds and pass through certificates all rely upon the cash flow from real estate investments. In the same way that it would be difficult to evaluate risky bonds without the value of the underlying stock and company, it is harder to value these mortgage related instruments without knowing something about equity real estate returns.

Thus, the real estate index is potentially useful throughout the investment management process. Ongoing research in this area includes the completion of the industrial property data base, installation of an ongoing data collection mechanism and continual updating and reestimation (when necessary) of the industrial real estate subindex. Further developments include an expansion of the data base and indexes to the other main areas of real estate returns and finally a link between all return subindexes to create an overall market index for investment real estate.

NOTES

[1] For a discussion of valuation with infrequently traded stock assets using similar techniques to those proposed in Section 2, see Hoag [1980]. Dimson [1978], Schwert [1977] and Scholes and Williams [1977] also propose techniques for estimating systematic risk for infrequently traded assets.

[2] One interesting question concerns the efficiency of the real estate market in processing fundamental information. Most real estate writers assert that the market is inefficient. The bulk of evidence for the stock market suggests that most public information is processed rapidly and efficiently. Of course, no evidence exists for the real estate market because no measures of return are available. Thus tests of market efficiency await completion of an index of market returns such as the one under construction herein. Until proven otherwise, a null hypothesis of efficiently established prices would seem prudent.

[3] The bulk of evidence in the stock market suggests that rewards for information processing are not consistently evident in returns to investment vehicles such as mutual funds. Thus, the null hypothesis is that if the model is adequately specified with fundamental characteristics, appraisals will *not* improve the valuation function.

[4] When the estimation of the valuation function is complete, an assessment of the value of appraisal information will be forthcoming. Given the breadth of the market data assembled for industrial properties plus

the objective nature of the estimation procedure, it would seem unlikely that appraisers could have appraisals with consistently positive value.

[5] Under certain assumptions, detailed in Lintner [1975], this market return is a value weighted index of the compound rates of returns for individual properties.

[6] The relationship of common stock risk and return to fundamental characteristics has been demonstrated in the stock market (see, for instance, Beaver, Kettler, Scholes [1970] and Rosenberg and McKibben [1973]).

[7] Later, it should be possible to value packages of properties or buildings with mixtures of property types in the same way that it is possible to value a conglomerate merger using value additivity.

[8] For excellent analyses of this effect in the stock market, see Litzenberger and Ramaswamy [1978] and Rosenberg and Marathe [1979]. An analysis of the overall effect of taxation on relative asset prices appears in Hoag and Rosenberg [1979].

[9] Interpretation of individual coefficient standard errors should be made with great care due to the multicollinearity of the independent variables. In Hoag [1980] as in Rosenberg [1974] factor analytic techniques are used to produce independent predictors of value. Alas, intuitive explanations of these factors are not possible and, hence, these techniques are not presented herein.

[10] Another use of techniques of this paper which is related to the index issue is obtaining estimates of return for any large stock which includes assets (such as real estate or OTC stocks) which trade infrequently (or nonsynchronously). This problem was first pointed out by Fisher [1966]. Our method calls for the introduction of fundamental factors into the valuation process coupled with smoothed time varying generalized least squares estimates (for a review of these techniques, see Rosenberg [1973]) of the logarithmic returns. Contrast this technique with those of Dimson [1978], Schwert [1977], and Scholes and Williams [1977] who use limited descriptor sets consisting of historical β and OLS estimates for nonsynchronous assets. Efficient, unbiased estimates can be obtained from the technique proposed in Hoag [1980].

REFERENCES

Beaver, W., P. Kettler and M. Scholes. "The Association Between Market Determined and Accounting Determined Risk Measures," *The Accounting Review,* Vol. XLV, No. 4 (October 1975), pp. 654–682.

Dimson, E. "Risk Measurement when Shares are Subject to Infrequent Trading," *Journal of Financial Economics,* Vol. 7, No. 2 (June 1979), pp. 197–226.

Fisher, L. "Some New Stock-Market Indexes," *Journal of Business,* Vol. 39 (January 1966), pp. 191–225.

Hoag, J. "The Fundamental Determinants of Risk and Return for Industrial Real Estate," unpublished manuscript, University of California, Berkeley, June 1979.

Hoag, J. "The Estimation of Return and Risk for Thinly Traded Assets Utilizing Fundamental Determinants of Relative Asset Value," *Berkeley Research Program in Finance Working Paper* (January 1980).

Hoag, J. "A New Real Estate Return Index: Measurement of Risk and Return," *Proceedings of the Seminar on the Analysis of Security Prices,* University of Chicago, Vol. 24, No. 1 (May 1979), pp. 223–259.

Hoag, J. and B. Rosenberg. "Tax Induced Inflation Sensitivity of Relative Asset Values," unpublished manuscript, University of California, Berkeley, September 1979.

Ibbotson, R. and R. Sinquefield. "Stocks, Bonds, Bills and Inflation: Historical Returns (1926–1978), *Financial Analysts Research Foundation Monograph,* 1979.

King, B. "Market and Industry Factors in Stock Price Behavior," *Journal of Business,* Vol. 39 (January 1966), pp. 139–190.

Lintner, J. "The Lognormality of Portfolio Returns, Portfolio Selection and Market Equilibrium," unpublished manuscript, 1975.

Litzenberger, R. and K. Ramaswamy. "The Effect of Personal Taxes and Dividends on Capital Asset Prices: Theory and Empirical Evidence," *Journal of Financial Economics,* Vol. 7, No. 2 (June 1979), pp. 163–196.

Rosenberg, B. "Extra Market Components of Covariance Among Security Returns," *Journal of Financial and Quantitative Analysis,* Vol. 9, (March 1974), pp. 263–274.

Rosenberg, B. "A Survey of Stochastic Parameter Regression," *Annals of Economic and Social Measurement*, Vol. 2, No. 4 (October 1973), pp. 381–397.

Rosenberg, B. and V. Marathe. "Common Factors in Security Returns: Microeconomic Determinants and Macroeconomic Correlates," *Proceedings of the Seminar on the Analysis of Security Prices*, Vol. 21, No. 1 (May 1976), University of Chicago, pp. 381–397.

Rosenberg, B. and V. Marathe. "Tests of Capital Asset Pricing Hypotheses," in Haim Levy, Ed., *Research in Finance*, Vol. 1, 1979 (JAI Press), pp. 115–223.

Rosenberg, B. and W. McKibben. "The Prediction of Systematic and Specific Risk in Common Stocks," *Journal of Financial and Quantitative Analysis*, Vol. 8 (March 1973), pp. 317–333.

Sand, O. "Industrial Parks in California and Their Value for Modern Portfolio Managers," unpublished MBA Thesis, University of California, Berkeley, May 1978.

Scholes, M. and J. Williams. "Estimating Betas from Nonsynchronous Data," *Journal of Financial Economics*, Vol. 5, No. 3 (December 1977), pp. 309–328.

Schwert, G. W. "Stock Exchange Seats as Capital Assets," *Journal of Financial Economics*, Vol. 4, No. 1 (January 1977), pp. 51–78.

Sharpe, W. "The Capital Asset Pricing Model: A 'Multi-Beta' Interpretation," *Stanford Graduate School of Business, Research Paper* #183, September 1973.

Wendt, P. and A. Cerf. *Real Estate Investment Analysis and Taxation*, (McGraw-Hill, 1979).

Wendt, P. and R. Haney. "The Prospects for a National Real Estate Market," unpublished manuscript, University of California, Berkeley, 1979.

10 The Historical Perspective of Real Estate Returns

And a comprehensive review of the literature

G. Stacy Sirmans and C. F. Sirmans

This study provides a review of the literature on the risk and return performance of real estate relative to alternative assets. The paper also examines the ability of real estate and these other assets to serve as a hedge against expected and unexpected inflation.

In summary, results of studies examining real estate returns and risk relative to other assets have found that, in general, when variation in return is used as the measure of risk, equity investments such as common stocks have been riskier than debt securities such as corporate or government bonds. The comparisons of real estate returns and risk to other assets is mixed. More than half the studies find that absolute returns on real estate have been higher than returns on either stocks, bonds, or other assets. Some studies show that real estate outperformed debt securities but not common stocks on an absolute rate of return basis. On a risk-adjusted basis (return divided by risk), most of the studies indicate that real estate earned a higher return per unit of risk than common stocks and the other assets included in the studies.

In examining the absolute risk of the asset returns, the results are mixed. Most of the studies show a higher standard deviation for common stocks than for real estate, while only a few studies show a higher variation for real estate. One study reports equal standard deviations for real estate and common stocks. In several cases, the reported standard deviations for real estate are even less than those reported for either corporate or government bonds. Later sections of this study will discuss the problems that are encountered in measuring real estate returns and risk and the smoothing and inaccuracy that may result from measurement error.

We also discuss several studies that examine real estate and other assets as hedges against inflation. Some studies find that real estate has been a good hedge against both expected and unexpected inflation. Other studies show that some types of real estate have provided an excellent hedge against expected inflation but not against unexpected inflation. The results of studies examining the value of financial assets as an inflation hedge are also mixed.

From *The Journal of Portfolio Management*. This copyrighted material is reprinted with permission from *The Journal of Portfolio Management*, 488 Madison Avenue, New York, NY 10022.

MEASURING RETURNS ON REAL ESTATE

The results of studies to measure the historical rate of return on real estate are shown in Table 1.

Miles and McCue (1982) examine the unleveraged rates of return on properties held by sixteen REITs over the period 1972–1978. They find average returns ranging from 8.44% to 9.62% for different types of properties.

A study by Webb and Sirmans (1982) presents expected returns on various types of real property over the period 1966-1976. These returns are shown in Table 1 and Table 4. The lowest average annual return is 9.54% for office buildings, while the highest return is 9.64% for retail properties. Risk for the properties is similar with the standard deviations ranging from 0.74% for non-elevator apartments to 1.05% for shopping centers.[1]

Edwards (1984) indirectly measures the return and risk on real estate investments by examining the performance of wholly-owned service corporations of savings and loan associations. As of December 1983, real estate, such as unimproved land and commercial properties, comprised 31.4% of service corporation assets. Edwards measured the average annual return for service corporations to be 17.4% over the 1979–1983 period. The standard deviation of the service corporation returns was 40%.[2]

The National Council of Real Estate Investment Fiduciaries in conjunction with the Frank Russell Company provides an index of returns on various types of income properties. The index begins in 1977. As of December 1983, 845 properties are included. Table 1 and Table 4 (the NCREIF report) show the average annual returns over the 1978–1983 period. The returns range from 11.58% for retail properties to 24.62% for hotels, with hotels being riskiest.

At this point, the limitations and problems of a real estate return series such as the Frank Russell Company (FRC) series should be acknowledged. The index uses appraised values to measure the "capital gain" component of returns. The use of appraised values rather than actual observed market values may produce inaccuracies and smoothing of returns, thereby underestimating standard deviations. For example, the FRC properties are appraised independently once a year. This appraisal value is used to calculate the rates of return and can obviously vary from the actual market value were the property to be sold. Also, indexes, such as the FRC index, include a diversified group of properties from various geographic regions throughout the United States. Rates of return on an index of this type may not be representative of returns prevalent in a specific geographical area.

Returns on Real Estate and Other Assets. A number of studies have attempted to measure return and risk on real estate investments relative to other assets. These studies are presented in Tables 2 and 3. The results are mixed, in that real estate performs sometimes better, sometimes worse than other assets in a risk-return analysis. Brueggeman, Chen, and Thibodeau (1984), for example, show that real estate held in two large commingled real estate funds performed well compared to common stocks and corporate bonds. The Hoag study (1980) shows that real estate outperformed other assets such as stocks and bonds, not only with a higher average return but also with greater return relative to risk. Hoag's conclusions are based on a real estate index using such variables as location, size, age, and demographics.

Table 1 Studies Examining Returns on Real Estate Investment

Author(s)	Title	Source	Time Period	Summary
M. Miles and T. McCue	Historic Returns and Institutional Real Estate Portfolios	*Journal of the American Real Estate and Urban Economics Association,* Summer 1982	1972-1978	Examines property values of properties held by sixteen REITs. Return estimates are derived for the unlevered cash yields by property size, type, and location. REIT portfolios are compared to commingled fund portfolios. Using a regression equation to estimate the cash yield of the portfolios, the study finds the average returns on office, residential, and retail properties to be 8.62%, 9.62%, and 8.44%, respectively. Comparison of REIT and CREF portfolios would suggest that CREF portfolios should contain more residential property.
J. R. Webb and C. F. Sirmans	Yields for Selected Types of Real Property vs. the Money and Capital Markets	*The Appraisal Journal,* April 1982	1966-1976	Using real estate data from the American Council of Life Insurance, the study calculates investment yields of specific property types for fifteen companies. The average overall yields by property type were: elevator apartment, 9.57%; nonelevator apartment, 9.59%; retail, 9.64%; shopping center, 9.56%; office building, 9.54%; and medical office building, 9.63%.
D. G. Edwards	Rates of Return from S & L Investments in Service Corporations, 1979-83	Research Working Paper, Office of Policy and Economic Research, Federal Home Loan Bank Board, November 1984	1979-1983	Data from over 1,000 S & Ls with investments in service corporations are analyzed to obtain estimates of the rates and variability of returns from these investments. Many investments by service corporations are in areas such as unimproved land, land development, commercial properties, etc. In December 1983, real estate comprised 31.4% of service corporation assets with the remainder being cash and securities, receivables, fixed assets, first mortgage loans, other loans, and unconsolidated subsidiaries. The annual rates of return on service corporations for the sample S & Ls averaged 17.4% with a standard deviation of 40% over the 1979-1983 period. Of the sample firms, 67% reported returns below the industry's average rate on new conventional single-family mortgage loans closed for the period (13.35%).
National Council of Real Estate Investment Fiduciaries	The NCREIF Report	National Council of Real Estate Investment Fiduciaries and the Frank Russell Company	1978-1983	The Frank Russell Company publishes real estate returns on an index of income-producing properties that are completed and non-leveraged. As of December 1983, there were 845 properties in the index. The returns are based on net operating income plus change in property value. Changes in property value are determined by appraisal where appropriate. The average annual returns by index and type of property over 1978-1983 are: index, 15.6%; apartments, 18.28%; retail, 11.58%; hotels, 24.62%; industrial, 14.97%; office, 18.02%.

Table 2 Studies Examining Returns on Real Estate Relative to Other Assets

Author(s)	Title	Source	Time Period	Summary
C. Froland, R. Gorlow, and R. Sampson	The Market Risk of Real Estate	*Journal of Portfolio Management,* Spring 1986	1970-1984	Constructs and index of returns and risk based on valuation of average NOI using an average market capitalization rate for office buildings in four major cities. Results show that the office index outperformed the S&P 500. The variability of real estate was much greater than the S&P 500 index. Washington had the lowest absolute return for real estate while San Francisco had the highest. On a risk-adjusted basis, Washington and San Francisco outperformed the stock index. Results also show in general that negative correlations exist between cities and the index. This implies certain benefits for real estate geographical diversification as well as diversification across other assets.
W. B. Brueggeman, A. H. Chen, and T. G. Thibodeau	Real Estate Investment Funds: Performance and Portfolio Considerations	*Journal of the American Real Estate and Urban Economics Association,* Spring 1984	1972-1983	Estimates rates of return on two CREFs using cash returns and unit values. Unit values are proxies for market values of the underlying real estate. Unit values are based on appraisals. Results show an average annual yield of 11.73% for the entire period. Subperiods of 1972-1977 and 1978-1983 show average annual yields of 8.37% and 15.09%, respectively. When measuring return relative to risk, the real estate investment funds performed very well compared to common stocks and corporate bonds.
J. W. Hoag	Toward Indices of Real Estate Value and Return	*Journal of Finance,* May 1980	1973-1978	Examines returns based on income and price changes (as determined by a valuation model) for 463 industrial properties that are primarily warehouses with some light manufacturing and distribution. The average returns are weighted by property size and are unleveraged and pretax returns. The average annualized return over the study period was 14.2%.
R. G. Ibbotson and C. L. Fall	The United States Market Wealth Portfolio	*Journal of Portfolio Management,* Fall 1979	1947-1978	Examines returns based on income and changes in index values (USDA and Home Purchase Indexes) for farm real estate and residential housing. The returns are weighted by component size. The average annual return for farms was 11.7% and 6.9% for housing over the study period.
H. R. Fogler	20% in Real Estate: Can Theory Justify It?	*Journal of Portfolio Management,* Winter 1984	1915-1978	Estimates the returns on various assets over a long time period by adding historical risk premiums to the prevailing Treasury bill rate. Two proxies for real estate returns are estimated—Proxy 1 follows the Ibbotson and Fall study above, and Proxy 2 was calculated using a construction cost series and a rent series. The mean return on real estate is shown to be 11%. In a portfolio context, the results make a strong case for a 20% minimum investment in real estate.

Table 2 Studies Examining Returns on Real Estate Relative to Other Assets *(continued)*

Author(s)	Title	Source	Time Period	Summary
R. G. Ibbotson and L. B. Siegel	Real Estate Returns: A Comparison with Other Investments	*Journal of the American Real Estate and Urban Economics Association,* Fall 1984	1947-1982	Examines the return and risk for various types of real estate along with stocks, fixed-income assets (bonds, preferred stocks, commercial paper), government securities (bills, notes, bonds) and municipal bonds. The results show that real estate had an average return of 8.33% and was substantially less risky than other investments. The authors concede, however, that the real estate series may be smoothed thus creating artificially low standard deviations.
J. McMahan Associates, Inc.	Institutional Strategies for Real Estate Equity Investment	*Pension Trust Investment in Realty,* November/December 1981	1951-1978	Examines return based on income and price change as determined by changes in the construction cost index for mortgage commitments on multi-family and nonresidential properties as reported by fifteen life insurance companies. The returns are unleveraged and pretax. The average annual return on real estate over this period was 13.9%.
M. Brachman	Rating Commingled Funds	*Pension World,* September 1981	1970-1979	Examines the return on three commingled funds. Total return is based on income and changes in market value as measured by appraisals. The returns are pretax and are 10.3% for real estate over the study period.
A. A. Robichek, R. A. Cohn, and J. J. Pringle	Returns on Alternative Investment Media and Implications for Portfolio Construction	*Journal of Business,* July 1972	1951-1969	Examines return based on income and changes in market value as indicated by index values for farm real estate. Uses the Department of Agriculture Index of Average Value of Farm Real Estate per acre. Returns are unleveraged and pretax. The average return on real estate over this period was 9.5%.

The Ibbotson and Fall study (1979) shows that, although real estate had a lower average return than common stocks, it substantially outperformed other investments on a risk-adjusted basis. The same is true for the Ibbotson and Siegel study (1984) and the Robichek, Cohn, and Pringle study (1972). Studies that show that real estate performed better than other assets, not only with a higher average return but also a higher return on a risk-adjusted basis, are McMahan (1981) and Brachman (1981).

On the other hand, the Fogler study (1984) shows that real estate had outperformed by common stocks on an absolute return basis and also on a risk-adjusted basis over the 1915–1978 period. On a risk-adjusted basis, real estate was also outperformed by bonds and Treasury bills.

Returns on Real Estate Measured by REIT Performance. Some of the previous studies use appraised values in determining real estate returns (Brueggeman, Chen, and Thibodeau; Brachman; and Ibbotson and Siegel, for example). Because the use of appraised value instead of actual market value may tend to reduce the variability in real estate returns, these results may be biased in favor of real estate.

Table 3 Studies Measuring Real Estate Returns Using Data of Real Estate Investment Trusts (REITs)

Author(s)	Title	Source	Time Period	Summary
W. L. Burns and D. R. Epley	The Performance of Portfolios of REITs plus Common Stocks	*Journal of Portfolio Management*, Spring 1982	1970-1979	Examines the returns on thirty-five REITs relative to other investment trusts (closed-end and mutual funds) and the Standard & Poor's Composite Index. In a portfolio context, results show that portfolios of all assets outperform portfolios of just REITs. The average return on real estate (REITs) is 16% over the study period. In subset time periods, the return is 3% for 1970-1974 and 37.4% for 1975-1979.
H. A. Davidson and J. E. Palmer	A Comparison of the Investment Performance of Common Stocks, Homebuilding Firms, and Equity REITS	*The Real Estate Appraiser*, July/August 1978	1972-1977	Calculates the return and variance on each of eleven equity REITs, the Standard & Poor's 500 Index, and ten homebuilding common stocks. Over the period examined, the equity REITs outperformed both building firms and the S&P 500 on a systematic risk-adjusted basis. On a total risk-adjusted basis, the REITs outperformed the S&P 500. The average annual return on the REITs was 8.8%.
K. V. Smith	Historical Returns of Real Estate Equity Portfolios	*The Investment Manager's Handbook*, 1980	1965-1977	Examines the rate of return based on purchase price, quarterly cash distributions, and the sale price at the end of the holding period for fourteen equity REITs. The returns are pretax. The average return over this study period was 9.8%.

In order to avoid this problem, other studies have used data for real estate investment trusts (REITs). These studies are shown in Tables 3 and 4. The returns on REITs can be calculated using the income accruing to the REITs and the change in the market price of the share. As the principal underlying assets of the REITs are either real estate or mortgages or both, then, to the extent that the market price reflects the true value of the underlying assets, the returns on the REIT may serve as a proxy for the return on the underlying real assets. A caveat is that pension real estate studies usually measure unleveraged (fully-owned) properties; thus, while having REIT market prices instead of appraisals is a plus, one loses in terms of purity of the portfolio.

The studies using REIT data show that real estate has had higher absolute returns than other assets such as common stocks and bonds. Burns and Epley (1982), for example, show a 16% average return on thirty-five REITs from 1970 to 1979. On a risk-adjusted basis, this outperforms stocks but not bonds.

Davidson and Palmer (1978) compare the performance of eleven equity REITs to the S&P 500 Index and ten homebuilding common stocks over the period 1972–1977. On an absolute return basis, the REITs outperformed the S&P 500 but not the homebuilding stocks. On a risk-adjusted basis, the REITs outperformed the homebuilding stocks but not the S&P 500.

The Smith study (1980) shows that fourteen equity REITs outperformed stocks and bonds on an absolute return basis. On a risk-adjusted basis, the REITs outperformed common stocks but not bonds over the study period 1965–1977.

Table 4 Summary Statistics of Returns on Real Estate Relative to Returns on Other Assets

Study	Time Period	Type of Assets	Average Annual[°] Rate of Return (%)	Standard Deviation (%)
Froland, Gorlow, and Sampson	1970-1984	Office		
		Chicago	25.4	53
		Manhattan	32.9	66
		Washington	19.0	29
		San Francisco	34.8	34
			8.8	15
		Treasury Bills	7.8	3
Miles and McCue	1972-1978	Office Real Estate	8.62	—
		Residential Real Estate	9.62	—
		Retail Real Estate	8.44	—
Webb and Sirmans	1966-1976	Elevator Apartments	9.57	0.76
		Non-elevator Apartments	9.59	0.74
		Retail	9.65	0.80
		Shopping Centers	9.56	1.05
		Office Buildings	9.54	0.78
		Medical Office Buildings	9.63	0.77
Edwards	1979-1983	Investment in Service Corporations by S&Ls	17.4	40
NCREIF Report	1978-1983	Index	15.6	3.91
		Apartments	18.28	6.99
		Retail	11.58	8.08
		Hotels	24.62	24.82
		Industrial	14.97	3.28
		Office	18.02	5.95
Brueggeman, Chen, and Thibodeau	1972-1983	Properties of 2 CREFs (1972-1983)	11.73	8.35
		Properties of 2 CREFs (1972-1977)	8.37	4.14
		Properties of 2 CREFs (1978-1983)	15.09	9.99
		Common Stocks (1972-1983)	9.71	34.99
		Corporate Bonds (1972-1983)	6.54	26.50
Hoag	1973-1978	Real Estate	14.2	17.2
		Common Stocks	3.7	20.8
		Bonds	6.4	8.0
		Treasury Bills	6.2	1.0
Ibbotson and Fall	1947-1978	Real Estate	8.1	3.5
		Common Stocks	10.3	18.0
		Bonds	2.9	5.5
		Treasury Bills	3.5	2.1
Fogler	1915-1978	Real Estate	11	4
		Common Stocks	13	4
		Bonds	8	2.6
		Treasury Bills	6	0

Table 4 Summary Statistics of Returns on Real Estate Relative to Returns on Other Assets *(continued)*

Study	Time Period	Type of Assets	Average Annual* Rate of Return (%)	Standard Deviation (%)
Ibbotson and Siegel	1947-1982	Real Estate		
		Farms	11.32	7.89
		Residential	7.5	3.89
		Business	8.1	3.78
		Total	8.33	3.71
		Common Stocks	12.42	17.52
		Fixed-Income Corporate Securities	3.76	6.47
		U.S. Government Securities	4.09	4.92
		Municipal Bonds	2.24	10.83
McMahan	1951-1978	Real Estate	13.9	3.8
		Common Stocks	11.4	18.3
		Bonds	3.5	6.7
		Treasury Bills	3.9	1.9
Brachman	1970-1979	Real Estate	10.3	4.9
		Common Stocks	4.7	19.6
		Bonds	5.6	8.0
		Treasury Bills	6.3	1.8
Burns and Epley	1970-1979	Real Estate	16.0	28.5
		Common Stocks	4.7	19.6
		Bonds	5.6	8.0
		Treasury Bills	6.3	1.8
Davidson and Palmer	1972-1977	Real Estate	8.8	17.0
		S&P 500	5.5	10.0
		Homebuilding Firm Stocks	9.2	39.0
Robichek, Cohn, and Pringle	1951-1969	Real Estate	9.5	4.5
		Common Stocks	11.9	17.4
		Bonds	1.3	5.0
		Treasury Bills	3.0	1.5
Smith	1965-1977	Real Estate	9.8	22.1
		Common Stocks	4.6	18.4
		Bonds	4.2	8.7
		Treasury Bills	5.4	1.3

* Some rates of return are calculated and presented in R. H. Zerbst and B. R. Cambon, "Real Estate Returns and Risks," *Journal of Portfolio Management* (Spring 1984), pp. 5-20.

The problem in using returns on REITs to measure real estate returns is that, in some periods, the REIT returns in the market may not match actual property returns. In the early 1970s, for example, REITs had poor returns while the underlying property values were relatively robust. Ibbotson and Siegel suggest that a possible reason for this divergence may be that high inflation increases the tax shelter attribute of real estate relative to REITs. Factors such as confidence in management's ability and the effects of leverage on REIT returns also may cause differences to arise.

REAL ESTATE RETURNS AND INFLATION

Real estate has received increasing attention in recent years as one of the few assets that provided an adequate hedge against inflation during the 1970s. To be a complete inflation hedge, an asset must adequately protect the investor from both expected and unexpected inflation. Expected inflation would be reflected in interest rates, while unexpected inflation would not be incorporated in market rates—although it might show up in *changes* in interest rates.

Several studies have attempted to measure the inflation hedge value of real estate relative to other assets such as common stocks and government or corporate bonds. These studies are shown in Table 5, where we can see that the results are mixed. Fama and Schwert (1977) find that real estate provided a good hedge against both expected and unexpected inflation from 1953 to 1971. Hartzell, Hekman, and Miles (1985) find that property types such as industrial and office properties provided complete protection from expected inflation but not unexpected inflation over their study period of 1973–1983.

Table 5 Studies Examining the Inflation Hedge Value of Real Estate and Other Assets

Author(s)	Title	Source	Summary
R. G. Ibbotson and L. B. Siegel	Real Estate Returns: A Comparison with Other Investments	Journal of the American Real Estate and Urban Economics Association, Fall 1984	Examines the total returns on a general index of real estate and compares those to other asset returns over the period 1947-1982. The purpose is to compare real estate returns to other returns over a long period of time to reduce statistical noise and eliminate temporary trends. Finds that common stocks had the highest return at 11.0% annually. Real estate had an unleveraged average return of 8.3%. All fixed-income securities had average returns below the inflation rate.
			A caveat of real estate returns is that they are based on appraised values. This causes smoothing and inaccuracy, thus reducing standard deviations. Also, real estate is not readily marketable as are stocks and bonds. In the case of these assets, reported returns are close to realized returns. Real estate is different in that it cannot necessarily be sold instantaneously at the quoted (appraised) value.
			Regression of asset returns on inflation shows that the real estate was an excellent, although not perfect, hedge against inflation. The comovement of real estate to inflation was 85%. Stocks and bonds reacted negatively to inflation.
E. F. Fama and G. W. Schwert	Asset Returns and Inflation	Journal of Financial Economics, November 1977	Estimates the extent to which private residential real estate, common stocks, Treasury bonds, Treasury bills, and labor income provided hedges against expected and unexpected inflation over the 1953-1971 period. Found real estate to have been a complete hedge against both expected and unexpected inflation. Treasury bills and bonds were complete hedges against expected but not unexpected inflation. Estimation problems made generalization about labor income difficult. Stock returns were found to have been negatively related to expected inflation and also, to a lesser extent, unexpected inflation. Thus, stocks could not be considered an inflation hedge over this period.

Table 5 Studies Examining the Inflation Hedge Value of Real Estate and Other Assets
(continued)

Author(s)	Title	Source	Summary
R. G. Ibbotson and R. A. Sinquefield	Stocks, Bonds, Bills, and Inflation: Year by Year Historical Returns (1926-1974)	*Journal of Business*, January 1976	Analyzes returns on common stocks, corporate bonds, Treasury bonds, and Treasury bills over 1926-1974 period. Finds that over this period Treasury bills provided a zero real rate of return, i.e., the average nominal return matched inflation at 2.2%. Government and corporate bonds earned nominal rates of 3.2% and 3.6% per year, respectively. Stocks earned an average nominal yield of 8.5% per year.
D. Hartzell, J. S. Hekman, and M. E. Miles	Real Estate Returns and Inflation	Unpublished paper, October 1985	Examines the ability of real estate to hedge against anticipated and unanticipated inflation. Uses quarterly returns for 300 properties of a large CREF over the 1973-1983 period. Develops two models of expected and unexpected inflation: one that uses a constant real rate and one that allows it to vary. The results show that real estate compensated the investor for both types of risk. By proper type for the entire period, industrial and office properties provide complete protection from expected inflation while retail properties were much weaker. Retail properties, however, seemed to be a better hedge against unexpected inflation. For the most recent five years of the sample period, industrial and office properties show complete protection from expected and unexpected inflation.
H. R. Fogler	20% in Real Estate: Can Theory Justify it?	*Journal of Portfolio Management*, Winter 1984	Identifies three types of periods over 1915-1978: inflation, deflation, and normal. Finds eight periods of significant inflation and deflation. Examines what happened to real estate and other assets in these periods. There were six periods when the inflation rate exceeded 5%. Common stocks seemed to do well until the later periods of 1960s and 1970s. Real estate did well in the 1960s and 1970s and also over the period 1915-1919. For other periods between these, real estate increased slightly, and there were mixed returns on stocks. In periods of deflation during the 1920's, there were several real estate booms in regional areas. Bonds did well at these times. In deflation in the 1930s, rents dropped, bonds did well, and common stocks did poorly. In normal periods, stock returns averaged higher than bond returns. Real estate returns seemed to be about the same as common stocks.
R. B. Peiser	Risk Analysis in Land Development	*Journal of the American Real Estate and Urban Economics Association*, Spring 1984	Examines risk analysis, including inflation risks, as it relates to land development. Income property development raises a number of risks not present in existing income property such as cost overruns, construction interest rate changes, delays, rent concessions, and absorption rates. Also, land development does not offer the tax benefits of income properties.

Table 5 Studies Examining the Inflation Hedge Value of Real Estate and Other Assets *(continued)*

Author(s)	Title	Source	Summary
			Inflation in construction costs was found to be somewhat higher than average inflation in all commodities as measured by the CPI. Using an internal rate of return model, finds that project returns are significantly more sensitive to changes in sales price, sales price inflation, and sales rates than to changes in construction costs, construction cost inflation rates, and interest rates.
H. R. Fogler, M. R. Granito, and L. R. Smith	A Theoretical Analysis of Real Estate Returns	*Journal of Finance*, July 1985	Estimates inflation betas for real estate, stocks, and bonds over several periods since 1952. While the data provide some support for the hedge demand hypothesis, the results are not strong enough to conclude that a rising inflation beta and declining required return on real estate was a cause of above-normal real estate returns in recent years. Thus the hypothesis cannot be rejected that there has been no change in expected returns on real estate because of an increase in its demand as an inflation hedge.
			The data used are Census Bureau index on new single-family houses sold, Livingston survey of farm prices, the CPI, S&P 500, and returns on twenty-year U.S. Treasury bonds.
			The study also addresses the problem of high returns on real estate but low variances. One solution proposed was that high unexpected rates of inflation lead to high realized returns on assets that are highly correlated with inflation such as real estate. The second solution was high realized returns on real estate as a result of changing investor perceptions about the degree of sensitivity of real estate returns to inflation. This could cause investors to bid up real estate prices.
J. B. Kau and C. F. Sirmans	Changes in Urban Land Values: 1836-1970	*Journal of Urban Economics*, 1984	Develops a model for measuring the return to land and examines these returns using a random coefficient estimation procedure for land in Chicago over specific periods from 1836 to 1970. A mean rate of return for land for each time period is derived from the model. The results suggest that the long-term rate of return on land is no higher than the rate of return on high-grade bonds over this period. The results also suggest that the rental income on land does not exceed, on average, the holding costs attached to the property.

Fogler examines the reaction of real estate to inflationary and deflationary periods from 1915 through 1978. He finds that real estate did well in the later inflationary periods (1960s and 1970s) and had slight increases in all inflationary periods. Common stocks did well until the later periods of the 1960s and 1970s. In normal periods, real estate and common stocks seemed to average about the same returns with both being greater than bonds.

Fogler, Granito, and Smith (1985) examine inflation betas for real estate, stocks, and bonds over various periods beginning in 1952. Their primary concern was whether there has been a significant change in expected returns on real estate as a result of its increased demand as an inflation hedge. While the data provided some support, the hypothesis that there has been no change could not be rejected.

Ibbotson and Siegel find that, over their study period of 1947–1982, common stocks had the highest annual return of 11% compared to 8.3% for real estate. Fixed-income assets had average returns below the inflation rate. While real estate seemed a good inflation hedge, they find that stocks and bonds reacted negatively to inflation.

While they find real estate to be a good hedge against expected and unexpected inflation over 1953–1971, Fama and Schwert find Treasury bills and bonds to be good hedges against expected but not unexpected inflation. On the other hand, they show common stocks to be negatively related to both expected and unexpected inflation.

Ibbotson and Sinquefield (1976) find that, with an average inflation rate of about 2.2%, common stocks earned an average return of 8.5% over the 1926–1974 period. Government and corporate bonds earned 3.2% and 3.6%, respectively, while the average Treasury bill yield equaled the inflation rate, thus yielding a zero real rate of return.

A study by Peiser (1984) that analyzes inflation risk and land development finds that inflation in construction costs was higher than average inflation as measured by the CPI. Peiser also finds that the returns on land development were much more sensitive to sales price inflation than to construction cost inflation.

A study by Kau and Sirmans (1984) examines changes in urban land values over the period 1836–1970. Using a model to measure rate of return, they determine that the long-term return to land was no higher than the rate of return on high-grade bonds over this period.

SUMMARY AND CONCLUSIONS

This study has analyzed the literature covering the returns and risk on real estate relative to other assets and the value of real estate as an inflation hedge.

In general, these studies indicate that common stocks have been riskier than debt securities such as government or corporate bonds. The results are mixed for real estate, in that some studies show real estate to be riskier than either stocks or bonds, some say real estate is riskier than bonds only, and others argue that it is less risky than either stocks or bonds. Some studies concede, however, that measurement errors in real estate returns may result in those returns appearing to be less risky than returns on other assets when actually that may or may not have been the case.

On the question of hedging against inflation, all studies found that debt securities were either not a good inflation hedge or allowed protection only for expected inflation. Common stock returns were, in general, negatively related to inflation rates, indicating that this asset did not serve as a good hedge against inflation. Some studies showed real estate has been a good hedge against both expected and unexpected inflation. Taken together, the studies seem to indicate that real estate served as a better inflation hedge over the time periods studied than common stocks and corporate or government bonds.

NOTES

[1] These results seem a little peculiar. Typically, income returns may be this stable; capital gains returns, however, would be expected to be more variable than these estimates indicated.

[2] It should be noted that the reliability of these data as a source of real estate returns depends on the accuracy of information reported to the regulating agencies.

REFERENCES

Brachman, W. O. "Rating Commingled Funds." *Pension World*, September 1981, pp. 25-38.

Brueggeman, W. B., A. H. Chen, and T. G. Thibodeau. "Real Estate Investment Funds: Performance and Portfolio Considerations." *AREUEA Journal*, Fall 1984, pp. 333-354.

Burns, W., and D. Epley. "Performance of Portfolios of REITs and Stocks." *Journal of Portfolio Management*, Vol. 8, No. 3 (Spring 1982), pp. 37-42.

Davidson, H. A., and J. E. Palmer. "A Comparison of the Investment Performance of Common Stocks, Homebuilding Firms, and Equity REITs." *The Real Estate Appraiser*, July/August 1978, pp. 35-39.

Edwards, D. G. "Rates of Return from S & L Investments in Service Corporations, 1979-83." Research Working Paper Series, Office of Policy and Economic Research, Federal Home Loan Bank Board, November 1984.

Fama, E. F., and G. W. Schwert. "Asset Returns and Inflation." *Journal of Financial Economics*, Vol. 5 (November 1977), pp. 115-146.

Fogler, H. R. "20% in Real Estate: Can Theory Justify It?" *Journal of Portfolio Management*, Vol. 10, No. 2 (Winter 1984), pp. 6-13.

Fogler, H. R., M. R. Granito, and L. R. Smith. "A Theoretical Analysis of Real Estate Returns." *Journal of Finance*, Vol. 40, No. 3 (July 1985), pp. 711-719.

Froland, Charles, R. Gorlow, and Richard Sampson. "The Market Risk of Real Estate." *Journal of Portfolio Management*, Vol. 12, No. 2 (Spring 1986), pp. 12-19.

The Handbook of Basic Economic Statistics. Bureau of Economic Statistics, Inc., Economic Statistics Bureau of Washington, D.C., Vol. 34, No. 11 (November 1985), pp. 97-101.

Hartzell, D., J. S. Hekman, and M. E. Miles. "Real Estate Returns and Inflation." Unpublished paper, October 1985.

Hoag, J. W. "Toward Indices of Real Estate Value and Return." *Journal of Finance*, May 1980, pp. 569-580.

Ibbotson, R. G., and C. L. Fall. "The United States Market Wealth Portfolio." *Journal of Portfolio Management*, Fall 1979, pp. 82-92.

Ibbotson, R. G., and L. B. Siegel. "Real Estate Returns: A Comparison With Other Investments." *AREUEA Journal*, Vol. 12, No. 3 (Fall 1984), pp. 219-242.

Ibbotson, R. G., and R. A. Sinquefield. "Stocks, Bonds, Bills, and Inflation: Year by Year Historical Returns (1926-1974)." *Journal of Business*, Vol. 49 (January 1976), pp. 11-47.

Kau, J. B., and C. F. Sirmans. "Changes in Urban Land Values: 1836-1970." *Journal of Urban Economics*, Vol. 15 (1984), pp. 18-25.

McMahan, J. "Institutional Strategies for Real Estate Equity Investment." *Pension Trust Investment in Realty*, Practicing Law Institute, November/December 1981.

Miles, M., and T. McCue. "Historic Returns and Institutional Real Estate Portfolios." *AREUEA Journal*, Vol. 10, No. 2 (Summer 1982), pp. 184-199.

The NCREIF Report. Published by the National Council of Real Estate Investment Fiduciaries. Washington, D.C.: Issue III (Spring 1984).

Peiser, R. B. "Risk Analysis in Land Development." *AREUEA Journal*, Vol. 12, No. 1 (Spring 1984), pp. 12-29.

Robichek, A. A., R. A. Cohn, and J. J. Pringle. "Returns on Alternative Investment Media and Implications for Portfolio Construction." *Journal of Business,* July 1972.

Smith, K. V. "Historical Returns of Real Estate Equity Portfolios." *The Investment Managers Handbook.* Homewood, Ill.: Dow Jones/Irwin, 1980.

Webb, J. R., and C. F. Sirmans. "Yields for Selected Types of Real Property vs. the Money and Capital Markets." *The Appraisal Journal,* April 1982, pp. 228-242.

Zerbst, R. H., and B. R. Cambon. "Real Estate Returns and Risks." *Journal of Portfolio Management,* Vol. 10, No. 3 (Spring 1984), pp. 5-20.

11 What Does the Stock Market Tell Us About Real Estate Returns?

Joseph Gyourko and Donald B. Keim

This paper analyzes the risks and returns of different types of real estate-related firms traded on the New York and American stock exchanges (NYSE and AMEX). We examine the relation between real estate stock portfolio returns and returns on a standard appraisal-based index, and find that lagged values of traded real estate portfolio returns can predict returns on the appraisal-based index after controlling for persistence in the appraisal series. The stock market reflects information about real estate markets that is later imbedded in infrequent property appraisals. Additional analysis suggests that the differences in the return and risk characteristics across different types of traded real estate firms can be explained in part by appealing to real estate market fundamentals relating to the degree of dependence of the real estate firm upon rental cash flows from existing buildings. These findings highlight the heterogeneity of securitized real estate-related firms.

Due to infrequent trading of properties and the absence of a centralized exchange for transactions, market-determined prices of commercial real estate are not readily available. This has led researchers to estimate real estate returns and risks. A number of methods have been used. Some of the earliest work employed hedonic techniques to estimate transactions prices for broader sets of properties that are not actually changing hands (e.g., see Hoag 1980; Miles, Cole and Guilkey 1990). In addition to normal misspecification concerns, the samples of transactions often are so small that trait price coefficients generally cannot be allowed to vary through time. There may be added worries about the representativeness of the sales prices. The issue is not whether the prices are accurately recorded, but whether they are typical arms-length transactions. With small samples, even a few extraordinary transactions (e.g., distressed sales) can affect estimated trait prices and the resulting property return index.

From *Journal of the American Real Estate and Urban Economics Association*, Vol. 20, No. 3 (1992), pp. 457–485. This is a revised version of a paper previously entitled, "The Risk and Return Characteristic of Stock Market-Based Real Estate Indexes and Their Relation to Appraisal-Based Returns." Much of this paper was done while Gyourko was visiting the Anderson Graduate School of Management at UCLA. We thank Marshall Blume, David Geltner, Peter Linneman, Rex Sinquefield, Sheridan Titman, a referee, and participants at presentations and workshops at the Winter 1989 AREUEA meetings, the 1990 Wharton Conference on Investment Management, UC-Berkeley, UCLA, and UC-Santa Barbara for helpful comments. Ed Nelling and Lixin Wang provided able research assistance. Financial support has been provided by the Wharton Real Estate Center and the Geewax-Terker Research Program in Financial Instruments. The usual caveat applies.

Beginning in the late 1980s, efforts were made to construct synthetic return series by applying cap rate data to rental income series (e.g., see Firstenberg, Ross and Zisler 1988; Wheaton and Torto 1989; Liu, et al. 1990). The property-level income data appear to be reliable so that the quality of these indexes rests on the quality of the cap rate series. Small errors in cap rates, either in the level of or in the timing of a change in the cap rate, can substantially alter return behavior.

Appraisal-based return series such as the Russell-NCREIF Property Index have also been widely studied.[1] These returns are suspect because of their low volatility relative to their significantly positive means. Ross and Zisler (1987a,b) and Geltner (1989b) were the first to detail the weaknesses of these data and to suggest ways to cleanse the returns of alleged appraisal-induced smoothing.

An alternative data source is equity real estate investment trust (REIT) returns.[2] Widely used by financial economists, stock market-based data often are viewed with suspicion in the real estate field. This is because REIT return volatility is materially higher than that for appraisal-based property series and REIT returns tend to be far more correlated with the stock market than with appraisal-based property return series (e.g., see Hartzell and Mengden 1986; Ross and Zisler 1987a,b).

This paper reexamines the returns of real estate stocks because we believe the stock market-based data provide more useful information on the nature of real estate returns than the existing literature suggests. Trading in the stocks of real estate-owning firms represents transactions-based data on the firms' values. Absent a huge upsurge in commercial property sales that would make hedonic indexes more reliable, the stock market is the only other source of such transactions-driven data. Ross and Zisler (1987b, 1991) note that, for a variety of reasons, not all stock price information bears directly on the value of the underlying properties owned by the firms. Nevertheless, our empirical findings provide convincing evidence that real estate stock returns contain much economically important and timely information about changing real estate market fundamentals.

Our first key finding deals with the ability of lagged equity REIT returns to predict current Russell-NCREIF returns. Because appraisals occur infrequently, appraisal-based series incorporate new information about market fundamentals with a lag. We document that the predictive impact of the lagged stock returns is particularly strong when they occur prior to the fourth quarter, which is the period of greatest appraisal activity. Our lagged REIT returns are constructed as compound annual returns so that a lagged end-of-the-year REIT return includes property market information that was known earlier in the year. The strong explanatory power of this particular lagged return almost certainly arises because the relatively high level of fourth quarter appraisal activity also is incorporating into the Russell-NCREIF Property Index much information that was public prior to the fourth quarter. This implies that the stock market signals changes in real estate values prior to the end of the year when large amounts of information are impounded into appraisal-based series such as the Russell-NCREIF Property Index.

The predictive power of the lagged REIT returns remains even after controlling for the well-known serial correlation in the Russell-NCREIF Property Index. We provide evidence that serial correlation at the fourth quarterly lag (i.e., one year out) is intimately related to an appraisal-induced fourth quarter effect. Research attempting to adjust appraisal returns for smoothing needs to control for this influence more precisely in order to obtain a better estimate of the 'true' variance in real property returns.

Our conclusions about the timeliness of the stock data are strengthened by the finding that equity REIT returns are *contemporaneously* correlated with the National Association of Realtors' (NAR) existing home price appreciation rate. The NAR series also is a transactions-based series. If performance in the housing and commercial property markets is partially driven by common factors, one might expect transactions-based returns from the two sectors to be contemporaneously correlated.[3]

The reliability of stock market-based data is reinforced by analysis of the risk and return characteristics of different types of traded real estate firms. While the equity REITs are owner-operators, others such as residential home builders and commercial developers primarily are builders, not owners, of property. With long-term leases on many commercial properties making rents a fixed cost for tenants, we would expect the cash flows of owner-operators to be less variable than those of their tenants over the business cycle. As producers of an extremely durable good, the builders' cash flows should be very cyclical. The different risks these two types of real estate firms face imply that the market *betas* of the builders should be much higher than those of the owner-operators. The data strongly confirm this intuition.

The outline of the paper is as follows. Section two details data sources, reports summary statistics, and documents a significant relation between lagged real estate stock portfolio returns and current returns on the Russell-NCREIF Property Index. The third section describes how changes in real estate market fundamentals and stock price behavior are likely to be related, reports summary statistics about the real estate stock indexes we create to test this relation, and analyzes the cross-sectional heterogeneity in the real estate stock index returns. A brief summary concludes the paper.

THE RELATION BETWEEN MARKET- AND APPRAISAL-BASED REAL-ESTATE INDEXES

Data Description and Summary Statistics. The Russell-NCREIF Property Index is a widely known appraisal-based series. Quarterly total returns are available beginning in the first quarter of 1978 [78(1)]. We use these data through 90(4), which corresponds to the final quarter for which we have stock return information. The *Annual Data Supplement to the NCREIF Real Estate Performance Report* (1989) provides details about this appraisal index.

The real estate stocks examined in this section are equity REITs. These stocks are investment trusts run by firms that own and operate real properties. Trust status allows escape from the corporate income tax in return for following rules dealing with issues such as income pass-throughs to investors. The National Association of Real Estate Investment Trusts' (NAREIT) *REIT Fact Book* details these provisions. Equity REITs are a subset of standard industry classification (SIC) 6799 which is used to identify them on the monthly return files of the Center for Research in Security Prices (CRSP). Standard and Poor's *Handbook of Real Estate Securities* and various issues of the *REIT Fact Book* and *REIT Source Book* also were employed to guide us in separating the equity REITs from the mortgage and hybrid REITs. Our equity REIT portfolio is composed of all qualifying firms with stock trading on the NYSE and AMEX, including those that were delisted for any reason. The number of stocks in the portfolio ranges from a low of fifteen in 1978 to a high of forty-seven in 1989 and 1990. For comparison with the

Russell-NCREIF series, quarterly returns are created by compounding the monthly returns from the CRSP files. All stock returns employed in the paper incorporate both dividends and capital gains.

Another real estate series that we examine is the NAR's monthly existing home price series obtained from The WEFA Group. These data run from January 1966 to December 1990. Prices are based on transactions in a large number of metropolitan statistical areas throughout the United States. This is not a quality-adjusted price series. Note also that this series is based solely on the appreciation rate and does not represent the total return because the implicit rent on owner-occupied housing is not observed. Quarterly appreciation rates are created by compounding the monthly observations.

Data were also collected on equity market movements, interest rate and term structure movements, and inflation. The S&P 500 index and a small stock index capture the broader equity market. The small stock series is based on the returns of the NYSE- and AMEX-listed firms that are among the smallest 20% in market capitalization on the NYSE only. Bond market variables include the returns on a portfolio of long-term Treasury bonds and on one-month and three-month Treasury bills. With the exception of the three-month Treasury bill which is from the CRSP government bond file, the stock and bond index variables are from Ibbotson and Sinquefield (1989) for the 1962–1987 period. Updates through 1990 are from Ibbotson & Associates. Monthly observations are compounded to produce quarterly returns.

The inflation variables in this section are derived from consumer price index (CPI) data. Expected inflation is based on an ARMA model estimated with quarterly CPI data. Experimentation showed that the structure of the process is not stable over time. Consequently, we estimated rolling quarterly forecasts with a new ARMA model specified each quarter. Unexpected inflation is the difference between actual inflation and the ARMA forecast.

Table 1 reports summary statistics for the quarterly excess returns for the asset categories described above. There are several interesting findings. Consistent with previous research, excess returns on the Russell-NCREIF index exhibit no significant contemporaneous correlation with the REIT portfolio or with other stock returns. The same is true with respect to housing appreciation. The appraisal-based returns are significantly negatively correlated with the excess return on long-term bonds, but not with inflation stocks.

Equity REIT returns are significantly positively correlated with the housing appreciation index ($\rho = .41$), providing evidence of a contemporaneous linkage between our two transactions-based real estate series. Also, equity REITs display a high correlation with stock market returns, especially the small stocks ($\rho = .82$), a finding that may reflect the fact that equity REITs themselves are small stocks. It is interesting to note, however, that the small stocks are also significantly related to the housing returns ($\rho = .48$). Such strong contemporaneous comovement between the small stocks and residential housing suggests a common factor in their returns. It is also noteworthy that the NAR's appreciation series is significantly positively correlated with unexpected inflation. This is consistent with the early finding by Fama and Schwert (1977) that residential real estate provides a relatively good hedge against unexpected inflation.

Market-Determined Variation in the Russell-NCREIF Property Index. The transactions-based (i.e., REITs and homes) and appraisal-based (i.e., Russell-NCREIF) real estate returns appear to have no relation to each other, but that appearance is mis-

Table 1 Summary Statistics
(Quarterly Data: 1978(1)–1990(4), n = 52)

Asset Category	Quarterly Percentage Excess Returns (Std. Dev.)	Russell-NCREIF	S&P500	Small Stocks	Long Bonds	Home Apprec.	Unexpected Inflation
Equity REITs	1.36 (8.46)	.10 (.49)	.65 (.00)	.82 (.00)	.43 (.00)	.41 (.00)	−.20 (.18)
Russell-NCREIF	.39 (1.40)		−.04 (.76)	.07 (.63)	−.35 (.01)	.16 (.27)	.07 (.65)
S&P500 Index	1.64 (8.26)			.83 (.00)	.39 (.00)	.28 (.04)	−.08 (.60)
Small Stock Index	1.94 (11.82)				.23 (.10)	.48 (.00)	−.00 (.98)
Long Bond Index	0.41 (7.52)					−.02 (.88)	−.44 (.00)
NAR Home Appreciation	−.85[a] (2.80)						.36 (.01)
Inflation	1.49[b] (1.03)						
90-day Treasury Bills	2.24[b] (0.70)						

Notes: [a]While the mean excess existing home appreciation rate is negative, the average quarter total appreciation rate over the 13-year period is 1.39%.

[b]Raw return or inflation rate.

Source: refer to text

leading. A key reason is that the appraisal process causes the Russell-NCREIF series to lag changes in property values. Appraisals can occur as frequently as every quarter, but often occur only every six or twelve months. Even with accurate appraisals, changes in real estate market conditions will only slowly be incorporated into the index if appraisals are infrequent and do not occur at the same time for all properties tracked in the index. This implies that *lagged* real estate-related stock returns and housing appreciation may be correlated with current period Russell-NCREIF returns.

To investigate this issue, current period Russell-NCREIF index returns (RNC_1) are regressed on current and lagged stock index returns while controlling for the well-known persistence and seasonality of the appraisal index. All regressions in the section use excess returns—total returns from which the three-month Treasury bill return has been subtracted. This reduces the persistence, but not the seasonality of the appraisal-based index.

It is important to control for appraisal-induced persistence in the Russell-NCREIF returns because regressing a series with strong persistence on lagged variables may spuriously indicate economically significant explanatory power for the right-hand side variables. Using the work of Ross and Zisler (1987a, 1991) and Geltner (1989b) as guides, experimentation with our longer time series determined the lags of the appraisal data controlled for below in equation (1). The impact of the fourth lag (RNC_{t-4}) always is strong and significant. Controlling for RNC_{t-4} weakens the otherwise strong first-order serial correlation. Longer lags were not found to be important.

With the Russell-NCREIF quarterly series available only since 1978, we use compounded lagged stock returns to preserve valuable degrees of freedom. A lagged return for stock index i ($I_{i,v(-1)}$) is defined to be the return over the four quarters constituting the calendar year immediately preceding current quarter t. Given Table 1's finding of a strong contemporaneous positive correlation between the returns on the equity REITs (I_{er}) and the small stock index (I_{ss}), we include current and lagged values of both these indexes in order to help assess whether any ability to explain the appraisal series is due to the influence of real estate versus that of the stock market in general.

The top panel of Table 2 reports estimated coefficients from equation (1),

$$RNC_t = \alpha_0 + \alpha_1 I_{er,t} + \alpha_2 I_{er,v(-1)} + \alpha_3 I_{ss,t} + \alpha_4 I_{ss,v(-1)} + \gamma_1 RNC_{t-1} + \gamma_2 RNC_{t-4} + \varepsilon_t, \quad (1)$$

where α_1 and γ_1 are coefficients and ε_t is the standard error term.

The findings indicate no independent influence for either the current or lagged small stock index after controlling for equity REIT returns.[4] Contemporaneous REIT returns ($I_{er,t}$) are not significantly correlated with the Russell-NCREIF returns, but the prior calendar year's equity REIT return ($I_{er,v(-1)}$) is a significant predictor of the current period appraisal return even after controlling for serial correlation in the appraisal se-

Table 2 Regression of Russell-NCREIF Returns on Current and Lagged Transactions-Based Series (1979(1)–1990(4); n = 48)

Panel 1
(1) $RNC_t = \chi_0 + \chi_1 I_{er,t} + \chi_2 I_{er,v(-1)} + \chi_3 I_{ss,t} + \chi_4 I_{ss,v(-1)} + \gamma_1 RNC_{t-1} + \gamma_2 RNC_{t-4} + \varepsilon_t.$

Intercept	Equity REIT Return ($I_{er,t}$)	Lagged Equity REIT Return ($I_{er,v(-1)}$)	Small Stock Return ($I_{ss,t}$)	Lagged Small Stock Return ($I_{ss,v(-1)}$)	Adjusted R^2	D–W Statistic	ρ_1
−.0034°°	−.0076	.0474°°	.0096	−.0057	.48	1.96	.01
(.0016)	(.0304)	(.0180)	(.0238)	(.0137)			

Panel 2
(2) $RNC_t = \chi_0 + \chi_1 I_{er,t} + \chi_2 (I_{er,t} \cdot QTR4) + \chi_3 I_{er,v(-1)} + \chi_4 (I_{er,v(-1)} \cdot QTR4) + \gamma_1 RNC_{t-1} + \gamma_2 RNC_{t-4} + \varepsilon_t.$

Intercept	Equity REIT Return ($I_{er,t}$)	Equity REIT Return, 4th Qtr. Impact ($I_{er,t} \cdot QTR4$)	Lagged Equity REIT Return ($I_{er,v(-1)}$)	Lagged Equity REIT Return, 4th Qtr. Impact ($I_{er,v(-1)} \cdot QTR4$)	Adjusted R^2	D–W Statistic	ρ_1
−.0025	−.0016	.0293	.0300°°	.0385°°	.54	2.06	−.04
(.0016)	(.0191)	(.0366)	(.0094)	(.0177)			

Panel 3
(3) $RNC_t = \chi_0 + \chi_1 (I_{er,t} \cdot QTR4) + \chi_2 I_{er,v(-1)} + \chi_3 (I_{er,v(-1)} \cdot QTR4) + \chi_4 I_{h,v(-1)} + \beta_5 I_{lb,t} + \gamma_1 RNC_{t-1} + \gamma_2 RNC_{t-4} + \varepsilon_t.$

Intercept	Equity REIT Return, 4th Qtr. Impact ($I_{er,t} \cdot QTR4$)	Lagged Equity REIT Return ($I_{er,v(-1)}$)	Lagged Equity REIT Return, 4th Qtr. Impact ($I_{er,v(-1)} \cdot QTR4$)	Lagged Housing App. Index ($I_{h,v(-1)}$)	Long Bond Return ($I_{lb,t}$)	Adjusted R^2	D–W Statistic	ρ_1
.0017	.0623°°	.0249°°	.0383°°	.0836°°	−.0227	.61	2.11	−.06
(.0021)	(.0300)	(.0092)	(.0162)	(.0336)	(.0174)			

Notes: Standard errors in parentheses; °°denotes significance at the .05 level or better.
Source: refer to text

ries. No additional lags were found to be influential. We believe that the differential predictive ability of the REIT portfolio is due to the fact that those firms own commercial properties similar to those tracked in the Russell-NCREIF Property Index.[5] This predictive relation is evident even though data limitations prevent us from controlling for REIT leverage.

While informative, the specification in (1) does not fully illuminate the timeliness with which the stock market impounds information about real property markets. Seasonality in the Russell-NCREIF returns, apparently induced by the nonuniform distribution of appraisal activity over the calendar year, can be exploited to increase the REITs' predictive power. There typically is increased fourth quarter appraisal activity, possibly for financial-reporting reasons. This implies that a relatively large amount of information available to market participants prior to the fourth quarter is being impounded into the Russell-NCREIF series via end-of-the-year appraisals. It also means that lagged compound returns occurring just prior to the fourth quarter should be especially influential predictors of the appraisal index. To test this hypothesis, we estimate equation (2) with the equity REIT returns retained from (1), and include interaction terms to control for differential fourth quarter effects (QTR4 is a 0 1 dummy variable for the fourth quarter),

$$RNC_t = \alpha_0 + \alpha_1 I_{er,t} + \alpha_2 (I_{er,t} \cdot QTR4) + \alpha_3 I_{er,v(-1)} + \alpha_4 (I_{er,v(-1)} \cdot QTR4) + \gamma_1 RNC_{t-1} + \gamma_2 RNC_{t-4} + \varepsilon_t. \quad (2)$$

The results are presented in the second panel of Table 2. There still is no significant contemporaneous correlation between REIT stock and appraisal returns. The α_2 coefficient on the current period interaction term ($I_{er,t} \cdot QTR4$) is positive, but is not significantly different from zero. The significantly positive α_3 ($t = 3.20$) indicates that, on average, equity REIT returns over the previous calendar year ($I_{er,v(-1)}$) do help explain current period Russell-NCREIF returns. Particularly interesting is the α_4 coefficient ($t = 2.17$) on the lagged interaction term that implies lagged returns are even more influential when the predicted return occurs in the fourth quarter. This is precisely the result one would expect if the stock market was incorporating information about real estate market fundamentals in a more timely manner than possible for the Russell-NCREIF series given the lags and seasonality in the appraisal process.

These returns do not appear to be the result of spurious correlations with other market-determined variables whose own returns also are correlated with the appraisal returns. Table 1 reported that Russell-NCREIF excess returns have a significantly negative contemporaneous correlation with excess long bond returns ($I_{lb,t}$). Investors may view a more steeply sloped yield curve as indicative of higher real rates. If so, appraisers would capitalize future rental flows at higher discount rates, lowering property values. Table 1 does not report correlations with lagged returns, but it is the case that the previous year's housing appreciation rate ($I_{h,v(-1)}$) is significantly positively correlated with the current period Russell-NCREIF return. This correlation may reflect the same forces that lead the previous year's equity REIT returns to forecast the Russell-NCREIF return. Alternatively, the housing appreciation index may proxy for different aspects of business cycle conditions than do changes in the returns on commercial property-owning firms.

To investigate the independent influences of these factors, we estimated equation (3) which modifies equation (2) by dropping the always insignificant $I_{er,t}$ term and adding the yield curve (I_{lb}) and lagged housing ($I_{h,v(-1)}$) variables that had significant simple correlations with the appraisal-based return.

$$RNC_t = \alpha_0 + \alpha_1(I_{er,t}°QTR4) + \alpha_2 I_{er,v(-1)} + \alpha_3(I_{er,v(-1)}°QTR4) \\ + \alpha_4 I_{h,v(-1)} + \alpha_5 I_{lb,t} + \gamma_1 RNC_{t-1} + \gamma_2 RNC_{t-4} + \varepsilon_t. \qquad (3)$$

The results are presented in the third panel of Table 2.[6] The size of the coefficient on current REIT portfolio returns realized in the fourth quarter ($I_{er,t}°QTR4$) more than doubles from that in the second panel and is now highly significant. The estimated value of .0623 implies that a 10% increase in the contemporaneous fourth quarter equity REIT return about its mean of 1.36% is associated with six-tenths of a basis point increase in the excess Russell-NCREIF index return. The mean excess return in the Russell-NCREIF index over all quarters is .39%. For the thirteen fourth quarters in our sample, the mean Russell-NCREIF excess return is .98%. (The standard deviation is also higher in the fourth quarter.)

Coefficients on the lagged REIT portfolio returns are little changed and remain significant at standard confidence levels. The estimated α_2 = .0249 implies that a 10% increase about the mean lagged compounded annual REIT return of 8.58% is associated with a 2-basis-point rise in the Russell-NCREIF index return. Based on the significant estimate of α_3 = .0383 on $I_{er,v(-1)}°QTR4$, a 10% increase in lagged returns occurring prior to the fourth quarter is associated with an additional 2.5-basis-point rise in the Russell-NCREIF index return. The results in panel 3 of Table 2 also show a significant independent influence for lagged compounded housing appreciation ($I_{h,v(-1)}$). Its relative marginal impact is similar to that for lagged REIT returns. The estimated α_4 = .0836 implies that a 10% increase in existing home sales price appreciation is associated with a 2-basis-point rise in the appraisal-based return. Increasingly steep yield curves depress Russell-NCREIF returns, but the estimated coefficient on $I_{lb,t}$ is significant only at the .20 level. Including the housing and bond market variables raises the adjusted R^2 by about 13% to .61. Finally, if a modified version of (3) is estimated that includes only predetermined variables (that is, only lagged and lagged interaction terms on the right-hand side), the adjusted R^2 = .58. Controlling for the serial correlation of the Russell-NCREIF index, much of its variation can be explained by transactions-based information that is available *prior* to the quarter during which the Russell-NCREIF return is measured.

BEYOND REITS: EXTRACTING MORE INFORMATION ABOUT REAL ESTATE FROM THE STOCK MARKET

It should not be surprising that stock market and real estate returns are related since common factors probably influence returns in both markets. Zeckhauser and Silverman (1983) report that roughly one-quarter of corporate value is real estate-related in nature. This suggests that at least part of the variance in stock returns should be related to changes in the value of corporate-owned land and structures. Some of this real estate-induced variance may be orthogonal to the firms' core business risk, but some almost certainly is correlated with that risk. In general, that part of property market risk associated with the health of the economy should result in a positive correlation between property returns and returns on the broader market.

For office and industrial property markets in particular, institutional factors such as multi-year leases are likely to limit the strength of the positive correlation between property and stock market returns. Gyourko and Linneman (1990) argue that rental flows from buildings with good quality tenants should be smoother than their tenants' own cash flows (not necessarily their smoothed earnings or dividends) over the business cycle. The reason is that rents are a fixed cost to tenants and cannot easily be altered in the short run. Even a building with tenants in cyclical industries will have a relatively stable rental income flow as long as the probability of tenant bankruptcy over the cycle is low and the exercise of space options on the upside of the cycle is limited.[7] The fixities introduced by long-term leases suggest that the strength of the covariance of a real estate stock with the market should be a decreasing function of the degree of the real estate firm's dependence on the cash flows from tenants in existing properties.

Contrast contractors and developers who only build structures with owner-operators of structures who do no building. One would expect the pure builders to have higher stock market betas. Building activity should be strongly positively correlated with corporate cash flows because businesses' demand for added space falls when equity prices drop. Construction activity is a leading indicator with a high amplitude. Purely property owning firms should have lower stock market betas because their cash flows are more closely linked with the rental income flows from existing buildings. Tenants have to pay rents even when the demand for their product drops, and they do not have to pay higher rents when the demand for their product increases.

The remainder of this section analyzes the cross sectional heterogeneity in the returns of three portfolios of real estate stocks. Evidence of significant heterogeneity in covariances with the market along the lines just suggested would strengthen our conclusion that the stock market accurately reflects information about real estate. For comparison purposes with previous research, we also briefly discuss interest rate and inflation impacts on real estate stock returns.

Data. Portfolios of real estate-related stocks trading on the NYSE and the AMEX are constructed with data from the CRSP monthly return files. We began with a masterlist of real estate-related firms drawn from Standard and Poor's *Handbook of Real Estate Securities* and then searched through the CRSP data, identifying additional real estate stocks via four-digit SIC codes for three different categories of real estate firms.

The first group of firms is general contractors (SIC 1521-1542). This category includes mostly residential builders who build for contract, not on their own account as speculative builders.[8] Our second category contains land subdividers and developers (SIC 6552). If these firms do own properties, they tend to relinquish them soon after development is finished. The equity REITs described in section 2.1 comprise the third category examined.[9] Each portfolio includes firms that failed or were delisted for other reasons. A complete list of firms is available upon request.

These three groups do not include all traded real estate-related firms. Many restaurant and vacation businesses have quite valuable real property holdings. Real estate industry suppliers such as lumber and wood products firms might also be considered real estate-related firms. We focus on the three groups noted above for two reasons. First, we can identify them in the CRSP files via their SIC codes as being primarily in the real estate business. More importantly, our strong priors about the relative strength of the relation between these stocks and the stock market provide an appropriate foundation for further examination of whether the stock market accurately reflects information about real estate fundamentals.[10]

Portfolio returns are constructed by combining securities within the same SIC groups. We compute equal- and value-weighted monthly portfolio returns from August 1962 to December 1990. The results using both value-weighted and equal-weighted returns are quantitatively and qualitatively similar since there is relatively little cross sectional diversity in market capitalization across firms within a given real estate category. The simple correlation between any pair of the three groups of equal- and value-weighted portfolio returns ranges from .8 to over .9. Unfortunately, market capitalization data are missing for many of our firms over the first ten to fifteen years of the sample. Consequently, we report results based only on the equal-weighted portfolio returns.

Table 3 lists the maximum and minimum number of stocks in any portfolio throughout the sample period. Due to the very limited number of traded real estate firms prior to the mid-1970s, we present results in the text only for the post-1974 time period. Tables providing analogous findings for the full 1962–1990 period and for the 1962–1974 subperiod are available upon request.

Summary Statistics. Summary statistics for the three real estate stock portfolio returns, the existing home appreciation rate, and for various stock and bond indexes are reported in Table 4. The statistics are based upon monthly excess returns defined as total returns less the one-month T-bill return, unless noted.

There is substantial variation in mean excess returns across the real estate stock portfolios, with the contractors' returns exceeding even the small stock index return. The general contractor and commercial developer portfolios have coefficients of variation higher than those found for the two broad stock indexes. The simple correlations also reported in Table 4 document the substantial comovement of the different real estate-related stock portfolio returns. Note that each real estate stock portfolio's return is also significantly positively correlated with existing home appreciation, albeit less strongly than with securitized real estate.

The returns on the real estate series are also strongly positively correlated with the broader stock market. The real estate stock portfolio return correlations with the small stock index are particularly high, ranging as high as .89 for the developers. Most of the real estate firms are relatively small in terms of market capitalization as Figures 1–3 illustrate for each real estate stock portfolio. Figure 1, for example, plots the annual capitalization values for the median general contractor firm against the analogous values for the 10%, 20%, and 50% fractiles of the market capitalization distribution for all NYSE and AMEX firms.

Table 3 Minimum and Maximum Number of Stocks in Real Estate Portfolios

Real Estate Stock Portfolio (SIC Codes)	Aug. 1962–Dec. 1974 Minimum (Date)	Maximum (Date)	Jan. 1975–Dec. 1990 Minimum (Date)	Maximum (Date)
General Contractors (1521–1542)	2 (12/62)[a]	14 (1/73)	11 (1/76)	26 (5/88)
Subdividers/Developers (6552)	16 (2/68)	45 (11/72)	22 (11/90)	38 (1/75)
Equity REITs	3 (8/62)	16 (8/73)	15 (1/76)	47 (8/90)

Notes: [a]Numbers in parentheses are the dates with the month listed first and then the year. This is the first date at which the relevant minimum or maximum occurs.

Source: refer to text

Table 4 Summary Statistics: Various Asset Categories
(January 1975–December 1990: 192 observations)

Asset Category (SIC Code)	Monthly Percentage Excess Return (Std. Dev.)	6552	Equity REITs	Existing Home Appreciation	LTGOV	S&P500	Small Stocks	Unexpected Inflation
General Contractors (1521–1542)	1.48 (11.88)	.85 (.00)	.77 (.00)	.26 (.00)	.27 (.00)	.66 (.00)	.82 (.00)	−.23 (.00)
Subdividers/ Developers (6552)	.85 (9.64)		.85 (.00)	.27 (.00)	.20 (.00)	.63 (.00)	.89 (.00)	−.17 (.02)
Equity REITs	.80 (5.17)			.26 (.00)	0.23 (.00)	.59 (.00)	.83 (.00)	−.24 (.00)
Existing Home Appreciation	−.12 (1.51)				−.01 (.89)	.26 (.00)	.30 (.00)	−.03 (.72)
Long-term Treasury Bond Index (LTGOV)	.17 (3.50)					.37 (.00)	.21 (.00)	−.26 (.00)
S&P500 Index	.64 (4.64)						.78 (.00)	−.19 (.01)
Small Stock Index	1.10 (6.65)							−.19 (.01)
30-day Treasury Bills	.66[a] (.22)							
Inflation (π)	.50[a] (.34)							

Notes: [a]Raw return or inflation rate
[b]Numbers in parentheses convey probability of observing stronger correlation under $H_0: \rho = 0$.
Source: refer to text

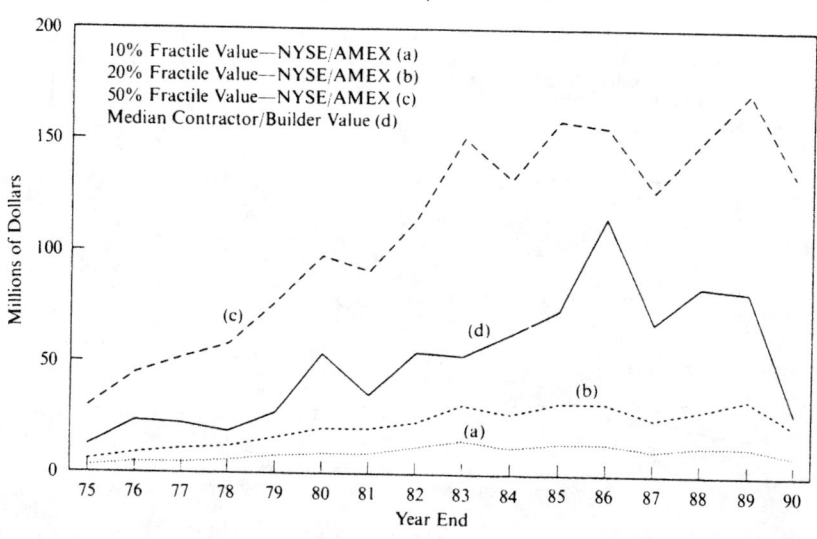

Figure 1 Market Capitalization Values
General Contractors and Builders (1521–1542)

Figure 2 Market Capitalization Values
Developers and Subdividers (6552)

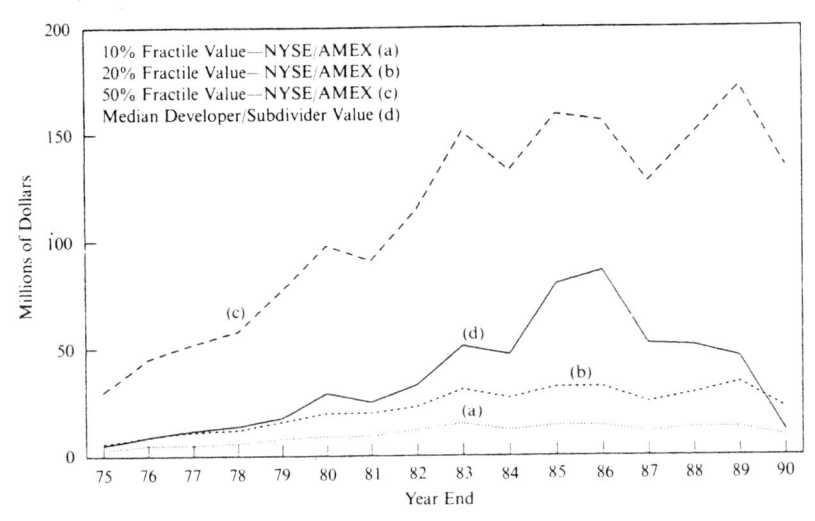

Given that our real estate securities are stocks and that many are small capitalization issues, the strong correlation with the S&P 500 index and the small stock index is expected and, therefore, need not represent any linkage between real estate market fundamentals and stock market valuation. However, the significantly positive correlation of the other transactions-based (but nonsecuritized) real estate return measure, existing home appreciation, with both the S&P 500 index return ($\rho = .26$) and the small stock index return ($\rho = .30$) suggest that common forces influence both real estate and corporate value in qualitatively similar ways.[11]

Figure 3 Market Capitalization Values
Equity REITs (6799)

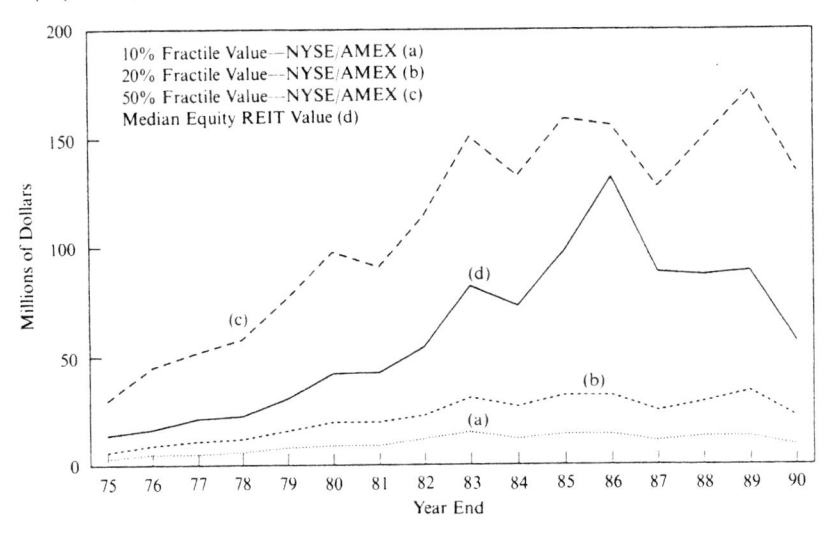

Table 4 also provides information about the relation of real estate returns with the bond market and inflation. The three real estate stock portfolio returns exhibit significantly positive correlations with excess returns on Treasury bonds. Those correlations are lower than the simple correlation between the bond market and S&P 500 returns. Unlike the real estate stocks, the housing market series is almost completely uncorrelated with the long bond excess returns. Finally, the excess returns on each of the real estate stock portfolios are negatively correlated with unanticipated inflation. The NAR's home price appreciation series is only slightly positively correlated with unexpected inflation in these monthly data.[12]

Return Variability Patterns Across Different Real Estate Sectors. To analyze the heterogeneity in real estate return covariances with the market, we estimated the following market equation for each real estate portfolio.

$$I_{i,t} = \beta_0 + \beta_1 I_{sp,t} + \beta_2 I_{sp,t-1} + \delta_{t,f}, \tag{4}$$

where $I_{i,t}$ is the monthly excess return on real estate portfolio i in period t, $I_{sp,t}$ is the monthly excess return on the S&P 500 index in period t and $\delta_{t,f}$ is the standard error term. Lagged market returns ($I_{sp,t-1}$) are included because the real estate stocks are small and likely trade infrequently (see, e.g., Scholes and Williams 1977; Dimson 1979).[13] The results are presented in Table 5. Note that the specification was estimated over the complete 1975–1990 sample period as well as for two eight-year long subperiods, 1975–1982 and 1983–1990. This was done to determine whether the pattern of decreasing betas over time, reported for equity REITs in Hartzell and Mengden (1987), persists in our longer sample period. We find a similar pattern for both REITs and other real estate stocks. Changing the breakpoint in the data as much as a few years does not alter the pattern of results.

Before examining the heterogeneity in market betas, it is interesting to note that the previous month's market excess return tends to help predict this month's return for the real estate portfolios. The significant influence of the lag arises primarily in the second subperiod. Evidence of significant *monthly* cross-autocorrelations is unusual. We are not precisely sure why this pattern holds for most real estate or why it gained strength in the mid-1980s. One possibility is the addition of more relatively small capitalization stocks in our sample in the 1980s. Such firms are most likely to exhibit non-trading. The mid-1980s did see a marked increase in REIT initial public offerings, many of which were relatively small capitalization issues (see Figure 1 on p. 22 of Nelling, et al. 1992).

More important for the purposes of this paper, the rank ordering of the strengths of the different firms' covariance with the market is precisely as anticipated. For the full sample period, the general contractors and developers who produce very durable real properties have *betas* significantly in excess of one. The REIT portfolio's market *beta* is significantly less than one. The appropriate F-statistics allow us to conclude with very high confidence that the contractors' and developers' market *betas* (both for the current period alone and for the sum of the current period plus lagged *betas*) are larger than that for the equity REITs. While the estimated *betas* for all three portfolios fall over time, the rank ordering of the covariances and conclusions about statistically significant differences between the builder and REIT *betas* hold for each subperiod.[14]

With respect to the absolute levels of the portfolio *betas*, the contractors' and developers' *betas* are at least equal to the consumer durables industry β of 1.29 and the

Table 5 Market Model Regressions:

(4) $I_{i,t} = \beta_0 + \beta_1 I_{sp,t} + \beta_2 I_{sp,t-1} + \delta_{i,t}$

	General Contractors			Subdividers/Developers			Equity REITs			Housing Appreciation		
	1975–1990	1975–1982	1983–1990	1975–1990	1975–1982	1983–1990	1975–1990	1975–1982	1983–1990	1975–1990	1975–1982	1983–1990
Intercept (%)	.16	2.08°°	−1.75	−.13	1.61°°	−1.87°°	.33	1.10°°	−.45°	−.19	.03	−.43°°
	(.65)	(1.02)	(.68)	(.55)	(.90)	(.51)	(.31)	(.51)	(.26)	(.11)	(.15)	(.15)
S&P 500 Excess Return ($I_{sp,t}$)	1.68°°	2.14°°	1.28°°	1.29°°	1.71°°	.94°°	.66°°	.93°°	.43°°	.08°°	.07	.09°°
	(.14)	(.22)	(.14)	(.12)	(.20)	(.10)	(.07)	(.11)	(.05)	(.02)	(.03)	(.03)
Lagged S&P 500 Excess Return ($I_{sp,t-1}$)	.39°°	.29	.50°°	.24°°	.25	.26°°	.08	.06	.11°°	.03	−.00	.06°°
	(.14)	(.22)	(.14)	(.12)	(.20)	(.10)	(.07)	(.11)	(.05)	(.02)	(.03)	(.03)
No. of obs.	192	96	96	192	96	96	192	96	96	192	96	96
Adj. R^2	.45	.49	.50	.40	.44	.48	.35	.41	.41	.07	.03	.11
DW	1.66	1.76	1.81	1.66	2.04	1.20	1.90	2.20	1.67	1.82	1.72	1.97
ρ_1	.05	.03	.09	.07	−.12	.38	.02	−.22	.13	.09	.14	.01

Notes: ªStandard errors in parentheses

°°denotes significance at the .05 level or better; °denotes significance at the .01 level or better

Source: refer to text

construction industry β of 1.20 estimated with respect to the value-weighted CRSP index in Breeden, Gibbons and Litzenberger (1989). This is true even in the 1983–1990 period if the developers' current and lagged *betas* are summed. The equity REIT portfolio's β is quite small relative to the other industry β's reported in Breeden, Gibbons and Litzenberger (1989). They find that utilities have a $\beta = .75$ with the food and tobacco industry having $\beta = .76$. The long-term leases on real properties apparently do substantially reduce the covariance with the market.

The subperiod analysis indicates that Hartzell's and Mengden's (1987) conclusion about the fall in equity REIT covariance with the broader market still holds. The REIT portfolio *beta* in the 1975–1982 period is insignificantly different from 1. The null of $\beta = 1$ can be confidently rejected for the 1983–1990 period (even if current and lagged *betas* are summed). The number of equity REITs increases substantially over time so that greater diversification is being achieved. Accumulated investor experience with equity REITs and the relative stability of their underlying rental flows also may have played a role in the declining covariance with the market. Moreover, the 1975–82 period immediately follows an interest rate-related downturn in the mortgage REIT market that was so dramatic that it negatively impacted equity REITs, too. Note that covariance with the market has also fallen substantially for the two builder portfolios. Part of the reason may be that the 1983–1990 period does not contain any recession years, which always are times of substantial drops in construction activity. It also may be the case that both the listed homebuilders and commercial developers took deliberate actions to reduce their return variance over the business cycle. There may be increasing ownership of real properties and the rental flows associated with ownership that is indicated by the contractor and developer classifications. Other factors not closely related to real estate also may be at work. This possibility is indicated by the fact that the covariance with the S&P 500 of our small stock index also falls through time. The sums of the current and lagged market *betas* if the small index is the dependent variable in (4) are 1.42 and 1.14 for the 1975–82 and 1983–90 subperiods, respectively.

We are unable to determine precisely how much of the explanatory power of the stock market is due to common factors affecting both the real estate and general business markets versus purely stock market trading-related factors (i.e., program trading of broad market baskets of stocks that include real estate-related firms). That some is due to common factors driving both markets again is suggested by the significant stock market *beta* for the appreciation rate on existing homes, even though the explained variation is much smaller for this nonsecuritized real estate measure (see the far right-hand side columns of Table 5).

Another interesting pattern in the results of estimating (4) is the significance of the intercept terms, often interpreted as measuring abnormal performance relative to the market. After controlling for covariance with the market, all the real estate stock portfolios earned significantly positive "abnormal" returns in the 1975–82 period, with the general contractors earning an added 2.08% per month. This pattern reverses itself in the 1983–1990 period. Both stock and housing portfolios earn relatively low returns in the 1980s given their comovement with the broader market. Over the entire 1975–1990 period, these patterns counterbalance each other so that there are no statistically significant intercept terms.[15]

Inefficiency explanations aside, the large and significant estimated intercepts over periods as long as eight years intimate that other factors may play a role in determining real estate stock returns. The empirical literature cited in footnote 2 has investigated the influence of various other factors (primarily with respect to REITs). For comparison purposes with the existing literature, we estimated a multifactor model that expanded (4) to include term structure, inflation, and risk premium variables similar to those used in Chan, Hendershott and Sanders (1991) recent study of equity REITs.[16]

The regression results are not presented for space reasons, but we close with a brief discussion of the pattern of findings. First, there is no evidence of any significant influence, independent of the stock market, for changes in the term structure. The same holds for a default-risk premium variable defined as the return difference between a junk bond portfolio and the long-term Treasury index. Increases in unexpected inflation depress excess returns in each real estate portfolio, with the impacts being significant at the .10 level for the general contractors and the equity REITs. However, the R^2's from the multifactor model are only marginally higher than those reported in Table 5 for equation (4).

It is noteworthy that some of these findings are at variance with those reported in Chan, Hendershott and Sanders (1991). The key difference between the specifications is our use of a stock market variable in lieu of industrial production. The inclusion of the stock index results in substantially higher R^2's. Consistent with their results, the statistical significance of the term structure and inflation variables increases when we exclude the stock market variable. Both expected and unexpected inflation variables become statistically significant in such a specification. However, the risk structure variable never has a significant impact on any real estate stock portfolio's returns. The R^2 for a regression including only term structure and inflation variables typically is about .10.[17]

CONCLUSIONS

The stock market provides a ready and useful source of transactions-based data with which to analyze real estate market risk and returns. Important information about changing market fundamentals appears to be incorporated into equity REIT returns before appraisers impound the information into the Russell-NCREIF Property Index. This probably is due to lags and seasonality in the appraisal process. Lagged equity REIT returns are particularly strong predictors of the Russell-NCREIF series' fourth quarter returns. The stock market also appears to accurately reflect information about the risks and returns faced by different types of real estate firms. The market *betas* of firms specializing in construction were significantly higher than those of firms that specialized in owning and operating existing properties. This is what one would expect given that long-term leases make rents a fixed cost over the business cycle for many tenants.

NOTES

[1] The letters NCREIF stand for the National Council of Real Estate Investment Fiduciaries. Prior to the fourth quarter of 1989, this index was called the Frank Russell Company (FRC) Property Index.

[2] There has been a substantial amount of research into REITs. General studies of REIT investment performance date back at least to Smith & Shulman (1976) and Davidson and Palmer (1978). Building upon these efforts have been Patel and Olsen (1984), Kuhle, Walter and Wurtzebach (1986), Hartzell and Mengden (1986, 1987), Titman and Warga (1986), Kuhle (1987), Chen and Tzang (1988), and Sagalyn (1990). Lee and Kau (1987) study REIT dividend policies. Allen & Sirmans (1987) investigate REIT performance in takeover settings. Chan, Hendershott and Sanders (1991) and Liu and Mei (1991) are among the most recent investigations into REIT return behavior.

[3] We say 'might' here because, even with common factors, one could justify a lack of contemporaneous correlation with an imperfect information story. Sellers of homes and/or office buildings rationally may not adjust prices equivalently in response to exogenous shocks to the economy. The optimal solution to many signal processing problems is to wait until more knowledge is available. If optimal waiting periods are different across markets, no contemporaneous correlation need exist even with high quality transactions data.

[4] The results are virtually identical if the excess return on the S&P 500 index is used in place of the small stock excess return.

[5] It is noteworthy that Geltner (1989b, 1991b) finds no significant correlation with lagged stock returns. Not only do we find a significant influence for lagged equity REIT returns, but if I_{ert} and $I_{ert(-1)}$ are dropped from (1), both the lagged small stock ($I_{ss,v(-1)}$) and S&P 500 ($I_{sp,v(-1)}$) index returns are statistically significant predictors of the Russell-NCREIF returns. There are a number of potential reasons for the different findings. (We appreciate Geltner's help via private correspondence in identifying the differences.) Foremost among the differences is time series length. Our relatively small number of 48 usable observations represents a one-third increase over Geltner's (1989b) sample size and a doubling of his 1991b sample. We also use excess returns while Geltner created real returns deflated by the consumer price index. The specifications are also different in that Geltner used six individual quarterly lags of the stock index returns on the right-hand side of (1) in lieu of our single lagged compound return. (His 1989b work also investigated the correlation with a consumption series, but not with the small stock index.) When we estimated Geltner's lag structure with our longer series, we could not reject the null that the sum of the *betas* on the current and lagged S&P 500 returns was zero. However, we could reject at high confidence levels the same null with respect to current and lagged small stock returns. The sum of the *betas* for the current and lagged small stock returns was .20. The analogous sum when only current and six lagged equity REIT returns are used on the right-hand side is .21. Giliberto (1990) does report significant correlations between lagged equity REIT residuals and current Russell-NCREIF returns. However, he does not control for any persistence in the appraisal series and he also purged the real estate indexes of all correlation with the stock and bond markets. In the next section, we argue that common factors are likely to influence both corporate and real estate returns. Thus, we are wary of purging the real estate returns of all stock and bond market influences.

[6] Dropping the I_{ert} variable does not alter any other coefficient in a material way. Experimentation also showed there not to be differential fourth quarter impacts for the bond market and housing variables.

[7] Special features of leases on retail properties help to make their rental flows more procyclical. In addition to the base rent tenants pay, retail leases typically contain 'overage' clauses that make total lease payments an increasing function of store sales. Retail sales themselves are procyclical.

[8] Major contractors for bridges and other infrastructure are not in this group. The government classifies them elsewhere.

[9] There are other forms who primarily are owner-operators of properties but are not organized in the trust form. They have SIC codes ranging from 6512–6519. Unfortunately, very few traded owner-operators choose to organize without trust status. From 1975–1979, there is only one firm in the sample. Until 1987, the number always is less than ten. While we do not report results for this portfolio because of the very small sample size, it turns out that the returns on this small sample of non-REIT owner-operators behave very much like those on the equity REITs. This gives us added confidence that the special REIT provisions with regard to pass-throughs of accounting income are not masking the true performance of the underlying properties that would occur if they were managed unhindered by trust restrictions.

[10] Knowledge of the differences in return behavior for different types of real estate firms is scarce. Davidson and Palmer (1978) and Sagalyn (1990) have analyzed the investment performance of different types of real estate firms. Our sample is much larger than that studied by Davidson and Palmer (1978), whose early to mid-1970s sample focused on homebuilders in addition to equity REITs. Sagalyn's (1990) sample of non-REIT firms combines homebuilders, developers, and investment companies. However, her sample is composed exclusively of firms that survived over a fifteen-year period.

[11] The NAR appreciation series contains significant seasonals as has been observed for small stocks. There are peaks in January and in June, with the summer seasonal slightly stronger. We investigated whether the significant positive correlation with the small stock index return is due solely to common seasonality by regressing the small stock excess return on excess housing appreciation, a dichotomous dummy variable for January, and the interaction of the excess appreciation rate with the January dummy. The excess appreciation variable remains significant even when the January dummy is included. The interaction term's coefficient is small

and insignificantly different from zero. Thus, existing home appreciation is contemporaneously positively correlated with the small stock index throughout the year. The same holds for the S&P 500 index which, of course, does not contain a January seasonal.

[12] Because the Treasury bill return has been subtracted to compute excess returns, we do not report correlations with expected inflation. The one-month Treasury bill returns should reflect expected inflation.

[13] Many attribute the ability of this period's large stock returns to predict next period's stock returns to the relatively slower assimilation of information into the prices of small stocks that trade less frequently. Others have argued that such lead-lag effects cannot be caused by the levels of nontrading observed in the data (Lo and MacKinlay 1990).

[14] The rank ordering of market *betas* is preserved if the small stock index is used as the market proxy in lieu of the S&P 500. Conclusions about statistically significant differences in *betas* also remain unchanged. Given that the real estate firms tend to be small capitalization issues, the small stock index has greater explanatory power. The R^2's rise by 40%–50% depending upon the real estate portfolio. Lagged small stock index returns are significant at the .05 level only for the general contractors and that coefficient is less than half of its lagged S&P 500 coefficient of .39 in Table 5.

[15] This pattern does not hold if current and lagged values of the small stock index are used on the right-hand side of (4) in lieu of the S&P 500 index. In that case, there are no significantly positive intercept terms in the 1975–82 period. In the 1983–90 period, only the subdivider-developer and housing appreciation intercept terms still are significantly negative. Even they are smaller in absolute value (i.e., subdivider/developer intercept is −1.11% per month; housing appreciation is −.33% per month).

[16] Multifactor specifications were estimated in which the bond market, risk premium, and inflation variables were constructed to be orthogonal to the stock market variables. Others were estimated without being orthogonalized. The findings do not vary across specifications. It is also the case that adding variables not constructed to be orthogonal to the stock market still leaves virtually unchanged the estimated stock *betas* and their standard errors.

[17] Chan, Hendershott and Sanders (1991) and Barker (1990) also find that REIT returns are related to changes in the discount on closed-end funds. Equity REITs being small stocks may be a key part of the story behind the result. The discount is defined as the difference between the price of the fund and the net asset value of the fund's underlying securities. Relying on the investor sentiment hypothesis of Lee, Shleifer and Thaler (1991), the papers attribute the relation between REIT returns and discounts on closed-end funds to changes in investor sentiment. Lee, Shleifer and Thaler (1991) report that changes in the discount on closed-end funds are significantly related to small stock returns movements. One likely reason for this is the fact that closed-end funds themselves can almost always be classified as small stocks. Therefore, it is not surprising that the behavior of closed-end fund prices relative to their net asset values (which are dominated by larger capitalization stocks) should mimic the behavior of the small stock premium. In fact, Brauer and Chag (1990) document a January seasonal in the time series of discounts for closed-end funds.

REFERENCES

Allen, P. R. and C. F. Sirmans. 1987. An Analysis of Gains to Acquiring Firm's Shareholders: The Special Case of REITs. *Journal of Financial Economics* 18 (March): 174–84.

Barker, D. 1990. Small Investor Sentiment in Financial Markets. Working paper, University of Chicago.

Brauer, G. A. and E. Chang. 1990. Return Seasonality in Stocks and Their Underlying Assets: Tax Loss Selling Versus Information Explanations. *Review of Financial Studies* 3(2): 255–80.

Breeden, D., M. Gibbons and R. Litzenberger. 1989. Empirical Tests of the Consumption-Oriented CAPM. *Journal of Finance* 44 (June): 231–62.

Chan, K. C., P. H. Hendershott and A. Sanders. 1990. Risk and Return on Real Estate: Evidence from Equity REITs. *Journal of the American Real Estate and Urban Economics Association* 18(4): 431–52.

Chen, K. C. and D. D. Tsang. 1988. Interest Rate Sensitivity of Real Estate Investment Trusts. *Journal of Real Estate Research* 3(3): 13–22.

Davidson, H. A. and J. E. Palmer. 1978. A Comparison of the Investment Performance of Common Stocks, Homebuilding Firms, and Equity REIT. *Real Estate Appraiser* 44 (July/August): 35–39.

Dimson, E. 1979. Risk Measurement When Shares Are Subject to Infrequent Trading. *Journal of Financial Economics* 7: 197–226.

Fama, E. and W. Schwert. 1977. Asset Returns and Inflation. *Journal of Financial Economics* 5 (November): 115–46.

Firstenberg, P., S. Ross and R. Zisler. 1988. Real Estate: The Whole Story. *Journal of Portfolio Management* 14 (Spring): 22–34.

Gau, G. W. and K. Wang. 1990. A Further Examination of Appraisal Data and the Potential Bias in Real Estate Return Indexes. *Journal of the American Real Estate and Urban Economics Association* 18(1): 40–48.

Geltner, D. 1989a. Risk and Returns in Commercial Real Estate: An Exploration of Some Fundamental Relationships. Ph.D. thesis, Department of Civil Engineering, Massachusetts Institute of Technology (February).

———. 1989b. Estimating Real Estate's Systematic Risk from Aggregate Level Appraisal-Based Returns. *Journal of the American Real Estate and Urban Economics Association* 17(4): 463–81.

———. 1991a. Smoothing in Appraisal-Based Returns. *Journal of Real Estate Finance and Economics* 4(3): 327–45.

———. 1991b. Real Estate and the Diversifiability of Stock Market Noise. Working paper, University of Cincinnati (September).

Giliberto, S. M. 1990. Equity Real Estate Investment Trusts and Real Estate Returns. *Journal of Real Estate Research* 5(2): 259–64.

Gyourko, J. and P. Linneman. 1990. Analyzing the Risk of Income-Producing Property. *Urban Studies* 27(4): 497–508.

Hartzell, D. and A. Mengden. 1986. Real Estate Investment Trusts—Are They Stocks or Real Estate? Salomon Brothers *Real Estate Research* (August 27).

———. 1987. Another Look at Equity Real Estate Investment Trust Returns. Salomon Brothers *Real Estate Research* (September 22).

Hoag, J. 1980. Toward Indices of Real Estate Value and Return. *Journal of Finance* 35(2): 569–80.

Ibbotson, R. and R. Sinquefield. 1989. *Stocks, Bonds, Bills, and Inflation: Historical Returns (1926–1987)*. Down Jones-Irwin, Institute of Chartered Financial Analysts.

Kuhle, J. L. 1987. Portfolio Diversification and Return Benefits—Common Stocks vs. Real Estate Investment Trusts (REITs). *Journal of Real Estate Research* 2(2): 1–9.

——— and C. H. Walther. 1986. REIT vs. Common Stock Investments: An Historical Perspective, *Real Estate Finance* 3 (Spring): 47–52.

——— and C. H. Wurtzebach. 1986. The Financial Performance of Real Estate Investment Trusts. *Journal of Real Estate Research* 1(1): 67–75.

Lee, C. F. and J. B. Kau. 1987. Dividend Payment Behavior and Dividend Policy on REITs. *Quarterly Review of Economics and Business* 27 (Summer): 6–19.

Lee, C., A. Shleifer and R. Thaler. 1991. Investor Sentiment and the Closed-End Fund Puzzle. *Journal of Finance* 46(1): 75–110.

Lo, A. W. and A. C. MacKinlay. 1990. When Are Contrarian Profits Due to Stock Market Overreaction? *Review of Financial Studies* 3(2): 175–206.

Liu, C., D. Hartzell, T. Grissom and W. Grieg. 1990. The Composition of the Market Portfolio and Real Estate Investment Performance. *Journal of the American Real Estate and Urban Economics Association* 18(1): 49–75.

Liu, C. and J. P. Mei. 1991. The Predictability of REITs and Their Comovement With Other Assets. Working paper, New York University (May).

Miles, M., R. Cole and D. Guilkey. 1990. A Different Look at Commercial Real Estate Returns. *Journal of the American Real Estate and Urban Economics Association* 18(4): 403–31.

National Association of Real Estate Investment Trusts (NAREIT). Various years. *REIT Fact Book*. NAREIT.

———. 1989. *Annual Data Supplement to the NCREIF Real Estate Performance Report.* NCREIF and the Frank Russell Company.

Nelling, E., J. Mahoney, T. Hildebrand and M. Goldstein. 1992. The Liquidity of Real Estate Investment Trusts. Working paper, The Wharton School.

Patel, R. C. and R. A. Olsen. 1984. Financial Determinants of Systematic Risk in Real Estate Investment Trusts. *Journal of Business Research* 12(2): 481–91.

Ross, S. and R. Zisler. 1987a. Managing Real Estate Portfolios. Part 2: Risk and Return in Real Estate Addendum. Goldman, Sachs & Co. *Real Estate Research* (November 16).

———. 1987b. Managing Real Estate Portfolios. Part 3: A Close Look at Equity Real Estate Risk. Goldman, Sachs & Co. *Real Estate Research* (November 16).

———. 1991. Risk and Return in Real Estate. *Journal of Real Estate Finance and Economics* 4(2): 175–90.

Sagalyn, L. B. 1990. Real Estate Risk and the Business Cycle: Evidence from the Security Markets. *Journal of Real Estate Research* 5(2): 203–20.

Scholes, M. and J. Williams. 1977. Estimating Betas from Nonsynchronous Data. *Journal of Financial Economics* 5(2): 309–27.

Smith, K. V. and D. Shulman. 1976. The Performance of Equity Real Estate Investment Trusts. *Financial Analysts Journal* 32 (September/October): 61–66.

Standard and Poor's. 1989. *Handbook of Real Estate Securities* Standard and Poor's.

Titman, S. and A. Warga. 1986. Risk and the Performance of Real Estate Investment Trusts: A Multiple Index Approach. *Journal of the American Real Estate and Urban Economics Association* 14(3): 414–31.

Wheaton, W. and R. Torto. 1989. Income and Appraised Values: A Reexamination of the FRC Returns Data. *Journal of the American Real Estate and Urban Economics Association* 17(4): 439–49.

Zeckhauser, S. and R. Silverman. 1983. Rediscover Your Company's Real Estate. *Harvard Business Review* 61 (January/February): 111–17.

12 Transactions-Driven Commercial Real Estate Returns: The Panacea to Asset Allocation Models?

R. Brian Webb, Mike Miles, and David Guilkey

> A transactions-driven commercial real estate return series is generated in this study to determine whether the reliance on appraised values in the estimation of real estate returns is the source of the reported underpricing of real estate relative to stocks, bonds, and bills when analyzed in a traditional mean-variance setting. The reported underpricing of commercial real estate would be rational if transactions-driven returns exhibit more variance than appraisal-driven returns. While we find that transactions-driven real estate returns have greater variance than appraisal-driven returns for individual properties, most of the individual property risk is idiosyncratic and diversified away at the portfolio level. Real estate continues to be a dominant asset class in mean-variance allocation models even when represented by transactions-driven indices.[1]

Existing real estate returns literature consistently reports that commercial real estate has provided higher risk-adjusted returns than stocks or bonds, and has exhibited low or negative correlations with these more liquid investment media.[1] Whether viewed within an equilibrium pricing setting such as the Capital Asset Pricing Model (CAPM), a Markowitz efficient portfolio setting, or simply in isolation, these results suggest that real estate has been underpriced relative to stocks and bonds over an extended period of time.

Arbitrage theory indicates that such persistent underpricing should not exist in a world with efficient markets. One possible explanation for the apparent underpricing of real estate is that existing returns data for this asset class are inadequate for comparison pricing with market-determined stock and bond returns.[2] As real estate is a heterogeneous asset class in which individual properties trade infrequently, reported returns are often based on appraised rather than market transaction values. The professional litera-

---

From *Journal of the American Real Estate and Urban Economics Association*, Vol. 20, No. 1 (1992), pp. 325–357. The authors appreciate the support and comments of the National Council of Real Estate Investment Fiduciaries (NCREIF) and participants in seminars at the University of North Carolina, Indiana University, the Homer Hoyt/Weimer School for Advanced Studies, and the Institute for Quantitative Research in Finance (Q-Group). The authors especially appreciate the comments and contribution to the data collection process of Rebel Cole. Any errors are the responsibility of the authors.

ture provides evidence that appraised values are unbiased estimates of transaction prices (on average, across time), but have much less variance than their market counterpart.[3] It follows that appraised values will generate unbiased estimates of mean returns over time,[4] but downwardly biased estimates of variance and correlations with market-determined returns for other assets. The low correlations are the statistical artifact of the low variances and the lagged nature of appraisal-driven returns.[5]

Edelstein and Quan (1991) demonstrate that the impact of appraisal-smoothing on the variance and correlations of real estate *portfolio* returns is not a straightforward extrapolation from the above-described impact on individual property returns. Using an appraisal model that appropriately assumes information imperfections, heterogeneous expectations, and varying search costs and bargaining abilities of market participants, they suggest that appraisal-smoothing arises when appraisers follow an optimal updating strategy in an imperfect world rather than from flaws in appraisal methodology. As appraisals are performed at the individual property level, appraisal-smoothing will only affect the estimated variance of portfolio returns to the extent that smoothing is systematically in the same direction across the properties in the portfolio. When the appraisal-smoothing process causes values to be underestimated on some properties and overestimated on other properties at any particular point in time, then the effect of smoothing will be reduced through diversification in large portfolios. The extent that appraisal-smoothing affects estimates of portfolio variance is a question that requires empirical evidence to answer.

Existing evidence provided by Hoag (1980) and Miles, Cole and Guilkey (1990) suggests that smoothing is predominantly systematic and therefore impacts measures of variance at the portfolio level. They construct quarterly "transactions-driven" real estate return indices that are based on market transaction prices from small samples of properties. They find transactions-driven indices have substantially more variance than appraisal-driven indices. This is an intuitively pleasing result, as it provides a reasonable explanation for why real estate appears to be underpriced (i.e., why mean-variance asset allocation models do not provide reasonable solutions when quarterly appraisal-driven returns from real estate are combined with market-determined returns on other asset classes).

Hoag and Miles, Cole and Guilkey (MCG) caution, however, that their results are sensitive to the data available at the time the research was performed, and that "as more information becomes available, the estimates of real estate return and risk will change, perhaps dramatically" (see Hoag, page 574). This warning was prophetic, as results using a similar methodology applied to a larger sample of properties, over a longer time period, and with more detailed property-specific information show that transactions-driven real estate returns have greater variance than appraisal-driven returns *for individual properties,* but that most of the individual property risk is idiosyncratic and diversified away at the portfolio level. The major finding of this study is that real estate continues to be a dominant asset class in mean-variance allocation models even when represented by transactions-driven indices. Other reasons for the reported underpricing of real estate must be explored.[6]

The finding that most of the quarterly property risk is idiosyncratic (i.e., nonsystematic) is not surprising when the degree of segmentation in commercial real estate markets is considered. Note, however, that the nonsystematic nature of *quarterly* property returns does not preclude commercial real estate from having a large systematic component when viewed over annual (or longer) time periods. Significant regulatory changes exacerbate the long-term systematic risk of commercial real estate and create periods of time when real estate markets in general are either robust or depressed. For example, the deregulation of financial institutions in the early 1980s helped to create a boom period for commercial real estate, and the tax law changes in 1986 helped to create the current bust period. The boom and bust periods began at different points in time for different markets, however, as suggested by the popular notion that current markets reflect a "rolling real estate recession" that began in the Southwest in the mid-1980s, moved to the Northeast in the late-1980s, and on to the West Coast in the early-1990s.

The organization for this paper is as follows. A model of commercial real estate value that provides guidelines for the selection of variables to be included in the value equation is derived in the next section. A description of the data on sold and unsold properties is provided in section three. Econometric concerns of the methodology used to generate the transactions-driven values are discussed in section four.[7] Results from the value equation regressions are presented in the fifth section, and characteristics of the derived transactions-driven real estate indices are discussed in section six. Section seven then summarizes the implications of the empirical results.

MODELING COMMERCIAL REAL ESTATE VALUE

The modeling of commercial real estate value provides a way to simulate continuous trading of infrequently traded commercial real estate properties. Modeled values may be used in the place of subjective appraised values to generate "transactions-driven" returns. Transactions-driven values help to alleviate the problem of appraisal-smoothing by using "comparable sales" both before *and after* the time periods the unsold properties are being valued, and by replacing the appraisers' subjective estimates of value with the model's objective estimate of value.

The purpose of the valuation model derived in this section of the paper is simply to establish guidelines as to the appropriate variables to include in the value equation. Theories from the fields of economics (on markets of homogeneous products), urban economics (on hedonic valuation of heterogeneous products), and finance (on discounted cash flow analysis) are integrated to generate the necessary valuation model.[8]

Financial and Urban Economic Theories of Value. Financial economic theory indicates that the value of an income-producing asset is a function of its expected future cash flows and an appropriate discount factor (i.e., appropriate adjustments for time and risk). Rent primarily determines the cash flow on commercial real estate, and is a function of the supply and demand for rentable space. Two significant problems are encountered when attempting to model commercial real estate rents, however. First, since commercial real estate takes from two to five years to "produce," supply is at least partly determined by the expected future demand. Demand, on the other hand, is determined in the current period as prospective tenants search the market for desired location and constructed amenities at the best possible price. To the extent that the expectations that drive supply are not precisely met (and given relatively inelastic demand for space), commercial real estate markets often go through periods with either excess supply or excess demand.[9] The "natural vacancy rate" of real estate has been shown to be unstable over time and across markets,[10] rendering simple adjustment for vacancy rates within an equilibrium setting invalid, and suggesting a more complex model.[11]

Second, since location is an important attribute of real estate (and no two properties can occupy the same space at the same time), commercial real estate is by its very nature a heterogeneous product. Therefore, standard homogeneous product models are not appropriate for commercial real estate. Heterogeneous attributes of specific properties must be incorporated. In consideration of these two problems, real estate is initially modeled as a homogeneous product trading in a market characterized by a laborious search for equilibrium. The model is then simplified to a single reduced-form equation of real estate value prior to the recognition of the heterogeneity of real estate and the specification of the final reduced-form equation for the empirical work that follows.

A Homogeneous Asset Model. Using discounted cash flow analysis, the value of a homogeneous unit of commercial real estate is a function of expected market rental rates and various exogenous capital market factors that determine the appropriate required rate of return (equation 1 that follows). Market rents are determined by the supply and demand for rentable space (equation 2). The supply of commercial real estate space is determined by the stock of existing real estate, as well as the flow from new construction. Supply of rentable space is therefore partially determined at time t as a function of rent and exogenously determined general economic activity,[12] and partially determined at the time $t - q$ as a function of exogenously determined *expected* future market rents (rents at time t) and a vector of exogenous cost factors (at time $t - q$) which include construction costs as well as the cost of obtaining capital (equation 3).

Demand for rentable space is determined at time t and is a function of current market rent and a vector of exogenous variables that include the general level of economic activity and any expected changes in the level of economic activity (equation 4). Quantity of space utilized, which is theoretically observable, is the minimum of supply or demand (equation 5). The five-equation disequilibrium model of real estate value is therefore as follows:

$$V_t = f(R_t CMF_t) \quad (1)$$
$$R_t = f(S_q, D_t) \quad (2)$$
$$S_t = f(R_q, EA_q, R^e_{t-q}, C_{t-q}) \quad (3)$$
$$D_t = f(R_q, EA_t) \quad (4)$$
$$Q_t = \operatorname{Min}(S_q, D_t) \quad (5)$$

where:

V_t = value at time t,
R_t = market rent at time t,
S_t = supply of rentable space at time t,
D_t = demand for rentable space at time t,
Q_t = quantity of space rented at time t,
CMF_t = a vector of capital market factors at time t,
EA_t = a vector of economic activity factors at time t,
R^e_t = expected market rent (at time $t - q$) of commercial real estate space (at time t),
C_{t-q} = a vector of construction cost factors (including the cost of capital at time $t - q$).

Reduced-Form Pricing Equation for Homogeneous Real Estate. This general model assumes a national market for a homogeneous product. Simplifying this general model to the following reduced-form pricing equation allows the inappropriate homogeneous product assumption to be eased in a manageable and testable fashion. Momentarily maintaining the homogeneous real estate product assumption, the reduced form of the general model specifies that the value of commercial real estate is a function of four vectors of exogenous variables.

$$V_t = f(CMF_t, EA_t, R^e_{t-q}, C_{t-q}), \qquad (6)$$

where all vectors are as previously defined.

Capital market factors (CMF_t) include required real returns (influenced in the 1980s by foreign, pension, and other "hot" investment money flowing into real estate) and inflation expectations.[13] The general level and future direction of economic activity (EA_t) in a homogeneous real estate product world is an indication of how close the economy is to full capacity, and therefore of the restrictiveness of the existing space market. Expectations of future rent (R^e_{t-q}) are based on general market rent histories and expectations about the business cycle (the level and future direction of economic activity). Construction costs (C_{t-q}) include both the cost of physical construction (land, legal limitations on land utilization, materials, labor, etc.) and the cost of obtaining capital.

Reduced-Form Pricing Equation for Heterogeneous Real Estate. Recognizing that both national and local location, quality of construction, differences in amenities, and intensity of management distinguish one property from another, the above homogeneous pricing equation is not sufficient to model commercial real estate value.[14] The field of urban economics has long recognized the heterogeneity of real estate, and hedonic pricing models have been developed to deal with this difficult problem.[15]

Incorporating hedonic theory into the homogeneous product pricing equation allows the unique characteristics of individual properties (such as their location within the nation and within their particular metropolitan area, their functionality, and their particular rent histories) to be included. In a heterogeneous product world, capital market factors (CMF_t) that determine the appropriate required rates of return not only include variables that affect all properties in a systematic fashion, but also include cross-sectional differences in the risk premiums associated with each property. These risk premiums are determined at least in part by the physical and locational characteristics of the property in question.[16]

The general level and future direction of economic activity (EA_t) in a heterogeneous world pertains to the specific primary metropolitan statistical area (PMSA) in which a property is located rather than the United States economy in general.[17] EA_t includes such variables as the level (and changes in the level) of per capita wealth and population in the PMSA. Rent expectations (R^e_{t-q}) now refer to the individual properties rather than to a generic unit of space, and are formed from the rent histories of the individual properties. Costs of construction (C_{t-q}) are likewise PMSA- and property-specific.

In addition to these determinants of value, specific attributes (A_t) of a property (such as its location within the PMSA, the quality of construction, and the level of amenities) materially affect value. These attributes are important to include in a heterogeneous model of commercial real estate value. The heterogeneous reduced-form pricing equation in vector notation then becomes,

$$V_{i,t} = f(CMF_{i,t}, EA_{i,t}, R^e_{i,t-q}, C_{i,t-q}, A_{i,t}), \qquad (7)$$

where $A_{i,t}$ represents the specific attributes of property i, and all other variables are property-specific (but defined as in the homogeneous pricing equation). Following the above discussion of the specific factors that comprise each vector, the pricing equation to be utilized in the empirical analysis is,

$$V_{i,t} = f(RP_i, PersInc_{i,t}, CPop_{i,t}, NISF_{i,t}, NIPotntl_{i,t}, Locate_i, Funct_i, \beta, \varepsilon_{i,t}), \quad (8)$$

where

- RP_i = variable that partially captures the cross-sectional differences in risk premiums,
- $PersInc_{i,t}$ = personal income per capita in the PMSA of property i at time t,
- $CPop_{i,t}$ = change in population in the PMSA of property i at time t,
- $NISF_{i,t}$ = net income per square foot for property i at time t,
- $NIPotntl_{i,t}$ = highest potential net income for property i as demonstrated by its rent history,
- $Locate_i$ = quality of location within the PMSA for property i,
- $Funct_i$ = functionality as a measure of quality of construction and amenities,
- β = vector of estimated regression coefficients,
- $\varepsilon_{i,t}$ = error term.

While some of the independent variables are observable across time for each property, the dependent variable (value) is only observed at one point in time—the time period the property is sold.

This model is necessarily different from models utilized by researchers to construct value indices in housing markets for several reasons. First, commercial real estate is an asset that produces directly observable income, thus a discounted cash flow model is more appropriate than the pure hedonic models (models of attributes that are valued by consumers) used in the housing literature. Second, housing data often contain repeat sales that are useful in constructing return indices. As noted above, only single observations of prices are available on the properties in this commercial real estate data. Finally, housing data contain sufficient observations to allow for time-varying estimates of the value of various attributes. At this time, commercial real estate transactions data are sufficiently limited that parameter estimates must be assumed constant over the time period that data are available. The validity of this assumption is tested in the empirical work that follows.

The selection of proxies for the independent variables allows for considerable discretion on the part of the authors. Hoag and MCG take advantage of this discretion by selecting the set of variables that maximize the R^2 of the regression equations. The danger of this approach is that the data will be "over-fitted" within sample and drive the results that are obtained when the parameter estimates are applied out-of-sample. Precautions are taken against over-fitting the data in this research by using only those variables suggested by the above derived model that proved to be significant at the 5% level and of the theoretically correct sign over several independent subsamples of the data (i.e., subsamples by property type, geographic region, and/or time period). The following describes the variables that met this criterion.

The cross-sectional measure of the appropriate risk premium (RP) proved to be a significant capital market factor (CMF). A time-series capital market factor should reasonably be included as well, but was omitted from the empirical analysis due to the lack of an adequate observable proxy. Finding time-series capital market factors for real estate proved to be empirically difficult for two reasons. First, most of the transactions prices used in this research occurred over the relatively short 1980–1988 time period. Time-series capital market factors, such as real required rates of return and expected inflation, did not go through a complete cycle over this time period. Second, the dual effect of inflation on real estate values (negative due to its impact on nominal required rate of returns, and positive due to the inflation-hedging abilities of real estate) necessitates adequate proxies for both property-specific required rate of returns and economy-wide expected inflation. Finding two proxies that satisfactorily interacted over this time period proved to be impossible.

Because the omission of a general time-series capital market factor that simultaneously affects the value of all real estate would impact the measurement of systematic risk (the primary measure of concern in this paper), an extensive search for a proxy that met the above-described criterion was initiated. Potential proxies that were examined include the dollar-to-yen exchange rate, the price earnings ratio on S&P 500, the price of oil in real terms, the Michigan Survey of Consumer Sentiment, the U.S. capital utilization rate, the unemployment rate, the trade deficit in real terms, the Dow Jones industrial average, the dividend yield on the S&P 500, the long-term Treasury yield (ten and twenty years), the yield on Treasury bills, the Baa Corporate Bond yield, the market risk premium as measured by the difference in the Baa yield and the Treasury bond yield, the yield curve as measured by the difference in the Treasury bond and Treasury bill yields, the survey of expected long-term price changes as reported by the General Motors survey research center, capitalization rates on commercial mortgage commitments by twenty life insurance companies as reported by the American Council of Life Insurance, returns on real estate (by property type) as reported by Russell-NCREIF, quarterly GNP growth, U.S. net exports of goods and services, U.S. savings percent, and total retail sales per quarter. This list includes macroeconomic variables that are often significant systematic factors in stock and bond research.[18] Of all these variables, only the yen/$ exchange rate proved to be significant in the pricing equation. The results that follow do not change significantly when this variable (or any other capital market proxy) is included in the pricing equation: thus it has been omitted for fear of over-fitting the data from this exhaustive search.

Personal income per capita in the PMSA (*PersInc*) and the change in population (*CPop*) reflect the level and direction of change of economic activity respectively (*EA*). Real net income per square foot (*NISF*) and the highest potential net income (*NIPotntl*) reflect expectations about rent (R^e). Subjective estimates of the quality of a property's location (*Locate*) and functionality (*Funct*) reflect individual attributes of the properties that affect value.[19]

Changes in the cost of construction proved to be difficult to observe, as adequate proxies for the relevant construction costs over time at the PMSA level are not readily available. The costs of labor and materials, while potentially observable, are relatively stable over time and thus not particularly useful. Data are unavailable for the costs of land and capital over time at the PMSA level. The variance of the error term in the value equation will thus be larger due to the omission of cost of construction variables.

A discussion on how all included variables are constructed for empirical tests is presented in Table 1. Due to the differences in the expected magnitude of the impact of the variables on the value of office, retail, and industrial properties (e.g., location is

Table 1 Description of Variables

RP_t:	High-rise office buildings have lower risk premiums than garden office buildings, requiring a dummy variable that distinguishes between the two. This variable takes on the value of –1 for all single-story office properties, 0 for all office buildings 2 to 6 stories tall, and a value of 1 for all office buildings that are 7 stories or taller.[a]
$PersInc_t$:	Personal income per capita in the PMSA is an indication of the level of economic activity.
$CPop_t$:	The change in population in the PMSA is an indication of the direction of changes in future economic activity, and is expected to have a positive coefficient. Increased economic activity generates increased demand and therefore real estate values.
$NISF_{t-q}$:	Average of preceding three, and current quarter's real net income. This variable reflects a stabilized level of cash flows generated by the property.
$NIPotntl_{t-q}$:	NIPotntl is calculated as the difference between the highest historical four-quarter average real net income and the current stabilized income. A property is partially valued on current income and partially valued on potential future income increases (or decreases). Any current vacancy gives the potential for more income in the future.
$Funct_t$:	As available descriptive characteristics of the properties are inadequate for complete measurement of the properties' relative functionality, each of the respective managers were requested to rank the properties on a scale of 1 (least functional) to 10 (most functional). The discrete variable (FUNCT) takes on the value of –2 for properties ranked 1–5, 0 for properties ranked 6–8, and 1 for properties ranked 9–10.
$Locate_t$:	Observable characteristics (such as distance to major highways, airports, etc.) of a property's location are not adequate in modeling the quality of that location. Subjective estimates of the properties' locations (again scaled from 1–10) were collected from the respective property managers.

[a]The critical difference for retail properties is the size of the property, rather than the height of the property. For industrial properties, the percentage of space finished out for offices is the distinguishing cross-sectional risk premium variable.

Source: Authors

more important to retail space, functionality is more important to office space), empirical tests of these property types are performed independently. The discussion in Table 1 pertains to office properties, but any differences for the other property types are explained in the footnotes.[20]

DATA COLLECTION ON SOLD AND UNSOLD PROPERTIES

The property-specific data necessary for the implementation of this methodology have been provided by the National Council of Real Estate Investment Fiduciaries (NCREIF) and the Frank Russell Company (FRC). NCREIF is comprised of forty-seven of the largest pension fund real estate managers who quarterly report net income, capital expenditures, sales (when applicable), and appraised values to the FRC on the properties they manage. The FRC constructs an appraisal-driven real estate returns index that is published quarterly in "The NCREIF Real Estate Performance Report" and has become the industry benchmark for institutional investment in this asset class.

Recognizing the limitations of an appraisal-based returns index in making asset allocation decisions across broad asset classes, the FRC provided all the quarterly information it presently has on the sampled properties, and the individual NCREIF members provided the additional property-specific information that is required for this study.

The resulting database includes 592 commercial properties valued at over $5.2 billion, with 270 sold and 322 unsold over the sampled time period. These properties are well-diversified geographically (forty of the forty-eight continental states are represented in this sample), by property type (151 office, 120 retail, and 321 industrial properties) and by investment manager (twenty-two different investment managers). The sample increases in size through time as NCREIF members' portfolios grew and as NCREIF membership grew, but the observed sales are reasonably spread across the 1980–1988 time period. This compares favorably to the 469 properties over the 1973–1978 time period available to Hoag and the 347 properties over the 1982–1986 time period available to MCG.

There are three types of information in the database: property-specific fixed characteristics such as location (state and county where property is located), property type (office, retail, industrial), net square feet, lease maturity, tenant quality, quality of location, functionality, and net sale price (one price for each sold property in the quarter it sold); property-specific quarterly characteristics such as net income, capital improvements, appraised value, and partial sales; and metropolitan area characteristics such as population and personal income.[21] As previously mentioned, quality of location and functionality are two critical variables that have been unavailable to previous researchers.[22]

PRICING OBSERVABLE CHARACTERISTICS OF VALUE: ECONOMETRIC ISSUES

With the necessary data in hand, the reduced-form equation of real estate value derived earlier in this paper can be used to "price" the modeled characteristics of value for the sold sample, and these characteristic "prices" can then be used to value each of the unsold properties in the sample at several different points in time. These property-specific point estimates of value are then used (along with the reported net income from the property) to calculate *individual* property returns. Two econometric problems, however, prevent the use of simple least squares regression analysis with the stated variables on the sample of sold properties. The first problem involves the attempted inference of values for an unsold sample of properties from a sold sample, and the second involves the fact that choice-based sampling is utilized (all sold properties were included, while only a sample of unsold properties are utilized in this analysis).

Correction for Bias Due to Use of Transacted Properties. It is likely that a sample consisting only of sold properties is biased relative to the set of all properties from which it is drawn, as this transacted subset of properties is clearly not chosen randomly by investment managers. If the bias is due to observable characteristics of the properties, the bias can be corrected by including these characteristics directly in the regression equation. For example, if small properties are more likely to be sold and are less highly valued, a variable indicating the relative size of the properties should be included in the value equation.

The correction for bias is more complicated when it is hypothesized that the bias is due to property characteristics that are not measured in the data set. For example, architecturally unique properties may be less likely to be sold and may also be more highly valued. If some measure of architectural quality is not available in the data set, coefficient estimates in the value equation will be biased unless statistical procedures are employed to correct for the bias.

The statistical procedures that are used to correct for bias due to unobservable variables fall under the heading of selectivity correction procedures. Selectivity correction procedures, applied to the problem at hand, involve determining the level of correlation between the error terms of the previously derived value equation and an equation with a discrete dependent variable that indicates whether a property has been sold or not. A non-zero correlation indicates that there is overlap in the unobservable variables that affect both whether or not a property is sold and its value, and that a simple regression on the value equation will lead to biased results. The likelihood function for the selectivity correction model we employ can be found in many textbooks (see, for example, Maddala 1983).

The suggested joint estimation procedure involves specifying the two equations of interest,

$$S_i = X_i\alpha + \mu_i \qquad (10)$$
$$V_i = Z_i\beta + \varepsilon_i, \qquad (11)$$

where S is a dichotomous indicator with a "1" indicating that property i has been sold and a "0" indicating that it has not been sold, X represents a set of independent variables that are hypothesized to affect a manager's decision to sell a property, α represents the set of unknown regression parameters to be estimated, and μ is an unobserved disturbance term that represents variables that affect the manager's decisionmaking process that are not available in the data set and may not be observable at all. Equation 11 is simply a restatement of the previously derived value equation (equation 8) in vector notation for ease of exposition (i.e., the Zs represent the set of observed variables that are hypothesized to affect the price of property i, β represents the set of unknown regression parameters to be estimated, and ε represents the unobserved disturbance term that reflects variables that affect price but are not available in the data set).

It is important to note that V_i is only observed for property i when $S_i = 1$. Such a sample of properties is not a random set of all properties in the data set and is in fact a biased sample. Standard regression methods will not allow a correct assessment of the impact of the Z variables in the equation of primary interest. To some extent, bias can be controlled by including appropriate variables in the set of regressors. As mentioned previously, if one expects that smaller properties are more likely to be sold and that size also affects V, then the solution is to simply include size in the Z-vector. Unfortunately, just as there is overlap in the set of observable variables that affects both S and V, there may be overlap in the set of unobservable variables. This means that there is a non-zero correlation between ε and μ and that,

$$E(\varepsilon_i \mid S_i = 1) = \rho\phi(X_i\alpha) / \Phi(X_i\alpha), \qquad (12)$$

where ρ is the correlation between ε and μ, ϕ and Φ are the standard normal distribution function and density function respectively, and the variances of ε and μ have been normalized to 1 to keep the notation simple.

The fact that the conditional mean of ε is not equal to zero implies that standard regression methods will yield biased estimates of β. The solution to the problem is the joint estimation of equations (10) and (11) by maximum likelihood method where the likelihood function is constructed under the assumption that ε and μ follow a multivariate normal distribution.[23] To implement this methodology, a probit equation that indicates whether a property has been sold must be specified.

Guilkey, Cole and Miles (1989) examine the motivation for institutional sales of specific properties and determine that smaller, less accessible properties are more likely to be sold, as well as properties in locations with current excess demand but future increasing supply of space. It is also reasonable to believe that anything that affects value might affect the decision to sell. Variables selected for the sales equation therefore include the net square feet of the property relative to the average net square feet of the other properties held by the same manager and of the same property type ($Size_t$), the number of sampled properties in the PMSA where the property is located ($Remote_t$) as a measure of the accessibility of the property, the number of tenants ($Ntenants_t$) as a measure of the diversity of the cash flows from the property, and all variables in the pricing equation. The probit equation is specified in reduced form as,

$$Y_{i,t} = f(RP_i, PersInc_{i,t}, CPop_{i,t}, NISF_{i,t}, NIPotntl_{i,t}, Locate_i, Funct_i, Size_i, Remote_i, Ntenants_i), \qquad (13)$$

where all variables are as previously defined. The joint estimation of the value equation (8) and the sales equation (13) will test and correct for selectivity bias in the value equation due to unobservable variables.

Correction for Choice-Based Sampling. The estimation procedure is further complicated by the fact that while all eligible sold properties are included in the database, only a chosen subset of the unsold properties are included.[24] Choice-based sampling methods must be used to correct for the non-random nature of the sample. Essentially, this estimation procedure involves the use of a weighted likelihood function, where the weights for the sold and unsold properties are determined by their actual frequencies in the set of all properties.[25] The purpose of sample weights is to adjust for over-sampling certain strata in a population; sample statistics can then be considered representative of the population.

Results for the probit-based, two-step estimator are presented in Table 2. For all three property types, the joint estimation failed to reject the null hypothesis of no selectivity bias. The test for selectivity is a simple t-test on the coefficient of the inverse Mills ratio that is included in the value equation as the sample selectivity correction factor. The inverse Mills ratio is insignificant for all property types, indicating the correlation of the error terms of the value and sold equations is not statistically different than zero. These results suggest that there is no significant bias introduced into the value equation from running ordinary least squares (OLS) regressions. Therefore, results from OLS regressions are used to perform the additional analysis reported below.[26]

It is important to note that the sample selectivity test results discussed here are different from the ones obtained by Guilkey, Cole and Miles (GCM) (1989), where significant selectivity bias was found. GCM did not have adequate proxies for the functionality or the quality of location of the properties, however, and these omitted variables are probably the source of the selectivity bias in their results.[27]

Table 2 Joint Estimation of Real Estate Value

	Value Equation[a] (Probit-Based Two-Step Estimator)					
	Office		Retail		Industrial	
Adjusted R^2	.89		.88		.82	
Variables	β	T-Stat	β	T-Stat	β	T-Stat
Intercept	2.42	.40	−6.58	−1.43	−5.46	−3.12
Personal Income	6.94	8.23	.71	1.34	1.22	4.88
Change in Population	1.85	6.20	.51	1.97	.35	4.00
Net Income	2.53	8.88	3.58	6.42	2.61	9.09
Net Income Potential	.88	3.92	.29	.77	1.29	5.24
RP	9.01	4.18	1.74	1.89	9.37	5.60
Quality of Location	1.90	2.87	1.42	2.14	.85	3.42
Functionality	5.00	5.12	−.04	−.04	−.29	−.29
Other	NA	NA	5.49	1.58	4.22	2.56
Inverse Mills Ratio	−6.53	.98	7.89	.96	1.63	.65

	Sales Equation[a] (Maximum Likelihood Probit Estimation)					
	Office		Retail		Industrial	
Variables	β	T-Stat	β	T-Stat	β	T-Stat
Intercept	−1.06	−1.10	1.34	.94	1.59	2.86
Personal Income	−.04	−.49	−.06	−.71	.10	1.80
Change in Population	−.00	−.02	−.03	−.77	−.00	−.18
Net Income	−.03	−1.39	.07	1.23	.16	3.29
Net Income Potential	.01	.33	−.00	−.09	−.08	−1.36
RP	−.18	−.81	.01	.03	−.24	−.56
Quality of Location	−.05	−.77	−.10	−1.29	−.12	−2.45
Functionality	−.05	.12	.05	.31	−.46	−3.26
Other	NA	NA	−.48	−1.49	.92	1.86
Size	.12	.64	.22	.62	−.19	−1.82
Remoteness	.55	1.97	.10	.24	.00	.01
Number of Tenants	−.06	−1.20	−.14	−1.24	−.07	−.76

[a]The dependent variable for the value equation is the real price per square foot of the sold properties. The dependent variable for the sales equation is a dummy variable that takes on the value of 1 if the property sold over the sampled time period, and a value of 0 if the property did not sell.

Source: Authors

VALUING THE UNSOLD SAMPLE

Table 3 presents the estimates of the parameters of a linear valuation function for all property types over the 1980–1988 time period.[28] All variables are constructed to have a positive expected effect on value. Section A provides results when all modeled variables are included, and section B when variables significant at the 5% level are included.[29] The fact that the results are not materially affected by the deletion of the insignificant variables provides support for the stability of the pricing equation. The adjusted-R^2s are high, ranging from .82 for industrial properties to .89 for office prop-

Table 3 OLS Estimation of Real Estate
$(V/SF)_{i,t} = \alpha + \beta_1(RP_i) + \beta_2(PersInc_{i,t}) + \beta_3(C\ Pop_{i,t}) + \beta_4(NISF_{i,t}) + \beta_5(NIPotntl_{i,t}) + \beta_6(Locate_i) + \beta_7(Funct_i) + \varepsilon_{i,t}$

(A)

Value Equation
(Ordinary Least Squares—All Variables)

	Office		Retail		Industrial	
Adjusted R^2	.89		.87		.82	
Variables	β	T-Stat	β	T-Stat	β	T-Stat
Intercept	−.72	−.13	−4.98	−2.14	−5.17	−2.97
Personal Income	6.89	7.54	.56	2.24	1.13	5.21
Change in Population	1.86	5.76	.39	3.45	.35	3.91
Net Income	2.40	8.69	3.19	16.42	2.75	13.57
Net Income Potential	.89	3.61	.29	1.25	1.34	5.44
RP	8.01	3.92	1.12	3.21	9.63	5.69
Quality of Location	1.67	2.54	1.04	3.61	.94	4.43
Functionality	5.08	4.82	.15	.27	.25	.42
Other[a]	NA	NA	2.93	2.59	3.59	2.66

(B)

Value Equation
(Ordinary Least Squares—Significant Variables)

	Office		Retail		Industrial	
Adjusted R^2	.89		.88		.82	
Variables	β	T-Stat	β	T-Stat	β	T-Stat
Intercept	−.72	−.13	−4.22	−2.19	−5.40	−3.29
Personal Income	6.89	7.54	.63	2.64	1.14	5.23
Change in Population	1.86	5.76	.39	3.45	.35	3.94
Net Income	2.40	8.69	3.16	16.48	2.75	13.61
Net Income Potential	.89	3.61	NA	NA	1.34	5.46
RP	8.01	3.92	1.10	3.17	9.56	5.69
Quality of Location	1.67	2.54	1.04	3.94	0.97	4.84
Functionality	5.08	4.82	NA	NA	NA	NA
Other[b]	NA	NA	3.11	2.79	3.57	2.65

[a]"Other" for retail properties is a dummy variable that takes the value of 1 if the property is a regional mall and 0 otherwise. [b]"Other" for industrial properties represents the percent of office space to total space in the property.

Note: Variables that are insignificant at the 5% level in panel A of this exhibit are omitted from the regression reported in panel B.

Source: Authors

erties. All modeled variables are significant for office properties, while net income potential is insignificant for retail, and functionality is insignificant for both retail and industrial properties.

The relative importance of variables in explaining office value can be examined by multiplying the average value of each variable across the properties in the sample by the parameter estimate from the value equation. Historical net income (NISF) is an important variable in explaining value due to the long-term commitments (leases) of rental income. NISF explains slightly less than 50% of the total value of office properties, slightly more than 50% of the total value of industrial properties, and almost 75% of the total value of retail properties. This difference in importance can be explained by looking at the average lease maturities for the sampled properties across the various property types. Whereas the average lease maturities for office and industrial properties are 3.4 and 3.1 years, respectively, the average lease maturity for retail properties is 10.6 years. When total value from future cash flows is separated into cash flows from existing leases and cash flows from leases to be negotiated in the future, it is easy to see why the value of retail properties is more predictable from historical cash flows.

The stability of cash flows and the unique structure of retail leases (which often include percentage rents) also explain why net income potential is not significant for retail properties. Due to the shorter duration of outstanding leases, office and industrial values are more dependent on characteristics that will determine the terms of leases to be negotiated in the near future, such as the submarket quality and the expected PMSA economic activity. Finally, functionality varies more for office buildings than for the other property types in the sample and is more critical due to the expense of the mechanical systems (e.g., elevators) that make an office building more functional. It is thus not surprising that functionality is a more important factor in determining office value than in determining industrial or retail value.

Tests of the Valuation Model. To test the stability of the results over time, the transacted sample for each property type is divided into two subsamples that have approximately the same number of properties. The first subsample spans the third quarter of 1980 to the third quarter of 1985, while the second spans the fourth quarter of 1985 to the second quarter of 1988. Table 4 presents the results from these two time periods. While the reduced sample sizes lower the significance of the parameter estimates in general, the estimates themselves are similar across the different time periods for all property types, with quality of location for retail properties in the earlier time period the only variable that changed signs.[30] While the differences in the parameter estimates across these time periods suggest that rolling regressions allowing parameter estimates to vary through time might be desirable, the reality of limited sample sizes prohibits this possibility. The differences are small enough to suggest that the assumption of constant values of the modeled characteristics across the 1980–1988 time period is not an unreasonable approximation.

An additional test of the valuation model is performed by comparing the differences in actual transaction prices of the sold properties to values that are generated by the pricing model. The valuation model does a reasonable job compared to appraised values, given that the appraisals are done on site and with first-hand knowledge of the property. The mean absolute percentage difference between the actual sales price of the property and the transactions-driven estimate of value is 17%, while it is 9% for the difference between the actual price and the appraised value. The standard deviations of the transactions-based differences are 25% higher than the appraisal-based differences. Valuing industrial properties proved to be the most difficult, as this property type includes everything from basic warehouses, to office/showroom structures, to research and development facilities. While percentage office space (RP) controls for some of these differences, the quality of improvements can vary dramatically.[31]

Note that the appraised value used in this comparison is the one reported to the FRC just prior to the actual sale. The appraised value in the quarter the property sold

Table 4 OLS Estimation of Real Estate Value—Subperiods

$(V/SF)_{i,t} = \alpha + \beta_1(RP_i) + \beta_2(PersInc_{i,t}) + \beta_3(C\ Pop_{i,t}) + \beta_4(NISF_{i,t}) + \beta_5(NIPotntl_{i,t}) + \beta_6(Locate_i) + \beta_7(Funct_i) + \varepsilon_{i,t}$

(A)

	\multicolumn{2}{c}{Office}	\multicolumn{2}{c}{Value Equation (OLS 80-3 to 85-3) Retail}	\multicolumn{2}{c}{Industrial}
Adjusted R^2	.81		.91		.83	
Variables	β	T-Stat	β	T-Stat	β	T-Stat
Intercept	13.75	1.19	2.84	.88	−5.61	−2.11
Personal Income	7.67	3.83	.36	.99	1.50	4.14
Change in Population	1.18	2.26	.54	2.79	.32	2.68
Net Income	1.97	3.44	3.33	13.55	2.55	8.94
Net Income Potential	.02	.03	.05	.16	1.48	4.00
RP	5.50	1.54	1.17	1.21	11.69	5.30
Quality of Location	1.36	1.10	−.22	−.53	1.09	3.30
Functionality	6.84	4.08	1.37	1.78	.15	.19
Other	NA	NA	2.80	1.54	1.85	1.12

(B)

	\multicolumn{2}{c}{Office}	\multicolumn{2}{c}{Value Equation (OLS 85-4 to 88-2) Retail}	\multicolumn{2}{c}{Industrial}
Adjusted R^2	.92		.91		.81	
Variables	β	T-Stat	β	T-Stat	β	T-Stat
Intercept	−6.20	−1.03	−9.05	−3.19	−5.07	−2.17
Personal Income	8.19	6.71	.66	2.34	.98	3.19
Change in Population	2.11	5.06	.26	1.83	.30	2.03
Net Income	2.35	7.21	2.80	10.44	3.17	9.80
Net Income Potential	1.04	3.94	.41	1.22	1.28	3.73
RP	10.38	4.03	.97	2.93	5.49	1.93
Quality of Location	1.67	2.08	2.08	6.35	.81	2.79
Functionality	3.64	2.69	−1.11	−1.80	.90	.97
Other	NA	NA	1.63	1.31	4.04	1.46

Source: Authors

is often exactly the sales price, as this information is available at the time of the report. Appraisers are often aware of ongoing negotiations on the properties in the preceding quarter, biasing the above test in favor of the appraised values. Given the strong bias in favor of appraised values, the transactions differences seem reasonable.

CONSTRUCTION OF THE TRANSACTIONS-DRIVEN SERIES

The industry benchmark Russell/NCREIF Property Index is derived from *individual* properties' total returns using appraised values. These quarterly returns are calculated as,

$$\text{Total Return} = [EMV - BMV + PS - CI + NI]/[BMV - .5PS + .5CI - .33NI], \quad (14)$$

where *EMV* is the end-of-quarter and *BMV* is the beginning-of-quarter appraised market value, *PS* represents any partial sales that occurred during the quarter, *CI* represents capital improvements made during the quarter, and *NI* represents net income for the quarter. This formulation assumes that capital improvements and partial sales occur at the midpoint of each quarter, while net income is received monthly (as is the case for most properties in the index). Returns are calculated according to this formula for each property in each quarter and then weighted by their appraised values to produce the Russell/NCREIF Index (see NCREIF 1988).

In this study, transactions-driven values are estimated for each unsold property on a quarterly basis by taking the estimates of the value of each of the modeled property characteristics (presented in Table 3(B)) and applying them to the observed characteristic of each property at every point in time the property is in the database. This provides a time series of values for each of the unsold properties. These *transactions-driven* values are then substituted for the appraised values in the Russell/NCREIF calculation of quarterly returns to estimate a time series of transactions-driven returns for each of the unsold properties. Portfolios of these unsold properties are formed to provide transactions-driven real estate return series for the eight-year period from the third quarter of 1980 to the second quarter of 1988 on a value-weighted (VW-T) and equal-weighted (EW-T) basis. As the same appraised values that are used to construct the RN-Index are available for the unsold properties on a quarterly basis, appraisal-driven indices (VW-A and EW-A) are also constructed for comparison purposes.

Note that transactions-driven values generated in this research are estimates that are absent any motivation to artificially smooth reported values through time, and are not subject to time lags since "comparable sales" both *before and after* the time periods the unsold properties are being valued are utilized. This corrects problems that may cause appraisal-driven returns to have less variance and lower correlations with contemporaneous stock and bond returns. For example, appraisers may be hesitant to make large adjustments to their previous estimates of value (as suggested by Edelstein and Quan), and they only have *prior* sales of comparable properties they are familiar with upon which to base their estimates.

Table 5(A) indicates that *property-specific* transaction-driven returns are more volatile, on average, than appraisal-driven returns. The standard deviations reported in panel A are the average standard deviations of the returns on individual properties; diversification benefits are thus suppressed. While individual property transactions-driven returns are more volatile than appraisal-driven returns, the transactions-driven *portfolio* returns in Table 5(B) have approximately the same volatility as appraisal-driven returns. Table 5(B) presents the means and standard deviations of the transactions-driven and appraisal-driven return *indices* from the sampled properties, along with the Russell/NCREIF Property Index. The only difference between the Russell/NCREIF Property Index and the value-weighted appraisal-driven series (VW-A) is sample size. VW-A is constructed from the unsold sample of properties used in this research (a subset of the properties used in the Russell/NCREIF Property Index). The means and standard deviations of these indices are similar across all property types, with the VW-A series having slightly higher returns with greater standard deviations. The slightly higher mean returns from the unsold sample of properties in the VW-A series are consistent with the belief that property managers are selling off their poorly performing properties on average. The greater standard deviations are consistent with the smaller sample sizes and the corresponding reduction in diversification benefits.

Table 5

(A) Individual Property Return Moments

		Appraisal	Transactions
Total	Mean	2.5	3.1
	Std. Dev.	5.0	6.9
Office	Mean	1.7	3.0
	Std. Dev.	5.3	7.5
Retail	Mean	2.9	2.8
	Std. Dev.	4.1	7.9
Indust.	Mean	2.8	3.3
	Std. Dev.	5.1	6.2

(B) NCREIF, Appraisal, and Transactions Indices
(Value and Equal Weighted, 80-3 to 88-2)

		NCREIF	VW-A	VW-T	EW-A	EW-T
Total	Mean	2.6	2.8	2.8	2.8	3.1
	Std. Dev.	1.2	1.5	1.0	1.2	.9
Office	Mean	2.4	2.6	2.9	2.2	2.9
	Std. Dev.	1.9	2.1	1.5	2.2	1.9
Retail	Mean	2.9	3.1	2.3	3.1	3.0
	Std. Dev.	1.0	1.6	1.9	1.4	1.5
Indust.	Mean	3.1	3.1	3.1	3.0	3.2
	Std. Dev.	1.3	1.4	1.1	1.2	.9

Source: Authors

Means and standard deviations of the VW-A index are also quite similar to the value-weighted, transactions-driven index (VW-T). Note that the omission of a time-series capital market factor may result in an underestimation of mean returns and the variability of returns over the time period analyzed. For example, required rates of return are believed to have declined on "trophy" office properties desired by foreign investors and domestic pension funds, causing an increase in value over the time period examined. The constant in the pricing equation absorbs this affect, on average, but appreciation rates (and therefore the mean and variance of total returns) are underestimated. This omission can be factored into the interpretation of the final results, however, and intuition about the return characteristics of commercial real estate can still be achieved. Consistent with this belief, office appraised values increased dramatically relative to transactions values during 1980–81, again in 1984, and then decreased steadily during 1985–88. This causes the VW-T series to underestimate the standard deviation of individual office property returns, as reflected in the low 1.5% standard deviation of the office index returns over the sample time period. Retail appraised values increased steadily relative to transactions values during 1983–87, and unlike office properties, never decreased relative to transaction values. This causes the VW-T series to underestimate the mean return of retail property returns, as it ignores the appreciation of retail values due to the declining required rate of return. Industrial property required rate of returns remained fairly constant over this time period, and the VW-A and VW-T series are very similar.

Correlations of the transactions-driven indices and their appraisal-driven counterparts range from .07 for retail to .55 for office properties, with the overall indices having a .41 correlation. The overall appraisal-driven series has a .95 correlation coefficient with the Russell/NCREIF index, while the transactions-driven index has a .36 correlation.

Comparing the VW-A series to the equal-weighted appraisal-driven series (EW-A) reveals that the larger office properties outperformed the smaller office properties, as the value-weighted mean return is substantially greater than the equal-weighted mean return. Comparing the VW-T series to the equal-weighted transaction-driven series (EW-T) further reveals that the larger office properties outperformed the smaller office properties due to declining required rates of return on large "trophy" properties (not due to changes in rents). As the transactions-driven series does not reflect value changes due to required rate of return movements, the mean returns of VW-T and EW-T for office properties are quite similar. The differences in mean returns of VW-T and EW-T for retail properties are primarily a function of sample size. Two of the larger retail properties performed below average, affecting the value-weighted series more than the equal-weighted series.

In summary, Table 5 indicates that appraisal-driven real estate returns understate the true variance of real estate returns for individual properties, but that most of the property-by-property quarterly volatility is diversifiable within the real estate asset class.[32] Diversifying quarterly risk is not the same as diversifying risk over longer time periods, however, and does not preclude the majority of real estate properties having depressed prices at a given point in time. The quarterly results reported here are quite consistent with the belief that commercial real estate in general declined in value over the 1985–1988 time period, and imply that the idiosyncrasies of commercial property (primarily due to different tenant mixes and lease structures) dominate property-specific returns on a quarterly basis, while systematic influences are felt over longer periods of time.

CONCLUSIONS

Commercial real estate is often reported to have high risk-adjusted returns and negative correlations with stocks, bonds, and other asset classes when estimated with quarterly data. Zerbst and Cambon (1984) and Sirmans and Sirmans (1987) survey the literature on commercial real estate returns and suggest that these results are due to the reliance on appraised values in the estimation of real estate returns, and that if market values were observable real estate returns would exhibit more volatility and possibly higher correlations with stocks and bonds. Hoag and MCG support this contention by modeling real estate values and estimating real estate returns from their modeled values. Both find their return series to have more volatility than any of the appraisal-driven return series used in past studies. Their findings are intuitively pleasing, but both caution that data limitations are a concern and further study is warranted as more data become available.

The database used in this research contains better information on the quality of location and functionality of the respective properties, as well as providing a larger sample of properties over a longer period of time than has previously been available to researchers. The analysis supports three general conclusions about commercial real estate returns in the 1980s:

1) Appraisal-driven real estate returns understate the true variance of real estate returns *for individual properties.*

2) Most of the individual property risk (estimated on a quarterly basis) is diversifiable *within* the real estate asset class.

3) The correlation between real estate returns and stock and bond returns is low.

The transactions-driven returns utilized to draw these conclusions are based on the theoretical model of value derived earlier in this study. Since no proxies were found to be significant for a time-series capital market factor, one might suppose that systematic risk is understated. However, since there should be some noise in market prices, and over 80% of the variation is explained by the value equations (as measured by the adjusted R^2 for the different value equations) without these hypothesized systematic factors, it is likely that the amount of systematic risk induced by capital market factors (should they exist across all real estate) would be quite small. The combination of this argument with the results in Table 5 which show significant reduction in variance moving from individual property averages to index returns, supports the diversifiability of individual property risk.

The hypothesis is further supported by the fact that when the yen/$ exchange rate (the only general capital market factor that was found to be significant in the pricing equation after an extensive search) and/or other selected capital market factors such as the S&P 500 were included, measurements of the mean and standard deviation of the resulting return series were essentially the same as when these variables were omitted. Also note that some of the systematic component of real estate returns will be reflected in the transactions-driven return series through any systematic movements in the modeled characteristics of value (such as net income or change in real personal income).

Our inability to find an acceptable proxy for a time-series capital market factor (and the lack of impact that selected capital market factors had on the time-series characteristics of the resulting real estate return series) also provides insight into the degree of diversification possible across asset classes. In looking for empirical proxies for a capital market factor, numerous possibilities were examined (including all of the typical macroeconomic variables found to be significant in stock and bond studies). Since none of these potential capital market proxies were significant in the value equations, it is unlikely that any capital market factor that systematically affects real estate returns (again, should one exist) would be highly correlated with stock and bond returns. Since the value equations work well, and the resulting returns are essentially uncorrelated with stocks and bonds, it follows that if the primary omitted variable (the capital market effect) from the value equation is also uncorrelated with stock and bond returns,[33] then quarterly real estate returns do in fact have a very low correlation with quarterly stock and bond returns.[34]

NOTES

[1] See Zerbst and Cambon (1984) or Sirmans and Sirmans (1987) for a summary of these results.

[2] The possible lack of comparability suggested here is not due to the differing degrees of financial leverage, and/or the differing tax implications of real estate investments as compared to stock and bond investments. Over the last twenty years unlevered real estate returns dominate leveraged corporate returns, and real estate returns to tax-free institutions (i.e., investors that are not utilizing any tax advantages real estate might offer) dominate corporate returns to both taxable and tax-free investors. Even after controlling for these structural differences, real estate appears to be underpriced when viewed in a mean-variance pricing framework.

[3] See Cole, Guilkey and Miles (1987).

[4] Giliberto (1988) uses a discrete time model of the appraisal process to show that even if real estate appraisals are unbiased estimates of the true market values, the mean *return* on a portfolio of real estate investments based on appraised values will be a positively biased estimate of the true portfolio return if the covariances of the real estate *values* are serially independent. Subsequent work by Geltner (1989) with a continuous time model, however, shows that under most market conditions, any bias is economically trivial and can be safely ignored.

[5] The direction of the correlation bias is theoretically unknown. However, if relevant information (i.e., some macroeconomic variable that affects asset prices) enters markets as random shocks, then these shocks would be expected to impact stock and bond prices immediately. Their effect upon real estate values would be spread over several periods due to the nature of the appraisal process (i.e., the use of "comparable" sales transacting at different points in time to estimate value). This would lead one to believe that the covariance of real estate returns with the returns of assets such as stocks and bonds would be biased toward zero. The effect on the correlation would depend on whether the reduction in variance in the denominator or the reduction in covariance in the numerator dominates.

[6] Liquidity premiums that are not captured in mean-variance calculations and/or investment horizons that are longer than three months are plausible explanations to pursue.

[7] The selected methodology is similar to that employed by Hoag and MCG, but with the following critical differences: 1) Hoag and MCG appear to utilize all available data and simply select models that "fit" the data the best (i.e., the models with the highest R^2). The problem of over-fitting the within-sample data is discussed. 2) A larger sample, over a longer period of time, and with important measures of the quality of location and functionality, are important differences in the data utilized in this research and the data available to Hoag and/or MCG.

[8] There are several interesting aspects to a comprehensive modeling of the commercial real estate market sector that are beyond the requirements of the valuation model needed for this research, including filtering, fast money, oligopolistic influences, and cross-over uses. The handling of these complex but interesting issues will be left for future research.

[9] As supply comes in lumpy increments, even if expectations were perfectly met one would not expect real estate markets to clear at all times.

[10] Empirical investigation suggests that highly regulated Boston and San Francisco have a far lower "natural" vacancy rate than relatively unregulated Houston or Phoenix. See Hendershott and Haurin (1988) for a discussion of this issue. See Voith and Crone (1988) and Wheaton and Torto (1988) for historic vacancy rates in the office market.

[11] The fact that real estate markets persist in "disequilibrium" is first analyzed by Fair and Jaffee (1972). Bowden (1978) shows that the dynamics of the disequilibrium process are complex, and that the simple flow models considered by Fair and Jaffee do not do justice to the application they have in mind. A complete model of real estate value should recognize both the stock and flow of rentable space. For a discussion of disequilibrium models in general, see Maddala (1983).

[12] Depending on current rental rates and level of economic activity, space may be used to differing degrees of intensity. When rates are high, or economic activity is low, existing space may be made available to the market by the users. In addition, when rates are high, temporarily vacant space may be approved and made available to the market.

[13] As real estate is believed to provide a hedge against inflation, real estate prices are affected in conflicting ways by expected inflation—negatively due to inflation's influence on required rates of return, and positively due to real estate's hedging abilities. Expected inflation should therefore be modeled independently of nominal required rates of return.

[14] Under the homogeneous product assumption, the error term in any empirical applications would pick up the impact of heterogeneity and would be unsatisfactorily large.

[15] Note that a true hedonic model is not developed in this paper, but instead the underlying concept of hedonic theory is used to deal with the heterogeneity of commercial real estate in the construction of the valuation model. Hedonic models use strictly cross-sectional differences in the assets being modeled and often estimate the *aggregate* change in price for the sample of assets using time-series dummy variables. The valuation model in this paper uses time-varying, property-specific variables and estimates *individual* property values at different points in time.

[16] For example, risk premiums vary by property type and are lower on "trophy" properties in general.

[17] The primary metropolitan statistical area (PMSA) is the preferred unit of location in economic studies such as this, as it subdivides geographic MSAs into smaller areas that have economic (rather than strictly geographic) ties.

[18] See Chen, Roll and Ross (1986) for example.

[19] Adequate proxies for the quality of location and functionality were not available to Hoag or MCG and these two variables were specifically collected to correct this apparent problem.

[20] Apartments and hotels are two other commercial property types that are not analyzed here due to insufficient observations in the available sample.

[21] Information on the data collection process, detail on the characteristics of the properties in the sample, and summary statistics of the variables are provided in the doctoral dissertation of R. Brian Webb written under the supervision of Mike Miles at the University of North Carolina at Chapel Hill. The data collection process was initiated in 1985 for the Miles, Cole, Guilkey (1990) paper, and updated and expanded for this research. The authors personally visited many of the NCREIF member firms to obtain the level of property-specific data needed for this project.

[22] Hoag and MCG had to rely on age as a proxy for functionality and a suburb versus CBD dummy variable to proxy for the quality of location. The insignificance of these variables in the valuation equations of Hoag and MCG provided the motivation to collect the subjective estimates of location and functionality used in this research. Results suggest that these were critical missing variables in the Hoag and MCG research.

[23] The specific procedure used is a two-step estimation strategy in which the determinants of whether or not a property is sold are estimated by the probit method, and the results of the probit regression are used to calculate a correction factor for the value equation.

[24] The cost to gather the property-specific information on all unsold properties was prohibitive, so while we have all properties that sold from the Russell/NCREIF database, we only have a sample of the unsold properties.

[25] To obtain the correct covariance matrix for the parameter estimates from this weighted estimation, the following procedure is used: the negative inverse of the Hessian of the weighted log likelihood function (H) and the summed outer products of the first derivatives of the weighted log likelihood function (G) are calculated. The correct covariance matrix (V) is calculated as $[GHG]^{-1}$. See Maddala (1983) for a more complete treatment of this commonly used correction procedure.

[26] Parameter estimates for the value equation are consistent whether OLS or joint estimation is utilized, and are quite similar as can be seen by comparing Tables 2 and 3.

[27] Hoag did not attempt to control for the potential sold sample bias. Quality of location and functionality were missing from this database, creating concerns about a missing variables problem with his work as well.

[28] With the sold sample of properties providing market transaction prices, this linear valuation equation is utilized to "price" observed factors of each of the seven characteristics of value. The general theoretical model does not specify a particular functional form for the reduced-form pricing equation. The typical functional forms utilized in the literature have been linear or log linear. While Table 3 presents the model in linear form for ease of exposition, both forms are examined through the use of the Box and Cox power function. The interaction terms among the independent variables are also examined as an additional specification check.

[29] Regressions are run with significant variables only since parameter estimates from this valuation equation will be applied out-of-sample (to the characteristics of the unsold properties) causing the concern of over-fitting the data with insignificant variables as discussed in the text.

[30] The limited number of retail properties that sold in this shortened time period probably explains this result.

[31] Percentage differences for industrial properties are 20% for transactions-driven values, and 9% for appraised values; differences for office properties are 18% and 11%; and for retail, 12% and 6% respectively. The standard deviations of the transactions-driven differences were nearly double the appraisal differences on office properties, but essentially the same for retail and industrial.

[32] Non-diversified (geographically or by property type) portfolios of office properties were constructed for PMSAs where there were enough observations to reasonably do so. For example, a portfolio of nine Houston office properties was constructed. This non-diversified portfolio has a standard deviation of .10, with a −.20 correlation with a S&P 500 over the 1980–1988 time period.

[33] The transactions-driven index has a −.01 correlation with the S&P 500, and a −.06 correlation with the twenty-year Treasury bond index over the 1980–1988 time period.

[34] Once again note that this conclusion does not imply that real estate returns are not affected by the same macroeconomic variables that affect stock and bond returns, just that the timing of the effect is muted within the real estate asset class. Possible reasons for this difference in timing include the effect that long-term leases have on the cash flows of property, a willingness of real estate owners to trade liquidity for lowered volatility in property values, and greater imperfections in real estate markets relative to stock and bond markets due to market segmentation and greater information costs.

REFERENCES

Bowden, R. J. 1978. Specification, Estimation and Inference for Models of Markets in Disequilibrium. *International Economic Review* 19(3): 711–26.

Chen, N.-F., R. Roll and S. A. Ross. 1986. Economic Forces and the Stock Market. *Journal of Business* 59(3): 383–403.

Cole, R., D. Guilkey and M. Miles. 1986. Toward an Assessment of the Reliability of Commercial Appraisals. *Appraisal Journal* 54(3): 422–32.

Edelstein, R. and D. Quan. 1991. Appraisal Bias. Working paper, University of California at Berkeley.

Engle, R. F., D. M. Lilien and M. Watson. 1985. A Dynamic Model of Housing Price Determination. *Journal of Econometrics* 28:307–26.

Fair, R. C. and D. M. Jaffee. 1972. Methods of Estimation for Markets in Disequilibrium. *Econometrica* 40(3): 497–514.

Froland, C. 1987. What Determines Cap Rates on Real Estate? *Journal of Portfolio Management* 13(4): 77–82.

Geltner, D. 1989. Bias in Appraisal-Based Returns. *Journal of the American Real Estate and Urban Economics Association* 17(3): 338–52.

Giliberto, M. 1988. A Note on the Use of Appraisal Data in Indexes of Performance Measurement. *Journal of the American Real Estate and Urban Economics Association* 16(1): 77–83.

Griliches, Z. 1971. *Price Indexes and Quality Change.* Harvard University Press.

Guilkey, D., R. Cole and M. Miles. 1989. The Motivation for Institutional Real Estate Sales and Implications for Asset Class Returns. *Journal of the American Real Estate and Urban Economics Association* 17(1): 70–86.

Hendershott, P. H. and D. R. Haurin. 1988. Adjustments in the Real Estate Market. *Journal of the American Real Estate and Urban Economics Association* 16(4): 343–53.

Hoag, J. W. 1980. Towards Indices of Real Estate Value and Return. *Journal of Finance* 35(2): 569–80.

Ibbotson, R. G. 1988. *SBBO 1988 Yearbook.* Chicago.

——— and L. B. Seigel. 1984. Real Estate Returns: A Comparison with Other Investments. *Journal of the American Real Estate and Urban Economics Association* 12(3): 219–42.

Ibbotson, R. G., J. Diermeir and L. Siegel. 1984. The Demand for Capital Market Returns: A New Equilibrium Theory. *Financial Analysts' Journal* 40: 22–33.

Kain, J. and J. M. Quigley. 1975. Housing Markets and Racial Discrimination: A Microeconomic Analysis. Urban and Regional Studies. Columbia University Press.

Linneman, P. 1980. Some Empirical Results on the Nature of the Hedonic Price Function for the Urban Housing Market. *Journal of Urban Economics* 8(1): 47–68.

Maddala, G. S. 1983. *Limited Dependent and Qualitative Variables in Econometrics.* Cambridge University Press.

Mehra, T. A. and E. C. Prescott. 1985. The Equity Premium: A Puzzle. *Journal of Monetary Economics* 15(2): 145–62.

Miles, M. 1989. Real Estate as an Asset Class: A 25 Year Perspective. *Salomon Brothers Bond Market Research* (January).

———. 1990. What Is the Value of All U.S. Real Estate? *Real Estate Review* 20(2): 69–77.

———, R. Cole and D. Guilkey. 1990. A Different Look at Commercial Real Estate Returns. *Journal of the American Real Estate and Urban Economics Association* 18(4): 403–30.

Miles, M., D. Guilkey, D. Hartzell and D. Sears. 1989. Toward a Transactions-Based Index. Salomon Brothers.

National Council of Real Estate Investment Fiduciaries. 1988. The NCREIF Real Estate Performance Report. Frank Russell Company (Winter).

Robichek, A. A., R. Cohn and J. Pringle, 1972. Returns on Alternative Investment Media and Implications for Portfolio Construction. *Journal of Business* 45: 427–43.

Rosen, S. Hedonic Prices and Implicit Markets. 1974. Product Differentiation in Pure Competition. *Journal of Political Economy* 82(1): 34–55.

Shulman, D. 1986. The Relative Risk of Equity Real Estate and Common Stock: A New View. *Salomon Brothers Bond Market Research* (June).

Sirmans, G. S. and C. F. Sirmans. 1987. The Historical Perspective of Real Estate Returns. *Journal of Portfolio Management* 13(3): 22–31.

Stambaugh, R. F. 1982. On the Exclusion of Assets from Tests of the Two Parameter Model: A Sensitivity Analysis. *Journal of Financial Economics* 10(3): 237–68.

Voith, R. and T. Crone. 1988. National Vacancy Rates and the Persistence of Shock in U.S. Office Markets. *Journal of the American Real Estate and Urban Economics Association* 16(4): 437–58.

Wheaton, W. C. and R. G. Torto. 1988. Vacancy Rates and the Future of Office Rents. *Journal of the American Real Estate and Urban Economics Association* 16(4): 430–36.

Zerbst, R. and B. Cambon. 1984. Real Estate: Historical Returns on Real Estate Investment. *Journal of Portfolio Management* 10(3): 5–20.

Zisler, R. and R. A. Feldman. 1985. Real Estate Report. Goldman Sachs & Company.

13 Some Additional Evidence on the Performance of Commingled Real Estate Investment Funds: 1972–1991

W. B. Brueggeman, A. H. Chen, and T. G. Thibodeau

This paper examines the investment performance of two commingled real estate investment funds (CREFs) over the past twenty years. Results indicate that these funds: (1) offered very good portfolio diversification potential by reducing risk and increasing return; and (2) provided a good hedge against (anticipated) inflation over the entire period of study. Risk-adjusted performance for these CREFs generally remained superior to stock and bond performance because of the lower volatility in CREF returns. While CREFs provided a significant hedge against inflation during the 1972–1991 period, this hedge was significantly diminished during the 1984–1991 period, a period when the rate of inflation was relatively low.

INTRODUCTION

During the 1980s, pension funds increased both the absolute dollar amount and the share of income-producing real estate included in their investment portfolios.[1] A common vehicle used by these funds to invest in real estate during the period was to acquire investment units in open-ended, commingled real estate funds (CREFs). These funds were established with the objective of purchasing and overseeing the operations and disposition of a diversified portfolio of income-producing properties on behalf of pension fund investors. Like mutual funds, pension investors purchase investment units in these funds. Fund managers also stand ready to redeem such units as cash flow from the operation and sale of properties allow.

Investor interest in income-producing real estate during the eighties was the partial result of expected diversification benefits obtained from real estate when added to portfolios containing bonds and common stocks. One reason why portfolio managers have become aware of these benefits is because of numerous real estate investment performance studies that were conducted during the decade. While there is some disagreement among these studies over performance measurement, most have consistently pointed out that real estate does provide the potential for diversification gains. These studies

From *The Journal of Real Estate Research*, Vol. 7, No. 4 (Fall 1992). The authors gratefully acknowledge assistance from Pension Real Estate Services, Encinitas, California and the Folsom Institute for Development and Land Use Policy. The authors also thank S. Michael Giliberto for providing useful comments on an earlier draft. The usual disclaimer applies.

have also indicated that, unlike stocks or corporate bonds, real estate may be a significant hedge against inflation (see Fama and Schwert [4], Brueggeman, Chen and Thibodeau [1], Gyourko and Linneman [10], Hartzell, Hekman, and Miles [11], [12], Firstenberg, Ross and Zisler [5], and Liu, Hartzell, Grissom and Grieg [15]). See Chan, Hendershott and Sanders [2] for an alternative view of real estate's inflation-hedging performance.

Using data obtained from the two oldest CREFs in existence, Brueggeman, Chen and Thibodeau [1] (BCT) compared returns on real estate investments with returns on common stocks and long-term corporate bonds over the 1972–1983 period. They examined the risk-adjusted performance of these investments as derived from the traditional capital asset pricing model (CAPM) and the CAPM modified to include the effects of uncertain inflation (CAPMUI). Performance was also judged by using an arbitrage pricing theory (APT) model in which real estate returns are related to a more inclusive macroeconomic factor representing large numbers of substitute investments. BCT examined investment returns from the 1972–1983 period and reported that real estate had: (1) generally outperformed stocks and bonds on a risk-adjusted basis; and (2) offered very good portfolio diversification benefits reducing risk and increasing return. Results also indicated that returns were highly correlated with inflation thereby providing a good inflation hedge. Results obtained by BCT were reported with two qualifications. First, quarterly data over the twelve-year period examined in the study was a relatively brief length of time to compare historical investment return data. Second, the period examined may have favored real estate investments relative to stock and corporate bond alternatives because of features in the federal tax code. High marginal income tax rates and accelerated depreciation schedules stimulated investment demand for income properties, driving up the prices of these assets particularly during the latter part of the 1972–1983 period.

The purpose of this paper is to update the 1984 study and to reconsider these concerns by examining CREF performance for the entire 1972–1991 period. In addition to increasing the sample size by over 50%, the additional eight years (1984–1991) include a period when: (1) real estate investments lost much of their tax-favored status (as a result of the Tax Reform Act of 1986); (2) common stock and corporate bond performance was vastly improved; and (3) the rate of inflation, as measured by the Consumer Price Index (CPI), was significantly lower.

Section two describes the data. Section three presents historic risk and return data for CREFs, common stocks, and long-term corporate bonds. Performance is measured using variations of CAPM (section four), CAPMUI (section five), and a two-factor Jensen index (section six). The seventh section examines investment performance measured against a broader range of substitute investments that include plant and equipment, human capital, and other assets held in investors' portfolios. Section eight provides summary remarks.

THE DATA

Investment return data used in this study are holding period returns based on quarterly index values for real estate, common stocks, long-term corporate bonds and Treasury bills. The real estate return data are obtained from two CREFs. One CREF (labeled RE1) is an affiliate of a commercial bank. At the end of 1989, this relatively small fund had assets of $413 million consisting of investments in industrial-warehouse properties (56%), land (31%), office properties (10%), and research and development facilities

(3%). Liquidation of all assets from this fund began during 1990 and results thereafter are not available. Investments were geographically distributed across the western (28%), midwestern (31%), and southern (41%) regions of the United States. The second CREF (labeled RE2), affiliated with a life insurance company, is much larger and more diversified both geographically and by property type. This fund had real estate investments of approximately $3.5 billion at the end of 1989. These investments were categorized as follows: 26% office space, 9% retail, 48% industrial-warehouse, 8% residential, 4% hotel, 2% land and 3% other. The investments were nearly uniformly distributed across the United States with 7% in the East, 32% in the South, 36% in the Midwest, and 25% in the West. Assets in these two CREFs represented about 10% of all real estate assets held by pension funds at the end of 1989; however it appears that a very broad spectrum of real estate investments are represented.

Holding period returns for common stocks are based on the Standard and Poor's 500 stock index. This index, holding period returns for long-term corporate bonds and T-bills, and changes in the CPI, are reported in Ibbotson Associates [13] based on their compilation of investment returns over the last fifty years. For the modified two-factor model, GNP data was obtained from the most recently available, internally consistent, GNP series.[2]

Caveats regarding the use of results from this study should be made clear. We have chosen to use ex-post data from only two CREFs because they provided the longest continuous quarterly returns available. In spite of this, the reader should be cautious in generalizing results to other CREFs or to other real estate investment vehicles. Real estate returns,[3] as calculated in this paper, are based on transactions into and out of the fund at the values shown in Exhibit 1. Like mutual funds, CREF unit values are based on the net asset value of all assets in the fund which may include properties, cash and other assets owned by the fund at the end of each quarter. While the net asset values of most properties in the fund are based on appraised values, these values also reflect prices for properties acquired or sold by the fund during each quarter. The unit values are the prices that willing investors must pay to purchase units in the CREF and prices at which funds will redeem such units. In spite of the redemption feature of these CREFs, the possibility of large-scale redemptions would make CREF liquidity risk a major component of total risk that investors must assess when contemplating the purchase of a CREF unit.[4]

Exhibit 1 lists CREF unit prices and actual transaction volume for the insurance company-affiliated CREF (RE2) over the 1972 through 1989 period. During the first four years of the fund's existence investors were, on balance, buying into the fund. This pattern generally continued through 1984 although there were occasional periods when redemptions exceeded purchases. However after 1984, redemptions have systematically exceeded purchases. Transactions occurred in sixty-seven of the seventy-two quarters during the study period.

Recently, several papers have indicated that a potential bias exists when real estate returns are computed from appraised values (Giliberto[9], Geltner [8], and Gau and Wang [7]). These criticisms are certainly appropriate for real estate return indexes computed from appraised values (i.e., the Frank Russell Company Index and the Evaluation Associates Property Index).[5] However, because the returns used in this study are computed from prices that investors must pay to acquire CREF units and prices that they receive when redemption requests are satisfied, the value of these units should behave more like that of a security, or claim on assets, rather than an opinion of value.

Exhibit 1 CREF Unit Prices and Transactions

Quarter	Assets	Purchases	Redemptions	Quarter	Assets	Purchases	Redemptions
71:4	$1,102.35	20,955	0				
72:1	$1,114.52	9,107	0	81:1	$3,369.84	47,067	826
72:2	$1,129.96	9,195	0	81:2	$3,512.77	47,996	6,548
72:3	$1,149.36	20,029	17	81:3	$3,655.45	178,993	356
72:4	$1,167.69	29,845	0	81:4	$3,774.22	48,646	7,366
73:1	$1,184.76	13,555	0	82:1	$3,846.32	14,273	0
73:2	$1,208.61	12,502	0	82:2	$3,900.77	18,560	0
73:3	$1,251.16	29,397	48	82:3	$3,935.85	5,640	17,709
73:4	$1,275.17	51,915	0	82:4	$3,939.45	5,635	25,384
74:1	$1,298.30	16,822	0	83:1	$4,002.21	6,771	10,869
74:2	$1,328.12	62,412	0	83:2	$4,119.08	138,186	48,166
74:3	$1,360.32	32,228	59	83:3	$4,240.03	28,538	7,099
74:4	$1,387.79	37,830	0	83:4	$4,347.02	40,534	27,720
75:1	$1,409.62	26,482	0	84:1	$4,538.10	20,141	8,682
75:2	$1,447.84	0	0	84:2	$4,665.72	10,031	29,170
75:3	$1,477.62	27,531	555	84:3	$4,813.19	4,201	22,314
75:4	$1,502.45	0	0	84:4	$4,933.54	9,265	34,302
76:1	$1,529.38	0	10,475	85:1	$5,059.45	3,360	27,256
76:2	$1,562.13	0	3,796	85:2	$5,125.60	2,419	38,396
76:3	$1,598.05	0	2,972	85:3	$5,226.79	17,303	29,339
76:4	$1,629.87	0	503	85:4	$5,321.05	4,022	40,003
77:1	$1,666.73	0	7,548	86:1	$5,413.54	4,903	38,005
77:2	$1,715.06	37,427	17,510	86:2	$5,422.94	6,808	34,350
77:3	$1,757.72	0	4,233	86:3	$5,535.53	824	54,542
77:4	$1,804.48	0	2,006	86:4	$5,596.34	929	54,198
78:1	$1,856.16	0	4,536	87:1	$5,603.69	3,549	22,960
78:2	$1,932.16	0	57	87:2	$5,610.84	1,297	43,304
78:3	$2,002.55	0	0	87:3	$5,766.21	1,953	43,014
78:4	$2,156.79	0	0	87:4	$5,853.00	3,448	33,593
79:1	$2,253.83	0	1,384	88:1	$5,943.13	2,975	27,371
79:2	$2,435.28	31,865	0	88:2	$6,058.61	1,327	24,334
79:3	$2,551.55	0	43	88:3	$6,227.82	4,490	29,588
79:4	$2,673.03	24,695	4,482	88:4	$6,374.57	8,868	33,039
80:1	$2,885.13	43,707	0	89:1	$6,476.09	10,840	17,846
80:2	$3,020.45	92,635	1,225	89:2	$6,627.69	1,101	13,869
80:3	$3,147.17	55,288	0	89:3	$6,747.75	6,648	18,058
80:4	$3,260.52	0	0	89:4	$6,907.30	479	16,373

INVESTMENT RETURNS

All investment return data are based on quarterly holding period returns beginning in 1972. This paper includes investment returns for the small bank CREF (labeled RE1) through 1989, for the larger insurance company CREF (labeled RE2) through 1991, and for an equally weighted combined synthetic CREF (labeled RE3) through 1989. The RE1 and RE3 series are provided to facilitate comparison with our earlier analysis (Brueggeman, Chen and Thibodeau [1]).

Exhibit 2 lists the annual nominal returns for these CREFs, for the S&P 500 series, and for the long-term corporate bond series as published in Ibbotson [13]. The

Exhibit 2 CREF Annual Nominal Returns

Year	RE1 %	RE2 %	RE3 %	Stocks %	Bonds %
1972	9.09	5.93	7.51	18.98	7.26
1973	7.07	9.19	8.13	−14.67	1.14
1974	9.70	8.77	9.24	−26.45	−3.06
1975	7.15	8.35	7.75	37.21	14.64
1976	5.29	8.45	6.87	23.85	18.65
1977	13.53	10.81	12.17	−7.18	1.71
1978	11.29	19.52	15.41	6.57	−0.07
1979	20.31	24.07	22.19	18.44	−4.20
1980	17.89	21.95	19.92	32.42	−2.61
1981	26.07	15.75	20.91	−4.91	−0.96
1982	11.45	4.36	7.91	21.41	43.79
1983	8.55	10.27	9.41	22.51	4.70
1984	8.67	13.53	11.10	6.27	16.39
1985	15.37	7.81	11.59	32.16	30.90
1986	7.17	5.19	6.18	18.47	19.85
1987	5.09	4.55	4.82	5.23	−0.27
1988	6.34	8.98	7.66	16.81	10.70
1989	−1.83	8.35	3.26	31.49	16.23
1990	NA	4.46	NA	−3.35	6.74
1991	NA	−7.14	NA	30.57	19.57

Summary Statistics (1972–1989)

	RE1 %	RE2 %	RE3 %	Stocks %	Bonds %
Arithmetic Mean	10.46	10.88	10.67	13.26	9.71
Standard Deviation	6.22	5.68	5.36	17.09	12.67
Geometric Mean	10.28	10.74	10.54	11.83	9.03

Summary Statistics (1972–1991)

	RE2 %	Stocks %	Bonds %
Arithmetic Mean	9.66	13.29	10.05
Standard Deviation	6.77	17.08	12.24
Geometric Mean	8.98	11.29	8.95

twenty-one year annual arithmetic average nominal return was 9.7% for RE2, 13.3% for stocks, and 10.1% for long-term corporate bonds. Annual standard deviations were 6.8% for RE2, 17.1% for stocks and 12.2% for bonds. The geometric mean for RE2 (9.0%) is approximately equal to the arithmetic mean. However, the higher volatility in the stock and bond funds produced significantly lower geometric mean returns for these investments (11.3% for stocks and 9.0% for bonds).

Exhibit 3 summarizes descriptive statistics for the nominal quarterly holding period returns for the CREFs, stocks, and long-term corporate bonds. The mean holding period returns, the standard deviation of those returns and the coefficients of variation are presented for the 1972–1989 period as well as for the 1984–1989 period.

Exhibit 3 Quarterly Nominal Returns

	RE3	(1972–1989) Stocks	Bonds
Mean	2.555	3.136	2.317
Standard Deviation	1.894	8.709	6.315
Coefficient of Variation	.741	2.777	2.726
		(1984–1989)	
Mean	1.800	4.524	3.679
Standard Deviation	1.043	8.448	5.347
Coefficient of Variation	.580	1.867	1.453
		(1972–1983)[1]	
Mean	2.932	2.427	1.636
Standard Deviation	2.088	8.748	6.626
Coefficient of Variation	.712	3.605	4.051

[1] results previously reported in Brueggeman, Chen and Thibodeau

Results in Exhibit 3 indicate that, as expected, mean quarterly returns for stocks and bonds exceeded real estate returns by a significant margin during the 1984–1989 period. Comparing returns for the 1972–1983 period to the returns for the 1984–1989 period, we find that quarterly nominal real estate returns declined from 2.9% to 1.8%. Concurrently, stock returns increased from 2.4% for the 1972–1983 period to 4.5% for the 1984–1989 period. Similarly, long-term corporate bond returns increased from 1.6% to 3.7%. For the entire eighteen-year period, quarterly nominal holding period returns are highest for stocks (3.1%), followed by the combined CREFs (2.6%), and then by bonds (2.3%).

The risk associated with these investment alternatives, as measured by the standard deviation of the nominal quarterly holding period returns, decreased by over 50% for the CREFs (down from 2.1% for the 1972–1983 period to 1.0% for the 1984–1989 period). Total risk was essentially unchanged for stocks (8.7% for the 1972–1983 period and 8.4% for the 1984–1989 period), and decreased slightly for bonds (down from 6.6% to 5.3%).

The coefficients of variation, a measure of risk per unit of return, decreased substantially for all three investment alternatives during the 1984–1989 period. For CREFs, the percentage decrease in the standard deviation exceeded the decline in returns, consequently the coefficients of variation decreased from .71 for the 1972–1983 period to .58 for the 1984–1989 period. Coefficients of variation for stocks decreased from 3.6 for the 1972–1983 period to 1.9 for the 1984–1989 period because mean stock returns increased while stock volatility remained unchanged. Finally, bond coefficients of variation decreased from 4.1 for the 1972–1983 period to 1.5 for the 1984–1989 period. For the entire 1972–1989 period, coefficients of variation for stocks and bonds were equal (2.7), while the CREF coefficients of variation were significantly lower (.7 for the combined CREF).

In sum, the descriptive statistics indicate that although real estate returns declined substantially during the 1984–1989 period, real estate investments again provided less risk per unit of return (relative to stocks and long-term corporate bonds) because of a greater decline in the variability of those returns.

Exhibit 4 contains the correlation matrix for nominal quarterly returns for the CREFs, common stocks, bonds, Treasury bills and the Consumer Price Index (CPI).

Exhibit 4 Correlation Matrix: Quarterly Nominal Returns

	RE1	RE2	RE3	(1984–1989) Stocks	Bonds	T-Bills	CPI
RE1	1.000	−.008	.879	−.012	.043	.002	−.089
RE2		1.000	.469	−.244	−.021	.623	.154
RE3			1.000	−.126	.003	.298	−.005
Stocks				1.000	.151	.073	.219
Bonds					1.000	.279	−.340
T-Bills						1.000	.132
CPI							1.000

	RE1	RE2	RE3	(1972–1989) Stocks	Bonds	T-Bills	CPI
RE1	1.000	.408	.927	−.154	−.247	.404	.312
RE2		1.000	.722	−.152	−.230	.496	.619
RE3			1.000	−.179	−.310	.510	.492
Stocks				1.000	.420	−.103	−.233
Bonds					1.000	−.056	−.387
T-Bills						1.000	.410
CPI							1.000

	RE2	Stocks	(1972–1991) Bonds	T-Bills	CPI
RE2	1.000	−.171	−.287	.498	.604
Stocks		1.000	.432	−.116	−.265
Bonds			1.000	−.069	−.404
T-Bills				1.000	.425
CPI					1.000

Separate tables are provided for the 1984–1989 period, for the 1972–1989 period (which includes RE1 and RE3), and for the entire 1972–1991 period. These results confirm that the negative correlation between the CREFs and stocks, reported in the earlier study, continued after 1984. Although negative correlation existed between CREFs and bonds during the previous study period, the correlation between the CREFs and bonds was essentially zero for the 1984–1989 period. These results imply that diversification benefits from adding real estate to a stock and bond portfolio continued during the 1984–1989 period. For the 1984–1989 period, the correlation between real estate and the rate of inflation was negative for the bank CREF, positive for the life insurance CREF, and small for both CREFs. Contrary to results showing positive correlations in the previous study, the return for the combined CREF was uncorrelated with inflation for the 1984–89 period.[6] However, as will be seen later in this paper, real estate continued to be a good hedge against anticipated inflation over the entire study period after controlling for market risk.

The correlation coefficients for the entire 1973–1989 period continued to generally support the results obtained for the 1973–1984 period. Namely, there was a negative correlation between the CREFs and both stocks and bonds, as well as a positive correlation between the real estate funds and inflation as measured by the CPI. This suggests that real estate: (1) offered significant diversification benefits when included in a stock and bond portfolio; and (2) provided a hedge against inflation over the eighteen-year period, although the inflation hedge is not evident for the 1984–1989 period.

PERFORMANCE MEASURES

To further examine the risk-adjusted performance of CREFs, we computed Sharpe's reward to variability ratio and Jensen's measure of differential return. Recall that Sharpe's index [21] evaluates investment performance using total risk and is defined as:

$$SI = (R_j - R_f)/s_j, \qquad (1)$$

where

SI = the Sharpe index of performance;
R_j = the average return on portfolio j;
R_f = the risk-free rate of interest; and
s_j = the standard deviation of excess returns.

The ninety-day Treasury bill rate was used to proxy the risk-free rate. A positive index indicates that average returns exceed returns provided by riskless investments. Also, the higher the index, the greater the risk-adjusted return.

Exhibit 5 summarizes the Sharpe indexes calculated for the twenty-one year period 1972–1991, for the eighteen-year period ending in 1989, and for three six-year subperiods: 1972–1977, 1978–1983, and 1984–1989. The results indicate that the combined CREF performance decreased significantly over the 1984–1989 period (down from .54 for the 1978–1983 period to .03 for the 1984–1989 period). Stock performance increased from .19 during 1978–1983 period to .33 for the 1984–1989. Bond returns also exhibited a significant increase—up from −.10 for the 1978–1983 period to .36 for the most recent six-year period. While results for the most recent six-year period (1984–1989) indicate that stocks and bonds outperformed real estate, results for the entire 1972–1991 period suggest that CREFs outperformed stocks and bonds on a total risk-adjusted basis. The Sharpe indexes for the entire period are .27 for RE2, .15 for stocks, and .09 for long-term corporate bonds.

Jensen's [14] measure of abnormal return was also calculated and the results are summarized in Exhibit 6. This return is measured by the extent to which the return on the portfolio in excess of the risk-free rate of return differs from the excess return on the market portfolio, as suggested by the Capital Asset Pricing Model. Jensen's index of performance is the intercept (χ) in the following regression equation:

$$R_{jt} - R_{ft} = \chi_j + \beta_j(R_{mt} - R_{ft}) + \mu_{jt}, \qquad (2)$$

where

R_{mt} = the rate of return on the market portfolio, and
μ_{jt} = the random error term.

Exhibit 5 Performance Measure Based on Sharpe's Index
(Quarterly Data: 1972-1991)

Type of Investment	21-Year Period (1972–1991)	18-Year Period (1972–1989)	1st 6-Year (1972–1977)	2nd 6-Year (1978–1983)	3rd 6-Year (1984–1989)
RE1	na	.2327	.3439	.3539	−.0656
RE2	.2700	.5162	1.3481	.6107	.2276
RE3	na	.3994	.6567	.5384	.0309
Stocks	.1469	.1413	−.0401	.1851	.3268
Bonds	.0868	.0665	.0564	−.0975	.3636

Exhibit 6 Performance Measure Based on Jensen Index
(Quarterly Data: 1972–1991)

Type of Investment	21-Year Period (1972–1991)	18-Year Period (1972–1989)	1st 6-Year (1972–1977)	2nd 6-Year (1978–1983)	3rd 6-Year (1984–1989)
RE1	na	.6811	.6933	1.5342	–.1127
		(2.147)	(1.645)	(2.098)	(.272)
RE2	.4703	.7272	.6718	1.3155	.2770
	(2.613)	(4.497)	(6.561)	(3.061)	(1.651)
RE3	na	.7041	.6825	1.4248	.0822
		(3.597)	(3.151)	(3.010)	(.379)
Bonds	.1306	.0339	.3423	–1.7581	1.6712
	(.209)	(.049)	(.599)	(1.118)	(1.460)

t-statistic is in parenthesis

The market return (R_{mt}) is represented by the S&P 500 index. A positive α implies superior (abnormal) performance relative to an unmanaged portfolio of similar risk while a negative α indicates inferior performance.

The results in Exhibit 6 indicate that the market risk-adjusted investment returns for the 1984–1989 period were not statistically different from zero (for a two-tailed test conducted at the 10% level of significance) for both CREFs and long-term corporate bonds. For the entire 1972–1991 period, however, RE2 provided positive market risk-adjusted returns. The risk-adjusted performance of corporate bonds could not be statistically distinguished from zero over either the most recent six-year period or over the entire period.

PERFORMANCE IN INFLATION HEDGING

To further investigate the inflation-hedging performance of these CREFs, we modified the one factor CAPM to incorporate the influence of uncertain inflation (CAPMUI). Proponents of CAPMUI (Roll [19], Long [16], Chen and Boness [3] and Friend, Landskroner and Losq [6]) argue that market risk (measured by the covariance between the asset return and the market portfolio) and inflation risk (measured by the covariance between the asset return and the rate of inflation) are both determinants of the equilibrium rate of return. CAPMUI provides useful insights as to the real estate investment funds' diversification and inflation-hedging potential. The two-factor return-generating model is:

$$R_{jt} = \gamma_0 + \gamma_1 R_{mt} + \gamma_2 \pi_t + \mu_{jt}, \qquad (3)$$

where π_t is the rate of inflation in period t as measured by the CPI.

The results in Exhibit 7 indicate that RE2 had low market risk over the entire 1972–1991 period; that long-term corporate bonds had significant market risk; that RE2 provided a good hedge against inflation while bonds were a negative inflation hedge. Hence, in addition to providing diversification benefits to institutional investors holding common stocks, CREFs provided a good inflation hedge over the entire period.

To gain further insight into CREFs' inflation-hedging ability, we separated inflation into anticipated and unanticipated components. Anticipated inflation was measured using the one-period, lagged-three-month T-bill rate (Fama and Schwert [4]). Unanticipated inflation is the difference between the actual inflation rate, as measured by the CPI, and the anticipated inflation rate defined above. Exhibit 8 summarizes the results

Exhibit 7 Regression Results from the Two-Factor Model

	(1972–1989)				(1972–1991)	
Parameter	RE1	RE2	RE3	Corporate Bonds	RE2	Corporate Bonds
γ_0	1.2157	1.0047	1.1102	4.7259	.5086	4.73333
	(1.788)	(3.279)	(2.699)	(3.489)	(1.470)	(3.842)
γ_1	−.0285	−.0138	−.0149	.2525	−.0025	.2453
	(.737)	(.079)	(.639)	(3.279)	(.124)	(3.481)
γ_2	.8843	1.0149	.9496	−2.0381	1.1785	−2.0365
	(2.492)	(6.347)	(4.424)	(2.884)	(6.375)	(3.094)
Adjusted R-squared	0.327	.3652	.2242	.2433	.3480	.2579
DW	2.5269	1.2454	1.7990	2.4157	1.0019	2.4134

t-statistic is in parenthesis

of the market and anticipated inflation two-factor model; Exhibit 9 summarizes the results of the two-factor market model with unanticipated inflation. The results indicate that during the 1972–1989 period real estate provided a good hedge against anticipated inflation but did little to hedge against unanticipated inflation. This result is consistent with Fama and Schwert [4], Gyourko and Linneman [10], Hartzell, Hekman and Miles [11], [12], Firstenberg, Ross and Zisler [5] and Liu, Hartzell, Grissom and Grieg [15] but is at variance with Chan, Hendershott and Sanders [2].

The result that real estate hedges against anticipated inflation may be because many real estate leases have relatively short maturities and are frequently renegotiated, others are tied to the CPI, and most provide for a full or partial pass-through of future operating expenses relative to the level in existence at the time a lease is made or renegotiated. Because of these provisions, the income streams reflect anticipated inflation to a greater or lesser degree for most properties. However these provisions are based on ex-post, not ex-ante, measures of inflation which may partially explain why real estate was not a good hedge against unanticipated inflation. The estimated coefficient of unanticipated inflation in the bond equation was negative and statistically significant implying that investors should have reduced their bond holdings as the variance around expected inflation increased.

Exhibit 8 Regression Results of the Two-Factor Model with Anticipated Inflation

	(1972–1989)				(1972–1991)	
Parameter	RE1 %	RE2 %	RE3 %	Corporate Bonds %	RE2 %	Corporate Bonds %
γ_0	.1071	1.0555	.5813	−.0721	.5068	.2092
	(.109)	(2.010)	(.926)	(.034)	(.845)	(.107)
γ_1	−.0501	−.0266	−.0383	.3047	−.0344	.3040
	(1.345)	(1.342)	(1.619)	(3.860)	(1.559)	(4.230)
γ_2	1.3644	.8629	1.1136	.7623	1.0189	.6607
	(2.775)	(3.297)	(3.561)	(.731)	(3.372)	(.670)
Adjusted R-squared	.1218	.1315	.1588	.1586	.1320	.1706
DW	1.9536	.8154	1.5902	2.2158	.6327	2.2074

t-statistic is in parenthesis

Exhibit 9 Regression Results of the Two-Factor Model with Unanticipated Inflation

	(1972–1989)				(1972–1991)	
Parameter	RE1 %	RE2 %	RE3 %	Corporate Bonds %	RE2 %	Corporate Bonds %
γ_0	2.7125	2.7945	2.7535	.8767	2.5634	.9097
	(7.347)	(14.681)	(11.523)	(1.260)	(12.10)	(1.433)
γ_1	−.0469	−.0149	−.0309	.2524	−.0199	.2466
	(1.171)	(.720)	(1.191)	(3.340)	(.861)	(3.568)
γ_2	.1617	.4955	.3286	−2.0949	.5957	−2.1004
	(.471)	(2.797)	(1.477)	(3.234)	(2.916)	(3.430)
Adjusted R-squared	−.0013	.0970	.0347	.2638	.1029	.2762
DW	1.7226	.7552	1.3339	2.4477	.5993	2.4394

t-statistic is in parenthesis

THE TWO-FACTOR JENSEN INDEX

To further examine the market and inflation risk-adjusted performance of real estate investment funds, we computed a modified Jensen index for the two-factor model. The modified Jensen index examines excess portfolio return (the portfolio return in excess of the risk-free rate) relative to the excess return on the market portfolio and the rate of inflation. The index is the intercept in the equation:

$$R_{jt} - R_{ft} = \gamma_0 + \gamma_1(R_{mt} - R_{ft}) + \gamma_2(\pi_t - R_{ft}) + \mu_{jt}. \quad (4)$$

Exhibit 10 contains a summary of the performance for real estate investment funds and corporate bonds based upon the modified two-factor Jensen index. The results of the 1984–1989 period indicate that neither RE2 nor long-term corporate bonds provided superior performance after controlling for both market and inflation risk. For the entire twenty-one year period, however, CREFs provided superior performance while long-term corporate bonds did not.

AN ALTERNATIVE TWO-FACTOR MODEL

Many would argue that when investigating the investment performance and the inflation hedging potential of real estate, the market index (i.e., S&P 500) is inadequate.

Exhibit 10 Performance Measure Based on Two-Factor Jensen Index
(Quarterly Data: 1972–1991)

Type of Investment	21-Year Period (1972–1991)	18-Year Period (1972–1989)	1st 6-Year (1972–1977)	2nd 6-Year (1978–1983)	3rd 6-Year (1984–1989)
RE1	na	.7609	1.0353	1.7650	.0126
		(2.265)	(2.008)	(2.216)	(.017)
RE2	.7108	.9389	.6804	1.9285	.2314
	(4.037)	(6.167)	(5.273)	(6.135)	(.751)
RE3	na	.8499	.8579	1.8468	.1220
		(4.234)	(3.237)	(3.997)	(.306)
Bonds	−.4888	−.5519	.5798	−2.8562	−2.1038
	(.764)	(.789)	(.812)	(1.768)	(1.134)

t-statistic is in parenthesis

Many have suggested that the performance of these investment alternatives should be measured against a broader range of substitute investments that include plant and equipment, human capital, and other assets held in investors' portfolios. Liu, Hartzell, Grissom and Grieg [15] evaluate investment performance using a market index that combines stock returns with a variety of other assets (cash equivalents, corporate bonds, U.S. government bonds, mortgage-backed bonds, commercial real estate, farm real estate, and single-family homes. They conclude that superior investment performance may result when assets are omitted from the market portfolio.

Following this rationale, we further investigated the inflation-hedging potential of CREFs by modifying the two-factor regression model. We substituted nominal changes in GNP in place of the S&P 500 as one factor and retained the CPI as the second factor. This alternative model follows directly from Ross's APT [20]. Ross argues that the return on a portfolio is influenced by several factors that influence economic activity. The condition for equilibrium in this model is that no arbitrage profits can exist between securities on a risk-adjusted basis. The reasons for including GNP as a factor are: (1) GNP is a composite macroeconomic variable that reflects real economic activity; and (2) GNP contains the returns on assets (such as human capital) that are excluded from the market portfolio.

The regression results for the alternative two-factor model, shown in Exhibit 11, are consistent with those reported earlier in this paper and provide additional evidence that real estate continued to provide a good hedge against inflation while common stock and corporate bond investments provided virtually no protection against inflation.

Exhibit 11 Regression Results of GNP-Inflation Model
(Quarterly Data: 1972–1989)

Parameter	RE1 %	RE2 %	RE3 %	S&P %	Corporate Bonds %
γ_0	1.6160	.7697	1.1928	8.0919	9.7248
	(1.961)	(2.077)	(2.381)	(3.160)	(5.866)
γ_1	−.3541	.1368	−.1086	−.9647	−2.0316
	(1.100)	(.945)	(.555)	(.964)	(3.137)
γ_2	1.0662	.9712	1.0187	−1.8107	−1.8847
	(2.956)	(5.987)	(4.645)	(1.615)	(2.597)
Adjusted R-squared	.0872	.3733	.2231	.0399	.2346
DW	1.9024	1.2305	1.8031	1.8403	2.4417

(Quarterly Data: 1972–1991)

Parameter	RE2 %	S&P %	Corporate Bonds %
γ_0	−.0502	8.1435	8.9964
	(.13)	(3.61)	(6.31)
γ_1	.3737	−.8425	−1.7695
	(2.41)	(.92)	(3.04)
γ_2	1.0348	−2.1332	−1.9333
	(5.66)	(1.97)	(2.82)
Adjusted R-squared	.3936	.0561	.2333
DW	1.0586	1.8906	2.4136

SUMMARY

This paper contains the results of a study of real estate investment performance over the 1972–1991 period. Returns through 1989 are based on data from the two longest time series available for commingled real estate investment funds. This study indicates that real estate (1) continued to offer very good portfolio diversification potential by reducing risk and increasing return; and (2) provided a good hedge against (anticipated) inflation for the entire eighteen-year period. Conclusions regarding the diversification benefits from adding real estate to common stock portfolios remain the same, even though significant changes have occurred since 1986. During this most recent period: (1) markets have experienced disinflation; (2) significant changes in real estate volatility have occurred; and (3) major revisions in the tax code were made in 1986. Although common stock outperformed real estate on the basis of nominal returns during the eighteen-year period, CREFs involved less risk per unit of return relative to both stocks and long-term corporate bonds. Risk-adjusted performance for CREFs generally remained superior to stocks and bond performance because of the lower volatility in CREF returns.

The CREFs also provided a significant hedge against inflation during the entire twenty-one-year period. The CREFs hedged against anticipated, but not unanticipated, inflation. The CREFs ability to hedge against inflation was significantly diminished during the last six years of the study, a period when the rate of inflation was relatively low.

NOTES

[1] McKelvy [17] reported that in 1982 pension funds had $19 billion invested in real estate which represented 2.4% of total pension fund assets. Ring [18] reported that in 1989 pension funds had $102.6 billion (4.7% of total assets) invested in real estate.

[2] *Survey of Current Business* [22].

[3] The holding period return is generally computed as:

$$\frac{\text{Unit Value}_t - \text{Unit Value}_{t-1}}{\text{Unit Value}_{t-1}},$$

where unit value is equal to property value plus income earned during the period. Cash distributions are made at the option of the investor by redeeming units.

[4] Generally, CREF withdrawal requests are honored at the end of each quarter, subject to ninety days notice, and available cash. However, there is no obligation for a CREF to sell properties to meet liquidation requests. If the total amount of all liquidation requests in a quarter exceeds the amount of cash then available, cash is apportioned based on the proportionate unit value to total fund value. An unfulfilled liquidation request remaining after the cash is exhausted is automatically considered as a request for liquidation at the end of the next quarter. Requests that are carried forward do not have any priority in the next quarter and are considered in proportion with all other requests.

[5] However, sales data for the last eight quarters (Q2/90–Q1/92) compiled from 152 FRC-NCREIF properties indicate that appraised values were about 1.9% higher than net proceeds.

[6] The correlation between the combined CREF and the CPI was .47 for the 1972–1983 period.

REFERENCES

[1] W. B. Brueggeman, A. Chen and T. G. Thibodeau. Real Estate Investment Funds Performance and Portfolio Considerations. *AREUEA Journal* 12:3 (Fall 1984), 333–54.

[2] K. C. Chan, P. H. Hendershott and A. B. Sanders. Risk and Return on Real Estate: Evidence from Equity REITs. *AREUEA Journal* 18:4 (Winter 1990), 431–52.

[3] A. H. Chen and A. J. Boness. Effects of Uncertain Inflation on the Investment and Financing Decisions of a Firm. *Journal of Finance* (May 1975), 469–83.

[4] E. Fama and W. Schwert. Asset Returns and Inflation. *Journal of Financial Economics* 4 (November 1977), 115–46.

[5] P. M. Firstenberg, S. Ross and R. Zisler. Real Estate: The Whole Story. *Journal of Portfolio Management* (Spring 1988), 22–34.

[6] I. Friend, Y. Landskroner and E. Losq. The Demand for Risky Assets Under Uncertain Inflation. *Journal of Finance* (December 1976), 1278–97.

[7] G. Gau and K. Wang. A Further Examination of Appraisal Data and the Potential Bias in Real Estate Return Indexes. *AREUEA Journal* 18:1 (Spring 1990), 40–48.

[8] D. Geltner. Bias in Appraisal-Based Returns. *AREUEA Journal* 17:3 (Fall 1989), 338–352.

[9] S. M. Giliberto. A Note on the Use of Appraisal Data in Indexes of Performance Measurement. *AREUEA Journal* 16:1 (Spring 1988), 77–83.

[10] J. Gyourko and P. Linneman. Owner-Occupied Homes, Income-Producing Properties, and REITs as Inflation Hedges: Empirical Findings. *Journal of Real Estate Finance and Economics* 1:4 (December 1988), 347–72.

[11] D. Hartzell, J. Hekman and M. Miles. Diversification Categories in Investment Real Estate. *AREUEA Journal* 14:2 (Summer 1986), 230–54.

[12] ———. Real Estate Returns and Inflation. *AREUEA Journal* 15:1 (Spring 1987), 617–37.

[13] Ibbotson Associates. *Stocks, Bonds, Bills, and Inflation*. Chicago, IL: Ibbotson Associates, 1992.

[14] M. Jensen. The Performance of Mutual Funds in the Period 1945–1964. *Journal of Finance* (May 1968), 443–55.

[15] C. H. Liu, D. H. Hartzell, T. V. Grissom, and W. Grieg. The Composition of the Market Portfolio and Real Estate Investment Performance. *AREUEA Journal* 18:1 (Spring 1990), 49–75.

[16] J. B. Long. Stock Prices, Inflation, and the Term Structure of Interest Rates. *Journal of Financial Economics* (July 1974), 131–70.

[17] N. McKelvy, *Pension Fund Investments in Real Estate: A Guide for Plan Sponsors and Real Estate Professionals*. Westport, CT: Quorum Press, 1982.

[18] T. Ring. Assets Increase, but Lag Markets. *Pensions & Investments* (May 21, 1990), 1–3.

[19] R. Roll. Assets, Money, and Commodity Price Inflation Under Uncertainty. *Journal of Money, Credit and Banking* (November 1973), 903–23.

[20] S. Ross. The Arbitrage Theory of Capital Asset Pricing. *Journal of Economic Theory* (December 1976), 341–60.

[21] W. F. Sharpe. Mutual Fund Performance. *Journal of Business* 39:1 (January 1966), 119–38.

[22] U.S. Department of Commerce, Economics and Statistics Administration, Bureau of Economic Analysis. *Survey of Current Business* 71:11 (November 1991).

Part 5. Portfolio Management and Real Estate

14 Diversification Works in Real Estate, Too

Terry V. Grissom, James L. Kuhle, and Carl H. Walther

> The data here suggest that diversification, especially across property types, is even more effective in reducing variance than it is for stock portfolios.

This article examines the effects of portfolio diversification on the reduction of unsystematic real estate investment risk, using calculated returns of actual real estate assets in two geographically different markets. We hope this study will be a valuable innovation in the field, because inspection of the literature suggests that the solution to the fundamental problem of applying portfolio theory efficiently to real estate investment strategies—that is, the problem of gauging the benefits of portfolio diversification and the reduction of variance—has been elusive.

Sharpe [1970] suggests that the total return variation of a portfolio may be classified in two ways: 1) as systematic variation, resulting from the covariation of the returns of the individual asset with the returns of the market, and 2) as unsystematic variation, resulting from the individual asset but unrelated to the market. Empirical tests of modern portfolio theory confirm that equity investors can reduce 80% or more of the unsystematic risk through diversification without sacrificing expected return. This diversification benefit is based on the correlation between the returns of pairs of assets. Typically, the value of this correlation is less than 1.0 and ranges between 0.5 and 0.75 for the majority of common stocks.

To date, however, there has been little empirical evidence for reducing unsystematic risk by portfolio diversification of real estate assets. A lack of sufficient transactional data has made it difficult to calculate frequent real estate returns and return correlation values between pairs of assets. Most recent real estate studies focus primarily on comparing the rates of return of various real estate assets, while failing to give attention to the inherent risk of these returns (Wendt and Wong [1965]; Kelleher [1976]; Hoag [1980]; Cullen and Blake [1980]). Empiricists have been forced to use either simulated or estimated market values when calculating risk and rates of return for real estate assets.

The first section of this study presents the methodology we have employed for calculating rates of return for real estate assets, the data base, and the method for building

---

From *The Journal of Portfolio Management*. This copyrighted material is reprinted with permission from *The Journal of Portfolio Management*, 488 Madison Avenue, New York, NY 10022.

portfolios of real estate assets. This methodology for calculating rates of return is based on guidelines proven in local real estate markets and incorporates property-specific characteristics. In the second section, we examine the effects of portfolio diversification on risk reduction. In the final section, we compare the performance of real estate diversification to common stock diversification as reported in earlier studies.

MEASURING RETURNS

There have been a number of valuation methodologies to value real estate properties. Some are based on the notions of a risk/return trade-off and the risk averseness of investors. The capital asset pricing and arbitrage pricing models are examples of valuation methodologies that rely on market based macroeconomic factors in pricing individual assets.

The major problem with these valuation techniques is in estimating them for real estate. Unlike the common stock market, individual assets in the real estate market trade infrequently. As a result, it is not easy to estimate the market prices necessary to estimate variances in the properties' holding period returns and covariances between holding period returns and risk factors. Time series analysis of holding period returns therefore has been impractical in the real estate market, and analysts have been forced to generate sufficient data points through simulation (Pellatt [1972]; Phyrr [1973]; Findlay, et al. [1979]) or through estimation of market value (Friedman [1970]; Hoag [1980]; Miles and McCue [1984]).

Kuhle [1985] has developed a simulation method for generating sufficient data for the analysis of real estate based on the parameters of actual market data. This method accounts for all cash flows derived from the asset and deals effectively with several problems caused by the unique nature of the real estate market.

First, in accounting for the multi-period nature of real estate investment, the model reduces periodic expected cash flows to a single present value. Second, it recognizes the unique financing characteristics of each real estate asset. Third, it accounts for any equity buildup and appreciation of value occurring during the holding period. Finally, the values generated by the model are determined by market parameters, which allow us to generate a covariance matrix by simulating rates of return for each asset class examined and to calculate correlation coefficients of return between pairs of assets.

Mathematically, the model employed to calculate rates of return based on actual cash flows from the asset can be expressed as follows:

$$V = MV + \sum_i \frac{NOI_t - MV(R_m)}{(1 + Y_e)^t} + \frac{(1 \pm \Delta)V - (1 - P)MV}{(1 + Y_e)^n}, \quad (1)$$

where:

V = the selling price of the asset,
M = the loan-to-value ratio,
NOI_t = net operating income for period i,
P = the percentage of original principal paid off during the holding period,

R_m = the mortgage constant,
Y_e = the equity yield or internal rate of return,
Δ = the appreciation or depreciation of the asset over the holding period, and
n = number of years in asset holding period.

The major objective of Equation (1) is to determine the equity yield for the real estate asset once both the investor-specific variables (Δ, P, NOI, and V) and the lender-specific variables (M and R_m) are determined. Then, actual appreciation range values are calculated for each asset class. We can then use this range of appreciation values to determine a distribution of equity yield rates.

The distribution of actual appreciation values is different for each real estate asset class—apartments, office buildings, shopping centers, and industrial properties—which means that the calculated equity yield values will exhibit correlation coefficients that differ significantly from one. Therefore, we can study the performance of different portfolios of real estate assets based on mean portfolio returns and variances of returns.

THE DATA BASE

We collected ex post data from a total of 170 different income properties from two geographical markets in Texas between 1975 and 1983: Houston (40 assets) and Austin (130 assets). The data collected on each asset include:

1. Property type—apartment, office, industrial, or shopping center.
2. The dates each property was purchased and then sold.
3. The actual verified sales price for the two transactions.
4. Net operating income in each of the two transaction periods.
5. Financing terms established for the holding period (the time between the two transactions), including the loan-to-value ratio, interest rates, and the term of the loan.

CALCULATING RETURNS

We used the actual sales prices of each asset in the two markets to estimate the means and variances of the distributions of actual asset class appreciation rates in both geographical markets. The operating financial data collected for each asset in combination with the distribution of actual asset appreciation rates for each asset class were then transformed using Equation (1) into an asset equity yield distribution for each asset.

PORTFOLIO FORMATION

To test for the effects of portfolio diversification, we identified four types of assets in each market: apartments, offices, industrial properties, and shopping centers. Then we generated four categories of portfolios:

Category 1: Assets of the same category selected from the same geographical market.
Category 2: Assets in the same category selected from different geographical markets.

Category 3: Different asset types selected from the same geographical market.
Category 4: Different asset types selected from different geographical markets.

The size of each portfolio was limited to ten assets for two reasons. First, according to previous risk reduction studies, most unsystematic risk reduction occurs over the first ten assets; second, this procedure provides a greater number of real estate portfolios for subsequent analysis.

Next, we calculated the variance of each portfolio by using a mean—variance portfolio model similar to the one proposed by Findlay [1979]:

$$Z(e) = \min \left[\sum_i \sum_j (X_i C_i \sigma_i \rho_{ij} \sigma_j C_j X_j) / \sum_j (C_j X_j)^2 \right], \qquad (2)$$

where:

$Z(e)$ = the objective function that calculates the variance of a portfolio of indivisible assets,
X_i = either 0 or 1, representing the decision to either invest or not invest in the asset,
C_i = the cost of the ith asset,
C_j = the cost of the jth asset,
σ_i = the standard deviation of the ith asset,
σ_j = the standard deviation of the jth asset,
ρ_{ij} = the correlation coefficient between assets i and j, and
$C_j X_j$ = the total portfolio outlay.

Finally, we identified all minimum-variance portfolios that were Markowitz-efficient. The total number of efficient portfolios for the four categories was 2,267.

EMPIRICAL RESULTS

Naive portfolio diversification suggests that the simple combination of several assets causes the variance of such a portfolio to be lower than the variance of the individual assets. This reduction in variance occurs because the returns of different assets are less than perfectly correlated. Therefore, the variance of returns of real estate portfolios should decrease as a result of increasing the number of real estate assets in the portfolio.

Figure 1 shows the average reduction in portfolio variance for the four major categories of portfolios (detailed data are available on request from the authors). The graphs measure average variance of return on the vertical scale and number of assets on the horizontal scale.

The average portfolio variance for all portfolio categories decreases rapidly as the number of assets included in the portfolio increases from one to ten. The "portfolio" variance of return for one-asset portfolios is equal to the average variance of return of each single asset. The decrease in total variance of the average portfolio was 58.3%. The largest decrease in portfolio variance was 75.4% for industrial asset portfolios in the same market, while the smallest decrease in variance occurred within office-asset portfolios in different markets, where the reduction of total variance was 42.8%. The average decrease of variance from increasing the number of holdings for all categories of portfolios from one to two assets was 14.3%. An increase in the number of assets included in each portfolio from three to five assets reduces total average portfolio variance by 25.1%, while an increase in the number of securities from six to eight leads to a further reduction of variance of 20%.

Figure 1 Average Reduction of Portfolio Variance—Four Categories of Portfolios

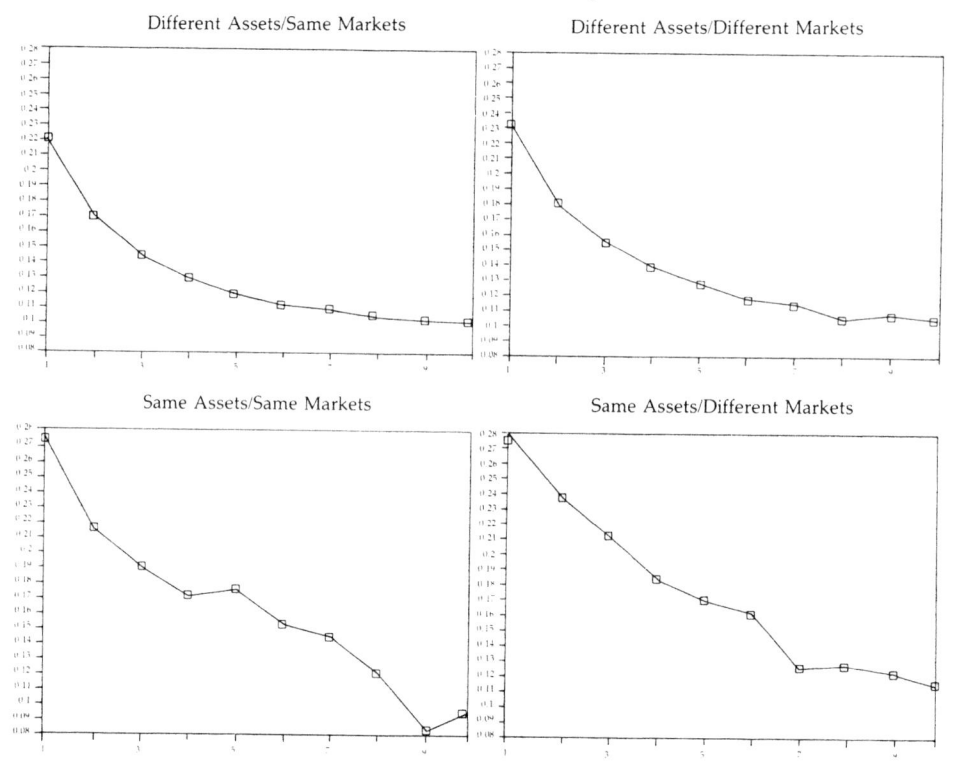

The largest average percent decrease of portfolio variance for all categories appears to occur over the first two to five assets; the rate of decrease of portfolio variance rapidly diminishes after six to seven assets. Independent of the degree of diversification in each category of portfolios, the reduction of the average variance of returns for all categories demonstrates the significant risk reduction benefits that an investor can obtain even from selecting small numbers of real estate assets in portfolios.

IMPROVING DIVERSIFICATION

Effective portfolio diversification is based on the existence of a systematic comovement between pairs of assets within a portfolio context. For example, when combining real estate assets into portfolios, we should expect a weaker comovement between returns from assets located in different cities, regions, or countries. By the same token, we should expect to obtain more effective diversification by combining real estate assets of different categories such as apartment, office, industrial property, or commercial property within a portfolio. If these two expectations about comovements of returns are justified, the diversification benefits for a real estate investment portfolio should be expected to increase even further when we combine real estate assets of different categories in different geographical locations.

Such expectations for diversification benefits are based on the assumption that the variables affecting real estate asset returns will be different for different categories of assets and or locations. We hypothesized in this study that benefits from diversification in the form of risk reduction can be obtained by diversifying real estate portfolios effectively across asset types and markets or a combination of both. Although the geographical diversification in this study is limited to two cities in Texas, the purpose of the study is to test for diversification benefits from asset type as well as from geographical diversification.

Unsystematic risk is defined as that portion of total portfolio variance that we can reduce or eliminate by including a mix of assets. From now on, by risk reduction we mean unsystematic risk reduction, so we can compare our results with previous studies on common stock risk reduction.

Portfolio Category 1 (same assets/same markets) was expected to show a more limited degree of unsystematic risk reduction than the other categories, because most of the assets in each portfolio would be likely to share common variables that would affect their overall performances. The highest degree of unsystematic risk reduction was expected to occur in portfolio Category 4 (different assets/different markets), because risk reduction in that category was expected to result from selecting these assets from different cities and different categories. We considered portfolio Categories 2 (same assets/different markets) and 3 (different assets/same markets) as moderately diversified, because in each case some return independence was expected either in the form of asset difference or different geographical location. In addition, we anticipated that Category 3 would offer greater unsystematic risk reduction benefits from diversification than Category 2, because we expected the effects of the geographic diversification to be less than those benefits obtained from different asset type.

Measures of the adequacy of this hypothesis, as well as that of our first two hypotheses, appear in Table 1 for the Austin-Houston market and the different categories of real estate assets. The percentages reported in the table represent the degree to which total unsystematic risk is reduced in each portfolio category.

The formation of portfolios from the same asset type and market caused an average reduction of 73.1% of total unsystematic risk for all subcategories of portfolios. The asset types in this group with the highest percent reduction of unsystematic risk (85.2%) are portfolios of apartment assets. Office asset portfolios show the lowest reduction in unsystematic risk (64.8%).

Effectively diversifying across either asset types or geographical locations leads to significantly lower amounts of unsystematic risk. The average reduction of total unsystematic risk was 92.5% for diversification across markets and 97.8% for diversification across assets. This represents an increase in risk reduction over portfolios of same asset

Table 1 Percentage Reduction of Unsystematic Risk From Effective Diversification

Same Assets/Same Markets		Same Assets/Different Markets	
Apartments	85.2	Apartments	88.8
Office	64.8	Office	96.6
Industrial	70.9	Industrial	92.3
Shopping Center	71.5	Shopping Center	92.1
Average	73.1	Average	92.5
Different Assets/Same Markets		Different Assets/Different Markets	
Average	97.8	Average	98.9

types and same markets of 26.5% for market diversification and 33.8% for asset type diversification. The increase in risk reduction from asset type diversification (33.8%) is greater than the increase from market diversification (26.5%), supporting the hypothesis that asset type diversification would prove more effective than market diversification. Although this result may not hold when more than two markets are involved, we expected it in this case, because the diversification across markets was limited by the city-pair chosen.

The reduction of risk obtained for each asset type from diversifying portfolios of the same asset type across different markets is especially interesting, because market diversification often is used as a marketing tool by real estate investment companies. The greatest reduction of unsystematic risk (49.1%) from market diversification is obtained for office assets, while it is a negligible 4.2% for apartment assets. The reduction of unsystematic risk for industrial and shopping center assets is 30.2% and 28.8%, respectively.

These findings suggest that market diversification may be superfluous for some types of assets such as apartments. On the other hand, diversification across asset types in the same market leads to significant risk reduction for office, industrial, and shopping center assets.

When combining asset type and market diversification, the improvement in diversification benefits, again, is a negligible 1.1% additional reduction in unsystematic risk over the risk reduction obtained from different asset types within the same markets. Expressed differently, asset type diversification, at least in this study, appears to be effective enough so that further efforts at diversifying lead quickly to superfluous diversification.

To the degree that these findings are representative of other real estate markets or time periods, they suggest that some of the diversification efforts of real estate investment companies might be questionable—particularly in view of the additional costs involved in the form of asset selection, professional specialization, transaction fees, and administrative costs connected with location diversification.

COMPARISON WITH PREVIOUS STUDIES

One of the earliest studies of risk reduction and portfolio size was performed by Evans and Archer [1968], who measured the risk of a portfolio by comparing the standard deviation of returns from the average return for that portfolio. Evans and Archer raise doubts concerning the economic justification of increasing an equity portfolio size beyond ten securities. In fact, the study concludes that 89.8% of unsystematic risk can be eliminated by diversifying across only eight equity assets.

In a second study, Fisher and Lorie [1970] performed an analysis similar to that of the Evans—Archer study, in that they created simulated distributions of returns for various portfolio sizes for all stocks listed on the New York Stock Exchange. Fisher and Lorie assumed equal investment in all securities in the portfolio, which is a rational assumption when the investor has no information about future return variances and covariances. If the investor were able to forecast further information on returns and variances/covariances, an unequal weight in the assets would reduce overall portfolio variance. Therefore, equally weighted assets with portfolios would result in the highest risk over a given set of return levels, which means that the Fisher and Lorie analysis represents an upper-limit study of portfolio variance reduction.

A major finding of the Fisher and Lorie study is that diversification by random selection reduces the average portfolio variance within each time period, but it does not affect the variance of returns. In addition, unsystematic risk was decreased by an average of 84.3% through diversifying from one to eight assets.

In a third study, Wagner and Lau [1971] created various types of common stock portfolios based on different stock quality ratings reported by the *S&P Stock Guide* earning and dividend rankings. The Wagner and Lau findings suggest that diversification causes greater reduction in unsystematic risk for lower-quality stocks than for higher-quality stocks.

Finally, a study by Elton and Gruber [1977] reported results similar to those of the previous studies. The effect of diversification on unsystematic risk from holding eight assets instead of one asset results in a decrease of 87.5%.

Table 2 summarizes the results of these common stock risk reduction studies and compares them with the findings of this study for real estate assets. The reduction of unsystematic risk by increasing the number of real estate assets in each portfolio category from one to eight assets ranges from 73.1% to 98.9%, averaging 90.1%. This reduction in risk may be compared with the possible reduction found for common stock portfolios, which ranges from 83.3% to 91.7% and averages 87.3%. Such findings lend support to a recent study by Miles and McCue [1984], who found diversification among real estate assets reduces unsystematic risk more than portfolio diversification does for common stocks.

REFERENCES

Brigham, Eugene F. *Fundamentals of Financial Management.* Chicago: The Dryden Press, 1983.

Burns, W. L. and D. R. Epley. "The Performance of Portfolios of REITs and Stocks." *Journal of Portfolio Management,* Spring 1982, pp. 37-42.

Cullen, T. F., and B. Blake. "How Does Real Estate as an Investment Compare with Stocks and Bonds?" *Trusts and Estates,* July 1980, pp. 18-22.

Draper, D. W., and M. C. Findlay. "Capital Asset Pricing and Real Estate Valuation." *Journal of the American Real Estate and Urban Economics Association,* Summer 1982, pp. 152-183.

Elton, E. J., and M. J. Gruber. "Risk Reduction and Portfolio Size: An Empirical Analysis." *Journal of Business,* October 1977, pp. 415-437.

Evans, E. J., and S. H. Archer. "Diversification and the Reduction of Dispersion: An Empirical Analysis." *Journal of Finance,* December 1968, pp. 761-768.

Table 2 Percentage Reduction of Unsystematic Risk Among Various Common Stock Studies Compared to Real Estate

Study	Unsystematic Risk Reduction Decrease Over First Eight Assets	
1. Evans and Archer [1968]	89.8	
2. Fisher and Lorie [1970]	84.3	
3. Wagner and Lau [1971]	91.7	— B Quality Common Stocks
	83.3	— A + Quality Common Stocks
4. Elton and Gruber [1977]	87.5	
5. Grissom, Kuhle, and Walther	73.1	— Same Assets/Same Markets
	92.5	— Same Assets/Different Markets
	97.8	— Different Assets/Same Markets
	98.8	— Different Assets/Different Markets
	90.1	— Averge Real Estate Study

Findlay, M. D., R. D. McBride, S. D. Messner and J. S. Yormark. "Optimal Real Estate Portfolios." *Journal of the American Real Estate and Urban Economics Association,* Fall 1979, pp. 298-317.

Fisher, L., and J. H. Lorie. "Some Studies of Variability of Returns on Investments in Common Stocks." *Journal of Business,* April 1970, pp. 99-134.

Fogler, H. R. "20% in Real Estate: Can Theory Justify It?" *Journal of Portfolio Management,* Winter 1984, pp. 6-13.

Francis, J. C., and S. H. Archer. *Portfolio Analysis.* New Jersey: Prentice-Hall, 1979.

Hoag, J. "Toward Indices of Real Estate Value and Return." *Journal of Finance,* May 1980, pp. 569-580.

Johnson, K. H., and D. S. Shannon. "A Note on Diversification and the Reduction of Dispersion." *Journal of Financial Economics,* Winter 1974, pp. 365-372.

Kelleher, D. G., "How Real Estate Stacks Up to the S&P 500." *Real Estate Review,* Summer 1976.

Kuhle, J. L. "A Decision-Theoretic Portfolio Model for the Selection of Real Estate Assets." Ph. D. dissertation, University of Texas, Austin, 1985.

Markowitz, H. M. *Portfolio Selection.* New York: John Wiley and Sons, 1979.

Miles, M. and T. McCue. "Commercial Real Estate Returns." *Journal of the American Real Estate and Urban Economics Association,* Fall 1984, pp. 355-377.

Pellatt, P. G. K. "A Normative Approach to the Analysis of Real Estate Investment Opportunities Under Uncertainty and the Management of Real Estate Investment Portfolios." Ph.D. dissertation, University of California, Berkeley, 1970.

Sharpe, W. F. *Portfolio Theory and Capital Markets.* New York: McGraw-Hill, 1970.

Wagner, W. H., and S. C. Lau. "The Effect of Diversification on Risk." *Financial Analysts Journal,* November-December 1971, pp. 48-53.

Webb, J. R. and C. F. Sirmans. "Yields and Risk Measures for Real Estate, 1966-77." *Journal of Portfolio Management,* Fall 1980, pp. 14-19.

Wendt, P. F. and S. N. Wong. "Investment Performance of Common Stocks Versus Apartment Houses," *Journal of Finance,* December 1965, pp. 633-646.

Zerbst, R. H., and B. R. Cambon. "Historical Returns on Real Estate Investments." *Journal of Portfolio Management,* Spring 1984, pp. 5-20.

15 Institutional Portfolios: Diversification through Farmland Investment

David A. Lins, Bruce J. Sherrick, and Aravind Venigalla

This article demonstrates that farmland can enhance the overall performance of institutional portfolios which are currently dominated by stocks, bonds, and business real estate. Unlike previous articles on farmland returns, this article addresses the issue of "smoothing bias" associated with appraisal-based farmland returns. Improved measures of income returns to farmland are also used in developing the estimates of optimal portfolios. Parametric testing revealed that farmland continues to enter the optimal portfolios even for large increases in the variance or for large reductions in the annual returns to farmland.

Managers of pension funds face the constant challenge of maximizing returns on their investment portfolios, subject to risk and liquidity constraints. Traditionally, institutional investors have selected portfolios that are dominated by stocks and bonds, with a much smaller percentage of the portfolio invested in real estate. Despite the recent problems encountered in commercial real estate, there have been signs of interest on the part of institutional investors in moving into other nontraditional real estate investments such as farmland (Speidell 1990).

In addition to diversifying across financial holdings, the complexities and magnitude of managed funds typically necessitates a type of "manager diversification" as well. That is, the total fund may first be allocated among asset classes in given proportions and then managers with specific expertise are selected to manage particular asset classes. Thus, one manager, for example, may be optimizing his/her holdings in an asset class that is already assigned a specific weight in the total portfolio. The possibility exists that this two-step process (first allocating proportions of the fund to asset classes and then allowing managers to optimize individual asset group portfolios as though they were stand-alone) may result in a significantly different aggregate fund composition than had the fund selected all holdings simultaneously.

From *Journal of the American Real Estate and Urban Economics Association*, Vol. 20, No. 4 (1992), pp. 549–571. The authors thank two anonymous reviewers for helpful comments and suggestions. The usual disclaimers apply.

The purpose of this article is to first evaluate the attractiveness of investments in farmland from the perspective of an institutional investor and to provide guidance on the composition of the farmland portion of the portfolio. Unlike previous studies of farmland returns, this article addresses the issue of "smoothing bias" associated with appraisal-based farmland returns. Further, a more appropriate measure of current return is used to more accurately reflect the true income to a fund for holding farmland. State and regional diversification issues are considered and restrictions are imposed to help limit the estimation bias that often accompanies historic data. Differences that arise from optimizing the farmland portion of the portfolio separately from the selection of the assets in the remainder of the portfolio are also discussed.

PREVIOUS STUDIES

Early studies of the addition of farmland to an investor's portfolio focused on the reduction in risk available by diversifying across asset types. Farmland as an aggregate asset class has been shown to have the favorable characteristics of a positive correlation with inflation and low or even negative correlation with many other equity classes and corporate debt (Ibbotson 1991). In addition, farmland tends to have very stable returns for its level of expected total return.

Kaplan (1985), using data from 1947 through 1980, considered six classes of assets including farm real estate, large capitalization stocks, small capitalization stocks, long-term corporate bonds, long-term government bonds, and Treasury bills for an investment portfolio and established the desirability of including farmland in the investment portfolio. In particular, the low coefficient of variation and the low correlations with other assets such as large capitalization stocks made farmland appear to be highly attractive as an asset class.

Webb and Rubens (1988) derived efficient portfolios with NYSE common stocks, corporate bonds, small stocks, government bonds, residential real estate, and farmland. They note that the transactions costs associated with less liquid assets are much greater and that the true risk of farmland ownership is likely understated using only historic data. Hence, to test the sensitivity of their results to the model formulation, variances of returns were inflated and the results compared across different risk estimates (variance quintupled) for farmland and residential real estate. Even when the variance was quintupled, they found that farmland constituted a substantial portion of the optimal portfolio across a wide range of tax and income scenarios.

Moss, Featherstone and Baker (1988), using real rates of returns and a multiple-year investment horizon model, determined the extent to which agricultural assets enter the risk-efficient investment portfolios for investors who have stocks, bonds, Treasury bills, and farm assets as investment alternatives. They also tested the sensitivity of the results to increasing the variance of the farm assets by a factor of 4. They found that farm assets are a much larger portion of the efficient portfolios than the historical share of farm assets in the total capital market. For the five- and ten-year planning horizons the level of farm assets in the portfolio was fairly constant across risk-aversion levels. Their conclusions were also robust to increases in the estimated variance of returns on farm assets.

In their discussion of investments in real estate, Firstenberg, Ross and Zisler (1988) note that the real estate investment decisions are often made without regard for the impact on the remainder of the portfolio. And, they suggest that funds tend to be under-invested in real estate. They too increased the estimate of the variance of returns to test the sensitivity of their results and to account for the possible understatement of variance that accompanies historic data. Their findings imply that optimal portfolios contain a large portion of real estate, even with increased measures of the riskiness of real estate. In specific reference to pension funds, they advise that real estate holdings be diversified across geographic location and types of enterprise.

Though past studies have considered farm real estate as an investment medium, the measure of current income to the investment has been based on reported income from farming rather than cash rents. Most institutional investors, however, cash rent the farmland they own, raising possible concerns about the use of data from returns to farming. Also, except for Webb and Rubens (1988), there is no indication of having adjusted for property taxes in any of the previous studies. State and regional diversifications issues also were not adequately treated as U.S. aggregate farmland returns were typically used. None of the previous studies tested for "smoothness bias." Finally, the sensitivity of optimal portfolios to changes in the level of returns to farmland has not been addressed. This study attempts to rectify some of these shortcomings and gives evidence on the potential impact of selecting the optimal composition of one portion of the portfolio separately from the remaining asset classes.

INSTITUTIONAL APPROACH TO FARMLAND INVESTMENT

Soil and climatic conditions determine which crops can be grown most profitably on which type of land. The returns from the crops and thus the land depend on the vagaries of weather and other location specific events. As these natural determinants differ from one geographic location to another, the volatility of returns from farmland also differ. Besides the natural determinants, other factors such as industrial development and policy decisions of the local/state governments also play a significant role in the returns on farmland. In some states, urban pressure has created high farmland values, but low cash rents relative to market value. Investing in a single geographic location exposes an investor to those unique factors. However, it may be possible to reduce the overall volatility of the portfolio return by diversifying farmland investment among different geographic locations without sacrificing returns.

The process by which institutions manage investments in farmland varies from firm to firm. However, a fairly common approach is for the institution to select a farmland portfolio manager and initiate a separate rather than a commingled account with that portfolio manager. The portfolio manager in turn typically works with a set of geographically dispersed farmland brokers/managers. These brokers identify target properties for purchase with the portfolio manager providing "due diligence" in the selection process. Once properties are acquired, the portfolio manager relies on the local brokers/farm managers to find tenants and to manage the property. Most farmland properties are based upon an annual cash rental arrangement. For services provided, the portfolio manager may be compensated at an annual rate of ½% to 1% of the market value of the property under management.

METHODOLOGY

One implication of modern portfolio theory is that investors choose among portfolios that are on the "efficient frontier"; that is, portfolios that have the minimum level of risk for a given rate of return. Choices from the portfolios on this efficient frontier are made on the basis of risk preferences and the availability of a risk-free asset. This method of describing investment choices (popularly referred to as the E-V model), has been demonstrated to be quite robust to violations of the assumptions first used to derive its results (Kroll et al.), and is well accepted as a tool for portfolio selection guidance.

The standard quadratic programming model to minimize portfolio variance for any given level of return was used to "map" the efficient frontier across the feasible levels of return.[1] Algebraically, the model may be stated as min $\omega'\Sigma\omega$ subject to:

$\omega'I = 1$ (sum of portfolio weights equals one)
$\omega \geq 0$ (all weights non-negative)
$\omega'r \geq \Theta$, where Θ is parametrically varied from Θ_{min} to Θ_{max},

where ω is a choice vector of weights for the assets available for investment, Σ is the estimated variance-covariance matrix of returns, r is the vector of mean returns for the available assets, I is a vector of ones and Θ is a parametrically varied target level of portfolio return ranging from the minimum-variance portfolio's return to the maximum return available in the population of assets. Equivalently, the model could have been formulated to maximize return for a parametrically varied level of target risk. Either formulation gives the same risk-efficient frontier.

An important concern in the use of the standard portfolio model is quality of the estimated variance-covariance matrix. The issues of the stationarity of the data, and of simply estimating all the parameters are often raised.[2] In other words, the use of the estimates in a decisionmaking context depend on the accuracy of the predicted outcomes.

To examine the properties of the estimated covariance matrix and shed light on these issues, a Monte Carlo procedure was used. Basically, a large number of estimates of a variance-covariance matrix were generated that followed the hypothesized multivariate normal distribution used in the paper, with equivalent data limitations imposed. Then, the maximum, and variance of the deviations in the elements of the estimated variance covariance matrix are examined as an indication of the sensitivity of the estimates to the data used to generate them. Specifically, consider the lower triangle matrix l where $ll' = \Sigma$; and then generate a multivariate normal sample y where $y \sim MVN_n(0,I)$, where I is the identity matrix. Then, for a large number of "n-tuples" from y, generate a large number of observations from a multivariate normal $q \sim MVN_n(0,\Sigma)$ generated from $q = l'y$ and then repeatedly generate estimates of a covariance matrix with dimension n. These Monte Carlo replications can then be used to test the sensitivity of the estimated variance-covariance matrix to the data and procedures used. Note that, for example, if the asset returns were perfectly correlated, the procedure would be invariant to the sample size and number of observations, but as the degree of association among variables decreases, the degree of variability in the estimates of variance would likely increase.

The results indicate that the estimates of the variance-covariance matrix used are very robust to the data used. In particular, the maximum deviation over one thousand replications of any element of the estimated covariance matrix was approximately 8.9%. More importantly, the pseudo-"t" statistics formed across all observations by dividing the difference in estimates from the mean by their own standard deviation were all insignificant. Hence, the procedure used to generate the estimates of the variance-covariance matrix was judged to be very robust.[3] Although this test demonstrates the validity of procedures used to estimate the covariance matrix, it does not address the issue of potential appraisal bias. This issue is treated later.

DATA

The asset classes used in this study include common stocks, long-term corporate bonds, business real estate, and farmland on a state-by-state basis. Annual returns data on long-term corporate bonds, common stocks as reflected by the S&P 500, and business real estate were obtained from Ibbotson and Associates. These returns cover the period 1967 through 1988.

Annual returns on farmland for individual states were calculated from USDA data by adding cash rents and capital gains as percentages of land value and subtracting property taxes as a percentage of market value. The cash rent data are available for twenty-eight states from 1967 to the present (Table 1). These returns measure the returns institutional investors would get from their investment in farmland, except for management fees, which are not directly measurable.[4] A subsequent section considers arbitrary reductions in farmland returns to reflect management charges.

The risk-return performance of the farmland of the twenty-eight states compared with that of long-term corporate bonds, S&P 500, and business real estate are shown in Table 2. It is evident that farmland in many states had both a higher return and a lower standard deviation of return than the S&P 500 and long-term corporate bonds.

Table 3 gives the correlations among the various investment choices. Except for Michigan which had a correlation coefficient of 0.009 with stocks, farmland of every state had a negative correlation with bonds and stocks and positive correlation with inflation. For individual states, correlations with business real estate are mixed and weak, with some states being negatively and some being positively correlated (in the case of twenty-three states the correlation coefficient is less than .1). Farmland had a high positive correlation with inflation, while stocks and bonds have a strong negative correlation with inflation.

Table 1 Regions and States in Which Farmland Returns Data Are Available

Northeast	Corn Belt:	Southeast:
Maine	Ohio	South Carolina
Vermont	Indiana	Georgia
New York	Illinois	Florida
New Jersey	Iowa	Alabama
Pennsylvania	Missouri	
Delaware		Delta States:
Maryland	Northern Plains:	Missssissippi
	North Dakota	Arkansas
Lake States:	South Dakota	
Michigan		Southern Plains:
Wisconsin	Appalachia:	Texas
Minnesota	Virginia	
	North Carolina	
	Kentucky	
	Tennessee	

Table 2 Mean Annual Returns and Standard Deviations of Returns of Various Assets, 1967–1988

Asset Class	Average Annual Return(μ)	Standard Deviation (σ)
Farmland by State	%	%
Maine	15.6	6.5
Vermont	13.1	5.4
New York	12.4	6.2
New Jersey	9.2	6.8
Pennsylvania	11.8	9.3
Delaware	11.7	8.7
Maryland	10.1	8.7
Michigan	9.9	9.9
Wisconsin	12.9	10.6
Minnesota	13.6	14.5
Ohio	11.4	11.6
Indiana	12.0	13.3
Illinois	11.0	13.4
Iowa	12.8	16.0
Missouri	13.6	11.3
North Dakota	14.6	12.5
South Dakota	13.6	10.5
Virginia	12.6	7.4
North Carolina	11.7	8.7
Kentucky	13.5	8.8
Tennessee	13.7	8.2
South Carolina	11.5	8.7
Georgia	13.6	8.7
Florida	11.8	8.0
Alabama	13.8	9.2
Mississippi	13.2	11.9
Arizona	12.6	10.6
Texas	13.0	9.0
S&P 500	11.5	15.9
Business Real Estate	10.6	4.3
Long-term Corporate Bonds	8.1	12.5
Inflation	6.1	3.3

The negative correlation of farmland with stocks and bonds and the weak correlation of farmland with business real estate makes farmland a potential source for portfolio diversification. The high positive correlation with inflation makes farmland an important hedge against inflation. This inflation hedging ability is important for pension funds, especially for defined benefit plans where the employee benefits are tied to inflation via a cost-of-living adjustment.

TESTING FOR APPRAISAL BIAS

Two of the asset classes, farmland and business real estate, have the capital gain (loss) portion of their return estimated from appraisals rather than actual sales. However, sev-

Table 3 Correlations of returns on Farmland of Various States with Other Assets, 1967–1988

	Business Real Estate	S&P 500	Long-term Corp. Bond	Inflation
Maine	−.08	−.30	−.23	.08
Vermont	−.07	−.30	−.23	.08
New York	−.06	−.34	−.43	.31
New Jersey	−.37	−.23	−.29	.09
Pennsylvania	−.29	−.22	−.36	.21
Delaware	−.23	−.15	−.27	.42
Maryland	.06	.08	.63	.46
Michigan	.08	.01	−.42	.35
Wisconsin	.01	−.18	−.49	.46
Minnesota	−.07	−.23	−.54	.56
Ohio	−.17	−.05	−.33	.32
Indiana	−.13	−.06	−.35	.41
Illinois	−.24	−.05	.28	.31
Iowa	−.22	−.10	−.38	.37
Missouri	.01	−.05	−.44	.38
North Dakota	−.10	−.39	−.50	.60
South Dakota	−.11	−.29	−.49	.54
Virginia	−.09	.25	.31	.34
North Carolina	.16	−.02	−.35	.37
Kentucky	−.04	−.16	−.36	.41
Tennessee	−.07	−.22	.41	.38
South Carolina	.09	−.22	−.49	.45
Georgia	−.11	−.31	−.43	.28
Florida	−.02	−.27	−.47	.49
Alabama	.15	−.10	−.48	.56
Mississippi	.15	−.18	−.64	.60
Arizona	.25	−.12	.62	.47
Texas	.35	−.24	−.44	.37
Bus. Real Estate	1.00	.14	−.18	.52
S&P 500	.14	1.00	.43	−.32
Long-term Corp. Bonds	−.18	.43	1.00	−.51
Inflation	.52	−.32	−.51	1.00

eral studies have identified a "smoothing bias" associated with appraisal based returns (e.g., Firstenberg, Ross and Zisler 1988; Wheaton and Torto 1989; Liu et al. 1991; Geltner 1991). Therefore before proceeding with the estimation of returns it is important to either (1) correct for the smoothing bias, or (2) demonstrate that results are not significantly altered by this bias.

To begin this process the "corrected" means and variances of returns for farmland and business real estate were estimated using a procedure suggested by Firstenberg et al. Basically, the procedure is intended to recover a "true" mean return based upon the autocorrelation in reported returns and an assumed process of appraising that combines the "true" estimate with lagged returns. Further, the procedure assumes that true returns are not correlated over time, which may be an inappropriate assumption given the persistence of land price pressures over time. The results revealed that the difference in returns between the raw data and the "corrected" mean returns on farm real estate and business were less than one percentage point for twenty-four out of twenty-eight states and for business real estate. The differences for the other four states were less than two percentage points. For estimates of the variances, the differences between the raw data and the "corrected" variances were much larger. However, for all states and business real estate, the "corrected" variance was never more than four times as large as the "uncorrected" variance. Sensitivity analyses given later, demonstrate a rather small impact on optimal portfolios due to the understatement of variances of real estate returns in the case that appraisal based returns do follow the process suggested by Firstenberg et al.[5] Finally, it should also be noted that, in large part, the actual prices paid and received in farmland investments are based on appraisals of specific properties. If in fact, the appraisal bias does exist relative to the "fair" value that would result from the application of a discounted returns model, the data containing the appraisal bias are likely more appropriate in judging the performance of the investment, as that is likely to be the basis for acquisition or sale anyhow.

RESEARCH DESIGN

In the sections which follow, the optimal portfolios are estimated under a variety of conditions as a basis for examining the impacts of various restrictions and to demonstrate the likely impacts of different approaches for selecting optimal portfolios. First, optimal portfolios are examined where *only farmland* is considered. These results will be used to identify the states that enter optimal portfolios if farmland is considered as a separate class of investments to be managed independently from the remainder of the portfolio. Next, farmland is allowed to compete against stocks, bonds, and business real estate for selection in optimal portfolios. Comparisons of these two sets of results allow an examination of the role of farmland in an optimal portfolio, but also allow one to examine if the same states enter the optimal portfolios when farmland is treated as a separate investment class to be managed independently from the remainder of the portfolio.

The optimal set of portfolios where the proportion of farmland is restricted either by state or by geographic region is also determined. These results allow an examination of how the arbitrary restriction on the proportion of assets in a portfolio is likely to affect the risk/return combination of optimal portfolios. Finally, parametric variations in variance and returns are used to examine the impact on optimal portfolios.

FARMLAND ONLY OPTIMAL INVESTMENT PORTFOLIOS

In this section, optimal portfolios selected from only farmland are determined. The optimal farmland portfolios formed solely from the twenty-eight states are shown in Table 4.[6] Results are reported for the maximum return portfolio and the minimum variance portfolio with portfolios reported at ½% return intervals between these two "end points." Note that only five of the twenty-eight states enter the optimal portfolios and that the portfolios are dominated by the Northeast states. The highest risk-return combination occurs when 100% of the portfolio is invested in Maine. The annual return is 15.56% with a standard deviation of 6.49%. As the risk and return levels are lowered, farmland in South Dakota and Texas enter the optimal portfolios. These states differ

Table 4 Efficient Portfolios When Asset Classes Are Restricted to Farmland

Annual Return %	Standard Deviation %	Portfolio Composition				
		Maine %	Vermont %	New Jersey %	South Dakota %	Texas %
15.56°	6.49	100.0	0	0	0	0
15.50	6.40	96.7	0	0	3.3	0
15.00	5.99	76.1	8.7	0	7.7	7.5
14.50	5.66	55.7	26.8	.1	9.4	8.0
14.00	5.36	41.4	36.6	3.6	9.5	8.9
13.50	5.09	27.4	46.0	7.4	9.4	9.8
13.00	4.84	13.4	55.3	11.3	9.3	10.7
12.50	4.63	0	63.7	15.5	9.1	11.7
12.00	4.52	0	53.6	27.6	4.6	14.2
11.84	4.51°°	0	50.3	31.5	3.1	15.1

°Maximum Return Portfolio
°°Minimum Variance Portfolio

greatly from the Northeast states both in terms of geographic location and in the types of agricultural production that dominate in the state. The minimum standard deviation portfolio consists of investments in four states and allows the investor to generate an 11.84% average annual return with a standard deviation of 4.51%. These results illustrate optimal portfolios for a fund manager who approaches the farmland investment decision independently from the fund's other holdings.

FARMLAND AS PART OF A LARGER PORTFOLIO

Suppose that instead of optimizing among only farmland investment choices, the portfolio manager considers the simultaneous selection of farmland and more traditional asset classes. Table 5 shows the optimal portfolios when farmland, S&P 500, long-term bonds, and business real estate are considered as alternative investments.[7] As before, the highest risk-return optimal portfolio consists of 100% of the investment in farmland in Maine. As the return is lowered, a smaller proportion of the total portfolio consists of farmland. Only five different states enter the optimal portfolio. Four of the five states are the same as for optimal portfolios when only farmland was considered. It is interesting to note that farmland is always over 40% of the total portfolio, while common stocks and bonds either singly or in combination never exceed 15% of the total portfolio.

When stocks, bonds, and business real estate were allowed into the optimal portfolios, the composition of the farmland in portfolios changed.[8] Thus if portfolio managers invest in farmland, they should consider the effects of this investment on the entire portfolio. Hence, the institutional investors who assign a manager to acquire farmland should consider possible impacts of the farmland investments on the optimal composition of the remainder of their portfolio.

STATE CONSTRAINED INVESTMENT IN FARMLAND

It is unlikely that institutional investors would (or should) commit as high a proportion of their assets to farmland in any given state as the previous section indicated. Imposing upper

Table 5 Efficient Portfolios When Asset Classes Are Unrestricted

| | | \multicolumn{6}{c}{Portfolio Components} | | | |
| | | \multicolumn{5}{c}{Farmland} | | | | |

Annual Return %	Standard Deviation %	Maine %	Vermont %	New Jersey %	Maryland %	South Dakota %	Total Farmland %	S&P 500 %	Business Real Estate %	Long-term Corp. Bonds %
15.56°	6.49	100.0	0	0	0	0	100.0	0	0	0
15.50	6.31	98.4	0	0	0	0	98.4	1.6	0	0
15.00	5.33	84.4	0	0	0	3.5	87.9	12.1	0	0
14.50	4.72	73.0	0	0	0	5.8	78.8	12.0	9.2	0
14.00	4.17	62.7	0	0	0	6.6	69.3	10.8	19.7	.2
13.50	3.68	53.6	0	0	0	8.1	61.7	8.8	26.2	3.3
13.00	3.26	44.5	0	0	0	9.6	54.1	6.7	32.8	6.4
12.50	2.90	35.0	2.5	3.0	0	10.0	50.5	5.2	36.2	8.1
12.00	2.58	22.4	10.3	6.1	0	10.4	49.2	4.2	37.3	9.3
11.50	2.31	9.9	18.2	9.2	0	10.8	48.1	3.2	38.4	10.3
11.00	2.09	0	22.2	13.3	0	10.5	46.0	2.0	40.3	11.7
10.55	2.03°°	0	14.2	17.8	3.4	7.4	42.8	0	43.1	14.1

°Maximum Return Portfolio
°°Minimum Variance Portfolio

bounds (constraining portfolio weights) on portfolio weights can reduce the estimation bias, thus eliminating the problem of over-investment in securities/assets with favorable estimation bias and under-investment in securities/assets with unfavorable estimation bias.[9]

Hence, a constraint that investment in farmland of any single state not exceed 10% of entire investment was imposed and optimal portfolios were again formed with the S&P 500, long-term bonds and business real estate.[10] The portfolios representing the efficient frontier are given in Table 6.

When no more than 10% of the farmland is allowed to come from any one state, farmland still tends to be the dominant asset in the portfolios. With this constraint, fifteen different states appear in the optimal portfolios, although there are never more than eleven states reflected in a single optimal portfolio. Stocks and bonds continue to constitute a relatively minor proportion of optimal portfolios at different risk-return levels. Business real estate tends to replace farmland at lower levels of risk and return.

GEOGRAPHIC LOCATION AND STATE CONSTRAINTS

The USDA has grouped states into different geographic regions (refer to Table 1). States were placed into these regions to maintain contiguous states and to group similar types of agriculture, soil types, and climatic conditions that affect the inherent risks associated with agricultural production. There is a long history of using regional diversification to reduce the risks associated with lending to agricultural operations. For example, the Farm Credit System, a specialized lender for agricultural producers, was originally organized into twelve geographic districts. To the extent possible, these districts were chosen to obtain geographic diversity while maintaining contiguous state selections. In addition, the regulations surrounding a new secondary market for farm mortgage loans (Farmer Mac) stipulates that not more than 40% of the loans in any one pool can come from one of the ten farm production regions developed by USDA. Likewise, at least one well-known institutional investor in farmland has placed specific limits on the percent of farmland in its portfolio that can come from any one farm production region.

To reflect this concern over geographic diversity, the twenty-eight states were grouped into the USDA farm production regions and then a constraint imposed that not more than 10% of the portfolio could be invested in one region. Because only eight different regions are represented, this restriction will limit the proportion of farmland in the optimal portfolios to no more than 80%. Using this type of geographic constraint, efficient portfolios were again derived and are given in Table 7.

Constraining the investment by geographic region generates risk-return combinations in the optimal portfolios that are not dramatically different from those obtained when state-by-state restrictions were used. By taking a constrained regional approach to farmland investment, the institutional investors can not only alleviate the problem of over-investment in certain states but can also obtain a geographically diversified investment in farmland.

CONSTRAINTS ON THE PERCENTAGES OF FARMLAND AND BUSINESS REAL ESTATE IN THE TOTAL PORTFOLIO

It seems highly unlikely that institutional investors would be willing to invest a high proportion of their portfolios in farmland and business real estate in combination, even

Table 6 Efficient Portfolios When Farmland of Each State is Restricted to 10% of the Portfolio

Annual Return %	Standard Deviation %	ME %	VT %	NY %	NJ %	MN %	KY %	MO %	ND %	SD %	TN %	MD %	AL %	GA %	TX %	MS %	Total Farmland %	S&P %	BR %	CB %
13.88°	9.02	10.0	.5	0	0	10.0	10.0	10.0	10.0	10.0	10.0	0	10.0	10.0	0	9.5	100.0	0	0	0
13.50	5.87	10.0	10.0	10.0	0	0	6.0	0	10.0	10.0	10.0	0	10.0	10.0	10.0	0	86.0	14.0	0	0
13.00	4.58	10.0	10.0	10.0	0	0	0	0	10.0	5.0	10.0	0	0	8.3	10.0	0	73.3	15.5	11.2	0
12.50	3.63	10.0	10.0	10.0	0	0	0	0	3.0	10.0	10.0	0	0	2.9	6.3	0	62.2	10.8	23.8	3.2
12.00	2.85	10.0	10.0	10.0	0	0	0	0	0	10.0	9.2	0	0	0	1.5	0	50.7	6.0	35.5	7.8
11.50	2.38	10.0	10.0	8.3	6.8	0	0	0	0	10.0	0	0	0	0	1.2	0	46.3	3.7	39.6	10.4
11.00	2.18	6.5	10.0	2.0	10.0	0	0	0	0	9.6	0	3.1	0	0	0	0	41.2	0.8	44.0	14.0
10.57	2.12°°	0	10.0	4.7	10.0	0	0	0	0	7.4	0	10.0	0	0	0	0	40.1	0	43.9	16.0

S&P is S&P 500. CB is Long-term corporate bonds. BR is business real estate. Farmland states are denoted by the conventional abbreviations.

° Maximum Return Portfolio
°° Minimum Variance Portfolio

Table 7 Efficient Portfolios When Farmland of Each Region is Restricted to 10% of the Portfolio

		Portfolio Components																
		Farmland													Total			
Annual Return	Standard Deviation	ME	VT	NJ	VA	MN	MO	ND	SD	TN	AL	GA	TX	MS	Farmland	S&P	BR	CB
%	%	%	%	%	%	%	%	%	%	%	%	%	%	%	%	%	%	%
13.40°	7.02	10.0	0	0	0	10.0	10.0	10.0	0	10.0	8.7	1.2	10.0	10.0	80.0	20.0	0	0
13.00	5.52	10.0	0	0	0	6.6	10.0	10.0	0	10.0	0	10.0	10.0	0	66.6	17.6	15.8	0
12.50	4.10	10.0	0	0	0	0	1.2	10.0	0	10.0	0	10.0	10.0	0	51.2	13.3	35.4	0.1
12.00	3.22	10.0	0	0	0	0	0	4.9	5.1	10.0	0	10.0	3.7	0	43.7	6.8	41.2	8.3
11.50	2.73	9.8	0	.2	0	0	0	0	10.0	4.5	0	9.6	0	0	34.1	2.1	50.5	13.3
11.00	2.50	0	5.1	4.9	.3	0	0	0	10.0	2.6	0	10.0	0	0	32.9	1.2	51.6	14.3
10.64	2.41°°	0	0	10.0	1.4	0	0	0	10.0	0	0	8.3	0	0	29.7	0	54.4	15.9

S&P is S&P 500. CB is Long-term corporate bonds. BR is Business real estate. Farmland states are denoted by the conventional abbreviations.

°Maximum Return Portfolio

°°Maximum Variance Portfolio

though historical results suggest that both would have performed well. Lack of familiarity with these investments, liquidity concerns, and greater experience with other forms of investments are likely constraints. Therefore, the optimal portfolios with the constraint that not more than 20% of the farmland in the portfolio could come from any one region *and* that not more than 10% of the entire portfolio could consist of farmland were computed. Also, no more than 10% of the portfolio could be in business real estate. Results are shown in Table 8.

Comparisons of Tables 7 and 8 reveal that restricting the portfolio to no more than 10% farmland and business real estate reduces the risk/return combinations, as would be expected. The minimum variance portfolio has a standard deviation more than three times higher than when these restrictions were not imposed. Notice also that farmland in Iowa now enters optimal solutions while several other states (Vermont, Texas, New York, New Jersey, South Dakota, Missouri, and Kentucky) disappear. This result again suggests that decisions surrounding optimal investments in farmland should not be made independently from the portfolio investment decisions surrounding stocks, bonds, and business real estate.

TESTING CHANGES IN RISK/RETURN CHARACTERISTICS OF REAL ESTATE

In several previous studies (Webb and Rubens 1988; Moss, Featherstone and Baker 1988), the variance of returns on farm real estate and business real estate was arbitrarily increased to reflect a concern that standard risk measures (variance and standard deviation) do not capture the total risk in real estate. While our earlier tests revealed no inherent bias in the process used to estimate variance, it is useful to test the sensitivity of our results to changes in the levels of variance from historic data. There is also concern on the part of institutional investors that historical returns will not easily be achieved because of annual management fees and transactions costs associated with purchase and sale. To examine these issues, parametric changes were made to the variance of returns and the level of returns on both farm and business real estate.

The variance of returns on farm real estate and business real estate were doubled and optimal portfolio combinations again determined. Although the attainable frontier retreated relative to the unrestricted portfolios (Table 4), the proportion of farmland in the optimal portfolio actually *increased* for the same level of returns. However, as expected, the proportion of farmland decreased for the same level of risk. These results confirm that in an unrestricted portfolio, farmland is likely to remain a major component even if the historical variance has been understated.

To test the sensitivity of the results to reductions in farmland returns, the annual returns of farmland and business real estate were reduced by 300 basis points per year. The results, given in Table 8, reveal that this reduction in returns had very little impact on the proportion of farmland or business real estate in the optimal portfolios. A reduction of this magnitude should more than compensate for differences in management fees and liquidity costs between real estate and other asset classes. Over virtually the entire range of the E-V frontier, farmland continued to be included at the restricted maximum of 10%. When annual returns were reduced by 800 basis points per year, farmland continued to enter the optimal portfolio, while business real estate did not. These outcomes suggest that inclusion of farmland in the optimal portfolio is very robust across very wide ranges of returns.

Table 8 Efficient Portfolios When Farmland and Business Real Estate are Both Restricted to 10% of the Total Portfolio and No More Than 20% of the Farmland May Come from Any One Region

Total Return %	Standard Deviation %	Portfolio Components												
		Farmland												
		ME %	MD %	IO %	MN %	MS %	ND %	TN %	GA %	AL %	Total Farmland %	BR %	S&P %	CB %
11.73[*]	13.98	2.0	0	0	2.0	0	2.0	2.0	0	2.0	10.0	.5	89.5	0
11.50	12.03	2.0	0	0	2.0	0	2.0	2.0	2.0	0	10.0	10.0	75.7	4.3
11.00	10.62	2.0	0	0	2.0	0	2.0	2.0	2.0	8.0	10.0	10.0	60.9	19.1
10.50	9.54	2.0	0	0	2.0	2.0	2.0	0	2.0	0	10.0	10.0	46.4	33.6
10.00	8.90	2.0	0	0	2.0	2.0	2.0	0	2.0	0	10.0	10.0	31.7	48.3
9.52[**]	8.72	0	2.0	2.0	2.0	2.0	2.0	0	0	0	10.0	10.0	21.4	58.6

S&P is S&P 500. CB is Long-term corporate bonds. BR is Business real estate. Farmland states are denoted by the conventional abbreviations.

[*] Maximum Return Portfolio
[**] Minimum Variance Portfolio

CONCLUSIONS

Institutional investors in farmland are typically equity holders who acquire current income through cash rent from farmland. Previous studies in farmland portfolio diversification have tended to ignore this fact and instead measure the income part of the data as income for operating a farm.[11] This study used cash rents after property taxes to derive the income part of the returns on farmland for the period 1967–88 and showed that diversification enhances portfolio performance for institutional investors. The results were robust across wide variations in variance and annual returns to farmland.

For the period 1967–88, farmland exhibited a higher return than that of stocks and bonds. Further, returns on farmland were negatively correlated with stocks and bonds and positively correlated with inflation, while stocks and bonds had a negative correlation with inflation. Thus, investment in farmland not only was a good hedge against inflation but also provided diversification for those who included it in their portfolio.

The implication for institutional investors is that, by including farmland in their portfolio, they may be able to reduce the possibility of shortfall of their fund in times of higher inflation. This is even more beneficial if the earnings of the underlying company are negatively correlated with inflation. For such a company the earnings will be lower when it needs more money to make up the deficit in the pension fund which is caused by the fall in the value of the stocks and bonds in the fund.

This study determined the optimal portfolios on an ex-post basis. Efficient portfolios when formed using historical data may have their returns biased upwards and their risk biased downwards. This problem can be alleviated by constraining the portfolio weights. Even after restricting the investment in farmland of every state to 10% of the entire portfolio, states with similar cropping and climatic patterns seem to dominate the farmland portfolio. To overcome this problem states were grouped into regions and then a constraint that investment in any region should not exceed 10% of the entire portfolio was imposed. This new strategy provided better geographical diversification with no significant decrease in the return to risk performance of the efficient frontier. When ex-post returns are used as a guide for investment, this kind of strategy would enable the fund manager to optimize the portfolio.

Constraining the optimal portfolios to no more than 10% farmland and business real estate generates somewhat lower returns for the same level of risk. Parametric testing revealed that farmland continued to enter the optimal portfolio at the constrained level of 10% for large increases in the variance of farmland returns or for large reductions in the annual return to farmland. Thus results do not appear highly sensitive to the accuracy of the underlying measures of farmland returns. However, the results also caution against simply optimizing a portfolio consisting only of farmland independently from the remainder of the investment portfolio.

NOTES

[1] The General Algebraic Modeling System (GAMS) was used on an IBM compatible computer.

[2] In fact, if there are "n" assets, one would need to have at least $n(n + 1)/2$ observations on the set of returns to avoid the "negative degrees of freedom" problem of effectively estimating more parameters than data points. Further, it is often overlooked that the assumed multivariate distribution from which returns are observed is assumed to have particular properties for the variance-covariance matrix to adequately proxy for risk. For example, high degrees of co-skewness could affect the composition of the optimal portfolio for par-

ticular types of investors, and their choices could not be made on the basis of the variance-covariance and returns measures alone.

[3] The simulation was performed in Gauss-386 VM. Source code for the simulation and complete results are available from the authors upon request.

[4] Cash rent data used in this study are the percentages of cash rent to crop land value. In the case of Virginia, the value of cash rent to crop land was not available for 1986. The missing number was estimated by first regressing the remaining years' percentage of cash rent to crop land value against the percentage of cash rent to farm value and then estimating cash rent for 1986. For Florida, the cash rent data are unavailable for 1982, 1983 and 1985. These data were estimated by regressing the remaining cash rent data of Florida against that of Georgia and using the results to estimate the missing values. These approximations were very close as judged by the high R^2 values and should have no significant effect on the conclusions of this study.

[5] While Firstenberg et al. used quarterly data and found a fourth-order equation to fit well, annual data were used here with a first order specification typically fitting best. Again, source code and complete results are available from the authors upon request.

[6] The composition of the portfolios, the range of returns and standard deviation of the efficient frontier may differ from what is presented here, if one could consider all fifty states for portfolio formation.

[7] For portfolio formation, farmlands by state instead of the U.S. aggregate are used because in case of farmland, investment vehicles such as indexed funds, which offer shares of the aggregate fund, are not available. In contrast, for stocks and bonds these kinds of investment vehicles (stock and bond mutual funds) are available. However, this argument can also be made for business real estate, but regional data were not available for business real estate.

[8] This result is not surprising because the introduction of an asset into the optimal portfolio is partly determined by its correlation with other assets that are already part of the optimal portfolio.

[9] For a more complete treatment on this subject, refer to Frost and Savarino (1988).

[10] The 10% constraint is arbitrary. Investment managers can impose any upper bound they think appropriate. However, lowering the upper bound would make the constraint more severely binding and vice versa.

[11] Except the study by Kaplan, as mentioned earlier. However, the method of calculating rents assumed in that study is highly arbitrary and is not based on reported rent data.

REFERENCES

Firstenberg, P. M., S. A. Ross and R. C. Zisler. 1988. Real Estate: The Whole Story. *Journal of Portfolio Management* (14): 22–32.

Frost, P. A. and J. Savarino. 1988. For Better Performance: Constrain Portfolio Weights. *Journal of Portfolio Management* (15): 29–34.

Geltner, D. 1991. Smoothing in Appraisal-Based Returns. *Journal of Real Estate Finance and Economics* (4): 327–45.

Ibbotson Associates. 1991. *Stocks, Bonds, Bills, and Inflation: 1991 Yearbook.* Ibbotson Associates.

Kaplan, H. M. 1985. Farmland as a Portfolio Investment. *Journal of Portfolio Management* (12): 73–78.

Liu, C. H., D. J. Hartzell, T. V. Grissom and W. Grieg. 1990. The Composition of the Market Portfolio and Real Estate Investment Performance. *Journal of the American Real Estate and Urban Economics Association* (18): 49–75.

Moss, C. B., A. M. Featherstone and T. G. Baker. 1988. Agricultural Assets in an Efficient Multiperiod Investment Portfolio. *Agricultural Finance Review* (47): 82–94.

Speidell, L. S. 1990. Embarrassment and Riches: The Discomfort of Alternative Investment Strategies. *Journal of Portfolio Management* (17): 6–11.

Webb, J. R. and J. H. Rubens. 1988. The Effect of Alternative Return Measures on Restricted Mixed-Asset Portfolios. *Journal of the American Real Estate and Urban Economics Association* (16): 123–37.

Wheaton, W. and R. Torto. 1989. Income and Appraised Values: A Reexamination of FRC Returns Data. *Journal of the American Real Estate and Urban Economics Association* (17): 439–49.

16 Real Estate Portfolio Diversification Using Economic Diversification

Glenn R. Mueller and Barry A. Ziering

Previous work on real estate portfolio diversification by location began with geographic region diversification and moved to economically defined regions (a combination of economics and geography). This work takes the next step by removing the arbitrary geographic restriction and looking at the local economic drivers of individual metropolitan areas as the key determinant for more efficient diversification. The results show that economic diversification can be a more effective diversification strategy than previously used strategies that have geographic constraints.

INTRODUCTION

Research on the diversification benefits to enhance the performance of real estate portfolios has been studied by many authors. Miles and McCue [9] used property-specific data to calculate the holding period returns for the widely accepted division of the United States into four geographic regions: the East, Midwest, South, and West; as well as property type diversification. This geographic grouping of real estate remains today as the main determinant of diversification in major organizations such as the National Council of Real Estate Investment Fiduciaries (NCREIF). Additional work confirmed and expanded these findings giving real estate portfolio managers solid ground for reducing some of the unsystematic risk in real estate portfolio returns (Miles and McCue [9], Hartzell, Hekman and Miles [6]). Further work included diversification benefits for mortgage portfolios (Corgel and Gay [2]).

More recent work redrew the traditional four-region geographic boundaries of the United States from the (economically random) boundaries of contiguous state lines into geographic boundaries drawn on similar general economic-base conditions affecting long-term trends in real estate (Hartzell, Shulman and Wurtzebach [5], Mueller, Kapplin and Schwartz [11]).[1] This work improved the focus on economic location but still contained geographic limitations. Previous work also suggested that the best method for determining diversification effectiveness would be to compare movements along the efficient frontiers of portfolios, based on the different methods.

From *Journal of Real Estate Research*, Vol. 7, No. 4. The authors would like to thank Charles H. Wurtzebach and acknowledge his major contribution to the development of the economically based diversification strategy. Of course, responsibility for any remaining errors is ours. The authors also would like to express their appreciation to Donna Machi for the numerous hours of computer consultation she provided.

The most recent work by Malizia and Simons [8] used three real estate demand-side indicators (employment, personal income, and population) to test the effectiveness of three current geographic diversification strategies: the traditional geographic four regions used by Frank Russell Company/NCREIF; the U.S. Department of Commerce's eight regions, and the economically grouped eight regions developed by Hartzell, Shulman and Wurtzebach [5]. This study found the economically based diversification strategy superior because it was devised on historic economic relationships rather than political categorizations that strictly follow state geographic lines.

The purpose of this research is to take the next step, completely removing the contiguous geographic restrictions used in all previous studies and to compare a pure economically based approach on diversification to the previous geographic approaches. The basic premise for categorizing economic fundamentals comes from economic base theory. Any given urban metropolitan area in the United States can be characterized by the base industries that drive the growth of the local economy. These base industries export products and/or services to other parts of the country and/or world and thus support and enhance the growth of the local economy. The most vivid example is Detroit, Michigan where the auto industry is the major driver and barometer behind the local economy. Because real estate is one of the three major factors of production (land, labor, and capital), its returns are affected by trends in the local economy.

DESCRIPTION OF CATEGORIES

This study places U.S. urban metropolitan areas (MSAs) into five Dominant Economic Employment Categories (DECs) and five Employment Performance Zones (EPZs) following the method developed in the Prudential Portfolio Construction Process [15]. The DEC categories include: finance/service dominant (FIN), manufacturing dominant (MFG), government dominant (GOV), energy dominant (ENERGY), and diversified employment (DIV) (similar to the U.S. average). Each urban area is categorized by comparing employment sector representation (one-digit SIC code employment percentage) for the metropolitan area against the U.S. employment sector representation as a whole. If the employment category is statistically larger than the U.S. average as indicated by a modified *chi*-square technique at the .01 significance level, the area is considered to be dominated by the employment of that base industry and the market is placed in that category.

The difference between a geographically constrained grouping of cities versus an economic categorization is best illustrated when the DEC category "financial services" is examined. The cities of Fort Lauderdale, Florida; Phoenix, Arizona; San Francisco, California; Boston, Massachusetts; and Pittsburgh, Pennsylvania are all categorized in the Financial/Services employment area, yet each falls in a different economic region when defined by NCREIF or the Hartzell, Shulman and Wurtzebach method. The basic premise is that local economic conditions have a dramatic impact on real estate returns while geographic groupings provide only a rough clue as to economic character.

The EPZ categories include consistently higher employment growth (CH), recently higher growth (RH), recently lower growth (RL), cyclical growth (CYC), and consistently lower growth (CL). Each urban area is categorized by comparing the twenty-year metro area average to the U.S. average in two ten-year time frames. A *T*-test at the

.05 significance level is used to test for differences between averages. If the metro area employment growth is higher or lower over both ten-year time frames it is categorized as a consistently higher or lower market, respectively. If the metro area employment growth has been higher or lower only in the last ten years it is categorized as recently higher or lower. If the employment growth is not statistically different from the U.S. average it is categorized as cyclical (similar to the U.S. pattern of growth).

DATA

Previous academic studies used return series starting from 4th quarter 1973 through 2nd quarter 1987. The data for this study came from a large institutional commingled real estate fund and runs from 4th quarter 1973 through 4th quarter 1990. Thus, a full real estate cycle from bottom, to recovery, to boom, to decline is captured in this time period. A maximum of 411 and a minimum of 113 properties were held in this portfolio over the time period, with the number rising through 1982 and then declining to around 200 in 1986 and remaining relatively stable since that time.

The return series for each property consists of actual unleveraged quarterly net operating income and quarterly estimates of market value obtained from appraised values. Returns are annual rates for the overall period and quarterly rates for the subperiods. The individual property returns are weighted by market value for construction of the diversification category return series. The actual calculation for a quarterly weighted holding period return used the following formula (1):

$$Ri(t) = \frac{MV_i(t+1) + Ci(t)}{MV_i(t) + Ii(t)} - 1, \qquad (1)$$

where

$Ri(t)$ = holding period return,
$MV_i(t)$ = beginning of period market value,
$MV_i(t+1)$ = end of period market value,
$Ci(t)$ = cash flow earned,
$Ii(t)$ = additional cash investment during period.

The problems of an appraisal-based return series are well documented. However, in a market of heterogeneous assets and inactive trading, outside value opinions appear to be the best alternative in the absence of continuous market transactions. A recent study by Miles, Webb and Guilkey [10] compared the appraised values of 462 commercial properties in the Russell-NCREIF Property Index that were sold over its twelve-year history and found an average 1.6% difference between appraised value and sale value, lending support to the assumption that appraised values are a reasonable proxy for transactions prices. The data used in this study represent a "transactions flavored" time series, as this database includes appraised values and actual sales prices whenever available. The problem may be more serious when real estate is analyzed in a mixed-asset portfolio, but should present only a minor problem here where the focus is on within-real estate diversification questions.

To perform the analysis, each of the individual real estate investments in this study had the MSAs, where each property was located, placed into the diversification categories. The breakdown was as follows:

Four-Region Diversification (FRC-NCREIF)

Region	No. Properties
East	84
Midwest	220
South	147
West	62

Eight-Region Diversification (Hartzell, Shulman, Wurtzebach)

Region	No. Properties
New England	24
Midatlantic	52
Old South	70
Industrial Midwest	215
Farm Belt	16
Mineral Extraction	97
Southern California	138
Northern California	71

Dominant Employment Category

Economic Group	No. Properties
Diversified	170
Energy	82
Government	48
Manufacturing	298
Finance/Service	64
Unclassified	23

Employment Performance Zone

Economic Group	No. Properties
Consistently Higher	230
Recently Higher	31
Cyclical	187
Recently Lower	94
Consistently Lower	120
Unclassified	23

STATISTICAL PROCEDURES AND RESULTS

Correlations for each diversification strategy were run for the three time subperiods (recovery, growth and decline) plus the full cycle. The correlation matrix of returns for each diversification type are shown in Exhibits 1 through 4. Even though comparing correlations is difficult, a number of interesting points can be observed.

(1) In the four-region correlation matrix during the three subperiods, six out of eighteen (33%) of the correlation coefficients were significant within the three subperiods tested. Additionally 50% of the correlation coefficients were significant for the full cycle (1973–1990).

Exhibit 1

			Correlation of Returns			
Expected Return	Standard Deviation	Grouping	East	Midwest	West	South
Four Region 4Q73–4Q76 (Recovery)						
2.97	2.32	East	1.00			
1.90	.95	Midwest	−.407	1.00		
1.83	.87	West	.202	−.260	1.00	
2.31	1.49	South	.660[a]	−.285	.499[b]	1.00
Four Region 1Q77–2Q82 (Growth)						
6.21	6.24	East	1.00			
2.86	1.36	Midwest	.361[b]	1.00		
4.81	2.76	West	.103	.639[a]	1.00	
4.03	3.45	South	−.457[a]	−.159	−.218	1.00
Four Region 3Q82–4Q90 (Decline)						
2.78	1.82	East	1.00			
1.97	1.43	Midwest	.282[b]	1.00		
2.05	1.41	West	.122	.227	1.00	
.80	2.28	South	.194	.074	.216	1.00
Four Region 4Q73–4Q90 (Full Cycle) (Annual Return)						
17.53	8.38	East	1.00			
9.61	2.79	Midwest	.308[b]	1.00		
12.57	4.59	West	.282[b]	.459[a]	1.00	
8.73	5.93	South	−.938	.076	.199	1.00

[a]significant at 95% level
[b]significant at 90% level

(2) In the eight-region correlation matrix during the three subperiods, seventeen out of eighty-four (20.2%) of the correlation coefficients were significant within the three subperiods tested. Additionally 21% of the correlation coefficients were significant for the full cycle (1973–1990).

(3) In the DEC correlation matrix during the three subperiods, four out of thirty (13%) of the correlation coefficients were significant within the three subperiods tested. Additionally 20% of the correlation coefficients were significant for the full cycle (1973–1990).

(4) In the EPZ correlation matrix during the three subperiods, four out of thirty (13%) of the correlation coefficients were significant within the three subperiods tested. Additionally 20% of the correlation coefficients were significant for the full cycle (1973–1990).

Thus, comparison of correlations finds that using economic diversification produced lower correlations overall and fewer statistically significant correlations. Additionally, the four-region and eight-region correlation matrices had the significant correlations carrying over from one time period to another, which did not happen in the DEC or EPZ categories. These results lead to the conclusion that the move from geographic to economic diversification can reduce the non-systematic component of risk in this real estate portfolio's returns.

Exhibit 2

Group	Mean	SD	NE	MA	OS	IN	FB	ME	SC	NC
Eight Region 4Q73–4Q76 (Recovery)									
NE	2.55	3.33	1.00							
MA	1.45	1.82	NA	1.00						
OS	1.45	1.23	NA	−.093	1.00					
IN	2.29	1.02	NA	.232	−.322	1.00				
FB	2.29	2.24	NA	.473	.374	.274	1.00			
ME	2.92	1.63	NA	.086	.318	.158	.698[a]	1.00		
SC	1.43	1.23	NA	−.079	.211	−.184	.285	.177	1.00	
NC	2.05	1.08	NA	−1.43	.529[b]	−.554[a]	−.057	.156	−.174	1.00
NA—indicates too few observations to be meaningful									
Eight Region 1Q77–2Q82 (Growth)									
NE	3.50	2.78	1.00							
MA	5.16	4.74	−.315	1.00						
OS	3.41	2.64	.380[b]	−.057	1.00					
IN	2.93	1.07	.153	.442[a]	.054	1.00				
FB	2.88	2.65	.177	.380[b]	.045	.127	1.00			
ME	3.44	2.08	.198	.105	.068	.087	.473[a]	1.00		
SC	5.65	3.59	.204	.228	.084	.0667[a]	.283	.057	1.00	
NC	4.91	4.08	.113	.095	−.263	.377[b]	−.034	−.115	.108	1.00
Eight Region 3Q82–4Q90 (Decline)									
NE	4.07	4.07	1.00							
MA	2.60	2.60	−.297[b]	1.00						
OS	1.04	1.68	−.196	.290	1.00					
IN	1.97	1.37	−.128	.296[b]	.276	1.00				
FB	1.47	2.78	.054	.341[a]	.066	.375[a]	1.00			
ME	0.15	2.54	−.468[a]	.015	−.039	−.138	.285	1.00		
SC	3.02	2.07	−.034	.034[a]	.305[b]	.344[b]	.439[a]	.042	1.00	
NC	2.47	1.78	−.008	.096	.138	.129	−.078	.115	.018	1.00
Eight Region 4Q73–4Q90 (Full Cycle)									
NE	16.35	6.38	1.00							
MA	17.34	9.30	−.212	1.00						
OS	9.88	9.96	−.179	−.077	1.00					
IN	9.78	2.67	−.042	.306[a]	.025	1.00				
FB	9.28	5.51	−.013	.125	.167	.323[a]	1.00			
ME	7.04	5.77	−.238[b]	.070	.126	.177	.205	1.00		
SC	15.28	5.70	.045	.378[a]	.085	.473[a]	.361[a]	.102	1.00	
NC	13.18	5.23	−.007	.095	.139	.207	.139	.145	.371[a]	1.00

[a]significant at 95% level
[b]significant at 90% level

The next phase of analysis was to determine if an investor could receive higher risk-adjusted returns using the different diversification strategies. To accomplish this goal, the historical return information was fed into the OPTAMIX [12] asset allocation computer program. Optamix utilizes historical return information with capital market assumptions to determine the efficient frontier of risk-return with different mixes of each pre-defined sample grouping of assets. The relevant parameters entered into the program include the expected value and standard deviation for each asset class group

Exhibit 3

Expected Return	Standard Deviation	Group	DIV	ENERGY	FIN	GOV	MFG
			\multicolumn{5}{c}{Correlation of Returns}
\multicolumn{8}{l}{Dominant Employment Category 4Q73–4Q76 (Recovery)}
1.56	0.98	DIV	1.00				
3.31	1.97	ENERGY	−.222	1.00			
2.51	1.81	FIN	.150	.169	1.00		
3.96	5.18	GOV	.087	.547[b]	.133	1.00	
1.61	.79	MFG	.059	.554[a]	−.270	.343	1.00
\multicolumn{8}{l}{Dominant Employment Category 1Q77–2Q82 (Growth)}
4.11	4.09	DIV	1.00				
3.36	2.39	ENERGY	−.214	1.00			
7.60	9.81	FIN	−.155	−.327	1.00		
4.74	3.50	GOV	−.112	−.073	−.138	1.00	
4.16	2.17	MFG	−.114	.252	.127	.131	1.00
\multicolumn{8}{l}{Dominant Employment Category 3Q82–4Q90 (Decline)}
2.27	1.70	DIV	1.00				
0.18	2.59	ENERGY	−.215	1.00			
2.94	1.97	FIN	.356[a]	.153	1.00		
1.40	1.75	GOV	−.164	−.201	.017	1.00	
2.56	1.56	MFG	−.208	.070	.337[b]	.041	1.00
\multicolumn{8}{l}{Dominant Employment Category 4Q73–4Q90 (Full Cycle)}
11.95	5.21	DIV	1.00				
7.12	7.12	ENERGY	.032	1.00			
19.33	12.68	FIN	.014	.022	1.00		
13.40	7.17	GOV	.039	.250[b]	.180	1.00	
12.68	3.82	MFG	.200	.147	.290[b]	.114	1.00

[a] significant at 95% level
[b] significant at 90% level

and the correlation coefficient between each pair of grouped asset classes. A minimum and maximum allocation for each pre-defined group is selected (in this case a 0% minimum and 100% maximum was chosen to obtain the full range of possibilities). The program generates a range of returns and standard deviations with the optimum percentage mix of each asset grouping to achieve the lowest risk for a given return.

Exhibits 5 through 8 show graphically the efficient frontiers for each diversification strategy during the different time periods.

(1) In the 1973 to 1976 recovery period, the eight-region strategy started as the best strategy at low risk and return levels; the DEC strategy took over as the best strategy for higher returns (and risks)—the DEC strategy allowed for the highest overall returns.

(2) In the 1977 to 1982 growth period, the eight-region strategy started out as the best at low risk low return levels, DEC took over, then four-region, then eight-region, then DEC again for the highest return (and risk) potential.

(3) In the 1982 to 1990 decline period, the eight-region strategy dominated as the best strategy over all risk-return possibilities.

Exhibit 4

Expected Return	Standard Deviation	Group	CH	CL	CYC	RH	RL
\multicolumn{8}{l}{Employment Performance Zones 4Q73–4Q76 (Recovery)}
2.09	1.55	CH	1.00				
2.38	1.68	CL	.069	1.00			
1.57	.79	CYC	.076	.284	1.00		
3.30	4.29	RH	.710[a]	.250	.025	1.00	
2.44	1.23	RL	.384	−.021	−.032	−.092	1.00
\multicolumn{8}{l}{Employment Performance Zones 1Q77–2Q82 (Growth)}
4.02	3.38	CH	1.00				
6.69	8.38	CL	−.358	1.00			
4.21	2.21	CYC	−.058	.092	1.00		
4.24	3.62	RH	−.105	.194	.079	1.00	
4.11	3.14	RL	−.106	−.182	.234	.082	1.00
\multicolumn{8}{l}{Employment Performance Zones 3Q82–4Q90 (Decline)}
1.60	2.09	CH	1.00				
2.83	2.73	CL	.381[a]	1.00			
2.73	1.31	CYC	.198	.143	1.00		
2.62	3.15	RH	−.225	−.077	−.136	1.00	
0.55	1.89	RL	.311[b]	.171	.078	−.338[b]	1.00
\multicolumn{8}{l}{Employment Performance Zones 4Q73–4Q90 (Full Cycle)}
11.78	4.60	CH	1.00				
16.65	10.58	CL	−.025	1.00			
14.19	4.17	CYC	.130	.251[b]	1.00		
13.82	5.49	RH	.081	.192	.056	1.00	
7.41	1.89	RL	.258[b]	.171	.056	.014	1.00

[a] significant at 95% level
[b] significant at 90% level

(4) For the 1973 to 1990 overall time period, the eight-region strategy had the best efficient frontier for low to medium risk-return combinations up to a 15.8% return. The four-region strategy was best from 15.9% to 17.4%. Finally the DEC strategy allowed for the highest portfolio returns of 17.6% to 19.2%.

CONCLUSIONS

Utilizing economic versus geographic strategies provided superior diversification capabilities. Economic strategies had lower correlations between categories and fewer numbers of statistically significant correlations. While the comparison of the diversification strategies during different periods of the real estate cycle and over the entire time period does not lead to a conclusive result as to one superior diversification strategy to achieve the best efficient frontier, the economically based strategies (eight-region, DEC, and EPZ) clearly provided consistently better efficient frontiers than the geographic four-region technique. There is the possibility that more diversification categories will inherently allow for better efficient frontiers, because high return properties

Exhibit 5 Efficient Frontiers 1973 to 1976

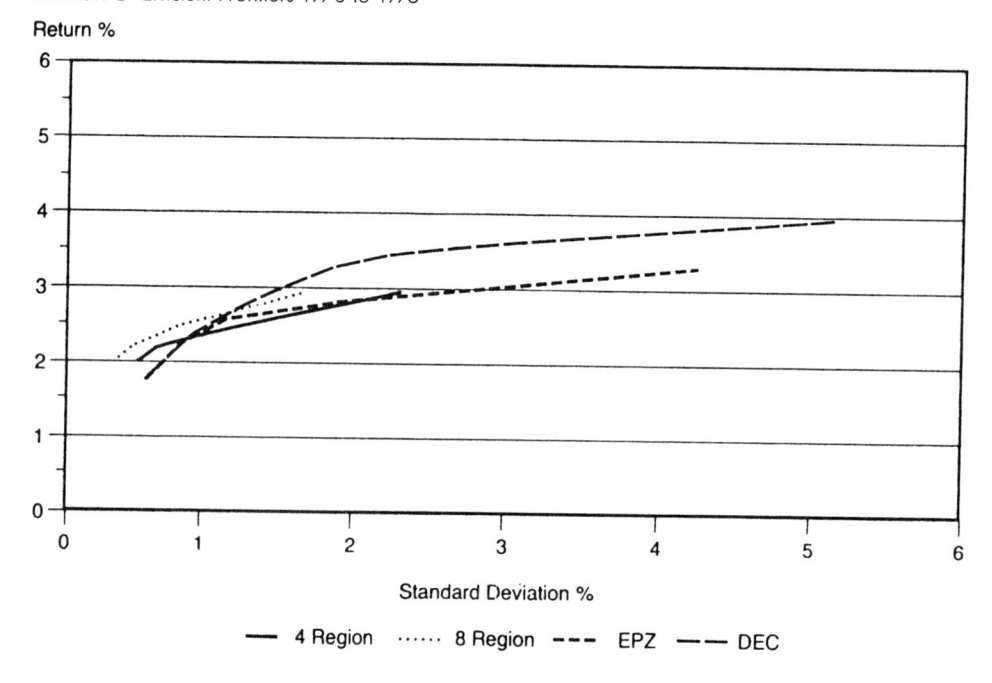

Exhibit 6 Efficient Frontiers 1977 to 1982

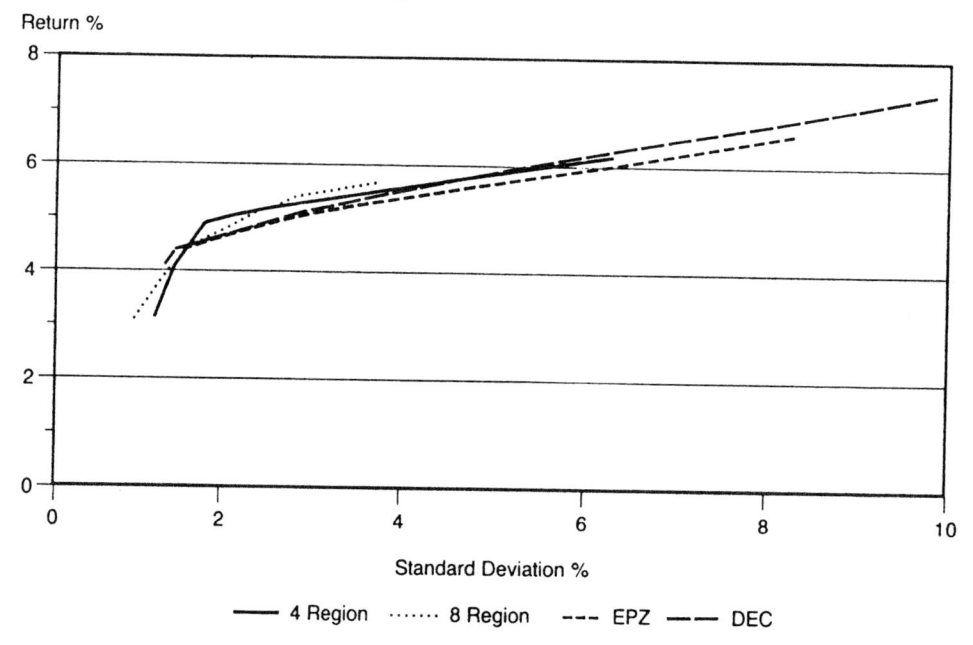

Exhibit 7 Efficient Frontiers 1982 to 1990

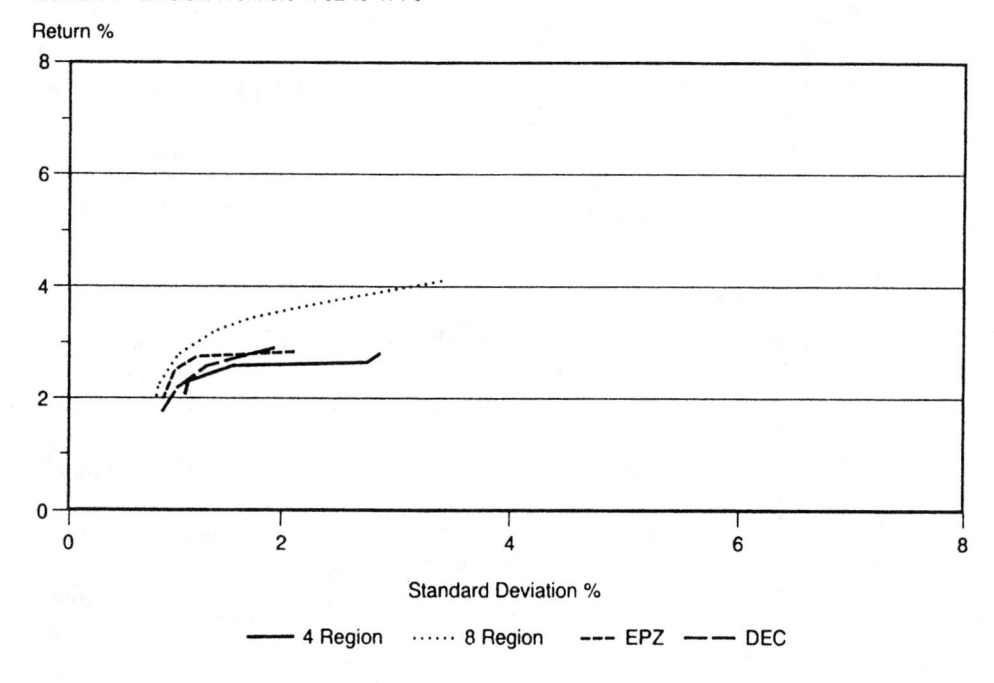

Exhibit 8 Efficient Frontiers 1973 to 1990

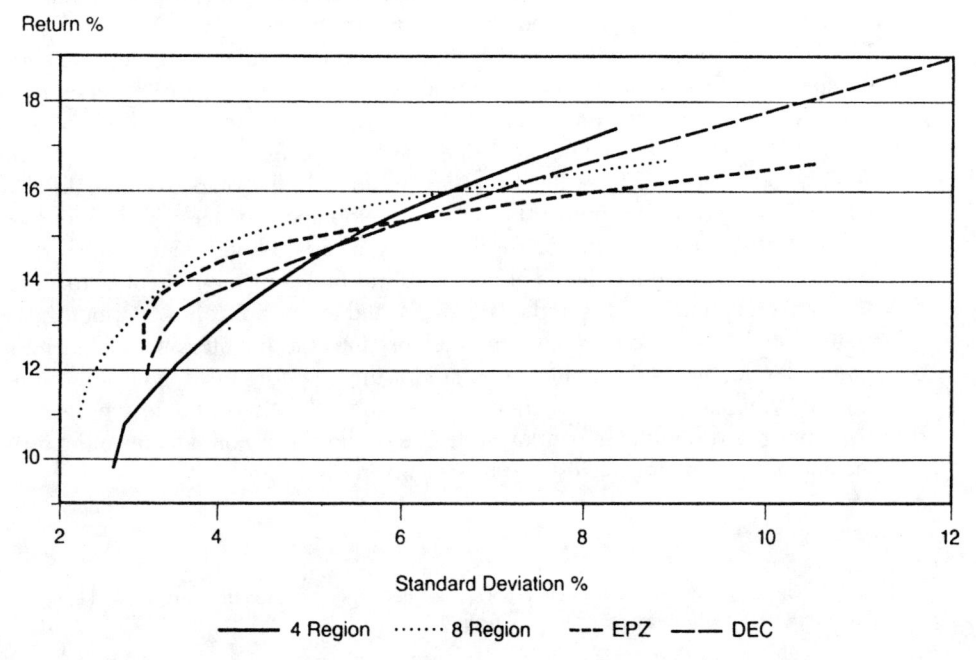

REAL ESTATE PORTFOLIO DIVERSIFICATION

will not be diluted in a group dominated by lower return properties (this may be one explanation for the eight-region diversification strategy doing well in this study).

It is interesting to note that the DEC category typically allowed for the highest possible return (albeit high risk) in the overall time frame and both the recovery and growth periods, but not in the decline period. Returns were highest in the Finance/Services diversification group during the high return time periods. This would suggest that future real estate investment strategies look toward areas dominated by industries that are expected to have the highest expansion during the next real estate cycle.

IMPLICATIONS FOR FURTHER STUDY

Removing the geographic constraints placed on diversification strategies of the past opens a new realm of possibilities to the real estate portfolio management community. Some researchers have already suggested new diversification strategies (see Cole, Guilkey, Miles and Webb [1]). However, a larger database of information is still required to accomplish further study that will utilize different property types and more sophisticated diversification strategies.

This study validates the theory that local economics is more important than geographic contiguity for achieving diversification. The priority for future research should be placed on more careful analysis of local economic factors and their impact on local real estate returns. Further work by property type should yield interesting results as certain industries affect particular property types more than others. Breaking dominant employment industry categories into increasingly homogeneous groupings may also provide better return correlations and increased predictive power. The cyclicality of some industries may also affect property returns differently. Individual markets may also have submarkets with different employment characteristics than the overall MSA, thus a more pointed analysis of submarket employment character may yield additional insight into specific real state return and diversification potential.

The authors are well aware that the demand for real estate is only one part of the equation and that the supply side of the equation can have a major impact on real estate returns as it did for office investments in the late 1980s (see Wurtzebach, Mueller and Machi [16]). However, the demand side plays the major role in forecasting real estate returns today in the U.S. and will continue to do so in the years to come, if future new supply is effectively constrained by lack of development financing, federal or local government constraints, and the logical economics of cost-to-build versus market return potential. The over-building boom of the 1980s was fueled by a variety of factors including tax laws, exceptional profits in the late 1970s, and oversupply of money, but the current state of real estate should put a long memory into the investors who financed uneconomic developments. Locating real estate for the investor's portfolio will be an increasingly difficult and complex task in the future. The utilization of the lessons learned from continuing portfolio theory work will be one of the major components of better strategic decisionmaking for real estate investments in the future.

NOTE

[1] The underlying economic region concept was developed from the theory delineated in the book, *The Nine Nations of North America*, by Joel Garreau [3].

REFERENCES

[1] R. Cole, D. Guilkey, M. Miles, and B. Webb. More Scientific Diversification Strategies for Commercial Real Estate. *Real Estate Review* (Spring 1989) 59–66.

[2] J. B. Corgel and G. D. Gay. Local Economic Base, Geographic Diversification, and Risk Management of Mortgage Portfolios. *AREUEA Journal* 15:3 (Fall 1987), 256–67.

[3] J. Garreau. *The Nine Nations of North America.* New York: Avon Books, 1981.

[4] S. M. Giliberto and R. E. Hopkins. Metro Employment Trends: Analysis and Portfolio Considerations. Salomon Brothers, Inc., May 14, 1990.

[5] D. J. Hartzell, D. G. Shulman and C. H. Wurtzebach. Refining the Analysis of Regional Diversification for Income-Producing Real Estate. *Journal of Real Estate Research* 2:2 (Winter 1987), 85–95.

[6] D. J. Hartzell, J. S. Hekman and M. E. Miles. Diversification Categories in Investment Real Estate. *AREUEA Journal* 14:2 (Summer 1986), 230–54.

[7] D. J. Hartzell and E. E. Malizia. Market Analysis for Investors. *Urban Land* 48 (January 1989), 6–8.

[8] E. E. Malizia and R. A. Simons. Comparing Regional Classifications for Real Estate Portfolio Diversification. *Journal of Real Estate Research* 6:1 (Spring 1991), 53–78.

[9] M. E. Miles and T. E. McCue. Historic Returns and Institutional Real Estate Portfolios. *AREUEA Journal* 10:2 (Summer 1982), 184–98.

[10] M. Miles, B. Webb and D. Guilkey. On the Reliability of Commercial Appraisals. Paper presented to the Spring NCREIF meetings. Orlando, Florida, March 1991.

[11] G. R. Mueller, S. A. Kapplin and A. F. Schwartz. A Study of Geographical Diversification on Real Estate Asset Management. Paper presented to Financial Management Association meetings, New Orleans, Louisiana, October 1988.

[12] OPTAMIX (Optimal Asset Mix and Allocation Analysis System). New York: Buck Pension Fund Services, Inc., 1984.

[13] D. Shulman and R. E. Hopkins. Economic Diversification in Real Estate Portfolio. New York: Salomon Brothers, Inc., November 1988.

[14] D. Shulman, et al. Real Estate Market Review. New York: Salomon Brothers, Inc. (1991).

[15] C. H. Wurtzebach. The Portfolio Construction Process. Newark, NJ: Prudential Real Estate Investors, 1988.

[16] ———, G. R. Mueller and D. Machi. The Impact of Inflation and Vacancy on Real Estate Returns. *Journal of Real Estate Research* 6:2 (Summer 1991), 153–68.

17 A Look at Real Estate Duration

David J. Hartzell, David G. Shulman, Terence C. Langetieg, and Martin L. Leibowitz

Duration is a function of lease contracts and market conditions.

The analysis of duration, or the sensitivity of an asset's value to changes in interest rates, has followed an interesting path since the development of duration concepts for investments outside the fixed-income area. The duration concept has been extended to common equities, liability structures, and the management of the pension surplus. In this article, we use the effective duration concept to analyze real estate, with a look toward consolidating the contractual differences between real estate holdings and the equity duration model.[1] This topic is particularly relevant in the measurement of total portfolio duration for portfolios with a significant real estate content.

Real estate duration can be determined using methods similar to those for common stocks, such as the dividend discount model (DDM). As with common equity, however, empirical estimates of duration vary considerably between the traditional dividend discount model and newer techniques. We analyze these differences, using examples that differ in their ability to pass through inflation to net income. In particular, we model the speed of adjustment to inflation in lease contracts. This factor determines how quickly total returns adjust to inflation-included changes in interest rates and, hence, the effective duration of the asset class.

We analyze duration under a number of scenarios, which differ by inflation adjustment assumptions. First, we define real estate as an investment vehicle, with a particular focus on the microfactors affecting real estate performance. Second, we describe the different rental adjustment processes used as inputs to duration calculations. The results show that different lease rollover assumptions result in different durations. Third, we discuss the impacts of a change in real interest rates. Finally, we present our conclusions and implications of the analysis.

REAL ESTATE DEFINED

Equity real estate has the same attributes as common stock and can be viewed as an industry segment within a broad securities index. As a result, the equity duration model is applicable. An investor receives a stream of payments called net rents and holds claim on the residual value of the asset.

From *The Journal of Portfolio Management*. This copyrighted material is reprinted with permission from *The Journal of Portfolio Management*, 488 Madison Avenue, New York, NY 10022.

Real estate is also characterized by three factors that differentiate it from common stock. Real estate represents an unusually large segment of the economy, which is subject to its own cycle and is a major factor of production in all industries. Hence, investors can diversify within real estate with relative ease, which is not possible for other given industry groups. For example, it is easier to diversify away unsystematic risk in real estate than in almost any of the S&P industry groupings. Even though there is a general real estate "cycle," the heterogeneity of local markets, as well as the different lease and economic characteristics of the various property types, creates the potential for risk reduction through diversification within the real estate portfolio (Hartzell et al., 1986).

Second, the contractual nature of the cash flows, which are determined by the property's leasing structure means that equity real estate embodies some debt aspects. We can generate differing maturities and bond-like cash flows by altering the terms of the portfolio of leases.

Finally, real estate rents and values are determined by replacement costs that approximate inflation. This offers investors the long-term potential to receive rates of return indexed to inflation.

Three factors affect the indexation of returns and, therefore, the duration of real estate: the lease structure, the supply and demand cycle for real estate, and product deterioration or enhancement over time. The two polar extremes for lease structure are fully-indexed leases and non-indexed leases. The former allows the full pass-through of inflation into rents on a periodic basis. The pass-through can be accomplished contractually by indexation clauses in leases or by rolling over short-term leases in markets where real estate supply and demand conditions remain unchanged. From this perspective, hotel leases provide the ultimate inflation sensitivity, because they can be adjusted overnight; such leases also create vacancy risk, because these short-term contracts are typically not renewed.

At the other extreme are financing leases, where lease rates remain unchanged for a decade or more. The only way to pass inflation through to the investor with this type of lease structure is to release the space at the expiration of the lease, at which time the capital value of the asset would adjust to reflect the new level of rents. The trade-off here is between a non-indexed rent stream and a guaranteed occupancy level for the term of the contract. Reality in the real estate marketplace is somewhere between the two extremes; even with indexed leases, there is sufficient friction to prevent a full pass-through of inflation.

Superimposed on the lease structure are market risks generated by real estate supply and demand conditions that historically have been more of a national, rather than local, phenomenon. These market risks require a fully-diversified real estate portfolio to have a time diversification dimension, as well as product and geographic diversification dimensions. Real rents fluctuate in response to local supply and demand conditions, which are influenced by national economic conditions.[2] Consequently, rents may increase at rates higher or lower than the underlying rate of inflation in the short run. This obviously influences the ability of real estate to pass through inflation-based returns to its owners. In the long run, however, competition erodes abnormal returns, as long-term supply adjusts to long-run demand. As a result of recent overbuilding, "long-term" in real estate could be very long indeed.

The third aspect of real estate risk lies in the notion of product obsolescence and enhancement. Although many financial models of real estate transactions make assumptions concerning these risks, obsolescence and enhancement exist and ultimately affect the residual value of the asset. If the product maintains its attractiveness over time, then its value in equilibrium will be its replacement cost. If there is obsolescence or deterioration, however, its value would be lower than its replacement cost, preventing the residual value from fully passing through the inflation increases. Conversely, if the product improves over time because its site value is enhanced, its replacement cost would increase at a rate faster than that of inflation (Corcoran, 1987).

RELATION TO PREVIOUS RESEARCH

The adjustment in real estate returns as a result of changing inflation rates has been discussed in prior studies (Hartzell et al., 1987; Brueggeman et al., 1984). A fundamental problem with these studies concerns the quality of data that they employ, and, in a more general sense, the unavailability of real estate return data with which to analyze theoretical finance issues.

The ability of real estate to provide hedges against inflation can be determined by testing for the empirical reaction of real estate returns to changes in the expected and unexpected components of inflation. In general, studies have found that real estate provides a strong hedge against expected inflation. On the other hand, only the Hartzell, Hekman, and Miles study (1987) found a strong hedge against unexpected inflation. This study categorizes the data sample by different property characteristics, which leads to similar conclusions for various property types (office, retail, and industrial) and property sizes. Most studies do not shed light on the way changes in inflation affect real estate returns, beyond a discussion of methodology and empirical results.

One problem in previous studies is the use of appraisals to calculate the holding-period returns. The typical appraisal process that commingled real estate funds—the source of data—follow includes at least annual external appraisals, with in-house employees updating these values in the quarters between reappraisal. It is likely that the in-house appraisers merely adjust for inflation in the values of the properties, which would lead to an obvious inflation hedge finding. Such a problem is inherent in the use of any data series that uses appraised values as proxies of transaction values to calculate holding-period returns. In tests of duration, with real estate returns measured by appraisals, we find duration levels of zero.

Returns exhibited by equity real estate investment trusts (REITs) have been suggested as proxies for measuring the performance of real estate portfolios. Given the possibility of induced stock-like price volatility and the use of financial leverage for this type of security, though, most observers believe that these returns are not an accurate reflection of the nature of the underlying properties. Estimates of duration using equity REIT returns over the 1980s range from two to four years, about two-thirds of the duration of the S&P 500 over the same time period.

Given the limitations of existing real estate data sources, we propose an analytical approach to measuring effective duration. Using a realistic valuation model of market rents and lease contracts, we analyze the impact of changing inflation rates on duration and real interest rates for several different contracting regimes.

THE VALUATION OF REAL ESTATE

We begin with the premise that the rate of increase in real estate income is a function of the inflation rate modified by lease structure, real supply and demand conditions, and the degree of product enhancement or deterioration that occurs over time. *In this form, real estate can be viewed as a bond whose principal is inflation-indexed and whose coupons range from zero to full indexation.* Thus, the price of real estate can be reduced to the following equation.[3]

$$\begin{pmatrix} \text{Current} \\ \text{Property} \\ \text{Value} \end{pmatrix} = \begin{pmatrix} \text{Present Value of} \\ \text{Net Rents Over} \\ \text{Next T Years} \end{pmatrix} + \begin{pmatrix} \text{Present Value of} \\ \text{Expected Market Price} \\ \text{in T years} \end{pmatrix}$$

$$P_0 = \sum_{t=1}^{T} \left(\frac{\overline{NR}}{(1+k_0)^t} \right) + \frac{E[NR_0(1+g_0+\bar{u}_1)(1+g_0+\bar{u}_2)\ldots(1+g_0+\bar{u}_T) \times \bar{M}_T]}{(1+k_0)^T} \qquad (1)$$

where:

- P_0 = present value of future cash flows generated by the property;
- T = term of lease;
- $\overline{NR}$ = net rental income on lease (fixed over T years);
- NR_0 = current level of market rents;
- g_0 = current expected growth rate in property value, which reflects the expected economywide inflation rate;
- $\bar{u}_T$ = unexpected growth rate in rents in year T that reflects unexpected inflation, local supply and demand imbalances, as well as obsolescence and enhancements, which are interrelated with local market conditions;
- $\bar{M}_T$ = price-to-rent multiple in year T;
- k_0 = current required rate of return; and
- $E[\cdot]$ = expected property value in T years.

The net rent variable in the equation is determined by the interaction of the structure of the contracts underlying the real property, the supply and demand conditions within local markets, and inflation. For the former, net rents will rise or fall depending on the ability of the landlord/property-owner to roll over leases, thereby adjusting for inflation. In our annual model, for example, the interval for which lease payments are fixed can range from one year to more than twenty years. At the short end, rents adjust as announcements of inflation are made. Over the long term, rents do not adjust at all to inflation and are held constant for the entire lease term. At lease renewal, rents adjust to "catch up" for all previous inflation during the fixed contract period. Thus, the interaction of inflation rates and speed of adjustment determines the effective duration of the asset class.

With this valuation equation, we can calculate the effective duration of real estate by measuring asset price changes in response to changes in interest rates under varying types of lease contracts. In this context, an asset with an effective duration of five years would experience a 5% decrease in value in response to a 1% increase in interest rates. We assume that there is direct and instantaneous transmittal of changes in the expected inflation rate to the discount rate. Initially, we assume that the expected real rate of return is constant and that there is no unanticipated rent growth. Later, we allow changes in the underlying real rate or real estate risk premium to cause changes in the nominal interest rate.

ALTERNATIVE LEASE STRUCTURES: PERFECT MARKETS VERSUS MARKET FRICTIONS

The limited availability of appropriate data to use in empirical tests of duration requires us to use an analytical valuation model. Our duration calculations are based on Equation (1), with five alternative contract terms:

- Continuous rent adjustment to the prevailing market rent;
- Rent adjustments every two years;
- Rent adjustments every five years;
- Rent adjustments every ten years; and
- Rent adjustments every twenty years.

In all five cases, we assume a ten-year holding period, which is typical for most real estate investment managers. In the case of a twenty-year lease, we have assumed a sale at the end of the tenth year, by discounting the net rents from years 11–20 and the residual value at the end of the period.

Our analysis assumes a 6% real rate of return for real estate, a rate real estate investment managers use frequently for quality assets. The real return consists of a general economic real interest rate plus a risk premium appropriate for real estate.[4] An initial 5% expected inflation rate is also assumed for the base case. This translates into an initial discount rate (k) of 11.3%. The expected growth rate of the rental stream at the beginning of the holding period is equal to the expected inflation rate.

With continuous rent adjustment, inflation over the next year is fully embedded into next year's rents and in every subsequent year's rents during the holding period, as well as in the terminal value of the property. For fixed-rent contracts, the adjustment to the new rate of inflation takes place at the end of the contract term. With a contract term of ten years, for example, there is no rent adjustment to inflation during the next ten years. Nevertheless, inflation is embedded in the growth of the property value, as represented by the second term in Equation (1). This case is similar to a ten-year bond with a fixed coupon and an indexed principal.

We analyze two generic types of leasing contracts. Both types assume that the contracting term is held constant throughout the holding period. That is, at the end of an initial lease term, a new lease is put into effect with the same term as the initial one. From that point forward, the contract rolls over every T years until the end of the holding period. Further, the property, after the assumed ten-year holding period, is sold under the condition that leases have been contractually set so that their maturities will equal T in the future.

The first contract regime, which we call the "market frictions regime," assumes an equal rent for all lease terms. Contracts with different terms are not present value equivalents unless the expected inflation rate is equal to zero, but the market frictions regime is typical of existing rent contracts in major markets where there is often little difference between rents on contracts with different terms. One explanation for this is the possible presence of substantial periods of vacancy, leasing commissions, and other contracting costs. The potential cost of those market frictions is much greater with short-term leases than with long-term contracts. Consequently, benefits arising from inflation may be reduced with a long-term fixed-rent contract, but substantial costs resulting from market frictions are avoided.

The second contract type, which we call the "perfect markets regime," sets the fixed rent such that the present value of the rent payments until the leases roll over is equal to the present value of the expected inflation-indexed rent payments over the same time period. At the end of the investment horizon, the property value is equal to the market value of a fully-indexed cash flow stream, which is also the value of a perpetual floating-rent contract. The assumption is that the two contracts have equivalent present values. Given information asymmetries and market frictions related to local market supply and demand conditions, as well as inflexibility in setting lease terms, this case is more theoretical than real.

A graphic example serves to clarify this cash flow generation process. Figure 1 shows the cash flows earned by the property for a floating-rent contract and a five-year fixed-rent contract in the perfect markets regime. Assuming the base case, where expected inflation is 5% throughout the holding period, the present value of the five-year fixed-rent contract is $114.84, which is equal to the present value of a five-year rental stream starting at $105 that increases annually at the 5% expected inflation rate. After the initial five-year contracting period, the fixed rent is increased to $146.56. The present value of this second five-year annuity is equal to the present value of the floating-rent contract, which starts at $134.01 in year six ($105 \times 1.05^5 = 134.01), and is again indexed to the 5% expected inflation rate. A similar process is employed for leases with terms not equal to five years.

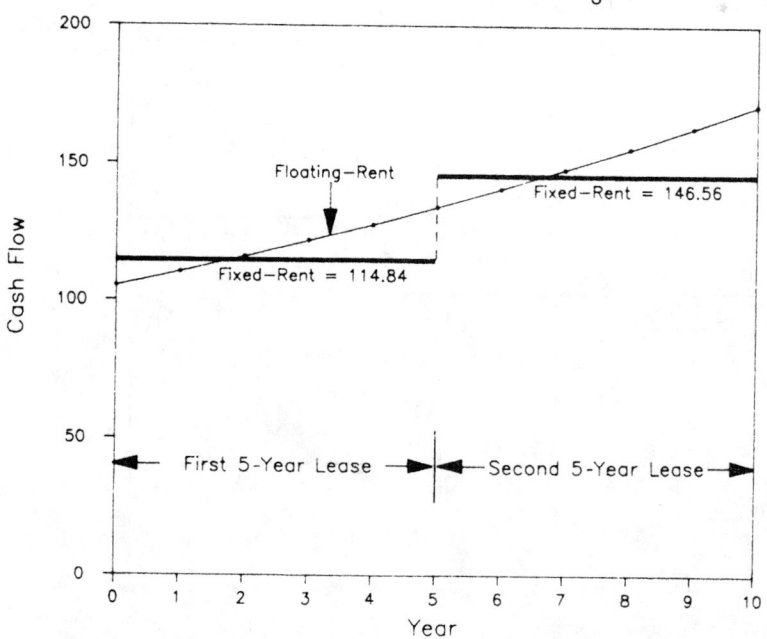

Figure 1 Cash Flows for a Five-Year Lease—Perfect Markets Regime

Figure 2 shows the rents for the fixed-rent and floating-rent leases in the market frictions regime. The fixed-rental stream is equal initially to the initial year's indexed-rent flow of $105. For the sixth year, the indexed rent rises to $134.01, and the fixed rent is set equal to this amount for the remaining five years of the holding period.

To illustrate the effect of a change in expected inflation, suppose that the rent contract is determined on the basis of a 5% inflation rate, and a shock occurs causing inflation expectations to increase to 6%. The effect of this change on the rental stream depends on the lease term, which determines how long it takes until rents can adjust to the inflation rate.

Figure 3 shows the rental stream for the market frictions regime before and after the instantaneous increase in inflation expectation from 5% to 6%. As the five-year contract is put into place prior to the shock, the base rent remains at $105 for the first five years. In year six, the new fixed rent—given that inflation has been rising at 6%—is $141.85. This is obviously higher than the fixed rent of $134.01, because the new contract adjusts to catch up to 6% versus 5% inflation. A similar adjustment takes place in the perfect market regime to preserve the "present value equivalence" in years 6–10.

PRICE SENSITIVITY TO CHANGES IN THE EXPECTED INFLATION RATE

A floating-rent or fully-indexed contract has a base payment in year zero of $100. With an expected inflation rate of 5%, the first-year payment is expected to be $105, the second-year payment $110.25, and so forth. The property value with a perpetual floating-rent contract is $1667 for our example, with a 5% expected inflation rate and 11.3% discount rate.[5] This translates into a capitalization rate—equivalent to a dividend yield—of 6.3% on income in year one.

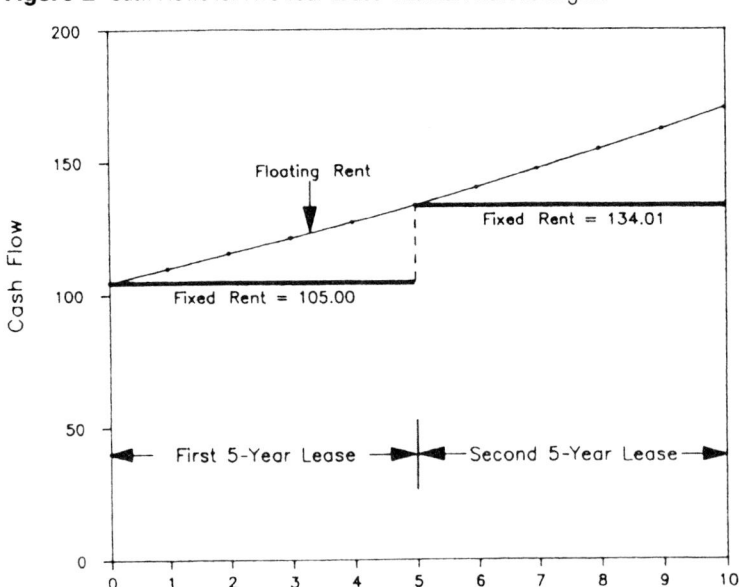

Figure 2 Cash Flows for Five-Year Lease—Market Frictions Regime

Figure 3 Cash Flow Effect from an Increase in the Inflation Rate from 5% to 6%—Market Frictions Regime

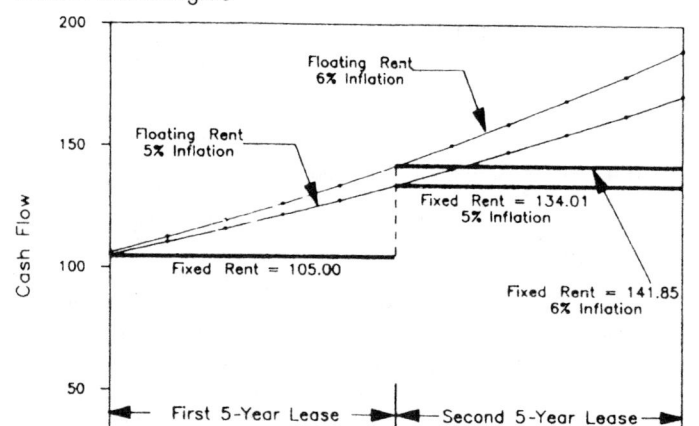

An instantaneous increase in the expected inflation rate to 6% after the lease contract is entered into would have no effect on value, because the lease is assumed to be fully and immediately indexed to inflation. This automatically increases income in year one to $106 and the discount rate to 12.36%. Consequently, there is no effect on asset value from a 100 basis point change in inflation, and the value of the property remains at $1667. Thus, the effective duration in the fully-indexed case is zero in both simulations.

A ten-year fixed-rent lease obviously leads to a different conclusion. In this case, the lease income remains unchanged at $105 during the life of the lease, but the residual value at expiration increases at the rate of inflation. This implies an initial value of the asset of $1383 and a residual value of $2253. The loss of coupon indexation results in a 17% diminution in value. We derive these values by assuming the capitalization rate in year ten is the same as in year zero.

If the expected inflation rate increases to 6%, the lease contract rents remain unchanged, but the discount rate increases by 106 basis points, and the resulting value falls to $1324. This represents a 4.26% drop in value and an effective duration of approximately 4.02 years for the market frictions case.[6] By contrast, the change in value for a ten-year lease contracting period in the perfect markets case is 1.8%.

DEVELOPING AN EQUIVALENT MEASURE OF INFLATION PASS-THROUGH

The inflation sensitivities that we find in these calculations can also provide some insights regarding the flow-through of inflation for real estate with different leasing structures. Given the indicated inflation sensitivities and the extension of the DDM incorporating inflation sensitivity, we can estimate an implied pass-through parameter. The price sensitivity of a floating-rent contract to a change in the expected inflation rate is equal to:[7]

$$\begin{pmatrix} \text{Price Sensitivity} \\ \text{to a Change} \\ \text{in the Expected} \\ \text{Inflation Rate} \end{pmatrix} = -D_{DDM}(1-\lambda)\Delta I \qquad (2)$$

where:

$D_{DDM} = \dfrac{1}{k-g}$ = duration of the divident discount model;
ΔI = change in the expected inflation rate; and
λ = inflation flow-through parameter.

D_{DDM} represents the duration in the traditional sense. It measures the price sensitivity to a change in the discount rate, holding the cash flow stream constant. A change in interest rates caused by a change in the expected inflation rate will also increase rents. For the floating-rent lease, we have assumed complete pass-through of inflation, hence λ is equal to one, and the price sensitivity to a change in the expected inflation rate is zero.

For the fixed-rent lease, we determine the price sensitivity to a change in the expected inflation rate as discussed above. Having determined the left-hand side of Equation (2), we then solve for λ to obtain a measure of the imputed inflation pass-through. Thus, we can determine an equivalent measure of inflation pass-through, which we then can use to compare contracts with level payments for fixed terms with contracts in which rents continuously adjust to reflect all or part of inflation.

Estimates of Inflation Sensitivity and Effective Duration. Given the methodology and assumptions underlying the valuation equation, the percentage change in value resulting from a 1% inflation-induced change in interest rates can be obtained for both the market friction and perfect markets cases. As mentioned above, estimates of the inflation flow-through measure are implied in these effective durations.[8]

The results, presented in Table 1 and Figure 4, are intuitively appealing. They show that effective duration, or the price change arising from a 1% increase in inflation rates, increases with the lease term. In what we consider our typical leasing arrangement, with a five-year term, the duration of real estate is 2.1 years in the more realistic market frictions case. By contrast, under the assumption of perfect markets, the dura-

Table 1 Changes to Value and Duration When a Discount Rate Increase Results from 1% Increase in the Expected Inflation Rate

	Market Frictions Regime			Perfect Markets Regime		
Inflation Rate	5%	6%		5%	6%	
Discount Rate	11.3%	12.4%		11.3%	12.4%	
Term	Value		Effective Duration[a]	Value		Effective Duration[a]
1 Year	$1,667	$1,667	0	$1,667	$1,667	0
2 Years	1,628	1,617	0.6	1,667	1,664	0.1
5 Years	1,524	1,490	2.1	1,667	1,656	0.6
10 Years	1,383	1,324	4.0	1,667	1,635	1.8
20 Years	1,191	1,114	6.1	1,667	1,592	4.2

[a] See Footnote 6 for the calculation of effective duration.

Figure 4 Effects of a Changing Lease Term on Duration

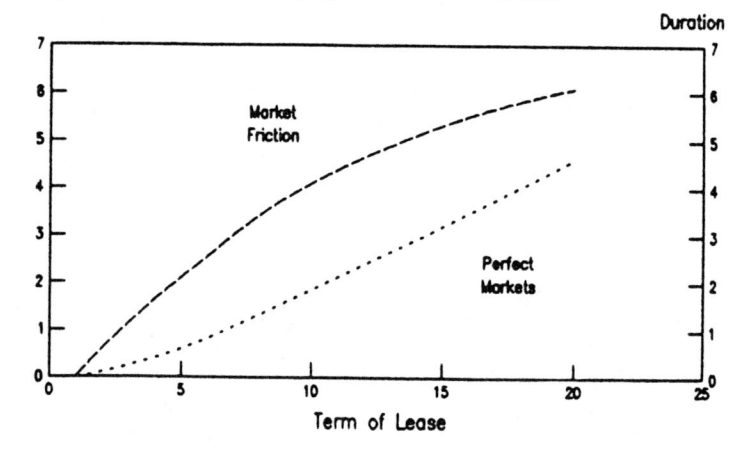

tion of real estate is only 0.6 year. This number is higher than what was found for appraisal-based returns, but at the low end of the range when REIT data were used to measure returns.

Next we look at the equivalent inflation pass-through, $\lambda°$, of a fixed-rent lease, which is defined as follows:

$$\begin{pmatrix} \text{Equivalent} \\ \text{Inflation} \\ \text{Pass-Through } (\lambda°) \end{pmatrix} = 1 + \begin{pmatrix} \text{Price Sensitivity} \\ \text{to a Change in the} \\ \text{Expected Inflation Rate} \end{pmatrix} / D_{DDM}$$

As an example, in the market frictions regime the current property value for the five-year lease is $1524. If the expected inflation rate increases from 5% to 6%, the price drops to $1490, a drop of 2.23%. Using Equation (2), this results in an equivalent inflation pass-through of:

$$\lambda° = 1 - (2.23/16.67) = 0.87.$$

In other words, a five-year fixed rate lease has an inflation pass-through that is equivalent to a floating-rent lease that passes through 87% of inflation.

Figure 5 illustrates the inflation pass-through for leases of different terms. Obviously, the amount of implicit pass-through decreases as the length of the adjustment period, or lease term, increases. Furthermore, the decrease occurs at a declining rate. The pass-through is also higher under the perfect markets assumption, because fixed-rent leases are assumed to compensate investors partially for expected inflation at the beginning of the lease term.

Price Sensitivity to Changes in the Real Rate of Return. In theory, the discount rate for real estate has three components: the expected inflation rate (I), the expected real interest rate (R), and the real estate risk premium (H). Up to now we have been

Figure 5 Estimates of Equivalent Inflation Pass-Through

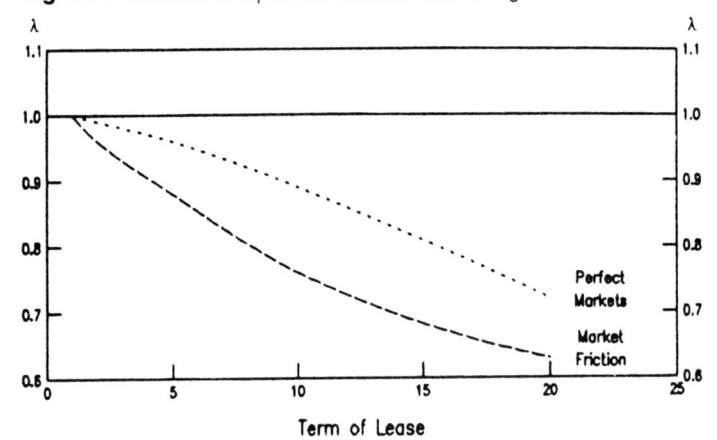

concerned only with inflation sensitivity. The underlying real interest rate and real estate risk premium, however, can change as well, and these effects can be far more powerful than changes in the inflation premium. For the floating-rent contract, the price sensitivity to changes in the expected real interest rate is equal to:

$$\begin{pmatrix} \text{Price Sensitivity} \\ \text{to a Change in the} \\ \text{Expected Real Rate} \end{pmatrix} = -D_{DDM}(1-\gamma)\Delta R \tag{3}$$

where:

ΔR = change in the expected real interest rate, and
γ = sensitivity of rents to changes in real interest rates.

In a similar way, we can determine the price sensitivity to changes in the risk premium, H:

$$\begin{pmatrix} \text{Price Sensitivity} \\ \text{to a Change in the} \\ \text{Risk Premium} \end{pmatrix} = -D_{DDM}\Delta H \tag{4}$$

where:

ΔH = change in the risk premium.

The real interest rate directly affects the discount rate and also may affect the level of rents as represented in the sensitivity parameter. On the other hand, a change in the risk premium affects only the discount rate. Together, the real interest rate plus the risk premium represent the expected real rate of return on real estate. Combining Equations (3) and (4), the price sensitivity to a change in the expected real rate of return is equal to:

$$\begin{pmatrix} \text{Price Sensitivity} \\ \text{to a Change} \\ \text{in the Expected} \\ \text{Real Rate of Return} \end{pmatrix} = -D_{DDM}[(1-\gamma)\Delta R + \Delta H] \tag{5}$$

where:

R + H = expected real rate of return.

In our calculations, the expected real rate of return is 6%. If a change in either the real interest rate or the risk premium caused the expected real return to increase from 6% to 7%, the value of our hypothetical real estate asset would fall from $1667 to $1429, a drop of 14.3%. As a result, changes in the discount rate caused by changes in the real rate introduce the potential for very high interest rate sensitivity or duration.

Furthermore, both floating-rent and fixed-rent contracts in either market regime have very high price sensitivities when the interest rate change is due to a change in the real interest rate or the risk premium. By comparison, a duration of 14.3 years is far higher than durations in the one-to-six range reported in Table 1 for interest rate changes caused by changes in expected inflation. In either case, however, real estate has a positive duration.

In addition, the level of real interest rates and the risk premium have implications for inflation pass-through. Table 2 and Figure 6 illustrate the impact of an inflation pass-through at 4%, 6%, and 8% real rates in the market frictions case. The higher the real expected rate of return, the lower the inflation pass-through for a given lease term, because the real rate has an inverse relation to D_{DDM}. A lower inflation pass-through is a result of discounting a given inflation-indexed residual value at a higher discount rate. Thus, a higher real rate per se diminishes the attractiveness of real estate as an inflation hedge.

CAN REAL ESTATE DURATION BE NEGATIVE?

Our analysis has shown that an increase in interest rates caused by an increase in the expected inflation rate or the real interest rate leads to a decline in real estate prices. Although this result is characteristic of a positive duration investment, it appears to be counterintuitive because real estate seemed to increase in value in the face of rising interest rates during the late 1970s and early 1980s. Two factors can explain this apparent contradiction.

First, although the economywide real interest rate increased during that time, the risk premium for real estate actually declined as investors switched from financial assets to other assets, such as real estate, that offered the potential for a high inflation flow-through. High and uncertain inflation increases the importance of assets that have a high inflation pass-through. The effects of rising real interest rates and declining risk premi-

Table 2 Estimates of the Equivalent Inflation Pass-Through with Varying Real Rates and Lease Contract Terms

Term	Market Frictions Regime Expected Real ROR[a]			Perfect Markets Regime Expected Real ROR[a]		
	4%	6%	8%	4%	6%	8%
1 Year	1.00	1.00	1.00	1.00	1.00	1.00
2 Years	0.97	0.96	0.95	0.99	0.99	0.98
5 Years	0.92	0.87	0.83	0.98	0.96	0.94
10 Years	0.84	0.76	0.68	0.94	0.89	0.83
20 Years	0.76	0.63	0.51	0.85	0.74	0.63

[a] The expected real rate of return (ROR) consists of the real interest rate plus the risk premium.

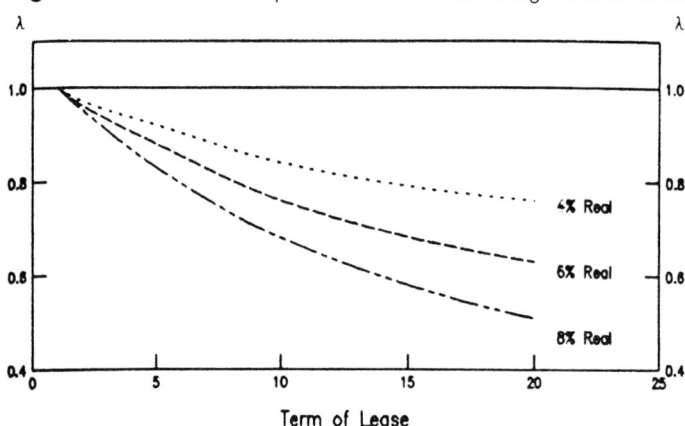

Figure 6 Estimates of the Equivalent Inflation Pass-Through—Market Frictions Regime

ums tend to offset one another to some degree. The net effect could even be a reduction in the expected real rate of return. This decreased return would cause investors to bid up the price of real estate as a result of their willingness to accept a lower real return. There can be a very significant price increase associated with declines in expected real rates of return.

Second, these events occurred during the period when net rents were increasing faster than the inflation rate because of very tight real estate markets. Thus, in the short run, real estate offered a pass-through factor in excess of one, which empirically gives the appearance of a negative duration. Consequently, two factors were at work that resulted in a price increase in the face of rising interest rates.

Rising real rents, rising real estate prices, and the willingness of investors to accept lower real returns became a clear signal to create more real estate. In the late 1970s and early 1980s, the development community responded with the greatest commercial real estate building boom in history. Within our framework, this reduces the growth rate of rents below expectations thereby lowering the value of real estate and limiting the ability of the asset to permit the flow-through of inflation. The negative duration aspects of real estate during the late 1970s and early 1980s were eroded by increased supply, which lowered both net rents and residual value. To protect themselves, both renters and owners also moved toward longer lease contracts, effectively lengthening the duration of real estate.

IMPLICATIONS AND CONCLUSIONS

This analysis has two implications. First, given market conditions, real estate investors have some control over the duration of the asset through the lease contracting process. Second, the duration of real estate is not always as low as investors implicity assume it to be. Duration is a function of lease contracts and market conditions. The longer the lease contract (excluding indexed leases), the longer the duration of the asset. Real estate investors who hold assets with long leases in reality own annuities with a claim on an inflation-indexed residual.

Market conditions influence the duration of real estate in two ways: The length of the lease term contract is market-determined to some extent, and the residual value of the asset, which affects inflation sensitivity, is determined not only by the cumulative inflation over the lease term but also by market conditions at the end of the lease. To the extent that the real estate investor can control the term of the lease, the investor has some control over the duration of the position. The management of real estate duration is further augmented by the ability to structure real estate financing in conjunction with the underlying lease contract.

NOTES

[1] See *A Total Differential Approach to Equity Duration*, Salomon Brothers Inc, September 1987.

[2] See *Rent Projections in the Context of a Rent Cycle*, Salomon Brothers Inc, October 22, 1986, and *Adjustment Mechanisms in Real Estate Markets*, Lawrence B. Smith, Salomon Brothers Inc, June 1987.

[3] We discuss the valuation model in detail in the Appendix to *A Look at Real Estate Duration*, Salomon Brothers Inc, December 1987.

[4] We initially assume the expected real return is invariant to the lease structure, which may not necessarily be the case; however, we examine the effects of changes in the expected real return later in this article.

[5] For a floating-rent contract, the price can be calculated from the familiar Gordon-Shapiro model

$$P_0 = \frac{NR_0(1+g)}{k-g} = \frac{105}{0.113 - 0.05} = \$1667$$

[6] The effective duration is equal to:

$$\frac{-\delta P/\delta k}{P} = \frac{-\Delta P/\Delta k}{P} = -\frac{(1324 - 1383)/0.0106}{1383} = 4.02$$

[7] Equation (2) shows the price sensitivity for a floating-rate contract with continuous, rather than discrete, rent payments. In this context D_{DDM} is equal to $1/(k^c - g^c)$, where k^c and g^c are interpreted as continuous rates. We set $k^c = 0.11$ and $g^c = 0.05$, which produces a property value of \$1667 and a D_{DDM} of 16.67 for the continuous floating-rent case. We focus on the continuous case so that our estimate of inflation pass-through is consistent with the concept of inflation pass-through developed for common stocks in *A Total Differential Approach to Equity Duration*, Salomon Brothers Inc, September 1987. For more detail, see the Appendix to *A Look at Real Estate Duration*, Salomon Brothers Inc, December 1987.

[8] The implied λ^* is not an instantaneous pass-through parameter. Rather, it is a pass-through equivalent parameter implied under the varying lease terms used in the simulations. The actual pass-through comes at the rollover of the leases.

REFERENCES

Brueggeman, W., A. Chen, and T. Thibodeau. "Real Estate Investment Funds: Performance and Portfolio Considerations." *AREUEA Journal*, Fall 1984.

Corcoran, Patrick. "Explaining the Commercial Real Estate Market." *Journal of Portfolio Management*, Spring 1987.

Hartzell, D., J. S. Hekman, and M. Miles. "Diversification Categories in Investment Real Estate." *AREUEA Journal*, Fall 1986.

———. "Real Estate Returns and Inflation." *AREUEA Journal*, Spring 1987.

Hartzell, D., D. G. Shulman, T. C. Langetieg, and M. L. Leibowitz. *A Look at Real Estate Duration*. Salomon Brothers Inc, December 1987.

Rent Projections in the Context of a Rent Cycle. Salomon Brothers Inc, October 22, 1986.

Smith, Lawrence B. *Adjustment Mechanisms in Real Estate Markets*. Salomon Brothers Inc, June 1987.

A Total Differential Approach to Equity Duration. Salomon Brothers Inc, September 1987.

Part 6. Inflation and Real Estate

18 Real Estate Returns and Inflation

David Hartzell, John S. Hekman, and Mike E. Miles

The ability of assets to protect an investor from purchasing power risk due to inflation has received a good deal of attention in the literature recently. The focus of much of this research has been on the properties of common stocks as inflation hedges. Bodie [1976] finds that the real return on equity is negatively related to both anticipated and unanticipated inflation; a similar result is obtained by Fama and Schwert [1977]. Bernard and Frecka [1983] examine individual common stock returns and find that the majority exhibit this negative relationship. This paper uses similar logic to examine the ability of a well-diversified portfolio of real estate to hedge against anticipated and unanticipated inflation.

INTRODUCTION

Real estate has received increasing attention in recent years as an alternative to stocks and bonds. The rapid growth of pension fund assets, accompanied by the passage of ERISA[1] and the relatively poor performance of the stock market through the 1970s, has resulted in an increased interest in real estate investment by institutions, especially through Commingled Real Estate Funds (CREFs). Several authors have tested the relationship of real estate returns and inflation (Ibbotson and Fall [1979]; Ibbotson and Siegel [1983]; Fogler [1983]). However, none of these authors has performed a rigorous test of the response of these returns to inflation using a portfolio of real estate assets. Rather, they have used various indices to proxy for returns such as the home purchase price component of the CPI (Fama and Schwert) or home prices plus the USDA farm index (Fogler; Ibbotson and Fall).

This study utilizes quarterly holding-period returns from over 300 properties that comprise the assets of a large CREF.[2] It provides a greater degree of regional and property-type diversity as well as property-specific detail than any data set used to date. Two alternative models of expected and unexpected inflation are estimated over the period 1974-83; the results indicate that real estate returns compensate the investor for both types of inflation, and that a portfolio composed of real estate and default-free bonds can reduce inflation risk substantially below that of a bonds-only portfolio. Finally, the nature of this inflation protection is investigated by looking briefly at the degree of hedging available by property type, property value, and urban growth rate.

From *AREUEA Journal*, Vol. 15, No. 1 (1987).

ASSET RETURNS AND INFLATION

The literature on stock market returns and inflation has found that monthly, quarterly and annual comparisons do not produce the presumed positive relationship (Fama and Schwert [1977]; Bodie [1976]). Schwert [1981] finds that stock prices react negatively, albeit modestly, to new information on inflation.

Interest rates are also presumed to provide inflation protection through the Fisher effect. Fama [1975] provides evidence that the bill market is efficient over the period 1953-71 in the sense that the market correctly uses all historic information in setting nominal rates of interest. However, this study assumed a constant real rate of interest. Subsequent work (Fama and Gibbons [1982]) has concluded that the expected real rate of interest is not independent of the expected rate of inflation, so that Treasury bills do have some amount of inflation risk.[3]

Studies of the Fisher effect have tended to show low and insignificant coefficients for the effect of inflation on nominal interest rates when periods before the 1970s were used. When the early 1970s are included, the effects are often unstable, suggesting that the equation has been misspecified by omitting important variables. More recently, Peek and Wilcox [1983] estimated a reduced-form equation for the nominal rate which included the effects of changes in effective marginal tax rates and aggregate supply shocks. They were able to reduce the instability of the expected inflation coefficient by a considerable amount over the postwar period 1952-1979. Fama and Gibbons [1983] adopted the alternative strategy of modeling expected inflation by allowing the real rate of interest to vary using a moving average process. As the period covered by this paper is considerably shorter than that covered by Peek and Wilcox, the approach used here is the Fama and Gibbons technique (which allows the use of pre-sample data to model the expected rate of inflation). Two measures of expected and unexpected inflation are presented, one with a constant real rate (following Fama and Schwert) and the other with a real rate that is allowed to vary using the Fama and Gibbons framework.

If the expected real interest rate is assumed to be constant, then nominal rates would increase on a one-to-one basis with expected inflation, and these nominal rates would provide an index of expected inflation. The one-period nominal interest rate realized in period t is that which is determined in the market at the end of period $t - 1$, or

$$R(t - 1) = r(t - 1) + EI(t - 1) \tag{1}$$

and so

$$EI(t - 1) = -r(t - 1) + R(t - 1) \tag{2}$$

The inflation rate in period t, $\Delta(t)$, is the sum of the expected rate $EI(t - 1)$ and the unexpected rate. Assuming the expected real rate of interest $r(t - 1)$ to be a constant means that $R(t - 1)$ is an index of expected inflation, and unexpected inflation ($UI(t)$), is the difference between actual inflation in t and the measure of expected inflation, $R(t - 1)$. Thus, following Fama and Schwert, the equation to be estimated for an asset return R_j as an inflation hedge becomes

$$\tilde{R}_j(t) = \alpha_j + \beta_j R(t - 1) + \gamma_j(\tilde{\Delta}(t) - R(t - 1)) + \tilde{z}_j(t) \text{ where } \tilde{z}_j(t) \tag{3}$$

is the random disturbance term.

Alternatively, if the real interest rate embedded in $R(t-1)$ is not constant over time, then $R(t-1)$ is not an accurate reflection of the market's expected rate of inflation. The procedure used here to allow for a non-constant real rate is that adopted by Fama and Gibbons [1983]. A Box-Jenkins model is used to forecast the real rate using moving average parameters. First the ex-post real rate of return series is calculated as

$$r(t) = R(t-1) - \Delta(t). \tag{4}$$

Applying the integrated moving average process and generating forecasts of the expected real return yields a time series resembling a random walk.[4] The expected rate of inflation is then the difference between the nominal interest rate and the forecast real rate $\hat{r}$:

$$EI(t) = R(t-1) - \hat{r}(t) \tag{5}$$

Unexpected inflation is the difference between actual inflation and expected inflation:

$$UI(t) = \Delta(t) - [R(t-1) - \hat{r}(t)] \tag{6}$$

The regression model to test for the inflation hedging ability of an asset j is

$$\tilde{R}_j(t) = \alpha_j + \beta_j[R(t-1) - \hat{r}(t)] + \gamma_j[\Delta(t) - (R(t-1) - \hat{r}(t))] + \tilde{z}_j(t) \tag{7}$$

The models represented by (3) and (7) provide two alternative tests of an asset as an inflation hedge.

The effectiveness of assets such as real estate in providing protection from inflation is determined by the extent to which they can be used to reduce the purchasing power risk of an investor's portfolio.[5] Default-free Treasury bills are free of all risk except that from purchasing power, so the effectiveness of real estate as an inflation hedge can be measured by the proportionate reduction of the variance of return on Treasury bills by the addition of a diversified portfolio of real estate.

Following Bodie and Bernard and Frecka (1983), two measures are used in the empirical work to gauge the diversification benefits of real estate. The first is W_1, the proportion of real estate which should be held in a portfolio of government bonds and real estate in order to minimize the variance of the portfolio. The other is S_1, the proportionate reduction in the variance of the portfolio gained by holding the fraction W of the portfolio in real estate.[6]

RELATIONSHIP TO PREVIOUS STUDIES

Most previous studies of real estate returns and inflation have used indices of the value of real property or portfolios which were limited in terms of the number of properties or property type.[7] The main problem involved with the use of an index is that it does not represent actual portfolio returns available to an investor. Further, it is not possible with a general index to estimate the diversification benefits of real estate by number of properties in the portfolio, property size, type, region or other characteristics.

The use of actual real estate portfolios in the literature is rather limited due to the lack of available data. Wendt and Wong [1965] look only at California apartment properties. Friedman [1970] uses a sample of 50 properties selected from two separate sources. Brueggeman, Chen and Thibodeau [1984], using commercial real estate, show no significant hedge against unexpected inflation. They use a two-factor CAPM to show low and insignificant correlations on their market index and significantly positive coefficients on inflation (the second factor). Following Fama, they derive a second two-factor model with expected and unexpected inflation and find no significance to the unexpected inflation factor. Unfortunately, they use two commingled funds' total return (non-property-specific data). Miles and McCue [1984] employ quarterly return data for a highly diversified portfolio of individual income properties for the period 1973-3 to 1981-3. Using the same method as Fogler [1981] to estimate the relationship of real estate returns to expected and unexpected inflation, they find a strong response to expected inflation as proxied by the average annual commercial paper rate and a weak relationship to unexpected inflation. One shortcoming of this study is the use of an annual interest rate with quarterly real estate returns, which tends to reduce the variation displayed by the expectations variable compared with the use of a quarterly interest rate. In addition, the sample period used may be unrepresentative, as the inflation rate rose more or less steadily from 1973 to 1981, so that the calculated real estate returns cover what could be considered a single period, and one which is far shorter than the spans used by Fama and Schwert, and Fogler.

THE DATA

The data set used in this study provides an opportunity to examine more closely the problem of measuring the potential of real estate investment as a hedge against expected and unexpected inflation. These data were supplied by a large financial institution from its commingled real estate fund. This portfolio begins within 113 properties in the fourth quarter of 1973, rises to a peak of 411 in 1982, and includes 382 properties in the last available quarter, 1983-3. The time period of analysis is a ten-year quarterly sample which exhibits both the increasing inflation of the late 1970s and the slowing inflation of the early 1980s.

In order to examine the response of returns to inflation by property type and other characteristics, holding period returns were developed directly from quarterly cash flow data and quarterly appraisals for individual properties. Previous studies (e.g., Brueggeman, Chen and Thibodeau) have used actual holding period returns calculated from CREF's unit values, i.e., from portfolios including near cash investments. In a strict sense, the property-specific data used here represent hypothetical holding period returns which could have been earned on portfolios formed from the total number of properties held by the CREF. However, these hypothetical returns bear a close relationship to the returns actually earned by pension fund investors in that the CREF's unit values (at which purchases and sales are made) are derived from the same cash flow and appraisal data. The use of property-specific CREF data yields a larger and more diverse sample of properties than has been available in previous studies. (Of course, it is possible that there are institutional biases in property selection which reduce the diversity of this particular CREF's portfolio despite its large aggregate size.)

Holding period returns (HPR) are calculated for each of the properties in the sample for each quarter in the sample period as follows

$$R_i(t) = \frac{MV_i(t+1) + C_i(t)}{MV_i(t) + I_i(t)} - 1$$

where $R_i(t)$ is the HPR for the ith property in the tth period. $MV_i(t)$ and $MV_i(t+1)$ are beginning-of-period and end-of-period market value. $C_i(t)$ is the cash flow earned in period t, and $I_i(t)$ is any change in cash investment which occurred in period t. The cash flow variable is total cash revenues net of operating expenses and property taxes. For properties which were purchased or sold during the sample period, no partial quarters of cash flow are included; the first full quarter for new properties and the last full quarter for sold properties are those used for the first and last quarters in the data set.[8]

Market values are determined by sales price when a property is sold and by appraised value for all other quarters. Pension funds can buy into or withdraw from the open-ended CREF at what is termed the net asset value. This value is determined each quarter, at which time market value estimates are made for each property and summed over all properties. Total market value is divided by the number of units held by the pension funds to arrive at the net asset value per unit, which serves as a price at which the units can be bought or sold.

Appraisals are done by an outside appraiser in each quarter for very large properties and annually for smaller properties. These small property estimates are updated quarterly by in-house staff. The income approach to valuation is used, meaning that an estimate of stabilized income is developed, and the net present value of this income stream is calculated using an appropriate capitalization rate. The resulting net asset value per unit is a market price in that pension fund trades are made on this basis.

A test of the accuracy of the appraised values can be obtained by comparing actual sales prices with the appraised value in the sale quarter. For the 89 properties that were sold over the sample period, the average premium sales prices over appraised value was 8.7%. This indicates that the calculated holding period returns may be biased slightly downward. However, the recorded sales prices do not include all the costs to the fund of the sales, so that this difference may be overstated somewhat. Also, it is not known at what point in the quarter the appraised values are done. A lag between the appraisal and the time at which the sale price is determined may also explain part of the premium.[9,10]

Two samples have been constructed from the CREF data. The first contains data from all properties in the fund for all 40 quarters from 1973-4 to 1983-3. The fund grew from 113 to 382 properties over this period, and many of the acquisitions were new rather than existing structures. As a result, cash flow for many acquisitions is artificially low for some time during the absorption period. In the latter half of the sample period a much smaller proportion of the sample was in this absorption stage, so the cash flow portion of the return is a better reflection of the long-run income-producing ability of the portfolio. To test for the influence of this acquisition bias, the second sample is composed of those properties for which data are available in all of the last 20 quarters of the period, from 1978-4 to 1983-3. This produces a sample of 220 properties that were neither sold nor acquired during this time (only 78 properties with this characteristic are available for the entire 10-year period). The two samples are referred to hereafter as the 40-quarter sample (with 113 to 411 properties per quarter) and the 20-quarter sample (with the same 220 properties in each quarter).

These two portfolios of real estate are used to evaluate the relationship of real estate returns to expected and unexpected inflation. The quarterly default-free interest rate used for this comparison in the models outlined in the previous section is the yield on 3-month Treasury bills. Prices for these pure discount instruments are taken from quotes provided in *The Wall Street Journal*. The rate for quarter t is the yield implied by the market price 92 days prior to the end of that quarter. The inflation rate in period

t is the percentage change in the Consumer Price Index (CPI) from $t-1$. The next section of the paper describes the results of the inflation tests for the entire 40-quarter and 20-quarter samples, as well as for portfolios differing by property type, property size and SMSA growth rate.

EMPIRICAL RESULTS

A test of the ability of real estate to hedge against inflation depends on a method of measuring expected and unexpected inflation, as described above. Fama and Schwert estimate the degree to which Treasury bills reflect expected inflation by testing the following model:

$$\tilde{\Delta}(t) = \alpha_0 + \alpha_1 R(t-1) + \tilde{\varepsilon}(t)$$

Their results for the period 1953-71, using 3-month bills are

$$\Delta(t) = -0.0023 + 0.93\, R(t) \quad R^2 = 0.48$$

which suggests that the T-bill rate compensates fully for inflation ($\alpha_1 \cong 1.0$), and the autocorrelations of this regression equation are insignificant.

The economic situation since 1971 has been considerably more turbulent, encompassing periods of low or even negative realized real returns during the inflation of the 1970s as well as the post-October 1979 period of fluctuating rates and higher realized returns. Table 1 represents estimates of the Fama-Schwert test for the 3-month bill rate as a measure of expected inflation over the period covered by this study.

Regression (1) shows that the fit is much poorer over the entire period than for the Fama-Schwert period, suggesting that the real rate of interest was not constant; this is also shown by the Durbin-Watson statistic, which suggests positive autocorrelation of the residuals. Regression (2) estimates the same relationship from the end of the wage and price controls period; the results here are substantially the same. Regression (3) covers the 20-quarter sample period from 1978-4 to 1983-3. Here the α_1 coefficient rises somewhat, but it is still insignificant, and there is still autocorrelation. It appears that real interest rates were low in the early part of the 1974-83 period and high at the end, so that this test, which assumes a constant real rate, produces estimates of α_0 which are biased upward and estimates of α_1 biased downward.

The alternative measure of expected inflation as outlined above allows the real rate of interest to wander using the integrated moving average process. Expected inflation is measured as the difference between the T-bill rate and the modeled real rate;

Table 1 3-Month Treasury Bills as Measures of Expected Inflation
$\Delta(t) = \hat{\alpha}_0 + \hat{\alpha}_1 R(t-1) + \tilde{\varepsilon}(t)$

	α_0	α_1	R^2	Durbin-Watson
1. 1973-4/1983-3	0.013	0.338	0.08	0.89
	(2.98)	(1.84)		
2. 1976-1/1983-3	0.010	0.393	0.11	0.89
	(2.05)	(1.93)		
3. 1978-4/1983-3	0.007	0.500	0.09	0.78
	(0.62)	(1.31)		

t-statistics are in parentheses beneath estimated coefficients

unexpected inflation is then calculated as actual inflation less this alternate measure of expected inflation. The results of the moving average estimation process indicate a highly significant positive coefficient, suggesting a good fit for the model. This model allows the real rate of interest to be lower during the mid and late 70s when unexpected inflation was running quite high, and on the other side of the cycle it has the real rate increasing in the early 80s. These two sets of estimates thus allow for two distinctly different sets of assumptions about the behavior of the capital market under which to test the ability of a real estate portfolio to hedge against the two components of inflation.[11]

INFLATION HEDGE RESULTS: ALL PROPERTIES

The first tests were performed on the entire portfolio of properties in the 40-quarter and 20-quarter samples with quarterly holding period returns, value-weighted using the market value of each property in that quarter. Table 2 presents the results of the hedge regressions for both samples and both measures of expected and unexpected inflation. The Bodie measure of the optimal proportion of the asset to be combined with the Treasury securities (W) is reported along with S, the percentage reduction of the bond portfolio inflation risk. Finally, the ratio W/S measures the efficiency of inflation risk reduction.

Using either the constant real rate assumption (hereafter Fama-Schwert) or the variable real rate (a variation of Fama-Gibbons), real estate appears to have provided complete protection from expected inflation over both periods ($\alpha_1 > 1.0$). The α_2 coefficients for unexpected inflation are greater than 1.0 for the 20-quarter sample and are within one standard error of one in the 40-quarter sample. All coefficients are significant at the 5% level except for the coefficient on the Fama-Schwert expected inflation measure in the 20-quarter sample. The measures of W and S vary widely, but it seems that real estate offers about a 20% reduction in inflation risk with a 20% share of real estate in the portfolio. These values are higher for the 20-quarter sample (1978-83) than for the entire 10-year period.

Table 2 Results of Inflation Hedge Regressions for Expected and Unexpected Inflation

Inflation Expectation Measures	α_1 (Expected)	α_2 (Unexpected)	W	S	W/S	R^2
40-Quarter Sample, 1973-4 to 1983-3						
1. EI1, UI1	1.44	0.76	32.7	19.1	1.71	.40
(Constant real return)	(4.85)	(3.24)				
2. EI2, UI2	2.23	0.98	14.6	6.3	2.31	.36
(Moving average real return)	(3.83)	(1.97)				
20-Quarter Sample, 1978-4 to 1983-3						
1. EI1, UI1	1.09	1.77	34.8	59.1	0.59	.56
	(1.69)	(4.67)				
2. EI2, UI2	1.65	1.63	20.7	24.8	0.84	.53
	(4.26)	(2.95)				

t-statistics in parentheses beneath estimated coefficients

These results contrast markedly with the inflation hedge results reported by others for common stocks (Bodie; Fama and Schwert). The results continue to hold for the more recent years, a turbulent period for interest rates in which old relationships have broken down in the wake of the Federal Reserve System's move away from interest rate targeting in 1979 and the deregulation of capital markets in the 1980s. In fact, the evidence presented here suggests that the ability of real estate to hedge against the risk of inflation has been greater since 1978 than before.[12]

RESULTS BY PROPERTY TYPE

The market value of real property and its cash flow may respond differently to inflation across property types. Many retail leases contain provisions tying rent to a percentage of gross revenue, so that lease revenues tend to vary directly with the general price level. In several types, there may also be a "pass-through" of operating expenses specified in the lease so that gross (but not net) revenue will increase automatically with cost.[13] Obviously, the response of occupancy rates to the causes of the unexpected inflation will also have a major bearing on the quality of the inflation hedge.

For the tests performed here, the samples are divided into portfolios by three property types: industrial, office and retail.[14] Differences in inflation protection by type are an indication of the degree to which property revenues and expected future revenues respond to inflation and on a quarterly basis. A priori, properties whose income is based directly on the sale of goods and services (which include retail in this sample) should provide better protection than those properties whose rents are not tied directly to the firm's sales (here, industrial and office).

Table 3 presents the results of the two inflation tests by property type for the 40-quarter and 20-quarter samples. In the 40-quarter sample the overall results are weak as indicated by the low R^2. Industrial and office properties provide complete protection from expected inflation (coefficients greater than 1.0), while retail properties are much weaker. Conversely, the retail properties appear to provide a better hedge against unexpected inflation (coefficients approximately equal to 1.0) presumably due to the prevalence of expense pass-through and percentage rents in retail leases.

For the 20-quarter sample (which uses the same 220 properties throughout), the results are stronger. Industrial and office properties show complete protection from expected and unexpected inflation, with generally significant coefficients and much higher R^2 values than those for the 40-quarter sample. This is consistent with a change in leasing strategy toward shorter leases with more expense pass-through which occurred as investment managers/property managers reacted to continued high inflation.

The modified Fama-Gibbons form of the equation ($EI2$, $UI2$) seems to result in markedly higher estimates of expected inflation protection. This $EI2$ measure allows the real rate of interest to change from quarter to quarter, and this feature is most useful in this period (1978-1983) when nominal interest rates were so volatile. However, retail properties do not show strong inflation protection using either the Fama-Schwert or the Fama-Gibbons measures, although the results are much stronger than for the 40-quarter sample. Overall, the results by property type tend to confirm the results for all properties together: real estate, as measured by the properties in this CREF, produced impressive inflation protection over the period 1973-1983.

Table 3 Results of Inflation Hedge Regressions by Property Type

Property Type	α_1	α_2	W	S	W/S	R^2
	40-Quarter Sample, 1973-4 to 1983-3					
Industrial						
1. EI1, UI1	3.57 (1.65)	2.07 (1.26)	2.52	1.63	0.94	.07
2. EI2, UI2	3.16 (1.87)	0.80 (0.37)	−0.20	0.005	−3.78	.09
Office						
3. EI1, UI1	1.45 (3.70)	0.55 (1.84)	16.37	6.50	2.52	.27
4. EI2, UI2	1.12 (3.73)	−0.03 (0.07)	−1.07	0.05	−23.50	.31
Retail						
5. EI1, UI1	0.54 (1.21)	0.75 (2.18)	24.39	22.55	1.08	.11
6. EI2, UI2	0.57 (1.62)	0.98 (2.21)	17.04	20.42	0.84	.13
	20-Quarter Sample, 1978-4 to 1983-3					
Industrial						
1. EI1, UI1	0.94 (0.92)	1.56 (2.59)	20.62	31.53	0.65	.28
2. EI2, UI2	1.41 (2.33)	1.61 (1.89)	11.93	15.83	0.75	.27
Office						
3. EI1, UI1	1.34 (1.11)	2.81 (3.96)	19.05	50.09	0.38	.48
4. EI2, UI2	2.53 (3.44)	2.65 (2.53)	8.48	13.75	0.62	.43
Retail						
5. EI1, UI1	−0.04 (0.04)	1.14 (1.95)	19.43	25.12	0.77	.20
6. EI2, UI2	0.92 (1.53)	0.97 (1.13)	10.13	10.26	0.99	.13

t-statistics are in parentheses

TESTS BY PROPERTY SIZE

Property size may have an effect on inflation risk mainly through both the nature of the tenant and the type of lease used. The relative proportion of single to multi-tenant properties decreases as property size increases. For the two largest size categories, 97% of the properties leased to more than one tenant.

If there is some variation in the effects of inflation on individual firms, then this will be transmitted to real estate returns through their demand for space. This factor appears to be borne out by the results of hedge regressions by property size reported in Table 4. The coefficients of expected and unexpected inflation generally rise with property size. The two smallest categories, representing properties under $2.5 million, provided less-than-complete protection (coefficients less than 1.0), the third category is mixed, and categories 4-6 (over $5 million) in general show more-than-complete pro-

Table 4 Inflation Hedge Regressions by Property Value

Property Value (000)	α_1	α_2	W	S	W/S	R^2
40-Quarter Sample, 1973-4 to 1983-3						
$0-999						
1. EI1, UI1	0.85 (1.65)	0.51 (1.26)	3.89	2.24	1.74	.02
2. EI2, UI2	0.61 (0.78)	0.54 (0.54)	2.62	1.96	1.34	.02
$1000-2499						
1. EI1, UI1	1.18 (2.35)	0.66 (1.72)	14.98	9.07	1.65	.14
2. EI2, UI2	0.94 (2.36)	0.43 (0.86)	16.15	24.44	0.66	.13
$2500-4999						
1. EI1, UI1	1.07 (3.27)	0.07 (2.92)	34.86	24.86	1.40	.26
2. EI2, UI2	0.89 (3.42)	0.63 (1.91)	19.95	13.92	1.43	.24
$5000-9999						
1. EI1, UI1	1.19 (4.41)	0.58 (2.81)	39.73	20.90	1.90	.35
2. EI2, UI2	0.91 (4.22)	0.30 (1.11)	17.26	6.54	2.64	.33
$10000-19999						
1. EI1, UI1	1.16 (1.97)	0.29 (0.64)	5.22	1.37	3.81	.10
2. EI2, UI2	0.70 (1.48)	0.04 (0.07)	2.42	0.59	4.12	.07
> $20000						
1. EI1, UI1	2.06 (3.54)	1.18 (2.58)	12.97	9.82	1.32	.28
2. EI2, UI2	1.66 (3.55)	0.79 (1.29)	4.28	1.84	2.32	.27

tection against expected inflation and stronger protection against unexpected inflation. These results suggest that portfolios made up of larger properties are superior inflation hedges. (Naturally this conclusion must be tempered by the possibility of selection bias inherent in a database whose properties were selected by one investment manager.)

TEST BY URBAN GROWTH RATE

Tests for inflation protection by city (SMSA) growth rate were also performed. Properties in fast-growing cities may have a greater potential to hedge against inflation because of the higher growth rate of demand for office space. Many slow-growing cities are burdened with unfavorable industrial structures that may lag behind the growth of the country as a whole and suffer disproportionately in recessions. Property owners, employing a strategy of writing short-term leases and incurring possible vacancy losses, may find it easier to locate new tenants in rapidly-growing areas. Some support for this idea

Table 4 *(Continued)*

Property Value (000)	α_1	α_2	W	S	W/S	R^2
		20-Quarter Sample, 1978-4 to 1983-3				
$0-999						
1. *EI*1, *UI*1	−2.22	1.46	8.39	16.39	0.51	.22
	(1.21)	(1.35)				
2. *EI*2, *UI*2	0.60	1.68	4.86	9.15	0.53	.06
	(0.56)	(1.00)				
$1000-2499						
1. *EI*1, *UI*1	0.62	0.95	11.55	11.57	1.00	.09
	(0.50)	(1.28)				
2. *EI*2, *UI*2	1.02	0.41	3.19	1.36	2.34	.11
	(1.40)	(0.39)				
$2500-4999						
1. *EI*1, *UI*1	1.87	1.22	27.52	29.21	0.94	.41
	(2.60)	(2.88)				
2. *EI*2, *UI*2	1.48	0.78	10.29	5.11	2.01	.43
	(3.58)	(1.32)				
$5000-9999						
1. *EI*1, *UI*1	2.10	1.34	34.09	38.85	0.88	.55
	(3.53)	(3.83)				
2. *EI*2, *UI*2	1.50	1.37	22.08	23.14	0.95	.51
	(4.13)	(2.64)				
$10000-19999						
1. *EI*1, *UI*1	2.29	0.67	10.42	4.88	2.14	.29
	(2.58)	(1.28)				
2. *EI*2, *UI*2	1.08	0.46	5.55	2.44	2.27	.19
	(1.94)	(0.57)				
> $20000						
1. *EI*1, *UI*1	0.58	3.33	14.08	45.54	0.31	.43
	(0.36)	(3.48)				
2. *EI*2, *UI*2	2.73	3.29	6.15	12.90	0.48	.34
	(2.68)	(2.26)				

t-statistics are in parentheses

is given in Table 5, which shows the lease maturity distribution by fast- and slow-growth SMSAs. Faster-growing SMSAs have a higher than average proportion of short-term leases, suggesting that leases may be written with the expectation that growth will continue and new tenants willing to pay higher rent will be found when leases expire.

On the other hand, the vacancy risk from shorter leases might dominate the price flexibility factor, so that returns on net may not compensate for inflation. In the older slow-growth areas, leases may be written to provide inflation protection for the lessor, passing the risk on to the lessee, whereas in fast-growth areas lease rate speculation may dominate inflation concerns. Thus the hypothesis to be tested is whether properties in fast-growth areas actually provide a better hedge against inflation (given the limitations imposed by the tendency toward shorter leases in these areas). The results of the hedge regressions for fast- and slow-growing areas are presented in Table 6, using the 20-quarter sample. Using any of the criteria—the estimated coefficients, reduction in inflation

Table 5 Lease Maturity for High-Growth and Low-Growth SMSAs*

	Low Growth		High Growth	
Lease Maturity	Number	Percent	Number	Percent
0-2 years	27	36	64	44
2-5 years	27	36	62	43
Over 5 years	21	28	19	13
Total	75	100	145	100

* High-growth areas (more than 2.5% per year employment growth): Anaheim, Houston, Denver, Miami, Dallas, Atlanta, Seattle, Washington, D.C., Minneapolis, New Orleans, Los Angeles, San Francisco; low-growth areas (less than 2.5% per year): Indianapolis, Stamford, Cincinnati, Boston, Newark, St. Louis, Philadelphia, Chicago, Detroit, Cleveland, Pittsburgh, New York.

risk (S) or relative efficiency of risk reduction (W/S)—the slow-growing cities show themselves to be a somewhat better hedge, but both groups of cities provide more or less complete inflation protection. The differences between them are not large enough to draw any firm conclusions about which is necessarily superior. Since slow-growing cities appear to provide, if anything, better inflation protection, there is no support for the idea that fast-growing cities perform better.

CONCLUSIONS

Real estate has become an increasingly popular vehicle for providing a new source of diversification in investor's portfolios. By the end of 1983, pension funds had placed over 20 billion of their nearly 1 trillion dollar aggregate portfolio in commercial real estate equities (see *Pension and Investment Age* [1984]). An important motivation for this trend has been the desire to provide protection from expected and unexpected inflation. The academic literature on inflation and real estate returns has not provided a clear answer about the degree of protection which can be afforded. In particular, tests for protection against unexpected inflation have obtained generally weak results.

The results reported here provide strong evidence that diversified portfolios of commercial real estate have been a complete hedge against both expected and unexpected inflation over the period 1973-83. The database supporting these conclusions is

Table 6 Hedge Regressions by Growth of SMSA: 20-Quarter Sample

	Inflation Measures: EI1, UI1					
Growth Rate	α_1	α_2	W	S	W/S	R^2
Fast	1.47	1.36	24.47	30.68	0.80	.33
	(1.73)	(2.71)				
Slow	0.63	2.18	20.59	44.30	0.46	.40
	(0.57)	(3.36)				
	Inflation Measures: EI2, UI2					
Fast	1.42	1.23	13.18	12.71	1.04	.33
	(2.85)	(1.73)				
Slow	1.88	2.00	9.67	13.49	0.72	.33
	(2.77)	(2.06)				

t-statistics are in parentheses

superior to those used in previous studies for a combination of reasons including diversification of property type, size and location; property-specific information; consistent accounting and relevant time period. The inflation rate was 5% or greater over this entire period, but real estate experienced both rising and falling values as the inflation rate accelerated and subsequently decelerated.

Returns by property type also show strong inflation protection with industrial properties holding an inconclusive edge. Larger properties performed better than smaller ones in this sample, which may have been due to the diversification which results from the positive relationship of size and number of tenants. Separating the sample into two portfolios by the growth rate of the SMSAs in which they are located did not reveal any advantage for rapidly-growing markets in hedging against inflation.

Several questions remain in judging the performance of real estate as compared to common stocks in inflationary periods. Quarterly holding period returns are a relevant measure to use for a CREF in that pension funds are allowed to buy and sell based on unit values calculated each quarter. However, one wonders if inflation protection is properly estimated on a quarterly basis. More needs to be done on the measurement of expected and unexpected inflation. Peek and Wilcox [1983] have shown that interest rates are affected by taxes and supply factors. This means that neither the Fama and Schwert nor the Fama and Gibbons approach to expected inflation correctly deals with the complex interaction of taxes, inflation and the real interest rate. Until some expected inflation formulation is generally agreed upon, it will not be possible to measure the risk-reduction benefits of commercial real estate precisely. Finally, the use of appraised values and difficulties with the return calculation continue to be troubling issues.

APPENDIX

Table One Number of Properties in the 40-Quarter Data Set*

Quarter	Industrial	Office	Retail	Residential	Hotel-Motel
Q473	95	9	4	2	3
Q174	97	9	5	4	3
Q274	99	14	5	4	4
Q374	105	15	7	4	4
Q474	114	17	8	5	4
Q175	123	18	8	5	4
Q275	129	21	9	6	5
Q375	130	23	9	6	5
Q475	134	26	10	6	5
Q176	139	31	11	6	5
Q276	141	31	11	6	5
Q376	140	32	11	6	5
Q476	143	32	24	6	5
Q177	144	36	24	6	5
Q277	143	37	26	6	5
Q377	144	37	26	6	5
Q477	206	36	26	6	5
Q178	209	35	26	6	5
Q278	211	35	26	6	5

Table One Number of Properties in the 40-Quarter Data Set* (continued)

Quarter	Industrial	Office	Retail	Residential	Hotel-Motel
Q378	213	36	26	6	5
Q478	215	37	20	6	5
Q179	213	40	20	6	5
Q279	212	43	21	6	5
Q379	212	44	21	6	5
Q479	211	44	23	6	5
Q180	211	46	23	5	6
Q280	212	50	24	5	6
Q380	218	51	26	5	6
Q480	233	56	35	5	6
Q181	244	60	36	5	6
Q281	244	59	39	5	6
Q381	250	61	40	4	6
Q481	265	71	46	4	7
Q182	267	82	46	4	7
Q282	269	85	46	4	7
Q382	268	86	46	4	6
Q482	267	82	45	4	6
Q183	265	80	44	4	5
Q283	259	79	44	4	5
Q383	254	78	42	3	5

° The number of residential and hotel-motel properties constitute subsamples which are too small to be meaningful.

Table Two Number of Properties in the 20-Quarter Sample

Total	East	Midwest	West	South
220	12	75	97	36

Ind°	Office	Retail	Res°	Hot/Mot°
176	23	15	3	5

Size 1	Size 2	Size 3	Size 4	Size 5	Size 6
76	73	35	20	12	4

Fast-Growth SMSA	Slow-Growth SMSA
145	75

Note: There are 220 properties in each quarter, therefore one quarter is representative of all. Property size is the only exception, as market values increase from quarter to quarter.

° Industrial, Residential and Hotel/Motel

NOTES

[1] The Employment Retirement Security Act of 1974 redefined the role of the fiduciary and has come to serve as an endorsement for diversification across asset classes.

[2] This CREF currently constitutes approximately 30% of pension fund equity investment in real estate.

[3] Note that the data for these studies is pre-DIDMCA (1980) which is widely believed to have increased real returns.

[4] See Box and Jenkins (1970), pp. 123-44, 144-46.

[5] Other possible definitions of an inflation hedge cited by Bodie are: (a) elimination of the possibility that the real rate of return will fall below some set minimum (see Reilly, Johnson and Smith [1971]); (b) the real rate of return on an asset is independent of the rate of inflation (see Branch [1974]; Fama and

Schwert [1977]). Definition (b) is consistent with the tests employed here, whereas (a) has not received a great deal of attention in the debate over inflation hedging, since it requires quite restrictive assumptions in any useful application.

[6] $W = [(1+R)(1+R+\alpha)]/[(1+r+\alpha)^2 + \text{var}(\tilde{\varepsilon})/\text{var}(\tilde{U}I)]$ and $S = [1+\text{var}(\tilde{\varepsilon})/(1+r+\alpha)^2 \text{var}(UI)]^1$, where $\alpha = \text{cov}(1+\tilde{r}_H, \tilde{U}I)/\text{var}(\tilde{U}I)$, $\tilde{r}_H$ = real return on portfolio of real estate and bonds, $\tilde{\varepsilon}$ is the part of the real return $(1+\tilde{r}_H)$ which is uncorrelated with inflation.

[7] Ibbotson and Fall use an index of residential and farm properties. Miles and McCue [1982] use portfolios of REIT properties. Fogler [1983] uses Ibbotson and Sinquefield data (in later years a combination of three indices) to show strong correlations of real estate returns with unexpected inflation.

Fogler uses annual commercial paper rates and constructs a proxy for unexpected inflation following Fama. In addition to the problems associated with annual data (note that Fama and Schwert had progressively better fits for real estate with longer time periods), the Ibbotson real estate index is a composite of three other composites: (1) Commerce Department residential homes (the rent component is typically neglected), (2) The Agriculture Department farmland series, and (3) The Frank Russell index.

[8] The assumption is that investment (which was paid for during the quarter) actually occurred near the beginning of the period but that the initial market value did not include the impact of said investment. In the case of "earnouts" and tenant finishes, which were the largest additional investments, this assumption is fairly reasonable. In the case of major repairs (new roof), such investments should be treated as a cash outflow in the numerator. The database did not always distinguish the types of incremental investment and we have thus chosen to go with the formulation which fits the bulk of the incremental investments.

Cash flows were taken to a separate account as received and the interest income not included in the numerator, so no adjustment in the denominator is required for these interperiod flows.

[9] Clearly the use of appraised values is not ideal; yet, appraisals (with some corroborating sales) are the best data available for this important asset class. The engagement letter to the outside appraiser clearly states that the estimate desired is "market value" according to the definition given in the eighth edition of the American Institute of Real Estate Appraisers' text. Therefore such risk factors as an increase in the probability of future vacancies is included and the market value estimated should be a function of all the factors affecting a typical investor.

[10] With any database, the estimation of appropriate transaction costs is a problem. With commercial real estate the problem is most difficult because there is no standard commission and related costs may vary dramatically depending on the particular situation. We admit the limitation, yet an examination of the sales from this database indicate that while transaction costs varied substantially across properties, they were never over 3% of the sales price.

[11] A table showing quarterly estimates of expected and unexpected inflation rates with the moving average real interest rate is available from the authors.

[12] Tests using equally-weighted portfolios produced substantially the same result.

[13] A major difference among property types can occur through variation in the average length of leases. Properties with longer leases which do not have CPI escalator clauses will clearly not see their cash returns increase immediately as inflation rises.

[14] See the Appendix for a complete description of these portfolios.

REFERENCES

[1] Bernard, Victor V. and T. Frecka. Evidence on the Existence of Common Stock Inflation Hedges. *Journal of Financial Research* 6(4): 301-312, 1983.

[2] Z. Bodie. Common Stocks as a Hedge Against Inflation. *Journal of Finance* 31(2): 459-470, 1976.

[3] G.E.P. Box and G. M. Jenkins. *Time Series Analysis, Forecasting and Control*, Holden-Day, 1970.

[4] B. Branch. Common Stock Performance and Inflation: An International Comparison. *Journal of Business* 47(1): 48-52, 1974.

[5] W. B. Brueggeman, A. H. Chen and T. G. Thibodeau. Real Estate Investment Funds: Performance and Portfolio Considerations. *AREUEA Journal* 12(3): 333-354, 1984.

[6] E. F. Fama. Short-Term Interest Rates as Predictors of Inflation. *American Economic Review* 65(3): 269-282, 1975.

[7] E. Fama and M. Gibbons. Inflation, Real Returns and Capital Investment. *Journal of Monetary Economics* 9(3): 297-324, 1982.

[8] ———. A Comparison of Inflation Forecasts. Working Paper, 1983.

[9] E. Fama and G. W. Schwert. Asset Returns and Inflation. *Journal of Financial Economics* 5 (2): 115-146, 1977.

[10] R. H. Fogler. A Mean-Variance Analysis of Real Estate. *Journal of Portfolio Management,* Winter 1983.

[11] H. C. Friedman. Real Estate Investment and Portfolio Theory. *Journal of Financial and Quantitative Analysis,* April 1970.

[12] J. W. Hoag. Towards Indices of Real Estate Value and Return. *Journal of Finance* 35(2): 569-580, 1980.

[13] R. G. Ibbotson and C. L. Fall. The United States Market Wealth Portfolio. *Journal of Portfolio Management* 7(1): 82-92, 1979.

[14] R. G. Ibbotson and L. B. Siegel. The World Wealth Portfolio. *Journal of Portfolio Management* 9(2): 5-17, 1983.

[15] R. G. Ibbotson and R. A. Sinquefield. Stocks, Bonds, Bills and Inflation: The Past and the Future. Financial Analysis Research Foundation, 1982.

[16] M. Miles and T. McCue. Commercial Real Estate Returns. *AREUEA Journal* 12(3): 355-377, 1984.

[17] ———. Historic Returns and Institutional Real Estate Portfolios. *AREUEA Journal* 10(2): 184-199, 1982.

[18] J. Peek and J. A. Wilcox. The Postwar Stability of the Fisher Effect. *Journal of Finance* 38(4): 1111-1124, 1983.

[19] *Pension and Investment Age,* January 1984.

[20] G. W. Schwert. The Adjustment of Stock Prices to Information About Inflation. *The Journal of Finance* 36(1): 15-30, 1981.

[21] P. Wendt and S. Wong. Investment Performance: Common Stocks vs. Apartment Houses. *Journal of Finance* 20(4): 633-646, 1965.

19 The Inflation-Hedging Effectiveness of Real Estate

Jack H. Rubens, Michael T. Bond, and James R. Webb

Inflation has become one of the predominant financial concerns of the late twentieth century. In the late 1970s, public opinion polls ranked inflation as the number one problem in the United States. While the rate of inflation has slowed since the late 1970s, inflation is still present and many investors expect a resurgence of inflation to higher levels in the near to immediate future. This continued concern about inflation has led to an increased search and evaluation of investments that will protect investors from inflation. Assets that have the ability to protect investors from the effects of inflation are generally labeled inflation hedges. Real estate has been regarded as one of the best inflation hedges of past years. While there has been research in the past evaluating this possibility and some recent research using only business real estate, no current research on residential real estate or farmland as inflation hedges exists. This study examines the inflation-hedging effectiveness of residential real estate, farmland and business real estate (with a different data set) as individual assets and in a portfolio context for 1960-86.

INTRODUCTION

One objective of holding an investment portfolio is to provide an investor with a positive real rate-of-return. During periods of inflation, certain financial instruments not only do not protect the investor, but actually perform as a perverse hedge, i.e., decrease in value as inflation increases. Nelson [25], Jaffe and Mandelker [19], and Stulz [29], among others, have shown that common stock has served as a perverse hedge in the United States. Others, such as Gultekin [12], Mandelker and Tandon [22], and Peel and Pope [26] have noted such a relationship between common stocks and inflation on an international basis. Other work has examined the inflation-hedging effectiveness of various other investment media including gold (Ritter and Ulrich [27]), commodities (Bird[2]), futures (Bodie [3] and Herbst [15]), and collectibles such as diamonds and art/antiques (Ferris and Makhija [9]), stamps (Taylor [30]), coins (Kane [20]) and comic books (Ang, et al. [1]).

Given the importance of the results and the wide variety of potential investment media analyzed, the relative dearth of research on the inflation-hedging effectiveness of real estate is surprising. Only studies by Fama and Schwert [8], Fogler, et al. [11], and Hartzell, et al. [13] have rigorously examined the effectiveness of real estate as an inflation hedge.

The purpose of this study is to examine the inflation-hedging effectiveness of three types of real estate (residential, business and farmland) as individual assets and as portions of mean/variance efficient portfolios. Further, the asset returns will be divided into the appreciation and income components as an expositional aid. All return measures will be regressed against actual, expected and unexpected inflation. By dividing inflation into the two return components, the hedging effectiveness can be better examined.

The next section will review the relevant literature. The third section discusses the data and develops the model used to test hedging effectiveness. The fourth section presents the results for individual assets as well as the portfolios. The final section contains the summary, conclusions and implications.

LITERATURE REVIEW

Fama and Schwert [8] test the hedging effectiveness of Treasury bills, government bonds, residential real estate, corporate bonds, labor income and common stocks against expected and unexpected inflation. Treasury bill rates are used as a measure of expected inflation. The return used for residential real estate is the rate of inflation of the Home Purchase Price component of the CPI. They conclude that private residential real estate is a complete hedge against both expected and unexpected inflation.

However, there are several problems with the Fama and Schwert residential real estate data. First, only appreciation returns are considered. Second, the sample includes only FHA-insured homes. Third, there is a one-month lag between when the FHA collects the data and when it appears in the CPI. A final criticism is that, as discussed by Fama [7] and Kaul [21], the results are due to a spurious correlation between the asset returns and the inflation rate. That is, the expected real rate of interest is not independent of the expected inflation rate.

Fogler, et al. [11] examine two possible explanations for the positive relationship between real estate returns and inflation. The first examines if it is the result of a true high correlation between the two factors. The second examines the result of changing investor expectations concerning the effectiveness of real estate as an inflation hedge. They find limited support for the first explanation, but not enough to reject the second. The data set used by Fogler, et al. is the Census Bureau quarterly price index of new single-family homes sold. The data is of limited value, since it only considers gains in appreciation and new home sales. Thus, it omits income returns and the stock of existing residential real estate.

Hartzell, et al. [13] perform two tests to examine the hedging effectiveness of a commingled real estate fund (CREF) from 1973 to 1983 that contains business real estate. Both tests involve using Treasury bill rates as the basis for expected inflation. One test is based upon Fama and Schwert [8], while the other involves using a nonconstant real rate that moves according to an integrated moving average process. Further, they construct portfolios consisting of real estate and government bonds to examine the benefits of including real estate in inflation-hedging portfolios. They find that commercial real estate acts as a complete hedge against both expected and unexpected inflation.

This study complements and extends these previous research efforts by updating the time period examined and including farmland in addition to residential and business real estate. Furthermore, we not only test total returns, but also the appreciation and income components of the returns. This division of the return stream helps ascertain the portion of the total return that determines the hedging effectiveness of the asset. Finally, mean/variance efficient portfolios are constructed to determine the additional hedging benefit accrued from including real estate in a portfolio.

DEVELOPMENT OF THE MODEL AND SOURCES OF THE DATA

Fisher [10] noted that the nominal rate of interest is comprised of an appropriate equilibrium real interest rate and an expected inflation premium. In efficient markets, the nominal rate-of-return on an asset incorporates the best possible estimate of expected future inflation. Fama and Schwert [8] test for hedging effectiveness of various financial assets against both expected and unexpected inflation. Assuming that Treasury bills are perfectly liquid, they use the rate on T-bills as a proxy for the expected rate of inflation. Their measure of unexpected inflation is the difference between actual inflation and the bill rate, calculated ex post. This study uses the Livingston price expectations (LPE) series as a measure of expected inflation.

The LPE series is a semiannual forecast by business economists that is conducted by Joseph Livingston. In each survey, respondents are requested to make six- and twelve-month predictions of many macroeconomic variables including inflation, GNP, unemployment, and stock prices. The survey has been conducted since 1946 and is now handled by the Federal Reserve Bank of Philadelphia.

There is no consensus on the best method to estimate inflationary expectations. Both survey-based data (such as the Livingston data) and regression-generated data appear to be acceptable proxies for expected inflation. The merits of each approach have been well developed in studies by Menil and Bhalla [23], Carlson and Parkin [5], Carlson [4] and Mullineaux [24]. In order to use as much ex-ante data as possible, the Livingston forecasts were used in this study.

The returns for the real and financial assets examined in this paper were obtained from Ibbotson and others [17, 18] and personal communications from Ibbotson and Associates for updates. For the business real estate returns, Ibbotson and Seigel [17] provide a detailed description of the data. The financial data composition is described in Ibbotson and Associates [16, 18].

Residential appreciation returns were calculated as the annual change in the home purchase component of the CPI. Residential income returns are net of operating expenses and were taken from Sprinkel and Genetski [28]. Business real estate returns were obtained from the First National Bank of Chicago CREF. The properties in the CREF are unleveraged, which makes these returns comparable to the unleveraged financial asset returns. Finally, the CREF returns are weighted, based upon census tract data, to reduce geographic bias. Farmland appreciation and income returns were taken from U.S. Department of Agriculture data for the annual percentage change per farmland acre and annual net farm operating income as a percentage of value, respectively.

Annual returns for the three types of real estate, S&P 500 and small capitalization stocks, government and corporate bonds, and Treasury bills from December 1960 through December 1986 were used. Furthermore, the appreciation and income component returns for the real estate, common stocks and government bonds were also included in the analysis. The component returns for the other asset types were not available.

The returns were then expressed as the log of 1 plus the return, as suggested by Fama and Schwert [8]. Actual inflation was taken from the Consumer Price Index data given by Ibbotson Associates [18] and also expressed as the log of 1 plus the inflation rate. Expected inflation data for each observation was defined as the log of 1 plus the Livingston observation. Unexpected inflation was defined as the log of 1 plus the difference between the CPI and expected inflation.

To test the effect of actual, expected and unexpected inflation on the asset returns, regression equations were estimated using the Cochran-Orcutt method to control for auto-regressive disturbances. For the three inflation types and for each of the assets, the following equations were estimated:

For actual inflation:
$$FA_{jt} = a_0 + b_1 CPI_t + e_t \qquad (1)$$

For expected inflation:
$$FA_{jt} = a_0 + b_2 LIV_{jt} + e_t \qquad (2)$$

For unexpected inflation:
$$FA_{jt} = a_0 + b_3(CPI_t - LIV_{jt}) + e_t \qquad (3)$$

where:

FA_{jt} = nominal return on asset j from time $t-1$ to t,
CPI_t = actual inflation rate as measured by the Consumer Price Index at time t, and
LIV_{jt} = expected inflation rate as estimated by the Livingston survey from $t-1$ to t.

EMPIRICAL RESULTS

Exhibit 1 presents the means and standard deviations of the annual nominal rates-of-return for the assets examined, as well as actual, expected and unexpected inflation rates. Component returns are also included and show that most of the variation in the asset return resulted from the appreciation portion of the return.

All total return measures provided a positive real rate-of-return. Furthermore, the market was fairly accurate in its assessment of inflation over the entire time period. Eighty-six percent of actual inflation was incorporated in the expected inflation estimates (.0411/.0476). However, as Exhibit 2 shows, the quality of the estimate of future inflation varied considerably over the time period examined. Unexpected inflation, the difference between the CPI and the Livingston data, shows that inflation was generally underestimated throughout the 1960s and 1970s, but overestimated in recent years.

Exhibits 3 through 5 show the results of the regression estimates for each type of inflation against the asset returns. Hedging effectiveness varied with the type of inflation. As implied by equations (1) through (3), the following definitions apply:

- A *complete positive hedge* against inflation is obtained when a positively-signed beta coefficient of an asset is not statistically different from positive one.
- A *complete negative hedge* against inflation is obtained when a negatively-signed beta coefficient for an asset is not statistically different from negative one.

Exhibit 1 Means and Standard Deviations of Annual Nominal Rates-of-Return: 1960-86

Return Type and Identifier	Mean (%)	Standard Deviation (%)
Treasury Bills Total Return (T Bills TR)	5.69	2.88
Government Bonds Total Return (G-Bonds TR)	5.88	9.83
Government Bonds Appreciation (G-Bonds App)	−0.94	8.19
Government Bonds Interest Yield (G-Bonds Div)	6.81	3.09
Corporate Bonds Total Return (C-Bonds TR)	5.66	11.29
S&P 500 Stocks Total Return (Com Stk TR)	8.78	12.55
S&P 500 Stocks Appreciation (Com Stk App)	4.76	12.01
S&P 500 Stocks Dividend Yield (Com Stk Div)	4.02	1.08
Small Stocks Total Returns (Sm Stk TR)	10.66	21.51
Residential Real Estate Total Return (Res TR)	8.44	3.78
Residential Real Estate Appreciation (Res App)	4.90	4.12
Residential Real Estate Income (Res Inc)	3.54	5.16
Business Real Estate Total Return (Bus TR)	8.43	4.03
Business Real Estate Appreciation (Bus App)	5.49	3.37
Business Real Estate Income (Bus Inc)	2.95	2.30
Farmland Total Return (Farm TR)	9.73	9.71
Farmland Appreciation (Farm App)	6.72	9.19
Farmland Income (Farm Inc)	3.01	2.11
Actual Inflation (Act Infl)	4.76	3.27
Expected Inflation (Exp Infl)	4.11	2.74
Unexpected Inflation (Unexp Infl)	0.65	2.24

Exhibit 2 US Unexpected Inflation 1960-86

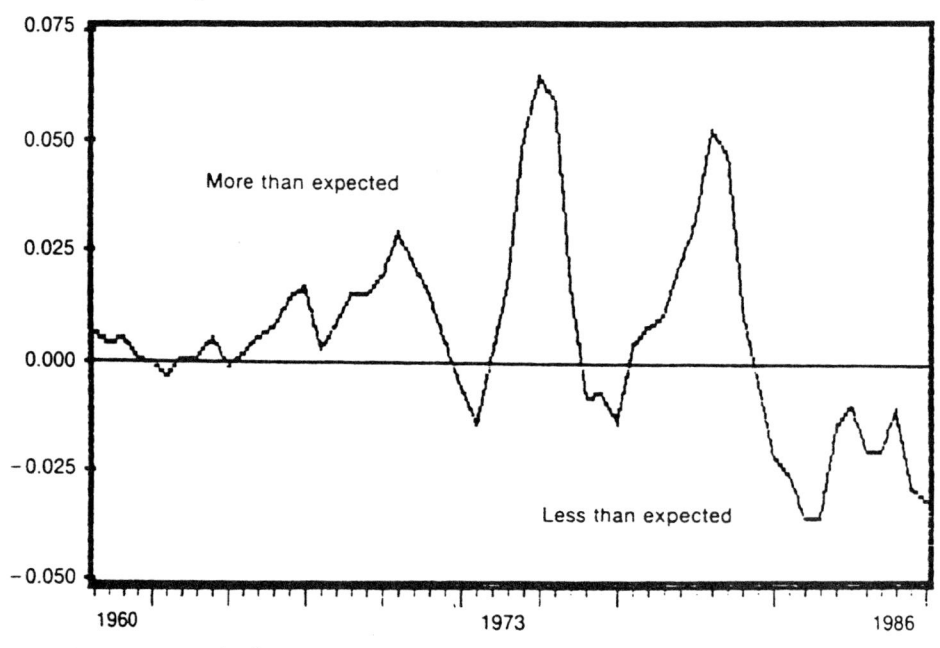

Note: Unexpected inflation = actual inflation minus Livingston data

- A *partial positive hedge* against inflation is obtained when a positively-signed beta coefficient for an asset is significantly different from both positive one *and* zero.
- A *partial negative hedge* against inflation is obtained when a negatively-signed beta coefficient for an asset is significantly different from negative one *and* significantly different from zero.
- An *indeterminant hedge* against inflation is obtained when the beta coefficient is not statistically different from zero.

A 95% confidence interval was used to test whether a particular investment instrument is a complete, partial or indeterminant hedge.

As indicated by Ang, et al. [1], since expected real returns are treated as a constant, the models should not be expected to explain a large portion of the variation in the rates-of-return. This is because the purpose of the present study is to examine hedging effectiveness and, necessarily, does not deal with the possible large variations in rates-of-return among the individual assets. Thus, the level of the coefficients of determination do not hold their normal importance in testing the hypothesis.

The hedging effectiveness of the return measures against actual inflation is shown in Exhibit 3. As can be seen, different assets yield differing levels of protection against inflation. Only residential real estate is a complete hedge against actual inflation. Treasury bills are the only other asset exhibiting at least some hedging effectiveness. All other financial and real assets have standard errors so large that their hedging effectiveness is indeterminant. The component results show that the income portion provided most of the hedging effectiveness for the Treasury bills and the residential real estate.

Exhibit 4 examines asset hedging effectiveness against expected inflation, as measured by the Livingston survey data. As with the results for performance against actual inflation, the results vary across asset types, although a few more positive hedges exist.

Exhibit 3 Hedging Effectiveness Against Actual Inflation: 1960-86

Asset Type	Constant	Beta Coefficient	Standard Error	R Squared	Type of Hedge
T Bill TR	0.0401	0.4795	0.1228	0.84	Partial Positive
G-Bonds TR	0.0900	−0.6824	0.6552	0.06	Indeterminant
G-Bonds App	0.0327	−0.9402	0.4676	0.15	Complete Negative
G-Bonds Int	0.1258	0.0744	0.0787	0.92	Indeterminant
C-Bonds TR	0.1024	−1.0221	0.7331	0.08	Indeterminant
Com Stk TR	0.1294	−1.1363	0.8085	0.08	Indeterminant
Com Stk App	0.0970	−1.2556	0.9375	0.11	Indeterminant
Com Stk Div	0.0351	0.0903	0.0491	0.72	Indeterminant
Sm Stk TR	0.1850	−2.1718	1.7900	0.10	Indeterminant
Res TR	0.0485	0.7470	0.2294	0.48	Complete Positive
Res App	0.0107	0.8150	0.2675	0.52	Complete Positive
Res Inc	0.0367	−0.0426	0.3259	0.70	Indeterminant
Bus TR	0.0794	0.1240	0.3039	0.44	Indeterminant
Bus App	0.0288	0.0238	0.2934	0.21	Indeterminant
Bus Inc	0.0570	0.1192	0.0947	0.84	Indeterminant
Farm TR	0.0256	0.9165	0.6061	0.69	Indeterminant
Farm App	−0.0035	0.4454	0.5262	0.70	Indeterminant
Farm Inc	0.0350	0.1370	0.1720	0.29	Indeterminant

Exhibit 4 Hedging Effectiveness Against Expected Inflation: 1960-86

Asset Type	Constant	Beta Coefficient	Standard Error	R Squared	Type of Hedge
T Bill TR	0.0218	0.8399	0.1643	0.81	Complete Positive
G-Bonds TR	0.0247	0.7716	0.7456	0.06	Indeterminant
G-Bonds App	−0.0068	−0.1109	0.2196	0.15	Indeterminant
G-Bonds Int	0.1369	0.4506	0.1164	0.95	Partial Positive
C-Bonds TR	0.0157	0.8961	0.8274	0.05	Indeterminant
Com Stk TR	0.0509	0.6003	0.9428	0.02	Indeterminant
Com Stk App	0.0247	−3.1772	0.9375	0.34	Complete Negative
Com Stk Div	0.0273	0.2578	0.0503	0.75	Partial Positive
Sm Stk TR	0.0210	1.4519	2.0050	0.07	Indeterminant
Res TR	0.0718	0.3090	0.4250	0.28	Indeterminant
Res App	0.0412	0.2249	0.5368	0.33	Indeterminant
Res Inc	0.0373	−0.0581	0.0613	0.69	Indeterminant
Bus TR	0.0477	0.8756	0.3031	0.51	Complete Positive
Bus App	0.0273	0.1093	0.3833	0.21	Indeterminant
Bus Inc	0.0390	0.4110	0.1643	0.41	Partial Positive
Farm TR	0.1171	−1.0848	1.2036	0.67	Indeterminant
Farm App	0.0300	−0.9534	1.0783	0.70	Indeterminant
Farm Inc	0.0507	−0.2189	0.2589	0.29	Indeterminant

Only Treasury bills and business real estate provide a complete positive hedge against expected inflation. All long-term financial assets, farmland and residential real estate are categorized as indeterminant hedges. The component returns indicate that the appreciation portion of the financial assets performed poorly against expected inflation.

As indicated in Exhibit 5, the results for hedging performance of the various financial and real assets against unexpected inflation are in direct contrast to the findings with respect to expected inflation. All stock and long-term bond total return measures were complete negative hedges. Only farmland and residential real estate provided complete positive hedges. Business real estate and Treasury bills are indeterminant hedges. As noted by Gultekin [12] and Hasbrouck [14] and confirmed here, the poor hedging performance of financial assets resulted from the unexpected portion of inflation.

Although the above results are of value to institutional real estate investors and selected others, most investors include real estate as only a portion of their portfolios. We address this mixed-asset portfolio consideration by creating four mean/variance efficient portfolios.

Portfolio 1 includes all five financial assets (S&P 500 stocks and small stocks, corporate and government bonds and Treasury bills) and farmland.
Portfolio 2 includes all five financial assets and business real estate.
Portfolio 3 includes all five financial assets and residential real estate.
Portfolio 4 includes all five financial assets and all three types of real estate.

Using a Markowitz variance/covariance model, we obtained the following vector of allocating fractions:

Exhibit 5 Hedging Effectiveness Against Unexpected Inflation: 1960-86

Asset Type	Constant	Beta Coefficient	Standard Error	R Squared	Type of Hedge
T Bill TR	0.0660	0.2679	0.1435	0.75	Indeterminant
G-Bonds TR	0.0690	−2.3607	0.6444	0.33	Complete Negative
G-Bonds App	−0.0007	−1.9035	0.5740	0.30	Complete Negative
G-Bonds Int	−0.0487	−0.0128	0.0780	0.91	Indeterminant
C-Bonds TR	0.0692	−3.0476	0.6309	0.45	Complete Negative
Com Stk TR	0.0949	−3.1772	0.9375	0.34	Complete Negative
Com Stk App	0.0566	−3.0896	0.9300	0.33	Complete Negative
Com Stk Div	0.0401	0.0439	0.0512	0.69	Indeterminant
Sm Stk TR	0.1079	−4.5116	1.9809	0.23	Complete Negative
Res TR	0.0813	−0.7674	0.3058	0.43	Complete Positive
Res App	0.0470	−0.8082	0.3195	0.48	Complete Positive
Res Inc	0.0346	−0.0226	0.0302	0.68	Indeterminant
Bus TR	0.0864	−0.1392	0.3083	0.45	Indeterminant
Bus App	0.0301	−0.0477	0.3241	0.21	Indeterminant
Bus Inc	0.0642	0.0203	0.0951	0.83	Indeterminant
Farm TR	0.0763	1.2177	0.5085	0.72	Complete Positive
Farm App	0.0139	0.9133	0.4784	0.73	Indeterminant
Farm Inc	0.0406	0.2463	0.1765	0.33	Indeterminant

$$Portfolio\ 1 = \begin{bmatrix} \times\ Common\ Stock & = 5.54\% \\ \times\ Small\ Stock & = 1.34\% \\ \times\ Government\ Bonds & = 3.69\% \\ \times\ Treasury\ Bills & = 69.25\% \\ \times\ Farmland & = 20.17\% \end{bmatrix} \quad (4)$$

$$Portfolio\ 2 = \begin{bmatrix} \times\ Common\ Stock & = 5.56\% \\ \times\ Treasury\ Bills & = 49.25\% \\ \times\ Business\ Real\ Estate & = 45.19\% \end{bmatrix} \quad (5)$$

$$Portfolio\ 3 = \begin{bmatrix} \times\ Common\ Stock & = 10.04\% \\ \times\ Government\ Bonds & = 3.20\% \\ \times\ Treasury\ Bills & = 32.44\% \\ \times\ Residential\ Real\ Estate & = 54.32\% \end{bmatrix} \quad (6)$$

$$Portfolio\ 4 = \begin{bmatrix} \times\ Common\ Stock & = 7.96\% \\ \times\ Government\ Bonds & = 3.44\% \\ \times\ Treasury\ Bills & = 51.20\% \\ \times\ Farmland & = 13.87\% \\ \times\ Residential\ Real\ Estate & = 23.53\% \end{bmatrix} \quad (7)$$

The portfolio mean returns, standard deviations and coefficients of variation are presented in Exhibit 6. The Markowitz algorithm allows the selection of the portfolios with the lowest coefficient of variation. These portfolios, of course, have lower CVs than any of the individual assets. The portfolios are then regressed against the three inflation types. These results are presented in Exhibit 7.

The farmland and "all three real estate types" portfolios (Portfolios 1 and 4) are partial hedges against actual and expected inflation. The business real estate portfolio

Exhibit 6 Portfolio Characteristics: 1960-86

Portfolio	Mean	Standard Deviation	Coefficient of Variation
Financial Assets (FA) and Farmland (Portfolio 1)	6.75%	2.14%	0.3170
FA and Business Real Estate (Portfolio 2)	7.10%	3.09%	0.4352
FA and Residential Real Estate (Portfolio 3)	7.50%	2.54%	0.3387
FA and All Real Estate Types (Portfolio 4)	7.10%	3.09%	0.4352

(Portfolio 2) is a complete positive hedge against expected inflation. The residential real estate portfolio (Portfolio 3) is a partial positive hedge against actual inflation and a complete positive hedge against expected inflation. None of the portfolios provide statistically significant protection against unexpected inflation. Thus, these mixed-asset portfolios provide better hedging effectiveness than any of the long-term financial assets. Further, the benefits of including real estate in portfolios include not only lower risk per unit of return, but greater inflation protection.

Exhibit 7 Hedging Effectiveness of Mixed-Asset Portfolios Against Various Inflation Types: 1960-86

		Actual Inflation			
Portfolio	Constant	Beta Coefficient	Standard Error	R Squared	Type of Hedge
Portfolio 1	0.0417	0.5514	0.0911	0.64	Positive Positive
Portfolio 2	0.0673	0.1571	0.1626	0.69	Indeterminant
Portfolio 3	0.0555	0.4031	0.1779	0.31	Partial Positive
Portfolio 4	0.0449	0.5577	0.0923	0.60	Partial Positive

		Expected Inflation			
Portfolio	Constant	Beta Coefficient	Standard Error	R Squared	Type of Hedge
Portfolio 1	0.0412	0.6133	0.1601	0.60	Partial Positive
Portfolio 2	0.0390	0.7415	0.2189	0.73	Complete Positive
Portfolio 3	0.0389	0.8208	0.1424	0.54	Complete Positive
Portfolio 4	0.0417	0.6889	0.1203	0.63	Partial Positive

		Unexpected Inflation			
Portfolio	Constant	Beta Coefficient	Standard Error	R Squared	Type of Hedge
Portfolio 1	0.0682	0.1379	0.1550	0.52	Indeterminant
Portfolio 2	0.0753	0.0241	0.1659	0.68	Indeterminant
Portfolio 3	0.0762	−0.0936	0.2569	0.27	Indeterminant
Portfolio 4	0.0726	0.0870	0.1688	0.47	Indeterminant

CONCLUSIONS

The purpose of this paper has been to test the hedging effectiveness of various financial and real assets against actual, expected and unexpected inflation. In addition, mean-variance efficient portfolios were derived and tested for hedging effectiveness against the various types of inflation. The results varied across both asset and inflation type for both individual assets and portfolios. The poor performance of the financial instruments against inflation was largely because of the unexpected, not the expected component of inflation.

The results obtained have several implications for investors. These results can be useful when used for personal forecasts of expected inflation—that is, to invest in asset types that provide at least some protection against inflation. In addition, as the returns are decomposed into the income and appreciation components, the hedging effectiveness differs using asset total returns versus the asset's income and appreciation returns. Use of stripped stock securities to at least hedge for the short term could be accomplished, although it would require constant portfolio revisions. Finally, the portfolio results also can be beneficial when considering types of assets to include in portfolios, when the investor is faced with a volatile inflationary environment.

REFERENCES

[1] J. Ang, J. Chua and W. Reinhart. Monetary Appreciation and Inflation-Hedging Characteristics of Comic Books, *Financial Review* 18 (May 1983), 196-205.

[2] P. Bird. Commodities as a Hedge Against Inflation. *Applied Economics* 16 (December 1984), 855-67.

[3] Z. Bodie. Commodity Futures as a Hedge Against Inflation. *Journal of Portfolio Management* 10 (Spring 1983), 12-17.

[4] J. Carlson. A Study of Price Forecasts. *Annals of Economic and Social Measurement* 6 (Winter 1977), 27-56.

[5] ——— and M. Parkin. Inflationary Expectations. *Economica* 42 (May 1975), 115-49.

[6] D. Cochrane and G. Orcutt. Application of Least Squares Regression to Relationships Containing Autocorrelated Error Terms. *Journal of the American Statistical Association* (1949), 32-61.

[7] E. Fama. Stock Returns, Real Activity, Inflation, and Money. *American Economic Review* 71 (1981), 545-65.

[8] ——— and G. Schwert. Asset Returns and Inflation. *Journal of Financial Economics* 5 (November 1977), 115-46.

[9] S. Ferris and A. Makhija. Tangible Assets as Investments: A Risk and Return Analysis. *Akron Business and Economic Journal* 18 (Fall 1987), 115-28.

[10] I. Fisher. *The Theory of Interest*. New York: MacMillan, 1930.

[11] R. Fogler, M. R. Granito and L. R. Smith. A Theoretical Analysis of Real Estate Returns. *The Journal of Finance* 40 (July 1985), 711-21.

[12] N. Gultekin. Stock Market Returns and Inflation Forecasts. *Journal of Finance* 38 (June 1983), 663-74.

[13] D. Hartzell, J. Heckman and M. Miles. Real Estate Returns and Inflation. *AREUEA Journal* 15 (Spring 1987), 617-37.

[14] J. Hasbrouck. Stock Returns, Inflation, and Economic Activity: The Survey Evidence. *The Journal of Finance* 39 (December 1983), 1293-1310.

[15] A. Herbst. Hedging Against Price Index Inflation with Futures Contracts. *Journal of Futures Markets* 5 (Winter 1985), 489-504.

[16] R. Ibbotson and L. Seigel. The World Market Wealth Portfolio. *Journal of Portfolio Management* 10 (1983), 5-17.

[17] ———. Real Estate Returns: A Comparison With Other Investments. *AREUEA Journal* 12 (1984), 219-44.

[18] Ibbotson and Associates. *Stocks, Bonds, Bills and Inflation: 1987 Year-book.* Chicago: Ibbotson Associates, 1987.

[19] J. Jaffe and G. Mandelker. The 'Fisher Effect' for Risky Assets: An Empirical Investigation. *Journal of Finance* 31 (May 1976), 447-58.

[20] A. Kane. Coins: Anatomy of a Fad Asset. *Journal of Portfolio Management* 10 (Winter 1984), 44-51.

[21] G. Kaul. Stock Returns and Inflation: The Role of the Monetary Sector. *Journal of Financial Economics* 18 (1987), 253-76.

[22] G. Mandelker and K. Tandon. Common Stock Returns, Real Activity, Money and Inflation: Some International Evidence. *Journal of International Money and Finance* 4 (June 1985), 267-86.

[23] G. Menil and S. Bhalla. Direct Measurement of Popular Price Expectations. *American Economic Review* 70 (May 1975), 178-79.

[24] D. Mullineaux. Inflationary Expectations and Money Growth in the U.S. *American Economic Review* 70 (March 1980), 158-59.

[25] C. Nelson. Inflation and Rates of Return on Common Stock. *Journal of Finance* 31 (May 1976), 471-83.

[26] D. Peel and P. Pope. Testing the Fisherian Hypothesis: Some Methodological Issues and Further Evidence for the UK. *Journal of Business, Finance and Accounting* 12 (Summer 1985), 297-311.

[27] L. Ritter and T. Ulrich. *The Role of Gold in Consumer Investment Portfolios.* Monograph Series in Finance and Economics. New York: Salomon Brothers, 1984.

[28] B. Sprinkel and R. Genetski. *Winning with Money.* Homewood, Ill.: Dow Jones-Irwin, 1977.

[29] R. Stulz. Asset Pricing and Expected Inflation. *Journal of Finance* 41 (March 1986), 209-24.

[30] W. Taylor. The Estimation of Quality-Adjusted Rates of Return in Stamp Auctions. *Journal of Finance* 38 (September 1983), 1095-1110.

Part 7. Finance Theory and Real Estate

20 Capital Asset Pricing and Real Estate Valuation

Dennis W. Draper and M. Chapman Findlay

This paper examines the Capital Asset Pricing Model with respect to its implications for real estate investment analysis and appraisal. The derivation of the CAPM, and theoretical problems with it, are discussed, along with its empirical validation. The similarities and differences between real estate and securities markets are evaluated. Alternative models to the CAPM are presented, followed by the conclusions.

INTRODUCTION

One artifact of recent inflationary periods is the price appreciation in real estate. Concomitantly, large institutions, in addition to small investors, have increasingly shifted larger proportions of their funds from financial assets into real assets. This attention has spurred the interest, not only of real estate experts but also of financial economists in search for applications of finance methodologies to real asset valuation.

Since the middle 1960s, the backbone of financial asset valuation has been the capital asset pricing model (CAPM). Originally offered as a stock valuation model, it was extended to numerous applications in corporate finance. Simply stated, the model posits that an asset's expected return, in excess of the risk-free rate, is a positive, linear function of its covariance of return with a portfolio of all risky assets. Recently, it has been suggested (see Miles and Rice [44], Gau and Kohlhepp [22], and Wofford and Moses [66], for example) that the CAPM be applied in real estate analysis. Though an appealing idea, some criticisms of the CAPM in financial theory suggest a cautious application of this model. The evaluation should begin with a thorough examination of its assumptions and include a critical analysis of the special nature of real estate with respect to the CAPM.

The purpose of this paper is to examine in detail the CAPM, its potential application to real estate, and its implications for real estate portfolio analysis. In the second section, the underpinnings for development of the CAPM are presented. General theoretical problems are discussed in the third. The fourth section reports empirical evidence on tests of the CAPM. And in the fifth section, a contrast of characteristics in the real estate market and the securities market is presented. The discussion considers the

From *AREUEA Journal* (Summer 1982). The authors would like to acknowledge the encouragement of William Brueggeman and the comments of James Hoag, David Dale-Johnson and Marc Reinganum. All errors are, of course, the authors' own.

similarities of the two markets, which would permit straightforward application of the CAPM, and dissimilarities, which cast doubt on the application of the CAPM. Next, alternative models are evaluated, followed by the conclusions. It is hoped that this synthesis and its conclusions will help bridge the gap between theories of finance, in particular the CAPM, and the demand for real asset valuation models.

RISKY ASSET VALUATION

The most common measure of an asset's performance is its rate of return. Regardless of the period over which an asset's return is calculated, the one-period rate of return is:

$$R = \frac{V_{t+1} - V_t + C_t}{V_t} \tag{2.1}$$

where

V_{t+1} = market value of the asset at $t+1$
V_t = market value of the asset at t
C_t = cash disbursements in period t

Though an easily stated concept, Equation (2.1) implicitly assumes that well-defined measures of market value and cash disbursements exist for all holding periods in order that any desired holding-period return can be calculated.

When asset returns are uncertain, anticipated returns for the next holding period are often expressed as the expectation of returns by placing the expectations operator in front of R, V_{t+1}, and C_t in Equation (2.1). At the same time, the existence of uncertainty about the return to be obtained suggests the need for a measure of the risk associated with an investment. Although concepts such as range of return or mean absolute deviation of return exist, variance (or its square root, standard deviation) is the most frequently used measure of dispersion (which is, in turn, commonly interpreted as risk). Variance of return is defined as:

$$\sigma^2 = E(\tilde{R} - \bar{R})^2 \tag{2.2}$$

Using these definitions, it is generally *assumed* that investors make choices among risky assets, or combinations of risky assets, using only the mean and variance of return.[1]

Extending the development of measures for individual asset returns, measures of expected return and risk can be derived for *portfolios* of risky assets. The expected rate of return for a portfolio is:

$$E(\tilde{R}_p) = \sum_{i=1}^{n} \alpha_i \, E(\tilde{R}_i) \tag{2.3}$$

where:

α_i = proportion of total investment in asset i $\left(\sum_{i}^{n} \alpha_i = 1\right)$
$E(\tilde{R}_i)$ = expected return on asset i

Similarly, the variance of the portfolio can be written as:

$$\sigma_p^2 = \sum_{i=1}^{n} \sum_{j=1}^{n} \alpha_i \alpha_j \rho_{ij} \sigma_i \sigma_j \tag{2.4}$$

where

α_i, α_j = proportions of total investment in asset i, asset j
σ_i, σ_j = standard deviation of return for asset i, asset j
ρ_{ij} = correlation of returns between asset i and asset j ($\rho_{ij} = 1$ for i = j)

with

$\rho_{ij}\sigma_i\sigma_j$ = covariance of returns between asset i and asset j = $\text{Cov}(\tilde{R}_i, \tilde{R}_j)$

Portfolio variance reflects not only the dispersion of the individual asset returns, but also the relationship between returns in the same portfolio through the correlation coefficient. As the correlation between asset returns decreases, the overall portfolio variance decreases, ceteris paribus.

If the concept of portfolio formation is extended to include all possible combinations of assets, the opportunity set of risk/return pairs can be represented in Exhibit 1. Selection of the optimal portfolio is achieved by imposing an individual's preferences on the risk/return choice set. Preferences are usually characterized as utility functions over mean return and variance of return. Iso-utility curves (i.e., constant utility curves) are represented as indifference curves in risk/return space, with utility increasing in a north-

Exhibit 1

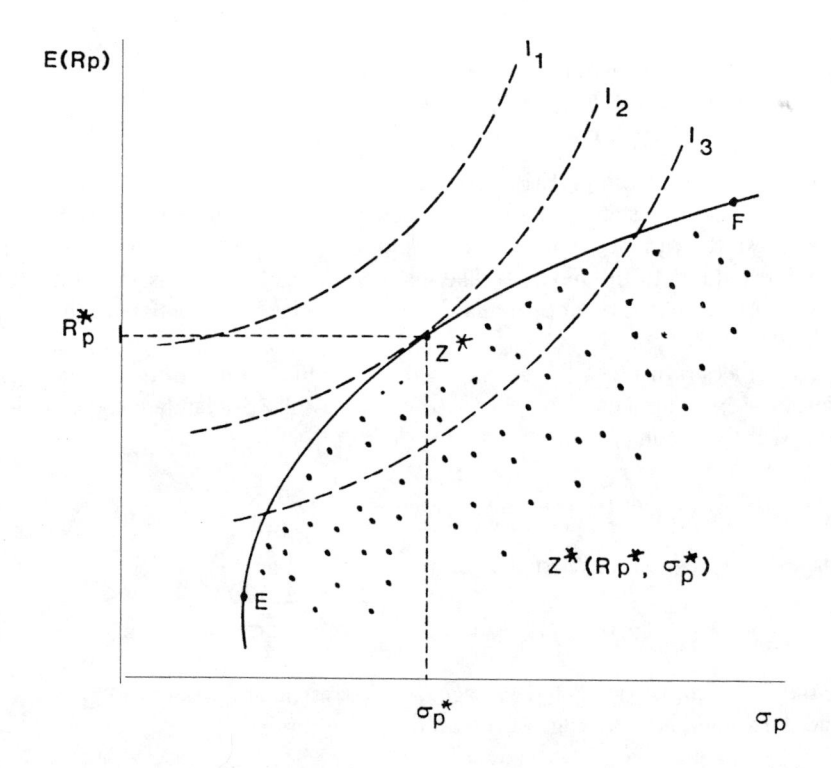

westerly direction. Exhibit 1 depicts iso-utility curves for an individual investor, such that $I_3 > I_2 > I_1$. Portfolio $Z°$ is optimal since it is determined as the tangency (or intersection of sets) of the opportunity set and the family of indifference curves.

Since investors are assumed to be risk-averse and to make portfolio choices considering only expected return and standard deviation of return, only portfolios on the outer edge of the opportunity set (noted as E-F in Exhibit 1) will be chosen. This subset is called the efficient frontier, with "efficiency" defining the concept under which it is impossible to obtain a lower variance for any given level of expected return. Practically, however, the necessary inputs and computational requirements present problems. In addition to computing the mean and standard deviation of return for each asset, the correlations, and the associated covariances, must be calculated for each distinct pair of assets. With these inputs, only parameters of the portfolios on the efficient frontier need to be calculated. The traditional formulation was first introduced by Markowitz [41] and solved as a quadratic programming problem.[2]

While recognizing the contribution of Markowitz, the need for covariances of individual assets remained. Sharpe [61], however, dealt with this problem by offering a simplified model which assumes that an asset's return relates only to a more general index (such as the Dow-Jones or the S&P 500). Since the assumption states that asset returns are related through the index return, the non-zero elements of the covariance matrix are reduced to those on the diagonal, lessening the computational burden. The model, commonly known as the Sharpe Diagonal Model, can be represented as:

$$\tilde{R}_i = a_i + b_i \tilde{R}_I + \tilde{e}_i \qquad (2.5)$$

where:

a_i, b_i = constants
$\tilde{R}_i, \tilde{R}_I$ = returns on asset i and on the index I
$\tilde{e}_i$ = error term with $E(\tilde{e}_i) = 0$, $\sigma_{e_i}^2$ (variance of e_i) equal to a constant, $\text{Cov}(e_i, e_j) = 0$, and $\text{Cov}(e_i, R_I) = 0$

The expected return on asset i, $E(\tilde{R}_i)$, can be calculated as $(a_i + b_i E(\tilde{R}_I))$. Given its form, Equation (2.5) permits statistical estimation of a_i and b_i by such methods as regression. In this context, the variance of the error term may be interpreted as the variation in return *not* attributable to the index. In like manner, the variance in asset i's total return minus the variance of the error term may be interpreted as the variation associated with the index.

Each asset's return can be decomposed into an index-related ($b_i \tilde{R}_I$) and an idiosyncratic ($a_i + \tilde{e}_i$) component. The portfolio return may likewise be depicted as a weighted average of these components:

$$\tilde{R}_p = \sum_{i=1}^{n} \alpha_i(a_i + \tilde{e}_i) + \left(\sum_{i=1}^{n} \alpha_i b_i \right) \tilde{R}_I \qquad (2.6)$$

Similarly, the expression for portfolio variation may be expressed in decomposed form:

$$\sigma_p \sqrt{\sum_{i=1}^{n} (\alpha_i \sigma_{e_i})^2 + \left(\sum_{i=1}^{n} \alpha_i b_i \right)^2 \sigma_I^2} \qquad (2.7)$$

where the first term is a weighted average of the idiosyncratic risk of the individual assets and the second is an average of their index-related risk.

The separation of terms in Equations (2.6) and (2.7) highlights the earlier discussion of diversification. If an asset's return depends on individual characteristics *and* on a general index (e.g., total market portfolio as a measure of the total performance in the economy), then it is unlikely that an unlimited addition of securities will continue to reduce portfolio standard deviation indefinitely. It is worth noting that since unsystematic risk (i.e., the first term in Equation 2.7) is diversifiable risk, it is unlikely that an investor will be paid a premium to bear such risk. Only systematic, or undiversifiable, risk (i.e., the second term in Equation 2.7) should be compensated with a market risk premium in equilibrium. Thus one should be careful in referring to unsystematic return variation as "risk" in a market where diversification opportunities exist.

An interesting extension of the paradigm presented above is the introduction of a risk-free asset, or an asset with a zero variance.[3] In a two-asset portfolio—asset 1 being risky, asset 2 being riskless—parameters of the portfolios are:

$$E(\tilde{R}_p) = \alpha_1 E(\tilde{R}_1) + \alpha_2 R_f \qquad (2.8)$$

$$\sigma_p^2 = \alpha_1^2 \sigma_1^2 \qquad (2.9)$$

where R_f = riskless rate of return

The return of the portfolio remains a weighted average of the assets' returns; the variance of the portfolio is the proportion-weighted variance of the risky asset only. Since α_2 represents an investment in a riskless security (e.g., a Treasury Bill), α_2 greater than zero implies a portfolio which purchased the risk-free security (also called a lending portfolio). Conversely, α_2 less than zero implies a portfolio with a short position in the risk-free security (i.e., a borrowing portfolio).

A natural extension of the risky asset case provides a reinterpretation of the development of the opportunity set and the efficient frontier. If a straight line emanating from the point defined as the risk-free rate (R_f) in Exhibit 2 is rotated clockwise until a tangency with the opportunity set is achieved, the intersection defines the optimal risk asset portfolio. The line itself represents the risk-return parameters of all possible combinations of the risk-free security and this portfolio, and, in turn, dominates (i.e., lies above) the old efficient frontier. Further, any risk-averse investor will hold his wealth in combinations of only these two portfolios—a concept which is known as *two-fund separation*.

If investors have homogeneous beliefs about returns and identical opportunity sets, the line in Exhibit 2 will be the same for all. The only risk asset portfolio which can be held by everyone is a microcosm of the market, called the market portfolio. With this interpretation, the line is known as the Capital Market Line (CML). Though all investors choose portfolios which lie on the CML, consisting of combinations of the risk-free asset and the market portfolio, the proportions of each of the two funds chosen will differ for individual investors. Portfolio A in Exhibit 3 represents a portfolio containing a portion of the market portfolio and lending a portion of its investment funds. Portfolio B is a portfolio containing borrowed funds, with all wealth (plus borrowed funds) in the market portfolio.

The CML is merely one simple linear relationship between risk and return, written as:

$$E(\tilde{R}_p) = R_f + \frac{E(\tilde{R}_m) - R_f}{\sigma_m} \sigma_p \qquad (2.10)$$

Exhibit 2

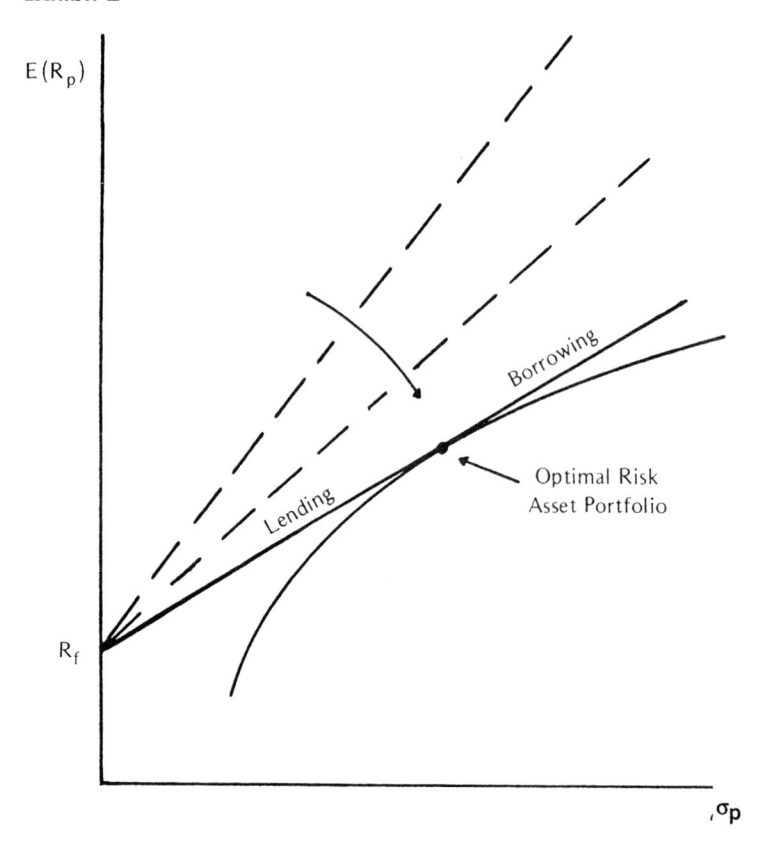

In Exhibit 3, the CML is shown to have a slope of $(E(\tilde{R}_m) - R_f) / \sigma_m$. Equivalently, this expression is the marginal rate of substitution between risk and return or can be viewed as *the market price of risk*.

Development of the price for risk by analyzing the risk/return relationship between efficient portfolios suggests an efficient pricing framework for individual assets. Sharpe [61] reasoned that the risk of a given asset should be viewed not as the risk of that asset held by itself but rather as the change in the total risk of a well diversified portfolio (e.g., market portfolio) caused by including that asset. That change is the nondiversifiable risk of the individual asset, which, as noted earlier, is captured in the covariance between the individual asset return ($\tilde{R}_i$) and the market return ($\tilde{R}_m$):

$$\text{Cov}(\tilde{R}_i, \tilde{R}_m) = \rho_{im} \sigma_i \sigma_m \qquad (2.11)$$

To see the importance of this measure of risk and the association between the CML and the individual asset pricing equation, consider a portfolio of an individual asset (i) and the market portfolio (m). The expected return and standard deviation of return parameters are:

Exhibit 3

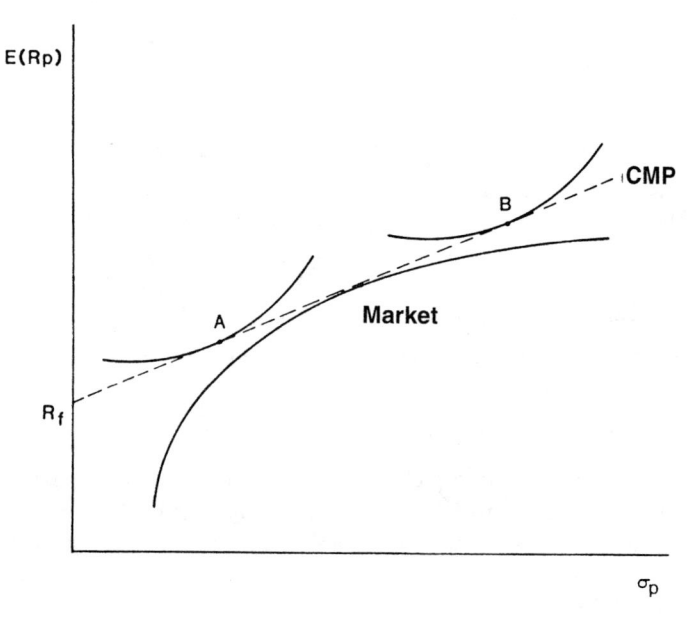

$$E(\tilde{R}_p) = \alpha E(\tilde{R}_i) + (1 - \alpha) E(\tilde{R}_m) \qquad (2.12)$$

$$\sigma_p = \sqrt{\alpha^2 \sigma_i^2 + (1 - \alpha)^2 \sigma_m^2 + 2\alpha(1 - \alpha) \rho_{im} \sigma_i \sigma_m} \qquad (2.13)$$

Sharpe pointed out that in equilibrium, the market portfolio already includes the "proper" proportion of asset i; thus, the *excess* demand for asset i is zero in equilibrium.

$$\left. \frac{\partial E(\tilde{R}_p)}{\partial \alpha} \right|_{\alpha = 0} = E(\tilde{R}_i) - E(\tilde{R}_m) \qquad (2.14)$$

$$\left. \frac{\partial \sigma_p}{\partial \alpha} \right|_{\alpha = 0} = \rho_{im} \sigma_i - \sigma_m \qquad (2.15)$$

Dividing (2.14) by (2.15) produces the slope of the risk/return line which must equal the slope of the CML in equilibrium:

$$\frac{E(\tilde{R}_m) - R_f}{\sigma_m} = \frac{E(\tilde{R}_m) - E(\tilde{R}_i)}{\sigma_m - \rho_{im} \sigma_i} \qquad (2.16)$$

Rearranging Equation (2.16) and solving for $E(\tilde{R}_i)$, the expected return on individual asset i produces:

$$E(\tilde{R}_i) = R_f + \frac{\rho_{im} \sigma_i \sigma_m}{\sigma_m^2} (E(\tilde{R}_m) - R_f) \qquad (2.17)$$

or

$$E(\tilde{R}_i) = R_f + \beta_i (E(\tilde{R}_m) - R_f) \text{ where } \beta_i = \frac{\rho_{im}\sigma_i\sigma_m}{\sigma_m^2} \quad (2.18)$$

Equations (2.17) and (2.18) are the Security Market Line (SML), or the Capital Asset Pricing Model (CAPM). They express the expected rate of return on an individual asset as the risk-free rate plus a risk premium based on the individual asset's covariance of return with the market return. The β_i term (or Beta coefficient) has become a popular measure of an individual asset's systematic risk. The sheer simplicity of and theoretical support for Equation (2.18) has made it acceptable not only in the academic literature but also to the professional investment community. Yet assumptions behind the development of the CAPM suggest cautious application of the valuation formula.

THEORETICAL CRITIQUE OF THE CAPM

The CAPM derivation in the second section presents a pricing model with an attractive formulation. Risk is separated into systematic (market) and nonsystematic (idiosyncratic) effects for individual assets. In addition, portfolio risk measures are linearly additive in the risk of the individual assets. The linearity of the risk/return relationship appears to lend itself to well-known statistical estimation procedures.

Despite these appealing properties, it is noteworthy that many of the assumptions required to derive the model appear to be violated in the real world. This raises questions of the model's validity and its use in empirical asset valuation. Research presenting alternative theories has been offered by Hakansson [24], Merton [43], Kraus and Litzenberger [32], and Ross [57]. Ball [1] and Reinganum [49] have published empirical results which cast doubt on the underlying framework. Finally, Roll [51] has offered criticism which questions the very ability to test the efficiency of the market portfolio.

Conflicting results and theoretical criticisms suggest a reexamination of the assumptions used in the second section to derive the CAPM, including:

1. All assets are tradeable (and therefore are traded) and are divisible;
2. All investors value end-of-period wealth and possess risk-averse preferences which can be summarized by mean and variance of returns only;
3. Markets for assets are frictionless with all information available to all participants;
4. Investors have homogeneous beliefs about the return distributions (assumed jointly normal); and
5. A risk-free asset exists and investors may either borrow or lend at the risk-free rate.

Each assumption, or combination of assumptions, is important (given the current status of financial research) in the CAPM derivation presented, and may seem unrealistic. Hence further examination is required.

In order to obtain simple, intuitive and logical valuation models, some degree of regularity in the market must be assumed. Restrictions are generally placed on either the preferences of the participants or the distribution of returns. These homogeneity assumptions are required because theories permitting all possible combinations of preference and return distributions would most likely result in valuation expressions too complex to be appealing, and in empirical validations too cumbersome to produce meaningful results.

In finance, these assumptions are directed toward assuring that individuals make choices between risky assets based solely on return and risk characteristics (i.e., mean and variance parameters). The usefulness of such assumptions is illustrated by the findings of Markowitz [40], who has shown that a quadratic utility function insures one-fund separation and that multivariate normal return distributions insure two-fund separation.

Furthermore, multivariate normality is sufficient for risk-averse investors to choose portfolios on the efficient frontier. Though a sufficient condition, a question arises as to whether returns are, in fact, jointly normal. One might argue that this appears inconsistent with actual return possibilities, since returns are bounded below at −100% (if liability is limited) and unbounded above. This inconsistency, however, may not be a problem if the probability of observing returns in the extreme "tails" is sufficiently small.

The implication that investors divide their investment portfolios between a fund of risky assets and a risk-free asset, which they can buy or sell (lend or borrow), requires the existence of such an asset. Black [2], however, demonstrated that, if no pure risk-free asset exists, an investor can obtain essentially similar portfolio characteristics by investing part of his wealth in the market portfolio and part of it in a portfolio with a zero beta (and thus no systematic risk).[4] All the implications of the CAPM hold and the separation result obtains.

The assumption of homogeneous beliefs about investment opportunities and returns is necessary to insure the choice of the market portfolio. Though restrictive in nature, the assumption has been slightly altered by Lintner [39] without severely changing the CAPM methods. The mean and covariance parameters become weighted averages of the divergent expectations in Lintner's special case—an expression more complicated in form, but possessing the same properties presented earlier. The more fundamental question relates to the impact of heterogeneity on empirical testing. Different individuals may be estimating different ex ante parameters for asset returns and, hence, for the market portfolio.

Even with homogeneity, however, the CAPM received devastating criticism from Roll [51]. He pointed out that linearity in beta, as derived in the CAPM, is equivalent to the market portfolio being mean variance efficient. Thus, any test of the CAPM is a statement of a joint hypothesis—the form of the CAPM and the efficiency of the market portfolio.

Further, use of the CAPM methodology to measure portfolio performance relative to an index will depend critically on which index is chosen. For any sample of observations, an infinite number of ex post mean-variance efficient portfolios (indices) will exist. If betas are calculated using an efficient portfolio, the linearity of the CAPM will be satisfied. If an inefficient index is chosen, *relative* rankings of portfolios will critically depend on which inefficient index is selected. Yet, the indices may be efficient while the market portfolio is inefficient, and vice versa. Roll argues that the only valid test is of the efficiency of the *market portfolio,* the portfolio which includes *all* assets. For practical purposes, this portfolio is only partially observable, leading Roll to comment that such tests may be impossible to accomplish. His critique has suggested great caution in application of the CAPM and has hastened the arrival of alternative pricing models, discussed in the section, *Alternative Asset Valuation Methodologies.*

EMPIRICAL TESTS OF THE CAPM

Despite the theoretical criticisms of the CAPM, the Security Market Line and the associated betas and alphas have been estimated during the past two decades. The general procedure involves obtaining historical (i.e., daily, weekly, or monthly) data for the risk-free rate (usually T-bill or commercial paper rate), the market return (usually calculated from an index such as the S&P 500), and individual security returns. The securities' betas might then be estimated using an equation such as (2.18); commonly the equation is transformed into an excess-returns form by substracting the risk-free rate from both sides of (2.18):

$$\tilde{R}_i - R_f = \beta_i(\tilde{R}_m - R_f) \qquad (4.1)$$

By subtracting R_f, nonstationarity due to a changing risk-free rate is reduced. The linear estimator of Equation (4.1) becomes:

$$(\tilde{R}_i - R_f) = \alpha_i + \beta_i(\tilde{R}_m - R_f) + \tilde{\varepsilon}_i \qquad (4.2)$$

or

$$\tilde{r}_i = \alpha_i + \beta_i \tilde{r}_m + \tilde{\varepsilon}_i \qquad (4.3)$$

where $E(\alpha_i) = 0$ and $E(\tilde{\varepsilon}_i) = 0$.

If the CAPM can be properly tested, the model should reveal the following:

A positive linear relationship between risk and return

Assets with higher systematic risk should earn higher returns

The intercept term should not be significantly different from zero

Unsystematic risk should have no predictive power for asset returns

Despite numerous econometric problems, these tests normally select a different (usually more recent) historical period and collect the same three sets of return data discussed above. The tests then involve regressing the excess (beyond the risk-free rate) return of a security (or, often, portfolio of securities having similar estimated betas) in the more recent period against its beta estimated from the earlier period:

$$\tilde{r}_i = X_0 + X_1 \beta_i + \tilde{\varepsilon}_i \qquad (4.4)$$

Statistical tests are then run to see if $X_0 = 0$ and $X_1 = \tilde{r}_m \equiv \tilde{R}_m - R_f$. Also, other risk measures (i.e., β_i^2, σ_i, σ_{e_i}) are sometimes added to the regression to test if their coefficients are zero.

Early studies (e.g., Jacob [27]) tested individual asset returns, not portfolios. Though the risk and return relationship was found to be positive, the slope of the SML was usually less than anticipated. Individual asset betas appeared unstable and returns showed some effects of unsystematic risk.

Studies (e.g., Black, Jensen, and Scholes [4], Blume and Friend [5], Fama and Macbeth [15], Fouse, Jahnke, and Rosenberg [20], and Levy [38]) employing portfolios of assets with similar betas exhibited more stability. Results indicated that portfolios betas, calculated as the market-value-weighted average of the betas of the underlying assets, explained most of the *future* return of the portfolio. In the paper by Fouse, Jahnke and Rosenberg, the predictive power of portfolio betas was tested for the period 1956-1973. At the beginning of each year, the universe of stocks was divided into ten groups based on beta calculated on the previous 60-months' returns. Each group was like a portfolio of different levels of betas. For the eighteen-year period, the predictive beta performed correctly in eleven years, indifferently in two years, and incorrectly in five years.

The use of portfolio assets, instead of individual assets, reconfirmed some of the early results and added stability to the calculated betas. The results from numerous studies suggest:

> A positive linear relationship between beta and returns does exist; yet the slope is less than the CAPM predicts
>
> Assets with higher systematic risk usually show higher returns[5]
>
> The intercept term is often significantly different from zero
>
> Tests which include the effects of both systematic and unsystematic risk usually reveal that unsystematic risk is unimportant in explaining returns beyond those explained by systematic risk (see Levy [37] for exceptions to this statement).

One nagging question was the use of historic betas to predict future ones. Subsequently, financial advisory services have marketed betas not only based on historical data but adjusted for recent fundamental changes in the economy. Conceptually, these "ex ante" betas were offered to reflect more accurately current *expectations* of asset performance by de-emphasizing long histories and emphasizing current trends. While conclusive evidence is not currently available, these predictive betas appear to offer little improvement over historical betas.

THE MARKET CHARACTERISTICS FOR REAL AND FINANCIAL ASSETS

As noted in the previous sections, valuation models have been rigorously developed for financial assets under some idealized assumptions. Although some of the assumptions are quite robust, other criticisms and empirical results have questioned the validity of the CAPM and its remaining assumptions. Another dimension of the criticism of the application of financial asset valuation techniques to real estate is the differential characteristics of the two asset classes.

Data. The second section of this paper began by reviewing basic measures of asset returns and risk. To calculate historical returns and variation of returns, these measures require asset values and cash flows for all possible holding periods. If markets for assets meet regularly (and in a centralized location), asset values and the associated cash flow data are easily acquired. For financial assets, such as common equity, such data are readily available. For real assets, such as grains and precious metals, organized markets provide continuous market prices from which return and risk measures can be calculated. The real property market, however, is not centralized or standardized. Individual properties trade infrequently and, thus, market prices do not exist for calculating holding period returns. One approach to solving this problem is the use of appraisal data for intervals in which market data do not exist. Use of appraisal data, however, adds an additional source of bias (due to the smoothing nature of the appraisal methodology) and error (due to the subjective nature of the process). Hoag [26] suggests that this may be responsible for the comments that real estate has return characteristics equivalent to common stock, but superior risk properties.[6]

Additionally, the lack of a centralized market for standardized property makes estimates of cash flows for each property difficult. Whereas quarterly dividend information is readily available for the common equity of major firms, monthly (or quarterly) cash flow for real properties is not regularly placed in the public record. Without these data, or "good" surrogates for market values, consistent comparisons of risk and return between two real assets or between a real asset and financial asset on a *pretax* basis are extremely difficult.

The basic models in financial asset valuation are driven by the trade-off between risk and return. To derive these expressions, investors are assumed to be risk averse with preferences over end-of-period wealth. Sufficient restrictions are placed on the utility function and/or the distribution of returns to ensure preferences over risk and return. These assumptions have already been questioned, as noted earlier, but many require further scrutiny before making any application to real estate valuation.

Characteristics. Real estate has two particular attributes which appear to separate it from financial assets or other real assets. First, it is generally believed that separate parcels of real estate are not completely comparable since each has its own innate characteristics (e.g., zoning, view). Second, owner-occupied real estate provides consumption flows as well as investment return.

The first attribute, that of the specific nature of each property, is also an attribute of the common equity for different firms. Each firm's asset base, product line, management, etc., differs from every other firm's, even from those in the same industry. In essence, the return of each firm (and its associated value) is dependent on the *individual* ability of one firm to surpass another in supplying its product or service to the market. But in contrast to the real estate market, the financial asset market has been amenable to mapping individual firm characteristics into a risk-return space. This should suggest a reexamination of the reluctance to seek common bases (e.g., risk-return) in real estate valuation; some of the models in the sixth section of this paper represent movement in this direction.

The second characteristic, that of owner-occupied real estate possessing both consumption and investment value, is a real difference. Corporate common equity ownership provides only investment return. In general, there are no benefits which subsidize an individual's consumption derived from ownership; thus, use of market asset value and cash flow is adequate to calculate pretax return for common equity. Comparable calculations for owner-occupied real estate require not only the market asset values and cash flows, but also a *market value* (i.e., imputed rent) for the consumption derived from the parcel. Not only is it difficult to measure the consumption component of owner occupancy, but problems are exacerbated by the fact that this component is untaxed.

Taxes. The holding period return measures upon which the CAPM computations are based are derived from prices and cash flows after corporate, but before personal, taxes. However, it is generally held in economic theory that investors evaluate returns after all taxes, including personal. Historically, it was felt that the tax effects on stocks and bonds were sufficiently simple that pretax relationships would be reasonable surrogates for the true after-tax relationships.

This blissful state has evaporated over the last few years, beginning perhaps with Miller [45]. If in the capital market there exists one class of securities (e.g., bonds) with a return deductible to the issuer but fully taxable to the recipient and another class (e.g., stocks) neither deductible nor (fully) taxable, then the former should bear a higher market (i.e., before personal tax) return at a given risk level than the latter. This implies, in equilibrium, that there may be multiple SMLs based upon the personal tax treatment of the return of the given security.

Even in the case of a given class of security, the return may be subject to differential tax treatment. In the case of common stock, dividends constitute ordinary income while capital gains are taxed at a preferential rate (to individuals) and only then when realized. This leads to the inference that shares of firms paying large dividends should offer higher market returns (i.e., to compensate for the adverse tax consequences to holders) than otherwise identical firms. One set of studies argues that such a differential exists and reflects a marginal tax rate of about 25% (Litzenberger and Ramaswamy [40]). Another set of studies, relying on dealer arbitrage on ex-dividend days, argues that no such effect exists (Miller and Scholes [46]).

Hence, the impact of taxation on equilibrium pricing relationships is quite unclear at present with respect to financial assets. Real estate assets are not only subject to the ordinary income and capital gain taxes of financial assets, but also to depreciation deductions (and recapture), investment tax credit, and other tax features. Furthermore, real estate assets are often held by foreign nationals, limited partnerships, REITs and other entities with differing tax situations. Thus, the impact of tax effects upon equilibrium pricing of real estate would seem an even bigger muddle than the case of financial assets.

Finally, even the simplest tax implications appear to be violated in the market. Black {3} has argued that tax-exempt investors (e.g., pension funds) should purchase those investments having the least advantageous personal tax treatment (e.g., bonds) so as to earn the tax premium (to which they would not, of course, be subject). Yet the trend of the last few years has been the movement of pension funds into real estate. For such acts to be rational, it must follow: that there are no significant tax advantages to real estate; or that the real estate market offers such high gross returns (e.g., because of inefficiency and segmentation from other markets) as to dominate other investment media even for tax-exempt investors; or real estate offers diversification opportunities not found in any other investment.[7]

Information and Efficiency. Even with market data available, additional information assumptions are usually invoked to permit efficient pricing of assets. Market efficiency (as opposed to portfolio efficiency—the efficient frontier concept) is implied if asset prices reflect *all* available information at any point in time. Fama [14] discusses this concept in varying degrees by segmenting what information is available to whom. He recognizes that "all public information" and "all information" are not equivalent in that some agents may possess superior information or "inside" information about asset returns. If differential information exists, agents may be able to earn returns in excess of the appropriate market risk premium and, thus, refute the presumption of market efficiency.

If informational asymmetries might exist in the financial asset markets (i.e., markets generally believed efficient), it seems quite easy to accept the existence of informational asymmetries in the real estate market. Without the existence of a centralized market and a standardized product, the availability and characteristics of individual assets may become "localized" in nature. Potential buyers and sellers will face a market in which supply and demand parameters are known in only a limited manner. Economists refer to such conditions as markets with limited information or with large information costs (e.g., research costs).

In a competitive economy, agents arise to fill the informational void; that is, they invest time and effort in augmenting their human capital to acquire an informational comparative advantage. Potential investors compensate the agents for the use of their human capital. In an institutional setting, one could say that these agents (e.g., real estate syndicators and brokers) perform an intermediation function in the market. As in any other labor market, the rewards are merely returns to human capital, with superior skills earning higher returns in equilibrium. Though real estate agents are often presumed to earn excess returns, it is well known that excess returns to human capital cannot persist in a market without access restrictions. Additional agents will arise and dissipate any excess returns at the margin. It is more appropriate to view the income as rewards to an agent's human capital investment in a market with large informational disparities.

If the real estate market were inefficient, the increasing presence of agents offering intermediation services may provide the market with one means to move toward efficient pricing. Note, however, that as the informational disparities are reduced, the return for the production of added information is reduced. It is, therefore, likely that a market equilibrium would be reached in which rewards to human capital are sufficient to produce some information, but not sufficient to produce perfect information.

From an economic perspective, it suggests that some real property might be inefficiently priced relative to its price under perfect information; but since perfect information is costly, it will not be produced. If the definition of efficiency is strictly interpreted as price reflecting all available information, and assuming real property agents have calculated the returns to human capital versus information production *optimally,* the presence of less than perfect information in the market does not imply inefficiency, and the market can maintain an equilibrium. In short, if the agent market clears on the information production side, the real estate market can still be efficient.

Divisibility. Another potential barrier to efficient pricing of real estate is the "lumpiness" of real property or the question of divisibility. If a potential investor perceives an asset to be "undervalued," he would purchase the asset in expectation of earning an excess return. To effect this purchase, the asset must be of the "proper" size to fit into the individual's portfolio. It is possible that though the asset is "mispriced," adding the entire asset would unbalance the risk and return characteristics of the investor's portfolio. It is also possible that the required investment exceeds the individual's wealth available for investment. Though a good investment, the indivisibility of the asset may prohibit the investor from adding it to his portfolio.

In general, this does not create a problem for an industrial firm's common equity since an investor can choose to purchase the number of shares which are consistent with his portfolio's risk and return characteristics and which also satisfy his wealth constraint. This observation provides a potential solution to the perceived indivisibility problem in real estate. If assets are mispriced in a market solely because no investor can perform the arbitrage, then one would expect the asset to be syndicated by a group of investors with shares (or a partnership) issued against the real asset. Indeed, this is the observed trend; it, again, suggests that excess profits due solely to market barriers or inherent properties of the asset will be arbitraged away by an investor or a syndicated formation of capital.

Market Portfolio Identification. Satisfying preconditions for the efficient pricing of individual assets does not, however, negate Roll's criticism of testing the CAPM and market efficiency. The methodology relies heavily on an optimized market portfolio or market index. Construction of such indices, and choice among them, is no small task. Further, use of a non-optimized index or portfolio is subject to Roll's criticism of the use of the CAPM as a choice criterion in selecting portfolios.

In theory, the market portfolio is a portfolio of all assets—including stocks, bonds, commodities, real estate, etc. Traditionally, it has been implemented for common stock using market indices, such as the S&P 500, as a surrogate for the market portfolio. This would be sufficient if there were no diversifying aspects to adding other assets to this portfolio. It is generally believed that real estate, for example, provides diversification characteristics not found in common stocks alone. If this is the case, a market portfolio consisting solely of stocks is misspecified. Consequently, if one includes real estate, or any asset, in a CAPM framework, problems with measuring return variance and covariance with the market portfolio must be solved.

ALTERNATIVE ASSET VALUATION METHODOLOGIES

Considering the characteristics of real property and the questions raised about the CAPM methodology, it appears ill advised to pursue real estate with this methodology. The importance of the "optimized" market portfolio only becomes more complicated when real estate is included. Just as the finance literature has reconsidered asset valuation, the real estate literature might also pursue other asset valuation methods which have been presented. Specifically, three alternative approaches are presented, each distinctly different, yet each employing a multifactor (in contrast to the single factor) model.

Arbitrage Pricing Theory (APT). The primary alternative to the CAPM currently being advocated in the finance literature is the arbitrage pricing theory (APT) first proposed by Ross [57]. Similar to the CAPM in its intuitive appeal, the APT assumes that asset returns are generated by a linear factor model. There are not restrictions on the specific form of individual utility functions except general monotonicity and concavity. More importantly, there is no central role for a mean variance efficient market portfolio. The equilibrium condition is merely asset pricing such that no arbitrage profits exist.

The APT, defined in a frictionless and competitive market, assumes individuals possess homogeneous beliefs about asset returns described as a common k-factor generating model:

$$\tilde{r}_i = \chi_i + b_{i1} \tilde{\delta}_1 + \ldots b_{ik} \tilde{\delta}_k + \tilde{\varepsilon}_i \qquad (6.1)$$

$$i = 1, 2, \ldots n$$

where

- $\tilde{r}_i$ = random returns on asset i
- $\tilde{\delta}_k$ = K (common) generating factors
- b_{ik} = individual response coefficients for each of the k factors
- χ_i = expected return on asset i
- $\tilde{\varepsilon}_i$ = random term idiosyncratic to asset i

Whereas the factors $\tilde{\delta}_k$, common to all assets, represent the systematic risk components, the $\tilde{\varepsilon}_i$ factor represents the unsystematic component particular to that asset. The values of the factors are assumed to follow:

$$E(\tilde{\delta}_k) = 0 \quad \text{for all } k$$
$$E(\tilde{\varepsilon}_i \mid \tilde{\delta}_k) = 0 \quad \text{for all } i, k$$

Further, the $\tilde{\varepsilon}_k$'s are assumed to be mutually independent.

Since the underlying presumption of the APT is that no arbitrage profits exist, the equilibrium relationship is found by forming all possible arbitrage portfolios (i.e., portfolios that have a zero net investment and no risk). No arbitrage profits implies that the portfolios' expected returns are zero. The following conditions define the choice of arbitrage portfolios.

i) $\Sigma \alpha_i = 0$ (6.2)

where α_i = proportion of wealth invested in asset i

ii) $\Sigma \alpha_i b_{ik} = 0$ for all k (6.3)

iii) Investment in each asset i is of the order 1/n, where n is the number of assets in the economy.

Condition (i) is the formal statement that the portfolio of assets contains zero net wealth. Condition (ii) insures that the portfolio is formed so there is zero systematic risk; the latter is embodied in the common factors. The last condition suggests that by forming a portfolio of assets, where noise terms are mutually independent and the amount invested in each asset is of order 1/n, unsystematic risk is diversified away (approximately). Thus the three conditions assure that an arbitrage portfolio has been formed. This portfolio return is:

$$\Sigma \alpha_i \chi_i = 0 \quad (6.4)$$

Equations (6.2)-(6.4) imply that an asset's expected return χ_i can be written as:

$$\chi_i = \omega_0 + \omega_1 b_{i1} + \ldots + \omega_k b_{ik} \quad (6.5)$$

where $\omega_0, \omega_1, \ldots \omega_k$ is a set of constant weights.

If a riskless asset with return χ_0 exists, then (6.5) can be written as:

$$\chi_i - \chi_0 = \omega_1 b_{i1} + \ldots + \omega_k b_{ik} \quad (6.6)$$

χ_0 is also the return on all zero beta assets.

Equation (6.6) is the crux of the APT. It is a linear multifactor model of asset returns which does not *require* use of a market portfolio as a factor. But as Roll and Ross [52] point out, the market portfolio is not *necessary* but may well be one of the factors predicting systematic return. Further, if a single-factor model using a market portfolio were a correct specification of asset return, Equation (6.6) would reduce to:

$$\chi_i - \chi_0 = \omega\, b_i \qquad (6.7)$$

Comparing Equation (6.7) and Equation (4.1), the CAPM can be seen as a special case (one-factor model) of the APT. Whether a one-factor or multifactor model is appropriate remains an empirical question. It is clear, however, that a multifactor theoretical specification admits a one-factor model in empirical tests while the converse is not true.

Given the recency of the model, relatively few direct empirical tests of the APT exist, with all of them performed on common stock returns. In a general setting, however, early work by Brennan [6], and more recent work by Gehr [23] testing the APT, and by Rosenberg and Marathe [56] testing an intertemporal CAPM find multiple factors generating asset returns. Langetieg [35] and Lee and Vinso [36] also find evidence of multiple factors present in describing security returns. In another recent test, Reinganum [48] found that a five-factor model fit common stock return data but that, even after such an adjustment, firms with small capitalizations still outperformed large firms; such a result raises questions as to whether the APT is misspecified or the market is informationally inefficient.

A recent direct test, however, is presented in Roll and Ross [52] which also suggests that a five-factor model generates security returns. In their paper, the b_{ik} coefficients in Equation (6.1) are estimated by factor analysis (the coefficients are merely the factor loadings). The coefficients are then employed to estimate the weights in Equation (6.5) using a generalized least squares technique. As noted, the results are consistent with five factors predicting security returns, suggesting not only a theoretical role but also an empirical role for the APT. It maintains the linear simplicity of the CAPM while admitting more than one factor generating returns and eliminating the dependence on an efficient market portfolio. Though the results are preliminary, the methodology appears to overcome *some* of the restrictions of the CAPM. Whether the APT will be of practical value, especially in a real estate setting, remains an open question.

Fundamental Valuation Model (FVM). The second alternative incorporates the "spirit" of the APT while developing a variation potentially useful in property valuation. Similar to models used in common stock evaluation (e.g., see King [31], Rosenberg [54], or Rosenberg and Marathe [55]), the model uses a set of underlying macroeconomic and firm-specific variables to determine the contribution of each factor to asset returns. This approach has been applied most recently by Hoag [26] in a preliminary study of risk and return for commercial real estate; the development below will follow his research.

To construct a measure of a property j's value at time t, define $\tilde{V}_{jt}$:

$$\tilde{V}_{jt} = \tilde{P}_{jt} + \tilde{CF}_{jt} \qquad (6.8)$$

where

$\tilde{P}_{jt}$ = Price of asset j at time t
$\tilde{CF}_{jt}$ = Cash flow from asset j during the period from t − 1 to t

Using this contrast, a multifactor model is then hypothesized to explain the market value of the asset:

$$\tilde{P}_{jt} = \ln(\tilde{V}_{jt}) = \sum_{k=1}^{k} b_{jk}\, \tilde{f}_k + \tilde{s}_j \qquad (6.9)$$

where

b_{jk} = weight for asset i and factor k
$\tilde{f}_k$ = kth factor
$\tilde{s}_j$ = component of specific value for asset j

$$Cov(\tilde{s}_j, \tilde{s}_i) = 0, j \neq i \text{ and}$$
$$Cov(\tilde{s}_j, \tilde{f}_k) = 0$$

Equation (6.9) prescribes a basic link between an individual property value and a set of basic factors which determines prices. It can be estimated cross-sectionally if these factors have the necessary stochastic properties (e.g., the conditions assumed for the factor covariances above). In reality, the conditions are usually violated; thus Equation (6.9) should be transformed and estimated using a generalized least squares method.[8] The coefficients of the factors (b_{jk}) not only provide a description of the valuation process but also suggest an *estimate* of each individual property's value during periods in which the property *does not* trade. In essence, values for non-traded properties are imputed for each holding period from process parameters determined by the traded properties. With these data, both return and risk measures can be estimated using the definition offered in Equations (2.1) and (2.2).[9]

Hoag extends the interpolated valuation data to construct return and risk measures for a market portfolio of real estate. First define the excess return on property j at time t as:

$$\tilde{r}_{jt} = \ln(1 + \tilde{i}_{jt}) - \ln(1 + i_{ft}) \quad (6.10)$$

where

i_{ft} = risk-free rate of interest at time t

and the associated market excess return ($\tilde{r}_{mt}$) as:

$$\tilde{r}_{mt} = \ln(\sum_j W_{jt} \exp(\tilde{r}_{jt})) \quad (6.11)$$

where

$$W_{jt} = P_{jt-1} / \sum_j P_{jt-1}$$

Equation (6.11) is merely a portfolio of real estate returns weighted by their market values. Using Equations (6.9)-(6.11) and adjusting for econometric problems noted earlier, estimates for the market rate of return and variance of return ($E(r_{mt} - E(r_{mt}))^2$) can be obtained. Hoag reports preliminary results constructing an industrial property portfolio (sample index of warehouses) for the ten quarters (quarterly holding period returns) from the third quarter of 1973 to the first quarter of 1976.

	Bonds	Stocks	Industrial Real Estate
Average Quarterly Compound Return	1.4%	.5%	3.0%
Standard Deviation of Quarterly Compound Return	4%	15%	17%

Source: Hoag [26]

Noting that the results are preliminary, Hoag suggests that real estate earned a higher return than stocks and bonds during the period; however, it also exhibited a higher standard deviation of return. Of the approximate 12% annual compound return, about 7% was cash flow return and 5% was price appreciation.

Hedonic Price Model (HPM). The third model, the hedonic price model (HPM), is a formulation which relates the price of a good to the implicit value of the characteristics (or factors) which are embodied in that good. Prevalent in the real estate and urban economics literature, most models of this form are based on the work of Lancaster [34] or Rosen [53].

The Lancaster approach presents consumers who have preferences over a set of product characteristics. Goods in the market possess these characteristics, are indivisible, but heterogeneous. Subject to a budget constraint, consumers choose bundles of goods to maximize the utility of the underlying characteristics. The consumption technology is linear and the hedonic pricing mechanism is linear in attributes.

$$P(\underline{z}) = \underline{p} \bullet \underline{z} \qquad (6.12)$$

where

$\underline{p}$ = vector of imputed prices
$\underline{z}$ = vector of characteristics
$P(\bullet)$ = total price of vector of characteristics

The vector $\underline{p}$ is the set of implicit prices or values the consumer places on the attributes $\underline{z}$. This equation is appealing because of its simplicity and the ability to estimate $\underline{p}$ by regressing the market value of real estate against its underlying attributes (e.g., size, number of bedrooms, etc.). Further, the form permits use of a representative consumer.

Criticism of this approach is often offered on several fronts. The assumption of linearity in the consumption technology may be unrealistic. Four bathrooms may not be worth twice as much as two bathrooms; that is, the marginal value of an attribute may depend on the level of the attribute. Additionally, the Lancaster approach subsumes the analysis of the supply of these characteristics. Without inclusion of the supply response to "valued" characteristics, the concept of equilibrium pricing is elusive.

Rosen's presentation of the hedonic price model results from a more extensive treatment of the market, considering both demand and supply. The consumption technology is unspecified and the hedonic price function is permitted to be nonlinear in attributes.

$$P(\underline{z}) = p(z_1, z_2, \ldots z_n) \qquad (6.13)$$

Equation (6.12) is a more restrictive form of Equation (6.13). Yet with the fewer restrictions in the Rosen model, the possibly nonlinear implicit prices may differ for individual consumers. Consequently, estimation of the model's implicit prices requires more data than estimates for Equation (6.12).

Empirical implications of the hedonic price model are numerous and use a broad category of factors. For example, Dewees [10] employs availability of rapid transit; Maser, Riker, and Rosett [42] investigate zoning effects; and Thaler [65] uses measures of crime control. Studies isolating a more diverse set of characteristics and their effects on market value include Edelstein [12] and Zerbst and Eldred [67].

The studies, in general, demonstrate the potential usefulness of the hedonic price approach; further, the literature recognizes that these implicit prices may differ if there are differences in submarkets. Kain and Quigley [28] and King and Mieszkowski [30] found such differences across submarkets. Later studies by Schnare and Struyk [60], Sonstalie and Portney [62], Straszheim [64], and Dale-Johnson [9] explicitly research the existence of submarkets or market segmentation and find evidence to support the segmentation hypothesis.

Though results of these studies are diverse, they suggest the hedonic price approach permitting market segmentation may provide insight into property valuation. More extensive investigation of the microeconomic foundations of the market supply and demand for characteristics seems warranted.

Summary. Though the models are quite distinct in intent and development, none requires the ex ante construction of a diversified portfolio and all admit the possibility of numerous factors predicting market values or returns. In both the HPM and the FVM, a set of factors or predictors is assumed. The set is then used to estimate weights or responsiveness coefficients for each factor relative to market value measures. In the APT, a common set of factors is assumed to generate all asset returns in the market, but the factors are not identified ex ante. Instead, a methodology similar to factor analysis is employed to isolate factor weights which are used to estimate asset returns. Though the factors are "located" statistically, they are not identified with real-world variables (i.e., the methodology of the APT is aimed at estimating return, not providing an exhaustive list of factors).

Each of the methodologies *assumes* a relationship between either asset values or returns and a set of underlying factors generating these values. The precise form of this generating process will depend on assumptions made about preferences on both the demand and supply side. Criticism can always be offered about such preference restrictions. Yet, often, simplicity of a resultant pricing function may be sacrificed if more general preferences are admitted.[10]

To obtain estimates for any of these models, an extensive data base is required. The non-linear HPM requires a much larger (in number of transactions) data base than the linear version. The FVM requires not only data on market value and cash flow but also a hypothesized set of data specific to each property, and a set of general measures of the economy. By comparison, the APT requires less data since it hypothesizes a common set of unknown factors and uses a statistical technique to isolate (not define ex ante) the factors. Thus, an application of the APT to real estate does not require all the individual property micro-data or the general economy data. Yet all three approaches share a common problem which plagues real estate pricing models. As noted in the fifth section of this paper, real estate does not trade on a regular basis or in a centralized market. Holding periods for real property may differ tremendously from investor to investor. Before asset values and characteristics (or factors) can be associated, a price or value series must be obtained.

In general, the HPM and FVM techniques invoke some level of cross-sectional (possibly serial) stability in the data to permit imputation of value when an actual property does not transact. This is done by assuming the pricing structure is similar across properties and estimating model parameters on the transaction subset for each period; parameters can then be used to impute values for the subset which did not transact. As

Hoag points out this process is similar to the appraisal process but can be accomplished in an objective fashion. For any period, the factor coefficient will estimate a property return. One benefit of such an implementation is the ability to "cross-check" appraisal values in distant markets. As the national real estate market expands, this objective framework will become more valuable.

Movement toward a national real estate market also reinforces the importance of "objectives" valuation for portfolio managers. As more institutional investment funds have moved into real estate, two problems have arisen. First, without the centralized market for real property, it is difficult to value portfolios on a regular basis. Second, without measures of return and risk, it is difficult to measure the risk-adjusted performance of two portfolios or evaluate portfolio managers. The ability to construct return and risk measures by use of fundamental characteristics, or factors, provides some resolution. Using the value series, individual covariances can be computed and real estate *portfolio* return and risk parameters can be calculated. With portfolios composed of stocks, bonds, or other assets, the correlation between portfolios can be computed. If real estate portfolios possess low correlations with portfolios of other assets, the addition of real estate investments will diversify risks contained in those other portfolios. Further, individual portfolio managers will be able to construct portfolios which include real estate and satisfy a desired risk/return profile. From an investor's perspective, the ability to calculate parameters for a diversified real estate portfolio (a real estate index) will provide a benchmark for evaluating the performance of portfolios, or of the portfolio managers, in choosing investments. The capability to assess real estate return and risk is a natural precursor to an integrated real estate market. To the extent that they permit investment on a geographically and economically broader base, market pricing models may find success in valuation.

CONCLUSION

This paper has surveyed the literature of portfolio theory and equilibrium asset pricing as it might relate to real estate analysis and valuation. Analysis has traditionally been considered part of the investment literature in real estate, while valuation has been dealt with by appraisal. This traditional distinction of functions takes on various meaning(s) in a context of different market equilibrium concepts. In particular, if a market is in equilibrium, the price is always "right." An appraiser, accustomed to capitalizing income streams at "appropriate" rates, would find that he would not estimate values which were more accurate in any consistent way than market prices. The analyst might expect to find projects which earned an acceptable return, but he would rarely expect to encounter windfall opportunities. The point which remains, however, is that the interpretation of the notion of the price being "right" (or the market being incapable of being "beaten") will vary with the equilibrium concept assumed.

In the financial economics literature, it has been recognized that tests of equilibrium asset valuation models (i.e., some benchmark of a "normal" return) are simultaneous tests of market efficiency; the problem is often referred to as a test of a joint hypothesis. Efficiency is invariably the first among equals (i.e., the maintained hypothesis in joint tests) such that empirical failures are often attributed to the valuation model employed. In this regard, the empirical discussion of the CAPM in the fourth section of the paper might be viewed as evidence of market inefficiencies rather than CAPM failures.

Interestingly, the opposite tradition has been followed in the HPM real estate literature; fit problems often give rise to claims of segmentation (an inefficiency) rather than model misspecification.

The traditional approach in real estate may be viewed as a rejection of the joint hypothesis. Markets can be observed (generally) to clear, but few assumptions are made about the level of information impounded into (or the long-run stability of) the observed prices. Data might be estimated from historic sources or directly (including simulation techniques as in Phyrr [47] and Findlay, et al. [19]). Analysts might take the circumstances of individual investors and try to pick good investments (perhaps using portfolio models—see Findlay, et al. [17, 18]). Appraisers can estimate value using direct (e.g., residential comparables) or indirect (e.g., capitalization rates) market comparisons. Any notions of efficiency embodied in this traditional approach are thus very simple (i.e., markets clear) and any equilibria imprecise. In the current state of the art, however, this rejection of the joint hypothesis is not unreasonable.

The latter two models in the sixth section of this paper may be viewed as efforts to impose a greater structure of equilibrium upon at least the real estate market (or submarkets). As such, the HPM is not really an income or return model at all, but an effort to price the tastes of consumers. Aside from the problem of whether two bathrooms are worth twice as much as one, it does not describe a valuation process or what might cause this to change. It, and to some extent FVM, will admit to price bubbles, for if everyone is bidding up bathrooms, the model will not signal the potential change in equilibrium or disequilibrium (unless used in conjunction with reproduction cost data). Hence, HPM might be viewed as a market comparison (hopefully, to be used in conjunction with a cost) approach.

The FVM, in this view, would be some hybrid of income and market comparison approaches. Potential difficulties here include stability of values and concepts of equilibrium pricing. Much cruder regressions were performed on share prices (or price-earnings ratios) during the 1960s; though the fit statistics were quite good over the data for which the regressions were estimated, the forecasting power was low (see Keenan [29]). It is also not clear whether the discovery of a "mispriced" property implies market inefficiency or model misspecification.

As a matter of logic, however, these models can only be way stations. As discussed above, an assumption of efficiency or equilibrium, given current methodology, requires the assumption of both. Once it is assumed that the real estate markets meet these requirements, then (absent some unpalatable assumptions of entry barriers) it becomes difficult to explain why a common equilibrium pricing scheme might not exist across several (and in the limit, all) real and financial asset markets. In sum, the partial equilibrium analysis of the real estate market alone can be expected to lead, over time, to an assumption of (general) equilibrium across all asset markets.

In this changing framework, some version of APT will hold virtually by definition, either in a one-factor (e.g., CAPM) or multiple-factor form. If the parameters are initially unknown, some adjustment process will result in parameter estimates converging. If information is costly and imperfect, "optimal" amounts of information will come to be produced over time, and a constrained (i.e., second-best) equilibrium will result. Finally, the introduction of taxes will imply that the same marginal tax rate clears all markets for taxable vs. sheltered vs. exempt income.

As the real estate market becomes fully integrated with the more traditional asset markets, many of the issues raised above would disappear through the joint influence of efficiency and equilibrium pricing. Even in the limiting case, however, at least three issues would remain important:

Taxes—Even if the same rate clears all markets (and would be the rate appraisers should use), only by chance will a given individual (for investment analysis purposes) have that as his marginal rate. Virtually everyone will be either sub- or supramarginal with respect to the market clearing tax rate and hence not indifferent as to whether he shelters his income.

Human Capital—Real estate agents can only expect to earn a normal return at the margin on their human capital in this world. This does not, however, imply that those with special talents cannot expect to earn more on average.

Project Analysis—Even if existing projects are fairly priced and windfalls are siphoned from new project proposals by brokers and promoters, infeasible projects (which, if undertaken, would generate less-than-normal returns) can still exist. These must still be identified and avoided (e.g., one could not expect to earn normal profits by randomly selecting from all deals proposed with no analysis).

Consequently, even in the highly idealized state of fully integrated markets in general equilibrium, these three factors (and possibly others) would still cause real estate to be somewhat "different" and specialized analysis and talent in this area to "matter."

NOTES

1. For the expected return and variance of return to be sufficient statistics in choosing among risky assets, investor's preferences are either quadratic or the return distributions are jointly normal. If the distribution is not symmetric (and the utility function not quadratic) other "shape" parameters (such as skewness measures) must be known for optimal choices among risky assets to be made. For a more extensive discussion of these and the other points in this section see Fama and Miller [16] or Copeland and Weston [8].

2. This methodology has been expanded to handle large sets of projects, all-or-nothing projects, and budget constraints in a real estate context. See Findlay, et al. [18].

3. Note that risk-free or zero variance usually means an asset whose return is fixed in *nominal* returns, not real returns, and which has no default risk.

4. Note from Equation (2.18) that a portfolio may have $\beta_i = 0$ by virtue of $\sigma_i = 0$ or $\rho_{im} = 0$. Black described *the* zero beta portfolio as that having the least variance among all such portfolios which could be formed.

5. Technically, one cannot reject the hypothesis that beta is priced in the market. Recent research (Reinganum [50]) has shown that one also cannot reject the hypothesis that beta is not priced.

6. An extreme example (Friedman [21]) involved simply interpolating prices for a given property. For a more detailed discussion, see Findlay, et al. {17].

7. Absent inefficiency or segmentation, it would be expected that means would be found to resell any tax benefits which might exist in the last case.

8. If the valuation process is stationary, a pooled cross-section regression also can be run.

9. The logarithm of individual property return is merely $\ln(1 + i_{jt}) = \ln(V_{jt} | P_{jt-1})$.

10. Recall the discussion which described the Lancastrian linear HPM and the Rosen nonlinear HPM. Linear relationships often have more popular appeal but at the cost of restrictions on the choice space.

REFERENCES

[1] Ray Ball, "Anomalies in Relationships Between Securities' Yields and Yield-Surrogates," *Journal of Financial Economics* 6 (June/September 1978) pp. 103-26.

[2] Fisher Black, "Capital Market Equilibrium with Restricted Borrowing," *Journal of Business* 45 (July 1972), pp. 444-455.

[3] ———, "The Investment Policy Spectrum: Individuals, Endowment Funds, and Pension Funds," *Financial Analysts Journal* 32 (January-February 1976), pp. 23-31.

[4] Fisher Black, Michael Jensen and Myron Scholes, "The Capital Asset Pricing Model," "Some Empirical Tests," in: M. C. Jensen, ed., *Studies in the Theory of Capital Markets* (New York, NY: Praeger 1972), pp. 79-121.

[5] Marshall Blume and Irwin Friend, "A New Look at the Capital Asset Pricing Model," *The Journal of Finance* 28 (March 1973), pp. 19-33.

[6] Michael Brennan, "Capital Asset Pricing and the Structure of Security Returns," Unpublished manuscript, University of British Columbia (May 1971).

[7] David Cass and Joseph Stiglitz, "The Structure of Investor Preference and Asset Returns, and Separability in Portfolio Allocation: A Contribution to the Pure Theory of Mutual Funds," *Journal of Economic Theory* 2 (June 1970), pp. 122-160.

[8] Thomas Copeland and J. Fred Weston, *Financial Theory and Corporate Policy*, (Reading, MA: Addison-Wesley Publishing Company, 1979).

[9] David Dale-Johnson, "An Alternative Approach to Housing Market Segmentation Using Hedonic Price Data," *Journal of Urban Economics* (May 1982).

[10] D. N. Dewees, "The Effect of a Subway on Residential Property Values in Toronto," *Journal of Urban Economics* (October 1976), pp. 357-369.

[11] Matthew Edel and Elliot Sclar, "Taxes, Spending and Property Values: Supply Adjustment in a Tiebout-Oates Model," *Journal of Political Economy* 82:5 (September/October 1974), pp. 941-954.

[12] Robert Edelstein, "The Determinants of Value in the Philadelphia Housing Market: A Case Study of the Main Line 1967-69," *The Review of Economics and Statistics* LVI:3 (August 1974), pp. 319-328.

[13] John Evans and Stephen Archer, "Diversification and the Reduction of Dispersion: An Empirical Analysis," *Journal of Finance* (December 1968), pp. 761-69.

[14] Eugene Fama, "Efficient Capital Markets: A Review of Theory and Empirical Work," *Journal of Finance* 25 (May 1970), pp. 383-417.

[15] Eugene Fama and James MacBeth, "Risk, Return, and Equilibrium: Empirical Tests," *Journal of Political Economy* 38 (May 1973), pp. 607-36.

[16] Eugene Fama and Merton Miller, *The Theory of Finance* (New York: Holt, Rinehart and Winston, 1972).

[17] M. Chapman Findlay, Carl Hamilton, Stephen Messner, and Jonathan Yormark, "Optimal Real Estate Portfolios," *AREUEA Journal* 7:3 (Fall 1979), pp. 298-317.

[18] M. Chapman Findlay, Richard McBride, Jonathan Yormark, and Stephen Messner, "Mean-Variance Analysis for Indivisible Assets," *Omega* 9:1 (February 1981), pp. 77-88.

[19] M. Chapman Findlay, Stephen Messner, and Rocky Tarantello, *An FMRR Simulation Model* (Storrs, CT: CREUES, University of Connecticut, 1980).

[20] William Fouse, William Jahnke, and Barr Rosenberg, "Is Beta Phlogiston," *The Financial Analysts Journal* (January/February 1974), pp. 70-80.

[21] Harris Friedman, "Real Estate Investment and Portfolio Theory," *Journal of Financial and Quantitative Analysis* 6:2 (March 1971), pp. 861-74.

[22] George Gau and Daniel Kohlhepp, "Estimation of Equity Yield Rates Based on Capital Market Returns," *Real Estate Appraiser and Analyst* 44:6 (November-December 1978), pp. 33-39.

[23] Adam Gehr, Jr., "Some Tests of the Arbitrage Pricing Theory," *Journal of the Midwest Finance Association* (1975), pp. 91-105.

[24] Nils Hakansson, "Capital Growth and the Mean-Variance Approach to Portfolio Selection," *Journal of Financial and Quantitative Analysis* 6 (January 1971), pp. 517-557.

[25] James Hoag, "A New Real Estate Return Index: Measurement of Risk and Return," *Proceedings of the Seminar on the Analysis of Security Prices*, 24:1, University of Chicago, May 1979, pp. 223-259.

[26] ———, "Towards Indices of Real Estate Value and Return," *Journal of Finance* 35:2 (May 1980), pp. 569-580.

[27] Nancy Jacob, "The Measurement of Systematic Risk for Securities and Portfolios: Some Empirical Results," *Journal of Financial and Quantitative Analysis* 6 (March 1971), pp. 815-834.

[28] John Kain and John Quigley, "Measuring the Value of Housing Quality," *Journal of the American Statistical Association* 65:330 (June 1970), pp. 532-548.

[29] Michael Keenan, "Models of Equity Valuation: The Great SERM Bubble," *Journal of Finance* (May 1970), pp. 243-273.

[30] A. Thomas King and Peter Mieszkowski, "Racial Discrimination, Segregation, and the Price of Housing," *Journal of Political Economy* 81:3 (May/June 1973), pp. 590-606.

[31] Benjamin King, "Market and Industry Factors in Stock Price Behavior," *Journal of Business* 39 (January 1966, supp.), pp. 139-90.

[32] Alan Kraus and Robert Litzenberger, "Skewness Preference and the Valuation of Risk Assets," *Journal of Finance* 31 (September 1976), pp. 1085-1100.

[33] Kelvin Lancaster, *Consumer Demand: A New Approach* (New York: Columbia Press, 1971).

[34] ———, "A New Approach to Consumer Theory," *Journal of Political Economy* 74:2 (March/April 1966), pp. 132-157.

[35] Terence Langetieg, "An Application of a Three-Factor Performance Index to Measure Stockholder Gains from Merger," *Journal of Financial Economics* 6 (December 1979), pp. 365-383.

[36] Cheng Lee and Joseph Vinso, "Single vs. Simultaneous Equation Models in Capital Asset Pricing: The Role of Firm-Related Variables," *Journal of Business Research* (1980), pp. 65-80.

[37] Haim Levy, "The CAPM and Beta in an Imperfect Market," *The Journal of Portfolio Management* 6:2 (Winter 1980), pp. 5-11.

[38] Robert Levy, "On the Short Term Stationarity of Beta Coefficients," *Financial Analysts Journal* 27 (November/December 1971), pp. 55-62.

[39] John Lintner, "The Aggregation of Investor's Diverse Judgements and Preferences in Purely Competitive Markets," *Journal of Financial and Quantitative Analysis* 4 (December 1969), pp. 347-400.

[40] Robert Litzenberger and Krishna Ramaswamy, "The Effects of Personal Taxes and Dividends on Capital Asset Prices: Theory and Market Equilibrium," *Journal of Financial Economics* 7:2 (June 1979), pp. 163-195.

[41] Harry Markowitz, *Portfolio Selection: Efficient Diversification of Investments* (New York: John Wiley, 1959).

[42] Steven Maser, William Riker, and Richard Rosett, "The Effects of Zoning and Externalities on the Price of Land: An Empirical Analysis of Monroe County, New York," *The Journal of Law and Ecomonics* 20:1 (April 1977), pp. 111-132.

[43] Robert Merton, "An Inter-Temporal Capital Asset Pricing Model," *Econometrica* 41:5 (September 1973), pp. 867-87.

[44] Mike Miles and Michael Rice, "Toward a More Complete Investigation of the Correlation of Real Estate Investment Yield to the Rate Evidenced in the Money and Capital Markets: The Individual Investor's Perspective," *Real Estate Appraiser and Analyst* 44:6 (November-December 1978), pp. 8-19.

[45] Merton Miller, "Debt and Taxes," *Journal of Finance* 32 (May 1977), p.261-75.

[46] Merton Miller and Myron Scholes, "Dividends and Taxes: Some Empirical Evidence," CRISP WP55 (University of Chicago, 1981).

[47] Stephen Phyrr, "A Computer Simulation Model to Measure the Risk in Real Estate Investment," *Real Estate Appraiser* 39:1 (January-February 1973), pp. 13-31.

[48] Marc Reinganum, "The Arbitrage Pricing Theory: Some Empirical Results," *Journal of Finance* 36:2 (May 1981), pp. 313-321.

[49] ———, "Misspecification of Capital Asset Pricing: Empirical Anomalies Based on Earnings, Yields and Forecasts," *Journal of Financial Economics* 9:1 (March 1981), pp. 19-46.

[50] ———, "A New Empirical Perspective on the CAPM," *Journal of Financial and Quantitative Analysis* 16:4 (November 1981), pp. 439-462.

[51] Richard Roll, "A Critique of the Asset Pricing Theory's Tests," *Journal of Financial Economics* 4 (May 1977), pp. 129-76.

[52] Richard Roll and Stephen Ross, "An Empirical Investigation of the Arbitrage Pricing Theory," *The Journal of Finance* 35:5 (December 1980), pp. 1073-1103.

[53] Sherwin Rosen, "Hedonic Prices and Implicit Markets: Product Differentiation in Pure Competition," *Journal of Political Economy* 81:1 (January/February 1974), pp. 32-55.

[54] Barr Rosenberg, "Extra Market Components of Covariance in Security Returns," *Journal of Financial and Quantitative Analysis* 9 (March 1974), pp. 263-274.

[55] Barr Rosenberg and Vinay Marathe, "Common Factors in Security Returns: Microeconomic Determinants and Macroeconomic Correlates," *Proceedings of the Seminar on the Analysis of Security Prices*, University of Chicago, May 1976.

[56] ———, "Tests of Capital Asset Pricing Hypothesis," Unpublished manuscript, University of California, Berkeley, (1977).

[57] Stephen Ross, "The Arbitrage Theory of Capital Asset Pricing," *Journal of Economic Theory* 13 (December 1976), pp. 341-60.

[58] ———, "The Current Status of the Capital Asset Pricing Model (CAPM)," *Journal of Finance* 33 (June 1978), pp. 885-900.

[59] ———, "Risk, Return, and Arbitrage," in Irwin Friend and James L. Bicksler, eds., *Risk and Return in Finance*, I (Cambridge, MA: Ballinger, 1977), pp. 189-218.

[60] Ann Schnare and Raymond Struyk, "Segmentation in Urban Housing Markets," *Journal of Urban Economics* 3:2 (April 1976), pp. 146-166.

[61] Willima Sharpe, *Portfolio Theory and Capital Markets* (New York, NY: McGraw-Hill, 1970), pp. 117-140.

[62] Jon Sonatelie and Paul Portney, "Gross Rents and Market Values: Testing the Implications of Tiebout's Hypothesis," *Journal of Urban Economics* 7:1 (January 1980), pp. 102-118.

[63] Mahlon Straszheim, *An Econometric Analysis of the Urban Housing Market*, (New York: NBER, 1975).

[64] ———, "Hedonic Estimation of Housing Prices: A Further Comment," *The Review of Economics and Statistics* 56:3 (August 1974), pp. 404-406.

[65] Richard Thaler, "A Note on the Value of Crime Control: Evidence From the Property Market," *Journal of Urban Economics* 5 (January 1978), pp. 137-145.

[66] Larry Wofford and Edward Moses, "Relationship Between Capital Markets and Real Estate Investment Yields: The Theory and Application," *Real Estate Appraiser and Analyst* 44:6 (November-December 1978), pp. 51-61.

[67] Robert Zerbst and Gary Eldred, "Improving Multiple Regression Valuation Models Using Location and Housing Quality Variables," *Assessors' Journal* 12:1 (March 1977), pp. 1-15.

21 Public Information and Abnormal Returns in Real Estate Investment

George W. Gau

This study performs empirical tests of the semistrong form efficiency of a real estate investment market. An asset pricing model is utilized to estimate the abnormal returns resulting from two types of public information, major changes in government tax shelter and rent control policies as well as unanticipated changes in interest rates. In both cases the results find an absence of significant abnormal returns and no evidence to suggest that real estate investors can utilize information concerning government policy changes or interest rate movements to earn higher returns on a risk-adjusted basis. In general the findings of this study conform to the semistrong form version of the efficient markets hypothesis.

INTRODUCTION

The objective of this study is to test the applicability to real estate investment markets of the semistrong form of the efficient markets hypothesis. Under this version of the hypothesis, it is argued that prices in an efficient market quickly capitalize publicly available information affecting the value of market assets [5]. Investors in such a market cannot earn abnormal returns on a risk-adjusted basis by trading on the basis of this public information. If real estate investment markets exhibit semistrong form efficiency, real estate investors cannot utilize such information to consistently earn higher returns than received by other investors in assets having equivalent risk levels.

In an earlier study of real estate market efficiency by the author [8], weak form versions of efficient market tests were applied to a time series of asset prices of income-producing properties located in a Canadian real estate market. These empirical tests evaluated whether past price information can be employed to predict the future prices of real estate assets. The results of these tests indicated support for a random walk-fair game model as a representation of price behavior in real estate markets.

The apartment return series analyzed in the weak form tests also are utilized in this study to examine the capitalization of public information in real estate investment mar-

From *AREUEA Journal*, Vol. 13, No. 1 (1985). This research received financial support from the Institute for Quantitative Research in Finance. Preliminary data collection and analysis was supported by grants from the Real Estate Council of British Columbia and the Real Estate Education and Research Fund Committee. The paper benefited from the comments of Jeff Fisher and the assistance of Judy Fountain.

kets. These series are based on apartment transactions in the City of Vancouver, British Columbia for the period of January 1971 through December 1980. Monthly series of continuously-compounded returns are derived for a "unit" of homogenous apartment investment, with "unit" scaled in terms of sales price per square foot (LR1), sales price per dollar of gross income (LR2) and sales price per suite (LR3).[1] Background information on the formation of these three return series as well as summary statistics describing the distributional properties of the apartment measures can be found in the earlier study.

To test the semistrong form of the efficient markets hypothesis, it is first necessary to define an abnormal return based on an asset pricing model for real estate investments. The next section of this paper explores the controversy surrounding the choice of an appropriate asset pricing model and the empirical procedures used in this study to derive such a model for real estate assets. Based on the results in the second section, the third section calculates the estimates of abnormal returns in the apartment series. Section four then examines the size and significance of any abnormal returns resulting from two types of public information, unanticipated changes in interest rates and major changes in two government policies affecting real estate investment, specifically the tax sheltering of income and rent controls. The final section contains concluding remarks.

ASSET PRICING FRAMEWORK

In most of the past studies of the semistrong form efficiency of security markets, a version of the capital asset pricing model (CAPM) has been applied to the estimation of abnormal returns.[2] This model relates the expected returns on an asset to the expected returns on a market portfolio.[3] The pricing framework generally is presented in the form of either a one-factor market model

$$R_i = \alpha_i + \beta_i R_m + e_i \qquad (1)$$

or a two-factor model

$$R_i - R_f = \beta_i (R_m - R_f) + e_i \qquad (2)$$

where R_i = expected return on asset i, R_m = expected return on the market portfolio, and R_f = rate of return on a risk-free asset. Articles in the real estate literature also have suggested that the CAPM might be an appropriate pricing model for real estate assets.[4]

However, recent articles in both the financial and real estate areas have questioned the applicability of the CAPM to both financial and real assets. As an example, Roll [17] argues that there are severe limitations on the testability of this model caused by the problem of identifying the market portfolio. Draper and Findlay [4] cite a number of reasons why the CAPM may not be applicable to real estate markets including the differentiating characteristics of real estate assets and the failure of the model to incorporate tax shelter benefits into the pricing framework.[5]

An alternative asset pricing model that has been formulated by Ross [19] is arbitrage pricing theory (APT). In this pricing framework asset returns are generated by a set of k-multiple factors which are common to all investment assets.

$$\tilde{r}_i = R_i + b_{i1}\tilde{\delta}_1 + \ldots + b_{ik}\tilde{\delta}_k = \tilde{\varepsilon}_i \qquad (3)$$

where:

$\tilde{r}_i$ = (random) return on asset i;
$\tilde{\delta}_k$ = a common factor that influences the returns on all assets;
b_{ik} = relationship of asset i's return to movements in the common factor $\tilde{\delta}_k$.
$\tilde{\varepsilon}_i$ = an idiosyncratic (unsystematic) effect on asset i's return.

The underlying argument of the APT is that in equilibrium no arbitrage profits can exist. Therefore, the return on a zero-investment, zero-systematic-risk portfolio is zero, assuming that the idiosyncratic effects are diversified away in a large portfolio. This argument implies that the expected return on any asset i can be expressed as:

$$R_i = \lambda_o + \lambda_1 b_{i1} = \ldots \lambda_k b_{ik} \qquad (4)$$

The term λ_o is the expected return on an asset with $b_1 = b_2 = \ldots = b_k = 0$; in other words, an asset, with no systematic risk. The weights $\lambda_1 \ldots \lambda_k$ can be viewed as factor risk premia with the b_i's showing the pricing relationship between the risk premia and the asset.

There are two primary differences between the APT and CAPM frameworks. First, the APT allows for more than one or two factors to be important in the return-generating process. Such a broader approach may be quite useful in an asset pricing model for real estate since it has been suggested that there are other factors beyond the market portfolio (e.g., tax shelter benefits) which may be significant in the pricing of real estate assets. Second, the assumptions required with the APT model are not as demanding. Unlike the CAPM, there is no requirement that the market portfolio be mean-variance efficient. The basic condition necessary for deriving the APT model is that there is an absence of riskless arbitrage profits in the market.

In Gehr [10], Roll and Ross [18], and Kryzanowski and To [12], factor analytical techniques are employed to estimate from stock return data the number of significant common factors and the b coefficients in the form of the factor loadings on the observed factors. The Roll and Ross study finds that at least three, and possibly four, common factors are present in the expected returns of stocks traded on the New York and American Exchanges. Also, this study notes that the market portfolio may be one of the observed factors determining asset returns.

The first question that must be empirically addressed in this study is how many common factors are present in the return-generating process for real estate assets. Following the procedure described in Reinganum [15], a sample of properties is randomly divided into thirty portfolio returns. A variance-covariance matrix is estimated and a factor analysis is then performed on this matrix. The real estate sample analyzed in this stage of the research consists of 251 Vancouver apartment buildings. The properties are selected because information is available concerning their sales transactions and annual gross income during the 1971-80 period as well as important property descriptors (age, square footage of building, number of suites, location). Similar to the approach taken by Hoag [11], valuation functions are estimated for each year and annual return measures (LR1, LR2, LR3) are calculated for each property in the sample. The estimated valuation functions are displayed in the Appendix.[6]

The eigenvalues found in a factor analysis of the thirty portfolio return series are presented in Table 1. As shown in this table a substantial portion of the variance in the real estate returns is accounted for by the first factor. This result is similar to the find-

Table 1 Factor Eigenvalues

		LR1	
Factor	Eigenvalue	Percent of Variance	Cumulative Percentage
1	26.080	86.9	86.9
2	1.983	6.6	93.5
3	.910	3.0	96.6
4	.497	1.7	98.2
5	.338	1.1	99.4
6	.097	0.3	99.7

		LR2	
Factor	Eigenvalue	Percent of Variance	Cumulative Percentage
1	26.030	86.8	86.8
2	2.306	7.7	94.5
3	.872	2.9	97.4
4	.427	1.4	98.8
5	.205	0.7	99.5
6	.099	0.3	99.8

		LR3	
Factor	Eigenvalue	Percent of Variance	Cumulative Percentage
1	25.672	85.6	85.6
2	2.258	7.5	93.1
3	1.010	3.4	96.5
4	.568	1.9	98.4
5	.257	0.9	99.2
6	.113	0.4	99.6

ings in Kryzanowski and To [12] where a large percentage of the sample variance of security returns was associated with one factor. Such a result offers empirical support for the proposition that a simple one-factor structure adequately describes the underlying return-generating process of real estate returns. While the identity of the economic force making up this factor cannot be ascertained from the empirical analysis, one definite possibility is that this factor is the market portfolio. If true, a one or two-factor CAPM could be the correct pricing model for real estate assets.

However, further examination of the eigenvalues also indicates additional factors explain small portions of the return variance. A standard selection criterion often employed in applied factor analysis is that all factors with eigenvalues greater than one are considered significant (see Rummel [20]). In Table 1 one or two additional factors beyond the first factor have eigenvalues satisfying this selection criterion. On this basis a three-factor APT model could be appropriate for the pricing of real estate assets.

In summary, the results found in the factor analysis of the property returns can be interpreted as empirically supporting either the CAPM or APT frameworks for the pricing of real estate assets. It is not clear how many factors are important in the return-generating process for real estate. Both pricing models, therefore, are considered in the next section in the derivation of the abnormal returns in the apartment series.

ABNORMAL RETURNS

The abnormal returns of an asset can be defined as the residual investment returns in a period after subtracting the returns earned on other assets of equivalent risk. To measure the residual returns observed in the apartment series, it is necessary to derive the risk-adjusted returns based on the asset pricing models.

Market Model. Under the market (CAPM) model, the risk-adjusted returns are determined by the relationship of the real estate returns to the returns on a market portfolio. Equations (1) and (2) can be utilized to estimate the parameters of the one-factor or two-factor market model. These parameters would then be entered into the following equations to measure the abnormal returns (ABR) present in an apartment price series i in month t.

$$ABR_{it} = R_{it} - (\alpha_i + \beta_i R_{mt}) \tag{5}$$

$$ABR_{it} = (R_{it} - R_{ft}) - \beta_i (R_{mt} - R_{ft}) \tag{6}$$

In the absence of a broader market index, the model parameters are estimated with the monthly return on the Toronto Stock Exchange (TSE) index as the proxy for the market portfolio.[7] The risk-free rate is represented by the monthly rate for short-term Canadian Treasury bills.

The resulting regression equations for each of the three apartment return series find very weak relationships between the real estate and TSE returns. As an example, the estimated equations for the log returns of price per square foot series are

$$LR1 = -.082 + .013 \, LR_m \quad R^2 = .001 \tag{7}$$
$$(.385) \quad (.054)$$

$$(LR1 - LR_f) = .006 \, (LR_m - LR_f) \quad R^2 = .001 \tag{8}$$
$$(.020)$$

In all the estimations little of the variation of the real estate returns is explained by the market return. The β coefficients are not significantly different from zero, indicating that the risk inherent in the apartment returns is essentially unsystematic with respect to the returns on the market portfolio.

These findings are similar to the results reported in Robichek, Cohn and Pringle [16] for assets such as commodity futures and farm real estate as well as in a recent study of stamp auctions by Taylor [23]. All of these studies found no evidence supporting a relationship between the alternative investment returns and market returns represented by a stock market index.

The results in this research (along with those reported in the above studies) are at least partially a reflection of weaknesses in using a stock market index as a proxy for the market portfolio. A more comprehensive index that directly included real estate assets (if available) may show a stronger relationship between the apartment returns and the market. Further, any measurement errors in the real estate returns create noise in the monthly series and contribute to a lower correlation with the TSE index. Yet, in the absence of accurate empirical evidence concerning the true relationship of the market portfolio to real estate assets, the market model can be utilized for estimating abnormal returns. In this study the residual analysis is therefore limited to the abnormal returns derived from the APT model.

APT Model. The three-factor APT model observed in the factor analysis is utilized to identify real estate assets of equivalent risk. The basic idea is to establish risk classes within the apartment sample from the variation of the asset's values across the three factors. The time series of apartment returns is then assigned to one of the risk classes. Any differences between the returns in the risk class and the apartment return series are considered to be abnormal returns.

The statistical methodology employed to form the risk classes is cluster analysis. This multivariate technique groups observations into a small number of mutually exclusive categories based on the similarity of the observation's values as measured through a distance function. Factor scores across the three factor dimensions are first calculated for the apartment return series and the returns of the 251 buildings in the Vancouver sample. These factor scores are utilized in the grouping of the properties into risk classes through the cluster analysis routine. The cluster containing assets with scores most similar to the apartment series is the equivalent risk class based on the APT model.

To determine the optimal number of clusters, the real estate assets are grouped at the three through nine cluster levels, applying the Euclidian distance between the properties and the minimization of Wilks' lambda ($\Lambda = |W|/|T|$) as criteria for cluster formation. Friedman and Rubin [7] recommend that changes in the ln($|T|/|W|$) be employed as an indicator of the optimality of the grouping structure at each cluster level. According to their guideline, a large change in the indicator when moving from a lower to a higher cluster level followed by a smaller change in moving to the next level would point to a high degree of structure at the previous level. As shown in Table 2, this criterion indicates that a seven-cluster level is the optimal group structure for the LR1 measure, while the six-cluster grouping is appropriate for LR2 and LR3.

Seven and six-group cluster analyses are performed on the data and the clusters containing the equivalent risk class are identified. The mean each month of the asset returns in the cluster ($\bar{R}_{it}$) is calculated and the abnormal returns are estimated in the form:[8]

$$ABR_{it} = R_{it} - \bar{R}_{it} \qquad (9)$$

Since the properties in the selected cluster have similar factor scores as the apartment return series, the mean cluster returns in a period are the returns earned on assets of equivalent risk given the three-factor APT model. Any residual returns in the apartment series would thus represent risk-adjusted abnormal returns.

EFFICIENCY TESTS

The abnormal returns resulting from the two types of public information are evaluated in this study. The first type of event is a change in government policies affecting real estate investment. Prior to 1972 in Canada there were no restrictions on the amount of income tax losses from property investment that could be applied to the sheltering of non-real estate income. In June 1971 the Canadian federal government announced that effective January 1, 1972 tax regulations were changed to severely restrict tax sheltering; specifically, capital cost allowances (depreciation) from a real estate investment could not be used to shelter from taxation income from other sources. Other minor tax revisions were also enacted at that time which further reduced the tax shelter benefits of Canadian real estate investment.[9] These changes in government taxation policies ad-

Table 2 Cluster Optimality Indicator

LR1		
Number of Clusters	Indicator Value	Change
3	.879	.183
4	1.062	.165
5	1.227	.168
6	1.395	.209
7	1.604	.055
8	1.659	.107
9	1.766	

LR2		
Number of Clusters	Indicator Value	Change
3	.782	.242
4	1.024	.134
5	1.158	.198
6	1.356	.103
7	1.459	.137
8	1.596	.113
9	1.709	

LR3		
Number of Clusters	Indicator Value	Change
3	.947	.143
4	1.090	.156
5	1.246	.208
6	1.454	.130
7	1.584	.117
8	1.701	.107
9	1.808	

versely affected the returns from real estate investment and, in an efficient real estate market, would be capitalized into the market value of real estate assets.

The introduction of rent controls is another government policy change that would be expected to be capitalized into the values of controlled apartment buildings. In May 1974, the Province of British Columbia announced legislation establishing controls over the percentage rent increases allowed for most apartment units.[10] These rent restrictions were substantially below market rates and significantly reduced the expected future rental income of Vancouver apartment properties. Similar to the tax revision, rent controls would be expected to adversely impact on the market values of these assets.[11]

The second type of public information considered in this study is unanticipated changes in mortgage interest rates. Given the importance of financial leverage to real estate investment, movements of mortgage rates should be reflected in the market values of apartment investments. In this case the specific events tested are unanticipated changes from one month to the next of Canadian interest rates that are greater than the .5% level during the period of 1971–80.[12] There are a number of monthly rate changes larger than .5% during this period; however, to avoid the mixing of favorable and unfavorable information and to isolate the impact of a specific interest rate change from others, this study only considers unanticipated rate decreases where no change of .5% or more occurred three months prior to and three months after the event. There are three interest rate changes during the 1971–80 period that meet this selection criterion.

The abnormal returns in the form of average residuals (AR) and cumulative average residuals (CAR) for one to five months before (t = −1,…,−5) and one to twelve months after (t = +1,…,+12) the two government policy changes are presented in Table 3. These results are the residuals based on the APT model. The residuals are adjusted for lags created in the apartment return series by the real estate transaction period. In a real estate transaction there is commonly a one to two month period from the establishment of a transaction price by the parties at the time the interim agreement is signed and the transfer of ownership at the closing or sales date. Since the apartment returns are estimated from sales dates, they actually reflect the information capitalized approximately two months earlier. Therefore, in the calculation of abnormal returns, the real estate returns series are shifted back two months to coincide with the actual price setting.

The average residuals indicate that adverse changes in government policies have an immediate impact on the market prices of apartment investments. The ARs in the announcement month (t = 0) are in the range of −.09 to −.11 depending on the return measure. From t = +1 to t = +12 the residuals are generally positive, causing higher CARs twelve months after the announcement month. There is no evidence in the pattern of the residuals of any delay in the market capitalizing the effect on investment returns of these government policy changes.

The large negative ARs in t = −1 suggest substantial capitalization of this information in the month prior to the announcement of the new policy.[13] An anticipation period preceding the announcements is quite possible for both changes in government policies.

Table 3 Government Policy Residuals
APT Model

t		LR1 AR	LR1 CAR	LR2 AR	LR2 CAR	LR3 AR	LR3 CAR
−	5	−.197		−.240		−.190	
−	4	−.018	−.215	.081	−.159	−.135	−.325
−	3	.040	−.175	.002	−.157	.047	−.278
−	2	.112	−.063	.044	−.113	.150	−.128
−	1	−.153	−.216	−.197	−.310	−.133	−.261
	0	−.109	−.325	−.107	−.417	−.089	−.350
+	1	.159	−.166	.203	−.214	.174	−.176
+	2	−.052	−.218	−.011	−.225	.068	−.108
+	3	.288	.070	.089	−.136	.093	−.015
+	4	−.278	−.208	.043	.093	−.214	−.229
+	5	.030	−.178	−.208	−.301	.024	−.205
+	6	−.002	−.180	.020	−.281	.019	−.186
+	7	.028	−.152	−.016	−.297	−.041	−.227
+	8	.015	−.137	.031	−.266	.055	−.172
+	9	.062	−.075	.085	−.181	.020	−.152
+	10	.029	−.046	−.061	−.242	.010	−.142
+	11	.009	−.037	.047	−.195	.022	−.120
+	12	−.117	−.154	−.071	−.266	.089	−.031

In 1969 the Canadian federal government published a report which advocated many of the tax revisions adopted in 1971. Also, the socialist party which formed the provincial government in British Columbia in 1974 had as a party platform the introduction of rent controls. Similar to investors in other capital markets, real estate investors may react to the expected contents of a pending budget of a majority government under a parliamentary system in anticipation of the likely announcement of the legislation.

To test the statistical significance of the abnormal returns, the ARs are standardized by dividing them by estimates of their standard deviations from the distribution of ARs during the months $t = +13$ to $t = +36$. The study then applies t-tests to determine if any of the average standardized residuals are significantly different from zero. In all months in both tables the resulting t-statistics are not large enough to reject the null hypothesis at the .05 level. This result supports the proposition that public information in the form of government policy changes does not create significant abnormal returns for real estate investors.

Table 4 presents the ARs and CARs for unanticipated changes in interest rates. The criterion for event selection limits the residual analysis in this case to the announcement month and two months after the event. Similar to the government policy results, the ARs are not significantly different from zero and the capitalization of this public information seems to take place at the time of announcement. No significant positive abnormal returns are found as a result of a large unanticipated decline in mortgage interest rates.

CONCLUSIONS AND CAVEATS

This study has performed empirical tests of the semistrong form efficiency of a real estate investment market with respect to two types of public information. In both cases the results find an absence of significant abnormal returns surrounding these events and no evidence to suggest that real estate investors can utilize information concerning government policy changes or interest rate movements to earn higher returns on a risk-adjusted basis. In general the findings of this study conform to the semistrong form version of the efficient markets hypothesis.

The importance given to these findings should be tempered by data problems inherent in this research. The issue of the appropriate pricing model for real estate assets has not been resolved in this study. The results of the factor analysis of real estate returns offered support for both the CAPM and APT frameworks. The absence of a comprehensive market index, however, restricted the weight that could be given to the market model parameters estimated from the data and did not allow the market model to be used in the estimation of the abnormal returns. Finally, the apartment return series analyzed in these efficiency tests are plagued by measurement problems in the forma-

Table 4 Interest Rate Residuals

	\multicolumn{6}{c}{APT Model}
	LR1		LR2		LR3	
t	AR	CAR	AR	CAR	AR	CAR
0	.009		.051		.111	
+1	−.007	.002	.023	.074	−.137	−.026
+2	.078	.080	.012	.086	.193	.167

tion of a time series of the prices of a real estate asset. While the present series are the best available data for performing such tests, any conclusions based on these series must be viewed as only preliminary, awaiting additional support or refutation with improved real estate data.

APPENDIX

Valuation Functions

1971: LP = 4.622 + .405LINC − .005AGE + .564LFAR − .329LFAS
(1.277)°° (.113)°° (.002)°° (.123)°° (.172)
+ .295LOC1 + .279LOC2 + .359LOC3 + .288LOC4
(.203) (.192) (.188) (.192)
R^2 = .971   SE = .127   F = 109.9°°   N = 35

1972: LP = 1.041 + .885LINC − .002AGE + .052LFAR − .220LFAS
(1.459) (.199)°° (.001) (.204) (.200)
+ .253LOC1 + .271LOC2 + .211LOC3 + .289LOC4
(.131) (.142) (.126) (.122)°
R^2 = .947   SE = .185   F = 67.6°°   N = 39

1973: LP = 3.649 + .590LINC − .006AGE + .335LFAR − .084LFAS
(1.147)°° (.156)°° (.002)°° (.149)° (.124)
+ .153LOC1 + .307LOC2 + .143LOC3 + .032LOC4
(.133) (.135)° (.146) (.110)
R^2 = .909   SE = .213   F = 54.7°°   N = 56

1974: LP = .826 + .859LINC − .008AGE − .003LFAR + .464LFAS
(2.542) (.291)°° (.004)° (.287) (.229)°
+ .095LOC1 + .005LOC2 − .097LOC3 − .153LOC4
(.315) (.327) (.279) (.262)
R^2 = .806   SE = .340   F = 12.4°°   N = 33

1975: LP = 2.934 + .832LINC − .005AGE − .003LFAR + .158LFAS
(.852)°° (.132)°° (.001)°° (.130) (.100)
+ .134LOC1 + .287LOC2 + .063LOC3 + .076LOC4 − .029LOC5
(.076) (.117)° (.100) (.085) (.147)
R^2 = .964   SE = .131   F = 71.8°°   N = 34

1976: LP = 3.582 + .670LINC − .003AGE + .224LFAR − .014LFAS
(.981)°° (.142)°° (.001)°° (.146) (.120)
+ .118LOC1 + .183LOC2 + .132LOC3 − .012LOC4
(.103) (.155) (.126) (.114)
R^2 = .961   SE = .148   F = 85.8°°   N = 37

1977: LP = 3.018 + .913LINC − .004AGE − .047LFAR + .095LFAS
(.997)°° (.121)°° (.001)°° (.113) (.112)
+ .005LOC1 − .015LOC2 − .013LOC3 − .161LOC4
(.080) (.088) (.077) (.083)
R^2 = .962   SE = .136   F = 111.5°°   N = 44

1978: LP = 3.416 + .737LINC − .004AGE + .180LFAR − .023LFAS
(.567)°° (.077)°° (.001)°° (.080)° (.073)
+ .044LOC1 + .086LOC2 + .121LOC3 − .034LOC4 + .213LOC5
(.041) (.048) (.043)°° (.039) (.121)
R^2 = .965   SE = .117   F = 278.4°°   N = 102

1979: LP = 7.359   + .378LINC   − .005AGE   + .463LFAR   − .410LFAS
       (.698)°°   (.051)°°   (.001)°°   (.058)°   (.091)°°
     + .181LOC1   + .182LOC2   + .090LOC3   − .020LOC4   + .312LOC5
       (.072)°°   (.085)°   (.078)   (.067)   (.159)°
     R² = .912   SE = .212   F = 136.3°°   N = 132

1980: LP = 2.642   + .900LINC   − .006AGE   − .043LFAR   + .200LFAS
       (.658)°°   (.063)°°   (.001)°°   (.063)   (.086)°
     + .023LOC1   − .008LOC2   − .016LOC3   − .142LOC4   + .244LOC5
       (.075)   (.097)   (.078)   (.068)°   (.183)
     R² = .943   SE = .174   F = 136.3°°   N = 84

Standard errors of estimate in parentheses
°   significant at .05 level
°°   significant at .01 level
LP   = natural log of sales price.
LINC = natural log of annual gross income of property.
AGE   = age of structure in years.
LFAR = natural log of gross floor area of structure.
LFAS = natural log of average floor area per suite.
LOC1, ..., LOC5 = dummy variable for location within Vancouver.

NOTES

1. It should be noted that these return measures are in terms of changes in scaled prices of the apartment investment units and do not include monthly operating flows in the return calculation. The quantities of operating expense information available from the data source are not sufficient to enable the net operating income (before-financing, before-tax cash flow) to enter into the formation of the return series.

2. Recent examples of semistrong form efficiency tests of financial markets which utilized the CAPM to derive abnormal returns are Charest [3], Brown [2], and Bjerring, Lakonishok and Vermaelen [1].

3. The seminal articles regarding the CAPM are Sharpe [21] and Lintner [13].

4. See Gau and Kohlhepp [9] and Miles and Rice [14].

5. Fisher [6] derives an after-tax CAPM that recognizes in the pricing framework the potential tax shelter benefits in real estate investment.

6. These yearly valuation functions are able to explain a substantial portion of the variation in the sales prices of Vancouver apartment buildings. Each of the explanatory variables has a statistically significant coefficient in at least one of the regressions, with the property's gross income clearly being the most important determinant of value. The age of the building (acting partially as a proxy for operating expenses) has the correct sign and is significant in all but one of the functions. The only variables creating statistical problems in the estimations are the gross floor area and the average floor area per suite where collinearity causes sign reversals and higher standard errors for these variables in the regression.

7. Miles and Rice [14] discuss the creation of a broader market index that includes not only common stock returns, but also returns on real property and human capital. The lack of time series data in Canada on the values of these assets prohibited the formation of such an index in this study and its application as a proxy for the market portfolio.

8. To estimate the monthly returns of the cluster assets, the yearly valuation functions presented in the Appendix are re-estimated with the addition of monthly dummies as explanatory variables. The monthly values of these properties are then derived from the regression results and the monthly return measures are calculated for each property.

9. Prior to 1972, the capital cost allowance (CCA) schedules of different assets could be pooled, allowing investors selling properties to substitute subsequent acquisitions in the CCA pool of the disposed property and thereby postponing the recapture and taxation of previous CCA claims. The pooling of assets having values greater than $50,000 was disallowed starting in January, 1972.

10. The only exemptions to rent controls were: 1) new residential premises constructed after January 1, 1974, for their first five years of occupancy; and, 2) units with rents greater than $400 per month. Non-controlled properties are excluded from both the formation of the apartment time series and the sample utilized to estimate the valuation functions and the APT residuals.

11. Smith and Tomlinson [22] argue that rent controls would be expected to significantly lower the value of rental apartment dwellings.

12. Unanticipated interest rate changes are defined to be movements of mortgage rates greater than the difference in market yields between Canadian Treasury bills maturing at the beginning and the end of a month.

13. If the transaction period for these properties was around one month rather than two months as assumed in the shifting of the return series, the ARs in t = 1 would then be the residuals in the announcement month. Yet, from market observation, the transaction period for apartment buildings is generally longer than one month.

REFERENCES

[1] J. H. Bjerring, J. Lakonishok, T. Vermaelen. Stock Prices and Financial Analysts' Recommendations. *Journal of Finance* 38: 187-204, March 1983.

[2] S. L. Brown. Earnings Changes, Stock Prices, and Market Efficiency. *Journal of Finance* 33: 17-28, March 1978.

[3] G. Charest. Split Information, Stock Returns and Market Efficiency. *Journal of Financial Economics* 6: 265-330, June/September 1978.

[4] D. W. Draper and M. C. Findlay. Capital Asset Pricing and Real Estate Valuation. *American Real Estate and Urban Economics Association Journal* 10: 152-183, Summer 1982.

[5] E. F. Fama. Efficient Capital Markets: A Review of Theory and Empirical Work. *Journal of Finance* 25: 383-417, May 1970.

[6] J. D. Fisher. Taxation and Real Estate Valuation. In C. F. Sirmans, editor, *Research in Real Estate*. JAI Press, 1982.

[7] H. P. Friedman and J. Rubin. On Some Invariant Criteria for Grouping Data. *Journal of the American Statistical Association* 62: 1159-1178, December 1967.

[8] G. W. Gau. Weak Form Tests of the Efficiency of Real Estate Investment Markets. *Financial Review* 19: 301-320, November 1984.

[9] G. W. Gau and D. B. Kohlhepp. The Estimation of Equity Yield Rates Based on Capital Market Returns. *Real Estate Appraiser and Analyst* 44: 33-39, November 1978.

[10] A. Gehr, Jr. Some Tests of the Arbitrage Pricing Theory. *Journal of the Midwest Finance Association* 5: 95-105, 1975.

[11] J. Hoag. Toward Indices of Real Estate Value and Return. *Journal of Finance* 35: 569-580, May 1980.

[12] L. Kryzanowski and M. C. To. General Factor Models and the Structure of Security Returns. *Journal of Financial and Quantitative Analysis* 18: 31-52, March 1983.

[13] J. Lintner. The Valuation of Risky Assets and the Selection of Risky Investments in Stock Portfolios and Capital Budgets. *Review of Economics and Statistics* 47: 13-67, February 1965.

[14] M. Miles and M. Rice. Toward a More Complete Investigation of the Correlation of Real Estate Investment Yield to the Rate Evidenced in Money and Capital Markets: An Individual Investor's Perspective. *Real Estate Appraiser and Analyst* 44: 8-19, November, 1978.

[15] M. R. Reinganum. The Arbitrage Pricing Theory: Some Empirical Results. *Journal of Finance* 36: 313-321, May 1981.

[16] A. A. Robichek, R. A. Cohn, J. J. Pringle. Returns on Alternative Investment Media and Implications for Portfolio Construction. *Journal of Business* 45: 427-443, July 1972.

[17] R. Roll. A Critique of the Asset Pricing Theory's Tests. *Journal of Financial Economics* 4: 129-176, June 1977.

[18] R. Roll and S. A. Ross. An Empirical Investigation of the Arbitrage Pricing Theory. *Journal of Finance* 35: 1073-1103, December 1980.

[19] S. A. Ross. The Arbitrage Theory of Capital Asset Pricing. *Journal of Economic Theory* 13: 341-360, 1976.

[20] R. J. Rummel. *Applied Factor Analysis.* Northwestern University Press, 1970.

[21] W. Sharpe. Capital Asset Prices: A Theory of Market Equilibrium Under Conditions of Risk. *Journal of Finance* 19: 425-442, September 1964.

[22] L. Smith and P. Tomlinson. Rent Controls in Ontario: Roofs or Ceilings. *American Real Estate and Urban Economics Association Journal* 9: 93-114, Summer 1981.

[23] W. M. Taylor. The Estimation of Quality-Adjusted Rates of Return in Stamp Auctions. *Journal of Finance* 38: 1095-1110, September 1983.

22 Capital Structure and the Cost of Capital for Untaxed Firms: The Case of REITs

Brian A. Maris and Fayez A. Elayan

> REITs offer the opportunity to examine the relationship between capital structure and cost of capital in the absence of corporate earnings taxes. The evidence supports the leverage clientele effect as the motivation for the use of financial leverage by REITs.

INTRODUCTION

The relationship between capital structure and the cost of capital is a major unresolved issue in finance. Real estate investment trusts, or REITs, provide a unique opportunity to examine this relationship in the absence of corporate taxes because qualifying REITs are exempt from corporate earnings taxes. This study presents a cross-sectional analysis to determine which factors influence the capital structure choice of a REIT and what effect debt financing has on a REIT's cost of capital.

The 1958 and 1963 articles by Modigliani and Miller [11, 12] focused the discussion of capital structure on the tax benefits and other costs of debt. As M&M showed in 1958, with perfect capital markets and in the absence of tax effects, there is no advantage to debt. Other factors, including the existence of personal taxes and bankruptcy costs, in fact create a disadvantage of debt. However, businesses used debt before the existence of corporate earnings taxes in the US, and most REITs, which are untaxed, now use debt financing. Bradley, Jarrell and Kim [4, p. 570, Table 1] report the mean value of the book value of long-term debt divided by the sum of the book value of long-term debt plus the market value of equity for twenty-five industries. The values for 1962–81 range from a low of 0.09 for Drugs and Cosmetics to a high of 0.58 for Airlines. By comparison, the mean value of the same measure of leverage for the REITs in the sample used in this study was 0.31. REITs are more highly leveraged than sixteen of the twenty-five industries considered by Bradley, Jarrell and Kim.

From *AREUEA Journal*, Vol. 18, No. 1 (1990). The authors wish to express their appreciation for financial support of this project provided by the Louisiana State University Real Estate Research Institute. This is a much revised version of a paper presented at the 1987 AREUEA meeting. This article has benefited substantially from suggestions by Patric H. Hendershott, George W. Gau, and an anonymous referee. The authors bear full responsibility for any shortcomings.

Furthermore, Howe and Shilling [6] report positive stock price responses to announcements of debt offerings by REITs. This implies advantages to the use of debt that are not related to taxes. The existence of agency costs and the financial leverage clientele effect are possible explanations. These factors are discussed below.

MODEL

According to Modigliani and Miller's Proposition I, with perfect capital markets and no corporate or personal income taxes, financial leverage has no effect on the value of a firm or its cost of capital. The value of the firm is totally dependent upon assets and the expected value and risk of the cash flow generated by those assets. Because the value of the firm is total earnings divided by the weighted average cost of capital, the weighted average cost of capital is likewise unaffected by financing.[1]

Once corporate earnings taxes are introduced, the tax shield provided by debt results in a gain from leverage:

$$V^L = V^U + t_c B \qquad (1)$$

The value of the leveraged firm, V^L, is equal to the value of the unleveraged firm, V^U, plus the tax shield from debt, which is the tax rate on corporate earnings, t_c, times the market value of bonds issued by the leveraged firm. This leads to M&M's 1963 conclusion that under conditions of perfect capital markets, no personal income taxes, and zero bankruptcy costs, the taxed firm should use 100% debt financing. Under these conditions the advantage of debt financing derives entirely from the tax shield associated with debt.

The introduction of personal taxes into the model was provided by Miller [10]. If the tax rates on income from stocks and bonds are equal, the advantage from leverage is zero, and the value of the firm is independent of the method of financing. Such a result is consistent with M&M Proposition I. However, if the tax rate on income from stock is lower than the tax rate on income from debt, which may be the actual case, leverage will affect the value of the untaxed firm negatively. Also, if bankruptcy costs are nontrivial, their introduction creates a negative impact of debt financing on the value of the firm. Therefore, the use of debt financing by nontaxed firms at best has no effect on the value of the firm and may have a negative impact on the firm's value.

As mentioned above, agency costs and clientele effects can explain the use of debt financing in the absence of tax advantages.[2] Jensen and Meckling [7] argue that if a firm uses external financing, there is an optimal ratio of debt-to-external equity that minimizes total agency costs. Because all REITs require external financing, it may be desirable for REITs to obtain some of that financing in the form of debt. Also, there will be one optimal capital structure for REITs that are otherwise similar.

The agency theory implications for capital structure have been extended by Titman [22], Myers and Majluf [16] and Titman and Wessels [24]. Titman includes the nature of the firm's product: if the bankruptcy of a firm will impose high maintenance costs on its customers (for example, an automobile manufacturer), the firm should use relatively little debt. "Conversely, firms (such as hotels and retail establishments) which impose relatively low costs on their customers and business associates in the event that they liquidate choose high debt/equity ratios" [22, p. 150]. Quite clearly, REITs fall into the latter category, and other things equal, the nature of their product would encourage the use of debt by REITs. Myers and Majluf show that if one is willing to assume that management acts in the interests of passive, current stockholders, the fact insiders have more and better information than outsiders causes corporations to "prefer debt to equity if external financing is required" [16, p. 189].

Titman and Wessels point out that the model of Myers and Majluf implies that "firms with assets that can be used as collateral may be expected to issue more debt to take advantage of this opportunity."[3] [24, p. 3.] Again, the nature of REIT assets is well suited for secured borrowing. However, given the tax shelter benefits of real estate investment, the effective tax rate on REIT equity returns is less than the tax rate on mortgage interest. This should discourage debt financing by equity REITs relative to mortgage REITs. It must be recognized, however, that equity REITs may have acquired debt as the result of mortgage assumptions rather than as the result of capital structure decisions. If assumed mortgages are at below-market rates, they may be retained for that reason.[4]

Kim et al. [9, p. 88] concluded that "investors in high tax brackets will prefer to hold shares of unlevered firms, while investors in low tax brackets will prefer to hold shares of levered firms." The result is that shareholder-wealth maximizing firms specialize "their capital structures in one or the other extreme" [9, p. 91] by being either completely unlevered or highly levered. Thus, while agency cost considerations and the leverage clientele effect both encourage the use of debt financing, these two factors have different implications for the pattern of debt financing that would exist in the industry. If agency costs are the more important consideration, there should be uniformity of capital structures within the industry. If the leverage clientele effect is dominant, the use of debt by firms will be bimodal, with few firms in the middle.

According to the 1985 REIT Fact Book, untaxed investors are attracted to REITs, suggesting a clientele favoring leveraged REITs. "Many tax exempt institutions—such as pension funds, profit sharing plans, endowment funds, IRA and Keogh accounts and charitable and religious organizations—realize income through REITs that is undiminished by federal income taxes at both the corporate and (investor) levels ... Many tax-exempt investors also benefit from an IRS ruling that distributions received from REITs with leveraged portfolios are not subject to taxation as unrelated income." [17, p. 11.] Restrictions against self-leveraging placed on many non-taxed investors, such as pension funds and IRAs, tends to reinforce the leverage clientele effect by creating a class of investors that wish to substitute corporate leverage for self-leverage. Because various REITs may seek different investor clienteles, some might opt for little or no debt financing while others choose to become highly leveraged.

Other firm characteristics that have been identified as important to a firm's capital structure decision are firm size and the growth rate and volatility of earnings. Ang, Chua and McConnell [1] and Warner [26] present evidence that bankruptcy costs are relatively higher for smaller firms and their leverage should be lower. On the other hand, the cost of issuing equity is inversely related to firm size [19]; thus smaller firms may favor more leverage than larger firms. Several studies have identified higher expected growth and volatility of earnings as factors that should lead firms to choose less long-term indebtedness.[5]

Equation (2) shows leverage as a linear function of the identified determinants and represents the first relationship to be estimated empirically:

$$LEV_i = B0 - B1 Growth - B2 STD + B3 Size - B4 MTG + e2, \qquad (2)$$

where the sign of each coefficient reflects the expected sign of the relationship. In the empirical section, the results of estimating this relationship for three measures of leverage are reported. *Growth* and *STD* are the average annual percentage growth rate and the standard deviation of the annual percentage growth rate of net cash flow, calculated as net income plus interest expense plus depreciation charges.[6] Size is measured as the log of total assets. *MTG* is the percentage of income from mortgages, and $e2$ is the residual for equation (2). Details on the data are provided in the next section.

The second relationship to be estimated empirically is shown in equation (3):

$$ACC = B5 + B6iLevi - B7Size + B8MTG + B9TBR - B10Growth + B11STD + e3, \qquad (3)$$

where *ACC* represents the average cost of capital and is defined as (new cash flow)/(market value of equity plus debt). Leverage is expected to increase the cost of capital in the absence of tax benefits. The relationship shown in equation (3) is estimated for three measures of leverage, defined in Table 1 as *LEV1*, *LEV2* and *LEV3*. Size is expected to have a negative sign if larger REITs have better access to capital markets or if there are other economies of scale in obtaining external financing. *MTG* is included as a proxy for the percentage of REIT assets held in the form of mortgages and was used because it was possible to get annual data for mortgage revenues for the entire sample, but it was not possible to get annual data on the composition of assets. Titman and Warga [23] found the systematic risk of mortgage REITs to be higher than that of equity REITs; thus *MTG* is expected to have a positive coefficient. *TBR* is the Treasury bill rate and is included to reflect changes in the risk-free rate. To the extent that the growth rate of cash flows corresponds to expected future growth, it should increase the market value of the shares and reduce the calculated cost of capital. The standard deviation of the growth rate of cash flows is a proxy for business risk and is expected to have a positive coefficient. The empirical results for equations (2) and (3) follow the next section, which describes the data.

DATA DESCRIPTION

The data for this study were collected from Moody's *Bank and Finance Manual,* Standard and Poor's *Stock Reports* and *Standard Corporation Descriptions* and the *Value Line Investment Survey.* The sample for this study includes all sixty-one qualified REITs for which data were available for any year during the period 1981 to 1987. (A list of the sixty-one firms, along with several characteristics of each, for the most recent year data were available, is provided in the Appendix.) A total of 310 observations were included in the analysis, an average of just over five years of data for each firm out of a possible seven years. Because data are less available in published sources for smaller REITs, the sample is weighted towards larger REITs. According to the 1985 *REIT Fact Book,* average total assets for all REITs as of year-end 1984 was $76 million, while average total assets for the sample in this study was $182 million. Variables included in the analysis and their descriptive statistics are in Table 1. Table 2 presents descriptive statistics for high- and low-debt REITs. The mean value of *LEV3* for the high-debt firms is more than four times the mean value for the low-debt firms. The market value of equity is surprisingly close for the two groups, but average total assets for the high leverage group is more than three times the average total assets for the low leverage firms.

Table 1 Descriptive Statistics of the Model Variables

Variable	N	Mean	Standard Deviation	Minimum Value	Maximum Value
ACC	310	9.72%	6.19%	−13.90%	86.07%
LEV1	310	1.16	1.96	0.00	19.11
LEV2	310	0.42	0.26	0.00	1.31
LEV3	310	0.36	0.26	0.00	1.00
Total Assets°	310	182.6	344.2	1.5	3,294.0
Debt°	310	98.9	227.3	0.00	2,166.0
MVEQ°	310	100.3	90.5	5.00	731.5
MTG	310	0.34	0.36	0.00	1.00
GROWTH	309	32.2%	100.5%	−141.2%	920.0%
STD	295	59.1%	129.6%	0.4%	1,132.0%
TBR	310	8.75%	2.29%	6.32%	13.40%

Variable Definitions

ACC = (Net Cash Flow)/(Debt + Market Value of Equity)
Net Cash Flow = Net Income + Interest Expense + Depreciation
LEV1 = Debt/(Market Value of Equity)
LEV2 = Debt/(Total Assets)
LEV3 = Debt/(Debt + Market Value of Equity)
Total Assets = Book Value of Total Assets
Debt = Book Value of Long-Term + Short-Term Debt
Market Value of EQ = (High + Low Share Price for Year) (#Shares)/2
MTG = (Mortgage Income)/(Total Income)
GROWTH = Average Annual % Change in Cash Flow
STD = Standard Deviation of Annual Change in Cash Flow
TBR = Treasury Bill Rate

°in millions of dollars

While theory dictates that the market value of debt and equity should be used to estimate the capital structure and the cost of capital, as a practical matter the market value of debt is unavailable for the majority of REITs because their debt is not traded. As a result, the book value of debt is used in this study. That may not be as serious a shortcoming as it appears, however. Baskin [2] and Bowman [3] both found that the correlation between the book value of debt and its market value is quite high, and, as pointed out by Titman and Wessels [24, p. 7], there is no reason to suspect that the cross-sectional differences between market values and book values of debt are correlated with any of the determinants of capital structure suggested by theory, so no obvious bias is introduced by using the book values as proxies for the theoretically correct market values. Similarly, while theory calls for expected values of earnings growth and volatility, actual values must be used as proxies.

In the preceding section, agency theory and the leverage clientele effect were offered as explanations of the use of debt by untaxed firms. If agency costs are the dominant consideration, leverage is optimized where agency costs are minimized. Firms that are otherwise similar should adopt similar leverage ratios. On the other hand, the leverage clientele effect is based on the concept that firms will specialize their capital structure to appeal to different investor clienteles, resulting in a bimodal distribution of capital structures. Figure 1 represents the distribution of capital structures of REITs as measured by LEV3, and as shown there, the distribution is bimodal.[7] There is no tendency for REITs to adopt similar capital structures. This may

Table 2 Descriptive Statistics of Model Variables for High-Debt and Low-Debt REITs. Variables are defined in Table 1.

Variable	N	Mean	Standard Deviation	Minimum Value	Maximum Value
		HIGH DEBT REITS			
ACC	142	10.09%	7.61%	13.90%	86.07%
LEV1	142	2.29	2.45	0.58	19.11
LEV2	142	0.64	0.16	0.13	1.31
LEV3	142	0.61	0.14	0.37	0.95
Total Assets	142	300.9	479.3	1.4	3,294.0
Debt	142	190.8	311.0	6.5	2,166.0
MVEQ	142	99.9	109.8	6.7	731.5
MTG	142	0.37	0.41	0.00	1.00
GROWTH	142	36.5%	135.9%	141.2%	920.0%
STD	124	65.5%	108.2%	3.6%	1,432.0%
		LOW DEBT REITS			
ACC	168	9.40%	4.65%	0.33%	41.74%
LEV1	168	0.20	0.16	0.00	0.56
LEV2	168	0.23	0.17	0.00	0.68
LEV3	168	0.15	0.11	0.00	0.36
Total Assets	168	82.6	57.8	4.80	366.0
Debt	168	21.2	25.7	0.00	193.2
MVEQ	168	100.9	70.6	5.00	389.6
MTG	168	0.30	0.32	0.00	1.00
GROWTH	167	28.52%	55.05%	52.50%	289.2%
STD	162	53.94%	80.95%	0.40%	457.8%

be interpreted as an indication that the leverage clientele effect has an important influence on the capital structure of REITs.

EMPIRICAL RESULTS

Determinants of Capital Structure. The first step in the analysis was to estimate the relationship between the three measures of leverage and other firm characteristics that have been identified as important determinants of firm leverage. These determinants include the nature of the firm's assets, firm size, and the growth and volatility of earnings. The model shown above in equation (2) was estimated for each of the three leverage measures. For each variable, the value entered in the regression is the value from each year for the period from 1981–1987. The time-series data from the sixty-one REITs were pooled to form the data set. As a result, it is probable that the error terms in the regressions are not independent, either across firms or over time. Furthermore, the number of time-series observations per firm is too small to allow for estimation of the autocorrelation coefficient for each firm. Because of this, the error components model, as described in Judge et al. [8, pp. 479–87], was used to estimate the model.

When time-series data from several firms are pooled, the intercept term can be characterized as

$$B_{0i} = \bar{B}_0 + u_i \qquad (4)$$

Figure 1 Frequency Bar Chart For Leverage (*LEV3*)
LEV3 = (Total Debt)/(Total Debt + Market Value of Equity)

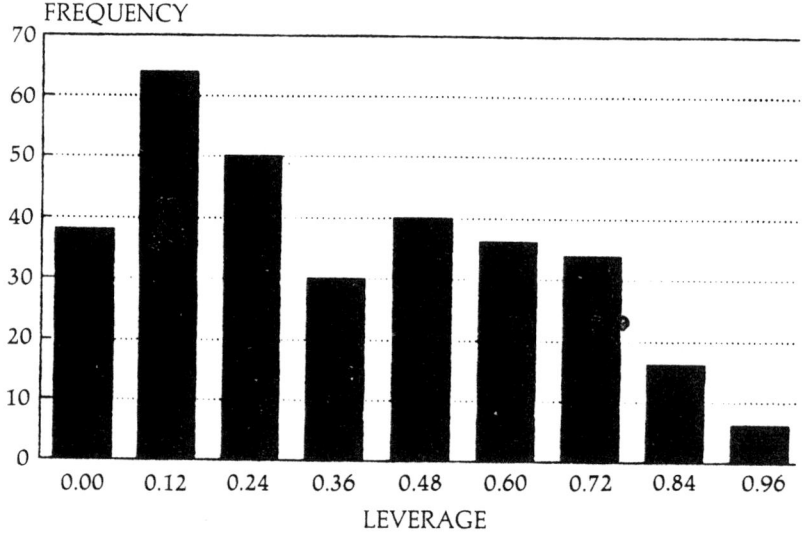

where $\bar{B}_0$ is the mean value of the intercept, u_i represents interfirm differences in the intercept and $i = 1 \ldots N$ firms. If the u_i terms are not estimated along with B, the resulting ordinary least squares estimates of the coefficients will be unbiased but inefficient if $u_i \neq 0$. To estimate the u_i vector, one alternative is to use firm dummy variables, in which case the u_i are treated as fixed parameters to be estimated. Another approach is to use error components, in which case the u_i are treated as a random sample from a larger population. The error components model is appropriate if one is interested in inferences about the larger population, rather than individual firms. As the number of time periods, T, approaches infinity for fixed N the two methods yield identical estimates. However, if N is large and T small (as is true in this study), the use of firm dummies is not asymptotically efficient. With the error components model, the population parameters can be characterized as independent random variables, rather than fixed coefficients.

If $u_i = 0$ the least squares estimator is best linear unbiased [8, p. 486]. This can be tested by using the dummy variable estimator and the F-test based on the restricted and unrestricted residual sums of squares.

Results of estimating equation (2) for each of the three leverage measures are presented in Table 3. At the top of Table 3 are the estimates for the entire sample (combining both equity and mortgage REITs). As shown there, the only coefficient that is statistically significant for all three leverage measures is the log of total assets, and the sign is positive as expected. Only one other coefficient is statistically significant (at the 10% level) in the combined results, that of *MTG* when regressed on *LEV*2. It, too, has the expected sign (negative).

To determine whether the use of leverage differs between equity and mortgage REITs, the sample was divided into those REITs that earned less than or more than 50% of revenue from mortgages. For equity REITs, *LEV*3 averaged 0.346, while for mortgage REITs, *LEV*3 averaged 0.408. The means test was used to determine whether the

Table 3 Dependent Variable is Leverage. Estimated With Error Components. Variables are defined in Table 1.*

Dep. Var.	Intercept	GROWTH	STD	Log of TOTAL ASSETS	MTG	Adj. R2
		EQUITY AND MORTGAGE REITS COMBINED				
LEV1	−1.5079	0.4950	0.1689	0.6445[a]	0.2914	0.244
	(−4.421)	(1.503)	(0.654)	(6.137)	(0.901)	
LEV2	0.0300	0.0425	−0.0283	0.0854[a]	−0.0906[b]	0.116
	(0.785)	(0.897)	(−0.763)	(6.085)	(−1.982)	
LEV3	−0.0619[a]	−0.0060	0.0101	0.1053[a]	−0.0100	0.176
	(−1.993)	(−0.125)	(0.267)	(7.954)	(−0.220)	
		EQUITY REITS ONLY				
LEV1	−0.6052[a]	−0.7451[a]	0.7852[a]	0.4492[a]	−3.0743[a]	0.190
	(−2.291)	(−2.568)	(2.450)	(5.628)	(−3.902)	
LEV2	0.1575[a]	−0.0597	0.0029	0.0533[a]	−0.7112[a]	0.111
	(3.589)	(−0.965)	(0.042)	(3.367)	(−4.523)	
LEV3	0.0040	0.1375[a]	0.1666[a]	0.0774[a]	0.4376[a]	0.157
	(0.115)	(−2.229)	(2.449)	(5.287)	(−3.019)	
		MORTGAGE REITS ONLY				
LEV1	−6.1444[a]	1.8894	−0.9464[b]	1.2905[a]	4.7104[a]	0.401
	(−3.647)	(2.720)	(−1.803)	(4.472)	(2.298)	
LEV2	−0.4399[a]	0.1625[a]	−0.1312[a]	0.1870[a]	0.3357[a]	0.510
	(−3.945)	(2.773)	(−2.958)	(8.262)	(2.059)	
LEV3	−0.3592[a]	0.1433[a]	−0.1178[a]	0.1857[a]	0.2292[b]	0.451
	(−3.478)	(2.107)	(−2.285)	(7.626)	(1.701)	

*Numbers in parentheses below coefficients are *t*-statistics.
[a]statistically significant at the 5% level
[b]statistically significant at the 10% level

difference is statistically significant, resulting in a Z statistic value of 1.75 indicating the difference is significant at the 10% level, but not at the 5% level. Equation (2) was estimated separately for equity and mortgage REITs. The Chow test was performed to determine if the results for the two groups are different. The F-value was statistically different from zero at the 5% level for all three measures of leverage, indicating that the hypothesis of no difference between the two groups must be rejected. Results of estimating equation (2) for the two groups separately are also reported in Table 3.

For equity REITs all of the variables are statistically significant at the 5% level for the equations with *LEV1* and *LEV3* as the dependent variable. For the equations with *LEV2* as the dependent variable, two of the four independent variables yielded significant coefficients. The growth variable is negative, as expected, in all three regressions, and significant at the 5% level in two. The standard deviation of the growth rate of cash flows is also significant in two of the three regressions, but the sign is positive, rather than negative, as expected. The size variable is positive and statistically significant, just as for the combined results, indicating that large REITs tend to be more heavily leveraged than smaller REITs. The coefficient for the percent of earnings resulting from mortgages (*MTG*) is negative, as expected, and significant at the 5% level for all three.

For equity REITs, leverage is negatively related to the growth rate and the percentage of earnings derived from mortgages and positively related to size and the volatility of cash flows.

In estimating equation (2) for mortgage REITs, all three leverage measures provided statistically significant coefficients (at the 10% or better level) for all four independent variables. The most interesting aspect of the results is that except for the size variable, the signs of all other coefficients are reversed from those for equity REITs. For mortgage REITs, leverage is negatively related to the volatility of cash flows (as predicted), but the growth rate of cash flows provides positive coefficients, as does the percentage of revenue from mortgages. The authors cannot explain why the signs of the coefficients for three of the four independent variables are reversed for equity and mortgage REITs, other than to suggest the obvious, that it is somehow related to the nature of the assets. Even that seems inadequate to explain why the percent of revenue from mortgage assets would result in a negative coefficient for equity REITs and a positive coefficient for mortgage REITs.

Cost of Capital. To estimate the weighted average cost of capital for REITs, the relationship shown in equation (3) was estimated for all REITs in the sample, and separately for equity and mortgage REITs. Results are reported for the three measures of leverage. For each variable, the value entered in the regression is the value from each year for the period from 1981–1987 for each firm. The time-series data for each REIT were pooled, and as in the case of equation (2), it is unlikely that the error terms of (3) are independent either across firms or over time for a given firm. However, for equation (3), the hypothesis that the u_i vector (as shown in equation (4)) is equal to zero cannot be rejected.[8] As a result, neither the use of dummy variables nor of error components is justified, and the least squares estimator is best linear unbiased [8, p. 486]. Therefore equation (3) was estimated with OLS.

The results of estimating equation (3) for the combined sample of equity and mortgage REITs is shown at the top of Table 4. For the combined sample, the coefficients for leverage are consistently positive as expected, but only two of the three measures of leverage are statistically significant, one of them only at the 10% level. The growth rate of net cash flow resulted in negative coefficients as expected, and all three are statistically significant at the 10% level. None of the other coefficients are significantly different from zero in the combined sample, and none of the three equations explain any meaningful amount of the variability of the cost of capital. When the sample is split into equity and mortgage REITs, the results are no better. Out of six regressions, only two of the independent variables resulted in coefficients significantly different from zero, and none of the equations explain as much as 7% of the variability of cost of capital.[9] The Chow test does not reject the hypothesis of no difference between the two groups. The results presented in Table 4 indicate that leverage increases the cost of capital for REITs, but the results are hardly overwhelming. As noted in the model section, leverage in the absence of corporate earnings taxes may increase the firm's cost of capital due to bankruptcy costs and/or due to tax effects at the investor level.

The inability of the regressions in Table 4 to explain differences in the cost of capital indicates that the cost of capital reflects firm-specific attributes not reflected in the variables included in the equation, or the data used to measure the variables are inadequate. For equity REITs in particular, it seems likely that the nature of the real estate

Table 4 Dependent Variable in the Average Cost of Capital. Estimate With OLS. Variables are defined in Table 1*

Intercept	LEV1	LEV2	LEV3	Log of Total Assets	MTG	TBR	GROWTH	STD	Adj R2
\multicolumn{10}{l}{*EQUITY AND MORTGAGE REITS COMBINED*}
0.1013[a]	0.0050[a]			−0.0027	−0.0009	0.0007	−0.207[a]	0.0090	0.000
(4.050)	(2.358)			(−0.665)	(−0.090)	(0.413)	(−1.969)	(1.096)	
0.0902[a]		0.0154		−0.0011	0.0017	0.0008	−0.0187[a]	0.0103	0.000
(3.654)		(0.969)		(−0.253)	(0.163)	(0.471)	(−1.778)	(1.246)	
0.0990[a]			0.0306[a]	−0.0035	0.0009	0.0006	−0.017[a]	0.0094	0.009
(3.939)			(1.916)	(−0.807)	(0.084)	(0.350)	(−1.690)	(1.148)	
\multicolumn{10}{l}{*EQUITY REITS ONLY*}
0.1066[a]	0.0103[a]			−0.0036	−0.0129	−0.0001	−0.0223	0.0141	0.022
(3.251)	(2.404)			(−0.664)	(−0.265)	(−0.060)	(−1.368)	(0.786)	
0.0922[a]		0.0148		0.0005	−0.0376	−0.0000	−0.2912[b]	0.0220	−0.003
(2.818)		(0.647)		(0.086)	(−0.737)	(−0.008)	(−1.786)	(1.228)	
0.0993[a]			0.0324	−0.0018	−0.0281	−0.0002	−0.0255	0.0169	0.004
(3.019)			(1.397)	(−0.322)	(−0.567)	(−0.083)	(−1.547)	(0.926)	
\multicolumn{10}{l}{*MORTGAGE REITS ONLY*}
0.1100[a]	0.0012			−0.0040	−0.0140	0.0026	−0.0042	−0.0009	0.066
(2.847)	(0.768)			(−0.960)	(−0.526)	(1.512)	(−0.471)	(−0.146)	
0.0910[a]		−0.0084		−0.0008	−0.0060	0.0029[b]	−0.0005	−0.0032	0.061
(2.210)		(−0.419)		(−0.142)	(−0.224)	(1.650)	(−0.053)	(−0.468)	
0.1063[a]			0.0064	−0.0039	−0.0115	0.0026	−0.0026	−0.0014	0.060
(2.550)			(0.337)	(−0.685)	(−0.428)	(1.508)	(−0.301)	(−0.212)	

*Numbers in parentheses below coefficients are t-statistics.
[a] statistically significant at the 5% level
[b] statistically significant at the 10% level

owned by the firm would have an impact. For mortgage REITs, however, that argument seems less convincing, and the results in Table 4 are only slightly better for mortgage REITs than for equity REITs. One aspect of the results for equation (3) that is surprising is the lack of significance for the size variable. Although all but one of the coefficients for firm size are negative, consistent with a lower cost of capital for larger firms (as expected), none of the coefficients are significantly different from zero.

CONCLUSIONS

This study has examined the factors affecting the capital structure and the cost of capital for REITs. Despite the lack of tax incentives, many REITs are highly leveraged.

Two non-tax factors that encourage the use of debt by REITs were considered: agency costs and the leverage clientele effect. According to both of these views, it may be rational for untaxed firms to borrow. Agency theory indicates that there is an optimum capital structure which is the same for firms that are otherwise similar. The leverage clientele effect, on the other hand, results in a bimodal distribution of capital structures within the industry. The capital structures of REITs are, in fact, distributed bimodally, which supports the leverage clientele effect as the motivation for the use of debt financing by REITs.

The results of this study indicate that the use of debt is somewhat higher for mortgage REITs than for equity REITs. Furthermore, while the use of leverage is positively related to firm size for both equity and mortgage REITs, the coefficients for the growth rate of and standard deviation of new cash flows, as well as the percent of revenues derived from mortgages, had opposite signs for equity and mortgage REITs.

The empirical results for estimating the cost of capital for REITs indicated that leverage may increase the firm's cost of capital. However, reported regressions explained only a very small percentage of the variability of the cost of capital.

APPENDIX

List of REITs in the sample, with key characteristics for the final year firm data were available.

Name	Year	Total Assets[a]	LEV3	MTG
Americana Hotels and Realty	87	107	0.29	0.95
Bank America Realty Investor	86	214	0.23	0.95
Bay Financial	87	298	0.72	0.06
California REIT	86	46	0.06	0.13
California Jockey Club	86	33	0.06	0.00
Cenvill Investors Inc.	86	184	0.38	0.88
Chicago Dock and Canal Trust	87	68	0.09	0.00
Clevetrust Realty Investments	87	61	0.49	0.24
Consolidated Capital Realty	87	85	0.67	0.00
Countrywide Mortgage Investments	87	1945	0.95	0.99
Del-Val Financial Corp.	86	109	0.51	1.00
East Group Properties	87	50	0.00	0.25

Eastover Corp.	86	21	0.07	0.00
Eastpark Realty Trust	87	12	0.37	0.15
Federal Realty Investment	86	306	0.43	0.10
Fifty Associates	84	9	0.20	0.00
First Continental REIT	87	73	0.66	0.99
First Union Real Estate Equity	87	371	0.37	0.15
Gould Investors Trust	87	109	0.62	0.02
HMG Property Investors	86	78	0.82	0.06
HRE Properties	87	155	0.09	0.19
Hallwood Group	87	141	0.20	0.50
Health Care Fund	87	182	0.54	0.11
Health Care International	87	370	0.91	0.00
Health Care Property Investments	87	307	0.43	0.06
Health Care REIT Inc.	87	157	0.53	0.05
Hotel Investors Trust	87	265	0.20	0.15
IRT Property Co.	87	191	0.48	0.23
International Income Property	87	198	0.47	0.00
JMB Realty Trust	87	31	0.11	0.54
L&N Housing Corp.	87	72	0.31	0.38
Lomas & Nettleton Mortgage Inv.	87	944	0.70	1.00
Lomas Mortgage	87	1126	0.79	1.00
Mortgage Investments Plus	87	119	0.37	1.00
MONY Real Estate Investors	87	204	0.49	0.62
Mortgage & Realty Trust	87	436	0.57	0.95
Mortgage Growth Investors	87	146	0.14	0.15
National Capital Real Estate	86	32	0.66	0.00
New Plan Realty Trust	87	189	0.06	0.25
Nooney Realty Trust	87	18	0.32	0.00
One Liberty Properties	87	30	0.00	0.16
Pennsylvania REIT	87	73	0.06	0.13
Presidential Realty Corp.	87	35	0.30	0.00
Property Capital Trust	87	192	0.22	0.30
Property Trust of America	87	59	0.23	0.09
REIT of California	87	107	0.14	0.21
Realty Refund Trust	87	70	0.74	1.00
Santa-Anita Realty Enterprises	87	148	0.21	0.04
Saul (BF) REIT	87	421	0.82	0.02
Sierra Real Estate Eq. Tr. 841	87	76	0.56	0.01
Southmark Corp.	87	3294	0.78	0.16
Storage Equities Inc.	86	245	0.32	0.07
Strategic Mortgage	87	356	0.71	0.98
Travelers REIT	87	23	0.00	0.88
Unicorp American Corp.	87	2823	0.71	0.13
United Dominion REIT	87	161	0.42	0.02
VMS Short-Term Income Trust	86	66	0.00	0.99
Washington REIT	86	79	0.06	0.06
Wedgestone Financial	87	79	0.23	0.99
Wells Fargo MTG and Equity Trust	87	500	0.70	0.56
Western Investment Real Estate Tr.	87	154	0.01	0.23

°$millions.

NOTES

[1] Similarly, the weighted average cost of capital can be calculated by dividing net operating income by the market value of the firm. As a result, it is not necessary to compute the cost of debt and the cost of equity separately to generate the cost of capital.

[2] A third explanation of debt in the absence of tax benefits might be signalling. The concept of signalling in this context is that management may use financial leverage to provide information about future performance of the firm. More debt is a sign of a better future for the firm, according to Ross [18]. While this may contribute to the use of debt by both untaxed and taxed firms, it is not clear what the implications of this hypothesis are for a cross-sectional analysis such as this.

[3] Titman and Wessels [24] found no empirical support for a connection between the collateral value of a firm's assets and its debt ratios, however.

[4] As pointed out by Myers [14] and Fischer et al. [5], observed leverage ratios are not optimal while the firm is adjusting toward the optimum. This is particularly relevant for equity REITs that have assumed below-market mortgages.

[5] See Titman and Wessels [24] and the references contained therein for a more detailed discussion of the factors affecting the capital structure decision.

[6] The standard deviation of the annual percentage change in net cash flow, rather than the standard deviation of the net cash flow, was used to reduce the problem of collinearity between the STD and $Growth$.

[7] The Kolomogorov D statistic, which tests for normality, has a value of 0.101 for the distribution represented by Figure A, indicating that the probability that it represents a sample from a normally distributed population is less than 1%.

[8] This was tested using the F-test on the firm dummy variables as described in Judge et al. [8, p. 486].

[9] The regressions shown in Table 4 calculate the average cost of capital as (net cash flow)/(market value of equity plus book value of debt). The relationships were reestimated by calculating the cost of capital as (net cash flow)/(total assets) where total assets were measured by book values. The results for this alternative were somewhat better, with adjusted R^2 ranging from a low of 0.07 up to 0.17. They are not reported because they are less justifiable theoretically, but are available from the authors upon request.

REFERENCES

[1] J. Ang, J. Chua and J. McConnell. The Administration Costs of Corporate Bankruptcy: A Note. *Journal of Finance* 37(1): 219–26, 1982.

[2] J. Baskin. An Empirical Investigation of the Pecking Order Hypothesis. *Financial Management* 18(1): 26–35, 1989.

[3] J. Bowan. The Importance of a Market Value Measurement of Debt in Assessing Leverage. *Journal of Accounting Research* 18(1): 242–54, 1980.

[4] M. Bradley, G. Jarrell and E. H. Kim. On the Existence of an Optimal Capital Structure: Theory and Evidence. *Journal of Finance* 39(3): 857–78, 1984.

[5] E. O. Fischer, R. Heinkel and Josef Zechner. Dynamic Capital Structure Choice: Theory and Tests. *Journal of Finance* 44(1): 19–40, 1989.

[6] J. S. Howe and J. D. Shilling. Capital Structure Theory and REIT Security Offerings. *Journal of Finance* 43(4): 983–93, 1988.

[7] M. Jensen and W. Meckling. Theory of the Firm: Managerial Behavior, Agency Costs, and Ownership Structure. *Journal of Financial Economics* 3(4): 305–60, 1976.

[8] G. C. Judge, R. C. Hill, W. E. Griffiths, H. Lutkepohl, T. C. Lee. *Introduction to the Theory and Practice of Econometrics.* John Wiley and Sons, second edition 1988.

[9] E. H. Kim, W. G. Lewellen and J. J. McConnell. Financial Leverage Clienteles: Theory and Evidence. *Journal of Financial Economics* 7(1): 83–109, 1979.

[10] M. H. Miller. Debt and Taxes. *Journal of Finance* 32(2): 261–75, 1977.

[11] F. Modigliani and M. H. Miller. The Cost of Capital, Corporation Finance, and the Theory of Investment. *American Economic Review* 48(3): 261–97, 1958.

[12] ——— and ———. Corporate Income Taxes and the Cost of Capital. *American Economic Review* 53(3): 433–43, 1963.

[13] Moody's. *Bank and Finance Manual*, Vol. 2, 1987.

[14] S. Myers. The Capital Structure Puzzle. *Journal of Finance* 39(3): 575–92, 1984.

[15] ———. A Comment. In B. M. Friedman, editor, *Corporate Capital Structure in the United States*. The University of Chicago Press, 1985.

[16] ——— and M. Majluf. Corporate Financing and Investment Decisions When Firms Have Information That Investors Do Not Have. *Journal of Financial Economics* 13(2): 187–221, 1984.

[17] *REIT Fact Book*. National Association of Real Estate Investment Trusts, 1985.

[18] S. A. Ross. The Determination of Financial Structure: The Incentive Signalling Approach. *Bell Journal of Economics* 8(1): 23–40, 1977.

[19] C. Smith. Alternative Methods for Raising Capital:Rights versus Underwritten Offerings. *Journal of Financial Economics* 5(4): 273–307, 1977.

[20] Standard and Poor's. *Standard Corporation Descriptions*, various issues, 1987.

[21] ———. *ASE, NYSE,* and *OTC Stock Reports*, 1987.

[22] S. Titman. The Effect of Capital Structure on a Firm's Liquidation Decision. *Journal of Financial Economics* 13(1): 137–51, 1984.

[23] ——— and A. Warga. Risk and the Performance of Real Estate Investment Trusts: A Multi-Factor Approach. *AREUEA Journal* 14, 414–31, 1986.

[24] S. Titman and R. Wessels. The Determinants of Capital Structure Choice. *Journal of Finance* 43(1): 1–19, 1988.

[25] Value Line. *Investment Survey*, November 13, 1987.

[26] J. Warner. Bankruptcy Costs: Some Evidence. *Journal of Finance* 32(2): 337–47, 1977.

Part 8. Real Estate Decision Models

23 Integrating Research on Markets for Space and Capital

Jeffrey D. Fisher

This article discusses the importance of recognizing that there are two distinct but interrelated real estate markets: the market for tenant space and the market for investment capital. The use decision is made in the space market whereas the investment decision is made in the capital market. The article points out that past research has tended to focus on a separate analysis of each of these two markets. That is, research historically has focused on understanding how changes in supply and demand affect equilibrium in either the space market or the capital market as if each market was autonomous. A graphical framework is illustrated that can be used to examine the effect of an exogenous shock to market equilibrium from either the market for space or the market for capital.

Arthur Weimer wrote an article in the *Harvard Business Review* in December 1966 entitled "Real Estate Decisions are Different." He stated that "Real estate resources are different from other resources used by companies" and "Real estate markets differ in many ways from other types of markets." He also made a distinction between use decisions vs. investment decisions and described situations where they might be different.

My hope is to add something to what Art Weimer was telling us twenty-four years ago. Real estate markets are different. In fact, there are two distinct but interrelated real estate markets: the market for tenant space and the market for investment capital. The use decision is made in the space market whereas the investment decision is made in the capital market. This distinction was also made in a "research framework" developed by the National Council of Real Estate Investment Fiduciaries (NCREIF) Research Institute and Homer Hoyt Institute joint task force.[1]

What I have attempted to do is identify ways in which these two markets are interrelated. I have developed two diagrams in an attempt to capture the factors that might impact equilibrium pricing in each market and the links between them. I also want to briefly review some of the models that have focused on a particular question in either the space market or the capital market. My emphasis will not be on what each author did—rather what we still do not know about real estate markets.

From *Journal of the American Real Estate and Urban Economics Association*, Vol. 20, No. 1 (1992), pp. 161–180. Presidential Address to the American Real Estate and Urban Economics Association, December 28, 1990. The author would like to thank William B. Brueggeman, Henry Pollakowski, Susan Wachter, and R. Brian Webb for comments on an earlier draft of this paper.

FACTORS AFFECTING SPACE AND CAPITAL MARKET EQUILIBRIUM

There are macroeconomic factors that affect all real estate markets as well as the rest of the economy. Although we still have much to learn about what the next most important ones are, the ones listed in Figure 1 are certainly likely candidates. I have put them into two categories—*spatial* and *non-spatial.* Non-spatial factors are those that primarily affect the capital market and therefore affect real estate through the capital market. These factors may cause differential performance of various capital assets and are factors often suggested for testing in an Arbitrage Pricing Theory (APT) framework.[2] However, these factors are not likely to affect different geographic areas differently, although I imagine arguments could be made that some of them might.

Spatial factors are those that are likely to differentially affect geographic areas. The ones I listed are those identified in a recent study by First Chicago (1990) that found these factors affected different regions of the country differently. For example, oil prices affected the income growth of some regions much differently than others—no surprise to our colleagues from Texas. There clearly are factors that differentially affect geographic areas. An implication of this is that we should diversify geographically or by different "economic areas" as Hartzell, Hekman and Miles suggest (1986). But, this does not mean that these factors are priced. Although these factors may affect rent levels and even ex-post rates of return in different economic areas differently, these effects may

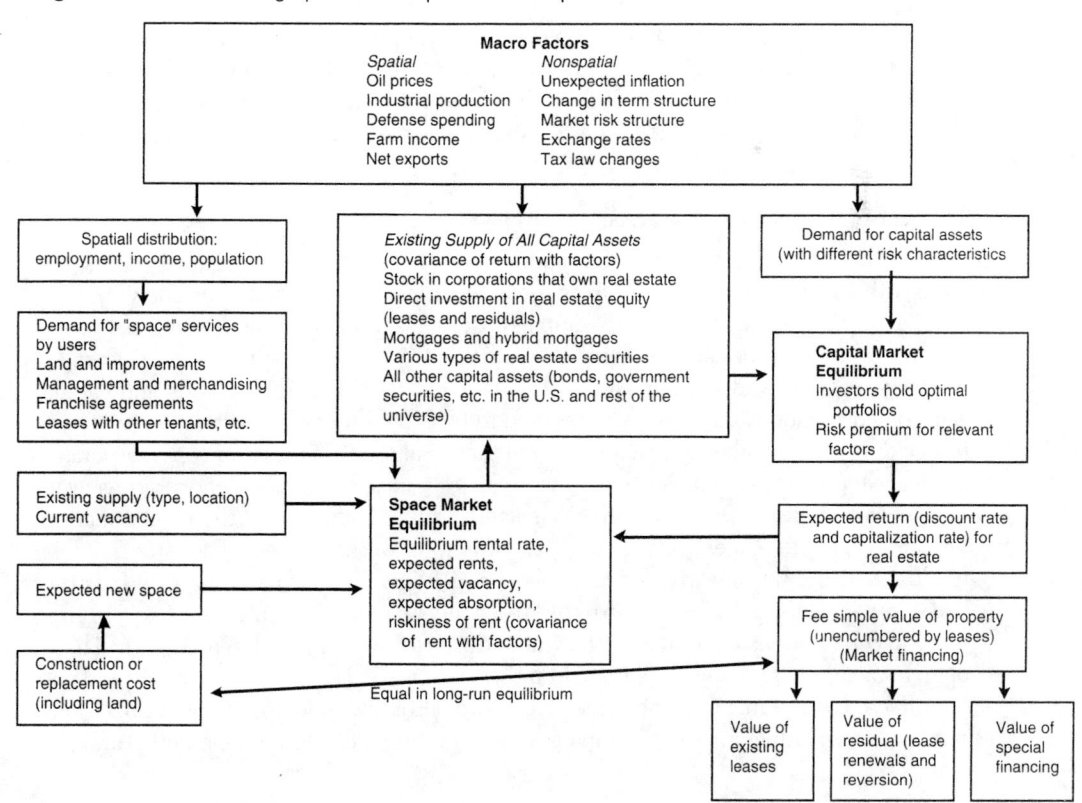

Figure 1 Factors Affecting Space and Capital Market Equilibrium

cancel in a well-diversified portfolio. Therefore, these factors may not be priced in ex-ante (expected) rates of return associated with investing in different geographic areas.

EQUILIBRIUM IN SPACE AND CAPITAL MARKET

Returning to Figure 1, I have attempted to capture the key relationships affecting supply and demand in each market, as well as the links between them. The left-hand side of the exhibit indicates demand and supply coming together to establish equilibrium in the market for space. The space (tenant) market is characterized by the supply and demand for space by *users* which results in an equilibrium (market) rental rate for each type of space. Rental rates may have a covariance with the macro factors, which leads to uncertainty in the income from real estate investments and uncertainty for users of space. But this risk may be systematic or unsystematic.[3] If the risk is unsystematic it may not affect the risk premia in real estate returns. Real estate appeared to outperform stocks and bonds during the 1970s and 1980s when evaluated using a single-factor model. More recent experience in real estate markets may suggest that there was, in fact, a risk premium for other factors that were priced.

It might be noted that I have avoided using the term "real estate" when talking about what is rented in the space market. As many of you know, Bill Kinnard and I have recently suggested in an article that users of space in operating properties like hotels and regional malls pay for more than the tangible real property.[4] Whether that portion of rent attributed to these other services should be capitalized into what we call "real estate" is a debatable issue.

The right-hand side of Figure 1 shows supply and demand coming together to establish capital market equilibrium. This is where the price of risk is established. That is, the amount and type of risk for real estate comes from the space market, whereas the premium for those risk factors that are systematic is determined in the capital market.

LINKS BETWEEN THE MARKETS FOR SPACE AND CAPITAL

The first link between the space and capital markets represented in Figure 1 represents the fact that promised rental rates from users become one of the many cash flow streams supplied in the capital market. It is supplied through the many creative ways that interests in real estate are made available in the market. Examples include lease payments, mortgage payments, dividends and capital gains on REITs, and dividends and capital gains on corporations that have also decided to be capital market investors in real estate by deciding to own rather than lease some of their real estate. This latter case (corporate-owned real estate) presents its own separate set of issues, some of which were reviewed in a recent article by Brueggeman, Fisher and Porter (1990). Does the capital market properly value the real estate or does it take a spin-off of the real estate for stockholders to ultimately get the reward, as Hite, Owers and Rogers (1984) have suggested? Is the decision to use the real estate separable from the decision to own real estate? I think there may be options associated with owning that may only have value to a given. These options cannot be sold and would be lost if the space were leased because they would not be reflected in the market rental rate. Thus, capital market and space market decisions may not be separable for some companies. Much more needs to be done in this area.

Once space exists in the space market, it tends to be securitized in some fashion and becomes just another income stream available to investors who, in theory, are concerned about how that income stream affects the risk and return of their portfolio.

The second link between the two markets is between the construction or replacement cost of supplying space and the value placed on that space in the capital market. This link was first identified in the "user-cost" literature.[5] The importance of this link to real estate markets has also been pointed out by Corcoran (1987). In the long run, the value of a real estate investment should equal its replacement cost; therefore rent levels (the cost of space to users) should provide a market rate of return on that replacement cost. This assumption was the basis for work by Brueggeman, Fisher and Stern (1982) and Hendershott and Ling, who examined tax-law changes (1985).

This link is probably one of the least understood components of this equilibrium process. In his presentation earlier today Atef Sharkawy commented that there was a "de-coupling of investment and tenant markets."[6] If we were always in equilibrium, appraisers would find that the value under the income approach equaled the value under the cost approach. Of course, in practice we might question an appraisal report where the numbers were exactly the same!

Another problem is that equilibrium is between fee simple value (unencumbered by existing leases and existing financing) and replacement cost. What we observe, when we can observe those infrequent real estate transactions, is usually the sale of encumbered property where we do not know all the details of the contracts.

GRAPHICAL ANALYSIS OF EQUILIBRIUM

Figure 2 shows another way of using graphs to link the market for real estate space and the market for real estate capital.[7] The left and right sides of the figure again describe, respectively, the space and capital markets. The top and bottom portions of the figure describe the short and long runs.

In the short run, the existing stock of space is fixed. This sets an upper limit on the supply of space that can be offered for rent. Some of this space will already be leased. The amount of remaining space that is offered for lease at a given point in time depends on the rental rate. The total amount of existing space that building owners have already leased or are willing to lease at different rental rates is expressed by the short-run curve in the upper left-hand quadrant of Figure 2. As the market rental rate rises, more space is supplied by building owners until the maximum amount of space that can be leased in the short term is reached.[8] In the long run, however, the supply of space is highly elastic as the stock of space increases due to construction (net of any demolition of existing buildings). For simplicity, the long-run supply of space is shown as completely elastic in Figure 2.

Figure 2 also shows the demand for space from users. As the rental rate falls firms are more willing to use additional space in their operations rather than other factor inputs such as labor and other types of capital (other than space in buildings). As shown in the figure, the intersection of the supply and demand curves determines the equilibrium market rental rate as well as the amount of space that is leased. The difference between the existing stock of space and the total amount leased at the market rate represents vacant space. This is a normal or equilibrium market vacancy rate.

Figure 2 Space Market-Capital Market Equilibrium

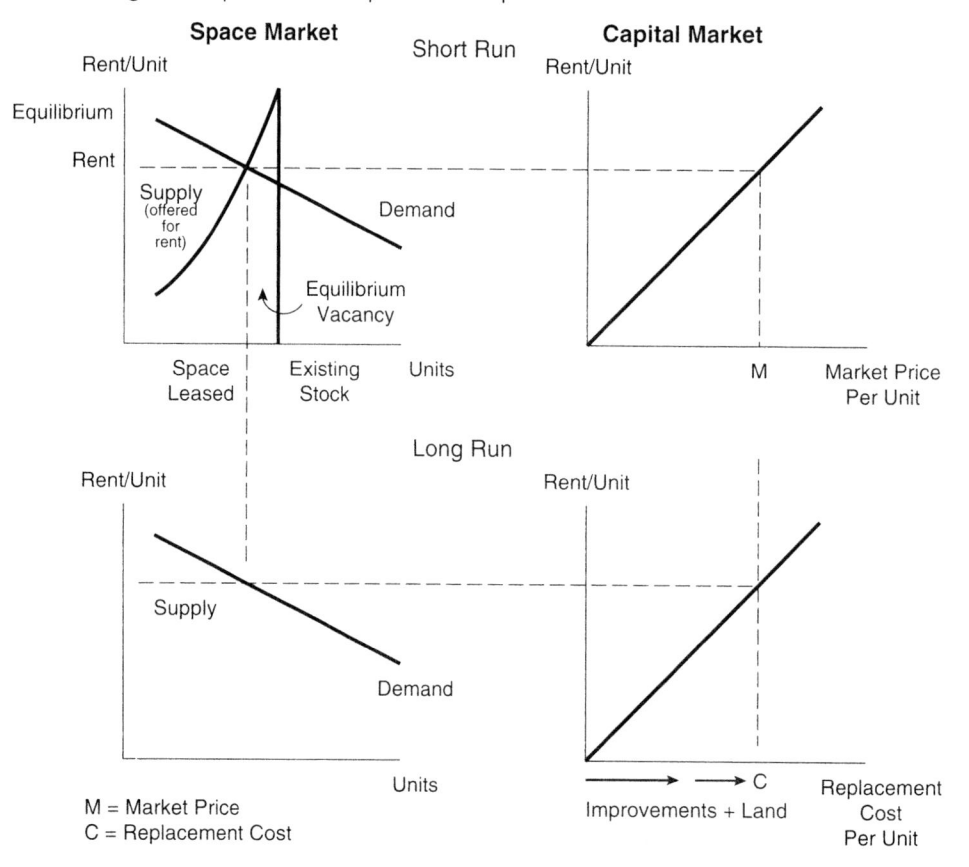

[Figure 2: Four-quadrant diagram showing Space Market (left) and Capital Market (right) in Short Run (top) and Long Run (bottom). Top-left quadrant shows Space Market with Rent/Unit on vertical axis, Supply (offered for rent) curve, Demand curve, Equilibrium Rent, Equilibrium Vacancy between Space Leased and Existing Stock on horizontal axis (Units). Top-right quadrant shows Capital Market with Rent/Unit vs Market Price Per Unit, with M marked. Bottom-left shows Long Run Supply and Demand curves (Rent/Unit vs Units). Bottom-right shows Rent/Unit vs Improvements + Land (Replacement Cost Per Unit), with C marked.]

M = Market Price
C = Replacement Cost

The upper right-hand quadrant illustrates the relationship between the rental rate and the market value per unit of space. The slope of the line is determined by the price that the capital market is willing to pay for the right to receive claims on the rental income from a unit of space. If we interpret the rent as net of all operating expenses, the slope of the line can be viewed as the market capitalization rate.[9] The capitalization rate for real estate at a given point in time depends on capital market factors such as the level of interest rates, the perceived riskiness of real estate, expected inflation, and the tax treatment of real estate relative to other investments.

As we discussed in the context of Figure 1, in long-run equilibrium the market price per unit of the real estate asset must equal the depreciated replacement cost of the asset ($M = C$ in Figure 2). Furthermore, the rent must be at a level that allows investors in the capital market to expect to earn the equilibrium rate of return based on the same capitalization rate. That is, the long-run rent level (bottom left-hand quadrant) is determined by the replacement cost (bottom right-hand quadrant) and the capitalization rate. Finally, if markets are in equilibrium, the net rental rate and the quantity of supply implied by the intersection of the long-run supply and demand curves should equal that implied by the short-run functions directly above.

The above framework can be used to examine the effect of an exogenous shock to market equilibrium from either the market for space or the market for capital. It should be evident that a change in rental rates can be induced by a change from either the space market or capital market. It should also be noted that the dynamics of changes in equilibrium depend on whether the change was induced by a change in a factor affecting the capital market or the space market. For example, an increase in the demand for space should result in a decrease in vacancy, followed by a lagged increase in rent and ultimately an increase in the existing stock of space, which will restore equilibrium. A decrease in the capitalization rate, however, should result in an immediate increase in the market value of real estate relative to construction costs.[10] This would induce new supply, leading to an increase in vacancy rates which would eventually led to lower rents. This is the scenario that occurred during the early 1980s when the capitalization rate for real estate (relative to the capitalization rate for other financial assets) fell because of the favorable tax benefits provided by the Economic Recovery Tax Act of 1981.[11] This lowered the real before-tax rate of return required for investment in real estate relative to other capital assets.

From the above discussion it should be clear that the relationship between new supply and changes in rents and vacancy rates can be quite complex. These relationships depend on the relative impact of the market for capital versus the market for space.

NEED FOR RESEARCH

Past research has tended to focus on a separate analysis of each of these two markets. That is, research historically has focused on understanding how changes in supply and demand affect equilibrium in either the space market or the capital market as if each market was autonomous.

Research related to real estate in the space markets by urban and regional economists tends to focus on how the demand and supply of space interact to establish market rental rates. Research related to real estate in the capital markets by financial economists tends to focus on how real estate should be priced based on its risk relative to other assets in the capital market, and the implication of this risk analysis for how much real estate should be held in a portfolio.

A "holistic" approach that simultaneously considers space and capital markets is the most logical next step in explaining real estate performance. Attempting to explain both of these markets in a single model is difficult, but ignoring the interaction of these two markets limits our ability to understand real estate performance in general.

CAPITAL MARKET RESEARCH

This research has dealt with pricing assets in general, with emphasis on modern portfolio theory (MPT). MPT tells us that unsystematic risk is reduced by including real estate in a portfolio, and perhaps by diversifying across economic areas and property types. This model assumes that there are no constraints on the amount of any given asset class.

The mathematical procedure for determining the optimal portfolio does not explicitly differentiate between different asset classes, e.g., stocks, bonds, and real estate. In theory, the optimal amount to allocate to each asset class should be determined simultaneously because all assets are inputs into the model. In practice, however, this has proven difficult due to the incomparability of data across asset classes. Real estate in particular lacks price data based on frequent transactions that are comparable to price data for publicly traded stocks and bonds. Therefore, results from combining appraisal-based real estate data with transactions-based stock and bond data in a single portfolio model are questionable.

Fund managers often follow a two-step process to develop portfolios. First, they constrain allocations to each asset class to a predetermined percentage, e.g., 40% stocks, 40% bonds, 15% real estate and 5% cash. Second, investments are selected within each asset class.

It has been assumed that it is appropriate to use the same portfolio approach to determine the optimal allocation to assets within a particular asset class. That is, it is assumed that minimizing variance within the asset class also minimizes variance for the entire portfolio. Cashdan, Fisher and Webb (1991) show that this may be suboptimal because real estate already includes a bond component due to existing leases.

Capital Asset Pricing Model (CAPM). The CAPM has nothing to say about real estate. It assumes that all that matters is the *beta* for real estate, and it suggests that everyone should hold a scale model of the "market portfolio," which implies we should hold some real estate. But we do not even know the answer to the most basic question: How much real estate is there?[12]

Assets that are correlated with uncertain inflation have less risk.[13] This suggests that real estate has less risk *if* real estate is still an inflation hedge. Inflation is one of the potential "factors" that might be priced. Because inflation is one reason real estate may be different in the capital market, it has received a lot of attention in the literature.

Several studies have attempted to look at whether real estate is different in the sense of providing an inflation hedge (Hartzell, Hekman and Miles 1986). Brueggeman, Chen and Thibodeau (1984) used a two-factor model to examine this issue. Chan, Hendershott and Sanders (1990) have taken a more recent look using REIT data in an arbitrage pricing theory (APT) framework and could not conclude that real estate is an inflation hedge or that it outperforms stocks in a multi-factor model. In general, I think the conclusion has to be that we still do not know if real estate is truly an inflation hedge. Is there something about real estate being a "real asset" and having a replacement cost that makes this so?

Arbitrage Pricing Theory (APT). As suggested above, although real estate appears to be underpriced relative to other asset classes when viewed within the CAPM, it may not be in a multi-factor model. The arbitrage pricing model (APT) formulated by Ross in 1976 allows more than a single factor to systematically affect investment required rates of return and risk, and may provide a more useful way to analyze real estate risk in the capital market. Although APT suggests that more than one factor may be relevant, it does not provide a theoretical basis for particular factors or indicate whether some factors would be spatial in nature. Chan, et. al. (1990) used the same five factors suggested by Chen, Roll and Ross (1986). However, we have talked about reasons several factors *might* be relevant, but much work needs to be done to settle this issue. A variation of the APT used by Dokko, Edelstein, Pomer and Urdang (1991) adds additional variables related to property type and location to explain returns in a disequilibrium framework.

SPACE MARKET RESEARCH

Research on the space market has attempted to develop and test models that explain the demand for space, the supply of new space, and rental adjustments. One of the first empirical studies was Rosen's office market study (1984). Demand, measured as square feet of occupied space, is expressed as a function of employment[14] and real rents. The supply of new space is expressed as a function of the vacancy rate, expected rent levels, construction costs, interest rates and tax laws. Change in rents is modeled as a function of the deviation in the actual vacancy rate from the optimal vacancy rate and the overall change in the price index. The average vacancy rate over the estimation period is used as a proxy for the optimal vacancy rate.

Hekman specifies the level of rent as a function of the vacancy rate, U.S. gross national product, total employment in the MSA, and the local unemployment rate (1985). He then estimates the new supply of office space as a function of rent (predicted values from the first equation), growth in office-using employment, construction costs and interest rates. The results show that the supply of new office space responds to rents and office-related employment. The cost and interest-rate variables are insignificant.

Hekman tests whether developers and investors favor "high-profile" cities with high growth rates. He finds no difference in estimated supply equations between the two groups. This would be expected if investors already expect to earn an appropriate risk-adjusted rate of return in each type of city.

Wheaton estimates a structural office market model that includes demand (absorption of space) and supply equations (1987). The determinants of demand (absorption) are the level of office employment, real rents, expectations about future space needs (measured by the ratio of current and previous period's office employment) and lagged occupied stock of office space.

On the supply side, the level of new permits is used to measure construction, which is a function of expected profits, as measured by rents, vacancies, construction costs, and the employment ratio. Real rent change as a function of the difference between the actual and the optimal vacancy rate (measured as the average vacancy rate) is included as a market clearing equation. Assuming that rents respond with a lag to the vacancy rate, the lagged vacancy rate is substituted for rents in the absorption and supply equations. Supply reacts more to vacancies than does absorption, which increases with cyclicality. The growth rate in employment enters both supply and absorption equations and links the office market cycle to the national macro cycle.

Wheaton and Torto confirm the existence of a strong rental adjustment mechanism in the market for office space (1988). They regress the change in real rents on the vacancy rate, using a national vacancy rate date series (from Coldwell Banker and BOMA) and an office rent series, constructed from Solomon Brothers. They find that real rents decline 2.3% per year for every 1% of "excess vacancy."

Shilling, Sirmans and Corgel focus on the determinants of natural vacancy rates, using data for seventeen cities for 1960 to 1975, by specifying the change in rent levels as a function of operating expenses and the difference between actual and normal vacancy rates (1987). The coefficients for the expense variable are insignificant for all seventeen cities. The vacancy variable is significant in eleven of the seventeen cities and has the expected negative sign in all cities.

Clapp, Pollakowski and Lynford extend the modeling of markets for office space to the metropolitan submarket level (1992). Suggesting that spatial patterns are strongly related to the office market dynamics modeled by Rosen, Wheaton, and others, the authors estimate a seven-market model for the Boston metropolitan area. To test the hypothesis that spatial concentrations by industry (agglomerations) are important determinants of growth in office demand, a measure of employment growth potential is constructed and found to be an important determinant of demand.

In summary, the space market research has shown a relationship between the demand for occupied office space and employment and real rental rates. The research has also shown a relationship between changes in rental rates and excess vacancy rates. On the supply side, however, the research has not been as conclusive. Specifications of supply determinants remains a weakness in office market research. The results of Rosen (1984) and Wheaton (1987) reveal a role for lagged vacancy rates and for employment in construction decisions. Neither, however, find expected rent or cost levels to be significant in explaining supply. Hekman finds supply responds to rent and employment, but also not to costs (1985). This can be attributed to an incomplete specification of the role of the capital market in supply decisions. Construction costs may not be as relevant as the value of the space in inducing new supply. This is because new supply is profitable when the value of the space exceeds the cost of developing the space.

WHY RESEARCH IS LIMITED BY NOT CONSIDERING THE LINK

The above discussion points out a potential weakness in modeling supply and demand and the rental adjustment process in the space market without adequately considering the role of the capital market. During most of the 1980s changes in rents and values were a response to increases in the demand for real estate as a capital asset rather than an increase in the demand for space. Also, factors affecting risk in the space market may or may not be the same factors affecting risk in the capital market. Focusing on the local space market alone may result in unsystematic factors appearing to be important when they are not. Or, perhaps unsystematic risk is important for real estate due to constraints on diversification. More work needs to be done to determine whether unsystematic risk is priced for real estate assets.

DATA PROBLEMS

Unfortunately, lack of data limits our ability to adequately pursue many of the areas of research suggested above. Either data does not exist in sufficient quantity (e.g., lack of real estate transactions) or market participants simply do not want it to be released to the public. Market participants want to know about everyone else's transaction but do not want to reveal the details of their own because of a perceived negotiating advantage. Or perhaps they think they are fooling the capital market and perhaps they are in the short run.

We currently have two primary sources of national historical data on real estate returns for capital market research: REIT data and Russell-NCREIF (FRC) data.

Several studies have used the REIT data to measure real estate performance in the capital market including Brueggeman, Chen and Thibodeau (1984) and Chan, Hendershott and Sanders (1990). One issue is whether REITs are representative of direct investment in real estate. REITs may not reflect the performance of the underlying real estate because they tend to trade like stocks.[15] On the other hand, the Russell-NCREIF Index is criticized for being appraisal-based.[16] Wheaton (1989) finds the appraisal-based Russell-NCREIF Index does not behave as his model would suggest it should. But does this mean the model is wrong or the appraisers are wrong?

The strongest evidence that something is wrong with the appraisal-based data is perhaps the fact that real estate appears to have had excess returns over a long period of time. But this could still be a model problem: there may be factors that are "priced" on an ex-ante basis but did not cause a shock in returns ex-post (or perhaps we are feeling the shock now).[17]

Ibbotson and Siegel (1984) suggest the apparent excess returns are due to transactions costs, liquidity, and other market imperfections. Cole, Guilkey and Miles (1986) examined appraisal values versus transactions prices of properties sold from the Russell-NCREIF Index. They found about a 6% difference when outliers were ignored. And as Edelstein and Quan suggest,[18] transactions prices are not necessarily equal to market value.

Miles, Webb and Guilkey developed a transactions-driven index using Russell-NCREIF data as well as additional data collected on each property in an attempt to improve the availability of real estate return measures and use this return series to see if the risk of real estate is really greater (1991). Real estate transactions prices are modeled as a function of general property and market characteristics, and these transactions-driven prices are used in the place of appraised values to compute a return index.

Geltner takes a slightly different approach by attempting to correct for the smoothing in appraisal-based return series (1989). Relying on the hypothesis that true returns are "unpredictable," he models the relation between observable appraisal-based returns and unobservable true returns and estimates the variance of true returns.

EFFECTIVE RENT (LEASE) INDEX AS A STEP TOWARD LINKING

Research on the space market has been hindered by lack of information about changes in rental rates. Brennan, Cannady and Colwell employ a pooled cross-sectional model that spans three years to explain lease rates within an urban office market (1984). They do not attempt, however, to measure changes in rental rates over time. A measure of changes in rental rates (changes in the price of space) is clearly important for modeling the supply and demand for space as well as for models of the rental adjustment process.

Fisher and Webb have developed an effective rent (lease) index based on lease transactions for selected properties in the Russell-NCREIF Index (1992). A lease index that controls for differences in the quality of space and terms of the lease indicates the price of a standard unit of space at a given point in time. It is a transactions-based index that captures changes in the price of space *currently* available in the market (unencumbered by existing leases). Thus, the lease index indicates rent variations in the space market that are important to identifying risk.

In future research, the rental index might be used as an explanatory variable in the transactions-driven price index (described earlier),which may improve our understanding of the performance of real estate in the capital market. Furthermore, a rental index can be used as the dependent variable in an attempt to identify the underlying determinants of changes in the space market, i.e., changes in national and local economic factors that impact market rental rates as reflected in the effective rent for leases signed at a given point in time for a given type of property in a given geographic area.

As discussed above, space market rental rates may be affected by different economic variables than discount rates and capitalization rates in the capital market. Furthermore, a property's income and appraised value as reflected by the Russell-NCREIF Property Index is affected by leases signed at various *past* points in time as well as expected future rental rates. This tends to "smooth" the return series. Although any national lease index has to be limited in terms of controlling for different lease terms, work in this area is critical to extensions of existing research on real estate behavior and is the first step towards a more refined lease index at the local level.

CONCLUSION

It is safe to say that much work needs to be done to refine the structure of the models as well as obtain better data to test the models. The existence and interaction of the space and capital markets should be kept in mind when developing and testing models. Real estate is different, if for no other reason, because there are two separate but linked markets worthy of study.

NOTES

[1] The purpose of this task force was to identify real estate research needs from an institutional investor's perspective. The NCREIF Research Institute is now called the Real Estate Research Institute.

[2] See Chen, Roll and Ross (1984).

[3] Systematic risk is due to factors that affect all assets and cannot be eliminated in a well-diversified portfolio.

[4] See Fisher and Kinnard (1990).

[5] See Jorgenson (1963).

[6] M. Atef Sharkawy, "The Role of Appraisal in Acquisition-Development-Construction (ADC) Loan Default," paper presented at the December, 1990 annual meetings of the American Real Estate and Urban Economics Association.

[7] See Fisher, Hudson-Wilson and Wurtzebach (1992) for a more complete analysis of the way that changes in the space market or the capital market affect equilibrium using this graphical approach.

[8] At lower market rental rates some of the existing space may not be made available for lease. This space may be deliberately held vacant by owners in anticipation of higher market rents in the future. Alternatively, they may prefer to convert the space to a different use rather than rent it under the existing use at the current market rate for that use. A certain amount of space will also always be vacant because of tenants moving and the time it takes for newly constructed space to be offered for lease.

[9] The capitalization rate is the ratio of net income (rent collected less operating expenses) to value.

[10] Construction costs may also increase due to an increase in land value. However, this is not likely to completely offset the increase in the market value of the real estate.

[11] There was also an increase in the demand for real estate capital from pension funds and foreign investors that viewed real estate as a way of diversifying their investment portfolios.

[12] See Miles (1990) and Miles, Pittman, et al. (1991).

[13] See Chen and Boness (1975).

[14] Total employment in finance, insurance and real estate.

[15] For example, see Giliberto (1990).

[16] I recently mentioned to a group of appraisers the criticism of that appraised real estate held by institutional investors, expecting them to dispute any "smoothing". Their reaction, however, was, "I can see how this would happen. We don't want to put all the weight on the most recent sale—it may be an outlier."

[17] Tax law change, excess supply that adjusts slowly, etc. are now lowering returns and may have been priced (ex-ante) years ago.

[18] Robert H. Edelstein and Daniel C. Quan, "Errors in Appraisal Based Return Indices," paper presented at the December 1991 annual meeting of AREUEA.

REFERENCES

Brennan, T. P., R. E. Cannady and P. F. Colwell. 1984. Office Rent in the Chicago CBD. *Journal of the American Real Estate and Urban Economics Association* 12(3): 243–60.

Brueggeman, W. B., A. H. Chen and T. G. Thibodeau. 1984. Real Estate Investment Funds: Performance and Portfolio Considerations. *Journal of the American Real Estate and Urban Economics Association* 12(3): 333–54.

Brueggeman, W. B., D. Fisher and D. M. Porter. 1990. Rethinking Corporate Real Estate. *Journal of Applied Corporate Finance* 3(1): 30–50.

Brueggeman, W. B., D. Fisher and J. Stern. 1982. Rental Housing and the Economic Recovery Tax Act of 1981. *Public Finance Quarterly* (April): 222–41.

Cashdan, D. M., Jr., J. D. Fisher and R. B. Webb. 1991. LOBs and RAREs: The Decomposition of Commercial Real Estate Returns. Working paper, Indiana University Center for Real Estate Studies.

Chan, K. C., P. H. Hendershott and A. B. Sanders. 1990. Risk and Return on Real Estate: Evidence from Equity REITs. *Journal of the American Real Estate and Urban Economics Association* 18(4): 431–52.

Chen, A. H. and A. J. Boness. 1975. Effects of Uncertain Inflation on the Investment and Financing Decisions of the Firm. *Journal of Finance* (May): 469–83.

Chen, N. F., R. Roll and S. A. Ross. 1984. Economic Forces and the Stock Market: Testing the APT and Alternative Asset Pricing Theories. Seminar on the Analysis of Security Prices, University of Chicago, May 1984.

Clapp, J. M., H. O. Pollakowski and L. Lynford. 1992. Intrametropolitan Location and Office Market Dynamics. *Journal of the American Real Estate and Urban Economics Association* 20(2): 229–57.

Cole, R., D. Guilkey and M. Miles. 1986. Toward an Assessment of the Reliability of Commercial Appraisals. *Appraisal Journal* 54(2): 422–32.

Corcoran, P. J. 1987. Explaining the Commercial Real Estate Market. *Journal of Portfolio Management* (Spring): 15–21.

Dokko, Y., R. H. Edelstein, M. Pomer and E. S. Urdang. 1991. Determinants of the Rate of Return for Nonresidential Real Estate: Inflation Expectations and Market Adjustment Lags. *Journal of the American Real Estate and Urban Economics Association* 19(1): 52–69.

Edelstein, R. H. and D. C. Quan. 1991. Errors in Appraisal Based Return Indices. Paper presented at the December annual meeting of the American Real Estate and Urban Economics Association.

First National Bank of Chicago's Economic Forecasting Division. 1990. Economic Issue Backgrounder (May).

Fisher, J. D. and W. N. Kinnard. 1990. The Business Enterprise Component of Operating Properties. *Journal of Property Tax Management* 2(1): 19–27.

Fisher, J. D., D. Geltner and R. B. Webb. 1991. Historical Value Indices of Commercial Real Estate. Working paper (July), 1–17.

Fisher, J. D., S. Hudson-Wilson and C. H. Wurtzebach. 1992. Equilibrium in Real Estate Markets. Working paper, Indiana University Center for Real Estate Studies.

Fisher, J. D. and R. B. Webb. 1992. Development of an Effective Rent Index for U.S. Office Space (1982–1990). Working paper (March 19), Indiana University Center for Real Estate Studies.

Geltner, D. 1991. Temporal Aggregation in Real Estate Return Indices. Working paper.

———. 1990. Return Risk and Cash Flow Risk With Long-Term Riskless Leases in Commercial Real Estate. *Journal of the American Real Estate and Urban Economics Association* 18(4): 377–402.

———. 1989. Bias in Appraisal-Based Returns. *Journal of the American Real Estate and Urban Economics Association* 17(3): 338–52.

Giliberto, S. M. 1988. A Note on the Use of Appraisal Data in Indexes of Performance Measurement. *Journal of the American Real Estate and Urban Economics Association* 16(1): 77–83.

———. 1990. Equity Real Estate Investment Trusts and Real Estate Returns. *Journal of Real Estate Research* 5(2): 259–63.

Hartzell, D., J. Hekman and M. Miles. 1986. Diversification Categories in Investment Real Estate. *Journal of the American Real Estate and Urban Economics Association* 14(2): 230–54.

Hekman, J. 1985. Rental Price Adjustment and Investment in the Office Market. *Journal of the American Real Estate and Urban Economics Association* 13(1): 33–47.

Hendershott, P. H. and D. C. Ling. 1985. Prospective Changes in the Tax Law and the Value of Depreciable Real Estate. *Journal of the American Real Estate and Urban Economics Association* 12(3): 297–317.

Hite, G. L., J. E. Owers and R. C. Rogers. 1984. The Separation of Real Estate Operations by Spinoff. *Journal of the American Real Estate and Urban Economics Association* 12(3): 318–32.

Hoag, J. W. 1980. Towards Indices of Real Estate Value and Return. *Journal of Finance* 35(2): 561–80.

Ibbotson, R. G. and L. B. Siegel. 1984. Real Estate Returns: A Comparison with Other Investments. *Journal of the American Real Estate and Urban Economics Association* 12(3): 219–42.

Jorgenson, D. W. 1963. Capital Theory and Investment Behavior. *American Economic Review* (May): 247–59.

Markowitz, H. M. 1952. Portfolio Selection. *Journal of Finance* 7 (March): 77–91.

———. 1959. *Portfolio Selection: Efficient Diversification of Investments.* John Wiley.

Miles, M. 1990. What is the Value of U.S. Real Estate? *Real Estate Review* 20(2): 69–77.

——— and T. McCue. 1984. Commercial Real Estate Returns. *Journal of the American Real Estate and Urban Economics Association* 12(3): 355–77.

Miles, M., B. Webb and D. Guilkey. 1991. On the Nature of Systematic Risk in Commercial Real Estate. Working paper (July), 1–33.

Miles, M., R. Cole and D. Guilkey. 1990. A Different Look at Commercial Real Estate Returns. *Journal of the American Real Estate and Urban Economics Association* 18(4): 403–30.

Miles M., R. Pittman, M. Hoesli, P. Bhatnagar and D. Guilkey. 1991. A Detailed Look at America's Real Estate Wealth. *Journal of Property Management* (July–August): 45–50.

Quan, D. C. and J. M. Quigley. 1991. Price Formation and the Appraisal Function in Real Estate Markets. *Journal of Real Estate Finance and Economics* 4(2): 127–46.

Rosen, K. 1984. Toward a Model of the Office Building Sector. *Journal of the American Real Estate and Urban Economics Association* 2(3): 261–69.

Sharkawy, M. A. 1990. The Role of Appraisal in Acquisition-Development-Construction (ADC) Loan Default. Paper presented at the December annual meeting of the American Real Estate and Urban Economics Association.

Shilling, J., C. F. Sirmans and J. Corgel. 1987. Price Adjustment Process for Rental Office Space. *Journal of Urban Economics* 22: 90–100.

Weimer, A. M. 1966. Real Estate Decisions are Different. *Harvard Business Review* (December): 105–12.

Wheaton, W. C. and R. G. Torto. 1989. Income and Appraised Values: A Reexamination of the FRC Returns Data. *Journal of the American Real Estate and Urban Economics Association* 17(4): 439–49.

Wheaton, W. C. 1987. The Cyclic Behavior of the National Office Market. *Journal of the American Real Estate and Urban Economics Association* 15(4): 281–99.

——— and R. Torto. 1988. Vacancy Rates and the Future of Office Rents. *Journal of the American Real Estate and Urban Economics Association* 16(4): 430–35.

Wurtzebach, C. H., G. R. Mueller and D. Machi. 1991. The Impact of Inflation and Vacancy on Real Estate Returns. *Journal of Real Estate Research* 6(2): 153–68.

24 The Markets for Real Estate Assets and Space: A Conceptual Framework

Denise DiPasquale and William C. Wheaton

In this study, we present a simple analytic framework that divides the real estate market into two markets: the market for real estate space and the market for real estate assets. After describing the size and character of flows and stocks in the U.S. real estate market, we use our framework to demonstrate the important connections between the space and asset markets. We illustrate how these real estate markets are affect by the nation's macroeconomy and financial markets, tracing out the impacts resulting from various exogenous shocks on rents, asset prices, construction and the stock of real estate.

Analyzing the market for real estate presents a formidable challenge because the market is comprised of two inter-related markets—the market for real estate space and the market for real estate assets. The distinction between real estate as space and real estate as an asset is most clear when buildings are not occupied by their owners. The needs of tenants and the type and quality of buildings available determine the rent for real estate space in the property market. At the same time, buildings may be bought, sold, or exchanged between investors. These transactions occur in the asset or capital market and determine the asset price of space. There are a number of important connections between these two markets, and the central objective of this article is to describe these links.

When space is owned by its occupant, such as occurs with single-family housing and much of the nation's industrial space, the notion of two separate markets is no longer applicable. Purchasing an asset and purchasing the use of space become one combined decision. The motives of participants and the forces governing market behavior are very much the same. In purchasing a home, the annual payments that a household can afford are determined primarily by its level of income. Conditions in the capital market, however, determine how a household converts these annual payments into a purchase price. If interest rates are low and inflation high, families will be willing to offer higher prices even though their annual ability to pay is unchanged. This investment motive of the homeowner is the same as that which motivates an investor in rental property.

From *Journal of the American Real Estate and Urban Economics Association*, Vol. 20, No. 1 (1992), pp. 181–197. This article is based on Chapter 1 of our book, *The Economics of Real Estate Markets*, forthcoming from Prentice-Hall in 1994. We thank Jean L. Cummings and Henry Pollakowski for helpful comments on an earlier draft. Of course, we are responsible for any errors that remain.

In this article, we begin with a brief discussion of the size and character of the U.S. real estate market, looking at residential as well as commercial real estate. We examine the value of the nation's real estate by type and ownership. We then present a simple analytic framework that illustrates the connections between the market for real estate space (the property market) and the market for real estate assets (the asset market). Distinguishing between these two markets helps to clarify how different types of forces influence this important sector. The framework we develop is a generic one, applicable to any type of commercial as well as residential real estate. Using comparative static analysis with this framework permits us to trace out the likely impacts on each market of changes in the behavior of investors, the macroeconomy or public policy. If there is a sudden demand by foreign investors to purchase U.S. office buildings, the impact on rents is very different than if firms suddenly decide that they wish to purchase more office space for their use. A reduction in long-term mortgage rates has just the opposite effect on house prices from that caused by a reduction in short-term interest rates for construction financing. Distinguishing between the property and asset markets helps to provide a clearer understanding of how such forces impact the real estate sector as a whole.

U.S. REAL ESTATE: FLOWS AND STOCKS

The flow of real estate is shown in Table 1, which breaks down the value of new construction put in place in 1990. Virtually all private construction was in the form of buildings, representing $301 billion (5.5% of Gross Domestic Product (GDP)). Residential buildings accounted for about 61% of private building construction, with office, industrial and other commercial structures representing 39%. In the GDP accounts for 1990, real estate (residential and nonresidential structures) represented 52% of total gross private domestic fixed investment ($803 billion).[1] The remaining $388 billion was investment by firms in machinery or equipment.

Over the years, government statistics have tracked the flow of gross investment into real estate (new building construction) with a high degree of accuracy. Valuing the total real estate stock at any point in time, however, is far more difficult (Miles 1990). A recent study by the IREM Foundation and Arthur Anderson (1991) has made a gallant attempt at estimating the value of all U.S. real estate, by type and owner, piecing together data from a variety of sources. The study employed standard government statistics, trade association data, and state and county property tax records to estimate statistically the value of real estate.

In this study, total real estate in the U.S. is estimated to be worth $8.8 trillion. As shown in Table 2, almost 70% of all U.S. real estate is residential, and almost 90% of the value of residential real estate is in the nation's stock of single-family homes. The 30% of U.S. real estate that is nonresidential is dominated by office and retail space—at least in dollar value. Using the Federal Reserve national net worth estimate of $15.6 trillion in 1990, the figures in Table 2 suggest that real estate constitutes roughly 56% of the nation's wealth.[2]

The legal ownership status of this wealth is shown in Table 3. Of residential real estate, 80% is owned by individuals, including individual ownership of personal residences and sole proprietor ownership of apartment buildings. The 61.5% of nonresidential real estate that is owned by corporations covers ownership of investment property as well as buildings occupied by their corporate owners. Partnerships own almost

Table 1 Value of New Construction Put in Place, 1990

	Billions of $s	Percent of GDP
Private Construction		
Buildings	301	5.5
Residential Buildings	183	3.3
Nonresidential Buildings	118	2.1
Industrial	24	0.4
Office	29	0.5
Hotels/Motels	10	0.2
Other Commercial	34	0.6
All Other Nonresidential	21	0.4
Non-Building Construction	37	0.7
Public Utilities	31	0.6
All Other	6	0.1
Total	338	6.1
Total New Construction	446	8.1
Total GDP	5,514	100.0

Source: U.S. Bureau of Census (1991). Gross Domestic Product from *Economic Report of the President 1992*.

equal shares of residential and nonresidential property, while corporations dominate the nonresidential market. Finally, the ownership of U.S. real estate by foreign entities is virtually nil, despite some considerable concern about this during the last few years.

In summary, U.S. real estate is the largest component of national wealth, and the largest component of annual net private investment. This huge base of assets, however, has been accumulated by devoting only about 5%–7% of each year's GDP to the construction and renovation of that base. It is, of course, the durability of real estate that allows us to devote such a small fraction of GDP to the accumulation and maintenance of such a large share of our assets.

THE MARKETS FOR REAL ESTATE ASSETS AND REAL ESTATE SPACE

Since real estate is a durable capital good, its production and price are determined in an asset, or capital, market. The price of houses in the U.S. largely depends on how many households wish to *own* units and how many units are available for such ownership. Likewise, the value of shopping centers depends on how many investors wish to own such space and how many centers there are available in which to invest. In both cases, all else equal, an increase in the demand to own these assets will raise prices while a greater supply of space will depress prices.

The new supply of real estate assets depends on the price of those assets relative to the cost of replacing or constructing them. In the long run, the asset market should equate market prices with replacement costs. In the short run, however, the two may diverge significantly because of the lags and delays that are inherent in the construction process. For example, if demand for the ownership of space suddenly rises, then with a fixed supply of assets, prices will rise as well. With prices now above construction costs, new construction takes place. As this space arrives on the market, demand is satisfied and prices begin to fall back towards the cost of replacement.

Table 2 Value of U.S. Real Estate, 1990

	Billions of $s	Percent of Total
Residential	6,122	69.8
Single-Family Homes	5,419	61.7
Multifamily	552	6.3
Condominiums/Coops	96	1.1
Mobile Homes	55	0.6
Retail	1,115	12.7
Office	1,009	11.5
Manufacturing	308	3.5
Warehouse	223	2.5
Total U.S. Real Estate	8,777	100.0

Source: IREM Foundation and Arthur Anderson (1991)

In the market for real estate use or space, demand comes from the *occupiers* of space, whether they be tenants or owners, firms or households. For firms, space is one of many factors of production, and like any other factor, its use will depend on firm output levels and the relative cost of space. The household demand for space depends on income and the cost of occupying that space relative to the cost of consuming other commodities. For firms or households, the cost of occupying space is the annual outlay necessary to use real estate—its rent. For tenants, rent is simply specified in a lease agreement. For owners, rent is defined as the annualized cost associated with the ownership of property.

Rent is determined in the property market for space, not in the asset market for ownership. In the property market, the supply of space is given from the asset market. The demand for space depends on rent and other exogenous economic factors such as firm production levels, income or the number of households. The task of the property market is to determine a rent level at which the demand for space equals the supply of space. All else equal, when the number of households increases or firms expand production, the demand for space *use* rises. With fixed supply, rents rise as well.

The link between the markets for assets and property occurs at two junctions. First, the rent levels determined in the property market are central in determining the

Table 3 Who Owns U.S. Real Estate in 1990 (billions of 1990 $s)

	All Real Estate $s	All Real Estate Percent	Residential Only $s	Residential Only Percent	Nonresidential Only $s	Nonresidential Only Percent
Individuals	5,088	58.0	5,071	82.8	17	0.6
Corporations	1,699	19.4	66	1.1	1,633	61.5
Partnerships	1,011	11.5	673	11.0	338	12.7
Not-For-Profits	411	4.7	104	1.7	307	11.6
Government	234	2.6	173	2.8	61	2.3
Institutional Investors	128	1.5	14	0.2	114	4.3
Financial Institutions	114	1.3	13	0.2	101	3.8
Other (includes foreign)	92	1.0	8	0.1	84	3.2
Total:	8,777	100.0	6,122	100.0	2,655	100.0
Percent of All Real Estate:		*100.0*		*69.8*		*30.2*

Source: IREM Foundation and Arthur Anderson (1991)

demand for real assets. After all, in acquiring an asset, the investors are really purchasing a current or future income stream. Thus, changes in rent occurring in the property market immediately affect the demand for assets in the capital market. The second link between the two markets occurs through the construction sector. If construction increases and the supply of assets grows, not only are prices driven down in the asset market, but rents decline in the property market as well. These connections between the two markets are illustrated in the four-quadrant diagram in Figure 1.

In Figure 1, the two right-hand quadrants represent the property market for the use of space, while the two left-hand quadrants represent the asset market for the ownership of real estate. Rents are determined in the short run in the NE quadrant. The NE quadrant has two axes: rent (per unit of space) and the stock of space (also measured in units of space such as square feet). The demand for space is drawn in the NE quadrant. In equilibrium, the demand for space, D, is equal to the stock of space, S. In Figure 1, taking the stock as given, rent, R, must be determined so that demand is exactly equal to the stock. Demand is a function of rent and conditions in the economy:

$$D(R, Economy) = S. \qquad (1)$$

In the NE quadrant of Figure 1, rent is determined by taking a level of stock on the horizontal axis up to the demand curve and over to the vertical axis.

The NW quadrant represents the first part of the asset market and has two axes: rent and price (per unit of space). The ray emanating out of the origin represents the capitalization rate for real estate assets: the ratio of rent to price. This is the current yield that investors demand in order to hold real estate assets. Generally, four considerations make up this capitalization rate: the long-term interest rate in the economy, the expected growth in rents, the risks associated with that rental income stream, and the treat-

Figure 1 Real Estate: The Property and Asset Markets

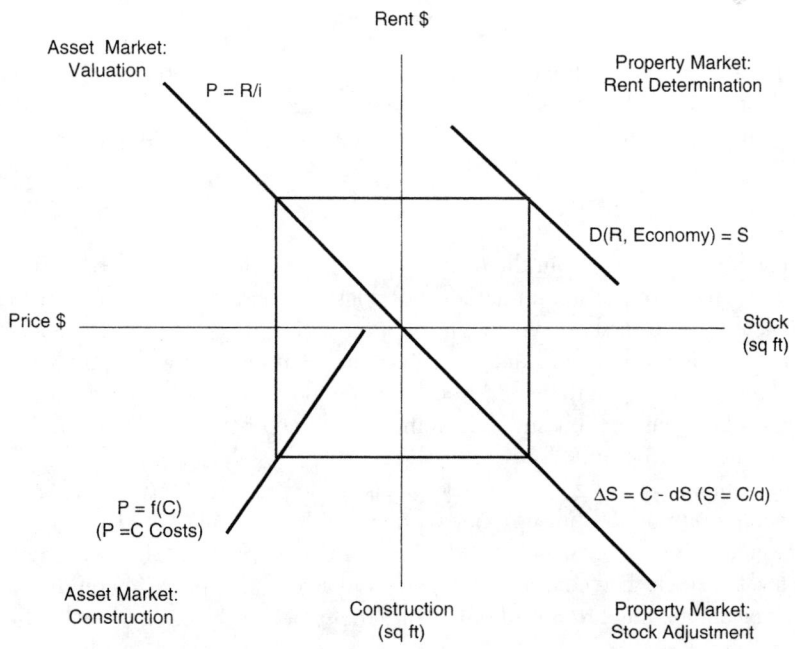

Asset Market: Valuation — $P = R/i$
Property Market: Rent Determination — $D(R, Economy) = S$
Asset Market: Construction — $P = f(C)$ ($P = C$ Costs)
Property Market: Stock Adjustment — $\Delta S = C - dS$ ($S = C/d$)

Axes: Rent $, Price $, Stock (sq ft), Construction (sq ft)

ment of real estate in the U.S. federal tax code. A higher capitalization rate is represented by a clockwise rotation in the ray, while a decline in the cap rate is represented by a counter-clockwise rotation. In this quadrant, the capitalization rate is taken as exogenous, based on interest rates and returns in the broader capital market for all assets (stocks, bonds, short-term deposits). Thus, the purpose of the NW quadrant is to take the rent level, R, from the NE quadrant and determine a price for real estate assets, P, using a capitalization rate, i:

$$P = \frac{R}{i.} \qquad (2)$$

In Figure 1, the price of the asset is determined by moving from the rent level on the vertical axis in the NE quadrant over to the ray in the NW quadrant, and then down to the horizontal axis (price).

The next (SW) quadrant is that portion of the asset market where the construction of new assets is determined.

Here, the curve, $f(C)$, represents the replacement cost, $CCosts$, of real estate. In this version of the diagram, the cost of construction is assumed to increase with greater building activity, and therefore the curve moves in a southwesterly direction. It intersects the price axis at that minimum dollar value (per unit of space) required to get some level of construction under way. If construction can be supplied at any level with almost the same costs, then the ray is almost vertical. Bottlenecks, scarce land and other impediments lead to inelastic supply and a ray that is more horizontal. Given the price of real estate assets from the NW quadrant, a line down to the replacement cost curve and then over to the vertical axis determines the level of new construction where replacement costs equal asset prices. Lower levels of construction would lead to excess profits while higher levels would be unprofitable. Hence, asset price, P, is equal to construction costs, $CCosts$, both of which are a function of construction level, C:

$$P = CCosts = f(C). \qquad (3)$$

In the final SE quadrant, the annual flow of new construction is converted into a long-run stock of real estate space. The change in stock, ΔS, in a given period is equal to new construction minus losses from the stock measured by the depreciation (removal) rate, d:

$$\Delta S = C - dS. \qquad (4)$$

The ray emanating from the origin represents that level of the stock (on the horizontal axis) that requires an annual level of construction for replacement just equal to that value on the vertical axis. At that level of the stock and corresponding construction, the stock of space will be constant over time since depreciation will equal new completions. Hence, ΔS is equal to 0 and $S = C/d$. It is important to note that the SE quadrant takes a level of construction and determines the value of the stock that would result if that construction continued forever.

In summary, starting with a stock of space, the property market determines rents which then get translated into property prices by the asset market. These asset prices, in turn, generate new construction that, back in the property market, eventually yields a new level of stock. The combined property and asset markets are in equilibrium when the starting and ending levels of the stock are the same.[3] If the ending stock differs from the starting stock, then the values of the four variables in the diagram (rents, prices, construction and the stock) are not in complete equilibrium. If the starting value exceeds the finishing, then rents, prices and construction must all rise to be in equilibrium. If the initial stock is less than the finishing stock, then rents, prices and construction must decrease to be in equilibrium.

In the case of real estate occupied by its owner, the four quadrants still hold, but there are not separate asset and property markets. The determination of prices and rents occurs with a single decision in a combined market. In the market for owner-occupied housing, for example, the stock of single-family homes, the number of households, and their incomes will determine an annual payment or willingness to pay by those households who purchase a home (NE quadrant). This is equivalent to a "rent." A rise in the number of households or a fall in available space means that to clear the property market, the annual payment to occupy a house must rise. The NW quadrant then translates this payment into a price actually paid for the home. Lower interest rates, for example, imply that for the same annual payment (rent), households can afford to pay a higher purchase (asset) price. With owner-occupied real estate, a single decision by the user/owner determines both rent and price. This decision, however, is influenced by the same economic and capital market conditions as with rental properties. Once the purchase price is determined, then construction and eventually the equilibrium stock of space follow in the other two quadrants (SW,SE).

It is important to realize that the four-quadrant diagram depicts a long-run equilibrium in the asset and property markets. The diagram is not as well suited to describing short-run market dynamics or the temporary disequilibria that often occur in the real estate sector.

COMPARATIVE STATICS

Using Figure 1, we can trace out the long-run impact of the broader economy on the real estate market. For illustrative purposes, we consider the impacts on the real estate market of changes in the macroeconomy (e.g., growth in income, production, or number of households), short-term or long-term interest rates, the tax treatment of real estate and the availability of construction financing. We identify which quadrant initially is affected by a specific exogenous change and trace the impacts through the other quadrants.

Increases in employment, production, or the number of households would increase the demand for space, shifting out the demand curve in the NE quadrant. For a given level of real estate space, rents must therefore rise. These higher rents then lead to greater asset prices in the NW quadrant which, in turn, generate a higher level of new construction in the SW quadrant. Eventually, this leads to a greater stock of space (SE quadrant). As shown in Figure 2, the new market equilibrium is the dashed box that in every direction lies outside of the box that connected the four curves in the original equilibrium. In the new equilibrium, neither rents, prices, construction, nor the stock can be less than in the initial equilibrium. The magnitude of the changes in these variables depends on the slopes of the various curves. For example, if construction were very elastic with respect to asset prices, then the new levels of prices and rents would be only slightly greater than before, whereas construction and stock would expand considerably.

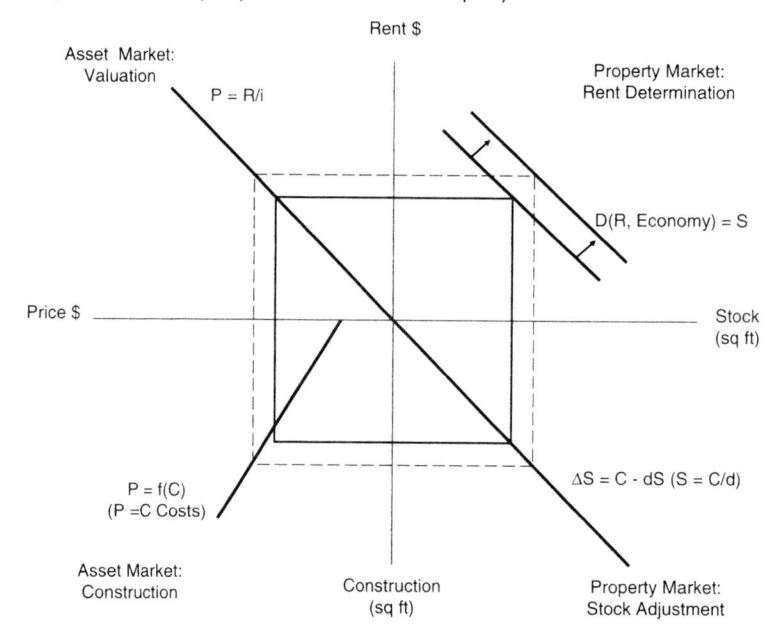

Figure 2 The Property and Asset Markets: Property Demand Shifts

Economic growth, then, increases all equilibrium variables in the real estate market, whereas economic contraction leads to decreases in all variables. Figure 3 compares the growth in total office employment in the U.S. with construction of office space and the overall office vacancy rate. It is clear that the national office market does move with the economy; during recession, vacancies tend to rise and construction falls whereas the opposite occurs during recoveries.

Figure 3 Office Employment Growth, Vacancy Rate and Construction

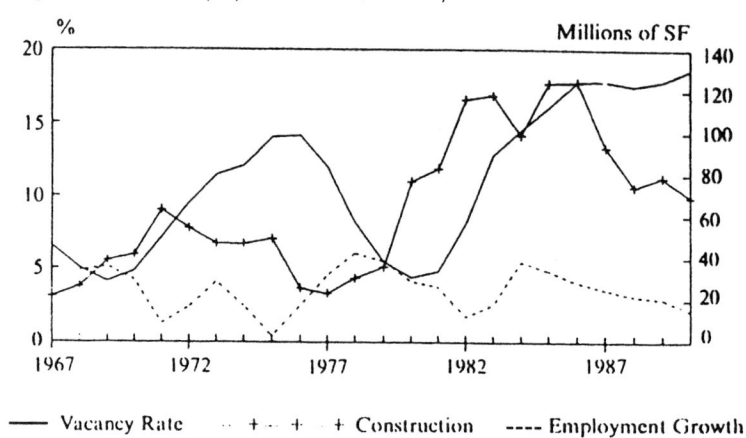

—— Vacancy Rate   + + + Construction   ---- Employment Growth

These data are aggregated from thirty metropolitan areas.

Source: CB Commercial.

If the demand to own real estate shifts, the impact on the combined markets is quite different than if the demand to use real estate changes. Shifts in the demand to own real estate assets may result from a number of factors. If interest rates in the rest of the economy rise (fall), then the existing "yield" from real estate becomes low (high) relative to fixed income securities and investors will wish to shift their funds from (into) the real estate sector. Similarly, if the risk characteristics of real estate are perceived to have changed, then the existing yield from real estate may also become insufficient (or more than necessary) to get investors to purchase real estate assets relative to other assets. Finally, changes in how real estate income is treated in the U.S. federal tax code can also greatly impact the demand to invest in real estate. Favorable depreciation rules for real estate (e.g., short tax life, accelerated deprecation schedule) increase the after-tax yield generated by real estate. This will increase the demand to hold real estate assets.

Reductions in long-term interest rates, decreases in the perceived risk of real estate, and generous depreciation or other favorable changes in the tax treatment of real estate all will cause a reduction in the income that investors require from real estate. As shown in Figure 4, in the NW quadrant, this has the effect of a counter-clockwise rotation in the capitalization rate ray that emanates out of the origin. Higher interest rates, greater perceived risk, and adverse tax changes rotate the ray in a clockwise manner.

Given a level of rent from the property market, a reduction in the current yield or capitalization rate for real estate raises asset prices and, in the SW quadrant, expands construction, as shown in Figure 4. Eventually this increases the stock of space (in the SE quadrant), which then lowers rents in the property market for space (NE quadrant). A new equilibrium requires that the initial and finishing rent levels be equal. In Figure 4, this new equilibrium results in a new solution that is lower and more rectangular than the original.

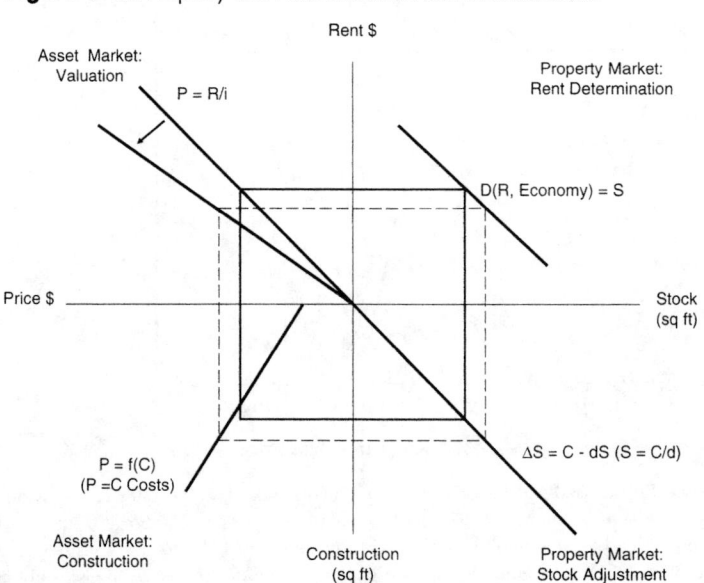

Figure 4 The Property and Asset Markets: Asset Demand Shifts

In the new equilibrium in Figure 4, asset prices must be higher and rents lower, while the long-term stock and its supporting level of construction must be greater. If rents were not lower, the stock would have to be the same (or lower) and this would be inconsistent with higher asset prices and greater construction. If asset prices were not higher, rents would be lower, and this would be inconsistent with the reduced stock (and less construction) which lower asset prices would generate. A positive shift in asset demand, like a positive shift in space demand, will raise prices, construction and the stock. It will, however, eventually lower rather than raise the level of space rents.

A negative relationship between commercial real estate values and interest rates has long been hypothesized, but the absence of a standardized asset price series makes this comparison difficult to test formally. Figure 5 examines this relationship in the housing market by tracking the historic movements in house prices and mortgage rates. The data in Figure 5 illustrate the generally inverse relationship between asset prices and long-term interest rates that is predicted by the model represented in our four-quadrant diagram.

The final exogenous change likely to impact the real estate market is a shift in the supply schedule for new construction. This can come about through several channels. Higher short-term interest rates will increase the costs of providing a given amount of new space, and lead to less construction. Even with modest interest rates, lending institutions may ration credit to selected real estate sectors. Throughout the early 1990s, commercial construction has been subject to a severe credit "crunch," despite lower short-term rates. Stricter local zoning or other building regulations also can add to development costs and reduce the profitability of new construction. As shown in Figure 6, these kinds of negative supply changes have the effect of causing a leftward shift in the

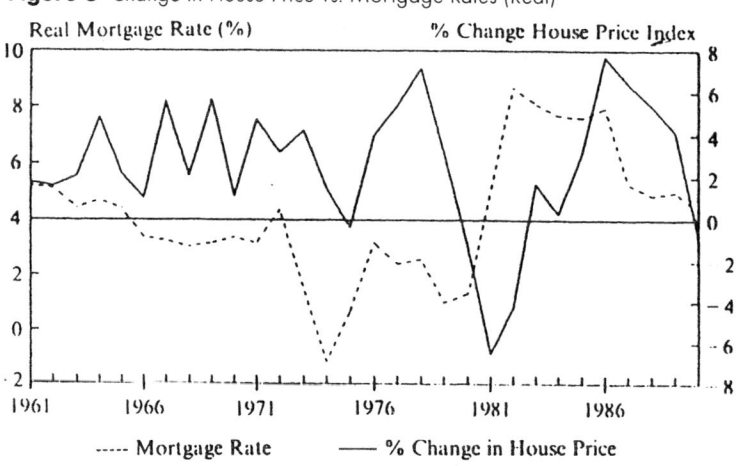

Figure 5 Change in House Price vs. Mortgage Rates (Real)

----- Mortgage Rate ——— % Change in House Price

Source: Price Index: 1960–69, Federal Housing Finance Board, 1990 Rates & Terms on Conventional Home Mortgages Annual Summary; 1970–1990, Federal Home Loan Mortgage Corp., Quality-Controlled Existing Home Price Index, unpublished report; Mortgage Rates: 1960–62, FHA insured rate plus .44 percentage points; 1963–90, Federal Housing Finance Board, 1990 Rates & Terms on Conventional Home Mortgages, Annual Summary.

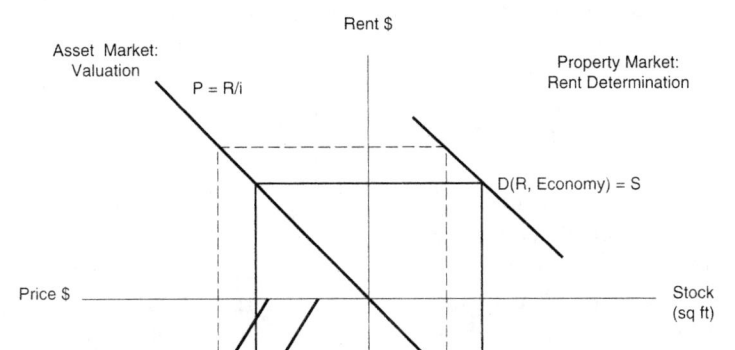

Figure 6 The Property and Asset Markets: Asset Cost Shifts

cost schedule of the SW quadrant: for the same level of asset prices, construction will be less. Positive changes in the supply environment, such as the easy availability of construction financing or a relaxation of development regulations, move the curve directly to the right and (for the same asset price) expand construction.

For a given level of asset prices, a negative shift in the new space supply schedule (SW quadrant) will lower the level of construction, eventually lowering the stock of space (SE quadrant). With less space in the NE quadrant, rent levels will have to rise, which in the NW quadrant will generate higher asset prices. When starting and finishing asset prices are equal, the new solution box will lie strictly to the northwest of the original solution. Rents and asset prices will increase, whereas construction levels and the stock will be lower. The magnitude of these changes, of course, will depend upon the slopes (or elasticities) of the various schedules.

Movements in the national economy can cause several shifts to occur simultaneously. As the national economy enters a slowdown, not only is there a contraction in output and employment (NE quadrant), but there are usually increases in short-term interest rates as well (SW quadrant). An economic expansion leads to the opposite combination. This combination of shifts can generate any pattern of new box solutions that lies between the two shown in Figures 2 and 6. Although the analysis gets more complicated in the case of multiple shifts, the net outcome is always some combination of the impacts from each individual change.

CONCLUSIONS

The distinction between the market for real estate assets and that for real estate space is an important one as we seek to improve our understanding of how this major sector operates. To this end, we have presented a simple analytic framework, illustrated by our four-quadrant diagram, which highlights this distinction and illustrates how real estate is impacted by both the nation's macroeconomy and its financial markets. This framework has proven to be very useful in the classroom as a way of introducing students to the operation of the real estate sector. With our four-quadrant analysis, we are able to trace out the impact on rents, asset prices, construction and the stock resulting from various exogenous forces.

This simple framework works well in illustrating the new equilibria that result as this exogenous environment changes. An important drawback of this framework is that it is not easy to trace out the intermediate steps as the market moves to its new equilibrium. Depicting the intermediate adjustments of the market would require a dynamic system of equations that would significantly complicate our analysis. Developing an intuitive framework similar to the one in this paper that traces the intermediate-term dynamic path to a new equilibrium remains a formidable challenge.

NOTES

[1] The figures on gross domestic product and gross and net private domestic fixed investment are from the GDP accounts as reported in the *Economic Report of the President 1992*. It should be noted that the methodology for estimating the value of structures is different in the GDP accounts and the Value of New Construction Put in Place reports. The structures components of GDP include value of new mobile homes sold, expenditures for drilling petroleum and natural gas wells, construction of mine shafts, real estate commissions on the sale of new and existing structures and the net value of used public sector structures purchased by the private sector. None of these are included in the Value of New Construction Put in Place estimates. The Value of Put in Place estimates include allowances for funds used in constructing public utility plants, which are excluded in the structures component of GDP (U.S. Bureau of the Census 1991, pp. 1–2).

[2] The estimate of national net worth is from the Board of Governors (1991). It should be noted that the Federal Reserve estimates the value of real estate at $10.7 trillion. Miles argues that the BEA/Federal Reserve estimates of the value of nonresidential real estate may be high because the data used for the stock estimates include special purpose fixtures in manufacturing plants which are certainly part of the nation's capital stock but really should not be included when measuring the value of real estate (see Miles 1990, p. 74).

[3] Our graph provides a simple, intuitive illustration of the solution to the simultaneous system of equations 1–4.

REFERENCES

Board of Governors of the Federal Reserve System. 1991. *Balance Sheets of the U.S. Economy: 1945–1990*. September.

IREM Foundation and Arthur Anderson. 1991. *Managing the Future: Real Estate in the 1990s*.

Miles, M. 1990. What Is the Value of All U.S. Real Estate? *Real Estate Review* 2(2): 69–77.

U.S. Bureau of Census. 1991. Value of New Construction Put in Place: May 1991. *Current Construction Reports*.

25 Modeling the Corporate Real Estate Decision

Mike Miles, John Pringle, and Brian Webb

The corporate real estate decision has been viewed traditionally in a capital budgeting context. Due to recent capital market innovations, it is now more useful to view this decision from a combined capital budgeting/corporate financing framework. With the new combined perspective, all corporate real estate decisions should be reviewed on a regular basis. Given this need for frequent review, and the large number of variables involved, a formal model is helpful.

The individual techniques needed for a model with this joint perspective are well known. The interactions between real estate valuation, accrual accounting and corporate valuation methodologies are quite complex, however, as demonstrated in this paper. Moreover, the application of the theoretical model to real life situations is a challenging task as shown in the analysis of recent corporate restructurings. Detailed information on a corporation's real estate holdings, and subjective estimates on the impact of changes in real estate holdings on the firm's cost of capital, debt capacity, systematic risk, and operating revenues and expenses are required.

INTRODUCTION

In June 1988, the market capitalization of listed securities in America was approximately $2.3 trillion,[1] with real estate believed to comprise over 25% of that value.[2] While real estate plays an important role on the corporation's balance sheet, Zeckhouser and Silverman [34] find that only 40% of American firms clearly and consistently evaluate the performance of their real estate, and only 20% manage their real estate for profit (i.e., try to match or exceed the rate of return they could achieve through alternative investments). Instead, corporations traditionally have treated real estate as a necessary cost of operations and, after careful analysis of the initial lease versus buy decision, have entered purchased real estate on the firm's balance sheet and thereafter largely ignored it. Given the magnitude of corporate real estate in both absolute and relative terms, the lack of management attention is a serious problem.

The normal sequence of events involved in a corporate real estate decision includes:

From *The Journal of Real Estate Research*.

- The corporation decides on a need for additional space. This is usually *part* of a larger capital budgeting decision tied to *operations*.[3]
- The space need is passed on to the corporation's real estate group for implementation.[4]
- Major builder/developers and/or real estate brokers are contacted about the need, and some subset of these professionals is hired to perform their services. This involves an investment decision (via discounted cash flow analysis), but with a focus on flexibility and the residual position of the corporate investor.[5]
- Either the real estate professional or the corporation brings in an investment banking firm to advise on financing. There are a few basic alternatives with innumerable bells and whistles as shown in Exhibit 1.
- The group then selects a financing alternative which best meets all *stated objectives*. Inevitably, without the kind of model described in this paper, this final selection will be an apples vs. oranges comparison with no good way to price alternative risks or to risk adjust alternative costs.
- The real estate is entered on the firm's balance sheet then largely ignored.

Exhibit 2 lists some of the possible objectives a corporation might pursue through the more exacting management of its corporate real estate after the initial acquisition and financing decision. The purpose of this paper (and a companion paper, *Information and Agency Issues in Corporate Real Estate Decisions*) is to help move real estate into the mainstream of corporate financial management by providing a vehicle for the systematic pursuit of these objectives. This point is particularly pertinent today since firms

Exhibit 1 Financing Alternatives

Type	Actions	Key Issues
Conventional-investor owned, corporate lessee, a bank construction loan, insurance company permanent financing	Swap for fixed rate prefund permanent, joint venture equity with tenant or long-term lender	Length of lease, maturity of debt
Special purpose corporation for financing, ownership financing, ownership flexible but the corporation takes the risk through a master lease	Rate commercial paper or domestic bond depending on maturity preference (backed by AAA letter of credit), privately placed lease payment bonds, construction period tranches	Long term financial and operating flexibility
Use some form of zero coupon to advance the realization of the expected appreciation	Combine lease payment bond with first mortgage	Size of residual and related risk
In all the basic approaches		Returns (and risks) to all three participants considering both current results and the expected residual values

Exhibit 2 Objectives for Corporate Real Estate Management[a]

- Cash Generation (but the related costs are again in apples and oranges unless a formal model is used).
- Takeover prevention (real estate financed to real estate motivated takeovers must be considered).
- More effective utilization of the tax laws.
- Minimizing agency cost (shareholder/bondholder and shareholder/manager).
- The use of real estate financing as a market signal.
- Playing the local real estate market by using the comparative advantage generated by the corporation's long-time horizon.
- Maintaining flexibility given the firm's current and expected space needs; flexibility is an important consideration while pursuing the objectives above.

[a]Objectives beyond the obvious desire to maximize the value of the firm

now enjoy additional flexibility in managing their real estate holdings due to (1) the creation of new financial instruments involving real estate; and, (2) the increased liquidity created by the presence of more institutional and foreign buyers in the market.

Due to this increased flexibility, the well-managed firm should view real estate decisions from a combined capital budgeting and corporate financing perspective *on an ongoing basis*. This paper identifies the potential gains from more active management of real estate, highlights some of the problems and issues, and models the corporate real estate decision process.

The interactions of real estate with many aspects of the firm's operations and financing decisions creates a level of complexity that requires careful analysis. This research approaches the task by first developing the logic for a corporate valuation model that focuses on real estate. The third section then makes the case for a "wholistic"[6] corporate valuation model, while the fourth section applies that model to data from several large corporations with recent large real estate transactions. A summary and conclusion follow in the last section.

THEORETICAL SUPPORT FOR A CORPORATE REAL ESTATE VALUATION MODEL

Lack of active management of real estate assets, along with changes in the environment surrounding corporate owned real estate, may result in significant value that is undetected by managers and investors alike. The potential hidden value in real estate is a function of (1) changes in capital market conditions, (2) changes in firm prospects, (3) changes in utilization of real estate, (4) tax and accounting changes, and (5) changes in factors affecting agency costs of the firm. Specifically, changes in the capital markets affect real estate values via changes in market capitalization rates on real estate relative to those of other assets.[7] Changes in a firm's operating prospects due either to changes in return prospects or changes in risk exposure have a similar impact. The expected return on real estate may justify ownership (as opposed to leasing) of real estate in periods when firm operating prospects are poor, but this relationship can reverse when firm prospects improve. The magnitude of the value increment created by changes in the use of a firm's real estate obviously depends on how much value the new use adds to the property. Changes in tax laws in 1984 and 1986 had a major impact on real estate values, and recent accounting changes embodied in the *Financial Accounting Standard* (FAS) #94 and #98 add to this impact.[8] Finally, a companion paper, *Information and Agency Issues in Corporate Real Estate Decisions,* explores the potential of corporate real estate to reduce the agency costs of the firm.

The potential to increase firm value (in addition to the threat of takeover) suggests that firms should consistently review the performance and the value of their real estate. Appraisal models of real estate value have been around for a long time, and these models do a satisfactory job of determining the market value of real estate in isolation. Knowing the value of real estate in isolation is not sufficient, however. A corporation must understand how its real estate holdings are affecting its *total* market value to determine how to utilize this asset, and this requires a valuation model of real estate *within* the corporate setting. The third section of this paper describes such a methodology.

AN INTEGRATED APPROACH TO THE CORPORATE REAL ESTATE DECISION

Techniques for valuing real estate separately from the remaining assets of the firm—the normal appraisal process—are well known. To value real estate within the context of the firm as a whole (and thereby properly account for interactions between real estate valuation, accrual accounting, and corporate valuation parameters) requires a comprehensive corporate valuation model that explicitly recognizes (and separately values) a firm's real estate holdings. Exhibit 3 presents the basic structure of such a model.

Valuing a corporation in this manner exposes the interactions of the corporation's real estate holdings with the overall financial structure of the firm. Real estate is shown

Exhibit 3 Model of Corporate Valuation with Real Estate Explicitly Considered

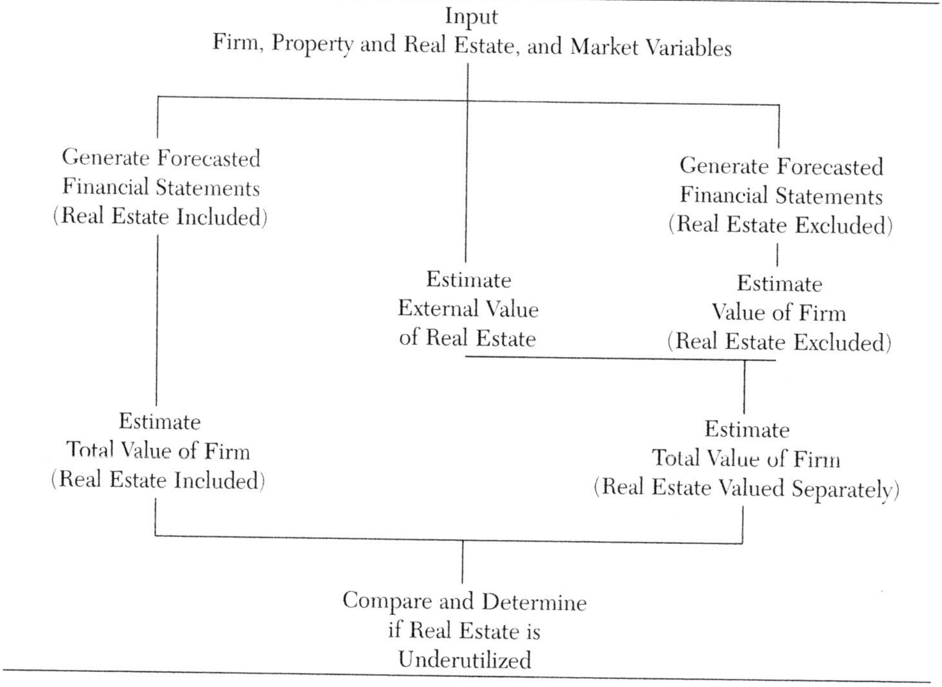

```
                    Input
     Firm, Property and Real Estate, and Market Variables
                      |
        ┌─────────────┼─────────────┐
        │             │             │
  Generate Forecasted         Generate Forecasted
  Financial Statements        Financial Statements
  (Real Estate Included)      (Real Estate Excluded)
        │             │             │
        │          Estimate        Estimate
        │        External Value    Value of Firm
        │         of Real Estate   (Real Estate Excluded)
        │             │             │
     Estimate                    Estimate
  Total Value of Firm         Total Value of Firm
  (Real Estate Included)      (Real Estate Valued Separately)
        └─────────────┬─────────────┘
                      │
              Compare and Determine
                if Real Estate is
                   Underutilized
```

to affect the cost of equity, cost of debt, debt capacity, systematic risk, and the book-to-market value ratio of the corporation. While it is not always obvious what the direction or magnitude of the changes in these attributes will be, this model clearly points out the minimum information that is needed by the market to value a firm independent of its real estate holdings.

Basic DCF Methodology.[9] Valuing an unlevered flow using DCF methodology is straightforward: cash flows expected in the future are discounted at a rate that reflects both the time value of money and the operating or business risk of the flows. When leverage is introduced, the valuation problem becomes more complex, for the process then must account for financial leverage and interest deductibility in addition to operating risk.

When a firm owns real property, valuation takes on yet another degree of complexity as real estate is different than other corporate assets from an accounting, tax, and appreciation/depreciation aspect.

In recognition of the potential for hidden value in company-owned real estate, a thorough financial analysis must specifically address the individual value of the firm's real estate, and incorporate the financing alternatives inherent in the real estate. This is of particular importance because the degree of financial latitude implicit in real estate is different from one firm to another. The next part of this section expands on this notion by separating the value of the firm into two distinct components, the value of the operating cash flows and the value of the real property. Each of these is independently evaluated with consideration given to whether separation of the components substantially alters the riskiness of either component in isolation.

Valuing a Firm. Consider the following hypothetical example in which privately held Alpha Manufacturing Company is being evaluated as an acquisition target by Omega Corporation. The problem at hand is to determine the value to Omega of Alpha's equity.[10]

A check of beta coefficients for comparable public companies might suggest a relevant market beta for Alpha.[11] Using publicly available data (as shown in the Atlantic Richfield example in the fourth section) for the bond rate and market risk premium yields an equity capitalization rate for Alpha as follows:[12]

$$K_e = Risk\ free\ rate + Market\ Risk\ Premium \times Beta$$

Assuming that Omega's management has determined the appropriate financing mix for the acquisition,[13] the weighted average cost of capital *(WACC)* is easily calculated using an estimate of the forward tax rate *(T)*.

The *WACC* takes into account three factors: operating risk, financing mix, and tax deductibility of interest. Since financing mix and interest deductibility are accounted for in the discount rate, the *WACC* should be applied to Alpha's expected after-tax *operating* cash flows for a period of years, with interest excluded completely.

The terminal value for the cash flow stream must also be calculated.[14] The nominal perpetuity approach to estimating terminal value is straightforward and is the method normally used.[15] Starting with expected earnings before interest and taxes *(EBIT)*, in the final year of the estimated period, one first multiplies by $1 - T$ to account for the tax liability on the operating flow. Assuming (1) that the flow is a perpetuity in nominal terms, (2) that depreciation is reinvested to cover capital expenditure requirements, and (3) that there is no additional investment in working capital, then cash flows from operations for all future years will be constant. Valuing this the *WACC* gives a terminal value for the operating flows.

After using the *WACC* to discount the operating flows, Alpha's interest-bearing debt at time t must be subtracted to determine the equity value of the firm. Note that the *market value* of the debt, rather than its book value, should be subtracted.

Valuing the Real Estate Option. A look at Alpha's fixed assets might reveal that the firm owns its headquarters building. By looking first at the office building as a separate asset and valuing it in an unlevered state, one begins to see the potential for hidden value in the real estate. It is hidden not because it is hard to find on the balance sheet, but because its effect is not specifically considered in the firm valuation methodology outlined in the previous section. In fact, most financial analysts estimating a firm's earnings do not consider operating or financing options inherent in the firm's real estate, mainly because they do not have access to the necessary information. This would not be a serious problem if all firms had the same proportionate option, but clearly that is not the case. Some firms have great flexibility in their real estate, while others have practically none.

The estimated future sale price might be derived by capitalizing the last-year net operating income *(NOI.)*. Note that *NOI* is defined here as *EBDIT* (earnings before depreciation, interest and taxes). The capitalization rate is empirical and not derivable theoretically. It is simply the typical ratio of *NOI* to market value for a local sample of real estate sales.

It should be noted that the general purpose nature of the office building in this example greatly facilitates a transaction. With special purpose buildings, an outside investor is less likely to see any appreciation potential.[16]

The operating flows are discounted at the required pre-tax return for unlevered real estate. This rate can be estimated from the mean *DCF* return actually realized on large national samples of properties. It can be calculated by relating ending market value plus cash flows received to beginning market value. Such a rate is analogous to the Ibbotson-Sinquefield data on common stock returns, both in its method of computation and in that it is post corporate (nonexistent in this case) pre-personal tax. This rate will exceed the *NOI* capitalization rate for the same reason that market required rates of return on common stocks typically exceed earnings/price ratios. That is, the capitalization rate is an earnings multiplier whereas the discount rate is a total return figure.[17]

Note carefully that the discount rate is derived from *historical* data.[18] Using this figure requires the same leap of faith required to use the Ibbotson-Sinquefield data, namely, an assumption that market risk premia will remain about the same in the future as in the past. It may often be advisable to adjust the historical data up or down to reflect current conditions; or, as in the corporate situation, one could use analysts' forecasts of future real estate returns such as those now available from both Salomon Brothers and Goldman Sachs.

Regardless of whether the buyer finances the purchase in some part with a mortgage, the corporation's capital structure will be affected by any real estate disposition. Since the real estate previously served as indirect collateral for corporate debt, it is logical to assume that part of the proceeds from sale would be used to reduce corporate debt. One could assume that the market values the real estate at its current value and that the firm is at its optimal debt ratio. In this case, one would reduce the corporate debt by the appropriate amount of mortgage debt (the optimal financing ratio for the property standing along, e.g., 80% of the market value of the real estate) and continue to use the original weighted average cost of capital.

Alternatively, if the market were totally ignorant of the real estate's value, one might reduce corporate debt by the book value change times the target percentage debt in the capital structure. In a world of imperfect information (i.e., the market does not have sufficient information to price the real estate), corporate debt might be reduced by the market value (rather than book) of the real estate times the target percentage debt in the capital structure. This intermediate position parallels the typical corporate load which requires a prorated debt reduction upon the sale of any major asset.

Operating Flow without Real Estate. Having valued the real estate to a potential buyer,[19] consider now the valuation of Alpha's operating flows with the real estate removed. If the real estate is separated from the company, the firm's operating flows are altered significantly. Specifically, when the real estate is removed, the firm:

- Loses rental income;
- Is relieved of all operating expenses associated with the real estate;
- Is relieved of all depreciation expense associated with the real estate;
- Now must pay rent at market rates for its employees that remain in the building.[20]

Revised WACC Cash Flows are calculated by starting with the revised EBIT and adjusting for depreciation, capital expenditures, change in working capital, and interest earned on investment of the cash netted from sale. Next, the revised operating flows of the company with real estate removed are valued. Caution is warranted here. Separating the real estate from the firm might significantly change the riskiness of the firm. If the real estate involved secure long-term leases, and operating expenses were subject to little uncertainty, the real estate flows might be less risky than the firm's operating flows. Pulling out the real estate flows would cause the firm's beta to rise. On the other hand, if leases were not long term and if uncertainty were high regarding local market supply and demand conditions, the real estate flows might be more uncertain than the operating flows.[21]

Original Unlevered Cost of Equity (K_o) is the starting point.

$$K_o = K_d + [K_e - Kd] \frac{E}{E + D(1-T)}$$

Using a revised target debt ratio (with a resulting level of debt ($D°$) and equity ($E°$)) after the real estate sale and corresponding loan payoff, the revised K_e and K_w are

$$K_e° = K_d + [K_o - K_d] \frac{E° + D°(1-T)}{E°}$$

$$K_w° = W_d° K_d(1-T) + W_e° K_e°$$

From these, the revised Terminal Value and the present values of the total cash flows are calculated. Finally, to arrive at a total value for the firm, the net cash realized from the real estate sale and assumed to be paid out as a dividend must be added back. This cash dividend can be estimated as follows:

Cash Dividend = Market Value of R.E. − Tax − (Market Value of R.E. × Target Debt%)

Summary Model Output. When the real estate is sold, the firm immediately captures both the income and appreciation components of value that are inherent in the real estate asset. Since traditional accounting, on which WACC is based, recognizes only the income side of real estate value, the firm might appear to be more valuable after the sale. If the analysis extended over a long period of time (say, fifty years), however, the difference would disappear as the firm experienced higher rent expense (and less rent income) as the long-term cost of recognizing the real estate's appreciation at the front end.

In "perfect" capital markets, there would be no change in value resulting from the separation except where 1) the separation was accompanied by an operating change such as a move of some workers to cheaper space or 2) a more advantageous set of tax rates were encountered as a result of the separation. (A loose translation of Miller [21] might even argue that rates of return would adjust to eliminate the potential tax benefit.) The argument here is information-, not market efficiency-, based. The information available to analysts is insufficient to properly value the appreciation component of the real estate return.

Using the Paradigm. The preceding model is no more than a combination of well-known accounting, finance and real estate methodologies. It is a challenging task because it requires an explicit combination of accrual accounting, actual after-tax cash flows and finance theory. (Traditionally, most analysts have focused on only one of these three areas at a time and hence ignored difficulties in the interfaces.) It is useful in practice because it facilitates sensitivity analysis on key variables. The completeness of the model allows a wholistic view of corporation finance not possible with any of the three methodologies in isolation. As market conditions change, the model helps the corporate financial officer continually reevaluate the firm's capital structure, particularly the real estate component, to maximize shareholder value.

APPLICATION OF THE EXPANDED MODEL USING PUBLICLY AVAILABLE DATA

The above analysis indicates that when real estate comprises a significant portion of the firm's assets and has more potential for real capital gains than most other corporate assets, it is important for corporations to independently value their real estate. To value the remainder of the firm independent of its real estate holdings requires the removal of all cash flows and financing related to these assets. The most enlightening aspects of valuing a corporation in this fashion are the observed interactions of the corporation's real estate holdings with the overall financial structure of the firm. Exhibits 4 through 8 present the application of data from Atlantic Richfield to the model. Exhibit 9 then presents in condensed form the results of similar analysis for Exxon, International Paper, and Time Incorporated. All of these firms, like Atlantic Richfield, experienced a major real estate restructuring in the past two years.

Specifically Exhibit 4 presents the necessary variables for corporate valuation when real estate is to be considered independently in a real life situation. Panel A of Exhibit 4 displays general firm variables, with Atlantic Richfield's 1986 data obtained from the firm's annual report,[22] and projections on most financial variables for the following four

Exhibit 4 Valuation Variables for Atlantic Richfield

Panel A: Firm Variables	1986	1987	1988	1989	1990
Sales ($MM)	14993.0	16000.0	17377.9	18874.5	20500.0
Annual Sales Growth	-0.333	0.067	0.086	0.086	0.086
Operating Margin	0.209	0.215	0.205	0.205	0.205
Depreciation ($MM)	1646.0	1630.0	1745.0	1868.2	2000.0
Non-Operating Income	781.0	781.0	781.0	781.0	781.0
Coupon Rate on Corporate Debt	0.113	0.113	0.113	0.113	0.113
Market Rate on Corporate Debt	0.093	0.093	0.093	0.093	0.093
Corporate Tax Rate	0.528	0.460	0.380	0.380	0.380
Capital Gains Tax Rate	0.280	0.380	0.380	0.380	0.380
New Profit ($MM)	615.0	910.0	993.7	1085.2	1185.0
Current Assets/Sales	0.316	0.316	0.316	0.316	0.316
Book Value of Land & R.E. ($MM)	130.0	120.0	110.0	100.0	90.0
Depreciation of R.E. ($MM)	10.0	10.0	10.0	10.0	10.0
Working Capital ($MM)	993.0	1000.0	1091.4	1191.1	1300.0
Long-Term Debt ($MM)	6969.0	5800.0	6085.7	6385.5	6700.0
Other L.T. Liabilities ($MM)	5626.0	5626.0	5626.0	5626.0	5626.0
Net Worth ($MM)	5259.0	5450.0	5740.0	6047.3	6370.0

Panel B: Real Estate Variables	1986	1987	1988	1989	1990
Square Footage Owned	1200000	1200000	1200000	1200000	120000
Market Rent per Sq. Ft.	34.50	35.54	36.60	37.70	38.83
Rent per Sq. Ft. (Leased Space)	43.00	44.29	45.62	46.99	48.40
% Change in Market Rent	0.03	0.03	0.03	0.03	0.03
Vacancy and Collection Losses (% of Gross Income)	0.05	0.05	0.05	0.05	0.05
Operating Exp. (% Gross Inc.)	0.45	0.45	0.45	0.45	0.45
% Building Occupied by Firm	0.80	0.80	0.80	0.80	0.80
Life of Building to New Investor	31.5	31.5	31.5	31.5	31.5
Land Market Value ($$MM)	110.00	110.00	110.00	110.00	110.00
Mortgage Interest Rate	0.0975	0.0975	0.0975	0.0975	0.0975
Mortgage Term (Yrs.)	30	30	30	30	30
Maximum Loan to Value Ratio	0.80	0.80	0.80	0.80	0.80
New Investor Personal Tax Rate	0.35	0.35	0.35	0.35	0.35
Transaction Cost of Sale (%)	0.08	0.08	0.08	0.08	0.08
Capitalization Rate for NOI	0.1025	0.1025	0.1025	0.1025	0.1025
Req. Return on Unlevered R.E.	0.1350	0.1350	0.1350	0.1350	0.1350
New Investor's Levered Req. Ret.	0.1723	0.1723	0.1723	0.1723	0.1723

Panel C: Valuation Variables	1986	1987	1988	1989	1990
20 Yr. U.S. Bond Rate (Rf rate)	0.085	0.085	0.085	0.085	0.085
Stock Market Return	0.145	0.145	0.145	0.145	0.145
Firm's Beta	1.0	1.0	1.0	1.0	1.0
Firm's Debt Ratio	0.520	0.520	0.520	0.520	0.520
Cost of Debt	0.044	0.050	0.058	0.058	0.058
Cost of Equity	0.145	0.145	0.145	0.145	0.145
Weighted Average Cost of Capital	0.092	0.096	0.100	0.100	0.100

Exhibit 4 *(Continued)*

WACC versus Equity Residual Method: Valuing an unlevered cash flow using basic discounted cash flow methodology is straightforward—cash flows expected in the future are discounted at a rate that reflects the time value of money and the operating risk of the flows. When leverage is introduced, the valuation problem becomes more complex as the process must account for financial leverage and interest deductibility as well. The two most commonly used approaches to this problem are the weighted average cost of capital (*WACC*) approach, and the equity residual (*ER*) approach. Under ideal conditions (where debt can be continuously adjusted so that it remains a constant percentage of the cash flows to be received), the two methodologies yield the same result. Under normal conditions, however, the two methodologies may yield substantially different results.[1] In light of the typical corporate situation of fairly decentralized investment decision making, but centralized financing, the *WACC* methodology will be used here. This methodology assumes a constant financing ratio rather than estimating specific amortization schedules for each project as the *ER* methodology requires. The cost of equity is estimated as the risk-free rate of return over the relevant time period (as measured by the 20-year Treasury bond rate), plus the market risk premium (6% over this time period) adjusted for the specific risk of the firm (estimated by the *Value Line* reported beta for the firm). The cost of debt is estimated as the holding period return on the corporation's bond issue with approximately 20 years to maturity, and relative weights are estimated by the current market value of equity and book value of debt.

Ex post versus Ex ante Risk Premiums: This analysis uses the Capital Asset Pricing Model (*CAPM*) to determine appropriate risk premiums for the individual firms. The *CAPM* has come under increasing criticism from academics and recently has been seriously questioned in regulatory rate of return testimony (see ATT Divestiture FCC Docket 84–800). A more forward-looking alternative is to estimate the risk premium from a composite of analysts' forecasts. Because derivation of the proper cost of capital is not the primary concern of this paper, the *CAPM* methodology is followed despite questions of its accuracy.

Terminal Values: Both the *WACC* and the *ER* methodologies require estimates of future cash flows for some time into the future, followed by an estimate of the terminal value of the project (or in this case, the firm). The following analysis estimates annual cash flows for four years, and then estimates a terminal value of the firm. Terminal values may be estimated by discounting an assumed perpetual cash flow at a nominal or real rate of return. In an inflationary world it is not certain whether cash flows assumed constant into perpetuity should be considered real or nominal cash flows. The nominal perpetuity approach is more straightforward, is the approach most frequently used in practice, and is therefore the approach used here. Starting with the ending year projections of cash flows, multiplying this figure by 1 minus the tax rate to account for the tax liability, assuming depreciation is reinvested to cover capital expenditure requirements and that there is no additional investment in working capital, and valuing this cash flow at the *WACC* yields a terminal value for the firm.

---

[1]For a thorough discussion of the issues that differentiate these two methodologies, see Salomon Brothers [12].

years (1987–1990) obtained from *Value Line*.[23] Information on the real estate is present in Panel B, as obtained from the report of the real estate's sales in the *Wall Street Journal*, private survey of local brokers, and/or estimates of the authors. Panel C displays general capital market variables that are required for the valuation analysis. These are obtained from the *Wall Street Journal*, *Value Line*, and estimated company annual reports. Finally, Panel D discusses some of the key underlying assumptions of the model.

Exhibit 5 presents expected financial statements (based on the data in Exhibit 4) for Atlantic Richfield, with real estate included in the estimates. Exhibit 6 presents these same

Exhibit 5 Expected Financial Statements for Atlantic Richfield (Real Estate included)

Panel A: Balance Sheet	1986	1987	1988	1989	1990
Current Assets	4743.00	5061.56	5497.47	5970.91	6485.13
R.E. (Single Property)	130.00	120.00	110.00	100.00	90.00
Fixed Assets	16731.00	15756.00	16251.17	16767.58	17306.00
Total Assets	21604.00	20937.56	21858.64	22838.49	23881.13
Current Liabilities	3750.00	4061.56	4406.07	4779.77	5185.13
Long-term Debt	6969.00	5800.00	6085.70	6385.47	6700.00
Other L.T. Liabilities	5626.00	5626.00	5626.00	5626.00	5626.00
Total Liabilities	16345.00	15487.56	16117.77	16791.24	17511.13
Net Worth	5259.00	5450.00	5740.87	6047.26	6370.00
Total Liab. + N.W.	21604.00	20937.56	21858.64	22838.49	23881.13

Panel B: Income Statement	1986	1987	1988	1989	1990
Sales	14993.00	16000.00	17377.93	18874.52	20500.00
CofGS and Op. Expenses	11853.00	12560.00	13815.45	15005.24	16297.50
EBDIT	3140.00	3440.00	3562.47	3869.28	4202.50
Depreciation	1646.00	1630.00	1745.03	1868.17	2000.00
EBIT	1494.00	1810.00	1817.45	2001.11	2202.50
Other Income/Expenses	781.00	781.00	781.00	781.00	781.00
Interest Expense	972.00	905.81	995.66	1031.86	1072.21
EBT	1303.00	1685.19	1602.79	1750.25	1911.29
Taxes	688.00	775.19	609.06	665.10	726.29
Net Income	615.00	910.00	993.73	1085.16	1185.00

Panel C: Financial Statistics	1986	1987	1988	1989	1990
Return on Assets	0.028	0.043	0.045	0.048	0.050
Return on Net Worth	0.177	0.167	0.173	0.179	0.186

expected financial statements with real estate omitted from the balance sheet and its effects on the financial and operational aspects of the firm removed from the income statement.

Exhibit 7 looks at estimates of the independent values of the real estate to both a tax-exempt and taxable investor. This analysis requires substantially more information than is publicly available for properties that have not recently been sold. To obtain the necessary information for this analysis, only corporations that had recent major real estate transactions (like Atlantic Richfield) were selected for this study, and only the specific properties sold (instead of all real estate as would be desirable) are analyzed. Although market transaction prices are available on the properties analyzed here making this analysis unnecessary, Exhibit 7 indicates how real estate that has not recently been sold could be evaluated by internal management using standard discounted cash flow methods.

Finally, Exhibit 8 presents the estimates of the value of Atlantic Richfield both with and without its real estate. Note that given the set of circumstances relevant to the 1986 time period, Atlantic Richfield's value is maximized by selling the real estate. This result is not obvious from casual observation, as removing the real estate from the financial state-

Exhibit 6 Expected Financial Statements of Atlantic Richfield (without Real Estate)

Panel A: Balance Sheet	1986	1987	1988	1989	1990
Current Assets	4743.00	5061.56	5497.47	5970.91	6485.13
Fixed Assets (Less R.E.)	16731.00	15876.00	16361.17	16867.58	17396.00
Land and Real Estate	130.00				
Total Assets	21604.00	20937.56	21858.64	22838.49	23881.13
Current Liabilities	3750.00	4061.56	4406.07	4779.77	5185.13
Long-term Debt	6969.00	5800.00	6085.70	6385.47	6700.00
Other L.T. Liabilities	5626.00	5626.00	5626.00	5626.00	5626.00
Total Liabilities	16345.00	15487.56	16117.77	16791.24	17511.13
Net Worth	5259.00	5450.00	5740.87	6047.26	6370.00
Total Liab. + N.W.	21604.00	20937.56	21858.64	22838.49	23881.13

Panel B: Income Statement	1986	1987	1988	1989	1990
Sales	14993.00	16000.00	17377.93	18874.52	20500.00
Original EBIT	1494.00	1810.00	1817.45	2001.11	2202.50
Lost Rent		10.10	10.40	10.71	11.03
Operating Expenses Saved		19.19	19.76	20.36	20.97
Lease Payment		42.52	43.79	45.11	46.46
Depreciation Saved		10.00	10.00	10.00	10.00
Revised EBIT	1494.00	1786.57	1793.02	1975.65	2175.97
Other Income/Expenses	781.00	781.00	781.00	781.00	781.00
Interest Expense	972.00	905.81	995.66	1031.86	1072.21
PBT	1303.00	1661.76	1578.35	1724.79	1884.76
Tax	688.00	764.41	599.77	655.42	716.21
Net Income	615.00	897.35	978.58	1069.37	1168.55
Gain From Sale of R.E.		33.48			
Revised Net Income	615.00	930.83	978.58	1069.37	1168.55

Panel C: Financial Statistics	1986	1987	1988	1989	1990
ROA	0.028	0.044	0.045	0.047	0.049
RONW	0.117	0.171	0.170	0.177	0.183

ments affects many aspects of the firm's financial operation—including the firm's cost of capital, debt capacity, and systematic risk—as well as its operating revenues and expenses.

The model of firm valuation examined here integrates real estate valuation, accrual accounting, and firm valuation in a consistent theoretical framework. Although this general model can provide a guideline for all firms, every corporate situation is unique and consideration must be given to the idiosyncrasies of each firm. To illustrate, Exhibit 9 shows the results of similar analyses of real estate transactions of four corporations: Atlantic Richfield with a $200 million sale, Exxon with a $305 million sale, International Paper with a $118 million purchase, and Time Incorporated with a $118 million sale. Relevant information for estimating the value of real estate was very difficult to obtain, even for real estate that recently sold. Similar public information is nearly nonexistent for real estate that has been held by the same corporation for any significant period.

Exhibit 7 Estimated Value of Atlantic Richfield Real Estate
(Sold 11/25/86 for $200m)

Panel A:	Value to Tax-exempt Investor			
Cash Flows from Real Estate:	1987	1988	1989	1990
Gross Income (Maximum)	42.64	43.92	45.24	46.60
Vacancy and Collection Loss	2.13	2.20	2.26	2.33
Gross Income (expected)	40.51	41.73	42.98	44.27
Operating Expenses	19.19	19.76	20.36	20.97
Net Operating Income	21.32	21.96	22.62	23.30
Terminal Value of Real Estate:				227.30
Ending Year NOI/Req. Ret. on NOI				
Total Cash Flow From RE	21.32	21.96	22.62	250.60
Present Value of Unlevered Real Estate	202.31			

Panel B:	Value To Taxable Investor			
Annual After Tax Cash Flows:	1987	1988	1989	1990
Net Operating Income	21.32	21.96	22.62	23.30
{Interest}	15.78	15.68	15.57	15.45
{Depreciation}	2.93	2.93	2.93	2.93
Taxable Income	2.61	3.35	4.12	4.92
{Taxes}	0.91	1.17	1.44	1.72
{Principal Payment}	1.03	1.13	1.24	1.36
Depreciation	2.93	2.93	2.93	2.93
Cash Flow After Tax	3.60	3.98	4.37	4.76
Terminal Value				227.30
Less Ending Period Loan Balance				157.08
Less Tax on Sale				12.85
Terminal Value Cash Flow				57.37
Total Cash Flow After Tax	3.60	3.98	4.37	62.14
Present Value of Levered Real Estate	41.58			
Debt on Real Estate	161.85			
Total Value of Real Estate	203.42[2]			

[2]In this case the value appears to be greater to the taxable investor. This result will vary, particularly with changes in the level of pension fund interest in real estate (causing the discount rate in Panel A above to change), changes in tax laws, and changes in mortgage interest rates.

The analysis presented here is done exclusively with public information and is for illustration purposes only. Application of this methodology in practice would rely on superior internal forecasts and records available only to management. The fact that management alone typically has access to this information gives rise to the agency issues discussed in Miles, Pringle and Webb [20]. This companion piece shows that interesting agency issues derive from the interplay of three factors: underutilized real estate, the asymmetric information sets in the hands of management

Exhibit 8 Estimates of Atlantic Richfield Value (with and without Real Estate)

Panel A:	Value with Real Estate Included			
Total Cash Flow:	1987	1988	1989	1990
Earnings Before Interest and Tax[3]	2591.0	2598.4	2782.1	2983.5
{Tax on EBIT}	1191.86	987.41	1057.20	1133.73
Depreciation	1630.00	1745.03	1868.17	2000.00
{Capital Expenditures}	645.00	2230.20	2374.58	2528.42
{Change in Working Capital}	7.00	91.39	99.75	108.86
Net Operating Cash Flows	2377.14	1034.48	1118.75	1212.49
Terminal Value of the Firm:				
Perpetuity—Ending Year EBIT(1−T)/Kw				26231.7
Total Cash Flow	2377.14	1034.48	1118.75	27444.1
Present Value (Discounted at Kw)	22639.6			
Less Beginning Period Debt	6969.0			
Present Value of Equity	15670.6			

Panel B:	Value with Real Estate Valued Separately			
Total Cash Flow:	1987	1988	1989	1990
Earnings Before Interest & Tax	2567.57	2574.02	2756.65	2956.97
{Tax on EBIT}	1181.08	978.13	1047.53	1123.65
Depreciation	1620.00	1735.03	1858.17	1990.00
{Capital Expenditures}	635.00	2220.20	2364.58	2518.42
{Change in Working Capital}	7.00	91.39	99.75	108.86
Net Operating Cash Flows	2364.49	1019.33	1102.96	1196.05
Gain from Sale of Real Estate	33.48[4]			
Terminal Value of the Firm				
Perpetuity—Ending Year EBIT(1−T)/Kw				26295.5
Total Cash Flow	2397.97	1019.33	1102.96	27491.5
Present Value (Discounted at Kw)	22713.5			
Less Beginning Period Debt	6969.00			
Present Value of Equity	15744.5			

[3] Operating earnings before interest and taxes plus other income.

[4] The gain from the sale of real estate is based on the actual market transaction as reported in the *Wall Street Journal* (11/20/88).

versus the markets, and management compensation plans that may exacerbate conflicts of interest.

CONCLUSIONS

Many corporations have the opportunity to increase their profitability through more effective management of their real estate. This entails evaluating real estate on an on-going

Exhibit 9 Value of Selected Corporations with and without Real Estate Holdings (millions of dollars)

	Real Estate Owned	Real Estate Sold and Leased Back	Difference
Atlantic Richfield	15670.6	15744.5	(73.9[5])
Exxon	54513.8	54517.7	(3.9)
International Paper	3162.4	3230.3	(67.9)
Time Inc.	4731.9	4756.6	(24.7)

[5] While the differences are large absolute numbers, they are small percentages of overall firm value. For perspective, the average difference in value is less than 1% of total value, while the market value of these firms differs from the theoretical value (model estimates) by an average of 14.66%. Hence the magnitude of the real estate card is often dwarfed by potential valuation errors. This only indicates the importance of the kind of detailed evaluation of each property that is only possible with inside information (e.g., lease provisions). Even with better internally available data, financial valuation models are not perfect and differences between theoretical and market prices may still be larger than the "real estate card". However, if the theoretical model generates values that are comparably biased for the firm with and without its real estate holdings, the differences may still be an accurate estimate of the magnitude of the "card."

basis using an approach that treats the interactions of real estate with the capital structure, debt capacity, cost of capital, and the overall operations of the firm. Real estate values so determined must be regularly compared to the external market value of the real estate in its highest and best use to determine whether it is being efficiently utilized.

Managers who evaluate their real estate and determine it to be undervalued have considerable flexibility in their actions. The market in general does not have the information to recognize underutilization, and the cost of obtaining the necessary information across a wide range of firms is often prohibitive.

Increased interest in real estate on the part of institutional investors adds another dimension to the problem. As pension funds and insurance companies become more active in this market, companies may find it increasingly attractive for others to own the real estate they occupy. It is now, more than ever, important for firms to view real estate as an asset that can and should be actively managed to achieve corporate goals.

NOTES

[1] Market Capitalization from *Anatomy of World Markets*, Goldman Sachs, September 1988.

[2] Zeckhouser and Silverman [34] survey major American corporations concerning their real estate holdings and find that buildings and land owned by corporations that are not primarily in the real estate business typically account for 25% or more of the firm's assets. Veale [32] updates this survey in 1987 and concludes that very little has changed in the six years since the Zeckhouser and Silverman study.

[3] Traditionally this operating decision is, itself, separate from the related financing decision.

[4] In corporations with higher-level real estate officers, the real estate group has been actively involved in the spatial aspects of the original capital budgeting decision.

[5] Important spin-off issues involve reputation, major client relations, and potential peripheral development profits.

[6] This idiom emphasizes that real estate holdings affect many aspects of both the financial and operating structure of the firm, and therefore cannot be isolated, but must be analyzed within the context of the "whole" firm.

[7] If required returns on real estate fall relative to required returns on other assets (as they have over the past several years due to an increased demand for investment grade real estate by foreign and institutional investors), firms may find superior alternative investments.

[8] FAS #94 requires consolidation of most real estate subsidiaries, potentially causing a major change in the firm's debt/equity position. FAS #98 curtails the use of sale-leaseback transactions by limiting the ability of a corporation to retain control of real estate while receiving off-balance-sheet treatment for the asset—unless the buyer has truly assumed the major risk position. These accounting changes, coming on the heels of the 1984 and 1986 tax law changes, clearly have the potential to affect the optimal structure of many corporate real estate financings.

[9] There are at least four different ways to apply standard discounted cash flow techniques to the valuation of either financial or real assets. Each of these approaches uses a different discount rate applied to a different stream of cash flows. The most widely used by corporate America in the evaluation of capital investments is the weighted average cost of capital (WACC) approach. WACC values operating cash flows at a calculated discount rate and then subtracts the value of debt to determine the market value of equity. A second methodology is called the "equity-residual" (ER) approach. This technique has been used in evaluating firms as well as individual projects. Under the ER methodology, the net cash flows to equity are valued after all debt service is subtracted. Two other approaches are less widely used. These are Stewart Myers' "adjusted present value" approach and a variation on the WACC technique suggested by Ardith and Levy. The WACC approach is described and utilized here. See any standard finance textbook for derivation of, and examples of the use of, the WACC methodology. For a technical discussion and critique of the strengths and weaknesses of WACC, see Myers [24] and Miles and Ezzell [17]. See Chambers, Harris and Pringle [1] for a detailed conversion of the four methods.

[10] For simplicity, it is assumed that there will be neither positive operating synergies in the combined firm (such as those that might result from previously overlapping distribution systems) *nor* negative organizational reactions to a merger (culture clashes, for example).

[11] Betas for many public companies can be obtained from the *Value Line Investment Survey*. The market portfolio used by *Value Line* in calculating its beta coefficients contains firms with financial leverage in their capital structures. For consistency reasons, levered betas and levered market risk premia are assumed throughout this note.

[12] This presentation uses the *Capital Asset Pricing Model* which has been the primary model in corporate finance textbooks since the early 1970s. It has come under increasing criticism from academics (see Roll [27]) and recently has been seriously questioned in regulatory rate of return testimony (see ATT Divestiture FCC Docket 84-800). A more forward-looking alternative is to estimate the risk premium from a composite of analysts' forecasts (see Harris [8]). Since derivation of the proper cost of capital is not the primary concern of this note, the CAPM methodology is followed. Note, however, that the use of analysts' forecasts to determine K_e is perfectly consistent with this overall presentation and would have no effect on the results shown later in this paper beyond the implications of using a different K_e.

[13] For a theoretical discussion of optimal capital structure, see Copeland and Weston [5]. In practical terms, the optimal capital structure is a function of the tradeoff between the lower after-tax cost of debt (interest, unlike dividends, being tax deductible) and the increased risk of insolvency as the required debt service payment is increased with increased debt. Theoretically the value of K_d used to calculate the WACC should be the interest rate applicable to Alpha.

[14] For a practical application of this discussion of terminal values, see Exhibit 4.

[15] To treat the terminal flow as a perpetuity in real terms raises some potentially tricky questions in dealing properly with debt flows.

[16] If a refinancing is undertaken using special purpose real estate, then the investor will be relying heavily on the corporate seller's promised lease payments. This presents difficult problems from valuation and tax standpoints. From the valuation perspective, an appraiser would have to estimate a residual value at the end of the lease period, which could prove difficult if the next most logical use were not readily apparent.

[17] As a comparison, in December 1987 the market RRR on the *Standard and Poors' 500 stock index* was about 14.5% (long-term government rate of 8.0% plus Ibbotson average historic risk premium), whereas the earnings/price ratio is 6%–7%. The RRR includes an expected growth component, whereas the e/p ratio does not.

[18] The FRC index returns, which are often used to estimate total returns for real estate, do involve the use of appraisals. For an empirical comparison of these figures with corresponding sales prices, see Cole, Guilkey and Miles [2, 3, 9].

[19] This real estate analysis makes a number of simplifying assumptions in order to facilitate the presentation of the main issues. This illustration assumes that all rents are at current market rates for both premium (executive) and lesser (clerical) office space. Also ignored is the possibility of long-term leases whose pay-offs might complicate a restructuring, as well as all the many important lease terms that can alter net rent over the years. Conceptually these complications are not difficult but the level of detail in the cash flow computations and financial reporting can be quite extensive. They can be very material and should clearly be included in any specific application of this methodology.

From a tax standpoint, the problem is doubly difficult since the tax reform act of 1984. Under the "original issue discount" rules, the buyer's basis cannot be inflated with artificially high lease payments or artificially low interest rates. For example, the IRS will not allow a firm to deduct above-market lease payments and then have the investor take higher depreciation write-offs from the higher tax basis in the building with that higher basis substantiated by the present value of the above-market lease payments.

[20] If the corporation chooses to move a less visible group to cheaper space, i.e., combine financial strategy with a real operating move, the value of the cash flows without real estate would obviously rise.

[21] To infer an unlevered equity rate, K_o, from observable, K_e and K_d, there are at least four possible valuation methods. The formula shown is based on MM [3]. See Harris and Pringle [9] for a fuller discussion.

[22] The compact disk data service "DATEXT" is the source for the annual reports.

[23] *Value Line* does not supply information concerning a firm's short-term interest-bearing debt, or the division of working capital into current assets and current liabilities. Information concerning nonoperating income and expenses is only reported as special information and not reported on a consistent basis. Actual values for these variables were obtained for 1986 from the annual reports and projected into the future by the authors.

REFERENCES

[1] D. R. Chambers, R. S. Harris and J. J. Pringle. Treatment of Financing Mix in Analyzing Investment Opportunities. *Financial Management* (Summer 1982), 24–41.

[2] R. Cole, D. Guilkey and M. Miles. An Assessment of the Reliability of Commercial Appraisals. *Appraisal Journal* (July 1986).

[3] ———, ——— and ———. Appraisals, Unit Values, and Investor Confidence in Real Estate Portfolios. *Real Estate Review* (Winter 1987).

[4] ———, ——— and ———. Toward an Assessment of the Reliability of Commercial Appraisals. *The Appraisal Journal* (1986).

[5] T. E. Copeland and J. F. Weston. *Financial Theory and Corporate Policy*. Reading, Mass: Addison-Wesley, third edition 1988.

[6] J. Franks and J. Pringle. Debt Financing, Corporate Financial Intermediaries and Firm Valuation. *Journal of Finance* (1982).

[7] S. Goldman. Collateralized Mortgage Obligations: Characteristics, History, Analysis. *Mortgage Securities Research Report* (1986).

[8] R. S. Harris. Return and Risk on Equity: Expectational Data and Equity Risk Premia. *Journal of Portfolio Management* (Spring 1986).

[9] ——— and J. J. Pringle. Risk-Adjusted Required Rate of Return—Extensions from the Average-Risk Case. *Journal of Financial Research* (Fall 1985).

[10] D. Hartzell, J. Hekman and M. Miles. Portfolio Diversification. *AREUEA Journal* (Summer 1986).

[11] ———, ——— and ———. Inflation Hedging with Commercial Real Estate. *AREUEA Journal* (Spring 1987).

[12] ———, ——— and ———. Diversification Categories in Investment Real Estate. *AREUEA Journal* (1986).

[13] G. Hite, J. Owers and R. Rogers. The Separation of Real Estate by Spin-off. *AREUEA Journal* (1984).

[14] R. G. Ibbotson and L. Siegel. Real Estate Returns—A Comparison with Other Investments. *AREUEA Journal* (Fall 1984).

[15] R. G. Ibbotson and R. A. Sinquefield. *Stocks, Bonds, Bills and Inflation—Historical Returns 1926–80*, Charlottesville, VA: The Financial Analysts Research Foundation, 1982.

[16] R. G. Ibbotson, L. Siegel and K. Love. World Wealth: Market Values and Returns. *Journal of Portfolio Management* (Fall 1985).

[17] J. A. Miles and J. R. Ezzell. The Weighted Average Cost of Capital, Perfect Capital Markets and Project Life: A Clarification. *Journal of Financial and Quantitative Analysis* (September 1980), 719–30.

[18] M. Miles, R. Cole and D. Guilkey. A Different Look at Commercial Real Estate Returns. Working paper, University of North Carolina, 1988.

[19] M. Miles, J. Pringle and A. Illinitch. An Integrated Approach To The Corporate Real Estate Decision. *Salomon Brothers: Bond Market Research Report*, 1987.

[20] M. Miles, J. Pringle and B. Webb. Information and Agency Issues in Corporate Real Estate Decisions. Working paper, University of North Carolina, 1989.

[21] M. Miller. Debt and Taxes. *Journal of Finance* (May 1977), 261–75.

[22] M. Moss and A. Dunan. The Location of The Back Officers. Monograph, New York University, 1988.

[23] F. Modigliani and M. Miller. Corporate Income Taxes and the Cost of Capital: A Correction. *American Economic Review* (June 1963), 433–43.

[24] S. Myers. Interactions of Corporate Financing and Investment Decisions—Implications for Capital Budgeting. *Journal of Finance* (March 1974), 1–25.

[25] D. Neidich and T. Steinberg. Corporate Real Estate: Sources of New Equity. *Harvard Business Review* (July–August 1984).

[26] J. J. Pringle and R. S. Harris. *Essentials of Managerial Finance.* Scott-Foresman and Company, second edition 1987.

[27] R. Roll. A Critique of the Asset Pricing Theory's Tests. *Journal of Financial Economics* (May 1977).

[28] S. Ross. The Arbitrage Theory of Capital Asset Pricing. *Journal of Economic Theory* (1976).

[29] R. Rutherford and H. Nourse. The Impact of Corporate Real Estate Unit Formation on the Parent Firm's Value. *Journal of Real Estate Research* (Fall 1988).

[30] Salomon Brothers. *Real Estate Market Review* (July 1986).

[31] C. Smith and L. Wabeman. Determinants of Corporate Leasing Policy. *Journal of Finance* (1985).

[32] P. Veale. Managing Corporate Real Estate Assets: A Survey of U.S. Real Estate Executives. MIT Laboratory of Architecture and Planning, 1988.

[33] C. Wurtzebach and M. Miles. *Modern Real Estate.* New York: John Wiley & Sons, third edition 1987.

[34] S. Zeckhouser and R. Silverman. *Harvard Real Estate Survey.* National Association of Corporate Real Estate Executives, 1981.

Part 9. Real Estate Derivative Markets

26 Mortgage-Backed Futures and Options

David C. Ling

This paper empirically tests valuation models for the mortgage-backed futures-options contracts that traded on the Chicago Board of Trade (CBOT) from June of 1989 until March of 1992. A simple contingent-claim model is shown to produce call option values on mortgage-backed futures (MBF) contracts that are unbiased estimates of actual futures-options prices. The ability of the MFG contract to hedge positions in current coupon Government National Mortgage Association (GNMA) securities relative to the effectiveness of cross-hedging GNMA positions with T-note and T-bond futures contracts is also examined.

This study examines futures and futures-options contracts written on mortgage-backed securities (MBSs). The size and importance of mortgage and MBS markets prompted the Chicago Board of Trade (CBOT) to introduce a new mortgage-backed futures (MBF) contract in June of 1989. The CBOT also simultaneously launched options trading on the MBF. This was done despite the failure of the original Government National Mortgage Association (GNMA) future contract, that was delisted in 1987 after a precipitous decline in trading volume.

The MBF and futures-options contracts were designed primarily for the mortgage securities industry. An originator of fixed rate mortgages could use the contracts as an alternative to the forward sale of GNMA securities or to hedge against variation in the percentage of outstanding mortgage commitments that actually went to closing. However, the new contracts never caught on with mortgage originators or traders, and the CBOT ceased to list new MFG and options contracts in March of 1992 because of insufficient trading volume.[1]

The primary purpose of this research is to empirically test some simple valuation models for the mortgage-backed futures-options contracts. The ability of the MBF to hedge positions in current coupon GNMA MBSs is also measured and compared to the effectiveness of cross-hedging GNMA MBS positions with T-note and T-bond futures contracts.

There has been a proliferation in recent years of new interest rate-dependent securities, such as bond futures, options on bonds, options on bond futures, swap agreements and MBSs. The valuation of these securities is a major concern of both practi-

From *Journal of the American Real Estate and Urban Economics Association,* Vol. 21, No. 1 (1993), pp. 47–67.

tioners and academics. The academic literature has been largely theoretical and has focused on the development of arbitrage-free valuation models.[2] While simulated model results are often compared to numerical results from alternative model specifications, few of these studies compare estimated model prices to actual transaction data.[3]

Schaefer and Schwartz (1987) developed a valuation model for debt options that uses the bond price as the single underlying state variable. A theoretical weakness of the approach is the assumption of a constant short-term rate of interest. The considerable advantages of the approach include a bond option model that is preference-free and that uses the observed market price of the underlying bond as an input rather than estimating the current price of the bond with an equilibrium term structure model. The numerical simulations of Schaefer and Schwartz indicate that their model produces Treasury bond option values that are broadly similar to those calculated with more complicated equilibrium term structure models. They acknowledge, however, that the only way to establish the reasonableness of bond option models that use the bond price as the single-state variable is through empirical tests of the model's ability to price debt options.

This paper includes such empirical tests and the results are supportive of the findings of Schaefer and Schwartz. In particular, the relatively simple model produces call option values on GNMA futures contracts that are unbiased estimates of actual futures-options prices. The results reported here also serve as benchmarks for subsequent empirical tests of futures-options pricing models that may employ more complicated assumptions about the stochastic processes governing interest rates and underlying bond and futures prices over time. The use of more complicated valuation models, whatever their enhanced conceptual appeal, can only be rationalized if they provide improved estimates of actual option prices relative to the simple model tested in this paper.

Section 1 of this paper contains a discussion of the institutional environment and contract details that likely contributed to the failure of the first MBS futures contract. The salient features of the MBF and options contracts are then examined. The data employed in the analysis and their limitations are discussed in Section 2, and in Section 3, the effectiveness of the MBF contract in hedging investment positions in current coupon GNMA securities is examined. These results are compared to the hedging effectiveness of Treasury-bond and Treasury-note futures contracts over the same time period. The conceptual framework for mortgaged-backed futures-option valuation is presented in Section 4. Section 5 contains the numerical simulations and empirical tests to determine whether model prices are able to explain actual transaction prices for a number of futures-options contracts that traded between June of 1989 and November of 1990. Concluding comments are offered in Section 6.

THE INSTITUTIONAL ENVIRONMENT

In 1975, the CBOT introduced the GNMA Collateralized Depository Receipt (CDR) futures contract. The GNMA CDR was a contract on mortgaged-backed securities and was actually the first interest rate futures contract available on the CBOT. The CDR contract was initially very successful: by 1980, annual trading volume had climbed to over 2.3 million contracts. However, after 1980, annual trading volume fell precipitously: during 1987, fever than 10,000 contracts were traded. This decline was occurring concomitantly with rapid growth in the secondary mortgage market and in the overall market for long-term interest rate futures.

Johnston and McConnell (1989) present a convincing explanation for the demise of the GNMA CDR contract. They document that during the late 1970s, the hedge provided by the CDR contract was effective for mortgages and MBSs issued at prevailing market interest rates. Thus, the contract provided an effective risk-management tool for mortgage originators and MBS dealers. However, the absolute quality of the hedge declined after 1982, and by 1983, Johnston and McConnell found that Treasury-bond futures contracts actually provided a superior hedge for current coupon mortgages.

Johnston and McConnell attribute the decline in the hedging effectiveness of the GNMA CDR to the value of the delivery options embedded in the contract. In short, the stated delivery asset for the CDR contract was $100,000 in remaining principal balance on GNMA securities bearing an 8% coupon rate. However, the seller of the futures contract could deliver GNMA securities with any available coupon rate, with the dollar amount of remaining principal balance to be delivered adjusted by predetermined "conversion factors." The conversion factors, however, assumed that mortgages underlying the various coupon rate securities would be prepaid by mortgage borrowers at identical rates. Thus, the factors understated the value of prepayment options embedded in higher rate securities and thereby overstated their value. This overstatement of value made them relatively "cheap" for the individual with the short position to deliver. This, in turn, caused the CDR futures price to follow the price of high coupon GNMA securities, even though most hedging demand was concentrated in lower coupon mortgages and securities.[4]

The MBF and Options Contracts. Trading in the CBOT MBF and futures-option contracts began in June of 1989. The most important features of these contracts are listed in Tables 1 and 2. The futures contract was designed to avoid the perceived problems associated with the GNMA CDR contract. Most importantly, pricing of the futures contract was based on a single, current coupon GNMA security. The current coupon was the GNMA coupon trading nearest to, but not greater than, par. Monthly coupon determination based on dealer surveys enabled CBOT futures to better track retail commitment rates. By eliminating conversion factors and associated "cheapest-to-deliver" complications, the short futures position no longer includes a quality option that requires valuation by market participants. The CBOT mortgage-backed futures and options also differed from traditional interest rate futures instruments (and the GNMA CDR contract) in that no physical GNMA certificates changed hands when futures positions were settled. Instead, each position was settled in cash at a survey price determined from median bid-side quotations of 15 randomly selected dealers. Cash settlement avoided the complications of delivering GNMA certificates and, perhaps more importantly, eliminated the "quantity" and "perpetuity" (timing) options associated with the GNMA CDR and many other interest rate futures contracts.[5]

A final feature of the MBF contract worth noting is that put and call options on the futures contracts traded alongside the futures contract and were exercisable into futures at any time before expiration. The futures and options contracts expired simultaneously.[6]

DATA SOURCES AND LIMITATIONS

Daily data on all MBF and options contracts, T-note futures and T-bond futures traded since the inception of the new market were obtained from the CBOT. Mortgage-backed futures and option prices and the prices of the underlying GNMA MBSs are only avail-

Table 1 CBOT Mortgage-Backed Futures

Trading Unit	$100,000 par value.
Coupons Traded	Each month, the CBOT will list a new coupon four months in the future. The coupon for that month will be the newest GNMA coupon; trading nearest to par (100) but not greater than par.
Price Quotations	In points and thirty-seconds of a point, e.g., 98-12 equals 98 and 12/32nds.
Trading Months	Four consecutive months.
Daily Trading Limits	3 points (or $3,000 per contract) above or below the previous day's settlement price (expandable to 4 ½ points).
Last Trading Day	At 1:00 p.m. on the Friday preceding the third Wednesday of the month.
Settlement	In cash on the last trading day based on the mortgage-backed Survey Price. The Survey Price shall be the median price obtained from a survey of dealers.
Trading Hours	7:20 a.m. to 2:00 p.m. (Chicago time).

Source: *Mortgage-Backed Futures and Options: An Introduction.* Chicago Board of Trade, June 1989.

able as closing prices. Nonsynchronous closing prices may effect the variability of the pricing errors that are calculated in this study, but it is difficult to determine ex ante the distribution of these errors or their approximate magnitude. The lack of transaction data would be a serious impediment if our study focused on issues such as market efficiency and the availability of arbitrage opportunities. However, our primary empirical objectives are to examine the hedging effectiveness of various futures contracts and to test the ability of a simple contingent-claim futures-option model to explain changes in actual market prices across securities and over time. For these purposes, the use of settlement prices is appropriate.

Daily settlement prices on the underlying GNMA securities were obtained from Knight-Ridder. Although specific mortgage-backed securities may be traded for immediate settlement (within five business days of the trade date), the vast majority of GNMA MBSs are sold into the forward delivery market with pool information details to be provided on a "to-be-announced" (TBA) basis. The uniform practices for good delivery and settlement are set forth by the Public Securities Association. Currently, the settlement date for GNMA MBSs with coupon rates less than 10 percent is the Tuesday before the third Wednesday of each month.[7] The GNMA MBS data provided by Knight Ridder are TBA prices and yields. In our sample, the time between the GNMA MBS trade on an observation date and the settlement of that trade ranged from three to 35 days, with an average of 18 days.

HEDGING EFFECTIVENESS OF THE MORTGAGE-BACKED FUTURES CONTRACT

A standard measure of hedging effectiveness is the reduction in price variation that results when the asset to be hedged is combined with a futures contract in such a way as to minimize the variance of the two-asset portfolio. Ederington (1979) and Figlewski (1985) demonstrated that the percentage reduction that can be gained by hedging is

Table 2 CBOT Mortgage-Backed Futures Options

Underlying Instrument	One CBOT MBF contract of a specified delivery month and coupon.
Strike Prices	Strike prices are set at multiples of one point ($1,000)
Price Quotations	Premiums are quoted in minimum increments of one sixty-fourth (1/64th) of 1% of a $100,000 MBF contract, or $15.625 rounded up to the nearest penny.
Tick Size	1/64 of a point ($15,625 or $15.63 per contract).
Daily Price Limits	Three points ($3,000).
Months Traded	Four consecutive months.
Last Trading Day	Options cease trading at 1:00 p.m. Chicago time on the last day of trading in MBF in the corresponding delivery month.
Expiration	Unexercised options expire at 8:00 p.m. Chicago time on the last day of trading. In the money options are exercised automatically.
Trading Hours	7:20 a.m. to 2:00 p.m. (Chicago time).

Source: *Mortgage-Backed Futures and Options: An Introduction.* Chicago Board of Trade, June 1989.

equal to the square of the correlation between the returns on the asset to be hedged and the returns on the futures contract over the same period. This quantity can be measured by the coefficient of determination from the regression

$$R_s = \beta_0 + \beta_1 R_f + \varepsilon \tag{1}$$

where R_s is the return on the asset to be hedged (the spot asset), and R_f is the return on the futures contract over the same period. Returns are calculated as the percentage change in the price of the asset over the time period that the hedge is in effect. The slope coefficient can be interpreted as the optimal (ex post) hedge ratio.

In the regressions, the dependent variable is the hedge period return on current coupon GNMA securities. The independent variable is the hedge period return on the corresponding futures contract. Three different futures contracts are considered as potential hedging instruments for the current coupon GNMA: the CBOT MBF, the five-year Treasury-note future and the Treasury-bond future. The GNMA MBF contract had twelve maturities per year. The Treasury futures contracts are written against non-callable (for at least fifteen years) debt instruments backed by the U.S. government and have four maturities each year: March, June, September and December. Only MBF contracts that matured in the same four months were examined. This procedure yields a single futures price for each day of the sample period. Hedge periods do not overlap but instead are assumed to be initiated sequentially, with a new hedge established simultaneously with the close of the preceding hedge.

The hedging effectiveness of the three futures contracts is estimated for hedge periods of five and ten trading days from June of 1989 to September of 1991; results are reported in Table 3. With a five-day hedge period, equation (1) is estimated with 115 observations. The coefficient of determination is 0.952 for the MBF contracts, 0.830 for the T-note contracts and 0.900 for the T-bond contracts. The ten-day hedge period results are not materially different. Given that mortgage interest rates were relatively stable over the majority of the sample period, these results likely understate the relative ability of the MBF to hedge the interest rate risk exposure associated with current coupon mortgages and MBSs.[8]

Table 3 The Effectiveness of Various Futures Contracts in Hedging GNMA Mortgage-Backed Securities

	Five Day Hedges - Number of Observations = 115	
Hedging Instrument	Coefficient of Determination°	β_1
GNMA Futures (MBF)	0.952	0.990
T-Note Futures	0.830	1.108
T-Bond Futures	0.900	0.761
	10-Day Hedges - Number of Observations = 55	
Hedging Instrument	Coefficient of Determination°	β_1
GNMA Futures (MBF)	0.965	0.972
T-Note Futures	0.828	1.028
T-Bond Futures	0.894	0.736

° Is equal to the R-squared from the regression $R_s = \beta_0 + \beta_1 R_f + \varepsilon$, where R_s is the five- or ten-day return on the GNMA MBSs (i.e., spot contract) and R_f is the corresponding return on the futures hedging instrument.

THE VALUATION OF GNMA FUTURES AND FUTURES OPTIONS

This section presents the conceptual framework for mortgage-backed futures-options valuation. An option on a futures contract is similar to an option on the spot in that it provides its holder with the right to buy or sell the underlying security at the exercise price of the option. However, unlike an option on the spot, a cash exchange in the amount of the exercise price does not occur when the futures-option is exercised; rather, the futures option holder merely acquires a long or short position in the futures contract with a price equal to the exercise price of the option. When the futures contract is marked-to-market at the close of the trading day, the option holder is entitled to receive in cash the payoff from exercising the futures option. This payoff equals the difference between the futures price and the exercise price.

Bond Price Dynamics. The valuation of options on futures contracts requires the specification of the stochastic process governing the evolution of the underlying asset's value and a process for the evolution of interest rates. The simplest approach to the valuation of debt options is a variant of the Black and Scholes (1973) option pricing model. This method assumes that the variance of the rate of return on the underlying asset (the bond or futures contract) is constant and that the short-term interest rate is constant. These assumptions may be plausible for common stocks, but appear to be contradictory to fundamental bond pricing principles. In particular, the variance of the underlying bond return is not constant, because the bond or GNMA price is constrained to converge to par at maturity. In addition, a driving force behind bond and bond-futures price changes is interest rate uncertainty.

A second approach to the valuation of debt options is derived from the equilibrium theories of the term structure of interest rates. Cox, Ingersoll and Ross (1985), Brennan and Schwartz (1982), Vasicek (1977), Courtadon (1982) and others have derived equilibrium models of the term structure assuming that one or two interest rates follow exogenously determined stochastic processes. There are substantial practical difficulties associated with the empirical application of the equilibrium approach (Schaefer and Schwartz

1987). First, it requires the estimation of the stochastic process for either one or two interest rates. Second, it requires the estimation of utility-dependent (i.e., unobservable) parameters of the interest rate process, such as the market price of short-term interest rate risk. Third, because the underlying bond or GNMA is not a state variable, the bond price in the boundary conditions (or in each node of a binomial lattice) must be computed from the interest rate variables in order to determine the value of the option. This adds both to the complexity of the models and to the probability of calculation error.

Moreover, the initial bond price generated as an output by the equilibrium pricing model must equal the readily observable current market price of the bond; otherwise, options on the bond will be systematically mispriced. This means that significant care must be taken to recalibrate the equilibrium interest rate model on each date for which a bond option value is desired.

This last shortcoming may effectively preclude the application of an equilibrium term structure model to the valuation of options on mortgage debt. While equilibrium term structure models can be calibrated to closely replicate the yield curve for non-callable, nondefaultable Treasury securities, they have not proven effective in accurately pricing mortgages and MBSs with embedded call and default options. Thus, even if the assumed term structure model can be calibrated to accurately price Treasury securities, MBS prices generated by the model may not match observed market prices.

Recognizing the complexities associated with incorporating equilibrium term structure models into bond option valuation models, Schaefer and Schwartz (1987) develop their relatively simple model for debt options that uses the bond price as the single-state variable. Simulations by Schaefer and Schwartz indicate that their model produces Treasury-bond option values that are broadly similar to those calculated with the more complicated Brennan and Schwartz (1983) model. Furthermore, Schaefer and Schwartz found that even the assumption of a simple lognormal process (in the spirit of Black and Scholes) for the evolution of the underlying bond price produces accurate option values, as long as the time to expiration on the option is short relative to the maturity of the bond. Note, however, that Schaefer and Schwartz use numerical results from the more complicated Brennan and Schwartz (1983) model, not actual market prices, as their benchmark for determining the model's "goodness of fit."

Assumptions and Notation. Following Schaefer and Schwartz (1987), our approach to the valuation of options on MBF contracts begins with the specification of a process for the evolution of the value of the MBF. By so doing, we avoid bringing preference assumptions explicitly into the valuation framework, and we are able to employ standard contingent-claims valuation techniques using observable and traded assets. Our principal assumptions are as follows:

(A1) Investors prefer more wealth to less and act as price takers. The MBF and futures-options markets are frictionless.

(A2) There are no taxes, and all margin requirements can be met by posting interest-bearing securities.

(A3) The short-term rate of interest on default-free securities is a constant, r.

(A4) Time is divided into a sequence of equal length discrete periods. All cash flows occur at these discrete points.

(A5) The MBF price is a random variable that follows a lognormal diffusion process with a constant variance.

Assumptions (A1) and (A2) are standard and fairly innocuous. Much empirical evidence suggests that investors behave rationally, and transaction costs are small for those making the market in the various financial assets. Assumption (A3) appears contradictory when valuing interest-sensitive contingent claims but is invoked for its simplicity and because the simulation results of Schaefer and Schwartz (1987) suggest that its effects on bond option values are minimal.

Although assuming a lognormal stochastic process for the MBF is appealing due to its simplicity and its implicit incorporation of the boundary conditions, the unbounded nature of the lognormal distribution seems inconsistent with the price of the underlying GNMA MBS converging to par at maturity and the bond price variance approaching zero at maturity. Schaefer and Schwartz (1989) address this issue by assuming that the standard deviation of return on the underlying bond over the life of the option is proportional to the bond's duration. They find, however, that differences between the values produced by their model and those produced by a constant variance model are "trivial" for short-term options on long-term bonds. The underlying asset in our option pricing model, the MBF, is written on a GNMA pass-through security that, in turn, is written against a pool of newly issued 30-year mortgages. Thus, the standard deviation of the MBF return is not adjusted, because the change in the maturity (or duration) of the underlying GNMA MBS over the life of the futures-option (which is less than four months) is inconsequential. This is consistent with Gay and Manaster (1990) and Hemler (1990), who also assume unbounded stochastic processes for the underlying bonds in their T-bond futures valuation models.

Note that (A5) defines the dynamics of the futures price movements with no reference to the relationship between the MBF price and the price of the underlying GNMA MBS. Whether the assumed stochastic process is more appropriate for the MBF price dynamics or for the GNMA MBS dynamics is an open empirical question. However, defining the underlying stochastic process for the futures price instead of the spot price increases the applicability of the option pricing model and may improve the results. Since under risk neutrality, the expected return on futures contracts is equal to zero, it is not necessary to consider the coupon payments to the underlying GNMA MBS. If the stochastic process were defined for the GNMA MBS, the expected drift in GNMA MBS prices would have to be adjusted for the coupon payments. The option pricing results should also be more accurate if the futures price is defined as the state variable, because errors between the model and actual futures price are avoided. Also, the volatility of the GNMA MBS and the MBF will be the same, because a nonstochastic short-term interest rate is assumed. In practice, however, it will probably be easier to obtain volatility estimates from future price data.

Generation of the MBF Price Lattice. In order to estimate the value of an option to exercise into an MBF contract, the evolution of MBF prices over time must be defined. Let U and D represent the ratio of MBF prices if prices rise or fall, respectively, from date $t-1$ to t. The logarithm of the ratio of MBF prices is assumed to follow a binomial distribution with an annual mean of

$$\mu = N[p\ln(U) + (1-p)\ln(D)] \tag{2}$$

and annual variance of

$$\sigma^2 = N[(\ln(U) - \ln(D))^2 p(1-p)] \tag{3}$$

where N is the number of periods or intervals per year, and μ measures the mean rate of drift in MBF prices. As the time interval between successive moves approaches zero, the discrete-time process approaches the continuous lognormal process. The term N is set equal to 365.

It is also possible to determine the values of U and D that are implied by a given set of values for μ, σ^2, p and N. Using equations (2) and (3), one obtains the following expressions:

$$U = \exp(\mu/N + (\sigma/\sqrt{N})\sqrt{N(1-p)/p}) \tag{4}$$
$$D = \exp(\mu/N - (\sigma/\sqrt{N})\sqrt{Np(1-p)})$$

U and D completely describe the movements of MBF prices over time. Note that the price lattice is constrained to be path independent; the value of the MBF after an up move-down move sequence is the same as that following a down-up sequence.

Futures Option Valuation. We focus on the valuation of call options on a futures contract: the treatment for puts proceeds in a similar fashion, with appropriate modifications of the maximization operator. Both the futures contract and the option contract expire at time T, at which time the value of the futures call option can be written as

$$C_{t,j}(F_{l-j}, \tau, r, K, \Theta) = \text{Max}[F_{l-j} - K, 0] \tag{5}$$

where the subscript j refers to the vertical position (or node number) in the futures tree at time T. The term F_{l-j} is the corresponding price of the MBF, τ denotes the time to expiration of the option (equal to zero at time T) and r is the annualized, default-free rate of interest. The term K is the exercise or strike price of the futures-option and Θ is a vector of parameters governing the evolution of MBF prices (i.e., μ, σ^2 and p). Note that at time T, there are $T+1$ nodes in the option price lattice to be "filled in." Thus, j will run from 1 down to $T+1$.

At time $t < T$, the individual who purchased the call option has two options to consider: exercise the option or hold the option for (at least) one more period. Let $I_{t-j} = F_{t-j} - K$ represent the intrinsic value of the call option (i.e., the payoff from immediate exercise). Let W_{1-t} be the value in period t of the decision to postpone exercise for at least one more period. It can be shown that it is always possible to establish a riskless hedge between the option and the underlying asset when the underlying asset follows a branching process, as we have assumed. Because the value of the call is therefore independent of investors' preferences, the price of the call in a risk neutral economy must be the same as the price of the call in an economy characterized by risk-adverse investors. The call must therefore be priced so that the expected return on the call is equal to the (assumed constant) riskless rate of interest over the period. Equivalently, the time t value of the call option is equal to

$$C_{t-j}(F_{t-j}, \tau, r, K, \Theta) = \text{Max}[I_{t-j}, W_{1-t}] \tag{6}$$

where

$$W_{t-j} = [pC_{t+1,j} + (1-p)C_{t+1,j+1}]/(1+r) \qquad (7)$$

Immediate exercise of the option results in the loss in value from possible future exercise. Thus, $I_{t,j} > 0$ is a necessary, but not a sufficient condition for an optimal exercise to occur. The excess of $W_{t,j}$ over $I_{t,j}$ (if positive) is usually referred to as the "time value" of the option. Option valuation proceeds in backward-time through the lattice until the value of the option at time zero is determined.

MODEL VERSUS ACTUAL FUTURES-OPTIONS PRICES

To compare calculated futures-option prices to observed prices, we analyze all call and put options contracts that were written on GNMA 9.5% futures contracts with expiration dates prior to December of 1990. Option prices are calculated for those days and contracts when actual trading occurred in *both* the MBF contract and the option contract. Requiring actual trading in the futures contract should reduce errors in the calculation of option values that are actually due to mismeasurement of the underlying futures price. Requiring trading in the cash, futures and futures-options markets results in a call option sample size of 216 and a put option sample size of 332.

Calculation of model prices for a particular option contract on a given day requires the following inputs: closing price of the 9.5% GNMA MBF; the short-term riskless rate of interest (r); the period of time until expiration of the future and option contracts (τ); the expected drift in MBF prices (μ); and the variance of MBF prices (σ^2). We assume r is equal to the contemporaneous yield on 3-month Treasury bills obtained from Salomon Brothers Inc. The value of τ is obtained by counting the number of days between the observation date and the expiration date of the option (which is always the Friday before the third Wednesday of the month). The value of μ is set equal to zero.

As in all option pricing models, a key input that cannot be directly observed is the expected volatility of the underlying asset. A daily time series of implied T-note volatilities was obtained from Salomon Brothers Inc. These volatilities are the standard deviations that are implied by the relationship between prices on T-note futures contracts and the prices of options written on these T-note futures. However, the price volatility of T-note futures contracts is known to overstate the price volatility of GNMA MBSs; thus, the implied T-note futures volatilities must be scaled down by an appropriate percentage.

To accomplish this, we calculate for each observation date a 70-day (moving) average of historical price volatilities on the 9.5% GNMA MBSs and on T-note futures contracts. Price volatility for both series is measured as the standard deviation of the log of the daily price relatives. The ratio of these historical volatilities becomes our scaler and is multiplied by the Salomon Brothers' implied T-note volatility to obtain our estimate of expected GNMA MBS and MBF price volatility for that day. The ex post ratio of GNMA MBS volatility to T-note volatility ranged from 0.684 to 0.912 and averaged 0.782 over the study period. That is, 9.5% GNMA MBS and MBF prices were expected to be only 78% as volatile as T-note futures prices, on average, over the time period of interest.[9]

Tests of the Call Option Pricing Model. With these assumptions, 216 model call option prices were calculated. Summary statistics are reported in Table 4. Measuring mis-

Table 4 Summary Statistics: Call Option Contracts on Mortgage-Backed Futures (MBF)

	Mean	Std. Dev.	Min.	Max.
Actual Option Price (p_0)	1.03	0.80	0.02	5.03
Model Option Price ($\hat{p}_0$)	1.01	0.79	0.00	4.97
Difference	0.01	0.09	−0.28	0.36
MBF Price-Strike Price	0.17	1.34	−4.59	5.03
Annual Volatility of MBF	0.05	0.01	0.04	0.08

Amounts are per $100 of current MBF price; the underlying GNMA MBS has a 9.5% coupon rate; the time period is June 1989–November 1990; the number of observations equals 216.

pricing as the difference between the actual call option price and the model price, the mean mispricing error is $0.014 per $100 of settlement price; that is, the average model price of a call option to acquire a long position in a $100,000 futures contract was $14 less than the actual settlement price. The annual standard deviation of the mispricing is 0.087 and the root mean square pricing error (RMSE) is 8.82%. Prices for call options were calculated with remaining time-to-expiration of 7 to 121 days. The assumed annual volatility of 9.5% MBFs averaged 0.053 and ranged from 0.039 to 0.075.

Regression analysis is used to statistically test the option pricing model's goodness of fit. The obvious choice for the test specification is $p_0 = \alpha + \beta \hat{p}_0 + \varepsilon$, where p_0 is the actual and $\hat{p}_0$ is the calculated or "predicted" futures-option price. If a sample period's model price is unbiased with respect to the actual price, a statistical null hypothesis that α equals zero and β equals one will not be rejected. However, $\hat{p}_0$ is known to be measured with some error; therefore, ordinary least squares (OLS) estimates of α and β will be inconsistent and the estimate of β will be biased downward. This problem can be remedied by reversing the dependent and independent variables and respecifying the test equation as $\hat{p}_0 = \alpha + \beta p_0 + \varepsilon$. This respecification is permissible because we neither hypothesize nor are we testing for the existence of an "economic" relationship between p_0 and $\hat{p}_0$. Thus, either may be used as the left-hand-side variable to measure whether $\hat{p}_0$ is unbiased.

The results of this first regression are reported in Panel A of Table 5 and suggest that the model explains a statistically significant proportion of the changes in actual call option prices across securities and over time ($R^2 = 0.988$). Moreover, the null hypothesis that the model price provides an unbiased estimate of the actual price cannot be rejected; the intercept is not significantly different from zero and the slope coefficient is not different from unity at the 5% significance level.

A somewhat stronger test is the model's ability to explain changes in the "time" (or "excess option") value of the option over the study period (defined as option price minus intrinsic value, or "IV"). The results of this regression are displayed in Panel B of Table 5. The intercept coefficient in this specification is not significantly different from one; however, the null hypothesis of $\beta = 1$ is narrowly rejected at the 5% level. Overall, the results are highly supportive of the model.

To determine if call option mispricing is systematically related to several key variables, we regress the dollar amount of the mispricing on: a constant; the dollar difference between the actual option price and the exercise price; the remaining time-to-expiration; and the assumed volatility of the underlying 9.5% GNMA MBF. These results are reported in Panel C of Table 5 and suggest that the amount of call option mispricing is not related in a systematic way to τ or to the amount that the option is currently in-the-money (IV). However, the assumed level of MBF price volatility is able to explain

Table 5 Regression of Model Call Option Prices on Actual Prices

Panel A: $\hat{p}_0 = \alpha + \beta p_0 + \varepsilon$

R^2	Variable	Coef	Std. Error	T-Stat
0.99	α	0.002	0.009	−0.2
	β	0.987	0.007	133.2

Panel B: $(\hat{p}_0 - IV) = \alpha + \beta(p_0 - IV) + \varepsilon$

R^2	Variable	Coef	Std. Error	T-Stat
0.91	α	0.004	0.010	0.4
	β	0.956	0.020	47.4

Panel C: $(p_0 - \hat{p}_0) = \alpha + \beta_1 IV + \beta_2 \tau + \beta_3 \sigma + \varepsilon$

R^2	Variable	Coef	Std. Error	T-Stat
0.23	α	0.299	0.037	7.9
	β_1	0.004	0.003	1.1
	β_2	−0.000	0.000	−1.1
	β_3	−5.112	0.637	−8.0

216 observations. Panel A contains the results of regressing the model option price ($\hat{p}_0$) on the actual option price (p_0). Panel B results are from regressing the time value of the option, as calculated by the model, on the actual time value of the option. Time value is defined as the option price minus intrinsic value (IV). The null hypothesis for both specifications is $\alpha = 0$ and $\beta = 1$. Panel C contains results from regressing the difference between the actual and model option price on IV; the number of days remaining until expiration of option (τ); and the annual standard deviation of MBF prices (σ).

a statistically significant portion of the call option mispricing. This suggests that the relatively small amount of mispricing that does occur could be further reduced by refining the estimates of expected MBF price volatility.

Tests of the Put Option Pricing Model. Three hundred and thirty-two put option values were calculated and compared to market prices; summary statistics are reported in Table 6. The mean mispricing error is $0.028 per $100 of settlement price, or $28 dollars less than the actual settlement price on a $100,000 futures contract. This mispricing error is twice that for call options. The standard deviation of the mispricing is 0.088 and the RMSE is 17.0%.

The regression results displayed in Panel A of Table 7 demonstrate that model put prices are able to explain 97.7% of the variation in actual put prices and the slope coefficient is not different from one at the 5% level of significance. However, a 95% confidence interval constructed around the estimated intercept does not contain zero. Calculated time values of the put options explain 91.2% of the variation in actual time values. The null hypothesis of $\alpha = 0$ and $\beta = 1$ cannot be rejected at the 5% level. Sim-

Table 6 Summary Statistics: Put Option Contracts on Mortgage-Backed Futures (MBF)

	Mean	Std. Dev.	Min.	Max.
Actual Option Price (p_0)	0.68	0.58	0.02	4.06
Model Option Price ($\hat{p}_0$)	0.65	0.59	0.00	4.01
Difference	0.03	0.09	−0.31	0.27
MBF Price-Strike Price	−0.54	1.22	−3.72	4.06
Annual Volatility of MBF	0.06	0.01	0.04	0.09

Amounts are per $100 of current MBF price: the underlying GNMA MBS has a 9.5% coupon rate; the time period is June 1989–November 1990; the number of observations equals 332.

Table 7 Regression of Model Put Option Prices on Actual Prices

Panel A: $\hat{p}_0 = \alpha + \beta p_0 + \varepsilon$

R^2	Variable	Coef	Std. Error	T-Stat
0.98	α	0.035	0.007	4.7
	β	1.009	0.008	120.0

Panel B: $(\hat{p}_0 - IV) = \alpha + \beta(p_0 - IV) + \varepsilon$

R^2	Variable	Coef	Std. Error	T-Stat
0.91	α	0.014	0.008	1.6
	β	0.966	0.017	54.6

Panel C: $(p_0 - \hat{p}_0) = \alpha + \beta_1 IV + \beta_2 \tau + \beta_3 \sigma + \varepsilon$

R^2	Variable	Coef	Std. Error	T-Stat
0.30	α	0.299	0.029	10.3
	β_1	0.014	0.003	−4.2
	β_2	0.000	0.008	0.6
	β_3	−5.064	0.937	−10.7

332 observations. Panel A contains the results of regressing the model option price ($\hat{p}_0$) on the actual option price (p_0). Panel B results are from regressing the time value of the option, as calculated by the model, on the actual time value of the option. Time value is defined as the option price minus intrinsic value (IV). The null hypothesis for both specifications is $\alpha = 0$ and $\beta = 1$. Panel C contains results from regressing the difference between the actual and model option price on IV; the number of days remaining until expiration of option (τ); and the annual standard deviation of MBF prices (σ).

ilar to call options, put option mispricing is correlated with the assumed price volatility of the MBF. The amount that the put option is in-the-money also explains a statistically significant portion of the option mispricing. Taken as a whole, these put option results are also supportive of the model.

SUMMARY AND CONCLUSION

The valuation of the many relatively new interest rate contingent claims has received much attention in the academic literature. This literature has been largely theoretical; few of these studies compare model prices to actual market prices. This paper empirically tests a simple valuation model for the mortgage-backed futures-options contracts that traded on the CBOT from June 1989 to March 1992. Theoretical futures-option prices are simulated numerically and then compared to observed transaction prices. The ability of the CBOT MBF to hedge positions in current coupon GNMA MBSs is also measured and is shown to be more effective than cross-hedging GNMA MBS positions with T-note and T-bond futures contracts.

The relatively simple call and put option models tested in this paper use the market price of the MBF as the single-state variable. Despite the conceptual limitations of this approach to debt option valuation, including the assumption of a constant short-term rate of interest, the null hypothesis that changes in the call model price provide an unbiased estimate of changes in the actual option price cannot be rejected. These results are especially encouraging given that the expected price volatility of the MBF is surely measured with some error. The accuracy of the model may be further improved by in-sample calculations to infer expected GNMA MBS price volatility.

The results of this paper provide empirical support for Schaefer and Schwartz (1987), who found that option pricing models that use the underlying bond as an input provide unbiased estimates of option prices as long as the maturity of the option is short relative to the maturity of the underlying bond. The results also serve as benchmarks for subsequent empirical tests of futures-options pricing models that may employ more complicated assumptions about the stochastic processes governing interest rates and underlying bond and MBS prices over time. The use of more complicated valuation models, whatever their conceptual appeal, can only be rationalized if they provide more accurate estimates of actual option prices than the relatively simple model tested in this paper.

NOTES

[1] Nothaft, Wang and Lekkas (1991) analyze the demise of the MBF contract.

[2] See Hull and White (1991), Kim (1990) and Turnbull and Milne (1991) for recent examples and further references.

[3] Ronn and Bliss (1990) and Ho and Lee (1990) are recent exceptions.

[4] Several individuals at the CBOT have suggested another explanation for the demise of the CDR contract. They point out that, unlike Treasury securities, mortgage securities selling at large premiums exhibit very little price volatility. Thus, when the GNMA CDR contracts began to track the higher coupon securities in the mid-1980s, the price volatility of the futures contracts was also reduced and traders/speculators lost interest in the contract.

[5] The valuation of the various delivery options afforded the short position in Treasury-bond futures contracts has received much attention in the literature. See, for example, Arak and Goodman (1987), Kane and Marcus (1986), Gay and Manaster (1984) and Hemler (1990).

[6] Mortgage-backed futures and options expired simultaneously on the Friday preceding the third Wednesday of the month. The Public Securities Association has designated the third Wednesday of the month as the day around which agency securities settlements are established. Settling the mortgage-backed contracts on the preceding Friday was meant to assure that the survey prices used to close out positions were determined while cash market trading in all securities was still active.

[7] See Bartlett (1989, pp. 136–141) for more information on delivery and settlement procedures for mortgage-backed securities.

[8] Batlin (1987) and Follain and Park (1989) discuss the problems and issues associated with cross-hedging MBSs with Treasury futures.

[9] This method of translating Treasury volatilities into GNMA MBS and MBF volatilities does not overstate or understate the volatility of mortgage-backed securities as T-note volatility changes. This was determined by regressing the ratio of GNMA price volatility to T-note volatility on the level of T-note volatility. The R^2 from this regression is 0.052.

REFERENCES

Arak, M. and L. Goodman. 1987. Treasury Bond Futures: Valuing the Delivery Option. *Journal of Futures Markets* 7: 269–286.

Batlin, C. A. 1987. Hedging Mortgage-Backed Securities with Treasury Bond Futures. *Journal of Futures Markets* 7(6): 675–693.

Bartlett, W. W. 1989. *Mortgage-Backed Securities: Products, Analysis, and Trading*. Prentice-Hall, Englewood Cliffs, New Jersey.

Black, F. and M. Scholes. 1973. The Pricing of Options and Corporate Liabilities. *Journal of Political Economy* 8 (May): 637–654.

Brennan, M. J. and E. S. Schwartz. 1982. An Equilibrium Model of Bond Pricing and a Test of Market Efficiency. *Journal of Financial and Quantitative Analysis* 17 (September): 301–329.

Brennan, M. J. and E. S. Schwartz. 1983. Alternative Methods for Valuing Debt Options. *Journal of Finance* 38 (October): 119–137.

Cornell, B. and K. R. French. 1983. Taxes and the Pricing of Stock Index Futures. *The Journal of Finance* 40 (June): 675–694.

Dietrich-Campbell, B. and E. S. Schwartz. 1986. Valuing Debt Options: Empirical Evidence. *Journal of Financial Economics* 16: 321–343.

Chicago Board of Trade. *Mortgage-Backed Futures and Options: An Introduction.* June 1989.

Courtadon, G. 1982. The Pricing of Options on Default Free Bonds. *Journal of Financial and Quantitative Analysis* 17 (March): 75–100.

Cox, J. C., J. E. Ingersoll and S. A. Ross. 1985. A Theory of the Term Structure of Interest Rates. *Econometrica* (March): 385–402.

Cox, J. C., S. A. Ross and M. Rubinstein. 1979. Option Pricing: A Simplified Approach. *Journal of Financial Economics* 7 (September): 229–263.

Ederington, L. H. 1979. The Hedging Performance of the New Futures Markets. *Journal of Finance* 34: 157–170.

Figlewski, S. 1985. Hedging with Stock Index Futures: Theory and Application in a New Market. *Journal of Futures Markets* 5: 183–199.

Follain, J. R. and H. Y. Park. 1989. Hedging the Interest Rate Risk of Mortgages with Prepayment Options. *The Review of Futures Markets* 8(1): 62–78.

Gay, G. D. and S. Manaster. 1984. The Quality Option Implicit in Futures Contracts. *Journal of Financial Economics* 13 (September): 353–370.

Gay, G. D. and S. Manaster. 1984. Futures Pricing in the Presence of Implicit Delivery Options: Theory and Applications to the Treasury Bond Futures Contract. Mimco (March).

Hemler, M. L. 1990. The Quality Delivery Option in Treasury Bond Futures Contracts. *Journal of Finance* 45 (December): 1565–1586.

Ho, T. S. Y. and S. B. Lee. 1990. Interest Rate Futures Options and Interest Rate Options. *The Financial Review* 25 (August): 345–370.

Hull, J. and A. White. 1991. Pricing Interest Rate Derivative Securities. *Review of Financial Studies* Vol. 4, 573–591.

Johnston, E. T. and J. J. McConnell. 1989. Requiem for a Market: An Analysis of the Rise and Fall of a Financial Futures Contract. *The Review of Financial Studies* 2: 1–23.

Kane, A. and A. J. Marcus. 1986. Valuation and Optimal Exercise of the Wild Card Option in the Treasury Bond Futures Market. *Journal of Finance* 41 (March): 195–207.

Kim, I. J. 1990. The Analytic Valuation of American Options. *Review of Financial Studies* 3(4): 547–571.

Nelson, D. B. and K. Ramaswamy. 1990. Simple Binomial Processes as Diffusion Approximations in Financial Models. *The Review of Financial Studies* 3: 393–430.

Nothaft, F. E., G. H. K. Wang and V. Lekkas. 1991. The Viability of the Mortgage-Backed Futures Contract. Mimco (December).

Ronn, E. I. and R. R. Bliss, Jr. 1990. A Non-Stationary Trinomial Model for the Valuation of Options on Treasury Bond Futures Contracts. Mimco (December).

Schaefer, S. M. and E. S. Schwartz. 1987. Time-Dependent Variance and the Pricing of Bond Options. *Journal of Finance* 42 (December): 1113–1128.

Schwartz, E. S. and W. N. Torous. 1989. Prepayment and the Valuation of Mortgage-Backed Securities. *Journal of Finance* 44 (June): 375–392.

Turnbull, S. M., and F. Milne. 1991. A Simple Approach to Interest-Rate Option Pricing. *Review of Financial Studies* 4(1): 87–120.

Vasicek, O. 1977. An Equilibrium Characterization of the Term Structure. *Journal of Financial Economics* 5 (November): 177–188.

27 Index-Based Futures and Options Markets in Real Estate

A big future for real estate in institutional portfolios, if ...

Karl E. Case, Jr., Robert J. Shiller, and Allan N. Weiss

Residential real estate and land in the United States account for about half of the national wealth. If we include also commercial real estate, we have the bulk of the national wealth.[1] The same is true in many other countries. Yet, at the time this is written, futures and options markets devoted to real estate, or index-based over-the-counter derivative real estate markets, are nowhere in operation.

A futures contract on real estate prices in the United Kingdom was initiated by the London Futures and Options Exchange (London Fox) in May 1991, but trading in this contract was suspended in October 1991, following news that the exchange had artificially supported trading volume. Now no price-index-based real estate futures contract exists in the world, nor are there good substitutes for such markets.

Futures and options markets should be established that are cash-settled on the basis of indexes of real estate prices, and there should be separate markets for each of the major geographic regions and for each of the major kinds of real estate: residential, commercial, and agricultural land. Index-based over-the-counter derivative markets in real estate are another worthwhile idea; these markets will allow more contract diversity and will augment and broaden the activities of the futures and options markets.

If all these index-based real estate markets came to be established and were liquid, institutional investors might often choose to put most of their portfolio, in effect, in such markets. Their clients would thereby enjoy better portfolio diversification. Individual and corporate owners of real estate could then hedge away most of the real estate risk that they bear, risk that has caused them enormous concern and trepidation in past years. That risk would be more efficiently borne by large institutional investors that can diversify over many regions and types of real estate, as well as over financial assets.

Nowhere in the world today are there markets that allow investors to invest in a widely diversified portfolio of real estate without incurring enormous transaction costs. Because they cannot invest in a widely diversified portfolio of real estate, they cannot invest in a truly diversified portfolio at all. The presumed diversification that is supposed to be practiced by all investors according to modern financial theory just isn't happening.

This copyrighted material is reprinted with permission from *The Journal of Portfolio Management*, 488 Madison Avenue, New York, NY 10022.

Nor are there markets that allow individuals and institutions with large exposure to specific real estate risk to hedge these risks. People for various reasons usually prefer to own their own homes, rather than rent them, and firms usually prefer to own real estate that they use in connection with their operations. But they cannot easily hedge the risk of these holdings.

In order to hedge their portfolios, these owners of real estate should go short in index-based real estate derivatives that are closely correlated with the real estate that they live in or operate. At the same time, everyone should invest in a broad portfolio of these real estate derivatives, which they can do by holding a portfolio of the opposite sides of the futures, options, forwards, and swaps contracts that those who own real estate concentrated in a certain area undertake.

The long sides of any given index-based derivatives real estate contract would be taken by a wide spectrum of investors, presumably primarily institutional, who invest in many contracts as a means of diversifying their portfolios. The short side would be taken by owners of region-specific real estate: individual homeowners, managers of rental properties, developers, corporations, and farmers.

The establishment of real estate futures and options contracts could spectacularly lower transaction costs for trading in real estate. The modern theory of transaction costs (see, for example, Demsetz [1968], Akerlof [1970], Gammill and Pérold [1989], and Gorton and Pennacchi [1991]) stresses the importance of superior or inside information. Dealers must announce bid-asked spreads wide enough that they are not routinely "picked off" by more informed traders. Baskets of corporate stocks and other financial assets are inherently subject to lower bid-asked spreads than are individual assets, because there is less informed trading in the aggregates.

The same would be true for the baskets of real estate on which an index used to settle real estate futures and options contracts would be based. Those who invest in real estate could be spared the concern that they are buying lemons by spreading the enormous costs and risks associated with buying individual properties.

EXISTING INVESTMENT AND HEDGING MEDIUMS

There have of course been previous institutional innovations that allow individuals and firms to invest in a broader portfolio of real estate than they could conveniently do by direct purchase of properties. And existing institutions offer some ways for real estate owners to hedge the risk of their real estate. Yet, no mechanism comes close to offering the investment and hedging capabilities that would characterize futures or options contracts, or well-designed index-based forwards or swaps.

Real estate investment companies grew out of an effort to provide a diversified portfolio of real estate. The idea of such a company dates back before the turn of the century: Old Dominion Land Corporation (New Jersey) was incorporated in 1880, Alliance Realty (New York) was incorporated in 1899.

There was an explosion of activity in real estate investment companies in the 1920s, and 1929 saw the establishment of the New York Real Estate Securities Exchange for the trading of stocks and bonds of real estate corporations. The exchange fell on hard times soon after, with the collapse of real estate securities prices, and the market was finally closed in 1941.

Real Estate Investment Trusts (REITs), created by an act of Congress in 1960, are a special form of real estate investment company with the ability to pass through profits without exposure to the corporate profits tax. As their shares are traded on exchanges, they have relatively liquid markets.

These investment companies allow individuals and institutions to invest in a broader portfolio of real estate than available through direct investment. They thus allow some benefits of portfolio diversification.

At the same time, they do not allow people to diversify their portfolios to include some important classes of properties, notably owner-occupied residential real estate, properties held by non-incorporated businesses, or land held by farmers. Only certain kinds of properties are suitable for holding by investment companies, and hence certain kinds of systematic risk are necessarily omitted.

REIT prices are substantially correlated with the prices of shares in the stock market. This fact is noted by Rabinowitz [1978], and is also apparent in data produced by the National Association of Real Estate Trusts (see Goetzmann and Ibbotson [1990]). Indeed, prices of real estate investment companies declined sharply in the crash of 1929, and the price of REITs declined sharply in the stock market debacle of 1973–1975 and the crash of 1987, while available data do not show any evidence of a sharp decline in real estate prices in any of those periods.[2]

This is evidence that the kinds of properties held in real estate investment companies are more like those held by other corporations. It is evidence that investors in REITs are not successfully diversifying their portfolios into a broad portfolio of real estate.

The existing real estate investment mediums might be used to hedge real estate risk. In principle, any owner of real estate in a given city could look for a real estate investing company whose holdings are mainly in that city, and hedge his or her risk by shorting stock in the company.

In practice, this will be very difficult to do. First, real estate investing companies rarely hold all their real estate in one city; one may have to pick a REIT that has substantial holdings elsewhere. Second, not many REITs are geographically concentrated, so the total number of shares in such REITs that are available for shorting is necessarily extremely small.

REITs are not geographically concentrated because those who create REITs do not have an incentive to create a hedging medium. Those who create hedging mediums can benefit only from the transaction fees that they receive when the medium is traded, but REITs are not the recipients, under current institutional arrangements, of these transaction fees. They are therefore promoted by their creators as investment, not hedging, mediums.

While some investors might short REITs as a means of hedging their risk in real estate, doing so is not an option for the great majority of owners of real estate. There are just not enough REIT shares available to short. Indeed, the total value of all qualified REITs in the United States in November 1991 was $45.4 billion, or a fraction of 1% of the value of all real estate.[3]

Even if the quantity of REITs outstanding were greatly expanded, the shorting of shares in REITs could never be a means of hedging real estate risk for the majority of real estate owners, because the value of REIT shares outstanding is limited by the value of real estate *owned* by REITs. As we have already noted, most residential real estate is owner-occupied, and hence not eligible for REIT holding.

We need instead some other medium, which allows real estate owners to hedge the risk of their real estate while at the same time owning the real estate. What is needed is some market that stands *between* individual property owners and broader portfolio investors, allowing the portfolio investors to share the risk of the property without owning it. What is needed, inherently, are futures and options markets cash-settled on indexes of real estate prices.

HOME EQUITY INSURANCE

Homeowners' equity insurance could be offered by financial institutions that take out hedging positions in the index-based real estate derivative markets and then repackage these positions into financial products designed for homeowners. The insurance would most likely be underwritten by an insurance company and sold either by the mortgage bank at the time of home purchase or refinancing, or sold by an insurance agent who also sells traditional homeowners' insurance policies.

The policy benefits could be based on the actual loss as measured by the purchase price and later sale price of an individual's home, in which case any benefits would be paid at the time of sale. Alternatively, the policy benefits could be based on the index for the metropolitan or geographic area, in which case any benefits would be paid at regular intervals, such as once per year.

If the policy were based on an index, the policy would pay the homeowner the percentage drop in house prices in his or her area, as measured by the index, less a deductible, times the amount of insurance purchased. For example, when Ms. Homeowner buys a policy for $10,000 worth of real estate with a 5% deductible, if prices drop 9% in her city, she receives the amount of drop beyond 5%; payment in this case is 4% times $100,000, for a total benefit of $4,000. If prices dropped less than 5%, she receives no benefit.

The benefits of the actual price scheme are that the homeowner is assured the maximum coverage of his or her particular home and runs no risk that the house value will move significantly differently from the index. This arrangement may also seem more natural to the homeowner because the coverage is based on events particular to the homeowner in the same way other types of insurance treat hospital stays, car accidents, and house fires.

There are several disadvantages of basing equity insurance benefits on the actual purchase and sale of the house. First, a person might be forced to sell the house in order to collect on the policy before it expires; otherwise there would be no price for the house on which to base settlement. Such forced sales of houses would be extremely inconvenient for homeowners, and the prospect of such sales could jeopardize the entire equity insurance market. (This disadvantage can be reduced somewhat if maturities of contracts are very distant.)

Second, the underwriting insurance company may be able to hedge only the entire metropolitan area traded on the house futures or options markets, which exposes the insurance company to the risk that homes protected under this policy could drop in value more than the index for the area. This may not be an unlikely event because of the problem of adverse selection; people who purchase this policy may know that they have a house in a deteriorating neighborhood, or a house built in an increasingly unpopular style or size, or that they paid too much for their house. These problems would be alleviated partially by a large deductible.

In addition, a moral hazard problem is created by settling the insurance policy on actual purchase and sale prices. Homeowners would have less incentive to maintain their homes and less incentive to sell them at the highest price.

For example, imagine that a homeowner buys her house at $100,000 and has a 5% deductible policy. If her house actually drops 5% in value, she is indifferent between getting $95,000 for it or any price below that, because the insurance company would make up the difference. This could be alleviated partially by creating a policy that pays only a percentage of the loss below the deductible.

Another problem with offering a policy on the selling price of the house is that the homeowner may be tempted to sell the house in a non-arm's length transaction. For example, the homeowner could sell the house to her brother at a discount of 50% off the market value and collect a huge insurance benefit. This problem could be resolved partially by requiring a sale price close to the appraised value. The insurance company could also impose deterrents such as the company's right-of-first-refusal to purchase the house at the agreed-upon sale price. These solutions are only partial, and significantly complicate the terms of the policy.

Although there are advantages to basing insurance benefits on actual purchase and sale prices, we believe that the complications do not merit doing so. A better alternative is to base insurance benefits on the index of the homeowner's geographical or metropolitan area. The policy could be purchased at any time for a fixed period of coverage such as one, two, or three years. The policy would pay off only at the end of this period, not upon sale of the house. If a homeowner moves and wishes an early settlement, this could be arranged, less perhaps an early settlement fee.

Such a policy could be offered as a stand-alone product or bundled with a traditional mortgage. In the latter case, any insurance benefits would be paid to the mortgage holder to pay down the homeowner's mortgage. Such an arrangement could lower the credit risk for the mortgage holder by helping to maintain a constant loan-to-value ratio, and therefore result in a lower interest rate to the homeowner. Home equity insurance may prove particularly useful to lenders who wish to offer riskier second mortgages or equity lines of credit.

MORTGAGE INSURANCE AND DEFAULT RISK

Index-based real estate derivative markets may be an attractive complement to private or quasi-public mortgage insurance for holders of residential mortgages. Mortgage insurers themselves (MGIC, General Electric, PMI, etc.) may find hedging in such markets to be an attractive form of reinsurance.

Mortgage default can occur for a variety of reasons. Individual homeowners may find themselves unable to service their debt because of changed economic circumstances (divorce, unemployment, and so forth). Thus, defaults can occur randomly whether or not property values change. As long as the equity in a property exceeds the unpaid balance of the mortgage plus the transaction costs of foreclosing and liquidating it, no loss is incurred by the mortgage holder or the insurer upon default.

Thus, in rising or even flat real estate markets, mortgage portfolios and insurers are insulated from all but truly random risk. Losses will, of course, occur when the value of an individual property that has not been maintained falls below the value of the secured debt.

Much larger and more systematic risk to mortgage portfolios and insurers occurs when real estate markets as a whole decline in value. The probability of default increas-

Exhibit Recent Housing Price Booms and Busts: Behavior of Median Price of Existing Houses (%)

Location	Time Period	Total Nominal Change	Annual Average Nominal Change	Annual Average Real Change
Booms				
San Francisco	1976–1980	106.9	19.9	9.3
Boston	1983–1987	114.5	20.6	17.7
New York	1983–1987	108.4	20.2	16.9
Washington, D.C.	1986–1988	30.4	14.2	10.2
San Francisco	1987–1989	53.2	23.8	19.1
Honolulu	1987–1990	101.6	26.3	21.2
Seattle	1988–1990	63.3	27.7	22.3
Busts				
Houston	1985–1987	−25.5	−12.0	−14.6
Iklahoma City	1986–1989	−22.2	−8.7	−12.2
New York	1988–1991	−14.2	−5.4	−10.1
Boston	1989–1991	−14.0	−8.3	−13.5

Sources: National Association of Realtors (median price) and U.S. Bureau of Labor Statistics (CPI-U).

es substantially during such periods, and losses will be incurred on foreclosure even of maintained properties.

In some states (such as Texas), there is no recourse for mortgage holders other than foreclosure. Where no recourse exists, homeowners would be expected to walk away from a mortgage whenever the unpaid balance exceeded current market value. Even in recourse states, the probability of losses rises when values fall because the mortgage will be the first obligation for a homeowner to default on, with no equity to protect. In addition, mortgage holders and insurers generally fail to exercise recourse because of very high transaction costs.

Mortgage holders can easily insure themselves against the risk associated with interest rate movements. Mortgage insurance provides a convenient but fairly costly way of insuring against the risk associated with higher-risk individual borrowers or higher-risk individual properties. But there is currently no way of insuring against the very large risks associated with movements in general market prices.

If the risk of losses on foreclosure to a mortgage holder or an insurer were truly random across individuals, they would indeed be holding widely diversified portfolios. But in fact, it is well-known that residential real estate prices move regionally, and that regional markets are relatively independent. The boom/bust cycles in the Northeast, the Southeast, and California occurred on very different timetables.

The behavior of home prices during regional boom/bust cycles also increases the systematic regional component of risk to mortgage holders and insurers. Prices tend to rise rapidly during booms, but are generally sticky when fundamentals would predict a decline (see Case and Shiller [1987, 1988, and 1989]). When decline finally occurs, that means that there were large numbers of transactions at or near peak prices.

For example, in Boston, prior to the recent sharp declines, peak prices held for nearly three years.

PRICE VARIABILITY AND REGIONAL CONTRACTS

There is substantial price variability through time in real estate, and there is sufficient variability across cities that there is room for a number of different city-specific futures and options markets.

Regionwide price cycles have clearly dominated housing price behavior in the last several decades, and those cycles have broadened in range over this period, as the Exhibit shows. While the first major California boom of 1976–1980 was a dramatic event, in real terms it was surpassed by what was to follow. The Boston and New York booms were similar to each other in magnitude, with real prices rising at 18% and 17% per year, respectively, over a four-year period. In both cities in the middle of the 1980s, prices were rising at nearly 40% per year.

The second California boom, at the end of the 1980s, was shorter-lived, but perhaps more dramatic near the peak. Realtors reported multiple offers and prices rising at 4% per month, or over 50% per year, in 1988.

The most recent booms have been in Honolulu and Seattle. In Honolulu, the median price jumped from $186,000 in 1987 to $375,000 in the third quarter of 1990. In Seattle, the median was up from $88,700 in 1988 to $144,800 in the third quarter of 1990.

In addition to booms, regions seem increasingly to be vulnerable to busts, and at different times in different regions. The Southwest experienced a dramatic decline in values that resulted in huge losses for mortgage portfolio holders and insurers during the mid-1980s.

More recently, there have been sharp region-wide declines in home values in the Northeast. Our own recent research reveals declines of 30% for condominiums and 22% for single-family homes in the Boston metropolitan area between mid-1988 and early 1992, and declines of 10% for condominiums and 11% for single-family homes in Los Angeles County between the second quarter of 1990 and the first quarter of 1992.

Because these enormous booms and busts occurred at different times in different parts of the country, a single national futures contract would not serve to insulate individual homeowners against risk in their particular market. We need regional futures contracts covering regions of sizes at least as small as some of the regions discussed above.

It has been documented that housing price movements in each region are relatively smooth through time (see Case and Shiller [1987, 1989] and Poterba [1991]). There is inertia in housing prices, which do not behave like near-random walks as do prices of liquid financial assets. This suggests that day-to-day movements in housing prices are not large.

Nonetheless, we would expect to see prices of futures or options tend to show day-to-day fluctuations more characteristic of financial asset prices. The futures and options markets should be immediately responsive to any news about the outlook for housing—and certainly there is no shortage of such news—even if the cash markets themselves are sluggish.

There is also the likelihood that the existence of futures or options markets will tend to make the cash market more efficient. Prices for real estate properties may in fact one day be quoted in terms of the prices in futures markets, as are many commodity prices today. A sales agreement for a single-family home may automatically be indexed for the change in the futures price between agreement and closing, thereby making the cash market more efficient.

HORIZONS OF CONTRACTS

In most futures markets, volume of trade tends to be concentrated in the contract with the shortest time to maturity, unless this time becomes very short, that is, close to the expiration date of the nearest contract. We think that there would be less concentration of trade in the nearest contract in the house futures and options contracts, and there may be substantial trade in very distant maturities.

Part of the reason for this is that there should be substantial long-run hedging demand by homeowners who will wish to sell a futures contract or buy a put with years to maturity. Institutional investors may also wish to hold a large part of these long-horizon contracts, or write a large number of long-horizon puts, as part of a long-term portfolio strategy.

Another reason is that in futures and options markets with a very illiquid cash market, rolling over short contracts may not hedge long-term risk. Suppose that information becomes available that real estate prices will decline over the next three years. Because the cash market is sluggish and inefficient, this information is not fully incorporated in real estate prices, and hence not in current short-term futures prices. As investors roll over the futures contract, in subsequent years, they will find that the futures prices will reflect the information, so that the risk is no longer insurable.

In short, holders of an existing short-term contract are not compensated for the fact that they must now confront very unfavorable terms when they roll over the futures contract. This factor may contribute to making index-based forwards and swaps, which are traditionally of a longer horizon than futures and options, a relatively more important factor (relative to futures markets) for real estate assets than they are for purely financial assets.

EFFECTS OF INDEX-BASED DERIVATIVE MARKETS ON CASH PRICES AND RENTS

Economic theory suggests that providing index-based derivative markets to hedge real estate risk should boost the aggregate price of real estate, at least initially. For example, people's demand for housing services is dampened by the necessity of undertaking financial risk specific to their neighborhood when consuming these services. Absent that necessity, other things equal, they should demand more.

To the extent that the supply of housing is limited by land or other restraints, greater demand will result in higher home prices. When a large derivative market is first established, this will provide a windfall to existing homeowners.

To the extent that real estate is reproducible with constant costs, its long-run price will be unaffected by the establishment of derivative markets. Instead, the quantity of real estate will be increased. The greater supply of real estate will mean that rents will tend to fall to clear the rental market. Thus, indirect beneficiaries of the real estate futures and options markets will be renters.

EFFECTS OF DERIVATIVE MARKETS ON CASH PRICE VOLATILITY AND THE BUSINESS CYCLE

There is a large literature on the effects of the establishment of futures markets on the volatility of the cash market. Empirical studies generally find that institution of a futures market reduces cash market volatility. This conclusion is reached by Gray [1963] and

Cox [1976] for the onions market, by Hooker [1901] for the wheat market, by Emery [1986] for the cotton market, by Powers [1970] and Cox [1976] for the cattle market, and by Schwert [1989] for the stock index futures market. (See also Turnovsky [1983] for other references.)

Theoretical analyses of the effects of institution of futures markets on volatility (as, for example, Peck [1976] and Turnovsky [1983]) suggest that the effect of instituting futures markets may be to reduce volatility, although researchers assert that the volatility of the cash market is not a good way to measure the welfare effects of the futures markets. Certainly, those who feel adversely affected by any increase in cash market volatility have the option of hedging this risk in the futures market.

Harris [1990] argues that an index alternative has effects on both "fundamental volatility" and "transactions" volatility. Fundamental volatility occurs in response to new public information, and here an index alternative is likely to have measurable but small effects.

"Transactions volatility" occurs because of the bid-asked spread and through uninformed order flow imbalances. At times of great order flow imbalances caused by uninformed investors, the bid-asked spread may become extremely wide. As market makers do not know that new orders are coming from uninformed investors, there may be great transaction-induced price movements.

As we noted in our introduction, the establishment of index futures markets may reduce bid-asked spreads, and this increased liquidity may therefore reduce the effects of order imbalances on prices. The same is true in a real estate market context; those who want to get out of their real estate holdings for reasons other than inside knowledge about the true value of their individual properties need not throw their lot in with people who are selling "lemons," so prices in the cash market need not drop as much from their selling pressure.

Case and Shiller have argued that the housing market in particular periods is driven by fads. (See Case [1986], Case and Shiller [1987, 1988, 1989], and Shiller [1989].) That is, there is a marked tendency for purely speculative price movements.

It is difficult to say from theory alone what will be the effects of the institution of real estate futures and options markets on such fad-driven price movements. The lower transaction costs will encourage much greater participation in the real estate market; the effects on price volatility will depend on the nature of the people brought into the market. Among those brought into the market will be professional institutional investors, so we would suspect the tendency will be to reduce speculative volatility in the market, but this result is not assured.

Some of this fad component is apparently in reaction to past price changes. One view of financial market price movements is that major speculative price movements may be triggered by large order flow imbalances, causing noticeable price changes, and that these initial price changes, if supported by public attitudes, may lead to further speculative price changes and a snowball effect.

Major stock market booms and crashes have been interpreted in these terms, and so might real estate booms and crashes. If this interpretation is right, the effect of institution of futures and options markets in real estate might be to lower price volatility, by preventing the initial order flow imbalance price changes.

Evidence suggests that upward volatility is in part driven by buyers who do not want to be "priced out" of a rising market. With an available futures market, buyers not really ready to buy could take a long position in the market of their choice and thereby be protected from price increases at much less cost than buying a house whose purchase is not warranted by their particular circumstances. The effect of a housing futures market may therefore be to reduce the severity of the very booms that we have seen in these markets.

Any acceleration of demand for housing futures will provide signals to the construction industry about potential future demand. Builders could embark on long-term construction projects on a hedged basis, thereby meeting any increased demand with an increased supply. This will mean a more rational supply response to speculative demand, which may interact with speculative behavior so as in the long run to reduce the volatility of house price movements.

If real estate prices become stabilized, there would be a tendency for stabilization of construction expenditure as well—a good thing, for a substantial portion of the aggregate business cycle has been related, in the past, to booms and busts in the construction industry.

DOUBTS ABOUT THE VIABILITY OF REAL ESTATE DERIVATIVE MARKETS

One argument against real estate derivative markets is that past efforts at establishing such markets, or similar markets, have failed.

The London Fox Property Futures Market closed in October 1991 after months of disappointing volume. That market included a residential real estate futures contract that was cash settled based on the Nationwide Anglia House Price Index, a regression-based hedonic price index; and a commercial real estate futures contract, which was cash settled on the Investment Property Databank (IPD) monthly index of prices in commercial real estate, on the basis of assessed values of properties owned by thirty-one funds.

Failures of other, analogous, futures markets may also be cause for concern. Of course, many efforts to establish new futures or options markets fail because the new market is very similar to an existing futures or options market. This is not a problem with the establishment of real estate futures or options markets; there is not now any market remotely resembling them. Some efforts to establish futures or options markets fail because the corresponding cash market is very small; this is certainly not a problem with real estate futures markets.

But, the analogy of these real estate futures and options markets with the consumer price index (CPI) futures market warrants more concern. The CPI futures market was proposed by Michael Lovell and Robert Vogel in 1973. A CPI futures market was instituted by the Coffee, Sugar and Cocoa Exchange in 1985. The market was unsuccessful; it shut down in 1989 because of inadequate investor interest.

When trading was first announced, the CPI futures market was heralded as a cure for much of the harms of inflation. There are some very important costs of inflation: the costs of nominal contracting due to substantial unexpected price level changes. Such costs can be hedged against in a CPI futures market. The claims made then that it would solve big, fundamental economic problems may sound analogous to the claims that we are making here for real estate futures contracts.

Why did the CPI futures markets fail? Horrigan [1987] cites three reasons. First, the aggregate CPI may not be the relevant measure of inflation for many who have different consumption or payment patterns. Second, inflation uncertainty dropped substantially by the time the contract was first traded. Third, there is no underlying asset for CPI futures. No one is storing the CPI market basket. Demand for a futures contract is thought to require that there are people holding stocks of the asset, who will want to hedge.

We are optimistic that none of these reasons applies to our proposed real estate futures and options markets. There would be many markets; for regions and types of real estate, real estate price uncertainty is still very large; and certainly prodigious quantities of real estate assets are held, and by a wide variety of types of individuals and businesses.

One fact that should be borne in mind is that innovative futures contracts often have a slow start; this was true of the Treasury bond futures market when it was first instituted, and it was ultimately extremely successful. One reason for slowness to start is that most traders are interested only in trading on *liquid* markets. But of course, establishing liquid markets is something that can eventually be done with time, money, and patience.

Slowness to start can also be attributed to unfamiliarity of the people who have reason to trade in these markets. Certainly, most individual homeowners do not have the familiarity with futures markets that would enable them to make ready use of them. The failure of the CPI futures market has also been attributed to the unfamiliarity of labor and management, the likely big users of these markets according to its proposers (Lovell and Vogel [1973]), with any futures markets. Similarly, the failure of the London Fox Property Futures Market could be attributed to a failure of the public to understand and appreciate such markets. In England, there was not, to our knowledge, any development of accessory institutions, such as residential real estate price insurance, that would encourage use of these markets by owners of real estate.

CONCLUSION

The economic significance of index-based real estate derivative markets, if they were to become well-established, could well be much greater than that of all financial derivative markets established to date combined. The reasons are that the reduced transaction costs caused by the introduction of these markets are of an order of magnitude larger than the reduction afforded by use of the other derivative markets, and that real estate represents the bulk of national wealth. The obstacles to investing in much real estate today are inherently prohibitive for portfolio managers, and truly diversified holdings of real estate are just not in their portfolios.

These markets could make life better for so many of us: homeowners who are worried about their concentrated investment in local housing; prospective homeowners who are worried about being one day priced out of the market; renters who are concerned about rental costs and availability of apartments; investors who want to diversify their portfolios to include real estate; builders who want to hedge the risk inherent in their business; users of commercial real estate; and farmers concerned about their costs and risks. The markets may well serve to smooth out the business cycle and allow more rational, even-keel planning in all walks of life.

What is needed is the establishment of such derivative markets by exchanges and underwriters that have the resources to see these markets through a trial period, with an education campaign to see to it that the general public understands and can use these markets. Given the enormous potential for efficiency, such markets should be established as soon as possible.

ENDNOTES

[1] The value of residential structures and land in the United States in 1990 was $8.35 trillion, or 51% of the domestic net worth of $16.24 trillion, according to *Balance Sheets for the U.S. Economy 1949–90*, Board of Governors of the Federal Reserve System, Washington D.C., September 1991.

[2] Real prices of houses did not fall much in 1929–1932 (see Shiller [1989]), nor was there any fall in single-family housing prices in 1973–1975 (see Case and Shiller [1987]).

[3] Data courtesy of the National Association of Real Estate Investment Trusts, Inc., Washington, D.C.

REFERENCES

Akerlof, George A. "The Market for "Lemons": Quality Uncertainty and the Market Mechanism." *Quarterly Journal of Economics*, August 1970, pp. 488-500.

Case, Karl E. "The Market for Single Family Homes in Boston." *New England Economic Review*, May/June 1986, pp. 38-48.

Case, Karl E., and Robert J. Shiller. "The Behavior of Home Buyers in Boom and Postboom Markets." *New England Economic Review*, November/December 1988, pp. 29-46.

———. "The Efficiency of the Market for Single Family Homes." *American Economic Review*, March 1989, pp. 125-137.

———. "Forecasting Prices and Excess Returns in the Housing Market." *AREUEA Journal*, Fall 1990, pp. 253-273.

———. "Prices of Single Family Homes Since 1970: New Indexes for Four Cities." *New England Economic Review*, September/October 1987, pp. 45-56.

Cox, C. C. "Futures Trading and Market Information." *Journal of Political Economy*, December 1976, pp. 1215-1237.

Demsetz, Harold. "The Cost of Transacting." *Quarterly Journal of Economics*, February 1968, pp. 33-53.

Emery, H. C. *Speculation on the Stock and Produce Exchange of the United States.* Columbia University Press, New York, 1986.

Gammill, James F., Jr., and Andre F. Pérold. "The Changing Character of Stock Market Liquidity." *Journal of Portfolio Management*, Spring 1989, pp. 13-18.

Goetzmann, William, and Roger G. Ibbotson. "The Performance of Real Estate as an Asset Class." *Journal of Applied Corporate Finance*, Spring 1990, pp. 65-76.

Gorton, Gary, and George Pennacchi. "Security Baskets and Index-Linked Securities." National Bureau of Economic Research, Working Paper No. 3711, May 1991.

Gray, R. W. "Onions Revisited." *Journal of Farm Economics*, 1963, pp. 273-276.

Harris, Lawrence. "The Economics of Cash Index Alternatives." *Journal of Future Markets*, April 1990, pp. 179-194.

Hooker, R. H. "The Suspension of the Berlin Produce Exchange and its Effects Upon Corn Prices." *Journal of the Royal Statistical Society*, 64 (1901), pp. 574-604.

Horrigan, Brian R. "The CPI Futures Market: The Inflation Hedge That Won't Grow." *Business Review*, Federal Reserve Bank of Philadelphia, May–June 1987, pp. 3-14.

Lovell, Michael C., and Robert C. Vogel. "A CPI-Futures Market." *Journal of Political Economy*, July–August 1973, pp. 1009-1012.

Peck, Ann E. "Futures Markets, Supply Response, and Price Stability." *Quarterly Journal of Economics*, August 1976, pp. 407-423.

Poterba, James. "House Price Dynamics: The Role of Tax Policy and Demographics." Brookings Papers on Economic Activity, No. 2, 1991, pp. 143-203.

Powers, M. J. "Does Futures Trading Reduce Price Fluctuations in the Cash Market?" *American Economic Review*, June 1970, pp. 460-464.

Rabinowitz, Alan. *Development of the Real Estate Investment Industry, 1925–1975.* University of Washington, Seattle, 1978.

Schwert, G. William. "Business Cycles, Financial Crises, and Stock Volatility." Carnegie Rochester Conference Series on Public Policy, No. 31, 1989, pp. 83-125.

Shiller, Robert J. *Market Volatility.* Cambridge, MA: MIT Press, 1989.

Turnovsky, Stephen J. "The Determination of Spot and Futures Prices with Storable Commodities." *Econometrica,* September 1983, pp. 1363-1388.

Index of Authors

Bond, Michael T., 19
Brueggeman, W.B., 13

Cannaday, Roger E., 5
Case, Karl E., 27
Chen, A.H., 13
Colwell, Peter F., 5

DeRosa, Paul, 8
DiPasquale, Denise, 24
Draper, Dennis W., 20
Dunn, Kenneth B., 6

Elayan, Fayez A., 22

Findlay, Chapman, 20
Firstenberg, Paul M., 2
Fisher, Jeffery D., 23
Follain, James R., 3

Gau, George W., 21
Goodman, Laurie, 8
Grissom, Terry V., 14
Guilkey, David, 12
Gyourko, Joseph, 11

Hartzell, David J., 17, 18
Hekman, John S., 18
Hoag, James W., 9

Jaffe, Austin J., 1

Keim, Donald B., 11
Kuhle, James L., 14

Langetieg, Terence C., 17
Leibowitz, Martin L., 17

Ling, David C., 26
Lins, David A., 15

Maris, Brian A., 22
McConnell, John J., 6
Miles, Mike, 12, 18, 25
Mueller, Glenn R., 16

Pringle, John, 25

Richard, Scott F., 7
Roll, Richard, 7
Ross, Stephen A., 2
Rubens, Jack H., 19

Sherrick, Bruce J., 15
Shiller, Robert J., 27
Shulman, David G., 17
Sirmans, C. F., 1, 10
Sirmans, G. Stacy, 10
Sunderman, Mark A., 5

Thibodeau, T. G., 13
Tucker, Michael, 4

Venigalla, Aravind, 15

Walther, Carl H., 14
Webb, R. Brian, 12, 26
Webb, James R., 19
Weiss, Allan N., 27
Wheaton, William C., 24

Zazzarino, Mike, 8
Ziering, Barry A., 16
Zisler, Randall C., 2

Index of Terms

actual inflation, 269
agency theory, 320
appraisal-adjusted series, 22
appraisal-based returns, 142, 226
appraisal-based return series, 131
appraisal-driven indices, 162
appraisal-smoothing, 162
Arbitrage Pricing Theory, 291
asset allocation, 30
asset pricing framework, 304
asset-type diversification, 202

base industries, 225
burnout multipliers, 95-98

call option, 81
call-option pricing model, 381
Capital Asset Pricing Model, 284, 304
capitalization rate, 334, 351
cash equivalence adjustment, 63
certainty models, 42
commingled real estate funds, 184, 267
commingled funds, 21
complete negative hedge, 269
complete positive hedge, 269
contemporaneous REIT returns, 146
corporate real estate decision, 358
correlation of returns with farmland, 211
cost of capital, 325
covariance matrix, 210
covariance of portfolio returns, 279
cross-correlation coefficients, 122
current coupon GNMA, 377

derivative markets, 395
Dominant Economic Employment Categories, 225
duration of real estate, 247

economic base theory, 225
effective duration, 244
effective rent index, 339
efficient frontiers, 231-232
embedded call and default options, 379
empirical duration, 110

Employment Performance Zones, 225
equilibrium asset prices, 351
equity REIT returns, 144
expected inflation, 269
expected rate of inflation, 251
expected real interest rate, 251

farmland returns, 271
farm production regions, 217
farm real estate, 220
farmland investment, 207
favorable estimation bias, 217
financed fee valuation adjustment, 63
financing environment, 8
financing premium, 70
fixed-rate mortgage, 39, 52
FRC return series, 128
fundamental characteristics of value, 119
fundamental valuation function, 120
fundamental valuation model, 293
futures and options markets, 388
futures and options valuation, 378
futures-options contracts, 373

generic bond pricing model, 75
geographic grouping, 224
GNMA mortgage-backed securities, 73
GNMA securities, 376
graphical analysis, 333
growth rate of earnings, 318

hedging effectiveness of MBF, 376
hedging mediums, 389
Hedonic Price Model, 295
heterogeneous reduced-form pricing, 165
historical perspective of real estate, 127
holding period returns, 196, 226
home equity insurance, 391
homogeneous asset model, 164

Ibbotson and Fall study, 131
index-related returns, 280
idiosyncratic return component, 280

industrial property subindex, 119
industrial real estate return index, 118
inflation hedge, 336
inflation hedge regressions, 255
inflation hedging, 192-196
inflation hedging effectiveness, 266
inflation pass-through, 243
inflationary expectations, 268
institutional farmland investment, 207

Jensen's index of performance, 194

lagged appraisal data, 145
lagged equity REIT returns, 156
lagged returns, 213
lease structures, 240
legal environment, 7
leverage clientele effect, 320
leverage-firm value, 317
loan to price ratio, 67, 68

market analysis, 5
market frictions, 240
market price of risk, 282
market rental rates, 333
market-determined returns, 162
Markowitz efficient, 201
mean-variance portfolio model, 201
minimum-variance portfolio, 214
modified duration, 107
moral hazard problem, 392
mortgage choice, 39
mortgage insurance and default risk, 392
mortgage REIT, 318
mortgage seasoning, 94
mortgage-backed futures and options, 375
MSA, 226

NCREIF fiduciaries, 224
net operating income, 360
net rent variable, 239
nominal Interest rate, 251
non-spatial factors, 331

one period rate of return, 278
optimal call policy, 76
optimal farmland portfolio, 222

partial negative hedge, 271
performance measures, 191
portfolio beta, 153-155
portfolio diversification, 198
positive abnormal returns, 000
premium burnout, 95
premium pool, 94

prepayment rate, 94
prepayment theory, 91
primary metropolitan statistical area, 165
property and capital markets, 348
property market prices, 345
property-specific data, 168
property type diversification, 28
put-option pricing model, 384

Real Estate Investment Trusts, 316, 390
real estate futures contracts, 389
real estate option, 360
real estate options contracts, 389
real estate return series, 128
real estate returns and inflation, 135
real estate valuation model, 357
refinancing incentive, 92
regional diversification, 25
rent, 348
rent controls, 309
replacement cost, 333, 345
residential appreciation returns, 268
risk reduction, 203
risk-adjusted performance, 194
Russell-NCREIF Property Index, 142, 176, 338

Security Market Line, 284
semistrong form efficiency, 303
Sharpe index of performance, 191
smoothing bias, 207
space and capital markets, 332
spatial factors, 331
specialized actors, 10
stylized facts, 40
suboptimal prepayment, 82

tax shield, 317
three-factor APT, 306
tilt problem, 49
transaction-driven returns, 161-162, 176
transaction-driven series, 175
transactions-based returns, 144
two-factor Jensen performance measure, 194

uncertainty models, 45
unexpected inflation, 257, 269
unleveraged-firm value, 317
unsystematic risk, 203
urban metropolitan areas, 225

vacancy rate, 337
valuation model, 174-178
valuation of real estate, 238

variability of derivative markets, 396
variable-rate mortgage, 39, 52
variance of portfolio returns, 278
variance of returns, 208
volatility of earnings, 318

volatility of MBF, 385

weighted average cost of capital, 361

List of Authors

Bond, Michael T.
Cleveland State University

Brueggeman, William B.
Southern Methodist University

Cannaday, Roger E.
University of Illinios

Case, Karl E.
Wellesley College

Chen, Andrew H.
Southern Methodist University

Colwell, Peter F.
University of Illinois

DeRosa, Paul
Eastbridge Asset Management Inc.

DiPasquale, Denise
Harvard University

Dunn, Kenneth B.
Carnegie Mellon University

Elayan, Fayez A.
Southwest Missouri State University

Findlay, Chapman
Findlay, Phillips & Associates

Firstenberg, Paul M.
Prudential Realty Group

Fisher, Jeffery D.
Indiana University

Follain, James R.
Syracuse University

Gau, George W.
University of Texas at Austin

Goodman, Laurie
Merrill Lynch & Co.

Grissom, Terry V.
Price Waterhouse

Guilkey, David
University of North Carolina

Gyourko, Joseph
University of Pennsylvania

Hartzell, David J.
University of North Carolina

Hekman, John S.
University of North Carolina

Hoag, James
James Hoag Associates

Jaffe, Austin J.
Pennsylvania State University

Keim, Donald B.
University of Pennsylvania

Kuhle, James L.
California State University at Sacramento

Langetieg, Terence C.
Salomon Brothers Inc.

Leibowitz, Martin L.
Salomon Brothers Inc.

Ling, David C.
University of Florida

Lins, David A.
University of Illinois

Maris, Brian A.
Northern Arizona University

McConnell, John J.
Purdue University

Miles, Mike
University of North Carolina

Mueller, Glenn R.
Alex Brown Kleinwort Benson

Pringle, John
University of North Carolina

Richard, Scott F.
Goldman, Sachs & Co.

Roll, Richard
University of California, Los Angeles

Ross, Stephen A.
Yale School of Organization & Management

Rubens, Jack H.
Bryant College

Sherrick, Bruce J.
University of Illinois

Shiller, Robert J.
Yale University

Shulman, David G.
Salomon Brothers

Sirmans, C. F.
University of Connecticut

Sirmans, G. Stacy
Florida State University

Sunderman, Mark A.
University of Wyoming

Thibodeau, T. G.
Southern Methodist University

Tucker, Michael
Fairfield University

Venigalla, Aravind
University of Illinois

Walther, Carl H.
California State University at Sacramento

Webb, R. Brian
Aetna Realty Investors, Inc.

Webb, James R.
Cleveland State University

Weiss, Allan N.
Case Shiller Weiss Inc.

Wheaton, William C.
Massachusetts Institute of Technology

Zazzarino, Mike
Eastbridge Asset Management Inc.

Ziering, Barry A.
Prudential Real Estate Investors

Zisler, Randall C.
Nomura Securities